OUR GAME, TOO

Edited by Andrew North

Associate Editors
Len Levin, Bill Nowlin, and Carl Riechers

Society for American Baseball Research, Inc.
Phoenix, AZ

Our Game, Too
Influential Figures and Milestones in Canadian Baseball
Edited by Andrew North
Associate editors: Len Levin, Bill Nowlin, and Carl Riechers

Copyright © 2022 Society for American Baseball Research, Inc.
All rights reserved. Reproduction in whole or in part without permission is prohibited.
ISBN 978-1-970159-81-3 ebook
ISBN 978-1-970159-82-0 paper
Library of Congress Control Number: 2022908748

Cover art and design: Sean Kane
Canadian-made bats portrayed in the cover art provided by the
Canadian Baseball Hall of Fame and Museum.

Book design: David Peng and Heidi Boyd
Copyright © 2022 Society for American Baseball Research, Inc.
All rights reserved. Reproduction in whole or in part without permission is prohibited.
Cronkite School at ASU
555 N. Central Ave. #416
Phoenix, AZ 85004
Phone: (602) 496-1460
Web: www.sabr.org
Facebook: Society for American Baseball Research
Twitter: @SABR

TABLE OF CONTENTS

INTRODUCTION

"**M**ake an endeavor to see more baseball; you need it." So urged journalist Jack Calder, writing in the *Chatham* (Ontario) *Daily News* on July 31, 1934. In various eras, and at diverse locations across Canada, such exhortation would not have been necessary. Not to the crowds as large as 10,000 who viewed the matches between London and Guelph in the 1870s, traveling between the cities on the newly-opened railroad, at a time when the combined population of the two cities was less than 27,000. Nor to the thousands who flocked to Vancouver's Powell Street Grounds in the 1920s and '30s to watch their local heroes, the Asahi. Not to the thousands more who jammed cramped ballparks hosting the big-money semipro tournaments on the Prairies for two decades in midcentury. And certainly not to the more than four million who packed the recently-opened SkyDome for the Toronto Blue Jays championship seasons of 1992 and 1993.

Canadian baseball has a rich, diverse, and deeply rooted history, one that spans fully two centuries. In its early days, baseball's development north of the border was shaped by the same social and economic influences, and the same competitive and entrepreneurial spirit, as was found south. The stories in this book tell the tales of the influential figures and milestone events that defined and directed the game's growth in Canada between the 1830s and the 1960s. While some names and subjects will be familiar to ardent baseball fans, these articles shine a spotlight on the movers and shakers, the pioneers, the leagues and games and tournaments, and the regions all across the country that hosted them.

The book is an initiative of the Centre for Canadian Baseball Research, and SABR's Hanlan's Point (Greater Toronto) Chapter. It is the collaborative effort of more than 30 SABR members, almost all of them Canadian: Richard Armstrong, Bob Barney, Gary Belleville, Warren Campbell, Patrick Carpentier, Stephen Dame, Michel Dugas, Eric Frost, Larry Gerlach, Gary Gillette, Tom Hawthorn, Martin Healy Jr., Colin Howell, William Humber, Heidi LM Jacobs, Maxwell Kates, Martin Lacoste, Bill Lamb, Len Levin, Chip Martin, David Matchett, Andy McCue, David McDonald, Peter Morris, Andrew North, Bill Nowlin, Riley Nowokowski, Bill Pruden, Carl Riechers, David Siegel, Paul Sinclair, Allen Tait, Dennis Thiessen, Christian Trudeau, Max Weder, and Daniel Wyatt. Original cover art was generously provided by Sean Kane of Guelph, Ontario.

Make an endeavor to read more Canadian baseball; you need it.

Andrew North
St. Marys, Ontario
December 2021

MAP OF BASEBALL LOCATIONS

Cities referenced in the text are shown on this map of the southern portion of Canada.

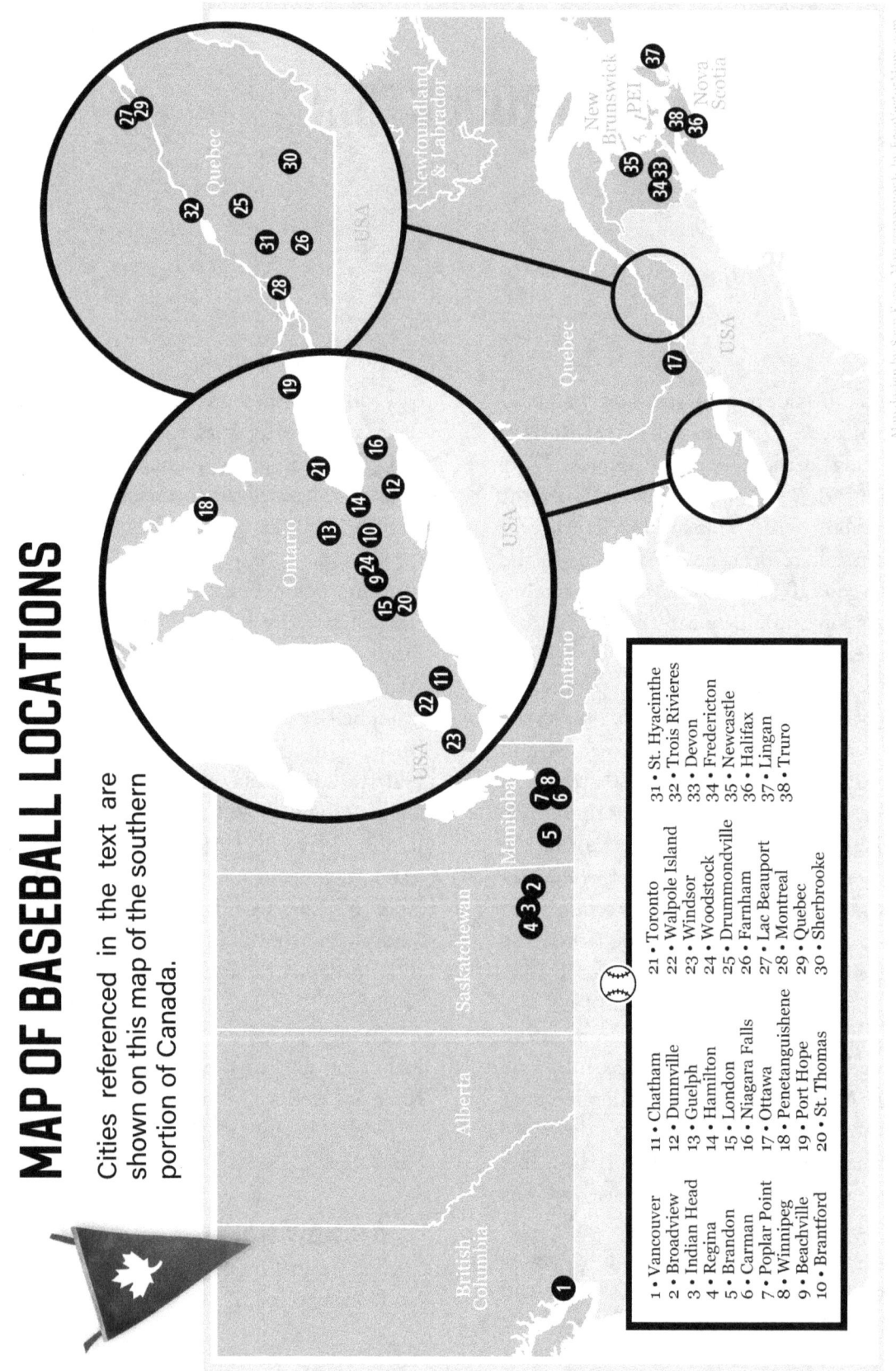

1 • Vancouver	11 • Chatham	21 • Toronto	31 • St. Hyacinthe
2 • Broadview	12 • Dunnville	22 • Walpole Island	32 • Trois Rivieres
3 • Indian Head	13 • Guelph	23 • Windsor	33 • Devon
4 • Regina	14 • Hamilton	24 • Woodstock	34 • Fredericton
5 • Brandon	15 • London	25 • Drummondville	35 • Newcastle
6 • Carman	16 • Niagara Falls	26 • Farnham	36 • Halifax
7 • Poplar Point	17 • Ottawa	27 • Lac Beauport	37 • Lingan
8 • Winnipeg	18 • Penetanguishene	28 • Montreal	38 • Truro
9 • Beachville	19 • Port Hope	29 • Quebec	
10 • Brantford	20 • St. Thomas	30 • Sherbrooke	

PART I:
THE NINETEENTH CENTURY

As the middle of the nineteenth century saw the rapid spread of baseball in the United States both westward and southward from its geographical hub in the Greater New York area, and Brooklyn in particular, so too did the game expand its footprint in Canada. From the 1850s through the 1870s, the game developed from its purely recreational folk roots to become more organized and structured. The ever-evolving rules gradually stabilized, as the New York game became more firmly established as the preferred style of play. The center of this Northern baseball universe, the Canadian equivalent to Brooklyn, if you will, was Southwestern Ontario.

The 30-year period beginning in the early 1850s encompassed all of these pioneering developments, virtually all of them happening in Southwestern Ontario. The first baseball club was formed (in Hamilton, Ontario, in 1854). The first international baseball match was played (in what is now Niagara Falls, Ontario, in 1860). The first Canadian player reached the major leagues (Bob Addy from Port Hope, Ontario, in either 1871 or 1876, depending on whether the National Association is considered major league). The first professional league in Canada was formed (the Canadian Association of 1876). Canada's first international championship was attained (by the International Association's London Tecumsehs in 1877). And the most extensive international tour to date by a Canada-based team was undertaken (by the St. Thomas Atlantics in 1882).

The nineteenth century not surprisingly featured various other firsts as well. The end of the century saw the formation of both the Montréal Royals and the Toronto Maple Leafs, two of Canada's most enduring and best-known franchises. And during the 1870s the rivalry between London and Guelph, driven by the civic boosterism of businessmen Jake Englehart of London and George Sleeman of Guelph, led to the increased use of imported professional players, reflecting a similar trend that had developed earlier south of the border. Oil baron Englehart left the greater legacy of the two outside of baseball, but it could be argued that brewer Sleeman is the single most important figure in Canadian baseball history.

Of course, there were numerous other colorful and influential characters involved with baseball in Canada in the nineteenth century. The aforementioned Bob Addy was the first star player developed in Canada, playing at various times with such luminaries as Al Spalding, Cap Anson, and Ross Barnes, but he oddly disavowed any link to his native Canada, claiming instead a birthplace of Rochester, New York. Al Spink left Quebec City to pursue a journalism career in the United States, eventually founding "The Bible of Baseball," *The Sporting News*, and later producing one of the earliest attempts at a comprehensive history of baseball, *The National Game*, in 1910. And William Galloway was a hockey and baseball star growing up in Dunnville, Ontario, at the mouth of the Grand River. When he played third base for the Woodstock Bains of the Class-D Canadian League in 1899, he became the first Black Canadian to play in Organized Baseball, and the last Black man to play in what was recognized as Organized Baseball until Jackie Robinson in Montréal in 1946. (Black baseball assumed a greater importance in Canada in the twentieth century, and is treated in greater detail in Part II.)

THE BEACHVILLE GAME

By Andrew North

Baseball in Canada has a deeply rooted history. We know of "a game of base ball" in Saint John, New Brunswick, in 1793,[1] as well as baseball-related games in the 1830s and 1840s in such diverse areas as Victoria, Manitoba's Red River Settlement, southwestern Ontario, and Nova Scotia.[2] During these decades, and the 1850s, the game's evolution in Canada paralleled that in the United States, as more organization and structure developed, and rules of play were formalized. The first teams were formed in Hamilton, Ontario, in 1854, and in London the next year. In 1860 the first international match was played in what is now Niagara Falls, Ontario, between the Burlington club of Hamilton and the Queen City club of Buffalo.[3] And Canadian teams have been part of Organized Baseball's structure since the entry of Guelph and London into the International Association in 1877. But it was a game apparently played in a farmer's field behind a blacksmith's shop, and not described until nearly 50 years afterward, that put Canada on the baseball map. Referred to today as the Beachville game, it has been celebrated by both the Canadian postal service and the Royal Canadian Mint, yet it remains a subject of debate among historians.

BACKGROUND

Beachville is a small farming community in Zorra Township, Oxford County, in southwestern Ontario, roughly 90 miles southwest of Toronto.[4] It was on the family farm just outside Beachville that Adam Ford was born to Irish immigrant parents in 1831. After local schooling, he travelled to Cobourg, Ontario, and Victoria College, where he studied medicine, obtaining his medical accreditation in 1855.[5] A subsequent job search took him to St. Marys, a mere 25 miles northwest of his family home (and now the home of the Canadian Baseball Hall of Fame and Museum).

Seemingly comfortable with his familiar surroundings, Ford settled in St. Marys as the local physician. He adopted a healthy and active lifestyle, befitting his profession, and became an enthusiastic advocate of both curling and horse racing, as well as maintaining the passion for baseball of his youth in Zorra Township.[6] He was a man of zeal and initiative, immersing himself in community affairs and sports administration, in addition to his professional duties. His office was established in one of the downtown's finest stone buildings.[7] Personable and gregarious, he infiltrated the town's higher social circles, aided somewhat by his marriage to the daughter of one of St. Marys' most influential and respected citizens, eventually being elected mayor. He was popular and successful, in his personal life, his business, and in politics. But he had also acquired a fondness for alcohol, a weakness that led to his temporary undoing.

The doctor fell into the habit of hosting late-night drinking parties in his downtown office, earning the disapproval of both the conservative elements of the community generally and the burgeoning local temperance movement in particular. After one such evening's festivities, a young man staggered into the street in obvious distress, claiming that Dr. Ford had poisoned him. Bizarrely, the man was a vocal temperance proponent. He later died, and Ford was held on suspicion of his murder. Ford spent time in jail, but was eventually released, primarily the result of lack of apparent motive, and was never formally tried or convicted. During the course of the investigations, an association was also revealed between the married Ford and a young woman of questionable repute. It was an altogether tawdry affair, and decidedly bad for business. In 1880 Ford decamped to Denver with his sullied reputation and his sons.

SPORTING LIFE

It was from Denver, on April 26, 1886, that Adam Ford penned a letter to the editor of the popular sporting weekly *Sporting Life* in Philadelphia. The letter was printed in the edition of May 5 under the heading "Very Like Base Ball – A Game of the Long-Ago Which Closely Resembled Our Present National Game."[8] In it, Ford describes in impressive (and surprising) detail a game played in his hometown of Beachville on June 4, 1838, and witnessed by a young Ford.

Adam Ford and his wife, the former Jane Cruttenden, ca 1872. Seated center is Jane's father Lauriston Cruttenden, one of the early settlers of St. Marys. Ford's marriage into the respected and influential family provided an immediate boost to both his social standing and his political aspirations. (St. Marys Museum and R. Lorne Eedy Archives, St. Marys, Ontario)

He recalls the day as a holiday, and that a passing detachment of Scottish volunteer soldiers stopped to view the proceedings. His memories include the names of many of the participating players and the location of the field within the town. He provides a layout of the diamond, and describes the equipment used, and their materials. The basic rules under which the game was played are outlined, as are the unwritten but apparently mutually understood responsibilities of batter and pitcher. Finally, Ford compares and contrasts his 1838 game with the more modern (1886) game, not surprisingly showing preference for the former.

The letter is an extraordinary feat of recall, particularly when one recognizes that Ford must have been only seven years old when he witnessed the game, and that nearly 50 years had passed between the witnessing and the writing. As historian Bill Humber has suggested, Ford's account suffers not from lack of detail, but rather from the opposite: it's almost too good to be true.[9]

INVESTIGATION

Perhaps not surprisingly, the letter was viewed with some skepticism. But the possibility of such a game piqued the interest and curiosity of Bob Barney, a professor in the Department of Kinesiology at the University of Western Ontario (now Western University). As a sport historian, he adhered to the prevailing belief that when southwestern Ontario had been visited by waves of American migrants following the end of the Revolutionary War, migrants westbound in search of land and better opportunities in such areas as what are now Michigan, Illinois, Wisconsin, and Minnesota, many of these migrants settled in Upper Canada, bringing with them their pastimes and recreations. He viewed a possible game in that area at that time as further validation of the belief, and decided to investigate.

With the assistance of one of his graduate students, Nancy Bouchier, Barney visited Beachville and its local museum. There, the two pored over everything they could find: the census records, the land records, the tax records, the geographical maps from the time, the headstone evidence, military histories. Everything they uncovered provided affirmation of Ford's account. Men of those names were residents of the area, and were of an appropriate age. The purported owner of the blacksmith shop was listed, his shop was where it

was stated to be, and behind his shop, where the game was said to have been played, was an open field. Sources of Oxford County military history revealed the presence of the Third Oxford Regiment in the area in the summer of 1838,[10] likely Ford's passing spectators. Descriptions of the equipment were consistent with the homemade manufacturing methods of the time: the ball of yarn and calfskin, the club of cedar.[11] The diamond layout described by Ford bears a striking resemblance to one shown in George Moreland's *Balldom*,[12] an early attempt at a history of the game; Moreland describes his "diamond" as "A Peculiar Shaped One Used in 1842," a mere four years after the Beachville game. And with one important exception,[13] the rules as set out by Ford were consistent with those codified in 1845 by members of the Knickerbocker Base Ball Club of New York.[14]

But perhaps the most telling feature of Ford's account was the game's date, June 4. By statute of Upper Canada, June 4 was indeed a holiday, Militia Muster Day, in recognition of the birthday of King George III. The day was to be set aside for military training and parades, much consumption of food and drink, and recreational pastimes of just such a nature as a game of baseball. Canadian historical artist Charles W. Jefferys described the festivities thus:

"The fourth of June, the birthday of King George III, was the most important holiday of the year in early Upper Canada. On that day, the annual muster of the militia was held. Every able-bodied male between the ages of eighteen and sixty was enrolled, and all were expected to turn out for the occasion. For most of them this annual muster was the only opportunity they had for receiving any instruction in military exercises. It was held in the most central or the most convenient place in each district; in an open field on the outskirts of the principal village, among the stumps of a forest clearing, or at a cross roads, known generally as 'The Corners.'

... Around the Training ground gathered the girls, the wives and mothers and children and old men, admiring or critical. The drill ended with three cheers for His Majesty. The warriors dispersed themselves among the houses of their neighbors. Many sought the tavern, the bar-room did the biggest trade of the year. There was a dinner for the officers and gentry, with a long toast list: toasts to the King, to the Duke of York, Commander-in-Chief, to the Army and Navy, to the Ladies, each accompanied by an appropriate sentiment, expressed in flowery language. ... The day was made the occasion of wrestling matches, horse shoe pitching contests, or the settling of old scores by a fight, which frequently ended in a general melee with plenty of black eyes, bloody noses and sore heads, but with general satisfaction to all concerned."[15]

Bouchier and Barney published their findings in 1988 in the *Journal of Sport History*.[16] The article served (almost literally) to put Canada on the early baseball map. The Beachville game was celebrated by Canada Post in 1988 with the issuance of a stamp, and was featured on a silver coin issued by the Royal Canadian Mint in 2018 in celebration of 180 years of baseball in Canada. It was a watershed moment in Canada's baseball history.

Or was it?

CREDIBILITY ISSUES

Despite the corroborative evidence supplied by the Bouchier and Barney paper, there are aspects of Adam Ford's account that invite skepticism. In fact, the credibility of the event as a whole has been questioned by some historians, among them some of the most respected of baseball's research community.

Researcher David Block is one who admits to needing further convincing. Block, an expert on bat and ball games, and baseball's origins in particular, discusses the Beachville game in his book *Baseball Before We Knew It*.[17] He finds Ford's memory "prodigious," particularly for a seven-year-old remembering 48 years after the fact. He would prefer a secondary reference, another account of the game from an independent source, before accepting its legitimacy: "The absence of direct corroboration that the game ever happened is probably the biggest reason for my doubts, but I don't dismiss the possibility that Ford could have remembered witnessing some sort of baseball-like contest at Beachville as a child. However, I still maintain that, unless he was an extraordinary savant, it is virtually impossible for a chronic drinker to remember with uncanny specificity the rules, the precise dimensions, and the exact names of the participants of an event he witnessed 48 years earlier when he was but seven years of age."[18]

Major League Baseball's official historian, John Thorn, is somewhat more blunt in his assessment. In a documentary film, *No Joy in Beachville*, produced for the Canadian television network Sportsnet in 2015, Thorn likened the Ford tale to the Doubleday myth, terming it "all baloney."[19] He states: "My principal objection to Ford's report is that it appeared in print nearly 50 years after the fact. In 1838 he would have been seven years old. The Beachville story, a game said to have been played in 1838 (with no contemporaneous reference) but recollected by Dr. Adam Ford almost 50 years later, may be filed with Abner Graves' recollections of Abner Doubleday inventing the game ... when Graves was five and Doubleday 19 or 20."[20]

It should be noted as well that some Canadian sources have done the game's credibility no service by overstating its significance. Misguided attempts at nationalistic one-upmanship have prompted the use of such phrases as "the first game ever played," "pre-dates Abner Doubleday at Cooperstown," and "pre-dates the first game played by the Knickerbocker Club, baseball's first club." Space does not permit discussion of the many flaws in these descriptions; suffice to say that statements that are demonstrably false do more harm than good.[21]

There are undoubtedly problems with Ford's account, the most obvious the suspicious clarity of the recollection. It's one thing to recall the names of some of the participants; after all, these families would have been among Ford's neighbors when he was a child. It's quite another to remember with exactitude such details as the distances between bases, distances that were likely not measured precisely to begin with. There are also identifiable errors. Although the game he claimed to have witnessed involved plugging (the practice of retiring a baserunner by hitting him with a thrown ball), and was therefore not the New York game, he does admit to having participated in a game played with that game's harder ball upon his return home from his university studies. Since he obtained his medical degree in 1855, this would have been shortly thereafter. But the first game known to have been played in Canada under the New York rules does not appear until May of 1859.[22] No matter their cause, the flaws in the 1886 account indicate that perhaps it is not quite so "too good to be true" as was first thought.

The delay between the 1838 witnessing of the game and the 1886 publication of its description seems less problematic. By 1886 Adam Ford was 55 years old. Memories, particularly fond ones, often prompt people of that age to share them in some way. Of greater import is a comparison with the writings of William Wheaton. Wheaton's unsigned history, entitled "How Baseball Began – A Member of the Gotham Club of Fifty Years Ago Tells About It," was published in the *San Francisco Examiner* on November 27, 1887.[23] In it, Wheaton describes the game as it was being played on the common areas of New York in the 1830s, and the founding of the Gotham Baseball Club (which he claimed to be the first) in 1837. It is noteworthy that Wheaton's memories, published 50 years after the fact, have not been questioned on that issue as have been Ford's.

As to a secondary source for the Beachville game, a smoking gun, it is unlikely that one will ever be found, and unreasonable to expect one will be. Why would a newspaper, for example, commit any of its presumably limited resources to the coverage of an event of so little importance as an informal bat and ball game played as part of holiday celebrations? Particularly if that event was considered in no way out of the ordinary? Nonetheless, there have in recent years been uncovered some documents providing additional support to the credibility of the Ford tale.

Two of the families mentioned in the *Sporting Life* account are Williams and Dolson. Author and historian Brian Dawe, in a post to MLB historian John Thorn's *Our Game* blog, notes that both of these families are part of an extended family named Burdick.[24] (Enoch Burdick was the owner of the pasture in which Ford's game was said to have been played.)[25] The Burdick family emigrated to the Beachville area in the late 1790s from Lanesborough, Massachusetts, the neighboring town to Pittsfield in Berkshire County. This is the same Pittsfield that enacted a 1791 bylaw prohibiting baseball play for fear of broken windows. The Burdicks and a number of other Berkshire families had accompanied Major Thomas Ingersoll (after whom the present-day town nearby is named) as Ingersoll set about assigning land to families for settlement. The movement of the families, and their accompanying social customs and traditions, provide a means by which baseball play became a part of recreational life in the Beachville area.[26]

Of more direct relevance to Dr. Ford's account is the discovery by Canadian historian Bill Humber of a game played in Hamilton, Ontario (then Upper Canada), in 1819. The game was first mentioned in the *Hamilton Times* in 1874, but reproduced in the *Woodstock Sentinel* later that year.[27] The full text of the *Sentinel*'s report is shown on the following page.

"Training Day" in 1819.

GEO. III'S BIRTHDAY AND ITS CELEBRATION.

An old resident of Hamilton furnishes the *Times* with a sketch of the 4th of June, "in Olden times when George the Third was King." He writes from memory and thought; his account is brief; it is none the less interesting, especially after the celebration of our own more modern and National Day, July 1st. He says :—

The 4th day of June, in the earlier days of Hamilton was decidedly the most lively of the whole year. On this day the general training (as it was called) of the "Men of Gore" took place. All the men liable to militia duty in this locality had to "fall in" in the morning and answer to their names and perform such Company drill, &c., as the officers might see fit to command or were able to give instruction in. The perliminary Company drill invariably consisted of the men of each Company clustering round the Captain, while he called over his list of names. The word "march" was then given, and a halt made in front of a store, when a pailful or more of "blackstrap" was compounded and passed around until all were satisfied. This delectable drink was made by mixing rye whiskey and West India molasses, and was altogether a most deceiving beverage. After all had partaken to their heart's content (and there were no laggards in this regard in those days), the real warlike aspect of the day came to the front. All disputes and quarrels during the past year were then settled by personal encounters. It has come to be understood that there was "no law on the 4th of June," and it seemed to be a fact, as no interference was ever attempted in the numerous pitched battles which took place all over the village on "training day." The old style of base ball, jumping and horse racing were also indulged in, and altogether a most jolly time was made of King George III.'s Birthday, for such it was.

Woodstock Sentinel, July 10, 1874

The report records a Hamilton old-timer's memories of what he refers to as Training Day, an alternate name for Militia Muster Day, in 1819. The old-timer describes the requisite military training in the morning, after which the fun began: fisticuffs and general belligerence, fueled by great quantities of potent drink. The "most jolly time" included as well the pursuit of various recreations, one of which was "the old style of base ball." Note especially the date of the festivities: June 4 again, King George III's birthday. Here is a record of another game of baseball of some form, again on the fourth of June, played 19 years before the Beachville game described by Dr. Ford. This report cannot be an attempt to verify, or substantiate, Ford's account, as it was published in 1874, 12 years before the *Sporting Life* letter of 1886. It represents what is likely the strongest corroborative support discovered to date.

It is true that none of the evidence provided above constitutes definitive proof that the game happened. However, the recent discoveries, particularly the recurrence of the June 4 date known to have historical significance in Upper Canada, provide support for those aspects of Adam Ford's letter already confirmed by the research of Bouchier and Barney. That a game of the type described should have been played in the Beachville area in 1838, and in Hamilton in 1819, fits nicely with the concept of the spread of migration following the Revolutionary War. Rather than being nurtured in Brooklyn and Philadelphia, and then exported to Canada as a finished product, we know that baseball evolved north of the border as it did south. If indeed those emigrating from the American Northeast to southwestern Ontario following the upheaval of the war, bringing with them the game's rudimentary aspects and fundamental tenets, were responsible for sowing baseball's seeds in the area, then the Beachville game could be considered the most substantial manifestation of early growth.

NOTES

1   *The Volunteer Review and Military and Naval Gazette*, Vol. III No. 7, February 15, 1869. The 1790s seem to have been fertile ground for baseball references. It was in 1791 in Pittsfield, Massachusetts, that an ordinance was passed prohibiting baseball play. See John Thorn, *Baseball in the Garden of Eden* (New York: Simon & Schuster, 2011), 23. And it was in 1798 in Hampshire, England, that Jane Austen wrote of cricket and base ball in *Northanger Abbey* (again see Thorn, 23).

2   William Humber, *Diamonds of the North* (Don Mills, Ontario: Oxford University Press, 1995), chapter 2.

3   *Buffalo Morning Express*, August 18, 1860.

4   Beachville is also only about five miles from both Ingersoll and Woodstock, two other sites of significant early baseball activity.

5   For more details on Ford's youth, his time in St. Marys, and the unfortunate events leading to his departure, see Brian Martin, *Baseball's Creation Myth* (Jefferson, North Carolina: McFarland & Co., 2013), chapter 4.

6   The *London Free Press* of August 13, 1869, describes a game between the visiting Tecumseh Club of London and the Young Atlantic Baseball Club of St. Marys. The box score shows the St. Marys center fielder as "Dr. Ford," who would have been approaching his 38th birthday at the time.

7   Ford's home, and the building that housed his business, still stand in St. Marys today.

8   For the complete text of Ford's letter, see Nancy B. Bouchier and Robert Knight Barney, "A Critical Examination of a Source of Early Ontario Baseball: The Reminiscence of Adam E. Ford," *Journal of Sport History* Vol. 15 No. 1, Spring 1988, 88-90, or Martin, *Baseball's Creation Myth*, Appendix C.

9   Humber, 18.

10 Bouchier and Barney: 80.

11 Humber, 17.

12 See Bouchier and Barney: 82, and George L. Moreland, *Balldom* (New York: The Balldom Publishing Co., 1914), 10.

13 Ford's rules include the use of plugging, or soaking, by which the baserunner could be retired by being hit by a thrown ball between bases. A feature of the early Massachusetts game, plugging was not part of the New York game played by the Knickerbockers and other early New York clubs.

14 Bouchier and Barney: 84.

15 Charles W. Jefferys, *Training Day.* https://www.cwjefferys.ca/training-day, accessed December 22, 2020.

16 Bouchier and Barney: 75-90.

17 David Block, *Baseball Before We Knew It* (Lincoln: University of Nebraska Press, 2005), 62-66.

18 Block, email correspondence with author, December 23, 2020.

19 https://www.sportsnet.ca/baseball/mlb/theres-no-joy-in-beachville-the-true-story-of-baseballs-origin-2/, accessed December 23, 2020.

20 Thorn, email correspondence with author, December 23, 2020.

21 There is no first baseball game: Baseball evolved, it wasn't born. Abner Doubleday was nowhere near Cooperstown in 1839, and had no involvement with baseball. And the Knickerbocker Baseball Club was not only not the first baseball club, it was not even the first baseball club in New York. For a good discussion of these and other misconceptions, see Thomas W. Gilbert, *How Baseball Happened* (Boston: David R. Godine, 2020), chapter 1.

22 *New York Clipper*, June 11, 1859.

23 https://ourgame.mlblogs.com/how-baseball-began-william-r-wheaton-tells-his-story-4b278edc172, accessed December 29, 2020.

24 https://ourgame.mlblogs.com/pittsfield-1791-and-beachville-1838-6b07d3f20497, accessed December 30, 2020.

25 Bouchier and Barney: 81.

26 As well, it fits nicely with Bob Barney's general theory of baseball migration northward and westward in the years following the Revolutionary War.

27 *Woodstock Sentinel*, July 10, 1874.

WILLIAM SHUTTLEWORTH: A MAN FOR HIS SEASONS

By William Humber

After quietly resting in the backroom of Canadian sports history for over a century, William Shuttleworth is now fully recognized for his role in establishing the country's first formal team, the Young Canadians (later Maple Leafs), in 1854. He had a distinguished playing career and organizational role beyond Hamilton, and contributed to the game's growth from umpiring to its promotion. He was inducted into the Canadian Sports Hall of Fame in 2015, and the next year into Canada's Baseball Hall of Fame and his local Hamilton sports hall.

William Shuttleworth was born in Brantford, Ontario (when the province was known as Upper Canada), in 1834. He lived most of his teenage and adult years in Hamilton, Ontario (when the province was known as Canada West before becoming Ontario following the country's July 1, 1867, Confederation), and spent his final years with a son in Geneva, New York, where he died in 1903. He was buried with his wife, Matilda, in a Hamilton cemetery, and then was almost forgotten. Shuttleworth, however, was more than an accomplished ballplayer in the game's primeval past. He was president of the Maple Leafs (after they changed their name from the Young Canadians) for over a decade. He assumed vice president and president

roles with the fledgling and original Canadian Base Ball Association in 1864 (when the game was still spelled with two words), as well as umpiring one of the most significant games of his era. He represents the overlooked independent identity of those playing baseball in Ontario in its formative years, almost exclusively Canadian- or British-born, and with negligible American input and content.

Baseball's formative stages had deep roots in the Hamilton area. The *Hamilton Times* newspaper in 1874 had described an old-timer's memory of locals playing the old-style game on the June 4 Militia Muster Day in 1819 in Hamilton.[1] The old-style game was best characterized by the use of a softer ball thrown at a runner between bases. If the ball connected, the runner was out. It was a practice called soaking or plugging. Alongside the contentious (well, only to some American baseball historians) June 4 game in Beachville almost 20 years later, these games are among the earliest examples we have of human agency driving the regular playing of baseball at an appointed time. No longer would they be part of an obligation to an old-world folk custom with diminishing but still significant roots in what had once been an exclusively religious-ordained or primitive cultural celebration. The Canadian June 4 games were an essential proto-modern innovation predating even American steps to leave behind a game embedded in this folk culture.

Given these circumstances, we can be fairly confident William Shuttleworth played some version of baseball as a child growing up in nearby Brantford. Brantford is only 25 miles west of Hamilton, admittedly a considerable distance in pre-railway Ontario, but a necessary journey for settlers, traveling salespeople, and emerging civic leaders.

There are, as yet, no reports contemporary to the time of the Hamilton Young Canadians' formation in 1854,[2] but near-in-time records exist to confirm the year and Shuttleworth's role. *Thomas Hutchinson's 1862-63 Directory for Hamilton*[3] stated that the Maple Leaf Base Ball Club (formerly Young Canadian) was organized in April 1854, and that its current officers (for 1862) included Wm. Shuttleworth, President; Chas. Waugh, Vice President; David Davies, Secretary; Thomas Carroll, Treasurer. They played on the grounds facing Central School, between Bond and Bowery Streets. The Burlington Base Ball Club was organized a year later. Its 1862 officers were J.C. Davis, President; P.W. Dayfoot, Vice President; J.J. Mason, Secretary; and George Black, Treasurer. They played on the grounds on Upper James Street at the corner of Robinson.

The second reference to the organization of Hamilton baseball was found in the *Hamilton Spectator's* report of December 4, 1865, regarding the Maple Leaf Base Ball Club Dinner. It said:

"Last evening the members of the Maple Leaf Base Ball club held their first Annual Dinner in their room on John Street, the President Mr. W. Shuttleworth, occupying the Chair and Mr. Thos. Carroll the Vice-Chair. About 30 persons sat down to the spread, which was provided by T. Young, saloonkeeper and was got up in the best style. The usual toasts of the Queen, the Royal Family, the Governor General, the press,

etc. were drunk with all the honors, and songs appropriate to these were sung by several members of the Club. The toast "Prosperity to the Maple Leaf Base Ball Club" having been proposed, the President replied in suitable terms, giving a short sketch of the Club, its organization in 1854, since which time it has been steadily increasing up to the present time. Toasts and speech making was kept up till a late hour, all apparently enjoying themselves."

A report on the same gathering in the *Hamilton Times* of December 2, 1865, said the team was "virtually the parent of all other organizations of the kind in Western Canada as it most assuredly is the first in the science of the game." It was then announced that the club was moving from its

William Shuttleworth and Harry Sweetman of the Maple Leaf Baseball Club of Hamilton, 1860. (*Toronto Globe*, August 15, 1903)

"old grounds upon Main Street" to new playing grounds on [Upper] James Street. In conclusion, the revelers in attendance declared, "For their efficiency in the game, and the general prosperity of the Maple Leaf, much is due to the President, Mr. William Shuttleworth. He has always manifested a deep interest in the same, and his encouragement of such manly recreations reflects creditably upon the character of the gentleman." They concluded with a rendition honoring a "jolly good fellow."

Finally, the *Hamilton Times* report of the Maple Leaf Base Ball Club's annual supper in its February 23, 1867, edition said that Mr. Wm. Shuttleworth, the President, was proud to boast that the Maple Leaf was the father of all Canadian Ball Clubs, that he himself was the paternal head of the Maple Leaf, and finally that it had organized 14 years earlier under the name of the Young Canadian Club.[4] The name change to Maple Leaf had occurred in the early 1860s.

The first, contemporary to its time, news coverage of baseball in Hamilton did not occur until 1858, when the team's executive, but one not including William Shuttleworth, was listed. His exclusion can be ascribed to his desire to play the game rather than manage its off-field needs. A very primitive box score in the same year speaks only of teams from Hamilton's East and West ends playing what might be a five-inning game, or maybe a game featuring five-a-side.[5] We do not know, and will likely never know. One thing we can be certain of is that they were playing the Canadian old-style plugging game, since this is what William's younger brother James, a shoemaker, introduced into Woodstock[6] when he moved there after a downturn in Hamilton's economy in the late 1850s.[7] Notably, an 1860 description of this old-style game in the *Ingersoll Chronicle*[8] also mentions its five-inning character, contrasting it with a two-inning version as played in London in 1856,[9] suggesting that even in Ontario variations of the game were played.

In 1859, two teams of tobacconists[10] from Hamilton and Toronto played the first game in this part of the world featuring the New York rules, and a year later Shuttleworth and Hamilton's two teams, the Young Canadians and the Burlingtons, met teams from Buffalo in the first international games played under those rules. Shuttleworth's team was preceded to the honor of being first by a few weeks, but the fate of both Canadian teams was the same.[11] They lost, perhaps a consequence of their recent adoption of the New York rules game with its harder ball, and the Canadians' unfamiliarity with this game's speed and physical challenges.

A critic of this independent Canadian role in the game's proto-modern and eventual modernization might cite this adoption of the New York rules game as proof of the Canadian subservience to American leadership, but in fact it proves the opposite. Baseball's folk and proto-modern popularity dated to times long before the New York rules came into vogue in a variety of regional variations throughout North America, including southern Ontario. The adoption by these places of the New York rules game ensured that it would flourish elsewhere rather than remain a locally distinct recreation for its geographically close enthusiasts such as, but not limited locally to, the Knickerbocker Club. These regional variations, though generally favoring the "soaking" version of the game, opted for the New York rules game because it was considered a better game. The ball could be hit farther, the game required a higher level of skill, it was more dangerous and therefore more entertaining, and, perhaps most significantly, its adoption allowed baseball to rival cricket as a more scientific and adult game.

At all stages throughout the 1860s, with the exception of a brief period in 1861 when the Young Canadians changed their name to the Maple Leafs, William Shuttleworth was president of the team.[12] No reason was given for the name change, though perhaps it was to avoid confusion with his brother James's namesake Young Canadians in Woodstock. It may also have provided an excuse for some of the players from the rival Burlingtons to join a more neutrally named team. In return, the Maple Leafs, as noted above, eventually adopted the Burlington grounds on Upper James Street near the "Mountain," forsaking the Young Canadians' first home near the city's Central School. Whatever laurels the Hamilton Maple Leafs had earned as Ontario's leading team, however, were not long lasting, as by the end of 1861 Woodstock reigned supreme, having defeated the Maple Leafs by two runs in their first encounter.[13] Never again would the Hamilton team come this close to defeating their southwestern Ontario rival.

One particularly notable aspect of its evolution further confirms the identity of baseball in Canada as a game developed alongside, rather than in subservience to, Americans during these formative years of transition from a proto-modern form to a fully modern game in the 20-year period from 1854 through 1873. That is a virtual absence of American participation and influence. William Shuttleworth is simply the best example of how this first generation of recognized Canadian baseball players were exclusively either Canadian- or British-born. While a few ballplayers had unclear birthplaces in either the British province of Canada, the United States, or Britain, with but one exception they were almost certainly raised from childhood in the British province of Canada before it became a formal nation in 1867.[14]

In the interest of full disclosure, the significant exception was an American immigrant and ballplayer, Charles L. Wood. Wood's role was important, persuading Woodstock to switch to the New York rules in 1861. By that time, however, Hamilton and Toronto had already adopted them. Wood was not even an apostle from New York City, but came from central New York state, where he might have been initially exposed to the New York rules at the same time as Toronto and

Hamilton players were experimenting with them. He came to Woodstock not as a baseball advocate but as an entrepreneur interested in running a hotel. He married into the ballplaying and tragic Douglas family[15] of Woodstock before spending his last years peripatetically moving west with his wife to the American Pacific coast. His advocacy for the New York rules game was as much about being able to play other Canadian towns, there being only limited competition with teams from south of the border until the 1870s. As well, Wood, along with Shuttleworth, would make up the first executive of the Canadian Base Ball Association in 1864;[16] Wood's presidency lasted only a few months when for unknown reasons he vacated the post in favor of Shuttleworth.

In 1862 William Shuttleworth married Matilda White of Hamilton, whom he likely met at a church bazaar. They raised five children, as William first depended on a clerking job with a dry-goods firm. Later he briefly ran his own retail operation, in which he promoted and sold tickets for games with visiting teams, most notably Bob Addy's famous Rockford (Illinois) squad in 1870. Eventually, however, he returned to employment under others. He thus lacked the personal wealth and the social position enjoyed by at least some of his teammates. Although an injury could have seriously jeopardized his ability to care for his young family, he nevertheless played the dangerous position of catcher throughout much of the 1860s. His limited protection was a piece of leather clenched between his teeth, and perhaps a small hand protector more like a thin glove than the trapper's mitts of today. Despite a continuing absence of financial security, he traveled to nearby Canadian towns and cities to play and later umpire the game. He went to Detroit with the Maple Leaf team in 1867 for what was ambitiously called a World Base Ball Tournament. In the premier level of the competition the team captured a gold ball in recognition of its third-place finish.[17] The prize remained in the family until at least the 1940s, in the possession of Shuttleworth's youngest son Harry. Its fate thereafter is unknown.

Shuttleworth's bravery and sense of civic duty were never better demonstrated than when he volunteered for the 13th Battalion in Hamilton in 1866, when Fenian raids from south of the border, aimed at freeing Ireland from Britain's control, threatened to bring the British province into conflict with a potentially larger American invasion force, fresh from its Civil War experience. One account says that a Private Shuttleworth was nearly killed by a bullet deflecting off his rifle.[18] We cannot be certain it was William, but his early volunteering and later status as the 13th Battalion's color sergeant argue forcibly for it being him.

In 1868 Shuttleworth umpired the raucous Canadian championship game between Guelph and Woodstock in the latter town before thousands of spectators, many of whom had come from Guelph by the early afternoon train. The game degenerated into chaos and brawling in the stands. Both sides applauded Shuttleworth's neutral oversight as Woodstock retained its Canadian championship and the silver ball trophy.[19]

A year later brother James died suddenly at the age of 29. He had rejoined William's Hamilton team in 1862. The papers sadly described the funeral procession for James, led by his Maple Leafs teammates, but gave no mention of what had brought about his premature end. A possible cause, however, might be found in a brief comment in a Bowmanville newspaper several days later.[20] Bowmanville is about as far east of Toronto as Hamilton is west, and the towns often met in friendly baseball competition. Without naming anyone, the newspaper article described a Dundas-based shoemaker who had killed himself, unhappy with his home life, and whose business was doing poorly. The profession fits that

of James Shuttleworth, and Dundas is a nearby urban adjunct to Hamilton. Imagining that another Hamilton-area shoemaker died under similar circumstances in the same week as James's untimely and unexplained end seems improbable. A verdict of suicide would be a strong reason for such a paucity of details in local papers, and why silence followed.

William, nearing 40, had disappeared from the team's executive by 1872, ironically, or perhaps not so, the same year Guelph began the process of bringing imported professionals into the country, in this case the former Boston Red Stockings player Sam Jackson. A few years later, however, William played in what is almost certainly the first-ever "Old Timer's Game" in Canada, an event that was caricatured in the *Canadian Illustrated News*.[21] He then departed the active baseball scene, perhaps because he was needed at home. In 1884 Matilda died, having been ill for some time from what was described as a brain disease. The widower William now relied increasingly on his grown-up children. His oldest son looked after the family's younger siblings. William moved to Geneva, New York, with a son James in the 1890s, undertaking an artisan role as an upholsterer before dying there in 1903.

It is possible we would still have little or no awareness of William Shuttleworth but for Dr. Bryan D. Palmer's book *A Culture in Conflict: Skilled Workers and Industrial Capitalism in Hamilton, Ontario*.[22] The book is a serious piece of academic research and analysis having little to do with baseball except for the story of the skilled workers who played the game in this nineteenth-century Canadian city. The Shuttleworth brothers were central to his account. For baseball's historians, it was an important example of why one's research should never be restricted to obvious sports-related materials.

NOTES

1   At first appearing in the *Hamilton Times*, but not available today. A short essay, "Training Day 1819: George III's Birthday and Its Celebration," was first discovered in an 1895 brochure entitled, *Souvenir book and programme for military encampment given by the Ladies' Committee of the Wentworth Historical Society*, edited and compiled by M.J. Nisbet, assisted by F.L. Davis (Hamilton: Griffin & Kidner, 1895), 44-45. Being so long after the events of 1819, there was concern for its reliability. Its later discovery in the *Woodstock Sentinel* (July 10, 1874), after being reprinted that year (1874) from the *Hamilton Times*, has put those concerns to rest, particularly because it appeared 12 years before Adam Ford's 1886 Beachville remembrance of baseball play, also on a June 4 occasion.

2   The pages of the *Hamilton Gazette* reviewed from 1854 and 1855 make no mention of baseball, but given that the game was new and the club as formed was likely only for intrasquad purposes, the lack of reporting either directly or incidentally is not surprising.

3   *Thomas Hutchinson's 1862-63 Directory* (Hamilton, C.W. [Ont.]: John Eastwood & Co., 1862), 224.

4   While 14 years does not line up neatly with 1854, the team may have been formed during the winter of 1853-54, and he simply subtracted 1853 from 1867. Or he could have included the year 1867 in his calculation, or simply been mistaken by a year. The year of 1854 is most plausible, however, given the other evidence.

5   *Hamilton Spectator*, August 14, 1858, with the barest of details, citing only East and West end clubs and what appears to have been a five-inning match, though it might also have been a five-a-side match lasting only one inning.

6   The source for this is a 1915 reminiscence by J. Henry Brown in the *Woodstock Sentinel Review* of April 12, 1915. "James Shuttleworth of Maple Leaf of Hamilton club came to work in Woodstock as a shoe maker [presumably in 1860 since he was in the games played that year against Ingersoll] and helped organize the team on a lot on Reeve St. back of the Post Office. Later a man named Wood [Charles L.] came to Woodstock and the old style game was given up and the regular American game adopted." The small problem with this chronology is that the Maple Leaf moniker would not be associated with Hamilton's team until 1861, but this may be due to a later confusion as to the timing of the club's naming. James's residence however is not in doubt. He appears in the 1861 census in Woodstock, though the name is misspelled as Suttleworth. One more frustration for later researchers!

7   "Then came the crisis of 1859, and with it financial disaster to Hamilton." In Herbert Lister, *Hamilton History, Commerce, Industries, Resources issued under the auspices of the City Council* (Hamilton: Spectator Printing Company, 1913), 25.

8   *The Chronicle* (Ingersoll), July 27, 1860: "Each side had five innings, the Young Canadians [Woodstock] taking the first. The total amount scored by the Young Canadians was 83; and the total score of the Rough and Readys [Ingersoll] 59 – the Young Canadians winning by 24."

9   *New York Clipper*, September 27, 1856 featured the box score for a game between the London base ball club and one from a nearby "suburban" adjunct, Delaware.

10   W.C.F. Caverhill, *Caverhill's Toronto City Directory for 1859-60* (Toronto: W.C.F. Caverhill, 1859); *Thomas Hutchinson's 1862-63 Directory* (Hamilton, C.W. [Ont.]: John Eastwood & Co., 1862).

11   On August 18, 1860 the Burlingtons of Hamilton lost to the Queen Citys of Buffalo 30-25 in what historian Joseph Overfield (*Niagara Frontier* magazine, Summer 1964: 59-60) described as the first ever international baseball match. It was played in Clifton, what is now Niagara Falls, Canada. In late August 1860, the Young Canadian Club of Hamilton were humbled in their first cross-border match with the Niagara Club of Buffalo, 87-13, and though the account is somewhat unclear, it appears the Hamilton team may have played with the additional men common to the "Canadian" game, while Niagara played by the New York rules. At a return match in Buffalo, the Young Canadians lost by a more respectable 45-13 score (Overfield).

12   *New York Clipper*, April 14, 1860. For the first time on the public record, William Shuttleworth is listed as president of the then Young Canadian Base Ball Club of Hamilton, C.W. (C.W. is Canada West, Ontario's name before the July 1, 1867, Confederation.) As late as 1870 (*New York Clipper*, May 7, 1870) it was reported that W. Shuttleworth had been reelected president of the (long since renamed) Hamilton Maple Leafs.

13   The Shuttleworth brothers confronted each other on the diamond on Tuesday, September 3, 1861, in Hamilton as the Young Canadians of Woodstock scored three in the top of the ninth to outlast the Maple Leaf of Hamilton, 24-22. As reported in the *New York Clipper*, September 21, 1861.

14   I reviewed, through Ancestry.com, players making up the lineups and administration of leading Canadian (really Ontario-based) teams in the 1854 through 1873 period. They included London Club and Delaware Club (1856), Hamilton Young Canadians (later Maple Leafs), Hamilton Burlingtons, Woodstock Young Canadians (old-style and New York game rules), Ingersoll Rough and Ready, Ingersoll Victorias, Dundas Independents, Guelph Maple Leafs, London Athletics and Tecumsehs, Kingston St. Lawrence, Bowmanville Victoria and Royal Oaks, Newcastle Beavers, Port Hope Silver Stars, Cobourg Travellers, Ottawa Mutuals, and early Toronto teams such as the Young Canadians and Dauntless. With one significant exception (Woodstock's Charles

Wood), these teams, both players and off-field leadership, consisted of those born in Canada or Great Britain, or having arrived at such a young age from the United States as to be considered essentially Canadian. They all learned the game in Canada. Even Bob Addy fit this mold. The 1854-1873 years were the beginning of baseball's regular media coverage, and the tail end of proto-modern experiments from which regularity and modernism emerged. What does this mean? From a reverse historical engineering process, based on Canadian independence of play and operation between 1854 and 1873, a Canadian claim to be co-evolving North American participants in the game's creative process is valid. If driven by American leadership in the proto-modern phase, we would not have expected to see that engagement so abruptly disappear in the 1854 to 1873 period. Recordings of the proto-modern era in Canada, though limited, show that the makeup of its baseball proponents generally matches the profile of those playing or organizing between 1854 and 1873. Finally, the remnants of the proto-modern period after 1854 consist largely of distinct but fading local interpretations of baseball. In one Canadian case it was even labeled as such. The roots of proto-modern games were in folk baseball play from England and Europe. Each region in North America experimented with variations on this play, from which the New York version ultimately succeeded. The arrival of itinerant American professionals in Canada only began in 1872 but was a significant minority until 1875. Canadian integration in a majority American baseball enterprise (the International Association) did not occur until 1877. Until then Canadians, except for adopting the New York game like everyone else, were creative masters in their own, and the larger, baseball domain.

15   Robert Douglas, the ballplaying and younger brother of Charles Wood's wife Joanna, was a Woodstock saddler and harness maker who died in early 1872, possibly as a result of complications arising from a baseball accident in 1870 (*London Free Press*, July 9, 1870). He crashed into a teammate and was concussed, and may have suffered other physical injury. He played for the Young Canadians throughout the 1860s and early '70s. His young widow, Sarah Jane, was just 25 and they had three young sons. The daughter of prominent local auctioneer and bailiff Samuel Burgess, she married Robert

when she was 17. Her older brother Marenus was in the lineup of the Woodstock team playing the 11-a-side Canadian game in 1860. Young people meeting at the baseball diamond was obviously a custom with deep roots. Sarah remarried a year and a half after Robert's death, and had three more sons, but she herself was dead by July 1878. She was buried under the Douglas name in Innerkip, northeast of Woodstock. Such are the short, marginally documented, but baseball-infused lives of long ago.

16   *Hamilton Evening Times*, August 24, 1864.

17   "The Base Ball Tournament at Detroit," *Hamilton Evening Times*, August 10, 1867.

18   John Alexander MacDonald, *Troublous Times in Canada: A History of the Fenian Raids of 1866 and 1870* (Toronto: W.S. Johnston and Co., 1910), 57. "Private Shuttleworth, of the 13th, had a narrow and extraordinary escape. While he was in the act of firing, the muzzle of his rifle was shot into by a Fenian musket ball and torn open."

19   Recalling the events of that season many years later (*Toronto Evening Telegram*, September 27, 1923), Guelph ballplayer William Sunley described for reporter C.O. Knowles the second of the two games in which Guelph and Woodstock met that year. Guelph, he said, lost 38-28 [actually 36-28]. He then described the unusual circumstances: "... the game was lost owing to the absence of Mr. Nichols, the catcher on account of family affliction." The box score of the game, noting Alfred Feast's role as Guelph scorer and William Shuttleworth's acclaimed duty as umpire, makes it clear, however, that James Nichols did play in the second game.

20   "A Shoemaker, Doing a Small Business in Dundas, Committed Suicide Because of Dull Trade and a Bad Wife," (*Canadian Statesman*, September 2, 1869).

21   The peculiar *Canadian Illustrated News* drawing (September 11, 1875) of the Hamilton old-timers game was probably the last game in which William Shuttleworth, then 41, played.

22   Bryan D. Palmer, *A Culture in Conflict: Skilled Workers and Industrial Capitalism in Hamilton, Ontario* (Montréal: McGill-Queen's University Press, 1979).

THE FIRST EVER INTERNATIONAL "BASE BALL" GAME

By William Humber

In a Niagara Frontier journal essay (Summer 1964), noted Buffalo historian Joseph Overfield described the first-ever international baseball match as being played between the Burlingtons of Hamilton C.W. (Canada West, or today's Ontario), and the Queen Citys of Buffalo, New York, on August 17, 1860. The Queen Citys were victorious 30-25 in a place called Clifton, as described in the Buffalo Morning Express. For many years, however, the location of Clifton remained uncertain.[1]

Historians in the Society for American Baseball Research initially wrestled with Clifton's location. A detailed survey of early games in upper New York state released in 2008 by Craig Waff described the place as Clifton, NY (for New York). Version 11 of SABR's full Protoball Chronology loaded in April 2010 in its working chronology for *Ballplaying in Canada* was more circumspect, noting, "Clifton NY is not a location found near Buffalo. Perhaps it was the former name of a section of the city. An area called Clifton Heights is on Lake Erie SW of Buffalo." Neither was definitive, however. Uncertainty surrounded the location until Canadian researchers looked within their own country and noted that until the 1880s Niagara Falls, Canada, went by the name of Clifton, a description still current today in the city's tourist enclave of Clifton Hill.[2]

The location should not have been hard to uncover. There had been several reports in the *New York Clipper* newspaper[3] the year before of cricket matches played by Clifton, C.W. One was against their nearby Canadian neighbor, Thorold, but more significantly, the *Clipper*, under the headline, CLIFTON VS ST. GEORGE, wrote, "… Clifton, C.W. defeated the latter of Buffalo, N.Y. in a match played at Clifton, on the 25th [July] … by three wickets."

Just as Canadians would later be surprised to discover that the first international game of their favorite sport, hockey, had been played in Burlington, Vermont,[4] so might the possibility of a non-American location for the first international game of their national game, baseball, have been a surprise to US-based researchers. Our deeply held belief systems do at times throw us a curve!

We must give some pause to this conversation, however, by clarifying our terms. While baseball's ultimately successful New York form barred the practice of soaking,[5] any game (whether a variation of the soaking game, or possibly one using a gradually harder ball), would have been a first for international recognition as long as it was played between formal teams from different national jurisdictions.

Two such games apparently meeting these criteria need, therefore, to be discounted. In 1859 a visiting team of prominent English cricketers had arrived in North America to play local squads in the Northeastern United States and in what today is eastern Canada.[6] The English were so good they often allowed their Canadian and American rivals to place 22 men in defensive positions when the Englishmen batted, rather than the normal 11, and still the visitors won. Near the end of their tour, there were proposals for them to play a team of Americans at baseball, but finances proved too big a hurdle.

Instead, the English split into two teams, then filled out their lineups with available local Americans and at least one Canadian, Godfrey Phipps Baker, an Ottawa cricketer and that city's postmaster.[7] They played a game of baseball in Rochester, New York. The result was immaterial, but English newspapers borrowing their box score from *Porter's Spirit of the Times* gave the match an international designation. While the nationality of the players was multinational, the teams were not formal baseball organizations, nor were they teams representing different national entities. For what it's worth, the Canadian Godfrey Baker hit the first home run in the game, an achievement more notable had this been the first such international baseball game.

The other candidate was a match in Schenectady, New York, on May 19, 1860, between teams described, by the *Sunday Mercury* sporting paper as New York vs. Canada, and which were listed as the Mohawk Club of Schenectady and the Union Club of Upper Canada. The Upper Canada appellation had been discarded geographically by the act of union between Upper and Lower Canada in 1841. At that time Upper Canada had become known as Canada West (Quebec was Canada East), a name later replaced by Ontario in 1867 following Canada's formal recognition as

The original Home Run Baker: Ottawan Godfrey Phipps Baker and his wife Elizabeth. (Author's collection)

a national entity. No record of this team exists in Canada, and if they had come from north of the border for this one encounter they would, as was the common practice of the day, have been known by a specific place, and not by an out-of-date generic locale.

SABR researcher Robert Tholkes finally set the record straight in 2014.[8] The *Sunday Mercury* item on the game involving the "Union Club of Upper Canada" in Schenectady on May 19, 1860, was also reported in the *Schenectady Daily News* of May 22, 1860. It stated, "THE MATCH GAME OF Base Ball played Saturday afternoon between the Mohawk club of this city and the Union Club of the Junior Class of Union College, resulted in the following score: Mohawk, 31 runs." Tholkes wrote, "The article then listed the players, [but] without the box score sent to the *Sunday Mercury*. These matched the names in the [earlier] box score. Why the college club decided to pretend to be from Canada is unknown. Perhaps one or more of the players were Canadian. So we can reject any claim for this game having been an international first."

None of this is particularly surprising. Most games were played in regionally confined outposts throughout North America, and significantly this includes locations in the "British Empire's Canadian Province." While such games would have featured players born in more than one country, they were either intrasquad affairs or between clubs specific to a shared territory, and within the same nationally defined jurisdiction. None was international. Likewise, expatriates from either country may have formed local squads to play other local teams, but since these would have been immigrants now residing in a host country, such games cannot be considered international. Finally, local squads of cricketers were known to often play simple games of baseball as a warm-up for their regular cricket match. Despite the possible international makeup of players, these were not formally defined baseball teams.

Our description requires that the two competing teams qualifying for status as participants in an international game must be formal baseball teams, whose primary identity is as such, and who each, in their name and regional location, represent a definable geographic territory distinct in national recognition from the other. It is/was not necessary that such places have formal status

Report of the match played at Clifton on August 17, 1860. (*Buffalo Morning Express*, August 18, 1860)

as independent national entities, but if they were a colony of another nation, they had to be distinct from the one against which they were playing. As such, the Hamilton Burlingtons game with the Queen Citys of Buffalo meets our criteria, in much in the same way as a game between a team largely but not exclusively of New York cricketers from the St. George's Club and a Canadian team from the Toronto club and the Upper Canada College eleven qualifies as the first ever international match for that sport in 1844.[9]

NOTES

1   Joseph Overfield, *Niagara Frontier*, Summer 1964: 59-60; *Buffalo Morning Express,* August 18, 1860.

2   "In October of 1881, at the request of its residents, the former Town of Clifton [Ontario, Canada] received permission to change its name to the Town of Niagara Falls. By 1881, the population of the Town of Niagara Falls was 2,623 citizens." From https://www.niagara-fallsinfo.com/niagara-falls-history.

3   *New York Clipper*, August 13, 1859.

4   https://www.mychamplainvalley.com/news/local-news/this-place-in-history-first-international-hockey-game/; or http://hockeygods.com/blog/hockeyhistory/The_1st_International_Ice_Hockey_Game_1886.

5   Soaking was the "old-style" practice of using a softer ball that could be thrown at a runner between bases. The runner was out if hit by the ball.

6   Fred Lillywhite, *English Cricketers' Trip [1859] to Canada and the United States* (London: F. Lillywhite, 1860).

7   *The Era*, December 4, 1859: 13. As sourced online through the British Newspaper Archives, https://www.britishnewspaperarchive.co.uk/viewer/bl/0000053/18591204/034/0013.

8   Email from Robert Tholkes to William Humber, April 16, 2014.

9   John I. Marder, *The International Series: The Story of the United States v Canada at Cricket* (London: Kaye & Ward, 1968), 16-25.

GEORGE SLEEMAN AND THE GUELPH MAPLE LEAFS

By Martin Lacoste

Baseball's rise in the nineteenth century featured a storied cast of characters in a variety of locales. It is perhaps a reflection of the prototypically humble Canadian persona that the early "dynasties" north of the border were not from the larger metropolitan areas, but rather from less populous centers, notably a town (not even a city) that ranked 14th in population.[1] And among the most significant figures was not a magnate or star player, but a young local businessman who later emerged as an influential leader in southwestern Ontario business, sport, and politics.

Nestled in the heart of southwestern Ontario, the town of Guelph was founded in 1827 and so was still in its infancy when the Sleeman family arrived in 1847. Among the newcomers was 6-year-old George Sleeman, the son of brewer John H. Sleeman and Anne Burrows. John was born in Cornwall, England, in 1805, and came to Canada in 1834 with his wife and three children. The family settled in St. David's, Ontario (near Niagara Falls), and it was here that John built the Stamford Springs Brewery in 1836.[2] George arrived five years later on August 1, 1841, their first and only child born in Canada.

In 1847, in search for a source of cleaner water, a crucial ingredient in the brewing process, John moved the family a full day's ride northwest to the town of Guelph.[3] After leasing a local brewery for three years, he purchased land in 1850 on Waterloo Avenue and built the Silver Creek Brewery, which opened the following year. He built a home near the brewery in 1859, and in this same year, son George took over the day-to-day operations of the brewery at the age of 18.[4] By 1862, the brewery was renamed Sleeman and Son, and George undertook an even more prominent role in the family business.[5] John retired from the brewery in 1867, and entrusted his son as sole owner. George's involvement in the brewing trade continued throughout his life, but this did not preclude his pursuing several other passions, notably a significant interest in sport, particularly baseball.

His initial involvement in baseball may have occurred as early as 1861, as he recounted in a magazine article in 1923: "I was always a member of the [Guelph] Maple Leaf team, from the time it was formed in 1861 by A.S. Feast, who came from Hamilton."[6] He pitched for the Leafs in the early 1860s, but as the decade progressed and the team became more competitive, George transitioned from the playing field to a more managerial role.

Baseball in southwestern Ontario had been expanding greatly in the 1860s, as teams formed

R. Emery (Centre Field).   W. Smiley (Left Field).   G. Sleeman (President).   W. Jones (Short Stop).   G. Keotl (Second Base).

The 1874 Guelph Maple Leafs, George Sleeman center.
(*Harper's Weekly*, September 12, 1874)

H. Myers (First Base).   J. Smith (Right Field).   C. Maddock (Catcher).   W. Smith (Pitcher).   H. Spence (Third Base).

THE MAPLE LEAF BASE-BALL CLUB, OF GUELPH, ONTARIO, CANADA.

in Hamilton, London, Toronto, and Ingersoll, but none could unseat the Woodstock Young Canadians as Canadian Champions from 1865 to 1868. But by 1869, the Guelph Maple Leafs had established a solid core of local players, including pitcher William Sunley, veteran catcher James T. Nichols, second baseman Charlie Maddock, third baseman William "Bunty" Hewer, and 18-year-old shortstop Thomas Smith. The 1869 Championship for the Silver Ball, the trophy for the Canadian victors, was held in London in August, and pitted Guelph against the Ingersoll Victorias and the reigning champions from Woodstock. The championship game, which had to be rescheduled to September 24, resulted in

a decisive 43-20 victory by the Maple Leafs over the London Tecumsehs. Woodstock was finally unseated as Canadian Champions, and Guelph retained this new title for another six years.

With the Maple Leafs as the new baseball dynasty into the 1870s, Sleeman was intent on further raising the profile of Guelph as the baseball capital of Canada. He also formed and managed a team "composed solely of home brews,"[7] called the Silver Creeks, for whom he occasionally pitched. Games were held on an empty lot behind Slee-man's brewery, and George paid for all expenses.[8] Meanwhile, the reputation of the Maple Leafs continued to spread, as they accepted challenges from all comers from southwestern Ontario and New York state, and defeated such teams as the Dundas Independents, London Eckfords, Toronto Dauntless, Rochester Flour Cities, and Ilion Clippers.

In 1873, the "largest crowd ever assembled on the Maple Leaf ground" witnessed a game on August 22 between the Canadian champions and the "celebrated Bostons (champions of America)."[9] The Boston Red Stockings were one of the top teams in the fledgling National Association of Professional Baseball Players, led by player-manager Harry Wright. It is perhaps ironic that the Leafs at this time were captained by former Red Stocking Sam Jackson, while the Boston team featured the first Canadian major leaguer, right fielder Bob Addy. Boston, with its legendary lineup that included no fewer than four future Hall of Famers (manager Wright in center field, his brother George Wright at shortstop, pitcher Al Spalding, and first baseman Jim O'Rourke), scored a decisive victory, 27-8, despite some "remarkably fine catches"[10] by Guelph's Tommy Smith and Johnny Goldie, and solid play by catcher Charley Maddock.

On April 7, 1874, the annual meeting of the Maple Leaf Base Ball Club was held, and George Sleeman was elected president of the club; as well, "motion was given for the creating of the office of Manager of the Nine, coupled with the name of Mr. Jas. T. Nichols,"[11] a new position for which the duties "should be explained at the next meeting."[12] As president, Sleeman devised the Club Rules, and found a way to reward his players while maintaining their amateur status: Though no salary was paid, profits were divided up among the team members.[13] The Leafs ventured successfully into international territory in 1874 on two fronts. In early July, at the Watertown (New York) tournament, they defeated all comers, including the Ku Klux Klan team from Oneida, New York, to take home the $500 prize. This success was due in no small part to the inclusion of a number of imports on the roster; Sleeman had signed several

American players (second baseman George Keerl, from Baltimore; first baseman Hank Myers, of Ilion, New York; outfielder William A. Jones, aka William A. Silkworth, from New York; and third baseman Harrison Leslie Spence, also of New York). He imported more players the following year (William Bevan Lapham of Cincinnati and Johnny Foley), ensuring that the team would retain the Silver Ball Trophy as Canadian Champions in 1875.

In the meantime, while maintaining his management of the brewery and with the Maple Leafs, Sleeman somehow engaged in several other pursuits. He was elected president of the Guelph Turf Club in 1872 and remained in that position for over 20 years. A proud Guelphite, he became increasingly invested in civic matters, and was elected to the town council in 1876. All the while, he and his wife, Sarah Hill (married in 1863), continued to fill the rooms of the Sleeman home; soon after the end of the 1874 season, they welcomed their sixth child. (They eventually had 12 children.)

Sleeman sought to further elevate the status of baseball in Ontario with the formation of the Canadian Association for 1876. He was elected president of the Association and managed the Maple Leafs through another strong season. The highlight for the club was an exciting 9-8 victory over the National League St. Louis Browns in an exhibition game on August 29, William Squire Smith allowing only two runs over eight innings; the *New York Clipper* was less than effusive in its praise of the Leafs, declaring that they "played very steadily."[14] But with strong competition from rivals 75 miles to their southwest, the Leafs' dominance came to an end as the London Tecumsehs were crowned champions of the Canadian Association.

Sleeman's practice of importing American professionals had fueled much controversy and debate over the previous two seasons, and these were exacerbated during the 1876 season, as

Sleeman continued to import more "amateur" players. This forced other teams to follow suit in order to remain competitive, and required teams and leagues to enact stricter rules to restrict the use of professionals in amateur leagues and contests.

With the success of the Canadian Association in 1876, Sleeman set his sights even higher in 1877; he sought to establish a fully international league that would also compete with the National League, then in its second year. Hence was born the International Association, wherein the London and Guelph clubs joined five American teams, but the Tecumsehs and Leafs followed very disparate paths. Though this did officially elevate the Guelph team to professional status (not to be confused with an amateur Guelph Maple Leafs team that also operated in the same season), the competition proved to be too much for both the team and Sleeman. He had to squash rumors in midseason of the team moving to Buffalo,[15] and it was all he could do to finish the season. The Leafs posted a dismal 4-12 record to finish last, not taking into account the record of the Lynn Live Oaks, who disbanded in midseason. Guelph played its last league game against the Tecumsehs (who eventually followed as champions of the Association) on August 29, and despite a promising 6-1 lead after five innings, could not hold on, its season ending ignominiously with a 6-6 tie. This marked the end of close to a decade of Guelph superiority and success, and it was time for the club and Sleeman to move on.

Guelph did not return to the International Association for 1878. (And despite their tremendous initial success, even the Tecumsehs were only able to continue into August of 1878 before disbanding.) Rather, the Leafs languished as an amateur club, playing only sporadically over the next two seasons. Sleeman did not appear to have much involvement with the club at this time, but he did play right field for the Leafs on July 31 against the Harriston Browns. Sadly, on this same day, his older brother William died of a morphine overdose. From this point, perhaps as a result of this family tragedy, George seemed to relinquish any role with the Maple Leafs; the Guelph papers made little mention of him or the club for the remainder of the season. He kept a low profile until he was named chairman of the inauguration committee when Guelph became a city on April 23, 1879.[16] He focused his energy more on civic matters, having gained such respect and popularity locally that he was elected the first mayor of the City of Guelph (by acclamation) in January 1880.

Mayor Sleeman returned to baseball for the 1880 season, as president of a new Canadian Association, which adopted the same constitution as the previous incarnation from 1876.[17] Teams from Galt, Toronto, and Woodstock, and a pair from Guelph (Maple Leafs and Athletics) vied for the Amateur Championship of Canada, but played only a handful of games. By season's end, both the Leafs and Woodstock Actives claimed they were entitled to the championship bat.[18] While the Actives' claim was justified by their 1-0 victory in the championship match on September 8, Sleeman and the Leafs asserted that "during the early part of the season, [they] vanquished all comers,"[19] and that the two losses they incurred at the end of the season (as well as a 3-2 loss on August 27 to the Harriston Browns) were under protest, as both the Actives and Browns had, in a stroke of irony considering Sleeman's prior management philosophy, "introduced professionals into their teams."[20] The final decision of the judiciary committee has not been found.

The Maple Leafs returned to independent amateur play in 1881, with Sleeman still as president. In an otherwise unremarkable season, another Sleeman signing caused yet another controversy. In early July, amateur pitcher John W. Jackson, known professionally as Bud Fowler, was engaged by the Maple Leafs, but "when he reached Guelph and the members of the club found he was a coloured youth, they snobbishly refused to play with him."[21] The *Guelph Herald* expressed its disappointment with the team's reaction, and could only take solace in finding "that it is only a few members of the team"[22] who objected to Fowler's engagement.

Over the next two years, Sleeman was more preoccupied with civic duties, having been reelected mayor of Guelph for both 1881 and 1882. He was asked to run yet again in 1883, but declined. The Maple Leafs saw little activity during this time, until 1884, when they resurfaced as a member of the Western Ontario Baseball League. This new amateur league consisted of 10 teams, including two from Guelph, and three each from Hamilton and London. Sleeman was elected a director of the league, but appears to have had little to do with league or team operations. But this set the stage for perhaps his most ambitious baseball project yet, when he was elected president of the newly formed Canadian League for 1885. The Leafs, with Sleeman returning as their manager, joined the Hamilton Clippers, Hamilton Primroses, London Cockneys, and Toronto Torontos to play out a full season of approximately 40 games.

However noble his intentions, Sleeman reignited the flames of controversy yet again when he signed Cincinnati pitcher George Washington Bradley. Bradley had been under contract with the Philadelphia Athletics since 1883, and was suspended for having left to join the Cincinnati Unions. And as the Canadian League constitution "[forbade] the employment by League clubs of players under contract with or expelled from any other club,"[23] other teams protested on the grounds that Bradley he was an ineligible player. But Sleeman insisted on putting Bradley in to pitch on July 9 against London, contending that he was indeed eligible, as the Canadian League was independent of the American Association. Regardless, the Cockneys refused to play, umpire Fred Goldsmith called the game, and a protest was filed. This scenario was repeated on July 11 in a scheduled game against Toronto. The Judiciary

Committee met on July 14 in Hamilton to decide the affair, and despite its feeling that Sleeman had "acted conscientiously for what he considered to be in the interests of the Leaf Club,"[24] it "could not endorse the club playing Bradley"[25] and ruled against the Leafs. Sleeman "gave it as his opinion that a mistake had been committed, and that the Leafs were dealt with unfairly and unconstitutionally, and in consequence he thought the Leafs would go out of the League."[26] Three weeks later, it was reported that the Leafs management had decided to disband. The *Hamilton Spectator* expressed its disappointment: "The Maple Leafs started out with a fine team of local players; but the other league teams were strengthened beyond the calibre of the local players, and it was principally to the endeavor to keep up with the procession that the Leafs owe their present position. Hard luck, too, had a great deal to do with it."[27] The announcement proved premature, because Sleeman resigned as manager, which left "the boys [to] run the machine themselves,"[28] but his "liberality and his love for baseball [were] again demonstrated"[29] when he allowed the Maple Leafs free use of his ground and stand in order to "finish the season with profit to themselves."[30] "In face of the fact that Mr. Sleeman lost a large sum of money on baseball this year, the generous offer shows that he is willing to make great sacrifices for the good of the sport in Guelph."[31] Third baseman James H. Hewer took over managerial duties, and the Leafs managed to finish the season. But despite players of major-league caliber such as Louis Bierbauer, Dennis Fitzgerald, Mickey Jones, and Edward Kent, they finished in a battle for last place (with a record of 8-28) with the equally hapless Hamilton Primroses.

Sleeman, still president of the Canadian League, sought to put the challenges of 1885 behind him, and at the annual meeting on November 30 in Toronto, was reelected league president as plans were made for the coming season. Meanwhile, the "formation of an International

League by affiliation with the New York State League was discussed,"[32] and this indeed came to fruition, with Toronto and Hamilton (Clippers) withdrawing from the Canadian League to join the newly renamed league. Sleeman filed suit against the Canucks and Clippers, to no avail, but, undeterred, secured a "first-class team for the coming season, and lovers of the game in Guelph may rely on having a good nine placed in the field."[33] Considering the success that was to come, it is worth taking a brief look at the players Sleeman brought together to form the most victorious team that Guelph ever fielded.

Two of those who remained with the club formed the catching tandem. A 21-year-old Guelph native, Andrew Dillon, worked as an upholsterer, and showed promise as a young catcher, touted as "one of the coolest and gamest catchers in the country"[34] by the *Kalamazoo Gazette*. He played in the Northwestern League in 1887 and for Lima in the Tri-State League in 1888, but died of typhoid and pneumonia only two years later.

James "Son" Purvis, from Port Hope, Ontario, had played with the Milwaukee reserve team in 1884, but returned to Canada in 1885 and played for both Guelph and London of the Canadian League. He enjoyed a lengthy career playing with Buffalo and London of the International League, as well as with clubs from Grand Rapids, Rockford, Peoria, and Des Moines. He finished with the Hartford Cooperatives of the Atlantic League in 1898, and thereafter, raised a family and worked as a cabinetmaker in Grand Rapids, Michigan. He died there in 1935.

Longtime Maple Leaf James Hewer played several infield positions with Guelph until 1896. A prominent businessman and merchant, he was elected mayor in 1897, and many Guelphites mourned his passing in 1916.

Sleeman brought in rising star Albert C. Buckenberger of Detroit to manage and play second base for the Leafs. He had been captain of the Cass Club of Detroit for three seasons, and had most recently played with Indianapolis, Terre Haute, and Toledo. He achieved greater fame as a manager for nine seasons in the majors, with Columbus of the American Association (1889-1890) and in the National League with Pittsburgh, St. Louis, and Boston between 1892 and 1904. He died in Syracuse in 1917.

As did Buckenberger, first baseman Wally "Jumbo" Millar, born in Jackson, Michigan, also played with amateur clubs in Detroit for several seasons. He impressed Sleeman very early on and was named Leaf captain. He returned to Sandusky in 1887 and managed the club several years later. He died in Detroit in 1935.

William George, born in Bellaire, Ohio, played primarily right field and shortstop with the Leafs, but also pitched in eight games. His brief turn on the mound got the attention of the New York Giants, who signed him as a pitcher for the following season. He pitched in 19 games in the majors with New York and the Columbus Solons of the American Association, then returned to the outfield in the minor leagues until 1899. His playing days over, he returned to Bellaire and operated a billiards parlor, then a saloon, before succumbing to peritonitis in 1916.

Benjamin Stephens of Pittsburgh (born Stephani in France) played first base and pitched on occasion for Guelph in 1886, having played the previous season with Macon of the Southern League. He spent the next several seasons playing in the Northwestern, Tri-State, and New York-Pennsylvania leagues, primarily as an outfielder. He continued to tend bar in Pittsburgh but troubles with alcohol led to a severe case of delirium tremens, and eventual death in 1906 at the age of 51.

Frank Scheibeck, from Detroit, also with the Sanduskys in 1885, was brought in by Sleeman to play shortstop and pitch for the Leafs. He enjoyed a lengthy career in baseball, including stints in London (International League) in 1888-89 and Montréal (Eastern League) from 1898 to 1901, and spent several years in the majors from 1887-1906 with seven teams. He was the last surviving member of the team when he died in 1956 in Detroit.

Scheibeck primarily alternated pitching duties with Harry Zell, who was born in Dayton, Ohio, and who, along with Stephens, had played with Macon in 1885, leading the Southern League in fielding. He played with Buffalo of the International League in 1887, then played for several other minor leagues before ending his career in Dayton in 1892. He owned and operated a saloon in his hometown, and died in 1912 after a long illness at the age of 47.

From the Sanduskys as well, Sleeman enticed third baseman Dan Mulholland, who had gained fame for his unassisted triple play against the National League Detroit Wolverines. He was one of the top hitters for the Leafs in 1886, but returned to play for Sandusky in 1887. He played a few more seasons before retiring to his hometown of Norwalk, Ohio, where he ran a saloon and later became a solicitor. He died in 1927.

Owen "Reddy" Williams had been a teammate of William George with the Bellaire Globes, and played left field for the Maple Leafs. He went on to play for Milwaukee of the Northwestern League in 1889, then played for several seasons in the Tri-State League. He spent his later years as a glassworker in Ohio and West Virginia, and died in 1929 in Fairmont, West Virginia.

The Leafs' stalwart center fielder was Charles "Count" Campau, who had played with Buckenberger on the Detroit Cass Club. He was an "itinerant minor-league star who played for teams in at least 19 cities, including three stops in the majors."[35] He had played with Erie, Pennsylvania, in 1885 until that club disbanded, then finished the season with the London Tecumsehs. His first major-league tour was with the Detroit Wolverines in 1888, but it was his second stint in the majors that was his most successful, when

he joined the St. Louis Browns of the American Association as player-manager in 1890. Despite an impressive record of 27-14 as manager, he was nevertheless replaced, but stayed on as a player. And although he hit an impressive .322 in 75 games and led the league with nine home runs, he was released by Browns owner Chris Von der Ahe with two weeks remaining in the season, in an effort to cut costs.[36] He returned to the majors four years later, but appeared in only two games with the Washington Senators. He umpired for a few seasons in the minors, then left baseball altogether to work at racetracks tracks across North America. He died of pneumonia in 1938.

With Sleeman's team in place, the Leafs barnstormed their way through Ontario and the United States, highlighted by an American tour in August that proved tremendously successful. They played top amateur clubs from Michigan, Indiana, Ohio, Virginia, and Pennsylvania, achieving a record of 23-1, and by September 1 their overall record stood at an exceptional 43-1. A mediocre final month still resulted in a formidable season record of 53-9, without question the greatest season enjoyed by the Maple Leafs.

Despite the successes, the Leafs underwent yet another dramatic transition, with an entirely new club in 1887. They merged with the Guelph Royal Oaks, and it was mostly former Oaks who comprised the 1887 Maple Leafs. Sleeman, essentially retired from the game by this time,[37] remained as honorary president, while former Guelph pitcher William S. Smith assumed the role of club president.[38] Considering the many changes, the local press was less than optimistic about the coming season: "Is the glory of the once champion Maple Leafs now allowed to be a thing of the past?"[39] This would prove prophetic, as the Leafs played only sporadically over the next several seasons.

Though honorary president, George Sleeman no longer held an active interest in the Maple Leafs.[40] Without his leadership, but with his blessing, the club soldiered on. It returned to organized play in 1893 as a member of the Canadian Amateur Baseball Association, then in 1894 finished first in the Western Ontario Baseball League, and repeated this the following year as a member of the Western League of the Canadian Baseball Association. A second iteration of a Canadian League was formed in 1896, including teams from Galt, Hamilton, London, and Guelph, and once again the Leafs finished first, with a record of 24-12. The 1896 roster featured two young local stars: Jimmy Cockman, younger brother of 1885 Leafs shortstop Tommy Cockman, played many years in the minors before finally reaching the majors in 1905 as a 32-year-old rookie to play 13 games at third base with the New York Highlanders; and William "Bunk" Congalton, who played with the Chicago Orphans in 1902, then with Cleveland and Boston from 1905 to 1907. His brief career was highlighted by a stellar season with the Cleveland Naps in 1906 in which he batted .320, which would have put him fourth in the AL had he had four more plate appearances. The Leafs and manager James Hewer returned to the Canadian League in 1897, but finished last of the three teams that remained by season's end. There is no trace of the Leafs during the 1898 season, but they rejoined the then Class-D Canadian League for the 1899 season. Manager George Black guided them to an unremarkable record of 42-48.

The heyday of the Maple Leafs now years behind them, they played in amateur versions of the Canadian League in 1904 and 1905. By 1908, the former International League (or Association) operated as the Class-A Eastern League, and this allowed four teams from Ontario and New York, including Guelph, to form a Class-D International League. But the Guelph franchise shifted to St. Thomas, Ontario, on June 12, and the league itself disbanded at the end of July.

Professional baseball returned to Ontario in 1911, as George "Knotty" Lee formed a new Class-D Canadian League. The league remained relatively healthy through 1915, by which time it had attained Class-B status. The Maple Leafs themselves achieved moderate success in the first three seasons, and after a sabbatical in 1914, returned, managed by Lee, to finish a very respectable second to the Ottawa Senators in the league's final season. This was the last year the Guelph Maple Leafs played at a professional level, though Lee once more brought professional baseball to Ontario in 1930 with the Class-D Ontario League; by this time, however, the Guelph team went by the nickname Biltmores.

With his role in baseball now relegated to that of an ardent fan, Sleeman became involved in several other areas of Guelph daily life. He had been an expert marksman, one of the best rifle shots in Guelph, and he was president of the Guelph Rifle Association from 1886 to 1906. He also delighted in winter sports, being named president of the Royal City Curling Club in 1888. When Mayor Thomas Goldie, also a former Guelph Maple Leaf, died suddenly in 1892, Sleeman agreed to take over and finish Goldie's term.[41] In 1894 George started the Guelph Railway Company, which constructed one of the first electric railways in Ontario.[42] His father, having returned to St. David's to enjoy a peaceful retirement working on his gardens, died early that year.

Sleeman returned to the mayor's office in 1905, elected by an all-time majority, a reflection of his stature in the community. By this time he had retired from the family business and erected the Springbank Brewery, which he conducted until his death.[43] He continued to be held in high regard in his city: He ran for mayor one last time in 1906, and won uncontested.

After his wife, Sarah, died in early 1917, George continued to surround himself with family and friends, being known by many for his hospitable nature.[44] Entering his 80s, he remained in excellent health, and his sense of citizenship and community pride never waned.

His passion for sport, notably baseball, remained undiminished: "It is worthy of note that in his last conscious moments his thoughts were about some of the men who were players of that famous baseball team."[45]

Sleeman died after an abdominal operation on December 16, 1926, in Guelph General Hospital, and was laid to rest in Woodlawn Cemetery, a few miles from where still stands the old Sleeman Manor, near the site of the original brewery and ballpark. His grave is perhaps fittingly modest and not a reflection of his impact, with only a simple flat stone marker that simply states "George Sleeman, husband of Sarah Hill," along with his dates of birth and death. Dubbed the "father of professional Canadian baseball for his role in the early organization of the game,"[46] he and his impact were more fully acknowledged when he was elected to the Canadian Baseball Hall of Fame as a builder in 1999.

SOURCES

In addition to the sources cited in the Notes, the author consulted:

Newspapers, including *Guelph Herald, Guelph Mercury, Hamilton Spectator, London Advertiser, London Free Press, Maple Leaf, New York Clipper, Toronto Globe,* and *Woodstock Weekly Sentinel.*

Ascenzo, Denise. "Niagara's History Unveiled: The Early Years," https://www.niagaranow.com/entertainment.phtml/1266niagarashistoryunveiledtheearlyyears, accessed July 7, 2021.

Bernard, David L. "The Guelph Maple Leafs: A Cultural Indicator of Southern Ontario," *Ontario History* (Toronto: Ontario Historical Society), September 1992.

Matchett, Micheal. "The Sleeman Family Brewery: 19th Century Paternalism to Prohibition-Inspired Myth," *Historic Guelph, the Royal City* (Guelph: Guelph Historical Society, 1993).

Genealogical and player data was obtained from a variety of sources, including Ancestry.com, Baseball-Reference.com, census records, FamilySearch.org, vital records, minor-league player files of Reed Howard, and the author's own player database and genealogical files.

Various ledgers and correspondence from the Sleeman Family Collection, Archives and Special Collections, McLaughlin Library, University of Guelph.

George Sleeman, email correspondence with Murray Inch (descendant), 2020-21.

NOTES

1   Census of Canada, 1870-71 (Ottawa: I.B. Taylor, 1873), 428.

2   "Timeline: Sleeman Family History and Events," https://www.lib.uoguelph.ca/archives/our-collections/regional-early-campus-history/sleeman-collection/timeline-sleeman-family.

3   "The Early Days: The Silver Creek Brewery," https://www.lib.uoguelph.ca/archives/our-collections/regional-early-campus-history/sleeman-collection/brewing-history/early-days.

4   "Timeline: Sleeman Family History and Events."

5   "Timeline: Sleeman Family History and Events."

6   "The Maple Leafs of Guelph," Maple Leaf, Guelph, January 1923: 13.

7   Old Timers Will Remember Those Famous Silver Creeks Who Played 'Way Back When Gloves, Masks and Pads Were Not Known," Guelph Mercury, July 20, 1927: 90.

8   "Old Timers Will Remember Those Famous Silver Creeks Who Played 'Way Back When Gloves, Masks and Pads Were Not Known."

9   "The Base Ball Match," Guelph Mercury, August 23, 1873: 1.

10 "The Base Ball Match."

11 "Maple Leaf B.B.C. Annual Meeting," Guelph Mercury, April 8, 1874: 1.

12 "Maple Leaf B.B.C. Annual Meeting."

13 Maple Leaf Baseball Club Ledger (1874-76), Sleeman Family Collection, Archives and Special Collections, McLaughlin Library, University of Guelph.

14 "St. Louis vs. Maple Leaf," New York Clipper, September 9, 1876: 186.

15 "Base Ball Notes," Guelph Mercury, July 19, 1877: 1.

16 "Death of Mr. George Sleeman Removes Prominent Pioneer Business Man of Royal City," Guelph Mercury, December 16, 1926: 1.

17 "Base Ball," Guelph Mercury, May 12, 1880: 1.

18 "The Return of the Actives," Woodstock Weekly Sentinel, September 17, 1880: 4.

19 "The Canadian Championship," Guelph Mercury, October 14, 1880: 2.

20 "The Canadian Championship."

21 "Base Ball," Guelph Mercury, July 27, 1881: 2.

22 "Guelph's Colored Pitcher," Hamilton Spectator, July 4, 1881.

23 "Bradley's Status," Hamilton Times, July 8, 1885.

24 "Meeting of Judiciary Committee," Guelph Mercury, July 14, 1885: 1.

25 "Meeting of Judiciary Committee."

26 "Meeting of Judiciary Committee."

27 "The Maple Leafs," Guelph Mercury, August 11, 1885: 1.

28 "The Maple Leafs."

29 "The Maple Leafs in Luck," Toronto Globe, August 25, 1885: 8.

30 "The Maple Leafs in Luck."

31 "The Maple Leafs in Luck."

32 "The Canadian Baseball League," Guelph Mercury, December 4, 1885: 1.

33 "Baseball," Guelph Mercury, March 8, 1886: 1.

34 "Baseball," Guelph Mercury, August 16, 1886: 1.

35 Stephen V. Rice, "Count Campau," SABR BioProject, https://sabr.org/bioproj/person/count-campau/.

36 Rice.

37 Lisa Bowes, "George Sleeman and the Brewing of Baseball in Guelph 1872-1886," Historic Guelph (Guelph: Guelph Historical Society, October 1988), 55.

38 "Guelph Baseballers," Guelph Mercury, May 10, 1887: 4.

39 "Local News," Guelph Mercury, April 30, 1887: 1.

40 Unattributed clipping from the Sleeman Family Collection, Archives and Special Collections, McLaughlin Library, University of Guelph.

41 "Death of Mr. George Sleeman Removes Prominent Pioneer Business Man of Royal City," Guelph Mercury, December 16, 1926: 9.

42 "Death of Mr. George Sleeman Removes Prominent Pioneer Business Man of Royal City."

43 "Death of Mr. George Sleeman Removes Prominent Pioneer Business Man of Royal City," Guelph Mercury, December 16, 1926: 1.

44 "Death of Mr. George Sleeman Removes Prominent Pioneer Business Man of Royal City," Guelph Mercury, December 16, 1926: 9.

45 "Late Geo. Sleeman," Guelph Mercury, December 16, 1926: 4.

46 "George Sleeman – Canadian Baseball Hall of Fame," http://baseballhalloffame.ca/blog/2009/09/17/george-sleeman/.

JAKE ENGLEHART

By Brian "Chip" Martin

A certain amount of mystery surrounds Jacob Lewis Englehart, an American whose never-say-lose attitude and substantial resources lay behind the stunning success of the London Tecumseh Base Ball Club in the 1870s. Under his leadership, the Tecumsehs finally bested the archrival Guelph Maple Leafs after years of frustration to become Canada's baseball champions, and one of the foremost clubs in North America, arguably the country's first major-league champions.

Defeat did not rest lightly on the mind of Englehart. He particularly disliked losing to Guelph, whose George Sleeman was a successful brewer, promoter of his town, and fiercely competitive driving force behind the Maple Leafs, Canada's championship team from 1869 to 1875. The rivalry that developed between London and Guelph was something to behold. London was a city of about 18,000, while Guelph was a town less than half that size. But games played between the two cities attracted as many as 10,000 spectators, many of whom joined their teams on excursion trains for what was then a four-hour journey between the communities. This was at a time when visits by either club to Toronto or Detroit resulted in lopsided wins against those

far bigger cities. London and Guelph sometimes defeated touring professional clubs from Chicago, Boston, and St. Louis. Southwestern Ontario was the hotbed for baseball in Canada throughout the 1870s, with games having been played in the region since at least the late 1830s. Major professional teams knew this, and regularly scheduled games in Guelph and London during road trips through neighboring New York and Michigan, knowing they would draw good crowds and play competitive teams.

Jake Englehart has an important place in Canadian baseball history, although his baseball exploits are less well known than his pivotal role in Canada's fledgling petroleum industry and his founding of the oil giant Imperial Oil. He also played a big part in opening Northern Ontario to development in the early 1900s, his success where others had failed resulting in a grateful community named after him. His achievements were many in business, philanthropy, politics, and railroading. When he died in Toronto, his funeral attracted headlines and attendance by many members of Canada's business and political elite. In the end, his important contribution to Canadian baseball was overshadowed by his many other accomplishments.

Englehart was born on November 2, 1847, in Cleveland, Ohio, one of three children of Joel and Hannah Englehart. Joel was a clothier, with the firm Deckand and Englehart. When Jake was about 13, his father relocated the family to New York City, where he pursued business opportunities. In time, the young Englehart became a salesman for clothiers Sonneborn, Dryfoos and Company, and eventually a partner of company principals Solomon Sonneborn, Abraham M. Dryfoos, and Leopold Beringer. The company switched from the manufacture of clothing to the "rectifying" of whiskey, a term used for the bottling of distilled spirits. By the time of the Civil War, America had developed a strong thirst for alcohol, and Englehart and his partners quickly changed their focus to profit from that trend.

Most whiskey rectifiers purchased spirits from a variety of distillers, then filtered and blended the spirits to produce their own distinct brands. Some, however, were after quick money by blending small amounts of whiskey with flavoring and neutral grain spirits to produce a watered-down beverage they called "blended whiskey."[1]

Consumption of alcohol in the United States had grown at an astonishing rate during the 1800s. By 1860, consumption had increased by 20 percent from 1850 alone, and it remained high during the Civil War. One factor in the increase was the desire for temporary escape from the economic, social, and political woes that plagued the country; another was increasing immigration from foreign lands where drinking was widespread, such as Germany and the British Isles, especially Ireland.[2] Whiskey was often used to dull the pain of wounded soldiers during the Civil War and to cleanse their wounds. The conflict also saw the destruction of some distilleries, so that prices began to skyrocket. A black market for whiskey boomed, and more than 1,000 whiskey distillers and rectifiers were operating by 1863. To fund the Civil War, President Abraham Lincoln introduced the Revenue Act of 1862, which

created an income tax and excise taxes on luxury items, including liquor and tobacco. Alcohol was taxed at 20 cents for each "proof gallon," which initially generated $3.2 million a year in revenue for Washington. The tax was raised to $2 a gallon, producing $30 million in tax revenue annually. This led to rampant moonshining and the creation of the "Whiskey Ring," a criminal operation that underreported actual production and used bribes and blackmail to influence federal agents and shopkeepers. To combat such tax avoidance, the government reduced the tax to 70 cents a gallon, but the practice continued.[3] Evidence suggests that the firm for which Englehart worked also participated in the widespread movement to dodge taxes.

For years, alcohol had also been widely used in illuminating lamps, but that market had gone flat with the growing use of kerosene derived from oil discovered in Pennsylvania and Ontario. Englehart's partners were intrigued by what they thought presented a new opportunity for them, and assigned the young man to look into it. After all, the process to create whiskey was similar to that used to produce kerosene: simply add heat to a liquid to produce a distillate of much greater value. Solomon Sonneborn, one of Englehart's partners, had family members who had put some money into Canada's oilfield based at Petrolia, Ontario. The city of London, little more than 35 miles to the east of Petrolia, had become the refining center for Petrolia and nearby Oil Springs in Lambton County. It was to London that Englehart was sent.

Meanwhile, the illicit practices of whiskey rectifiers Sonneborn and Company were attracting unwanted attention. The R.G. Dun credit rating agency found that the firm was prospering, but that company principals were "shrewd, sharp and unreliable" and "somewhat notorious in the whiskey trade," making more money than any similar operation. R.G. Dun went on: "They established themselves in Canada in 1869 and the move was regarded as the establishment of an asylum for the men who had hitherto been employed illicitly here, and for the investment of means which might otherwise [have] been pursued by the U.S. government."[4] Jacob Englehart had arrived in London in 1868 at the age of 20 to see what opportunities existed in the fledgling oil industry centered there. In effect, he became his company's front man in a cross-border money-laundering scheme. He traveled from New York City, more than 600 miles away, with money Washington would have otherwise taxed, just as R.G. Dun suggested.

Oil had been discovered west of London in 1857, transforming the city into a refining center for the next two decades. When he arrived in London, Englehart was already an agent for Carbon Oil Works, the leading producer, refiner, and marketer for the oil patch. The firm had been organized by J.M. Williams, who had established the first commercially viable oil well at Oil Springs. Englehart quickly teamed up with Isaac Waterman, another early refiner in London, and it was readily apparent that Englehart had money behind him. Soon afterward he established his own firm, Englehart & Company.[5] By 1870, Carbon Oil, Waterman Brothers (Herman and Isaac Waterman), and Englehart & Company accounted among them for fully one-third of the production from Ontario's oil patch. Englehart shipped kerosene to the Sonneborn firm in New York, making Sonneborn the fourth largest exporter of kerosene from that port.[6] In 1872, however, Sonneborn sued Carbon Oil for a claimed outstanding debt of $100,000. Carbon Oil was in deep trouble, its "big still" having been destroyed in an explosion; the firm soon collapsed, and Englehart acquired its assets cheaply at auction. Not long afterward, the Sonneborn company filed for bankruptcy following the widespread economic collapse of 1873. Englehart emerged unscathed, however, and had become a major player in the Canadian oil industry, which was beginning to face new competition

from cheaper and sweeter American crude from Pennsylvania.

Englehart, as did several other leaders of Canada's early petroleum industry, including the Waterman brothers, boarded at the Tecumseh House Hotel during his time in London. The new hotel was named after Shawnee Indian Chief Tecumseh, who fought alongside British General Sir Isaac Brock against the Americans during the War of 1812. Tecumseh (pronounced tuh-KUM-see) fell in battle along the Thames River about 60 miles west of London in 1813. The hotel featured a large painting of Tecumseh in its lobby. The Tecumseh House had been a popular refuge for some Southern families and for Confederate spies and buyers during the Civil War; London profited handsomely by selling to both sides in the conflict.

Operators of the hotel were among the directors of the Tecumseh Base Ball Club, which held its meetings there. At some point, Englehart became a follower of the club, then a director and eventually president, tapping into his personal or corporate funds to help attract to London some of the best baseball talent from south of the border. Englehart may have been surprised at the popularity of the game, which had been played in London since at least 1855, as revealed by an entry in the first city directory.[7] The following year, 1856, the May 1 edition of the *London Free Press* carried an advertisement saying that the London Base Ball Club would be holding its annual meeting the next day to elect officers and transact business. Afterward the newspaper reported that officers had been elected and that the club "intends to challenge any other Base Ball Club in the Province as soon as it gets into regular playing order."[8] Mention of an annual meeting and the apparent cockiness of the club suggest it was not new to the game. Later in 1856, the *New York Clipper* carried a report about a game London played in the village of Delaware, just west of the city, on September 12. London prevailed

34-33 in the two-inning game played under the rules of the day.[9]

Southwestern Ontario was developing into a hotbed of baseball activity at this time. The Hamilton Young Canadians (later renamed the Maple Leafs) had been playing since 1854, and not long afterward a team was fielded in Woodstock.[10] By 1861, the Woodstock Young Canadians were a formidable nine, that year defeating Hamilton twice, and by 1864 becoming Canadian champions. They were awarded the Silver Ball trophy, for which funds had been raised in Woodstock. Hamilton, Woodstock, and Ingersoll traveled to Detroit to compete in an international tournament, and met with success. Hamilton finished second, and Ingersoll took top honors in a junior division, but Woodstock struggled because of an injury to its pitcher.[11]

By 1868 it was becoming apparent that perennial Canadian champion Woodstock was slipping, and rivals old and new were anxious to topple the team from its perch. The town of Guelph had become baseball crazy and was determined to wrest the Silver Ball from Woodstock. The Guelph mayor declared a civic holiday in July so Guelphites could take the train to Woodstock to watch the Maple Leafs challenge the reigning champions. About 500 fans and a brass band journeyed west for the game, but were disappointed when Woodstock prevailed, 36-28. It wasn't until 1869 at the Provincial Exhibition in London that Guelph took top honors and $150 in gold, downing Woodstock, Ingersoll, and London in a three-day tournament.[12] It was a feather in the cap for the rapidly industrializing town of 5,900. Within a few years, brewer George Sleeman, who had operated and played on a ball team fielded by his Silver Creek Brewery, took control of the Maple Leafs and was determined to retain bragging rights as Canada's top team, even if he had to dig into his deep pockets to hire Americans to stay on top. Guelph reigned as Canadian champions until dethroned by London in 1876.[13]

Under Sleeman, the club traveled widely in the United States as it gradually drifted into professionalism, much to the chagrin of its traditional competition in Southern Ontario. Proceeds from surplus funds at the end of the season had been distributed to Guelph players as early as 1870.[14] At the time, sport was considered a gentlemanly and amateur pastime, so Guelph became the subject of criticism in other cities. By 1875 nearly the entire Maple Leaf roster was American and professional, which prompted the *London Free Press* to deride Sleeman's men (to whom the hometown London Tecumsehs continued to lose) as "The Guelph Foreign Legion."[15]

Englehart and Sleeman took their rivalry to a new level when the Tecumsehs and Maple Leafs became charter members of the International Association in 1877. The loop was established by baseball cities who felt excluded by the National League, which had been organized the previous season and tightly restricted its membership. Recognizing the Canadian entries in its name, the International Association easily attracted some of the best baseball talent of the day. Englehart had begun signing up topflight American players a few years earlier in a bid to wrest the claim of baseball supremacy in Canada from Guelph. Originally, London mocked Sleeman's fielding of a "foreign legion." But unable to dislodge Guelph as Canadian champions, London directors took a page from Sleeman's book and found the money (mainly in the deep pockets of Englehart) to lure north some of the best and brightest stars of the day. Among them were early curveball pitcher Fred Goldsmith, catcher Phil Powers, outfielder Joe Hornung, and others at the start of their careers. Team manager Harry Gorman traveled to Goldsmith's home in New Haven, Connecticut, to persuade the promising young hurler to play for London. Gorman was armed with gold bars provided by Englehart as an inducement. It worked; Goldsmith signed on for $100 a month.[16] At the time, the average workingman earned about $300 a year and had to work long hours for 12 months to do so. London finally took the championship of Canada in 1876, after which Englehart and the Tecumseh club directors were eager for a new challenge in a new league that was determined to challenge the supremacy of the one-year-old National League.

Management first determined that the Association venture justified a new ballpark. The Tecumsehs had been playing on grounds long occupied by the British Army at Victoria Park, but had to relocate late each summer to make way for the annual Provincial Exhibition. Temporary stands erected had proved to be flimsy, and had collapsed at least once. A piece of low-lying land was found across the Thames River from downtown, land where corn had been grown by First Nations people and where games, including baseball, had been played for years. The site was acquired by club supporter and downtown china merchant W.J Reid, and soon soil from road scrapings was used to help raise the elevation of the ground. In short order, a 600-seat grandstand was erected for spectators and boxes created for directors, including Englehart. The first game was played on May 3, 1877, when the Tecumsehs defeated the city's top amateur team, the Atlantics, 5-1. About $3,000 was spent to create the fine new ballpark, the *Canadian Illustrated News* reported a few months later.[17] The first game attracted 1,000 fans and began the ballpark's run as the world's oldest baseball grounds, still serving London baseball and its fans to this day as Labatt Memorial Park.[18]

By 1877 there were 54 professional baseball clubs in operation in North America. The National League was coming off an inaugural season that had failed to meet expectations. Two of its eight teams, the cash-strapped Mutuals of New York and the Athletics of Philadelphia, were expelled for failing to complete their schedules. Only Chicago turned a profit during the year; it was estimated that the remaining teams lost a

total of $17,300.[19] The future of the sport as a business venture seemed shaky. The National League fielded only six teams for 1877: the Chicago White Stockings, Boston, Louisville Grays, St. Louis Brown Stockings, Cincinnati Red Stockings, and the Hartfords of Brooklyn. The league was not interested in adding teams as it struggled to make the game a viable proposition. This led to complaints that it was an exclusive club consisting of Old Boys. For those complaining that the door was shut to them, the International Association was an attractive alternative. It appealed to smaller industrial cities during a time of rampant civic boosterism when anything seemed possible, and many of the baseball men were community leaders, including mayors and future mayors. Of the more than 20 cities that affiliated with the International Association for the 1877 season, seven clubs agreed to pay an additional fee of $15 to vie for its inaugural pennant. Aside from London and Guelph, the other contending teams were the Pittsburgh Alleghenys; the Columbus Buckeyes; Lynn (Massachusetts) Live Oaks; Rochester, New York; and Manchester, New Hampshire. Sixteen other clubs joined the IA but opted against competing for the pennant.[20]

London's first game against an International Association opponent came on May 5, 1877, when the Hartford Dark Blues appeared at Tecumseh Park. Fred Goldsmith puzzled the visitors with his curves for the first few innings until Hartford began to hit him freely. He was pulled after five innings, replaced by Foghorn Bradley, who had won 9 games and lost 10 during the previous season with Boston in the National League. Hartford disappointed the Opening Day crowd by winning the game 6-2. The following day, the visitors won again, 8-4, capitalizing on 13 Tecumseh fielding errors. Next in town were the Pittsburgh Alleghenys, who featured hard-throwing right-hander Pud Galvin, a future Hall of Famer. London committed three of the game's four errors, losing the official IA pennant-contesting game by a score of 2-0. On May 11 and 13 Rochester appeared at Tecumseh Park. Goldsmith's favored catcher, Phil Powers, saw his first game action after his return from a broken finger, and things immediately improved. London managed its first win, 7-2, and the following day, before 2,000 fans, won again, 9-8, powered by a ninth-inning hit and aggressive baserunning by shortstop Ed Somerville. On the May 24 holiday, a crowd estimated at from 6,000 to 8,000 saw an exciting game in which London came back from a 7-3 deficit with four runs in the ninth inning to tie the contest, although visiting Boston of the National League eventually prevailed 8-7 in 10 innings. In Guelph the same day, the Maple Leafs celebrated the Queen's birthday by downing the Syracuse Stars 5-4 before a crowd of 2,000.

The Tecumsehs made London fans and director Jake Englehart happy after a rough start when Goldsmith settled down and worked effectively with catcher Powers. Goldsmith managed to lead London to more successes than failures. For a good part of the season, the Tecumsehs occupied second place in the new loop, behind Galvin and the Alleghenys. The traditional rivalry with Guelph suffered; only 1,500 fans turned out in London for a June 21 game against the Maple Leafs that London won, 5-2. Things grew worse. By early July, rumors were circulating that the Maple Leafs were disbanding, and in August some of their professionals were indeed released as the team struggled to stay afloat. George Sleeman assured the International Association that his team would complete the season. The fight for the loop's inaugural pennant came down to games played at the beginning of October in London between the Tecumsehs and the Pittsburgh Alleghenys, who had not lost to London all season. On October 2, a Tuesday afternoon, Pittsburgh's Galvin faced off against Goldsmith in a battle of two of the best pitchers of the day. A crowd of between 1,600 and 2,000 witnessed the championship game, attendance less than expected because of the weekday contest that was arranged on short notice. Goldsmith and his

curves were effective, and behind him the Tecumsehs played errorless ball until the ninth inning, when several miscues allowed two Allegheny runs. But London prevailed, 5-2, for its first victory over Galvin and his mates, and consequent bragging rights as pennant winners.[21]

Guelph threw in the professional towel after the 1877 campaign, opting to play closer to home against Canadian opponents and American teams that passed through the area. After taking the IA pennant, London was invited to join the National League and seriously considered so doing, but after considering the potential costs of travel and other matters, directors declined.[22] London hoped instead to continue its success in the International Association. In December it was revealed that the club had signed Ross Barnes, the heavy-hitting former member of the Chicago White Stockings. He had missed several games with Chicago due to injury, had clashed with manager Albert Goodwill Spalding about his pay, and was looking for a new opportunity. Englehart and his fellow directors promptly announced that Barnes would captain the 1878 Tecumsehs.[23] The amount paid to induce Barnes to sign with London is not known, but doubtless it was significant, and showed that the club was willing to continue spending money for top talent.

For its 1878 season, the International Association featured a new team in Buffalo, led by former Allegheny star pitcher Pud Galvin. London was considered among the top teams at the beginning of the season, but its early schedule was an unfortunate one, as the Tecumsehs played on the road for four of the season's first five weeks, making it difficult to build and maintain a fan base locally. The consequent lack of home gate receipts also clobbered club finances. By July, crowds became light, amid grumbling about team performance and rumors of a fixed game or two. At a time when betting on games was heavy, any loss of trust in the home team hurt the gate. For his part, Englehart left the team after the

Jake Englehart in mid-life. (Glenbow Western Research Centre, University of Calgary)

With the time spent on his growing business and his subsequent move to Petrolia, Jake Englehart had little more to do with baseball in London. He soon became one of the founders of Imperial Oil, and was preoccupied with fending off competition from American refiners. He was the company's vice president and its largest shareholder. By 1893, Imperial had offices across Canada and was the country's leading refiner. In Petrolia, Englehart married Charlotte Eleanor Thompson, the daughter of a farmer from western Middlesex County. He was then 44 and a millionaire; she was 28. Englehart converted from Judaism to the Church of England and he and Charlotte, nicknamed "Minnie," became benefactors of Christ Church in Petrolia. For his bride he built a fine new red-brick mansion, which they called Glenview, and added a nine-hole golf course beside it. In Petrolia he became active in Conservative politics, and was a director of financial institutions there and in London. In 1908 Minnie died while pregnant at age 45. Glenview was given to the town of Petrolia for a much-needed hospital, and Englehart oversaw its conversion as he planned to move to Toronto, where his business interests had been pulling him for some time. Upon his own death, Englehart left money for the addition of two wings and equipment for a maternity ward and for X-ray equipment. It was later estimated that he put $200,000 into the hospital and its grounds, aside from the house itself, which was valued at $50,000.[24] The Charlotte Eleanor Englehart Hospital remains in Petrolia to this day, part of the Sarnia-based Bluewater Health Network.

In Toronto, Englehart remained active in Conservative politics. In 1905 the Conservative Party, led by James Whitney, swept into power. Englehart had helped elect friend and fellow Imperial Oil director W.J. Hanna to the Ontario legislature, and when Whitney was looking for someone to push a railway line into Northern Ontario, which the previous Liberal government

disappointing 1878 season, citing the pressures of tending to his refining business. Before he left, he and the directors released the high-priced American talent and finished the season with amateurs, ending London's connection to the IA. Buffalo, riding the arm of Galvin, took the second pennant of the International Association. Without any Canadian teams for 1879, the league renamed itself the National Base-Ball Association and struggled on, expiring after the 1880 season.

London and Guelph reverted to amateur status, in 1880 joining a newly formed Canadian Association under President George Sleeman. Sleeman continued in baseball for several more years, as London and Guelph focused on competition with other Canadian cities, including Toronto, which was relatively late to topflight competition.

had failed to do, Hanna recommended Englehart for the job. Whitney was anxious to exploit the north's riches in timber and newfound discoveries of silver and gold. Englehart was named chairman of the Temiskaming and Northern Ontario Railway Commission in 1906, and turned to his talents to opening up the north. His ability to get the job done saw a small railway community north of North Bay adopt his surname. This came after he had the railway help evacuate hundreds of people from the 1911 forest fire in Porcupine. He organized relief efforts and used his own funds to help refugees who fled with little more than the clothes on their backs. At the railway station in the small community which still bears his name, the railway chairman posted this sign: "No one need pass here hungry, J.L. Englehart."[25]

When Jake Englehart died on April 6, 1921, at the age of 73, he had accomplished much as a leader of a ball team, a major refining company, an Anglican church, and a railway. He had many friends and admirers. His funeral in Toronto drew a large number of business and political leaders in Ontario, his adopted home. Many words of praise were heaped upon him for his philanthropy, business acumen, and political deeds. Virtually nothing was mentioned about his propelling the London Tecumsehs to the top of the baseball world of the 1870s, even in the newspapers back in London. Upon his death, Englehart's estate was valued at $3.5 million. It was distributed widely to his nieces and nephews, and to Charlotte's family. Additional funds were allocated for the Petrolia hospital and to hospitals in Toronto. He set aside another $7,500 for Christ Church in Petrolia, to which he and Minnie had earlier donated a fine set of bells.[26] Their support of the church is memorialized on a brass plaque inside the entrance to the sanctuary. He was buried alongside wife Minnie in a fine marble vault at Hillside Cemetery just west of Petrolia. George Sleeman died in 1926 after becoming mayor of Guelph and incorporating the Guelph Street Railway, a venture far less successful than his Maple Leafs.

Englehart and Sleeman put London and Guelph on the baseball map at a time when the professional game was still struggling to survive in many places. Their determination to win and beat the other city led to one of the great rivalries in Canadian sport, decades before those between Toronto and Montréal in hockey, or Edmonton and Calgary in hockey and football. Englehart, an American shrouded by some mystery in his early days in business, became a significant contributor, not just to baseball, but to Ontario and Canada. His contributions were many – and invariably successful. Perhaps some day his important role in early baseball in Canada will be acknowledged by his induction into the Canadian Baseball Hall of Fame, where he would join his old rival George Sleeman.

NOTES

1   Gary Regan and Mardee Haidin Regan, *The Book of Bourbon and Other Fine American Whiskeys* (London, England: Mixellany Books, 2009), 40-41.

2   Clay Risen, "How America Learned to Love Whiskey," *The Atlantic,* December 6, 2013, accessed July 14, 2021, https://www.theatlantic.com/national/archive/2013/12/how-america-learned-to-love-whiskey/282110.

3   "The Whiskey Ring: The First Time Abraham Lincoln's Republican Party Lost Credibility," *History Daily,* accessed July 15, 2021, https://historydaily.org/whiskey-ring-facts-stories-trivia.

4   R.G. Dun Collection, New York City, Volume 348, 900, quoted in Hugh M. Grant, "The 'Mysterious' Jacob L. Englehart and the Early Ontario Petroleum Industry," *Ontario History* LXXXV, No. 1 (March 1993), 68.

5   *Monetary Times 5,* August 14, 1871, 85; *Monetary Times 5,* May 3, 1872, 864; *Monetary Times 6,* October 18, 1872, 308; R.G. Dun Collection Canada, Volume 25, 246, as quoted in Grant, "The 'Mysterious' Jacob L. Englehart and the Early Ontario Petroleum Industry," 69.

6   Hugh Grant and Henry Thille, "Tariffs, Strategy and Structure: Competition and Collusion in the Ontario Petroleum Industry, 1870-1880," *The Journal of Economic History* 61, No. 2 (June 2001), 391.

7   George Railton, *Railton's Directory for the City of London, C.W., 1856-1857* (London, Canada West: George Railton, Notary Public, 1856), 25.

8   "London Base Ball Club," advertisement, *London Free Press,* May 1, 1856; "London Ball Club," *London Free Press,* May 5, 1856.

9   "Ball Play," *New York Clipper,* September 27, 1856, 516. This game was played according to the rules of what is now referred to as the Canadian game. Teams were to consist of 11 men (although only nine were used in this game), and all of them were to be retired before the other team had its turn at bat. This helps explain why the game cited consisted of only two innings.

10 William Humber, *Diamonds of the North: A Concise History of Baseball in Canada* (Toronto: Oxford University Press, 1995), 23-24.

11 "The B.B. Match at Detroit," *London Free Press,* August 23, 1867; Humber, 28.

12 David L. Bernard, "The Guelph Maple Leafs: A Cultural Indicator of Southern Ontario," *Ontario History,* 84, No. 3 (September 1992), 214.

13 For details on Sleeman's involvement with the Guelph team, see Martin Lacoste's essay "George Sleeman and the Guelph Maple Leafs" in this volume.

14 Alan Metcalfe, *Canada Learns to Play: The Emergence of Organized Sport, 1807-1914* (Toronto: Oxford University Press, 1987), 90, quoted in Bernard, 214.

15 "The Ball Field," *London Free Press,* August 4, 1875.

16 Les Bronson, "History of Baseball in London," a paper delivered by the newspaperman and historian to the London and Middlesex Historical Society, February 17, 1972, 19.

17 *Canadian Illustrated News,* July 14, 1877, quoted in Pat Morden, *Putting Down Roots* (St. Catharines, Ontario: Stonehouse Publications, 1988), 47.

18 For a complete history of Tecumseh/Labatt Park, see Robert K. Barney and Riley Nowokowski's essay in this volume.

19 David Nemec, *The Great Encyclopedia of 19th Century Major League Baseball* (New York: Donald I. Fine Books, 1997), 98.

20 Brian Martin, *The Tecumsehs of the International Association: Canada's First Major League Baseball Champions* (Jefferson, North Carolina: McFarland, 2015), 118.

21 For a complete account of this game, and its significance, see Andrew North's essay "The 1877 International Association Championship Game" in this volume.

22 Martin, 149-152.

23 *New York Mercury,* quoted in "The Ball Field," *London Advertiser,* December 17, 1877.

24 "Petrolia Mourns the Death of Great Benefactor," *Petrolia Advertiser-Topic,* April 7, 1921.

25 Ian Sclanders, "The Amazing Jake Englehart," *Imperial Oil Review,* September 8, 1955.

26 Notarial Copy of Letters Probate of Will of Jacob Lewis Englehart, late of the Town of Petrolia, deceased. Located in Lambton Room of Lambton County Public Library, Wyoming, Ontario.

BOB ADDY

By Peter Morris

"A celebrated base ball character" was A. G. Spalding's succinct description of Bob Addy, who was his teammate on three separate clubs.[1] Others who knew Addy well referred to him as a philosopher or as a wag or as the "Honorable Bob." The reasons behind that last tag remain unknown, but it certainly sounds like the sort of inside joke that always swirled around Addy. Fred Cone recalled that his teammate "could say the funniest things while on the field without cracking a smile. Many a game he won for us by keeping up our spirits when the opposing team had a big bunch of runs to the good."[2] Another contemporary described him as "big hearted, bow legged, profane Bob Addy."[3]

For better or worse, everyone had a favorite memory and an opinion of Bob Addy, even when their views seemed contradictory. Cap Anson famously described him as an "odd sort of genius" because, to the horror of the single-minded Anson, Addy "quit the game because he thought he could do better at something else."[4] Yet others found his passion for baseball unsurpassed. "Bob Addy is the modern wonder," declared one sportswriter. "If base ball ever dies out, we believe Bob will want to die. His whole soul is wrapped up in the sport. To see him run in from the extreme field, and hear him beg for a high in-field ball, like a child begging for a bun, is amusing."[5] Cone agreed that Addy's "temperament was such that he could never miss seeing a game."[6]

On one point there was no dispute: that he was unforgettable. "Everybody remembers Bob Addy," declared a *Hartford Courant* reporter in 1886 – *twelve years* after Addy had spent a mere six months playing ball in that city.[7] More than three decades after Addy had played his last major league game, the nickname of rookie Shoeless Joe Jackson prompted a sportswriter to recall that "the famous second baseman, Bob Addy, did that very often, as he was much troubled with sore feet."[8]

But it was not just his eccentricities and his wit that made Bob Addy so memorable. For one thing, he was one of the best players of his era in spite of being very late to take up baseball. In addition, he played the game with a spirit of reckless abandon that led teammate George Bird to call him "about the toughest fellow I ever saw. He would go after anything, any way, and his hands were broken and battered out of shape."[9] Finally, Bob Addy was the first Canadian major leaguer and, unlike many early Canadian-born players, he had actually grown up there.

When and where Bob Addy was born has long been a disputed issue, with most sources indicating that he was born in Rochester, New York, in 1845. Addy seems to have given this information out in his later years, but there is overwhelming evidence that he was actually born in Canada. He was living in Port Hope, Ontario, when the 1861 Canadian census was taken – his birthplace was listed as Upper Canada (Ontario), and his age was given as 19. Nine years later, he was living in Rockford with many of his baseball teammates and was reported to have been born in Canada around 1842. It was not until the 1880 census that he was first listed as being born in New York.

While the census data points to a Canadian birthplace, it is other evidence that clinches the matter. A. G. Spalding, who knew Addy from their days on the Forest City Club of Rockford, described Addy as "originally a Canadian cricketer."[10] Canada was also given as Addy's birthplace in an 1874 book written by George Wright.[11] Finally, when the Forest City Club stopped in Hamilton, Ontario, during an 1870 tour, the locals learned of his Canadian birth and Addy became "the object of special pride on the part of the Canucks, they claimed him from the start as one of them." This made Addy the subject of kidding from his teammates and he finally declared: "I don't care nothing for them, I tell you I don't care nothing about 'em.'"[12]

Exactly when he was born remains unclear. Late in life he began claiming an 1845 year of birth, but the evidence suggests otherwise. His tombstone has 1838, which would be very intriguing if true, but the source of this information is not known. The 1860 and 1870 censuses suggest that he was born around 1842, and that seems most plausible.

Bob Addy reportedly "belonged to several cricket clubs in the Dominion," but any details are lost to history.[13] Nor is much known about his early years except that he was born shortly after

his parents emigrated from Ireland and that his father, whose name appears to have been James, had died by 1857.

It becomes easier to follow Addy's trail in 1861, when he appears in Port Hope on the Canadian census, already working in his lifelong profession as a tinsmith. Listed with him are his mother Ellen (age 44, born Ireland), his younger brother James (17, born Upper Canada, a saddler), and his older brother George (25, born Ireland, a clerk). George's presence in Port Hope is a bit odd, since he had been listed in Ogle County, Illinois, on the 1860 U.S. census and got married in that county in February of 1861. So perhaps he was still in the process of relocating to the United States.

By 1866 George Addy was a well-established Ogle County produce dealer with two young children, and Bob had followed him there. Both brothers also started playing on the Clipper Base Ball Club of the nearby town of Rochelle. While the club itself had limited success, Bob Addy made the sort of indelible impression that he so often did. A. G. Spalding would later recall paying a fateful visit to Rochelle in June of 1866 with the Forest City Club of Rockford, during which "Robert Addy startled the players of the Forest Citys by a diving slide for second base. None of us had ever witnessed the play before, though it may have been in vogue. Certainly we were quite nonplussed."[14]

On the basis of Spalding's comments, Addy has often been credited with inventing the slide. It would be nice to report that this was true, but baseball innovations are rarely that clear-cut. Slides seem to have gradually evolved from accidental slips while trying to make a sudden stop at a base into deliberate evasive maneuvers. While a slide in 1866 would still have been a novelty, there is no way to definitively pinpoint the first intentional slide.[15]

What we can be sure of is that Addy's play made a vivid impression the visiting players. "He showed wonderful ability as a ball player in this game," recollected Spalding, "by practically playing the whole game, captain of the team, pitcher, catcher, and, in fact, took every position where the player had developed weakness by making an error."[16] Both his standout play and his tendency to try to cover the entire field would become recurring themes of the career of the "celebrated base ball character."

Addy was soon offered a place on the Forest City Club and a job at a Rockford hardware store, both of which he accepted. It was a coup for the Forest Citys and the start of the club's highly successful policy of recruiting players from the surrounding countryside.

The Forest City Club was still experimenting with lineups, and Addy played all four infield positions during the remainder of the 1866 season. He began a two-year stint as a club director in 1867, and it was during these years that the Forest Citys began using a regular lineup in which Addy played second base and batted leadoff. The new stability paid off on July 25, 1867, when the Forest Citys traveled to Chicago to face the Nationals of Washington, a seemingly invincible club that was making a historic tour of the South and Midwest. Spalding recalled that "we were all frightened nearly to death, with possibly the exception of Bob Addy, who kept up his nerve and courage by 'joshing' the National players as they came to bat with witticisms."[17] Addy also launched his reputation as a clutch performer by scoring four runs and turning a key double play as the Forest Citys pulled off a stunning 29-23 upset that put the club on the national map.[18]

The Forest Citys made a gradual transition from amateurism to professionalism over the next three years, a process that entailed the replacement of several starters. Only three players remained fixtures in the club's lineup: Spalding, Addy, and a young protégé of Addy's named Roscoe Barnes. Spalding and Barnes went on to become superstars in the first major league, the National Association (1871-1875). Addy is much

less remembered today, in large part because his National Association statistics are not on a par with Spalding's and Barnes's gaudy numbers. But those who saw him play, especially during his years in Rockford, believed that he too was a star of the first magnitude.

George Wright wrote that Addy was "a thorough ball-player, and a most earnest worker; a splendid base runner, a good batter, and a lively fielder. He is a valuable member of any organization from the fact of his steady play having [a] tendency to infuse confidence into the minds of his fellow-players."[19] Anson recalled Addy as "a good, hard, hustling ballplayer, a good base runner and a hard hitter."[20] As late as 1876, he was still considered "one of the hardest working players and best run-getters in the country."[21]

Such judgments do not mean much when they are not supported by the statistical record, and a superficial look at Addy's National Association and National League statistics suggests that he was a run-of-the mill major leaguer. But such a conclusion can only be drawn by overlooking the key fact that by the time those leagues were formed, Bob Addy was already on the downside of his career – exactly how far past his prime he was again depends on the knotty issue of his correct age. While we have less extensive statistics from the 1869 and 1870 seasons, when Addy was in his prime, the available records show that he deserved to be regarded as one of the game's best players.

In 1869 Addy averaged well over five hits per game, a figure that ranked him first among all the players on the more than 400 clubs that were members of the National Association of Base Ball Players.[22] While the absence of at-bats make the comparison from club to club an imperfect one, he also easily topped a club that included Ross Barnes and many other future major leaguers in both hits per game and total bases.[23] Barnes was only 19 that year, but the following year, it was again Addy who led the star-studded Forest City Club in batting, collecting 204 hits in 56 games.[24]

The 1869 Rockford Forest Citys, Bob Addy sixth from left. His illustrious teammates include Ross Barnes (second from left) and Al Spalding (to Addy's left). (National Baseball Hall of Fame and Museum, Cooperstown, New York)

These two glorious seasons almost never happened. As the start of the 1869 season approached, Addy was talking seriously about heading west to "seek his fortune."[25] But in the end he decided to stay in Rockford for another summer, and he enjoyed a season that has to be ranked as the best of his career, since his five-plus hits per game were compiled while making the switch to the game's most demanding defensive position.

Forest City catcher George King had chosen to retire after the 1868 season, so Addy moved behind the plate. Catchers wore no equipment except a rubber mouthpiece, making the position extraordinarily dangerous, and they also needed great dexterity to prevent passed balls. Working with a hard-throwing pitcher like Spalding was especially onerous, but Addy made a seamless transition to the new position. Even more impressively, when he saw Doug Allison of the "Red Stockings" of Cincinnati standing close to the plate to catch, he immediately made the same decision.[26]

The 1869 season is remembered as the undefeated season of the "Red Stockings" of Cincinnati, but it was also a memorable campaign for the Forest Citys. The Rockford club, although still ostensibly amateur, lost only four games all season – all of them to the openly professional Red Stockings. In one of those contests, the Forest Citys came within two outs of pulling off an upset that would have changed baseball history.

The match was played in Cincinnati on July 24, and "Addy was the hero of the game in every way. Not only was he catching directly behind the bat, something he had done only at critical moments until two weeks before, but he allowed only two passed balls to [Cincinnati fill-in catcher Asa] Brainard's five, scored four runs in five times at bat, one a home run, and continued the game after having been knocked flat by a foul in the sixth inning."[27] Addy's insistence on remaining in the game after the gruesome injury led a Cincinnati paper to praise his "commendable pluck."[28]

More than half a century after the fact, Addy's brother-in-law Victor Wheeler still remembered the game vividly. "Bob was absolutely unafraid," he recalled. "He would step into the fastest ball and it didn't seem that anything could get away from those twisted fingers of his, strong as steel cables. Down in Cincinnati that day they carried him to the players' tent on the grounds, with part of his teeth knocked loose, and sent for a doctor. Addy wouldn't stay. He came back on the field and took up his place behind the batter. Then the game had to stop while Cincinnati stood up and cheered him for ten minutes."[29]

Led by Addy's heroics, the Forest Citys were clinging to a 14-12 lead as the game went to the bottom of the ninth inning. But after the first batter was retired, the Red Stockings mounted a three-run rally to preserve their undefeated season.

Bob Addy left Rockford at the conclusion of the 1869 season and announced that he would not be returning. But "the week before the election Bob was back again, swearing to locate permanently, and establishing himself in a tinning and jobbing shop opposite the court house."[30] He returned to second base in 1870 as the Forest Citys completed the transition to open professionalism. The club compiled a 42-13-1 record during a prolonged schedule that included Addy's previously mentioned return to Canada and that climaxed with an October 15 victory over the Red Stockings. On one of the club's few off-days, on August 13, Addy found time to get married in Rockford.

The winter following the 1870 season saw the birth of the National Association and the departure of three club stalwarts, as Spalding, Barnes, and Cone all chose to sign with Boston. The Forest Citys nonetheless decided to enter the new league, and Addy thus became the club's longest-tenured member (with the exception of Al Barker, who played sparingly). A much younger lineup resulted, with Addy the grizzled veteran among a group of newcomers who included the nineteen-year-old Cap Anson.

Scott Hastings is now listed in record books as the manager of the 1871 Forest Citys, but there seems to be no basis for this designation. Most baseball clubs of the 1870s did not have anyone whose role resembles that of today's manager, so listings of this sort are just an exercise in futility. Hiram Waldo, a Rockford bookseller, was the man who signed players and made player personnel decisions, while Addy was named the club's captain and made in-game decisions.[31]

Addy got off to a sizzling start, pounding Asa Brainard, the former Red Stockings pitcher, for four hits in the club's second National Association game and then collecting five hits two games later to lead the Forest Citys to a thrilling extra-inning come-from-behind victory over the Kekiongas of Fort Wayne. But then he cooled off, and so did his teammates. The season was not a success, but neither was it anywhere near as bad as the 4-21 record that appears in the record books – the club actually won eight of its 25 games but had to forfeit four wins when Hastings was ruled to have been ineligible.[32]

The Great Chicago Fire put a temporary halt to professional baseball in the region then known as the West and a permanent end to the brilliant career of the Forest City Club of Rockford. For a while, it appeared it would also mark the end of Bob Addy's career, as the newlywed elected to remain in Rockford and pursue business.

He returned to the diamond in 1873 with the White Stockings of Philadelphia (one of two National Association entries from that city that year). His new club won seventeen of its first nineteen games to grab a commanding lead in the pennant race. But in early June, Addy requested and received his release. Despite his short stay in Philadelphia, he had made such a vivid impression that he was "he was presented with a magnificent gold watch by the directors of the club, and was tendered a dinner."[33]

Business concerns were said to have been the reason for his return to Rockford, but a more personal matter may have been the determining factor. Bob and Ida Addy's only son was a boy named George. Following in the family tradition, George would later give contradictory information about his date of birth, but it appears most likely that he was born on August 1, 1873.

Shortly after that date, following a two-month absence, Bob Addy signed to join Spalding and Barnes with Boston. The Red Stockings were nine games behind his old team at the time of the signing, but he provided a much-needed spark. He batted .355 in 31 games, and Boston won twenty-six of those games to cruise to the pennant. Tim Murnane later credited Addy with having "pulled the Bostons through for the championship by his fine work at right field and timely hitting and baserunning in 1873."[34]

The hard-won pennant was jeopardized by claims that Addy was ineligible because of having played for a club in Rockford after leaving Philadelphia. But former Forest City Club officer A. N. Nicholds attested that Rockford had no club of any kind, and that Addy had merely taken part in a contest involving "little boys." The controversy simmered down, and Boston was awarded the pennant.[35]

Addy spent the 1874 season in Hartford, his last year as a regular infielder. At season's end, it was announced that he planned to organize a new professional club in Springfield, Massachusetts. But he was slow to sign players, prompting speculation that he would only enlist the services of a pitcher and catcher and would cover the rest of the field by himself.[36] Eventually plans for the Springfield Club were abandoned, and Addy instead returned to the White Stockings of Philadelphia where, according to one rather far-fetched retrospective article, he pretty much ended up fulfilling the prediction that he would have to cover the entire field.

The roster of the White Stockings was strewn with talented players who had suspect reputations. According to this article, "in one game eight

of the players were fixed to lose. The one true man was Bob Addy … It was thought by those who were engineering the 'skin' that it would not be necessary to buy Addy, and besides he had the reputation of being a square player." Throughout the contest, Addy did "great work in the field and was striving to win, covering a wonderful amount of ground," even while his teammates were conspiring to lose. Finally, at a pivotal moment Addy made a long run and saved the game by catching a ball that a teammate intended to let drop. When the teammate realized what had happened, "his disgust was supreme, and in a tone of contempt and scorn he remarked: 'Look here, Bob Addy, do you want to play the whole game?'"[37]

The story is at the very least exaggerated, and may be pure fabrication. Yet it is fascinating how well it captures two of the characteristics that were at the heart of Bob Addy's reputation as a "celebrated base ball character": his tendency to venture into the territory of teammates and his scrupulous honesty in an era when rumors of game-fixing were rampant. As Anson would say, "He was honest as the day is long."[38]

After the 1875 season the National League was formed as a successor to the National Association. The main motive for this coup was that it legitimized Chicago's William Hulbert's signing of Boston's four best players, the so-called "Big Four" of Spalding, Barnes, Jim "Deacon" White, and Cal McVey. From Rockford's perspective, the development was most ironic: five years earlier, the National Association had been launched when Boston had signed Spalding and Barnes, and the two young men who had grown up in Rockford had led Boston to four straight pennants. So their return to Illinois seemed a case of turn-about being fair play.

The demise of the National Association left the fate of many players, including Addy, up in the air. It was at first reported that he would remain in Philadelphia with a club that would combine some of the most talented and unsavory players from a city swarming with men who embodied both traits. The *New York Times* reported with dark irony that the managers of the new club had "engaged such able and honorable players as Dick Higham, John Nelson, George Zettlein, Billy Craver, Treacy, Meyerle, Bob Addy, and Shafer (sic). Mr. Bob Addy will officiate in the capacity of Captain. The one great advantage in having a nine of this kind is that they always play to win – perhaps. As an evidence of the high standing of this club, it is only necessary to state that at a recent election all the officers were required to subscribe an oath to the effect that they would not countenance the selling of a single game. Some people are curious to know why the imposing of such an oath was necessary."[39]

But as the *Chicago Tribune* was quick to point out, the *Times* had done an "injustice to Addy in classing him with such a gang."[40] Like many of his teammates, Addy was owed money at the end of the 1875 season and was anxious to leave Philadelphia.[41] Meanwhile, Spalding had been named captain of the new club in Chicago and Anson had been added to the club's contingent of Forest City alumni. Spalding soon offered Addy a spot on the team and the two men who had already been teammates in Rockford and Boston were reunited for the third time.

Upon his arrival in the Windy City, Addy made his usual indelible impression and displaying the now-familiar traits. An account of the team's home opener reported, "every man was where he belonged, from impassive White around to the agile Addy, and from the sure-handed Iowa infant [Anson] down through the grades of height to Capt. Bob Shorty, who teetered all over the infield as he thought there was occasion."[42]

His wit also remained conspicuous. When a July exhibition game to raise funds for an orphanage was rained out, the *Tribune* observed that "the orphans were unlucky – in fact, to use the words of that venerable philosopher, Robert Addy, it was to have been expected that they would be unlucky, for if they hadn't been unlucky they wouldn't have been orphans at all."[43]

Exactly how venerable Addy was by this time can only be estimated, but he was most likely nearing forty and now exclusively played the outfield. Nevertheless, he was as energetic as ever, and several game accounts describe slides like the one that had startled Spalding a decade earlier. According to one of these reports, "Addy opened the second inning and took his base on called balls. He at once stole second in his usual underground manner, and to the great detriment of his good clothes."[44]

Chicago won 36 of its first 43 games to take a commanding lead in the race for the National League's inaugural pennant. But Addy got off to a slow start at the plate and found himself sharing time in right field with Oscar Bielaski and Fred Andrus. His benching apparently was not Spalding's decision; a *Cincinnati Enquirer* sportswriter maintained after the season that "a higher authority than Spalding laid Addy off the nine and put Bielaski in his place – Bielaski, whose batting shows him eighty per cent weaker than Addy, and five per cent weaker as a fielder."[45]

But the pennant race suddenly tightened up in August when the White Stockings were swept at St. Louis. Addy was reinstalled in right field and again showed his knack for clutch performances. He pounded out four hits in a crucial game against St. Louis and continued to swing a hot bat as Chicago maintained its lead.[46]

In September, with the pennant within sight, Boston came to town for a game that featured numerous players from the old Red Stockings-Forest City rivalry. Addy, Spalding, and Barnes all took the field for the home side, while the visitors included Andy Leonard and both Wright brothers. For good measure the umpire was Fred Cone, the third player who had left the Forest Citys after the 1870 season to play for Boston.

Boston jumped to a six-run lead, but Chicago roared back and finally pushed across two decisive runs in the ninth inning for a 12-10 win. According to a game account, "Addy and White carried off the honors very easily, both in fielding, batting, and run-getting. The former made five wonderful catches, those off [Jim] O'Rourke, [Jack] Manning, and [Harry] Schafer being as fine bits of play as ever were seen in any game. Addy's base-running also drew out great applause." The dramatic win allowed Chicago, in the words of the *Tribune's* reporter, to reach "a step in the championship race which is next door to the absolute securing of the pennant."[47]

The labyrinthine phraseology was necessary because of some disputed games, but there was now little doubt about the league's first pennant-winner. Four days later, the last shred of doubt was eliminated when Chicago defeated Hartford. Once again, Addy was the hero in the clincher, making "a couple of extraordinary catches" in the ninth inning of the 7-6 nail-biter, one of which seemed "fairly impossible until taken."[48]

Bob Addy had now played an important role for championship teams in both the National Association and National League, but his mid-season benching still rankled, and he was not interested in returning to Chicago.[49] He instead signed with Cincinnati, prompting a reporter to offer this satirical warning to the fans of that city: "whatever happens on your ball-field the Hon. Bob will have part and lot in it; if a man is to be run out between third and home, Bob will show up and take a hand in it like as if he had been standing there all the while."[50]

Upon his arrival in Cincinnati, Addy made the same kind of impression that he had made throughout his career. Before played his first league game with his new team, it was reported that "The Hon. Bob Addy seems to be a sort of demi-god in Cincinnati; if he stubs his toe the fact is recorded with due solemnity; if he tumbles down while fielding the ball, it is immediately telegraphed throughout the entire country, headed,

'Sad disaster;' and if he makes a base hit, the local reporters spoil their entire reserve of lead-pencils, in making a half-column note of it."[51] Alas, it was Cincinnati's season that proved a sad disaster. After a 3-11 start, Addy took over as captain, only to see the team disband a few days later. Following a two-week hiatus, the team was reassembled, but the club finished with a dismal 15-42 record in a season that ended Addy's major league career. In an odd twist, he also played a role in the end of Spalding's pitching career – on June 5, Addy smashed a line drive that hit his old batterymate in the chest and literally knocked Spalding out of the box in what proved to be the final start of his illustrious major-league career.[52]

In November, Cincinnati announced that it was releasing Addy on the ground of drunkenness.[53] But whether this was the real reason remains open to doubt. A Chicago sportswriter quipped that the charge "sounds oddy" and pointed out that "Bob, though never a reliable player, has always been considered an honest man."[54] More to the point, Addy had a two-year contract, and the allegation enabled parsimonious Cincinnati owner "Si" Keck to avoid paying him for its second year.[55]

"Philosopher Bob" returned to Chicago that winter and opened a skating rink on the corner of Madison and Ada streets. To drum up business, he even organized a game of baseball on ice.[56] Addy's new enterprise prompted one reporter to quip that "Bob stands up better on ice than he does on land."[57]

But Addy soon gave up the skating rink business and finally did what he had so often talked of doing by heading out west, where he remained for the rest of his life. He brought along his young son George but not his wife Ida. She was still alive according to Bob's listing the 1880 census, but otherwise she remains a mysterious figure. Her marriage record gives her name as Ida Belle Seeley, while her son's marriage record says that it was Ida Enose, but she cannot be identified under either name. Nor is anything known about what became of her after Bob moved west.

Even after permanently settling in the West, Addy's doings continued to be chronicled in the eastern press. In 1879 he was reported to be playing baseball in Salt Lake City for a team known as the Gentile Club.[58] Seven years later, a claim that he had become a Mormon with twelve wives was widely reprinted.[59] Other unfounded reports had him in Oregon and California.

The reality seems to have been more prosaic. By the time of the 1880 census, he was living in Evanston, Wyoming, and he was still there at the end of the decade. Around 1891, he moved to Pocatello, Idaho, where he opened a hardware store and, on the first day of 1892, was remarried to a much younger woman named Louise Emma Clark. The marriage produced one child, a daughter named Ellen Louise, who was born on December 1, 1897.

As we have seen, Bob Addy continued to be remembered with great fondness in baseball circles long after his retirement. His feelings toward the game are more difficult to ascertain, but it certainly appears that he retained his passion for baseball. As late as 1890 he was still playing for the town team in Evanston.[60] His last known involvement with baseball came in 1899 when he took part in a "fat versus lean" game in Pocatello. Appropriately, the man who had been known for roaming the field at will started the contest with the "fat" side but ended it with the "leans."[61] One can imagine one of his fellow players exclaiming, "Look here, Bob Addy, do you want to play the whole game?"

Bob Addy died in Pocatello on April 9, 1910, after a severe attack of apoplexy.[62] His widow passed away in 1929, and their daughter died in 1974. At least one grandson was still alive as of 2009. His son from his first marriage moved to Spokane, Washington, and then to Oregon, where he is believed to have died in 1957. His brother George was last heard from in 1900, when he was living in Philadelphia and made news by making a desperate trip to England. The purpose of the voyage was to prevent his youngest daughter Arlan, a soprano who was singing with the D'Oyly Carte Opera, from marrying Dr. Henryk Arctowski, the Polish explorer who had recently returned from heading the celebrated Antarctic Expedition. But after meeting Arctowski, George Addy dropped his opposition and gave his blessing to the wedding.[63]

SOURCES

Coverage of the Forest City Club is usually based upon A. G. Spalding's fascinating but unreliable *America's National Game: Historic Facts Concerning the Beginning, Evolution, Development, and Popularity of Base Ball, with Personal Reminiscences of Its Vicissitudes, Its Victories, and Its Votaries* (1910) (reprint, Lincoln: University of Nebraska Press, 1992). I have instead relied primarily on two sources: an extraordinary 44-part history of the club that was written by Horace E. Buker and published serially in the *Rockford Republic* in 1922 and a five-part series by John Molyneaux that appeared in *Nuggets of History*, a publication of the Rockford Historical Society ("The Sinnissippi Base Ball Club," 43: 1 (March 2005); "The Forest City Base Ball Club: The Amateur Years," 45: 1 (March 2007); "No Longer Amateurs: The Forest City Base Ball Club in 1868," 46: 2 (June 2008); "'We Can Beat the Spots Off the Best Club That Ever Lived': The Forest City Base Ball Club in 1869," 46: 3 (September 2008); "The Eastern Tour – The 1870 Season of the Forest City Baseball Club," 47: 3 (September 2009)). Other sources that were of help included coverage of the 1896 Harry Wright Day celebrations in the *Rockford Register-Gazette* on April 13 and 14, 1896; the reminiscences of Fred Cone ("Baseball Thirty Years Ago," *Lima News*, July 15, 1899)

and Charles Page (E. C. Bruffey, "Bruffey Tells of Charles T. Page," *Atlanta Constitution*, August 10, 1919: A4; *Atlanta Constitution*, March 14, 1909); "Spalding's Start," *Sporting Life*, June 20, 1908, 16; Harriet Spalding, *Reminiscences of Harriet I. Spalding* (East Orange, New Jersey: Spalding, 1910*);* Peter Levine, *A. G. Spalding and the Rise of Baseball* (New York: Oxford University Press, 1909); a history of baseball in Rockford written by James McKee that appeared in *Sporting Life* on April 9, 1884: 4; Harvey T. Woodruff, "Forest Citys a Noted Team," *Chicago Tribune*, March 31, 1912: C2; Adrian C. Anson, *A Ball Player's Career* (1900: reprint, Amereon), and William J. Ryczek's *When Johnny Came Sliding Home: The Post-Civil War Baseball Boom, 1865-1870* (Jefferson, North Carolina: McFarland, 1998). Joe Overfield's profile of Addy in *Nineteenth Century Stars*, eds. Robert L. Tiemann and Mark Rucker, (Kansas City: Society for American Baseball Research, 1989) was also very valuable. Coverage of Addy's time in the National Association and National League is mostly based on contemporaneous newspaper accounts and on William J. Ryczek's *Blackguards and Red Stockings: A History of Baseball's National Association, 1871-1875* (Jefferson, North Carolina: McFarland, 1992). Specific sources are cited in the notes.

NOTES

1   *Chicago Inter-Ocean*, April 12, 1896.

2   "Baseball Thirty Years Ago," *Lima News*, July 15, 1899.

3   *Bismarck Daily Tribune*, July 7, 1891.

4   Adrian C. Anson, *A Ball Player's Career*, 51.

5   *St. Louis Globe-Democrat*, April 1, 1877: 7.

6   "Baseball Thirty Years Ago," *Lima News*, July 15, 1899.

7   *Hartford Courant*, July 27, 1886: 2.

8   *Sporting Life*, September 5, 1908: 7.

9   *Rockford Republic*, September 6, 1922: 10.

10 *Chicago Inter-Ocean*, April 12, 1896: 10.

11 George Wright, *Record of the Boston Base Ball Club, Since Its Organization: With a Sketch of All Its Players for 1871, 72, 73 and 74, and Other Items of Interest* (Boston: Rockwell & Churchill, 1874), 15

12 John Molyneaux, "The Eastern Tour – The 1870 Season of the Forest City Baseball Club," *Nuggets of History*, 47:3 (September 2009), 3

13 George Wright, *Record of the Boston Base Ball Club, Since Its Organization: With a Sketch of All Its Players for 1871, 72, 73 and 74, and Other Items of Interest*, 15

14 A. G. Spalding, *America's National Game*, 480.

15 See my *A Game of Inches* (Chicago: Ivan R. Dee, 2006), volume 1, entry 5.2.1, for an extended discussion of the origins of the slide.

16 *Chicago Inter-Ocean*, April 12, 1896.

17 A. G. Spalding, *America's National Game*, 111.

18 *Rockford Republic*, May 3, 1922: 1 and 10.

19 George Wright, *Record of the Boston Base Ball Club, Since Its Organization: With a Sketch of All Its Players for 1871, 72, 73 and 74, and Other Items of Interest*, 15.

20 Adrian C. Anson, *A Ball Player's Career*, 51.

21 *St. Louis Globe-Democrat*, December 12, 1876: 5.

22 Marshall D. Wright, *The National Association of Base Ball Players, 1857-1870* (Jefferson, North Carolina: McFarland, 2000), 241.

23 Wright, 241.

24 *Rockford Republic*, August 12, 1922: 9.

25 *Winnebago County Chief*, April 15, 1869.

26 *Rockford Republic*, June 21, 1922: 9.

27 *Rockford Republic*, June 21, 1922: 9.

28 *Cincinnati Dispatch*, quoted in *Rockford Republic*, June 21, 1922: 9.

29 *Rockford Republic*, June 21, 1922: 9.

30 *Rockford Republic*, June 28, 1922: 14.

31 *Rockford Republic*, August 16, 1922: 10.

32 William Ryczek, *Blackguards and Red Stockings*, 45-46.

33 Unspecified Philadelphia paper, reprinted in George Wright, *Record of the Boston Base Ball Club, Since Its Organization: With a Sketch of All Its Players for 1871, 72, 73 and 74, and Other Items of Interest*, 46.

34 *Sporting Life*, March 24, 1886: 5.

35 *New York Clipper*, February 21, 1874; William Ryczek, *Blackguards and Red Stockings*, 117-118.

36 *Chicago Tribune*, November 22, 1874: 16; *Chicago Tribune*, December 6, 1874: 2.

37 *Philadelphia Times*; reprinted in *St. Louis Globe-Democrat*, June 25, 1886: 5.

38 Adrian C. Anson, *A Ball Player's Career*, 51.

39 *New York Times*, January 30, 1876: 2.

40 *Chicago Tribune*, February 6, 1876: 12.

41 *Chicago Tribune*, February 27, 1876: 9.

42 *Chicago Tribune*, May 11, 1876: 8.

43 *Chicago Tribune*, July 18, 1876: 5.

44 *Chicago Tribune*, April 28, 1876: 5; for other instances of Addy sliding, see *Chicago Tribune*, June 9, 1876: 5, and *Chicago Tribune*, September 24, 1876: 3.

45 *Cincinnati Enquirer*; reprinted in *St. Louis Globe-Democrat*, February 4, 1877: 7.

46 *Chicago Tribune*, September 17, 1876: 7.

47 *Chicago Tribune*, September 23, 1876: 6.

48 *Chicago Tribune*, September 27, 1876: 5.

49 *St. Louis Globe-Democrat*, November 21, 1876: 5.

50 *St. Louis Globe-Democrat*, March 18, 1877: 7.

51 *Providence Dispatch*; quoted in *Chicago Tribune*, April 22, 1877: 7.

52 *Chicago Tribune*, June 6, 1877: 2.

53 *St. Louis Globe-Democrat*, November 11, 1877: 5.

54 *Chicago Inter-Ocean*, November 17, 1877: 8.

55 *New York Times*, November 15, 1877: 1.

56 *Chicago Inter-Ocean*, January 17, 1878: 8.

57 *Cincinnati Enquirer*, no date, quoted by Joe Overfield in *Nineteenth Century Stars*.

58 *St. Louis Globe-Democrat*, April 20, 1879: 10.

59 *Sporting Life*, August 4, 1886: 5.

60 *The Sporting News*, April 12, 1890: 5.

61 *Salt Lake Herald*, September 5, 1899: 3.

62 *Deseret Evening News*, April 16, 1910: 28.

63 "Face Which Won Arctowski: Portrait of Miss Caroline Addy, Party to the Romance of a Magazine Picture," *Chicago Tribune*, December 5, 1900: 7.

ROBERT "BOB" ADDY: AND NOW YOU KNOW THE REST OF THE STORY

by William Humber

Robert "Bob" Addy's Canadian baseball success story begs a really big question. Why are we only hearing about him now? In the last 10 years, thanks to researcher Peter Morris, Addy's Canadian roots have been highlighted, but this knowledge has taken its sweet time spreading to all corners of the baseball world.[1] Now additional details of the Addy story, of which Peter was uncertain, can be told.

Bob Addy was the first Canadian not only to play, but also to excel, at both the nascent professional game and its major-league startups in the United States.[2] He was the first Canadian to both umpire[3] and manage,[4] if only briefly, at the game's highest levels. Some accounts say he was the first ballplayer of any origin to slide into a base, but given how the game is filled with such myths, it is more likely he was among the first to popularize the move.[5] He even experimented with a version of baseball on ice.[6] It was a dismal failure, but not too offbeat for a guy from Canada, where he was born in 1842 in Port Hope, Ontario.[7] He not only learned to play baseball there, but his renown as a cricketer as well followed him throughout his later baseball career.[8]

Bob left Canada around his 20th year to join his older brother George in Rochelle, Illinois, near the Canada Settlement in Ogle County, Illinois, where he most likely hoped to pursue his career as a tinsmith, the training for which he had completed in Port Hope. Fortuitously, Rochelle was near Rockford, Illinois, home of one of the standout baseball teams of the 1860s and early 1870s, the Rockford Forest City.[9] Addy joined the team in 1866. It featured two Baseball Hall of Famers, Al Spalding and Cap Anson, though not at the same time, and a number of players with near equal proficiency, including Addy and Ross Barnes. When the Rockford team joined the National Association for its inaugural 1871 season, Addy immediately became the first Canadian to play professionally at the game's highest level. Bob Addy can therefore be considered Canadian baseball's "missing link," filling in the one gap (much of the 1870s) in the otherwise continuous record of Canadians playing the highest-caliber baseball in the United States. He flourished at that level while an increasing number of similarly gifted Canadian players elected to remain at home, their participation in the game in Canada enabling baseball to appeal to all ages, eventually in all parts of the country, and even to gain playing adherents among First Nations, women, and a small but enthralled African-Canadian population.[10]

To put the game in Canada into its historical context, we know that the ancestral "folk" nature of baseball-type games goes back thousands of years, long before their play in North America. These games were ritualistic, of a looking-back character, childlike in seriousness, and connected to religious custom or an associated culturally ordained celebration.[11] In most cases they were introduced from the United States into the Ontario (then known as Upper Canada) portion of the British Empire's territory of Canada through Loyalist and other settlement beginning in the 1790s.[12] Such play, however, came as an English or European custom, not as an American-developed or -owned one. Baseball would co-evolve as a modern sport in Canada alongside its development in the United States in the period roughly between the 1820s through the early 1850s. Despite being unabashed Anglophiles, Canadians opted for baseball over cricket because they had contributed to the former's evolution, and because it was seen by many as a better bat-and-ball game for participants.

While many additional examples of this process can be cited, of most significance to the career of Bob Addy were two reports from Upper Canada in 1803 demonstrating the manner in which the English and European, by way of the United States, folk game of "base ball" was becoming embedded in the emerging Canada. In 1878 H. Belden & Company's *Historical Atlas* carried the following account:

"The first Court of Queen's Bench that ever assembled in the counties of Northumberland and Durham was held in a barn on the premises of Mr. [Leonard] Soper, in Hope, on which occasion the judge (Major McGregor Rogers), lawyers and other officials, chose sides and played a game of ball, to determine who should pay the expenses of a dinner."[13]

Hope is the territorial jurisdiction surrounding Port Hope. The account concluded, however, by noting:

"This statement is made on the authority of a pamphlet issued by Mr. Coleman a few years ago. As will be seen, further on, it is contradicted by the accounts of the 'Town of Newcastle' and loss of the 'Speedy,' with the judge, crown prosecutor, &c., on their way to hold a court at Presque Isle."[14]

The contradiction was not regarding the game of ball, but the identity of the court proceedings on the 1803 premises of Mr. Soper as a Court of Queen's Bench, when in fact they were a district Court of Quarter Sessions.[15] The Belden Atlas description of the 1803 Court proceedings had essentially reprinted John Coleman's 1875 account.[16] Since the Coleman account had been published only three years earlier, long after the 1803 event, its legitimacy could be questioned. So from whom did Coleman get his account? On page 44 of his 1875 booklet, he lists people who helped him in his research. They included Timothy Soper. In 1803 Timothy Soper was the 14-year-old son of Leonard Soper, on whose property the court was held. A reasonable conclusion is that Timothy Soper either witnessed the play of ball firsthand, or learned about it from his father, Leonard. When Coleman published his account in 1875, Timothy Soper was still alive. He lived until 1878 and is buried in the Bowmanville Cemetery.

An additional validation is found in the diary of Ely Playter (1776-1858), a farmer, lumberman, militia officer, member of the Upper Canada House of Assembly, and in 1801-02 a tavern-keeper who lived in and around York (Toronto). Concurrent with the time of his writing, he described coming to town and joining, on Wednesday, April 13, 1803, "... A number of Men jumping & Playing Ball..."[17] We do not know definitively, and will never know, what "ball" they were playing, but Playter's connection to Major McGregor Rogers, who presided over the Hope Township Court Sessions, is captivating. Rogers married two of Playter's sisters, Sarah and Elizabeth (not at the same time, but after Sarah's death). Playter and Rogers thus had a close personal relationship. While distance would have ensured they met only occasionally, we can see the real likelihood of their sharing an interest in the game of ball.

It is not surprising that Bob Addy grew up playing cricket, the more advanced of the two bat-and-ball games, but given the above early reference to "ball" in the vicinity of Port Hope, we can reasonably conclude he was also exposed to and played "base ball" type games as a child, and into his teenage years. We have at least five accounts from the *Port Hope Guide* newspaper of his cricketing prowess.[18] His batting was a particularly strong point. But where is the baseball proof? At first glance it appeared to be found in a *New York Clipper* account (August 25, 1861) for a game that Addy's hometown Port Hope Mechanics played against the Live Oak of Bowmanville, and for which it was reported, "The pitcher of the Mechanics, Addie, is also a very fine player and a very powerful bat." Addy's name was misspelled, but this was not surprising in an era when such was common. There are no other names similar to Addy in the Port Hope Directories of the era.[19] There can be little doubt it is him but quibblers will still argue that the proof is tentative. It was confirmed however in the *Port Hope Guide*[20] of November 15, 1873, as found in the publication, *Doings of the Week the World Over*, describing Bob's one-time play with the Port Hope Mechanics beginning in 1858. The *Guide* story recognized the ballplayer's relation to a local man, his brother James Addy.[21] Most of the story, with the exception of his birth year, was correct, but researchers can't have everything.

Additional information has also come to light regarding Addy's family life. He appears to have met his wife, Ida, and married her when he was 28 and she was either 14 or 15. It was not a happy union. There was a boy, George, undoubtedly named after Bob's older brother. In a telling commentary seeking a divorce in 1880, Ida cited multiple cruelties, infidelities, and actual violence against her.[22] It later transpired that she probably needed a quick resolution of the matter, having become pregnant by her future husband. She withdrew the charges, the divorce went through, and eventually Ida and her new husband, Jerry Kinney, a railroad conductor, moved to Pocatello, Idaho, just down the street, as it turned out, from where Bob and his second wife settled.[23] Ida no doubt wanted to be near her son, whom Bob had taken to Wyoming. For Ida's part, she and Jerry had many more children and she lived long into the twentieth century, dying in 1938.

As he aged, Bob Addy made a point of disowning his past. The 1880 Wyoming census listed Bob and George with the misspelled last name of Addey, and Bob's birthplace as New York. Eventually he was more specific, claiming to have been from Rochester, New York, despite ongoing descriptions of him as a Canadian.[24] For years, baseball encyclopedias listed Rochester as his hometown, and even his daughter from his second marriage confirmed this heredity to the National Baseball Hall of Fame in Cooperstown. The reasons are complex, and possibly will never be known. However, when his Rockford team toured Canada on multiple occasions in the 1870s he tired of fans calling out his name as one of their own. "I care nothing for them," he is said to have mouthed on one occasion, and in this era of advanced American xenophobia, hiding even this small "national" difference from his teammates seemed appropriate.[25]

But Bob's connection to Port Hope was not quite severed. From a distance, he and George oversaw their younger brother's last will and testament in 1886, and then their mother's in 1889.[26] Both had died in Port Hope. Meanwhile

Bob continued to be listed locally as a possible returnee among Port Hope's network of "Our Wandering Boys," despite it being unlikely he would ever leave the American West.[27] He eventually died in Pocatello in 1910; the house he built there now has heritage acknowledgment.[28] Another side of his personality was revealed on jobs such as this. It was said "… boys would climb to roofs which he was tinning under an August sun to listen to his ceaseless chatter, which was more witty and clever than the routine of most professional monologuists."[29]

An intriguing element in this family story was his brother George's youngest daughter, and Bob's niece, Jane. George had sent Jane's older sister, Sara, to Port Hope in the late 1880s to marry a much older widower with whom she had six children in rapid succession.[30] Jane might have feared a similar fate. She was a talented vocalist and to forestall any repeat, she relocated to England near century's end, catching on with the D'Oyly Carte Opera company. Meanwhile, at the other end of the world, and with their research vessel,

the *Belgica*, entrapped in the ice of an Antarctic winter, the crewmates passed their days of endless darkness admiring the photos of females in the magazines brought along. Polish scientist Henryk Arctowski fell in love with an image of Jane Addy.[31] Eventually the freed boat made its way back to Europe, where Henryk pursued Jane to Paris. They married in London. The two became leading Polish intellectuals between the wars, Jane as a translator into English of Polish works, and Henryk as a respected academic.[32] Only because they were attending a conference in Washington in 1939 were they spared the fate of so many Poles when the Nazis invaded their country. They never returned. Following their respective deaths in the 1950s, their cremated remains were collected in the United States and shipped to Warsaw for burial as heroes of the nation.[33] Today, Henryk has a scientific base named after him in Antarctica, as well as a bi-annual award, while Jane's acclaim among Poles historically matches her illustrious uncle Bob's in the United States … and now in Canada!

NOTES

1   Despite Peter Morris's uncovering of Bob Addy's true identity, many online biographies of William Phillips from New Brunswick continue to list him as the first Canadian big leaguer, while Addy, despite his playing acclaim, had yet to make it into Canada's Baseball Hall of Fame in St. Marys, Ontario, as late as 2021. Editor's Note: This oversight was rectified in November of 2021.

2   Addy's statistical performance spans baseball's fully emergent time and as such encompasses a formal league (the National), another not always afforded full major-league identity (the National Association), tournaments, one-off encounters (such as with the famed 1869-70 Cincinnati Red Stockings), and games outside the purview of what we now call "Organized Baseball" (in Port Hope and Denver). Many of these games are today described as "exhibition," but unlike the contemporary understanding of such matches as marginal, preparatory, or frivolous, they were, in their day, the norm. Their recorded significance is closer to that of regulation games today, perhaps even greater given the fewer scheduled games played annually in the era as opposed to the number making up current league schedules. In fairness, there were often great disparities between teams in the early era, and players sometimes gave less than a full effort, hoping to "improve" the gambling odds for a return engagement. Encyclopedias and easily referenced online baseball sources provide statistics for Addy's League and Association career but do not include perhaps his most productive years with Rockford in the 1860s.

3   Robert Addy's umpiring appearance was in one of the last games ever played in the National Association (*New York Clipper*, November 6, 1875). The game in late October 1875 between the Athletic club of Philadelphia and the St. Louis Brown Stockings had been postponed several times. Addy was perhaps the only serious candidate remaining in town. He had played for the Athletics' crosstown rival White Stockings.

4   The *New York Clipper* of November 24, 1877, reporting details from a New York newspaper, said, "Robert Addy, former captain of the Cincinnati Club, was dismissed from the club on Nov. 10 on the charge of dissipated habits during the past season. The facts are that Addy was not only honorably released from his engagement to the Cincinnati Club, but he was given a bonus of $100." Other sources suggest he had assumed similar captain roles with the Philadelphia White Stockings. "Captain" was a means of describing an early manager role in this era.

5   Multiple sources over the years have fed the dubious story of Addy's "invention" of the technique of sliding into base. A cartoon illustration from the *Rockford* (Illinois) *Morning Star*, April 18, 1930, reprinted in multiple papers of the day, described him as "the first man ever to employ the slide in stealing a base in 1866." Al Spalding was the source, but the limited range of what was

then his teenage experience and travel argues against the claim's certainty. Intriguingly, at least two Canadian newspapers, the *Saskatchewan Daily Star* (September 24, 1921) and the *Winnipeg Tribune* (December 8, 1923), told the story of Addy's innovation, but went beyond "burying the lede" by failing to mention his Canadian identity.

6   "The second game of base ball on ice between the Franklins and picked nine [featuring Al Spalding] was played yesterday afternoon at Bob Addy's skating rink, on the corner of Madison Street and Ada," *Chicago Daily Inter Ocean,* January 17, 1878.

7   The 1861 Canadian census listed Robert Addy as a 19-year-old tinsmith. Addy's compulsory registration in 1863 for military service during the American Civil War shows him to be a 21-year-old tinner from Canada. His 1870 US federal census listing in Rockford describes him as a 28-year-old tinsmith from Canada. This documentation confirms three things: Addy's Canadian place of birth, birth year of 1842, and tinsmith profession.

8   In their famous 15-14 loss to the Cincinnati Red Stockings during Cincinnati's undefeated streak in 1869-70, Addy's cry of "how's that," sounding like "howzat," was an attempt to influence the umpire's call. See the Editorial Correspondence to the *Rockford Gazette* from Cincinnati, July 25, 1869. It owed much to the cricket playbook where that phrase is shouted to compel the cricket umpire to make a favorable call. In practice there is no call, since the verdict is either clear, or a player's integrity requires him to acknowledge a result unfavorable to him. If, in the latter case, he defers from doing so, the umpire can then be called upon for a ruling. Four years later, as reported in the May 24, 1873, *New York Clipper*, a game between the Atlantics and Philadelphia described a hot liner hit high over Addy's head, "but the cricketer jumped up and held it in splendid style with one hand."

9   George and Robert Addy played for the Clipper Club of Rochelle against the Rockford Forest City featuring the 16-year-old baseball prodigy Albert Spalding, as reported in the *Rockford Weekly Register-Gazette*, June 23, 1866. Rockford won easily, 49-16, but Robert Addy was so impressive that he was soon playing for the Forest City. George was nearing 30 and either was no longer a prospect or had no intention of becoming one.

10 African-Canadian baseball participation dates to at least 1869 with the Lincoln Nine team from London, Ontario. No doubt they were members of original Underground Railroad-fleeing Black families. It is possible that earlier accounts of such play within one of their communities will be found. Brantford's baseball tournament in late June 1874 featured the Foresters, an early First Nations team representing the Tuscarora, one of the Six Nations of the Grand River Territory (*Guelph Evening Mercury,* June 30, 1874). A female baseball club was formed in the

village of Dutton in the Ontario County of Elgin (*Guelph Evening Mercury*, May 26, 1876). A sense of the game's spread beyond Ontario was provided by a *Guelph Evening Mercury* (June 12, 1872) item entitled *Base Ball in Manitoba*, and by a *New York Clipper* item (May 3, 1873) entitled *Jacques Cartier B.B.C.* about a Montréal club composed of French-Canadians led by Charles Gauthier.

11 Thomas Gilbert's *Playing First: Early Baseball Lives at Brooklyn's Green-Wood Cemetery* (Brooklyn: Green-Wood Cemetery, 2015) presents Melvin Adelman's typology of folk and modern games. Adelman, however, did not include the crucial proto-modernity stage leading to the modern. Mike Huggins ("Associativity, Gambling, and the Rise of Protomodern British Sport, 1660-1800," *Journal of Sport History*, Vol. 47, No. 1, Spring 2020, 1-17) describes proto-modernity as the period preceding and preparing for "modern" sport. "It had some but not all of the features of the modern, but [was] not coherently linked in the ways described in its ideal types."

12 Brian Turner's "Sticks or Clubs: Ball Play Along the Route of Burgoyne's 'Convention Army,'" from Don Jensen, ed., *Base Ball: A Journal of the Early Game 11* (Jefferson, North Carolina: McFarland, 2019), describes "bat and ball" play by both Patriots and British Army regulars. Likewise, British soldiers could have brought early baseball-type games directly into Canada without an American intermediary stop. An account from the July 1, 1841, *Nova Scotian* newspaper says, "Quadrille and Contra dances were got up on the green – and games of ball and bat, and such sports proceeded."

13 *The Illustrated Historical Atlas of the Counties of Northumberland and Durham, Ontario*, released by H. Belden & Co. Toronto in 1878. Reprinted by Mika Silk Screening Limited, Belleville, Ontario 1972.

14 This is the spelling as given in the Belden atlas. Today the area near Brighton, Ontario, is named Presqu'Ile.

15 The *Dictionary of Canadian Biography* describes Rogers as clerk of the peace for the newly established Newcastle District (1802), registrar of the district Surrogate Court (1802), and clerk of the district Court of Quarter Sessions (1802). This appears to confirm the identity of the court on Mr. Soper's farm as that of a district Court of Quarter Sessions, and not the first Queen's Bench. Here the matter sat until the 100th anniversary of Canadian Confederation in 1967, and the publication of *The History of the Township of Hope*, by Harold Reeve (Cobourg, Ontario: *Cobourg Sentinel-Star*, 1967). Reeve confirms the Hope Township's court identity in his review of the minutes of the Quarter Sessions for Newcastle District as found in the Archives of Ontario [now located at York University in Toronto].

16 J. (John) T. Coleman, *History of the Early Settlement of Bowmanville and Vicinity* (Bowmanville, Ontario: West Durham Steam Printing and Publishing House, 1875).

17 Ely Playter's diary is available on microfilm in the Public Archives of Ontario at York University in Toronto. An item dated April 13, 1803, in his fulsome penmanship, reads "I went to Town see a number of my friends walk'd out and joined a number of Men jumping and Playing Ball perceived a Mr. Joseph Randall to be the most active." An excerpt is also found in Edith Firth, ed., *The Town of York 1793-1815: A Collection of Documents of Early Toronto* (Toronto: University of Toronto Press, 1962), 248.

18 A cursory review of the *Port Hope Weekly Guide* uncovered five cricket matches featuring Bob Addy; there are probably more. The July 21, 1860, issue featured Port Hope and Lindsay. Port Hope won by 12 runs with Addy scoring 39 of Port Hope's 187 runs. The July 25, 1860, *Guide* said of the game against Millbrook, "The batting of Mr. R. Addy of the Port Hope eleven was brilliant, his hits counting from two to four runs each." The August 10, 1860, *Guide* described a game against a Peterborough eleven featuring Henry Strickland, the son of an English cricketer and nephew of two of Canada's most noted nineteenth-century chroniclers, Catharine Parr Traill and Susanna Moodie. The August 11, 1860, *Guide* featured a match in which Port Hope's first 11 played 22 other members of the club; Addy scored 52 of the first eleven's 157 runs in a game they lost. The August 27, 1860, *Guide* described a game between the right- and left-handed members of the Port Hope club. The left-handed Addy did most of his team's bowling, not surprising given the general preponderance of right-handers.

19 The Port Hope Town Directory of 1856-57 lists Mrs. Addy (Ellen), a widow for at least 10 years, and her oldest son, George, a clerk, living in a house on Harcourt Street near today's main street, Walton, a heritage conservation district. The closest last names before and after them are Adams and Aikens. Robert and James were too young for listing. The Directory is available at the Port Hope history site at http://porthopehistory.com/1856directory/.

20 Michael Stephenson's online Ontario Lakeshore Records Database listed an item for purchase entitled "Addy Robert, Boston baseball player, born Port Hope, Bio 1873." The one-page sketch entitled "The Champion Right Fielder," described its original publication in *Doings of the Week the World Over* and then its republication in the *Port Hope Guide* of November 15, 1873. It said Robert Addy was the brother of Mr. James Addy of this town.

21 *The County of Durham Directory for 1869-70* (Toronto: Hunter, Rose and Co., 1869) listed James Addey [*sic*], occupation saddler, living in the Harcourt Street house in Port Hope. The misspelled "Addy" name was surrounded by last names of Adams and Aisthorp. James was a cricketer with the Port Hope Cricket Club and a baseball player with his town's Silver Stars team. The latter often played against leading Ontario teams from Guelph and Kingston.

22 Ida's divorce suit against the "well-known base ball professional" said they were married August 12, 1870, and had a six-year-old child. She alleged he had kicked her in 1873, threatened her life with a razor blade in 1876, and had committed "several distinct adulteries." The report in the *Rockford* (Illinois) *Daily Register* of March 12, 1880 said that if this was true, "Bob is a brute and villain and deserves to suffer something worse than separation from a bright, intelligent and long-suffering wife." Two years later the same paper (April 26, 1882) reported, however, that the suit had been dismissed by Ida at her costs.

23 We know about Ida's previous and subsequent life because of a fortuitous act of bravery by her second husband, Jerry Kinney, a conductor on the Oregon Short Line. Kinney's train struck a rancher, Mr. H.W. Leaden-wall, who was hurled into a nearby river. Conductor Kinney rescued Leadenwall, and the railroad man was said to be eligible for a Carnegie Medal for bravery. In reporting the incident, even from a great distance, the *Rockford Republic* of October 21, 1908, said, "The wife of Mr. Kinney is a former Rockford girl. Miss Ida Seeley having left here as the wife of Bob Addy, the celebrated ball player. ..." Now that her new name was known, follow-up investigation through Ancestry.com, Genealogy Bank, and Newspapers.com was straightforward. Her marriage to Kinney and the birth of a son soon after appear to have brought a quick, "no-fault" resolution to divorce proceedings against Addy. Her family, future prosperity, and long life are well documented.

24 *The Canadian Gentleman's Journal and Sporting Times*, November 23, 1877, stated, "The announcement recently made that Robert Addy, the Canadian ball player had been dismissed from the Cincinnati Club and that Foley was also to be thrown out, appears to be untrue." As late as 2004 in a reprint of *The Boston Braves 1871-1953*, by Harold Kaese (Boston: Northeastern University Press, 2004), but originally published in 1948, it was said of Addy's background on joining the Boston Red Stockings: "...Robert Addy, a Canadian, who had not played since 1872, but previously starred for the Forest Citys. ..." (page 11).

25 "The 10 man team departed Rockford May 17 [1870], accompanied by George Haskell as business manager (or traveling secretary); James Manny, Will Barbour, and C.M. Utter, all helping out rather than merely along for the ride. Also with the team was a reporter for the *Rockford Register* who signed himself only as 'N.' The first games were easy and overwhelming victories over the Hamilton Maple Leafs (Ontario, Canada) [May 18, 1870], the Buffalo Niagaras, and the Syracuse Eckfords. In Hamilton the locals discovered Bob Addy was Canadian-born 'and he was the object of special pride on the part of the Canucks, they claimed him from the start as one of *them*,' which immediately made the star the target of jibes from his teammates: 'I don't care nothing for 'em,' he exclaimed, 'I tell you I don't care nothing about 'em.'" From *Nuggets of History*, Volume 47, Number 3, September 2009: "The Eastern Tour of the 1870 Season for the Forest City Baseball Club" by John Molyneaux. The account originally appeared in the *Rockford Register* May 23, 1870. Perhaps Rockford's 65-3 victory over the Hamilton Maple Leafs was an additional factor in Addy's not wanting to be associated with a Canadian fandom.

26 The most definitive account of the Addy family's Port Hope connections is found in the *Surrogate Court Index of Ontario, Canada (1859-1900), Vol. 4 Northumberland and Durham Counties* on microfilm at the Ontario Public Archives, based at York University in Toronto, in Cabinet 2 of the Archives Reading Room. Robert Addy and George Addy (and their known locations) are principal executors for their mother Ellen Addy (Probate number 2593, Probate date 1889, reel number 569) and their younger brother James Addy (Probate number 2185, Probate date 1886, reel number 566).

27 Several exercises were undertaken toward the end of the nineteenth century to uncover the current location of men (women were noticeably absent from such lists) who had once lived in Port Hope. The July 5, 1889, issue of the *Port Hope Weekly Guide* featured an article under the heading "Our Wandering Boys," and subtitled *The Export of Blood, Brains and Bones, A Partial List of Our Young Men Who have Gone to Better their Condition in Uncle Sam's Domain*. Robert Addy was said to be in New York, but this was incorrect; by then he had settled in the American West. A second list of "Old Boys" claimed to name those who returned for a 1901 reunion. It was compiled by Joseph Hooper, and indicated where the "Old Boys" were apparently living at that time. It included the brothers George Addy from Philadelphia, and Robert Addy from Salt Lake City in the Utah Territory. By then, however, Robert was living in Pocatello, Idaho, and almost certainly he and George did not attend the reunion. Source for the latter: http://porthopehistory.com/1901reunion/.

28 Multiple sources listed Bob Addy's death on April 10, 1910, including the *Rockford Daily Register-Gazette* (April 11, 1910). Bob Addy's last home at 507 N. Garfield in Pocatello, Idaho, is today described as a two-story home combining Colonial Revival massing, low-pitched roof and eave overhangs reminiscent of the Prairie Style, and Victorian/Queen Anne features in its rounded bay, porch encircling two sides of the first story and fenestration. Recognized as the Addy House in a walking tour guide, it is included in the Pocatello Westside Residential Historic District, as listed by the US Department of the Interior National Park Service's National Register of Historic Places. Ironically, Bob's old house in Port Hope straddles that town's heritage district.

29 Frank Lander, "Bob Addy Was Talkative on Forest Citys," *Rockford Morning Star,* April 18, 1930.

30 Twenty-four-year-old Sara E. Addy of Illinois married 58-year-old George Reading of Port Hope on July 17, 1888, in Port Hope, as listed in the Schedule B of Marriages for the County of Durham, Division of Port Hope.

31 Frederick Cook, *Through the First Antarctic Night, 1898-1899* (New York: Doubleday, Page & Company, 1909), in which Arctowski and Roald Amundsen, the famed Norwegian explorer, provided a breakdown of their crewmates' votes for the most beautiful women. Henryk and Jane would later become close friends of Robert Scott and his wife, the sculptor Kathleen Bruce (*Cincinnati Post*, February 15, 1913). Scott was the ill-fated English adventurer who died on his return journey, having reached the South Pole shortly after Amundsen's historic first. Jane Arctowska (the feminine spelling in Polish) treasured the gift of a silk scarf presented to her by Scott (p. 295-296).

32 One of which was Antoni Choloniewski's *The Spirit of Polish History*, translated by Jane (Addy) Arctowska, The Polish Book Importing Co., Inc., 1918.

33 Correspondence between the US Department of State and the American Security and Trust Company dated April 6, 1960, discussed arrangements for sending the cremated remains of Jane Arctowska and her husband, Professor Henryk Arctowski, to Poland for a ceremony and burial. National Archives at College Park; College Park, Maryland, U.S.A.; NAI Number: *302021;* Record Group Title: *General Records of the Department of State;* Record Group Number: *Record Group 59;* Series Number: *Publication A1 205;* Box Number: *386;* Box Description: *1960-1963 Poland A–Z.* Available on Ancestry.com.

CANADA'S FIRST PROFESSIONAL BASEBALL LEAGUE

by Martin Lacoste

1876: A seminal year in baseball. Club owners and organizers recognized the necessity of providing increased stability and an opportunity to elevate the game of baseball on a national level by establishing a new professional baseball league. While meetings held early in the year in Louisville and New York laid the ground for the inception of the National League of Professional Baseball Clubs, similar meetings were held north of the border, in Toronto and Guelph, Ontario. These latter meetings resulted in the formation of the Canadian Association, the first professional league organized in Canada.

Organized baseball in Canada began in the 1850s, with the formation of teams in Hamilton (1854) and London (1855).[1] The first game on record played under Canadian rules took place on September 15, 1856, between the London and Delaware clubs from London, Ontario. Two innings were played before the London club was declared the winner by a score of 34-33.[2] Three years later, the first known game played under the New York rules[3] took place on May 24, 1859, between the Hamilton Young Americans and Toronto Young Canadians. Toronto bested Hamilton by a score of 68-41.

Baseball expanded throughout southwestern Ontario in the 1860s, as nines were organized in Burlington, West Flamboro, Ingersoll, Dundas, and Guelph. These clubs remained amateur and independent, as team managers and secretaries coordinated games by telegraph and by post, and teams traveled by train for spirited contests and entertaining postgame events. As competitiveness increased and with it a desire for baseball supremacy, it was the Young Canadian Club of Woodstock, Ontario, formed in 1860, which staked a claim as the best club in Canada during these early years.[4]

As baseball's popularity continued to grow, more teams emerged, and meetings were held in August 1864 in an attempt to establish an organized association of clubs from across Ontario.[5] Though this did not come to fruition, it continued instead to be more customary for a Canadian champion to be crowned, earning the coveted Silver Ball trophy, after a short series of matches between the top contenders. Woodstock's reign as champion lasted until 1869, when the Guelph Maple Leafs defeated the London Tecumsehs 43-20 in the championship match on September 24. In so doing, Guelph succeeded Woodstock as the new baseball dynasty in Ontario, as they kept possession of the Silver Ball as Canadian champions through 1875.

Baseball continued to expand in Ontario in the 1870s, resulting in larger crowds and increased coverage in the press. Teams from London, Guelph, Kingston, and Toronto scheduled more games in 1875, and team owners sensed the timing was right to proceed with another attempt at forming an organized association. On April 7, 1876, "a convention of Base Ball players was held at the Walker House, Toronto, for the purpose of forming an Association of the players of this game throughout the Dominion. There was a fair attendance, every leading club in Ontario being represented, with one noteworthy exception – the St. Lawrence, of Kingston."[6] Delegates from Guelph, London, Toronto, Dundas, and Dunnville were present, and the convention proved a success, as an "Association was formed as the Canadian Association of Base Ball players, and it was resolved that the entrance fee from each club contesting for the championship should be $10. The following officers were elected: – President, Geo. Sleeman, Guelph; Vice-President, Spaulding, Dunnville; Secretary, H. Gorman, London; Treasurer, W.F. Mountain, Toronto."[7]

As clubs deliberated whether or not to join the Association, many teams continued to organize practice or exhibition games throughout the month of May. Team managers signed players and assembled their rosters, searching for key acquisitions that would ensure their club's success. Several of these players had had prior major-league experience in the National Association, the precursor to the National League, while others attracted attention from major-league clubs during the season and in the years to follow.

The most notable player of the Canadian Association was undoubtedly the star pitcher for London, Fred Goldsmith. Before he joined the Tecumsehs, Goldsmith "played semipro and amateur ball in and around New Haven for several years, making a name for himself with his curveball. By 1875 he had drawn the attention of top-level professional teams, including the New Haven Elm Cities of the National Association."[8] The 19-year-old played one game at second base for New Haven on October 23, and achieved two hits and drove in a run in his debut. The Tecumsehs enticed Goldsmith north with an offer of $300 for 1876, and he proved himself worth every penny, as he led the team in batting and pitched every game for London, throwing at least nine shutouts in the process (in league and nonleague games). He remained with the club through 1878, then in 1879 played with Springfield of the National Association. Again, the major leagues sought him out, and he joined the National League Troy Trojans late in 1879, this time primarily as a pitcher. His brief sojourn with the Trojans drew the attention of Al Spalding and Cap Anson, secretary and manager respectively of the National League Chicago White Stockings, and they rushed to sign Goldsmith for the 1880 campaign. He starred with the White Stockings, winning 20 games each of the next four seasons. After a short stint with the Baltimore Orioles late in 1884, Goldsmith returned to London for the 1885 Canadian Association season, his last stint as a professional.

The Tecumsehs featured several other celebrated players, among them Goldsmith's batterymate in London from 1876-78, Phil "Grandmother" Powers. Originally from New York, Powers debuted in the major leagues late in 1878 with the Chicago White Stockings. He played with four other major-league clubs from 1880 to 1885, chiefly with the Cincinnati Red Stockings. London also possessed an all-star infield, most notably shortstop Joe Hornung from Carthage, New York, who spent 12 seasons in the major leagues from 1879 to 1890 with four clubs, primarily with the Boston Beaneaters. The major-league career of third baseman Mike Ledwith, from Brooklyn, was significantly shorter, as he had played a single game with the Brooklyn

Atlantics in 1874. First baseman George "Jumbo" Latham, from Utica, New York, had played in the National Association in 1875 with Boston and New Haven before he joined the Tecumsehs in 1876. Latham played with the National League's Louisville Grays in 1877, then returned to play in the majors from 1882 to 1884 with the American Association's Philadelphia Athletics and Louisville Eclipse. Two of London's outfielders also played in the major leagues. William Hunter, from St. Thomas, Ontario, played with Guelph, St. Thomas, and Saginaw, primarily as a catcher, before briefly joining Jumbo Latham for two games with the Louisville Eclipse in 1884. And Jack Leary, from New Haven, Connecticut, the consummate utility player, played at every position except catcher with seven different major-league teams between 1880 and 1884.

The Guelph Maple Leafs, in a bid to rival the Tecumsehs, coaxed several prominent players to join their roster, including third baseman Michael Brannock, from Massachusetts, and shortstop George Keerl, from Baltimore, each of whom had played briefly with the Chicago White Stockings in 1875. Infielder Harrison Spence, from New York, never played in the major leagues, but managed the Indianapolis Hoosiers to a seventh-place finish in the National League in 1888. Perhaps the most notable player to join the Leafs, however briefly, was Pete Hotaling, from Mohawk, New York. After several previous efforts had been made to sign Hotaling, the outfielder finally left the Ilion club in midseason and debuted in right field for Guelph on August 9, only to return to Ilion a few days later. Hotaling saw regular playing time as a major-league outfielder for six teams in the National League and American Association between 1879 and 1888, concluding his major-league career with a respectable .267 batting average.

The only other Canadian Association player to play in the major leagues was Dundas native Charles "Chub" Collins, who played a handful of games at second base for Hamilton in 1876 as an 18-year-old, then several years later played for the National League's Buffalo Bisons and Detroit Wolverines, and the American Association's Indianapolis Hoosiers, in 1884 and 1885.

With the players then in place, the first "Base Ball Match for the championship, between the Maple Leafs of Guelph and the Tecumsehs of London"[9] was touted as one of the most important events of "the fifty-seventh anniversary of the birth of Her Most Gracious Majesty Queen Victoria"[10] on May 24, 1876. Admission to the Exhibition Grounds in London was set at 25 cents a couple for seats nearest the entrance gates, and "for the balance of the seats ten cents will be the rate."[11] Ladies and club members were admitted free, and the Great Western Railway made special arrangements for visitors from Guelph, offering round-trip tickets for $2.[12]

After an estimated 6,000 spectators, nearly half of whom were ladies, "had been treated to the usual opening ceremonies of the ball game – such as throwing, striking and catching – the appearance of the Maple Leaf nine at the entrance gate of the grounds was greeted with cheers and welcomes from thousands of tongues."[13] The toss was won by the Maple Leafs, and the Tecumsehs went to bat first, with Mr. William McPherson, second baseman for the Toronto club, acting as umpire. London took an early lead with four runs in the second inning, courtesy of timely hitting by the Tecumsehs and errors by Guelph players Hewer, Maddock, and Myers. London expanded its lead in the fifth inning, scoring three more to run the score to 7-2 in its favor. But Guelph would inch back with two in the bottom of the inning, then one each in the seventh and eighth innings to close the gap to 7-6. In the bottom of the ninth, Guelph pitcher William Smith "made a clean hit for two bases and got third on Dinnen's misplay."[14] A wild pitch by London pitcher Fred Goldsmith brought in Smith for the tying run and forced the game into the 10th inning. In the top of that inning, London shortstop Dutch Hornung "planted a safe [hit] to right centre, reached second and third on passed balls and remained there unable to touch the goal,"[15] while Thomas Gillean and Thomas Brown were retired, the latter by a timely strikeout, the only one of the game by Smith. But with two outs, catcher Phil Powers drove a ball to center field that Lapham could not reach, plating Hornung for an 8-7 lead. In the bottom of the 10th, Guelph was put out by two groundouts and a foul tip by Emery "into Powers' unerring hands and the victory was won."[16] "Thus ended one of the best contested and most exciting games of base ball ever played in Canada."[17] In the evening "the players of both teams, with the officers of the Tecumsehs, enjoyed a pleasant social time at the Tecumseh House."[18] The organizers of the league could not have imagined a more thrilling beginning to their venture, one they hoped would kindle fervent enthusiasm for baseball among the citizens of the urban centers of southwestern Ontario.

With the Canadian Association season now officially underway, four clubs had by this point submitted the requisite entrance fee: The Maple Leaf Club of Guelph, Tecumsehs of London, Standards of Hamilton, and the St. Lawrence Club of Kingston. The final club to join, the Clippers Club of Toronto, entered into the competition for the Canadian championship in late May, despite not having a ground on which to practice, nor even a "representative nine."[19] Eventually these were both secured, and it was these five clubs that comprised the Canadian Association for 1876. Over the succeeding four months, they sought to ascertain whether Guelph could retain its Canadian championship or a new Canadian champion would be crowned.

The next league game, played on June 10, was a decidedly one-sided affair, with the London Tecumsehs defeating the Hamilton Standards in their first league game by a lopsided score of 27-1. The Toronto Clippers, often also nicknamed the Torontos, launched their season opener on June 17 against Hamilton. Though their belated entry into the league caused many to speculate that the Clippers would provide little competition, they nevertheless upset the Standards by a score of 5-3 for their first win.

Holiday celebrations in the nineteenth century often showcased a game of "base ball" as the centerpiece for the day's events. Dominion Day festivities in Kingston on July 1 were highlighted by the debut of the St. Lawrence club, in a league match with the Hamilton Standards. The St. Lawrence club, "the majority of whom display an unusual amount of flesh and muscle,"[20] were at a severe disadvantage with "the recent desertion of a couple of men occupying important posts."[21] And, "as ill luck would have it, the catcher did not arrive and the pitcher, Curtain, did not arrive in consequence of illness."[22] Hamilton, for its part, was more than a little apprehensive, admitting that "they represent amateur talent only."[23] Throughout the game their "weakness [was] apparent, especially in the batting and fielding,"[24] and it was perhaps merciful that rain curtailed the game after five innings. Those in attendance who braved the elements were rewarded with an 8-3 victory by the home team. Supporters were hopeful the win would give "hope of Kingston cutting a good figure in impending matches,"[25] but as the season progressed, this proved overly optimistic.

The long-awaited return match between London and Guelph took place in Guelph on July 20, with another sizable crowd of 5,000 in attendance. They were treated to another evenly-matched battle, but five runs in the fifth inning by the Tecumsehs and solid pitching by Fred Goldsmith secured another victory for London, 10-7. As it became evident that London and Guelph were the top contenders for the championship, the rivalry between them heightened, and this was both chronicled in and fueled by the press. It was, for instance, reported that the London citizens were more than enamored by the supremacy shown by their club:

The 1876 London Tecumsehs. Early curve baller Fred Goldsmith is seated front row, second from left. (*Canadian Illustrated News*, July 15, 1876)

"It is rumored they intend having the statues of their nine cast in bronze and placed to ornament some of the principal public buildings, such as the Court House, the Lunatic Asylum, etc."[26]

The third contest between the Tecumsehs and Leafs took place on the Civic Holiday, August 9, and was highlighted by another dominant performance by Goldsmith. He allowed only four singles as the Tecumsehs applied "what an on-looker called 'an everlasting coat of whitewash' to the Maple Leafs – something never before done,"[27] to a final score of 5-0. The Leafs did not recognize the loss, as Guelph President George Sleeman "handed to the Judiciary Committee of the Canadian Base Ball Association a protest against the game ... on the ground of erroneous and partial

decisions by the umpire."[28] Committee chairman Edwin M. Moore of London was "chosen at the request of the Guelph men [to provide a ruling], who knew him well, and they certainly should be the last to growl at any of his decisions,"[29] at least according to the *London Advertiser*. The *Guelph Mercury* unsurprisingly and unequivocally opposed this assertion, warning "all clubs against allowing him to act in such a position."[30] The committee, in what would prove to be a crucial ruling come season's end, sided in Sleeman's favor, and the game was eventually "struck out of the championship record for violation of rules."[31]

In between league contests, Canadian Association clubs engaged in exhibition games, typically with other Ontario teams such as the London

Atlantics, Guelph Silver Creeks, Woodstock Excelsiors, Cobourg Blue Stockings, and Stratford Maple Leafs. They also accepted challenges from American clubs, including several from New York (Ilion, Utica, Ogdensburg, Ithaca, etc.) as well as with nines from Detroit, Jackson, Indianapolis, and Fort Wayne, Indiana. The most notable exhibition games of the season occurred during the Canadian tour in late August by the National League's St. Louis Browns. The Browns, second in the League race at the time with a record of 35-17,[32] were nevertheless defeated by both London and Guelph in two thrilling contests on August 28 and 29 (10-9 in 10 innings, and 9-8 respectively). The following day, the National League-leading Chicago White Stockings, with a record of 42-12,[33] ventured to London as part of their tour to battle the Tecumsehs. "An immense number of persons were on the ground, probably over 3,000,"[34] and though London fandom was proud of its club's recent successes, there was not much hope held for victory: "The current opinion yesterday was that Chicago would win the game of base ball with the Tecumsehs by a score of about 12 to 3."[35] The White Stockings lineup featured legends Ross Barnes, Cap Anson, Cal McVey, Deacon White and pitcher-manager Al Spalding, and though Goldsmith held them scoreless for the first two innings, Chicago eventually collected 16 hits and almost "Chicagoed" the Tecumsehs, a single run in the bottom of the ninth making the final score 10-1.

By September, three Canadian Association clubs were decidedly out of contention for the championship. Kingston's league matches were all played at home, in eastern Ontario, evidence that the team presumably lacked the means to support extended travel to southwestern Ontario. This placed the burden on other clubs to travel a significant distance for any engagement, and the St. Lawrence club accordingly secured only a handful of matches. Guelph was able to head east in late September to complete its matches against

Kingston, and in two days the Maple Leafs easily took four games from Kingston, outscoring them 52-12 overall. Despite its promising debut on Dominion Day, Kingston finished the season 1-6. The Hamilton Standards and Toronto Clippers both concluded their dismal seasons with humiliating whitewashings (Hamilton lost to Toronto 15-0 on September 9, and Guelph defeated Toronto 33-0 on September 16), and joined Kingston at the bottom of the standings. (Hamilton finished 2-7; Toronto finished 2-9.)

It remained for Guelph and London to contend for the Canadian championship. The Guelph Maple Leafs concluded their season with a splendid 14-4 record, but as the four losses all came at the hands of the London Tecumsehs, it was apparent to most knowledgeable observers which team had secured the Canadian championship. However, the decision regarding the game from August 9 meant that the "official count stood in favor of the Tecumsehs by 3 games won and 0 lost,"[36] which was in violation of Article XIII, Section 3 of the Championship Code, which stated that "the series for the championship shall be four games, and each club shall play four games with every other contesting club."[37] As a result, "the Judiciary Committee of the Canadian Association met in Hamilton on October 22 and heard protests from the Maple Leaf Club against awarding the Championship to the Tecumsehs."[38] "Considerable discussion took place as to whether the protest should be sustained or not,"[39] and the majority of the Committee held that the remaining game was "not necessary to make their record valid."[40] The Committee therefore "declared the Tecumseh Base Ball Club, of London, champions of Canada for 1876, which entitles them to fly the championship pennant during 1877."[41] Also bestowed upon the Tecumsehs was "the Silver Ball offered by Mr. Wm. Bryce,"[42] awarded to "the club winning the greatest number of games in Canada during the season of 1876."[43] This offer was intended to "encourage the game of Base Ball among Canadian clubs,"[44] and was even sanctioned by the Canadian government when it was "entered according to act of Parliament ... in the office of the Minister of Agriculture at Ottawa."[45]

Who was this "Mr. Wm. Bryce"? William Bryce was born in Glasgow, Scotland, in 1846, to William Bryce, gardener, and Catherine Berry Speirs. The family emigrated to Canada in 1854, first to Toronto, then to London, where William Jr. set up a bookstore on Richmond Street in the early 1870s. He expanded the business to include the sale of stationery, "music, music books, fancy books, wrapping papers, twines, small wares, and all kinds of games."[46] His interest in games and sports further intertwined with his business interests when he became a shareholder in the Tecumsehs.[47] Then in April 1876, he published the *Canadian Base Ball Guide for 1876*, the "only book published that [contained] the Constitution, By-Laws and Rules of the Canadian Association of Base Ball Players."[48] For the price of 10 cents, readers could also consult a history of baseball in Canada, as well as statistics and club records from 1875 for Guelph and London. The guide served not only to publicize the Canadian Association, but also to promote Bryce's business, as full-page ads were also featured for Bryce's Ontario Game Emporium on Richmond Street, an outlet in which one could purchase fishing tackle, boxing gloves, and, predictably, baseball equipment, including balls, bats, and uniforms.

What inspired Bryce's enthusiasm for baseball is not evident, but of interest is that in 1871 he lived next door to Margaret Morrison,[49] whose 12-year-old son, Jonathan, later played for the Guelph Maple Leafs and Toronto Canucks, and also served two stints in the American Association in 1884 and 1887. Whether Bryce and Morrison had a more tangible baseball connection is not known, and though this is perhaps mere coincidence, it is at minimum a reflection of the widespread popularity of baseball in urban centers in southwestern Ontario during the 1870s.

Bryce continued to advocate for baseball in Canada with the publication of the *Canadian Base Ball Guide for 1877*. It followed a similar format to the previous edition, but printed instead the constitution and playing rules of the International Association for 1877. The guide also contained partial team statistics for Guelph, London, and Toronto from the year before, and A.G. Spalding granted permission to publish the National League team rosters for 1877.

Bryce's association with baseball appears to have ceased after the publication of this second volume. He moved his business to Toronto in 1886, but "was burned out in the great Toronto fire [of 1904], and [from then on] carried on business at King and Spadina."[50] He died in 1921, eulogized as "one of the oldest wholesale booksellers and stationers in Canada,"[51] having published a variety of magazines, games, maps, and books.

As mentioned, the primary focus of Bryce's 1877 guide was on the coming inaugural season of the International Association. It made no reference to a sophomore campaign for the Canadian Association, as by the time the guide was published, it was evident that no such campaign would take place. On the heels of their success in 1876, the Tecumsehs were keen on seeking out other top opponents, and "an unexpected opportunity arose in late 1876 when [London manager] Harry Gorman learned some American clubs were considering a new organization of professional clubs to rival the National League."[52] Gorman attended the International Base Ball Convention in Pittsburgh in February 1877 on behalf of the Tecumsehs, and "presented credentials from the Maple Leafs ... and was admitted to the Convention as [their] representative"[53] as well. "An organization was effected under the title of the International Association of Base Ball Players,"[54] with Gorman elected as vice president, and George Sleeman, Guelph manager, elected to the Judiciary Committee.[55]

At first, this development did not hinder plans to continue the Canadian Association for a second season. A "second annual convention of the Canadian Association of Base-ball players"[56] was held in Toronto on April 5, 1877, with representatives "from the Maple Leaf (professional), the Maple Leaf (amateur), and the Silver Creek, all of Guelph; the Athletic, of London; the Iroquois, of Markham; the Athletics, of Elora; and the Torontos, of Toronto; various other clubs in the Association being represented by proxy."[57] It was not a fait accompli that London and Guelph's admittance to the International Association would naturally preclude their participation in the Canadian Association, though "it was a noticeable fact that the Tecumseh Club, of London, did not think it worth while to send a representative."[58] This observation did cause some speculation and doubt as to the future of the Canadian Association: "Were the Tecumseh Managers of the opinion that by absenting themselves they would break up the association and thus hold the championship pennant for the season of 1877 without earning it? If such was the case, they were mistaken, as the Association is now on a sounder basis than ever."[59] This optimism was shared by the Guelph Maple Leafs and their owner, George Sleeman, as he was reelected president of the league for the coming season. However, by May 23, five clubs had entered the amateur championship of Canada, but "the only entry for the Professional championship of Canada [was] the Maple Leaf, of Guelph."[60] By then, both the Tecumsehs and the Leafs had commenced play in the International Association (headlined by an exciting 2-1 victory by London over Guelph on May 17 to launch the latter's season), and all hopes for the return of the Canadian Association for 1877 were extinguished.

The Canadian Association and National League, fraternal twins of a sort, each encountered their own respective struggles in their early years. Six of the eight charter members of the National League had folded or been expelled in the first four years of its existence, but the League persisted through its well-documented challenges and controversies, and has cultivated a legacy rich in history and lore. The Canadian Association embraced the game with comparable zeal and commitment, and though it did not survive infancy, its presence and impact on the sport at such a formative time helped solidify Canada's role and legacy in the evolution of baseball in the nineteenth century.

SOURCES

In addition to the sources cited in the Notes, the author consulted:

Newspapers, including *British Whig, Guelph Herald, Guelph Mercury, Hamilton Spectator, Hamilton Times, London Advertiser, London Free Press, New York Clipper, Pittsburgh Daily Post, The Globe* (Toronto), *Toronto Star,* and *Woodstock Weekly Sentinel.*

Genealogical and player data was obtained from a variety of sources, including Ancestry.com, Baseball-Reference.com, census records, city directories, vital records, minor-league player files of Reed Howard, Retrosheet.org, and the author's own player database and genealogical files.

Various ledgers and correspondence from the Sleeman Family Collection, Archives and Special Collections, McLaughlin Library, University of Guelph.

NOTES

1   William Humber, "It's Our Game, Too, Neighbor," in Jane Finnan Dorward, ed., *Dominion Ball* (Cleveland: Society for American Baseball Research, 2005), 7.

2   "Base Ball in Canada," *New York Clipper*, September 27, 1856: 183.

3   "Young Canadian vs. Young America," *New York Clipper*, June 11, 1859: 59.

4   William J. Ryczek, *Baseball's First Inning: A History of the National Pastime Through the Civil War* (Jefferson, North Carolina: McFarland & Co., 2014), 205.

5   "Base Ball," *Guelph Mercury*, August 26, 1864: 3.

6   "The Base Ball Convention," *Guelph Mercury*, April 8, 1876: 1.

7   "The Base Ball Convention."

8   David Fleitz, "Fred Goldsmith," SABR BioProject, https://sabr.org/bioproj/person/fred-goldsmith/.

9   "The Queen's Birthday," *Guelph Mercury*, May 23, 1876: 1.

10   "The Queen's Birthday."

11   "The Ball Field," *London Advertiser*, May 23, 1876: 1.

12   "The Ball Field."

13   "The Game in London or 'How's That?'," *Guelph Mercury*, May 25, 1876: 1.

14   "The Ball Field," *London Advertiser*, May 25, 1876: 1.

15   "The Ball Field."

16   "The Ball Field."

17   "The Ball Field."

18   "The Ball Field."

19   " Base Ball," *Guelph Mercury*, May 29, 1876: 1.

20   "Dominion Day," *British Whig*, July 3, 1876: 2.

21   "Dominion Day."

22   "Dominion Day."

23   "Dominion Day."

24   "Dominion Day."

25   "Dominion Day."

26   "Base Ball Field," *Guelph Mercury*, from the *Hamilton Spectator*, August 11, 1876: 1.

27   "The Championship Base Ball Match," *London Advertiser*, August 10, 1876: 1.

28   "Base Ball Field," *Guelph Mercury*, August 12, 1876: 1.

29   "The Championship Base Ball Match," *London Advertiser*, August 10, 1876: 1.

30   "The Base Ball Match," *Guelph Mercury*, August 10, 1876: 1.

31   *Bryce's Canadian Base Ball Guide for 1877* (London: Wm. Bryce, Publisher, 1877), 65.

32   Retrosheet.org.

33   Retrosheet.org.

34   "Yesterday's Game," *London Advertiser*, August 31, 1876: 1.

35   "Yesterday's Game."

36   *Bryce's Canadian Base Ball Guide for 1877* (London: Wm. Bryce, Publisher, 1877), 65.

37   *Bryce's Canadian Base Ball Guide for 1877* (London: Wm. Bryce, Publisher, 1877), 35.

38   *Bryce's Canadian Base Ball Guide for 1877* (London: Wm. Bryce, Publisher, 1877), 65.

39   "Tecumsehs, of London, the Champions," *Guelph Mercury*, October 28, 1876: 1.

40   "Tecumsehs, of London, the Champions."

41   "Tecumsehs, of London, the Champions."

42   *Bryce's Canadian Base Ball Guide for 1877* (London: Wm. Bryce, Publisher, 1877), 65.

43   *Bryce's Canadian Base Ball Guide for 1876* (London: Wm. Bryce, Publisher, 1876), 2.

44   *Bryce's Canadian Base Ball Guide for 1876* (London: Wm. Bryce, Publisher, 1876), 2.

45   *Bryce's Canadian Base Ball Guide for 1876* (London: Wm. Bryce, Publisher, 1876), 2.

46   *City of London Directory for 1876-77* (London: W.H. Irwin & Co., 1876-77), 115.

47   Brian Martin, *The Tecumsehs of the International Association* (Jefferson, North Carolina: McFarland & Co., 2015), 64.

48   *Bryce's Canadian Base Ball Guide for 1876* (London: Wm. Bryce, Publisher, 1876): 1.

49   Library and Archives Canada. *Census of Canada, 1871*. Ottawa, Ontario: Library and Archives Canada, n.d. RG31-C-1. Statistics Canada Fonds.

50   "William Bryce Dead/Was Long a Merchant," *Toronto Star*, October 3, 1921: 19.

51   "William Bryce Dead/Was Long a Merchant."

52   Martin, *The Tecumsehs of the International Association*, 86.

53   Correspondence from Harry Gorman to George Sleeman, February 26, 1877, Sleeman Family Collection, Archives and Special Collections, McLaughlin Library, University of Guelph.

54   Correspondence from Harry Gorman to George Sleeman, February 26, 1877.

55 "The Council of Ballists," *Pittsburgh Daily Post*, February 22, 1877: 4.

56 "Convention of the Canadian Association," *Guelph Mercury*, April 6, 1877: 1.

57 "Convention of the Canadian Association."

58 "Convention of the Canadian Association."

59 "Convention of the Canadian Association."

60 "Base Ball Notes," *Guelph Mercury*, May 23, 1877: 1.

A LONGEVITY MARVEL AND A CANADIAN NATIONAL TREASURE: TECUMSEH/LABATT MEMORIAL PARK

By Robert K. Barney and Riley Nowokowski

There resides in London, Ontario, across Queen's Avenue from the old early nineteenth century courthouse located above the confluence of the north and south branches of the Thames River (locally referred to as "The Forks"), one of baseball history's grandest historical legacies, the fabled Labatt Memorial Park, the oldest continuously operated baseball grounds found anywhere in the world. There it rests in all its contemporary luster, a luxuriant jewel in the Forest City's urban landscape.

We initially became interested in the historical lineage of Labatt Park in the face of an American challenge to the Park's embrace of the distinction "oldest and continuously operated." Hence, we resolved to carry out a mission to pursue a detailed history of Labatt Park's origin, and to examine the credibility of its unique longevity status. With regard to the latter, we carry out that exercise in the accompanying appended commentary. Beyond that secondary quest, however, we chiefly endeavor to leave to posterity a documented account of the Park's place in the cultural lineage of the city of London, the province of Ontario, the national state of Canada, and, perhaps above all, its place in the greater history of North America's long-standing preeminent team sport: baseball. Let us begin.

The record of baseball play in London predates the opening of Tecumseh Park/Labatt Park by two decades. In the *City of London Directory* for 1856, we note the establishment of a London Base Ball Club. One game of baseball appears to have been played in that year, a two-inning affair in which London edged a team from the nearby diminutive hamlet of Delaware by a score of 34-33.[1] Over the following two decades, 1856-1876, baseball play in London expanded rapidly, creating competition with the sport of cricket for players, fan followers, and, even more critically, for suitable practice and playing space. In general, cricket experienced a steady decline in the face of an ever-rising passion of public interest for baseball. By 1900 the sport of cricket hardly existed in London's sporting landscape.[2] Embedded in such passion for baseball rose the London Tecumsehs and the need for an exclusive playing venue. Hence, Tecumseh Park.

To recount Tecumseh Park's genesis authenticity, we turn to the pages of the *London Daily Advertiser* of the spring months March, April, and May of 1877. With knowledge that London's premier professional baseball aggregation, the Tecumsehs, had been accepted as a charter member of the new International Association, a genuine "major league" competitor to the equally new (1876) National Association of Professional Base Ball Clubs (today, Major League Baseball's National League) for urban franchises and baseball's best players, the *London Daily Advertiser* of March 31 sought to educate its readers on the forthcoming 1877 season's prospectus by offering for sale at 10 cents per copy the *Canadian Baseball Guide*, containing the "Constitution and Championship Code of the International Association," the "Playing Rules of the League," and "other valuable information connected with the Game."[3] There is little doubt that the prospect of the Tecumsehs playing in the new International Association sparked great interest among London's sporting public.

Two weeks and two days later, on April 16, in a column headed "The Ball Field," the *Advertiser* provided its readers with the "inside scoop" on reasons why a new baseball park was needed. Such a need was associated with limited Tecumseh practice and playing time on London's only viable fieldsports venue, today's greater Victoria Park area, which in 1877 served chiefly as the expansive parade grounds and drill field for the Crown's military garrison. Consequently, a new playing venue had to be secured, one with total Tecumseh control over its availability. Stated the *Advertiser*:

The vexatious delays in getting possession of part of the Park property, and the threatening attitude of certain parties who appear determined to have the ball ground at their own disposal, so as to benefit by the custom which large crowds invariably draw to people in their line of business, compelled the abandonment of the idea of utilizing the waste lands of the city for a ballfield. The conditions imposed by the Park Committee, one of which limited the size of the field to such narrow dimensions that it would be too small for either baseball, cricket or lacrosse, added another reason why it would be folly for the club to go to the expense of enclosing and preparing the portion of the Artillery Block set apart for its use.

After visiting London East, the northern suburbs of the city and the Petersville and Kensington Flats, the most convenient plot, taking everything into consideration, that could be secured, was a piece of meadow land adjoining the west end of Kensington Bridge, on the north side of the road, and an agreement has been effected by the owners of it for its lease or purchase. Work will be commenced on it at once, and the expectation is that it will be ready in ten days, or a fortnight at the furthest. It is nearer to the business centre of the city than the exhibition grounds, and when the Street Car Company extend their track to the brow of the Court House hill, which would be to their interest to do, it can be reached from all parts of the city readily and comfortably.[4]

With respect to the site choice made by the Tecumseh Base Ball Club ("a piece of meadow land adjoining the west end of Kensington Bridge, on the north side of the road") we are offered a then contemporary view of that particular piece of land that captured the favor of Tecumseh officials. There it lay, in its bucolic circumstance at the forks of the Thames River, the future site of Tecumseh Park, occupying a parcel of land that appeared to be endowed with a field of barley or winter wheat ready for harvesting, all painted in oils by the artist Charles B. Chapman in the late summer of 1875, a scant two years prior to the park's celebrative beginning.[5]

Returning our attention to a historic newspaper comment on the site selection of the park, published on Friday, April 20, the *Advertiser* was once again prompted to comment on developments at the new ballpark location:

The rain of the past two days has retarded the work of preparing the new grounds for the Tecumsehs, but an extra force is at work today endeavoring to make up for lost time. The contract for two thousand yards of sodding has been let to Mr. Murdoch. The fencing and stands for the accommodation of spectators will be rushed rapidly forward. There is a brisk competition for the lease of the refreshment stands on the grounds. Everything is expected to be in readiness by the first of May.[6]

As the new Tecumseh ball grounds, named appropriately Tecumseh Park, were being established, the professional Tecumsehs played a practice contest on the old Military Park grounds. The result, an 8-2 victory over the Atlantics, "an amateur team of this city," was played out before "a large attendance of spectators."[7] Baseball-fever-related activities surrounding the new Tecumseh Park under development continued to appear in the *Advertiser*, particularly with regard to the games planned for the gala inauguration of the facility:

The Great Western Railway have ordered reduced rates at all stations on their main line and branches for the 5th and 7th of May, to give people an opportunity of witnessing the base ball games between the Hartfords and Tecumsehs. Proposals are invited for leases of the refreshment stands on the Tecumsehs' new grounds; also for the privilege of decorating the fences with advertising announcements.[8]

On the last day of April, as the series against the Hartfords drew ever nearer, the *Advertiser* updated its readers on the new park's condition:

The Tecumsehs' ball grounds are beginning to look as pretty as a picture. The diamond is beautifully sodded and the clay paths around the bases serve to bring out the rich green surrounding them with double effect. The grandstand is a fine commanding building, and comfortably suited. The reporters and scorers, and telegraph operators are also well provided for. A large tier of open seats is being erected in the southeast angle. Though the grounds will be ready for playing on next Saturday, when the Hartfords open the season with the Tecumsehs, they will not be in their best condition for some weeks to come. The progress made during the past two weeks is something wonderful.[9]

But first, a critical moment in Tecumseh Park history – its first documented competition – a practice game between the Tecumsehs and London's amateur Atlantics on the afternoon of Thursday, May 3, 1877. The outcome, a 5-1 victory for the Tecumsehs, is inconsequential to our study here, but the *Advertiser's* commentary on Tecumseh Park itself is enlightening. On the eve of the "official" opening of the season against the Hartfords, one gets a full picture of the now classic baseball venue:

The new grounds are nearly complete in every respect of any of the kind in Canada, and but few American cities have such a convenient playing field. The place has been levelled under the management of Mr. Kitchen, who has worked hard in getting things into shape. The diamond and several feet around the borders are nicely sodded, while the base lines have been formed of clay, and are as hard as a rock. Mr. Murdock deserves a great deal of credit for the way he has done the sodding. A pipe well has been sunk, and a full supply of cool water is thus always in the ground; the well will also be useful in watering the grounds. A grandstand capable of seating 600 persons has been erected in the northeast corner of the field. This is for the use of members of the club and the seats have already been reserved for the entire season. At the southeast corner is the general stand, open to the general public in payment of a fee. To the south of the grandstand, which by the way is covered, is a Directors' Pavillion, erected at the expense of the President, Mr. J. L. [Jacob Lewis] Englehart, who with Mr. Plummer, has given a good deal of attention to overseeing the fitting up of the grounds and buildings.

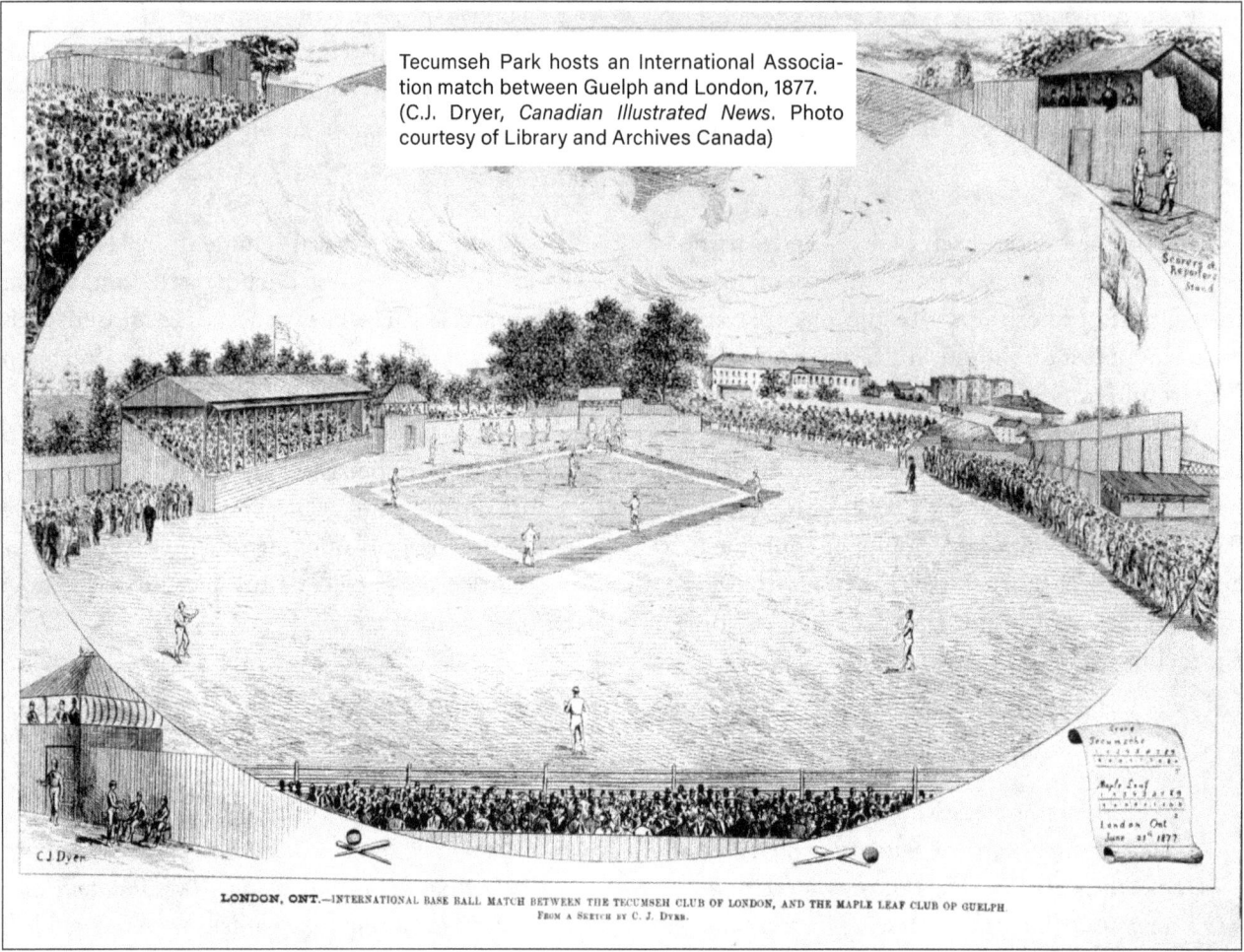

Tecumseh Park hosts an International Association match between Guelph and London, 1877. (C.J. Dryer, *Canadian Illustrated News*. Photo courtesy of Library and Archives Canada)

LONDON, ONT.—INTERNATIONAL BASE BALL MATCH BETWEEN THE TECUMSEH CLUB OF LONDON, AND THE MAPLE LEAF CLUB OF GUELPH. FROM A SKETCH BY C. J. DYER.

Directly behind the catcher is a booth to be used for a dressing and store room by the players, and above this is a point of observation for scorers, telegraph operators and reporters. It is hoped that they will be left alone by outsiders, as [they are] persons who have work to do and don't care to be bothered by people shouting, applauding or criticising the play.[10]

On the afternoon of Saturday, May 5, 1877, the Tecumsehs met and were defeated by the Hartfords by a score of 6-2. The *Advertiser* reported that "fully two thousand persons" attended.[11] Two days later, on the afternoon of Monday, May 7, the second game of the two-game series unfolded, an 8-4 series sweep victory for the Hartfords. The *Advertiser*, while reporting a crowd of "probably

fifteen hundred," extolled the visitors as "a fine body of men, quiet and gentlemanly in their manner, and never once in their two games did they question a decision or make a remark to which any exception could be taken."[12] There followed in London a two-game Friday/Saturday series against the Stars of Syracuse (New York), both contests of which the Tecumsehs won by scores of 7-2 and 9-8.[13] And then, scarcely two days later, on Tuesday afternoon, May 15, "at 3:00," Tecumseh Park spectators, among them "a large number of Maple Leafs" from Guelph, witnessed a 2-0 Tecumseh defeat at the hands of the Pittsburgh Alleghenys in "the first game of base-ball in this city in the international series."[14] And thus closed the first and earliest chapter in the history of what we know today as Labatt Park.

FLOODS, CYCLING, AND BASEBALL FEVER: TECUMSEH/LABATT PARK, 1877-1937

From the pages of the *London Advertiser* of the latter part of the nineteenth century[15] and the *London Free Press* for much of the twentieth century[16] comes the primary record that supports beyond all argument the record that preserves the distinction "continuously operating" that the hallowed park has rightfully earned. A thorough examination of two floods in question prove beyond a shadow of doubt that in both cases, the "one and the same" Tecumseh Park (1883) and John Labatt Memorial Park (1937) were in timely fashion renovated following the destructive inundations that in both cases interrupted scheduled activities. This study puts to rest the argument that the storied baseball park changed physical location.[17] Such findings provide further evidence undergirding the bona-fide heritage distinction the park enjoys.

For the first five years of its existence (1877-1882), Tecumseh Park was the hub of London's sporting activity. During that five-year period, not only was it the most active and prestigious venue for baseball, it also hosted the central activities of two other prominent sporting pursuits and their supporting constituencies, the "bicycle and lacrosse crowds." London, like much of North America in the late nineteenth and early twentieth centuries, embraced the period's cycling craze. The cycling pastime experienced phenomenal growth in the city and its surrounding areas during much of the 1880s and 1890s; in fact, few recreational sporting activities rivaled cycling in terms of numbers of participants, individual club organization, and investment in facilities.[18] London's Forest City Bicycle Club headquarters, located in a large three-floor warehouse on Dundas Street, formerly a wholesale dry-goods establishment, was the envy of most of the city's sporting aggregations. Referred to as "elegant and spacious,"[19] the top floor was fitted out as a club room, the lower two floors for riding activities.[20] Part of the club's activities focused on track racing, much of which was presented in Tecumseh Park before enthusiastic crowds.

Lacrosse, riding the pinnacle of its success in mustering Canadian sporting attention over that of other "national sport claimants" in the 1860s and 1870s, also focused squarely on Tecumseh Park for its main competitive attractions.[21] Members of the London Lacrosse Club, meeting on April 10, 1883, reported the *Advertiser*, "crowded into meeting rooms, showing that the national game has taken a strong hold on the lovers of sport in this city."[22] Club secretary Wylkie reported that the Management Committee had "... secured the entire [exaggerated] control of Tecumseh Park for the coming season. ..."[23] At a subsequent meeting, some two weeks later, the London Lacrosse Club announced an effort to "put Tecumseh Park in order, and have the stands moved and grounds scraped, so as to commence practice as soon as possible."[24] On May 3 the *Advertiser* reported that "the newly organized lacrosse club yesterday received a consignment of three dozen sticks from Brantford, where they are manufactured by the Indians. The sticks are pronounced in every respect first class. The first practice of the club will take place tomorrow morning on Tecumseh Park, and again on Saturday."[25] And on May 12: "The costume selected by the club consists of navy blue knickerbocker, blue and white striped shirt, blue stockings and polo dips. ..."[26] Learning of plans for a spectacular opening of the Lacrosse Club's 1883 competitive season, the May 14 issue of the *Advertiser* reported the following: "Between thirty and forty members assembled for practice Saturday afternoon on Tecumseh Park. After practice, the President, J.B. Vining called the members together for the purpose of electing a captain, which resulted in the choice of Mr. P.J. Edmonds, who is in every way qualified for the position, and a zealous lacrosse player."[27] The "Grand Opening" occurred on May 24 against the Brants of Brantford, an affair that drew a reported crowd of about 2,500 to "the Tecumseh grounds."[28]

Meanwhile, as Tecumseh Park played host to bicycle and lacrosse activity, it also accommodated the activities of London's foremost baseball nines. The city's 1882 champions, the Mutuals, determined to "retain the laurels won last year[,]" [were hoping] "to commence practice as soon as the state of weather permits" [while declaring an intent] to "secure, if possible, the Tecumseh Park."[29] During the month of May 1883 Tecumseh Park was the center of London's busy baseball activity. A number of local baseball aggregations featured the play of both young adherents to the game, for instance on teams such as the Young Athletes and Young Tecumsehs, as well as older experienced players on such baseball clubs as the Eurekas, Alerts, Atlantics, and, of course, London's "diamond pride," the senior Tecumsehs.

What appeared to be a rosy and active athletics life for Tecumseh Park for the season of 1883 was torn asunder by events occurring on the evening and early morning of July 10/11. In what the *Advertiser* proclaimed "a catastrophe altogether unknown at this season of the year," an "uninterrupted torrent of rain fell throughout the night, lasting until mid-morning the next day."[30] London West, and with it, Tecumseh Park, were hardest hit; the water was said to have reached the highest point ever known: "The whole of Tecumseh Park, fences, stands, and houses, together with Massie's boat house, all went down the river."[31] And it was not solely baseball that suffered the consequences of the disaster. As the *Advertiser* reported: "All the effects of the London Lacrosse Club were swept away by the flood, including sticks, clubs, balls, etc. They were stored at Tecumseh Park, and were carried away with the buildings."[32] Tecumseh Park, for the moment, ceased to function. The remainder of the 1883 outdoor sports season in

Tecumseh Park was suspended. London newspapers during that time were replete with reports of elite athletic contests normally contested in Tecumseh Park occurring instead on the grounds of rival teams.

Almost four months after the July 1883 flood, London city officials met on November 1 to decide on tax rates and priority expenditures, among which flood-related damage issues were prominent. The *Advertiser* reported that one subject of discussion was the plight of Tecumseh Park: "The baseball grounds should be looked after. The want of fence along the street renders walking after dark on the sidewalk a very dangerous matter."[33] A week later the London West Council met for further civic allocation purposes. No funds were allotted for Tecumseh Park, only a motion unanimously passed "that the Tecumseh Base Ball Club be notified to fence their property on Dundas Street, as it was in a dangerous condition."[34] As winter set in, thought and action toward rehabilitation of Tecumseh Park from the ravages of the great flood of July 1883 were put on hold until the following spring.

A decade after the 1883 flood, London's foremost baseball venue underwent significant change – a geographical alteration in the location of the park's baseball diamond. More than half a century later, in mid-December 1936, as the city rejoiced over the John Labatt family donation of Tecumseh Park to the City of London, the *Free Press* was moved to recall aspects of the park's history. Accordingly, the following notation appeared: "Originally the home plate was at the eastern section of the park and the players batted towards the west. In 1893 the diamond was rearranged and the home plate was close to Dundas Street, with the teams batting towards the north. Later the home plate was placed within a few feet of where it is now."[35]

Further documentation for this change from the park's original 1877 infield location has yet to surface, but if the *Free Press* revelation is true, then the diamond's infield position within the park property's confines changed from its original northeast location to a southwestern location in 1893. As seen in Figure 1, Dundas Street would have run somewhat parallel to the diamond's right-field foul line; Wilson Avenue (in 1893, Central Avenue) ran parallel to the left-field foul line. Moving home plate away from the consistently menacing overflow of the Thames River might have been the motivation for such action, as well as placing the setting sun in the west in the eyes of the outfielders rather than the batters.[36]

Probably the single most critical development in the park's diamond sport history evolved not from the impetus of baseball, but rather from

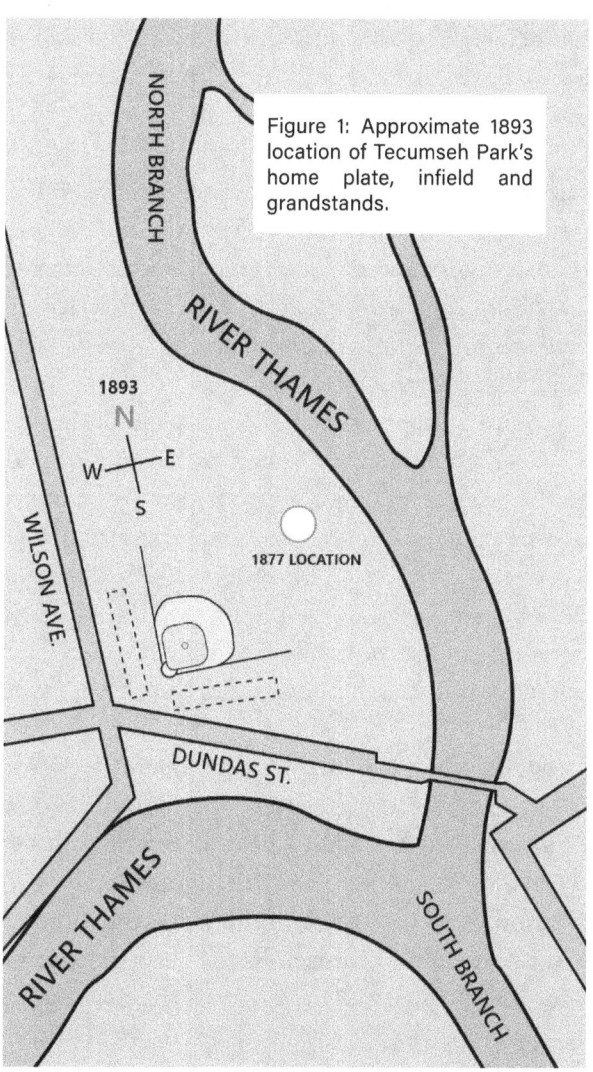

Figure 1: Approximate 1893 location of Tecumseh Park's home plate, infield and grandstands.

the widely popular late nineteenth-century sport of bicycling. We have previously noted the prominence of cycling affairs in London.[37] In the latter part of May 1895, the *London Advertiser* reported on the opening of the ball season, grumbling: "With decidedly uncomfortable weather, and a somewhat one-sided exhibition of baseball, the season of 1895 was opened at Tecumseh Park Saturday afternoon. Though the temperature was chilly and rain threatened to fall every minute the same old grandstand and the same old bleachers held about the usual number of cranks, who, however, owing to the tameness of the match, had little opportunity to whoop 'er up."[38]

And then, scarcely five days later, a startling *Advertiser* announcement: "It is a Go: The Much Talked of Bicycle Track Will be Built at Once."[39] An auspicious facility, "one of the best athletic parks in Canada" was projected to be finished in Tecumseh Park by late July.[40] Auspicious indeed: "... a third of a mile brick-dust and cement track, complete with proper banking on the turns, and a baseball diamond mapped out, the infield arranged inside the perimeter of the track itself, together with a grandstand seating 2,500 folks, all at a cost of $3,000."[41] [See Figure 2.]

There was more! Specific enhancements render a graphic picture of the park's new arrangement.[42] Representatives of the London Bicycle Club, among them W.J. Reid, the owner of Tecumseh Park, were the conceptual architects and exclusive financers of the entire endeavor. Throughout June and July, well into August, London newspapers, particularly the *Advertiser*, reported the progress of the grand project,[43] carried on without the need to curtail the park's baseball activities. And then, finally, the grand opening of Tecumseh Park's "new look." On Saturday afternoon, August 17, 1895, a procession of townsfolk and dignitaries led by the Musical Society Band formed at Richmond and Dundas Streets and marched to Tecumseh Park, arriving in pouring rain. A crowd of some 800

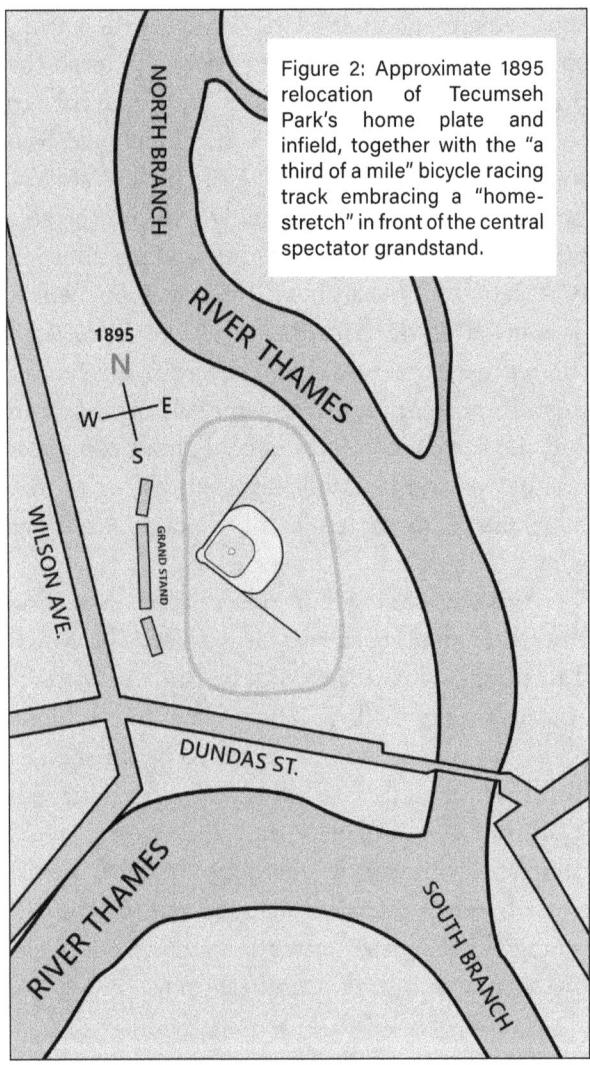

Figure 2: Approximate 1895 relocation of Tecumseh Park's home plate and infield, together with the "a third of a mile" bicycle racing track embracing a "home-stretch" in front of the central spectator grandstand.

souls, considerably short of the several thousand expected, braved the weather to attend.[44] London Mayor J.W. Little opened the formal ceremonies by orating on the prospective value of the cycling development to London youth and the debt owed to the facility's initiators: "The cultivation of these qualities and their application to our regular duties should certainly under ordinary circumstances, lead to success in any calling. (Applause) We are, therefore, under obligation to those who furnish facilities for the development of young people in this way."[45] Then, J.M. Reid spoke to the spectators and explained: "I trust … this is only the start of an era of bicycle riding in the city, and I will gladly do anything in my power to further

the sport. We will have in the near future, so Mr. Human has told me, a cricket club laying out their crease here. We already have a baseball diamond, and with a cricket crease and bicycle track we will have as good an athletic grounds as there is in the country."[46] Despite the August 17 attendance disappointment, subsequent bicycle race events held at Tecumseh Park's new cycling track generated robust spectator crowds witnessing races for prizes, often bestowed in the form of ornate rings set with diamonds.[47]

And so ended yet another chapter in the transformation of Tecumseh Park, one that brought the historic grounds closer to the perspective in which the park resides in these times. In closing this discussion of the bicycle club's installation of its racing track and subsequent relocation of the park's baseball diamond to the track's elongated oval infield in 1895, it should be noted that possibly by 1916, cycling activity, along with the celebrated racing track, had disappeared from the park's scheduled activities and physical landscape, the victim of a rapidly emerging preoccupation of Canadians and Americans alike with a relatively new technological fascination, the soon-to-be ubiquitous automobile.

Sometime prior to 1922, possibly dating to 1916, Tecumseh Park noted a reconfiguration of the park's expansive grounds, the installation of a new facility to accommodate the play of the Western University Mustangs football team. A 1922 aerial photograph of Tecumseh Park demonstrates that the football facility was laid out across the baseball diamond, directly in front of the spectator grandstand. In the late 1920s, the Western Mustangs abandoned Tecumseh Park to instead play their contests in the university's newly constructed J.W. Little Stadium, built on the campus proper and inaugurated in the autumn of 1929.[48] By the mid-1920s the football arrangement in Tecumseh Park no longer existed, and, for all intents and purposes, the park stood as a facility almost totally focused on London's ever-expanding baseball scene. Nevertheless, it remains ironic that one of the most significant "change agents" in the arrangement of the park's modern baseball playing field location was the sport of cycling and its spectacular racing track, which disappeared completely from the sporting scene, the victim, in part, of the development of and infatuation with the automobile.

The most devastating disaster in London's now two-century community history was the great flood of April 1937, an event that had repercussions for the city's premier baseball precinct. The catastrophic late April flood was preceded by an event occurring scarcely five months previous, the donation of the park property to the City of London by a recent purchaser, the John Labatt family. In mid-December of 1936 the *London Free Press* blared the good news: "City Is Given Tecumseh Park, $10,000: Famous Playground Donated by Labatt Family to Citizens."[49] Officially renamed the John Labatt Memorial Park, it became known by most folks as simply Labatt Park. The Labatt family gift of $10,000 came in the form of an endowment sum to be used for capital improvements. Little did London city fathers know at the time that the endowment sum would be pressed into needed service within a few months.

The December announcement and local celebration of the Labatt bequest had hardly subsided, when, once again, as was annually anticipated, the city began to brace itself for the fallout from melting snow and ice and the onset of heavy spring rainfalls. In early January of 1937, omens of approaching disaster were placed before London newspaper readers: "Nearly Five Inches of Rain in 15 Days," reported the *Free Press*.[50] And, approaching mid-February, continuing alarm: "Heavy Rains Flood River Flats."[51] And finally, the late April 1937 catastrophe: "... the swollen waters of the Thames River overflowed its banks in a wild rampage today...."[52] The preliminary flood damage cost rested at $3 million; newspaper descriptions underscoring the flood's consequence

detailed a great citywide tragedy,[53] from which Labatt Park was not exempt: "Flood Plays Havoc to Ancient Grandstand ... John Labatt Memorial Park now completely covered by water ... grandstand has been cracked and temporary bleachers have been washed away...."[54]

Unlike the July 1883 flood, which nullified any further sports activity at Tecumseh Park until the spring of 1884, the early April 1937 London flood disaster did not have such sustained consequence for the newly christened Labatt Park. On the eve of the flood's occurrence the *Free Press* reported on an inspection of Labatt Park by Frank Dark, construction superintendent of the Public Utilities Commission, and William Farquarson, London playgrounds supervisor. The property was "in bad condition. Fences need immediate attention, the roof of the grandstand leaks, fungus is growing on the grandstand seats."[55] Together with flood damage itself, pre-flood deterioration conditions added to a restoration urgency toward providing improvements and upgrading of the facility. Ultimately, the park remained unavailable for all activity for a little over a month. During that period alternative arrangements were made for previously scheduled contests. The *Free Press*, for instance, noted that the London Senior baseball team would "play [their] first six games away from home,"[56] the first home game to occur on June 19, 1937. Commencing in mid-June, the Seniors played the remainder of the 1937 season at Labatt Park.

LABATT PARK IN ITS MODERN FORM AND FUNCTION

After the flood, certainly by 1940, Labatt Park was once again transformed. The two spectator stands that previously extended from both sides of the central main grandstand (placed there originally to accommodate the homestretch of the bicycle racing track), were destroyed in the 1937 flood. Neither was resurrected in its original place. Instead, extended spectator stands were arranged contiguous to and behind the first base/right field and third base/left field foul lines. Home plate remained in roughly the same position as it did prior to the flood. A softball diamond was installed on the northern end of Labatt Park's grounds, a facility that particularly related to the explosion of ladies' softball in London and vicinity in the 1940s and early 1950s.[57]

Since the location of home plate in the park remains somewhat controversial, our research on the subject inclines us to argue that the home plate's location and its accompanying infield changed at least four times in its now almost century and a half of history.

After the 1937 flood, Labatt Park's baseball diamond remained generally located in its 1895 perspective, that is, with Wilson Avenue located directly west behind home plate, and batters hitting eastward. In 1937, too, at which time the city's representative in the Intercounty League was known as the London Silverwoods, the storied dressing-room building was erected that still remains today as a complementary Labatt Park reminder of London's baseball past. By 1940 the park was close to its present circumstance. Enlargements in spectator seating, dugout accommodation for players, and relocation of home plate to a slightly more northerly location were established in the decades of the 1950s, 1960s, and 1970s.

In 1989, just in time for the reemergence of professional baseball in Labatt Park, the City of London completed an important civic development that deflected on the historic baseball facility. The most important development between 1971 and 1989 was the extension of Queen's Avenue with its own bridge westward over the Thames River to intersect with Dundas Street running parallel to it, thus forming a junction from which Riverside Drive extends through London West. The Queen's Avenue extension necessitated removal of the small cluster of houses in the deep right-field corner, which in turn modified the dimensions

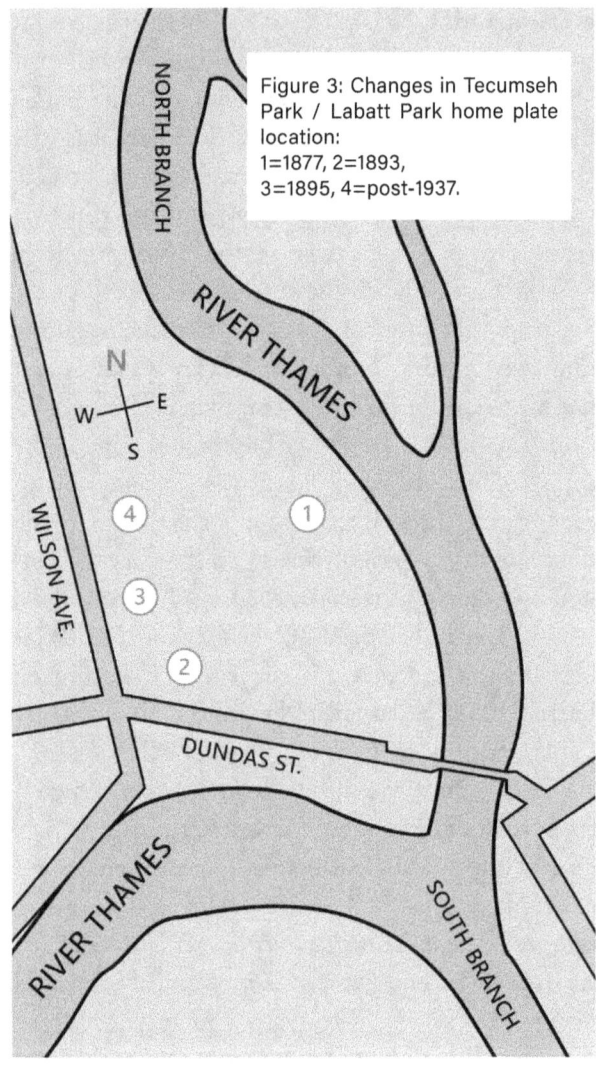

Figure 3: Changes in Tecumseh Park / Labatt Park home plate location:
1=1877, 2=1893,
3=1895, 4=post-1937.

of the right-field portion of the playing field. By 1989, too, the houses bordering Labatt Park on the east side of Wilson Avenue had been removed, greatly enlarging the park's main entry precinct. Other developments between 1971 and 1989 were the construction of extended bleachers along both foul lines, a warning track around the perimeter of the outfield, and impressive landscaping beautification.

Many of baseball history's luminaries have played in Tecumseh/Labatt Park at one time or another, including Hall of Famers Ty Cobb, Charlie Gehringer, and Canada's own Fergie Jenkins. The longest-standing baseball tenant of Tecumseh/Labatt Park has been the London representative in the Intercounty Baseball League, an enduring organization established in 1919. The first London entry in the Intercounty League, the London Braves, commenced play in 1925. Since then, depending on team sponsorship, London's Intercounty team has been known at various times as the London Winery (1934-1936), the London Silverwoods (1937-1938), the London Army Team (1942-1943), the London Majors (1944-1959), the London Diamonds (1960-1961), the London Majors again (1962), the London Pontiacs (1963-1969), the London Avcos (1970-1973) and the London El-Morocco Majors (1974). Since 1975 the team has stuck with the London Majors moniker.

Late in the twentieth century, professional baseball returned to Labatt Park, a first since the time of its earliest occupants, the London Tecumsehs. In 1989 the London Tigers, a Double-A Eastern League affiliate of the American League Detroit Tigers, took up residence in a much improved and beautified Labatt Park. Improvements made for the arrival of the Tigers cost in the vicinity of $1 million. They included new lighting, concession booth enhancements, a 40- by 19-foot electronic scoreboard (partially sponsored by Labatt Breweries), new dressing rooms, and new dugouts. The Tigers in London were short-lived. The franchise moved to Trenton, New Jersey, for the 1994 season. In 1999 the London Werewolves of the fledgling Frontier League arrived in London. Their tenure in Labatt Park ended in 2001, a victim of limited attendance and skyrocketing operating costs. And in 2003 Labatt Park became the home of the London Monarchs of the equally short-lived Canadian Baseball League, which folded in midseason due to financial difficulties.

EPILOGUE

Finally, what is in store for the storied park and its illustrious historic distinction? How might it be protected from the ravages of urban expansion and corporate development? One answer, of course, is heritage distinction reinforced by authority. We understand that "reinforced authority" is bestowed at three levels: municipal, provincial, and national. Labatt Park connotes much more than simply a venue for baseball activity.[58] It is a sanctified public space for the gathering of Ontarians, indeed greater Canadians, to experience and celebrate a national cultural pastime now approaching two centuries duration. The City of London, Ontario, realizes this fact. Since its ownership of the park commenced in 1937, it has poured millions of dollars into the park and its immediate surroundings. London fully realizes its value to the urban life of its citizens. On May 30, 1994, the City of London, under Part IV of the Ontario Heritage Act, named Labatt Park an Ontario Heritage Landmark Site. One month later, on July 1, 1994, in an act of civic heritage authority carried out at the park, a plaque was unveiled at Canada Day ceremonies presided over by Mayor Tom Gosnell.[59] Though Labatt Park's municipal and provincial heritage landmark distinctions are important barriers standing in the way of impacting urban growth/reconfiguration and corporate development expansion, the addition of Canadian National Historic Landmark Site distinction could well ensure a final measure for lasting preservation. Such a quest lies before federal consideration as this essay is written. Finally, if Lord Byron, the inimitable English poet, was on the mark when he asserted that "the best prophet of the future is the past," then perhaps Labatt Park has before it a glorious future in its service to London and Canadian citizens,[60] as well as to the annals of baseball history.

ACKNOWLEDGMENTS

Special thanks to Devin Lindsay, Stephen Harding, and the entire London Room staff of the London Public Library.

NOTES

1   We are indebted to Martin Lacoste for his penetrating compilations of baseball history's earliest published record of games played in Ontario. Lacoste has documented that, by 1865, some 80 games had been played, most carried out under New York rules, between teams established in the Toronto/Hamilton/Woodstock/London corridor. "Table of Baseball Games Played in Ontario, 1856-1865," email Martin Lacoste to Robert K. Barney, July 27, 2020. A full list of these games through 1870 is available at http://baseballresearch.ca/early-games/.

2   For a detailed examination of cricket play in London in the nineteenth century, and its jousts with baseball for public following and playing space, see Tony Joyce, "At Close of Play: The Evolution of Cricket in London, Ontario, 1836-1902," unpublished master's thesis, University of Western Ontario, 1988.

3   See "Ready," *London Advertiser*, March 31, 1877.

4   "The Ball Field," *London Advertiser*, April 16, 1877.

5   Charles B. Chapman, born Charles Trollope in Norfolk, England in 1827, emigrated to the New World in 1848, settling eventually in New York City, where he earned a living in the bookbinding business and dabbled in drawing and watercolors, an artistic bent he demonstrated in his elementary-school years in England. In New York he married a French-Canadian woman. Hearing that a town in "Canada West" offered a "good opportunity for a bookbinder," the couple left New York in 1855, crossed into Canada, and settled in London, Ontario. There, at the urging of his wife, he discarded the name Trollope, with its crude French connotation, and adopted the surname of Chapman, the maiden name of his wife's mother. Between 1855 and 1875 Charles Chapman graduated from being an amateur artist to one of noted professional qualification. His watercolors and oils, mostly of landscapes, won prizes at various competitions, fairs and exhibitions. An excellent example of his work was his classic 1875 oil painting of the "Forks of the Thames," displaying as it did the future site of Tecumseh/Labatt Park. For Chapman's place in Canadian art history, see Nancy Geddes Poole, *The Art of London: 1830-1880* (eBook Published by Nancy Geddes Poole, 2017), 25-26.

6   "The Ball Field," *London Advertiser*, April 20, 1877.

7   "Out-Door Sports," *London Advertiser*, April 23, 1877. The Atlantics, though a team composed of amateur players, were a formidable aggregation. By 1877 they deserved the distinction of being known as one of the top amateur baseball teams in the entire Dominion.

8   "Base Ball," *London Advertiser*, April 24, 1877. The Hartfords, a seasoned professional team from Brooklyn, New York, were not members of the International Association. Known as the Dark Blues of Hartford, Connecticut, they had been an original member of the National League in 1876, moving at season's end to Brooklyn for the National League's second season in 1877. They visited London after playing games in Chicago and Detroit.

9   "Summer Pastimes," *London Advertiser*, April 30, 1877.

10   "The Ball Field," *London Advertiser*, May 4, 1877. Brackets ours.

11   See "The Ball Field," *London Advertiser*, May 7, 1877.

12   See "The Ball Field," *London Advertiser*, May 8, 1877.

13   See "The Ball Field," *London Advertiser*, May 12, 1877 and May 14, 1877. See also Brian Martin, *The Tecumsehs of the International Association: Canada's First Major League Baseball Champions* (Jefferson, North Carolina: McFarland, 2015), 29.

14   "The Ball field," *London Advertiser*, May 16, 1877. The reference to "Maple Leafs from Guelph" refers to players and officials of the Guelph Maple Leaf Baseball Club, the London Tecumsehs' chief Canadian baseball rival, as well as a fellow member of the new International Association.

15   The *London Advertiser*, established by John Cameron in October 1863, was an evening newspaper, in contrast to the morning *London Free Press*. The *Advertiser*, an almost immediate success, proved an able competitor to the *Free Press*, right up to its eventual demise in the fall of 1936. It was born in the midst of the American Civil War, a landmark struggle between Union and Confederacy that captivated the attention of London citizens, particularly as hundreds and hundreds of fugitive Southern Negro slaves sought freedom in Canada, particularly in southwestern Ontario. See Fred Landon, *Western Ontario and the American Frontier* (Toronto: McClelland and Stewart, 1967 – Carleton Edition, original publication 1941), 215.

16   The *London Free Press*, an extension of the *London Canadian Free Press* (1849-1852), was established in 1856.

17   Admittedly, the position of home plate within the park grounds did indeed change, it would seem on at least four occasions over time, to its present position (2021).

18   For the importance of the safety bicycle in London, Ontario, see in particular Robert S. Kossuth and Kevin Wamsley, "Cycles of Manhood: Pedaling Respectability in Ontario's Forest City," *Sport History Review*, Vol. 34, No. 2, 170. For more, see Glen Norcliffe, *The Ride to Modernity: The Bicycle in Canada, 1869-1900* (Toronto: University of Toronto Press, 2001). Here, Norcliffe argues that "the bicycle carrier wave formed a small part of an even larger cultural movement in Canada known as modernity" (31). Further, in his "National Identity, Club Citizenship, and the Formation of the Canadian Wheelman's Association," *Journal of Canadian Studies*, Vol. 51, No. 2 (January 2018), Norcliffe argues that the *Canadian Wheelman*, an early magazine published in

southwestern Ontario, played a major role in the growth of the late nineteenth century Canadian bicycle craze (468). See also, Nancy Bouchier, *For the Love of the Game: Amateur Sports in Small-Town Ontario, 1838-1895* (Montréal: McGill-Queen's University Press, 2003).

19 "Sporting," *London Advertiser*, April 11, 1883.

20 For more on this elaborate facility, see *Wheelman* issues of December 1883 (Vol. 1, No. 4) and November 1883 (Vol. 1, No. 3).

21 The term "national sport" associated with lacrosse dates to an 1867 attempt by the Montréal dentist William George Beers to persuade Parliament in Ottawa to legislate the sport as Canada's official "national game." His attempt failed, but many in Canada, oblivious to Beers' failure, then and now, think that lacrosse is Canada's de facto national game. Beers himself was a noted lacrosse player in Montréal in the 1850s and 1860s. Further, he published the first standardized rules for lacrosse in 1860, was instrumental in expanding the number of lacrosse clubs in Ontario and Quebec in the decade following, formulated the National Lacrosse Association and its first annual convention, and helped organize the first international lacrosse tours to England in the 1870s. For this and more, he enters the annals of Canadian sport history as the "Father of Lacrosse." For more, see Donald M. Fisher, *Lacrosse: A History of the Game* (Baltimore: Johns Hopkins University Press, 2002).

22 "Sporting," *London Advertiser*, April 11, 1883.

23 "Sporting," *London Advertiser*, April 11, 1883. Brackets ours.

24 "Sporting," *London Advertiser*, April 28, 1883.

25 "Sporting," *London Advertiser*, May 3, 1883.

26 "Sporting," *London Advertiser*, May 12, 1883.

27 "Sporting," *London Advertiser*, May 14, 1883.

28 "Sporting," *London Advertiser*, May 25, 1883.

29 "Sporting," *London Advertiser*, April 6, 1883. Brackets ours.

30 "The Latest," *London Advertiser*, July 11, 1883. A prolonged subheadline told the tale: "Terrible Destruction by Water – London West and Low Points of the City Submerged – Immense Loss of Life Feared – Moving Tales of the Flood – The Damage to Property Incalculable."

31 "The Latest," *London Advertiser*, July 11, 1883.

32 "Sporting," *London Advertiser*, July 18, 1883. The July 1883 flood proved a disaster for the sport of lacrosse in London, especially lacrosse activity in Tecumseh Park. Shorn of its sticks, balls, and other equipment, which were carried away in the flood, the Lacrosse Club saw its membership dwindle, especially in the face of ever-increasing interest in cycling and baseball. In early August 1883, the London Lacrosse Club, now referred to as "The City Club," made a "last moment" arrangement for a game against London East, to be played on the Queen's Park grounds. The City Club "failed to muster a full team and were in consequence obliged to call upon London East for an additional supply." See "Sporting," *London Advertiser*, August 3, 1883. We could not find a record of lacrosse activity in Tecumseh Park after the 1883 flood.

33 "London West," *London Advertiser*, November 2, 1883.

34 "London West," *London Advertiser*, November 7, 1883.

35 "City Is Given Tecumseh Park, $10,000," *London Free Press*, December 15, 1936.

36 The logic here being that far fewer "sun affected" plays by outfielders occurred in comparison with "each pitch" experienced by batters in the course of the game.

37 We originally became interested in the orientation of a bicycle track in Tecumseh Park introduced in 1895 due to a reference made to us by Stephen Harding, for which we are grateful. Furthermore, there is a notation regarding the bicycle track in Daniel Brock's *Fragments from the Forks: London, Ontario's Legacy* (London, Ontario: London and Middlesex Historical Society, 2011), 147.

38 "The Green Diamond," *London Advertiser*, May 20, 1895.

39 "It is a Go," *London Advertiser*, May 25, 1895.

40 Discussions on building a bicycle racing track occurred as early as 1894, as noted in the *Canadian Wheelman Magazine*. For example: "The Meteor club has a membership now of about 70, and we are receiving applications for every meeting. We are growing fast, and, 'to put a flea in your readers' ears,' it is our intention to make a strong bid for the C.W.A. meeting of 1895. By that time we expect to have one of the best athletic grounds in the Dominion, including an up-to-date bicycle track. We are in the swim to stay." "London Meteors," *The Canadian Wheelman*, August 6, 1894.

41 "It is a Go," *London Advertiser*, May 25, 1895.

42 "Work Begun," *London Advertiser*, May 27, 1895: "... The track has been staked out. The home stretch is to be west of the baseball diamond and 30 feet wide. The course will gradually narrow, until on the east side, or near the breakwater, it will only measure 16 feet. ..."

43 See, for instance, daily copies of the *London Advertiser*, May 25 to August 16, 1895.

44 For an enlarged description of the entire grand opening, see "Wheelmen Happy," *London Advertiser*, August 19, 1895.

45 "Wheelmen Happy."

46 "Wheelmen Happy."

47 "The Diamond Meet," *London Advertiser*, August 29, 1895.

48 For more on this, see Robert K. Barney, *Mustangs 100: A Century of Western Athletics* (Straffordville, Ontario: Sportswood Printing, 2013), 12, 17.

49   "City Is Given Tecumseh Park, $10,000: Famous Play-ground Donated by Labatt Family to Citizens," *London Free Press*, December 15, 1936.

50   *London Free Press*, January 14, 1937: "Last night streets ran deep with water and small floods were reported at one or two city parks."

51   *London Free Press*, February 9, 1937: "Old Man River went on a rampage in London following heavy rains. ..."

52   *London Free Press*, April 26, 1937: "Scores of homes were menaced, streets were submerged, at least four district bridges were closed to traffic. ..."

53   *London Free Press*, April 27, 1937: "... mounting menace of disease, one man drowned, 6,000 without homes, South London completely isolated to motor traffic."

54   "Labatt Park Is a Young Lake," *London Free Press*, April 28, 1937.

55   "Labatt Park in Bad Condition," *London Free Press*, April 6, 1937.

56   Howard Broughton, "On the Sport Trail with Howard Broughton," *London Free Press*, May 14, 1937.

57   For a full treatment of this phenomenon and Labatt Park's role in the development, see Carly Adams, "Communities of Their Own: Women's Sport and Recreation in London, Ontario, 1920-1951," unpublished Ph.D. Dissertation, University of Western Ontario, 2007.

58   Better known, but similar circumstances, are associated with many original historic sporting precincts, for instance, the Kentucky Derby and Churchill Downs in Louisville, Kentucky; the Boston Red Sox and Fenway Park in Boston, Massachusetts; and the Indy 500 and the Indianapolis Speedway in Indianapolis, Indiana.

59   Co-author Dr. Bob Barney was present at those proceedings, and in fact rendered the keynote commemorative address.

60   Lord George Gordon Byron's notable quotation appeared in a letter written by him on January 28, 1821, composed in Greece, the country of his residence for the last three decades of his life. For the letter's transcription, see: https://www.gutenberg.org/files/16609/16609-h/16609-h.htm.

LABATT PARK'S
LONGEVITY CLAIM

There has been but one serious challenge mustered against Labatt Park's distinction: "baseball history's oldest continuously operating ball grounds." That challenger is Fuller Field in the town of Clinton, Massachusetts.

Clinton, nestled in bucolic surroundings some 40 miles west of Boston, nevertheless suffers from a long-embedded "tiredness." It was a bustling nineteenth-century town of world fame, but much of its present business landscape renders the impression of being in recession. Many of the town's streets and sidewalks are in disrepair. Though a fatigue-like mist appears to envelop today's Clinton, in its heyday in the nineteenth century, Clinton was a dynamic community, featuring some of America's best-known manufacturing firms, most especially those linked to a booming textile industry. In fact, Clintonian Erastus B. Bigelow rose to become one of the world's most important and best-known inventors/entrepreneurs with his invention and development of the power loom, including his subsequent scientific application of that loom to what we know today as the process by which screening for windows, doors, and porches is manufactured.

Then, too, Clinton was an enviable center of cultural flamboyance. Appearing in Clinton's civic halls and private salons for over a half-century were many of America's most celebrated writers, entertainers, cause-conscious lecturers, sports stars, even presidents of the United States, a legion of men and women that included such historical luminaries as Henry David Thoreau, Ralph Waldo Emerson, Frederick Douglass, Mark Twain, Carrie Nation, John L. Sullivan, Agnes Moorehead, and two Roosevelts, Franklin and Theodore.[1]

We are grateful to the librarians of the Bigelow Free Public Library in Clinton for providing us, during a research visit there in August 2018 with historical documents appropriate to Clinton's challenge to the Labatt Park distinction. Baseball has been a fixture in Clinton for nearly as long as some of the earliest historical records of the sport in American culture can attest. One can certainly pinpoint an 1865 Clinton newspaper notice offered by one of the local baseball aggregations, the "We'll Try Baseball Club," inviting ladies and gentlemen to attend its annual "baseball-sponsored ball."[2]

A "darkened and dog-eared by age"[3] four-by-five-foot oilcloth survey map of Clinton, dated 1878 and discovered by officials of the Clinton Historical Society in 2004, depicts a baseball

The art deco façade of the newly named John Labatt Memorial Park upon its reopening after the flood of April, 1937. (D.B. Weldon Library, Western University Archives)

infield diamond on property bounded by High and Allen Streets. Clinton's argument proposes that the infield diamond presently in place on Fuller Field, a "multi-purpose" facility operated by the town's Parks and Recreation authority, is situated in exactly the same place as the baseball diamond depicted on the 1878 "oilcloth survey map." Researching into the antiquity of baseball parks and diamonds, local Clinton historian Bastarache found no other claim equal to or offering an older date of baseball diamond origin and continuous use, with the exception of that of Labatt Memorial Park in London, Ontario.

Upon inquiry to London's Labatt Park historians,[4] Bastarache learned that Tecumseh Park (the park's original name), though predating Clinton's 1878 "origin claim" by one year (1877), was devastated by a flood in April 1937, causing it to cease to function for an interim, not to reappear until 1938 as Labatt Memorial Park, and, in Bastarache's incorrect conclusion, "moved" to a completely different location. To Bastarache, then, Labatt Park's "continuous use" claim could not be defended after the season of 1936. But apparently unknown to Bastarache was the fact that Tecumseh Park/Labatt Park was never moved. In the wake of the devastating 1937 flood, Kensington Flats, including Tecumseh Park, was inundated, and the park's playing surface and infrastructure severely damaged. Operations at the ball grounds ceased entirely. Over time, the flood waters receded; the Flats returned to normalcy. But the ground's ball field and supporting infrastructure were ruined.

Nevertheless, the John Labatt Brewing Company purchased the former Kensington Tecumseh Park ball field land and promptly deeded it to the City of London in perpetuity. Further, the Labatt family gifted $10,000 to the city for the restoration of the baseball park in the identical spot of its origin. Tecumseh Park rose in all its original splendor, renamed Labatt Memorial Park. But Bastarache was on a mission. Hence, to *Guinness World Records* and the National Park Service, he proceeded to launch a quest to have Clinton's Fuller Field ordained as the oldest continuously used baseball field in the world, dating to 1878. In fact, Bastarache went further, claiming that the Fuller Field baseball site "may actually date back to 1865 when baseball began in Clinton."[5] Had Bastarache consulted an 1876 Clinton map, he would have found that the Fuller Field baseball site was clearly not in place prior to 1878.

While *Guinness* certified Bastarache's claim, and accordingly in its 2007 annual edition affirmed the authenticity of Fuller Field's unique baseball antiquity, certification of the "Clinton distinction" failed in the halls of decision-making in the National Park Service's National Registry of Historical Landmarks.[6] We would suspect that the National Park Service's Registry of Historical Landmarks remains decidedly more rigorous in its survey of "origin evidence," to say nothing of the proof of "continuous use," than does a commercial press such as *Guinness*. The silence from government authority, the custodian of historical landmark claims, is a deafening commentary on the legitimacy of Clinton's assertion. On *Guinness's* website appears the following: "The claim (Clinton) is based on maps of the town that date as far back as 1878, and box scores from games played every year."[7] This is the only occasion where a reference to evidence of "continuous use" ("box scores") is offered, but it is merely a reference, rather than evidence itself. If such evidence exists, Bastarache would surely have brought it forth to support the "continuous use" aspect of his argument. We believe no such evidence exists, but if it does indeed exist, has never been examined relative to the Clinton claim. Finally, disastrous to Clinton's claim was the removal of Fuller Field from *Guinness World Records*, replaced in its 2009 edition by Labatt Memorial Park in London.[8]

NOTES

1   For more on this see A.J. Bastarache, *An Extraordinary Town: How One of America's Smallest Towns Shaped the World* (Clinton, Massachusetts: Angus MacGregor Publishing, 2005).

2   See Bastarache's chapter, "Making Sports History" (p. 95), in his *An Extraordinary Town*.

3   The phrase "darkened and dog-eared by age" is from Peter Schworm, "Fielding Dreams: A Central Massachusetts Town Hopes an 1878 Map Will Bring Visitors and Bragging Rights to a Spot in Baseball History," *Boston Globe*, August 14, 2005: 29. The phrase may in fact have been spoken directly to Schworn by his interviewee, A.J. Bastarache.

4   In this case, Barry Wells, as told to the authors by Wells himself during a tour of Labatt Park on November 10, 2018.

5   Bastarache, 95.

6   For the earliest notation of the National Park Service Submission, and actual *Guinness* submission, see Schworm, "Fielding Dreams."

7   https://www.waymarking.com/waymarks/wm5566_Worlds_Oldest_Baseball_Diamond_in_Continuous_Use_Fuller_Field_Clinton_MA.

8   Craig Glenday, ed., *Guinness World Records 2009* (New York: Bantam Books, 2009), 191.

THE 1877 INTERNATIONAL ASSOCIATION CHAMPIONSHIP GAME

By Andrew North

Mike Timlin scurried toward the first-base line, scooped up Otis Nixon's bunt, and tossed to a waiting Joe Carter at first base. The play retired the speedy Nixon, and the Toronto Blue Jays were World Series champions for the first time. The year was 1992, and the Toronto victory was hailed as Canada's first championship on the major-league baseball stage. Forgotten in the euphoria were the exploits of the London Tecumsehs, who 115 years earlier had won the championship of the International Association. The Association, and its 1877 champion Tecumsehs, have been relegated to the dustbin of history by a 1969 decision to deny the league major-league status, a decision with which not all baseball historians agree.[1]

BACKGROUND

The International Association was established on a basis different from that of its rival, the National League. The latter was controlled by the owners, and operated for their benefit. Many of the Association's teams, in contrast, were cooperatives, interested more in the social and political benefit to be gained from hometown glory than in financial profit. Some were even

player-led.[2] Twenty-three such teams comprised the Association for its inaugural season of 1877. Of these 23, seven paid the additional $15 fee required to contend for the championship pennant.[3] Only games played between pairs of these teams were to count toward the championship; all other games were the equivalent of exhibitions.

The Association season represented London's first opportunity for structured play against top-level competition. The highlight was the opening of Tecumseh Park as the Tecumsehs' new home.[4] The park hosted its first professional game on May 6, as the Tecumsehs fell 6-2 to the visiting Hartfords of Brooklyn of the National League.[5] A Victoria Day game against the League's Boston team drew a crowd estimated at between 6,000 and 8,000 on the national holiday; a late London rally went for naught as the Bostons prevailed 8-7 in 10 innings behind ace Tommy Bond, who would win a league-leading 40 games for the eventual league champions.[6] Any Guelph-London game was another highlight, as the rivalry between the two cities had intensified over the preceding years.[7]

The pennant race developed into a two-team affair, but it was a tight one. Tuesday, October 2, dawned with these championship standings, the Lynn Live Oaks having disbanded two weeks earlier:[8]

London	13-4
Pittsburgh	11-4
Rochester	8-8
Manchester	7-9
Columbus	4-8
Guelph	3-12

Since the Pittsburgh Alleghenys had only two games left to play (both against Guelph) after Tuesday, and London none, a win by London would give the Tecumsehs the title. But both London and Pittsburgh were still in contention.

THE GAME

Tuesday's cool, clear skies belied the Tecumsehs' sombre mood. Ed Somerville, the team's popular shortstop, had taken ill during the previous week. He died, a victim of pneumonia, on October 1, the day before the game. His teammates took the field wearing "crape [sic] bows on their breasts"[9] in his memory, having served as his pallbearers a mere 24 hours earlier.[10] No less daunting was the prospect of facing the Alleghenys' starting pitcher, Pud Galvin. The 20-year-old right-hander, the ace of the Pittsburgh staff, was early in a Hall of Fame career in which he would win 365 games, the fifth-highest total in baseball history.[11] Starting for London was the Tecumsehs' own ace, 21-year-old right-hander Fred Goldsmith. Goldsmith was a popular figure in London, having recently married a local woman and taken up residence there. He had also been instrumental in the team's success that year; he was credited with 46 wins in total, including a 13-4 record in championship games.[12]

As was the rule in the International Association that year, the Tecumsehs batted first. Galvin retired the side in order, shortstop Mike Burke being caught on a fine one-handed catch by center

fielder Russ McKelvy.[13] A single by McKelvy was the only damage off Goldsmith in the bottom half. Both pitchers quickly warmed to the task at hand. Through five innings, Galvin allowed no hits, the only batter to reach base doing so on an error. Goldsmith allowed only the McKelvy single over the same span, striking out the side in the third.

The Alleghenys threatened in the sixth. With one out, first baseman Jake Goodman singled to right, and McKelvy to center. Goldsmith escaped unscathed when shortstop Candy Nelson hit into a fielder's choice, and Galvin struck out for the third time. In the top of the seventh, the home side struck. With one out, Burke reached on an error by second baseman Chick Fulmer. Left fielder Joe Hornung singled past shortstop for the Tecumsehs' first hit. Both Burke and Hornung scored as first baseman George "Foghorn" Bradley[14] tripled into right-center, Bradley himself scoring on a subsequent sacrifice by Marshall Quinton. London led 3-0.

Goldsmith continued to dominate, allowing only a harmless single by Bill Holbert in the eighth. The Tecumsehs struck again in the top of the ninth. Phil Powers' double and Goldsmith's single with one out put runners on first and third, Powers scoring on a misplay near home plate by catcher Tom Dolan. Burke's single scored Goldsmith, and London led 5-0. A third single followed, by Hornung, but Galvin escaped further damage by inducing successive popups. To this point in the game, London had committed no errors, a remarkable display of fielding for the era. This changed quickly in the bottom of the inning, as a single, a wild pitch, an infield single, an overthrow and a subsequent outfield fumble allowed two Pittsburgh runs to score. It was too little, too late, for the Alleghenys, though, as London triumphed 5-2.

Pitching and fielding prevailed, as each team managed only six hits. Goldsmith in particular was excellent, his 10 strikeouts an impressive indication of his dominance.[15] That evening

George H. "Foghorn" Bradley, seated at left, with the Grafton Baseball Club in 1875. *Touch three out of four, George. You'll never hit a bigger triple in your life.* (Courtesy John Thorn)

Adams Bower   Bigelow Shattuck
Bradley Dorgan Stratton Sullivan Carpenter

the team was feted at the Tecumseh House Hotel downtown. The International Association pennant had been won by one of its two Canadian entries.

MAJOR LEAGUE?

The Tecumsehs' victory was acknowledged with approval at the time by no less than Henry Chadwick in the *New York Clipper*.[16] It has not been widely recognized as the first international baseball championship by a Canadian team,

however. This is primarily because the International Association has not been recognized as "major league," a distinction denied it by the 1969 decree. But is the reasoning behind that decision sound? Two of the more important characteristics of major-league status are stability and caliber of play. Let's look at these more closely.

Stability refers to strength of ownership, franchise retention from one year to the next, and the ability of teams to complete their schedules. In these respects, it is true that the International Association did not distinguish itself. For the

Association's 1877 season, not all of its seven original competing franchises completed their championship schedules. The Lynn Live Oaks disbanded before season's end. After the season two more franchises disbanded, and three new ones were added. The numerous cities comprising the Association for 1878, including the nonparticipants for the championship, included places as small as New Bedford, Massachusetts, and Hornellsville, New York. The Association was too large, scattered over too large a geographical area, and financially shaky. By 1880, it was out of business.

But what of the National League, the Association's only rival? Now regarded as a long-standing bastion of consistency, the National League of 1877 was all of one year old. In its first season, 1876, it consisted of eight teams. Here's how it evolved over the course of the next three years alone:

1877 (6 teams):
Drop New York, Philadelphia

1878 (6 teams):
Drop Louisville, Hartford, St. Louis
Add Providence, Indianapolis, Milwaukee

1879 (8 teams):
Drop Indianapolis, Milwaukee
Add Buffalo, Cleveland, Syracuse, Troy

Instability was the rule, as league founder William Hulbert struggled to find reliable competition for his Chicago franchise. During the first decade of the League's existence, 21 teams were members at one time or another. In fact, National League expansion and contraction, and replacement of franchises with others, was to be commonplace for the next few decades. It wasn't until the settlement of its dispute with the Western League at the turn of the twentieth century that the League settled into the largely stable structure that we know today.

So, yes, the International Association was unstable. But so was the National League. Rather than considering this a weakness peculiar to the Association, then, it's more reasonable to view this instability as a typical characteristic of the professional baseball landscape at that time. And when comparing the Association with the League, it's important that we focus on the League of 1877, rather than view the League as we know it today.

With respect to caliber of play:

One of the biggest issues facing baseball in its professional youth was the problem of "revolving," or contract-jumping. It was very common for players not to meet their contractual obligations, abandoning one team for another in the same league, or moving to another league, in midseason.[17] Such was the case between the Association and the League in 1877. The more players switched from one league to the other, the more homogeneous the player pool of the two leagues became. It therefore becomes hard to accept that either league could boast a caliber of play noticeably better than its rival's.

In 1877, the supposedly superior National League lost 72 games to outside clubs.[18] It has been noted that a number of these games were against semipro teams, competition that might not warrant the National League team's best lineups or efforts. This cannot be said of any games involving the two Canadian Association franchises. Both London and Guelph paid salaries, were stockholding companies, and had wealthy backers supporting them.

Collectively, the players on the top six International Association teams of 1877 accumulated more past or future seasons of major-league play than did the players of the top six National League teams.[19]

Clearly, then, the Association's caliber of play was at least the equal of the League's, if not better.

Evidence suggests that the Tecumsehs' league of 1877 was a viable competitor to the National League, in no way a poor cousin. The International

Association should be recognized as a major league, and its championship as a major-league championship. A number of baseball historians do so already. David Voigt, for one, discussing the financial problems faced by the National League in its early years, comments, "Although managerial austerity, salary cuts, and new stock issues lightened the burden somewhat, it was a discouraging picture. Ranged alongside the modestly profitable Association era, it goes far to debunk the myth of League superiority."[20] Author David Pietrusza, for another, opines that "a good caliber of ball was played by these nines. International Association and National League players were equally named to nationally recognized all-star teams."[21] And the *New York Clipper* obviously held the Association in high regard, referring to it early in the 1878 season as "the ruling professional association in the country – which it now unquestionably is."[22]

The London Tecumsehs' victory was Canada's first on the international baseball stage, and its only major-league championship until 1992. It deserves to be recognized as a significant milestone in Canadian baseball's historical development.

Note: A radio recreation of this game was a featured presentation at the 2018 Canadian Baseball History Conference in London. The Conference venue overlooked the outfield fences of Tecumseh Park (now Labatt Park).

ACKNOWLEDGMENT

A tip of the author's cap goes to London journalist and historian Chip Martin. His research for his book *The Tecumsehs of the International Association* provided the basis for much of the content of this article.

SOURCES

Statistics from Baseball-Reference.com and Retrosheet.org.

NOTES

1   In 1968, Commissioner William Eckert formed a Special Baseball Records Committee to determine (among other things) that portion of baseball's statistical record to be considered "major league." The committee's rulings the next year accorded six leagues such status; the International Association was not one of them. Questionable in particular are the designations of two leagues that could be considered little more than vanity projects: Henry Lucas's Union Association of 1884 and, to a lesser extent, John Montgomery Ward's Players' League of 1890. The special committee and its decisions were in the news again more recently, as Major League Baseball in 2020 granted major-league status to the Negro Leagues.

2   Brian Martin, *The Tecumsehs of the International Association* (Jefferson, North Carolina: McFarland & Co., 2015), 4.

3   The seven were the Columbus Buckeyes, Guelph Maple Leafs, London Tecumsehs, Lynn Live Oaks, Manchester, Pittsburgh Alleghenys, and Rochester. The Guelph and London teams were Canada's first professional league franchises. The rivalry between the two, fueled by civic boosterism, had been ongoing for several years.

4   The park is still in use for baseball today, having been renamed Labatt Park in 1937. It is the oldest continuous-use ballpark in the world.

5   Martin, 119.

6   Martin, 122.

7   The crowd for a holiday game in London the previous year, for example, had been estimated by a visiting Guelph reporter at between 9,000 and 10,000. See *Guelph Mercury*, August 10, 1876. While this may be an overestimate, note that attendance for National League games in 1877 was typically in the 1,500 to 2,000 range.

8   *London Advertiser*, October 2, 1877.

9   *London Advertiser*, October 3, 1877.

10   Martin, 142.

11   Galvin was baseball's first 300-game winner. He reached that milestone late in the 1889 season, although it was neither recognized nor celebrated at the time. Were Galvin's 36 wins in his two seasons in the International Association to be included, he would have reached 300 early in the 1888 season. His career wins total of 401 would then have been surpassed by only Cy Young and Walter Johnson in baseball history.

12   Goldsmith compiled a 112-68 record in his subsequent six-year major-league career. He is recognized as one of the earliest practitioners of curveball pitching. He formed what may have been baseball's first pitching rotation with teammate Larry Corcoran on the Chicago White Stockings teams of the early 1880s.

13   All play-by-play details are from the *London Free Press*, October 3, 1877.

14   "Foghorn" is George H. Bradley, not the George Washington Bradley who threw the National League's first no-hit game, in 1876.

15   To put this into perspective, strikeouts per nine innings for the entire National League in 1877 were just over 2.

16   *New York Clipper*, October 13, 1877.

17   Such frequent player movement was facilitated by the absence of anything resembling a reserve clause, which emerged only gradually during the next decade.

18   David Nemec, *The Great Encyclopedia of 19th Century Major League Baseball* (New York: Donald I. Fine Books, 1997), 102.

19   Nemec, 102.

20   The 1877 season was a particularly trying one for the League. Every League team lost money, even champion Boston. League magnates also had to deal with the Louisville Grays game-fixing scandal, the June disbanding and subsequent reorganization of the Cincinnati club, and the discovery that the latter franchise had never paid its membership dues, resulting in the nullification of all Cincinnati game results. (Most modern sources do include these results; see, for example, https://www.retrosheet.org/boxesetc/1877/Y_1877.htm.) See Martin, Chapter 9. Also see David Voigt, *American Baseball Vol. I* (State College: Pennsylvania State University Press, 1983), 76.

21   David Pietrusza, *Major Leagues: The Formation, Sometimes Absorption, and Mostly Inevitable Demise of 18 Professional Baseball Organizations, 1871 to Present* (Jefferson, North Carolina: McFarland & Co., 1991), 48.

22   *New York Clipper*, May 12, 1878.

ARTHUR IRWIN

By Eric Frost

Even for serious fans of early baseball, it can be difficult to know what to make of Canadian Baseball Hall of Fame member Arthur "Foxy" Irwin. On one hand, Irwin popularized the baseball glove, inspired a character in a Zane Grey novel, and served as a team captain, player-manager, manager, scout and minor-league owner during a career that lasted more than 40 years. On the other hand, few early baseball figures were as polarizing.

In *The National Game* (1910), Al Spink wrote that there was "no speedier or brainier fielder and batsman" in the 1880s and he said that Irwin was the best scout employed by the New York Highlanders.[1] Referencing Irwin's time as a manager, writer Roy Kerr described him as "a skinny, bug-eyed Canadian with large, protruding ears and a healthy ego. He was an impeccable dresser, and fancied himself to be a savant in the art of 'scientific baseball.'"[2] Daniel Levitt has characterized Irwin as "one of the slimier men in baseball,"[3] and pitcher Waite Hoyt said that he was "probably the most disgusting man [he] ever knew."[4]

Curiously, however, after it was reported in July 1921 that Irwin jumped off a passenger steamer to his death in the Atlantic Ocean, the discussion was not about differing opinions of Irwin's character. Instead, people argued over the basic facts. One man said that Irwin was still alive, others suspected murder, and two complete strangers each claimed to be his wife.

Arthur Albert Irwin was born in Toronto on Saint Valentine's Day of 1858. His father, who was born in Ireland in 1833 and who was also named Arthur, worked as a blacksmith. His mother, Elizabeth, was a homemaker; census records inconsistently describe her as a native of Ireland or Canada. By 1870, the younger Arthur had six siblings, all but one being younger than him.

The Irwin family moved to Boston when Arthur was six. He grew up playing sandlot baseball in South Boston, where his friends included future major-leaguer Tommy McCarthy.[5] Beginning in 1873 with the Aetna Club of Boston, Irwin spent several seasons as a shortstop in amateur baseball.[6]

On June 2, 1879, Irwin made his professional debut with the Worcester Worcesters of the minor-league National Association in an exhibition against the Chicago Cubs. Worcester pitcher Lee Richmond also debuted that day, throwing a no-hitter in a rain-shortened seven-inning game. Irwin played third base for that first game before he moved to shortstop, and he made two stellar plays that day.[7]

Boosted by a 47-win season from Richmond, who also hit .368, the Worcester club played well enough to move into the National League for the 1880 season. This meant that Irwin and the other players received major-league promotions without changing teams. A highlight that year came on June 12, when Richmond pitched the first major-league perfect game and Irwin scored the game's only run.[8] In 85 games, Irwin registered a league-leading 345 assists.

Irwin missed much of the 1881 season owing to an early-season illness and a broken leg later in the year. The leg injury occurred while Irwin was running the bases, and local sports equipment salesman Martin "Flip" Flaherty was inserted into the game in his only major-league appearance.[9]

The Worcester club folded after an 18-66 season in 1882. Irwin moved on to the NL's Providence Grays as a team captain. Gloves were only worn by catchers and first basemen at that time, but Irwin needed to play with two broken fingers one day in 1883. He fashioned a padded buckskin driving glove into a mitt and wore the glove even after his fingers healed. Monte Ward also started wearing the glove, and it was standard throughout the league by 1884. Sporting goods company Draper & Maynard produced a model based on "the Irwin glove" and they said that 90% of major leaguers wore its brand by the 1920s.[10]

The 1884 Grays won the precursor to the modern World Series – a best-of-three series against the AA champion New York Metropolitans. In 1885, the Grays folded after a fourth-place finish and Irwin was looking for a team again. He had not displayed his characteristic speed and defensive range since the 1881 leg injury. The introduction of overhand pitching in 1884 provided another challenge; already light-hitting, Irwin batted under .240 after that point in his career.[11]

In 1886, Irwin signed with Philadelphia of the NL. For the next three years, Irwin played at least 100 games per year; he only appeared in 100 major-league games one other time. Irwin posted mediocre offensive numbers in Philadelphia, but he led NL shortstops in 1888 with a career-high 204 putouts.

The *Philadelphia Inquirer* reported on May 27 that the Phillies had been benching Irwin.[12] He briefly returned to the field after an injury to Ed Delahanty, but his relationship with the team was irreparable after the initial benching. He was sold to the Washington Senators for $3,000 on June 8 and became a team captain.[13] Within a month of Irwin's arrival in Washington, he was named player-manager. It was Irwin's first major-league managerial opportunity and he was the team's fifth manager in only three years.[14] His predecessor had started the season with a 13-39 record and Irwin fared marginally better, finishing 28-45 as manager for the last-place team.

By this time, many players resented their controlling NL owners, and Irwin was becoming known as a key man in the players union called the Brotherhood of Professional Baseball Players. He helped to organize the Players' League and he purchased 12 shares of stock in the league's Boston club.[15] Irwin appeared in 84 games for the 1890 Boston Reds The team won the PL championship, but that league folded, and the Boston Reds joined the AA with Irwin as manager for 1891.

More than a year removed from playing in the NL, Irwin got on the bad sides of NL owners. In an era of competition among baseball leagues, a document known as the National Agreement of 1883 restricted how major-league and minor-league teams could pursue players from other leagues. Before the 1891 season, AA teams began disregarding the agreement in the pursuit of NL players. NL executives believed that Irwin had encouraged AA teams to break the agreement.[16]

If that wasn't enough to spark resentment, NL owners also felt that Irwin had convinced

The Philadelphia Phillies of the late 1880s. Arthur Irwin is seated to the left of manager Harry Wright. Fellow Canadian George Wood is standing, far left. (Canadian Baseball Hall of Fame and Museum)

Cincinnati Reds owner Al Johnson to move his team from the NL to the AA. Though Johnson sold the team before the 1891 season started and the club returned to the NL without having played in the AA, Irwin's reputation was damaged in baseball's most powerful league.[17]

Irwin also struggled for the approval of Reds players. In the middle of 1891, when Reds infielder Hardy Richardson was injured and Paul Radford would not play on Sundays, Irwin signed his younger brother, John Irwin, despite John's known fielding struggles. Teammates and local writers cried nepotism, but John struggled through 19 games over several weeks before the elder Irwin relented and dropped him from the team.[18] Irwin could focus on managing, as he played in only six games, and the 1891 Boston Reds won the AA.

That fall, Irwin made headlines after alleging game fixing in the NL pennant race. Irwin said that Cap Anson of the Chicago Colts had agreed to play Irwin's Reds in an AA-NL championship series if the teams won their leagues, but he said that the Giants had agreed to throw a late-season series to the Boston Beaneaters so that Boston could beat Chicago to the pennant. Irwin accused Buck Ewing of giving away the Giants' signs. No one on either team commented on Irwin's allegations.[19] Once the Beaneaters and Reds won their leagues, Beaneaters manager Frank Selee refused to play a postseason series against the Reds.[20]

In 1892, Irwin returned to Washington to manage the Senators when Billy Barnie had a disagreement with team owners after the second game of the season. The NL was using a split-season format to determine who would make the league championship. Washington was 35-39 in the first half, earning seventh place. This was the highest finish among the team's years in the NL, but fans disliked Irwin. When the team started poorly in the second half, he was fired.[21]

Irwin began managing the Philadelphia Phillies in 1894. He had not played in the major leagues since 1891; he played in one game for the 1894 Phillies, his last major league playing appearance. He had big shoes to fill as a manager; baseball pioneer Harry Wright had just managed there for ten seasons. Wright had been successful with other teams, but his contract was not renewed in Philadelphia because he had not secured any first-place finishes.[22] The team had led the league in hitting for in 1893 and again under Irwin in 1894 and 1895. The 1895 team brought in 474,971 fans, a 19th century single-season record.[23]

Despite that apparent success, the *Philadelphia Inquirer* reported in September 1895 that Irwin was thinking about leaving. The *Inquirer* called Irwin "the clearest sighted and coolest headed manager in the business to-day."[24] In early October, Irwin said he would not return to Philadelphia. He was trying to purchase the Toronto club in the Eastern League.[25]

Irwin had a 149-110 record with the Phillies, but he had irked their personnel and their fans. He meddled in the team's uniform decisions, resulting in unpopular red and black bars being placed on their leggings. Owner John Rogers criticized his lax handling of players, but even the players disliked Irwin, especially in comparison to his predecessor. On the field, Irwin introduced intricate strategy, but these tactics often confused his players.[26]

Irwin had also served as the University of Pennsylvania baseball coach from 1893 to 1895.[27] There Irwin coached future author Zane Grey. Grey's first baseball book, *The Short-Stop* (1914), is dedicated in part to Irwin; his second baseball book, *The Young Pitcher*, included a character known as Worry Arthurs, a fictionalized version of Irwin.[28][29]

In the mid-1890s, Irwin became very active outside of baseball. He invented a miniature football scoreboard to reproduce games in faraway cities and he started the short-lived American League of Professional Football, the country's first professional soccer league. He promoted boxing matches and organized roller hockey games and marathon bike races.[30]

Soon after leaving the Phillies, Irwin became manager of the New York Giants for 1896, working out a clause with owner Andrew Freedman to ensure that Irwin had complete control of the team.[31] Early on, Irwin showed aptitude for identifying talent, but he may have had less authority than promised. He had scouted future star Nap Lajoie in the minor leagues, and he attempted to convince Freedman to pay $1,000 for Lajoie and another player, but Freedman refused.[32]

Irwin created a farm team in Jersey City and he did have enough authority to name his brother John the manager of those prospects.[33] Irwin created a book of hand signs for his players to study on their own time.[34] He was fired after a 36-53 start, a record that looks worse when compared to the team's 28-14 finish under his successor, Bill Joyce.[35]

In 1897, Irwin became part-owner of the Toronto club in the Eastern League. During an 1898 dispute with the league's players over the length of the season and the players' compensation, Irwin was criticized by the *Buffalo Enquirer* for assuming "a know-it-all air which oftentimes gives his friends a very severe pain in the neck."[36]

In 1898, Irwin raised some suspicions by trading away several Toronto players to the Washington Senators before being announced as Washington's manager the next year.[37] Irwin and Toronto's co-owners hired future major-league executive Ed Barrow to manage that team for the 1900 season.[38] After leaving Washington in 1900,

Irwin never coached or managed in the major leagues again. He retained partial ownership in Toronto for at least a few more years.[39]

When the American League was being organized in January 1901, Ban Johnson and Connie Mack sought an AL site in Boston. Irwin owned a potential site known as Charles River Park. Mack visited Irwin's home to discuss the use of the park. Irwin, who was sick with the flu, hesitated to lease the park to the AL.[40] At the time, the AA was trying to revive itself as a major league and Irwin tentatively controlled the Boston AA team. Irwin said he might lease the park in exchange for a stake in the Boston AL club, but he hesitated to commit to anything. Mack tired of Irwin's indecisiveness and approached Hugh Duffy, who suggested land off Huntington Avenue that could house a baseball park. The AL signed a lease at the Huntington Avenue Grounds on January 16.[41] The NL and the Players' Protective Association reached an agreement a month later that refused to recognize the AA as a major league.[42]

In 1902, Irwin returned as the Penn baseball coach and then had a short stint in the NL as an umpire.[43] From 1903 to 1907, he was a minor-league manager for teams in Toronto, Rochester, Kansas City, and Altoona. He signed on as manager for the Washington club in the short-lived Union Professional League in 1908.[44] Reports as early as that year refer to Irwin as a New York Highlanders scout.[45] He was described as the team's "chief scout" by 1909.[46] He attempted to use binoculars to steal signs from New York's opponents that year, but it did not take long for the opposition to stop the behavior by bringing it to the attention of the league.[47]

As a scout, Irwin was persistent. For example, in 1910, he heard about young minor-league pitcher Ray Caldwell in Pennsylvania. Arriving the day after Caldwell had pitched, Irwin stayed until Caldwell's next appearance. Caldwell was knocked out of that game early, but Irwin liked Caldwell's mechanics and followed the team for a

few more days. Caldwell then threw a 14-inning shutout and Irwin signed him that day. The pitcher won 134 major-league games in 12 seasons, though his potential was somewhat stymied by a drinking problem.[48]

A 1912 *Harper's Weekly* piece called Irwin "the dean of scouts."[49] After that season, the Highlanders made Irwin business manager.[50] The next year, columnist Sam Crane wrote that Irwin was a good judge of talent, hampered only by managers who mishandled that talent.[51] Highlanders manager Frank Chance disagreed; he resigned in 1914 after two seasons and said Irwin had failed to find him any quality players. President Johnson seemed to side with Irwin, calling the manager "the biggest individual failure in the history of the American League… Chance failed to develop even one man of class."[52]

Irwin certainly thought outside the box in New York, establishing a spring training site on a cricket field in Bermuda in 1913.[53] Irwin resigned when the team was sold after the 1914 season. He became part-owner and manager of the minor-league Lewiston Eagles in 1915.[54] Three years later, he began a three-year stint managing the International League's Rochester Hustlers. In 1921, he managed the Hartford Senators of the Eastern League. He caused Lou Gehrig to lose a year of collegiate eligibility after convincing the Columbia University star to play some games with Hartford.[55]

Irwin had gained a lot of weight after his playing days, but in 1921 he had digestive problems and dropped 60 pounds in two weeks. The illness forced him to stop coaching and he was hospitalized with stomach cancer that June. The next month, he boarded a steamer from New York to Boston. He told other passengers that he was going home to Boston to die, but he never made it there, and he is thought to have jumped overboard on July 16.[56]

Things had gotten complicated when Irwin's son Harold visited him in the hospital and learned of an unknown brother, Herbert, who had also visited. It turned out that Irwin had married Elizabeth in Boston in 1883, and they had Herbert and two other children. While coaching at Penn in the 1890s, Irwin met May. They moved to New York, lived as husband and wife, and had a son named Harold.[57]

It would be an exaggeration to say that Irwin lived an intricate double life. Rather than rushing between two families in separate cities, Irwin spent almost all his free time and money on May and Harold, visiting Boston so infrequently that no one in New York suspected another relationship. When he visited Boston, he often misspoke, referring to Herbert as Harold. Elizabeth's family had long suspected that Irwin had another woman. Shortly before his death, Irwin sent Elizabeth $500 in revenues from his scoreboard enterprise, enclosing a note saying, "God bless you all." Irwin indicated that he could not send more money because his bills had been very costly, but the destitute Elizabeth had been surprised even by the money he did send. Finances aside, Elizabeth said she was happy to know that Irwin had been en route to Boston to be with her in the end.[58]

Elizabeth was accepting of suicide as her husband's cause of death, but the circumstances still inspired conspiracy theories. Some people wondered about the possibility of murder, and one player said that he saw Irwin in Oklahoma after he was said to have died.[59]

Irwin was posthumously inducted into the Canadian Baseball Hall of Fame in 1989.

AUTHOR'S NOTE

In addition to the sources listed below, the author consulted Irwin's file at the Baseball Hall of Fame and U.S. census records from the 1850s to the 1870s, and he utilized statistics from Baseball-Reference.com.

NOTES

1   Alfred Henry Spink, *The National Game* (St. Louis: National Game Publishing Company, 1910), 228.

2   Roy Kerr, *Sliding Billy Hamilton: The Life and Times of Baseball's First Great Leadoff Hitter* (Jefferson, North Carolina: McFarland, 2010), 93-94.

3   Daniel Levitt, *Ed Barrow: The Bulldog Who Built the Yankees' First Dynasty* (Lincoln: University of Nebraska Press, 2008), 37-38.

4   Levitt, 37-38.

5   Donald Hubbard, *The Heavenly Twins of Boston Baseball: A Dual Biography of Hugh Duffy and Tommy McCarthy* (Jefferson, North Carolina: McFarland, 2008), 35.

6   George Tuohey, *A History of the Boston Base Ball Club: A Concise and Accurate History of Base Ball from its Inception* (Boston: M.F. Quinn & Co., 1897), 211-212.

7   John Husman, "Lee Richmond's No-Hit Debut", in Bill Felber, Mark Fimoff, Len Levin, & Peter Mancuso (eds.), *Inventing Baseball: The 100 Greatest Games that Shaped the 19th Century* (Phoenix: Society for American Baseball Research, 2013), 114.

8   David Nemec, *The Great Encyclopedia of Nineteenth Century Major League Baseball* (Tuscaloosa: University of Alabama Press, 2006), 162.

9   Mike Passey, "Martin Flaherty," SABR Baseball Biography Project, http://sabr.org/bioproj/person/df77d4e0, accessed December 16, 2017.

10 Josh Leventhal, *History of Baseball in 100 Objects* (New York: Black Dog & Leventhal Publishers, 2015), 84.

11 David Nemec, *Major League Baseball Profiles, 1871-1900, Volume 1: The Ballplayers Who Built the Game* (Lincoln: University of Nebraska Press, 2011), 465.

12 "A Captain Will Win," *Philadelphia Inquirer*, May 27, 1889, 6.

13 "Captain Arthur Irwin Released," *Philadelphia Inquirer*, June 10, 1889, 6.

14 Norman Macht, *Connie Mack and the Early Years of Baseball* (Lincoln: University of Nebraska Press, 2007), 71.

15 Robert Ross, *The Great Baseball Revolt: The Rise and Fall of the 1890 Players League* (Lincoln: University of Nebraska Press, 2016).

16 "Base Ball Comment," *Philadelphia Inquirer*, March 15, 1891, 3.

17 "Base Ball Comment."

18 Nemec, *Major League Baseball Profiles, 1871-1900, Volume 1: The Ballplayers Who Built the Game*, 411.

19 Nemec, *Major League Baseball Profiles, 1871-1900, Volume 1: The Ballplayers Who Built the Game*, 465.

20 Marty Appel., *Slide, Kelly, Slide: The Wild Life and Times of Mike King Kelly* (Lanham, Maryland: Scarecrow Press, 1999), 164.

21 Brett Abrams, *Capital Sporting Grounds: A History of Stadium and Ballpark Construction in Washington, Part 3* (Jefferson, North Carolina: McFarland, 2009), 35.

22 Christopher Devine, *Harry Wright: The Father of Professional Base Ball* (Jefferson, North Carolina: McFarland, 2003), 162.

23 Nemec, *The Great Encyclopedia of Nineteenth Century Major League Baseball*, 697.

24 "Manager Arthur Irwin Contemplates Retiring from the Philadelphia Club," *Philadelphia Inquirer*, September 9, 1895, 5.

25 "Sporting Chat," *Philadelphia Inquirer*, October 8, 1895, 5.

26 Roy Kerr, *Sliding Billy Hamilton: The Life and Times of Baseball's First Great Leadoff Hitter*, 93-94.

27 "Penn Baseball in the 19th Century: From Student Origins to University Administration," Penn University Archives & Records Center, http://www.archives.upenn.edu/histy/features/sports/baseball/1800s/hist3.html.

28 Zane Grey, *The Short-Stop* (New York: Grosset & Dunlap, 1914).

29 Samuel Hughes, *Penn In Ink: Pathfinders, Swashbucklers, Scribblers & Sages: Portraits from The Pennsylvania Gazette* (Xlibris, 2006), 57.

30 Nemec, *The Great Encyclopedia of Nineteenth Century Major League Baseball*, 697.

31 "A Running Review of Sporting News," *Philadelphia Inquirer*, October 28, 1895, 5.

32 Ronald T. Waldo, *Characters from the Diamond: Wild Events, Crazy Antics, and Unique Tales from Early Baseball* (Lanham, Maryland: Rowman & Littlefield, 2016), 47.

33 "Giants to Play Mets," *The Journal*, April 10, 1896, 12.

34 Joshua Prager, *The Echoing Green: The Untold Story of Bobby Thomson, Ralph Branca, and the Shot Heard Round the World* (New York: Pantheon Books, 2006), 75.

35 Ronald Mayer, *Christy Mathewson: A Game-by-Game Profile of a Legendary Pitcher* (Jefferson, North Carolina: McFarland, 2008), 12-13.

36 "Manager Irwin Accuses President Franklin of Squaring Proper Authorities," *Buffalo Enquirer*, May 16, 1898, 6.

37 Kevin Plummer, "Historicist: Playing the Field," https://torontoist.com/2014/03/historicist-playing-the-field/, accessed December 16, 2017.

38 Daniel Levitt, *Ed Barrow: The Bulldog Who Built the Yankees' First Dynasty*, 37.

39 Plummer, "Historicist: Playing the Field."

40 Macht, *Connie Mack and the Early Years of Baseball*, 188-190.

41 Macht, 188-190.

42 "Baseball Rules Changed," *New York Times*, February 28, 1901.

43 Ronald Waldo, *Characters from the Diamond: Wild Events, Crazy Antics, and Unique Tales from Early Baseball* (Lanham, Maryland: Rowman & Littlefield, 2016), 64.

44 "Union League's Local Officers," *Washington Evening Star*, March 6, 1908, 15.

45 "New First Baseman for New Yorks," *New York Sun*, October 2, 1908, 8.

46 "World Series Doomed?" *Courier-Journal*, January 3, 1909, 30.

47 "Sign Stealing an Ancient Art in Majors," *St. Petersburg Times*, July 19, 1959, 3C.

48 Charles Faber and Richard Faber, *Spitballers: The Last Legal Hurlers of the Wet One* (Jefferson, North Carolina: McFarland, 2006), 98-100.

49 Edward Lyell Fox, "The Baseball Scout," *Harper's Weekly*, July 27, 1912, 11.

50 "Arthur Irwin is Business Manager of Highlanders," *Hartford Courant*, December 6, 1912, 18.

51 Sam Crane, "Yankees Scout is Valuable Asset," *El Paso Herald*, November 18, 1913, 7.

52 Ed Bang, "Frank Chance Without Peer as a Failure," *Pittsburgh Press*, November 28, 1914, 14.

53 "Yankees Will Have Hotel to Themselves," *Salt Lake Tribune*, January 10, 1913, 9.

54 "Irwin in Lewiston," *Fitchburg Sentinel*, February 18, 1915, 2.

55 James Lincoln Ray, "Lou Gehrig," SABR Baseball Biography Project, https://sabr.org/bioproj/person/ccdffd4c, accessed December 16, 2017.

56 "Irwin's Double Life Bared by Suicide," *New York Times*, July 21, 1921.

57 "Hid Double Life for 27 Years," *Gettysburg Times*, July 22, 1921.

58 "Irwin's Double Life Bared by Suicide," *New York Times*, July 21, 1921.

59 Nemec, *The Great Encyclopedia of Nineteenth Century Major League Baseball*, 697.

BLACK BASEBALL IN THE MARITIMES:
1880–1980

By Colin Howell

Although the origins of Black baseball in the Maritimes remain obscure, it is likely that the game was being played informally as early as the 1870s. Operating independently, but often in association with the African Baptist and Episcopal churches, black teams like the Eurekas, Victorias, and North-Ends of Halifax, the Dartmouth Stanleys, Truro Victorias, Amherst Royals, Woodstock Wanderers, Fredericton Celestials, and the Royals and Ralph Waldo Emersons in Saint John appeared in growing numbers in the following decade. These clubs were increasingly well-known by 1890, playing challenge matches for money prizes usually arranged through notices in local newspapers. Standout players like Joe Eatman, "crack catcher" of the Celestials, and Truro's hard throwing Vickery, who Eatman said "could throw a curve around a baseball," received accolades in the daily press. According to the *Fredericton Gleaner* on June 11, 1890, "it was worth walking some distance to see the playing of Joe Eatman alone."[1]

As challenges involving various teams increased, an annual Maritime Black Baseball championship was organized in the early 1890s – at the very least by 1894 – more than a year before the now well-known Nova Scotia Colored Hockey League began operations in 1895. Many ballplayers were also stars on the ice, including shortstop Eddie Martin of the Halifax Eurekas, who is credited with the introduction of hockey's slap shot to his Colored Hockey League club. Indeed, the development of Black hockey occurred on a solid foundation of inter-community and intra-regional competition already in place in baseball. The Eurekas won seven of eight Maritime baseball championships between 1894 and 1902.[2]

There were a number of prominent families involved in the early days of Black baseball in the Maritimes. The O'Rees, McIntyres, Gordons, and Eatmans in Fredericton, the Hectors, Skinners, and Washingtons in Saint John, the Dorringtons, Mentises, and Maxwells in Truro, and the Paris family in Westville, Halifax, and Three Miles Plains, were among the most acknowledged. Recent essays by historian Roger Nason and journalist Greg Mercer offer a detailed look at team rosters and lineups in New Brunswick, including those of the Saint John Resolutes and Alerts in 1886. The Alerts had four members of the Hector family in their lineup, led by curveball specialist Jamie "Jumbo" Hector, while Ned and Bob Washington anchored the Resolutes squad.

The Saint John Royals, Maritime Black Champions 1920. (New Brunswick Museum)

The latters' father, Thomas C. Washington, whose restaurant and saloon catered to sportsmen of various kinds, including cricketers and ballplayers, was an active promoter of sport and other forms of entertainment. In 1889 Thomas Washington was instrumental in the formation of the Saint John Royals, who won two games against a visiting Halifax club that year playing before an estimated crowd of 1,500. Beginning in 1905, under the leadership of coach and captain A.H. Skinner, the Royals began a dominant run as Maritime champions. Like the Eurekas before them, they were the team to beat in the years before World War I.[3]

Although regional baseball competition was interrupted by the war, it returned in earnest after that in response to a pent-up desire for pleasurable entertainment. Earlier, Black teams had only played each other, but by the 1920s there were occasional but increasingly frequent games between White and Black clubs. In 1921, for example, the Halifax Coloured Diamonds, winner of the provincial Black championship that year, drew over 6,000 spectators during a two-game series against a White all-star team from the city. Not surprisingly, the success of the Coloured Diamonds came to the attention of their New Brunswick counterparts. The *Halifax Herald* of June 7, 1922, reported that the Saint John Royals wanted to revive the Maritime championship: "G.E. Hope, business manager of the [Saint John] Colored Athletic Association … writes that his club is after games in Halifax with the Diamonds or any other colored team. The Saint John players are willing to meet in home and home games for the Maritime title."[4] By that time the Royals were also interested in playing against barnstorming teams from the United States for a shared portion of the gate. One of those series took place that same season when the Royals upset the touring Detroit Clowns. Over the next three decades, the Clowns were frequent visitors to the Maritimes, their final visit taking place in 1949.

Dressed in clown outfits and promising a circus-like atmosphere, the Detroit tourists had come to town that first time expecting to win handily, but lost two of three games to the Royals. Royals pitcher Fred Diggs, a rubber-armed fastballer, held the Clowns in check, while batterymate Ace Austin and first baseman Kid Tynes led the offense.[5] This series was but one of many against barnstorming Black teams in the interwar period. The Cleveland Colored Giants, New York's Black Yankees and Colored Giants, Chappie Johnson's Philadelphia All-Stars, the Broadway Stars, the Philadelphia Stars, the Zulu Cannibal Giants, the Ethiopian Clowns (earlier known as the Miami Clowns), the Black House of David, and even a team of Hawaiian players of Japanese descent – referred to derisively in the press as "the Japs" – helped turn the Maritimes into a baseball burned-over district over the years. In turn they exposed regional audiences to the exploits of great Negro League players like Newton Joseph of the Kansas City Monarchs, infielder Billy Yancey of the New York Lincolns and a number of other clubs, and Gus Gadsden and Judy Johnson of the famous Hilldale club. Two players in particular, catcher Burlin White and his batterymate, Bill "Cannonball" Jackman, a lanky submarine stylist, became household names. For a few years White and Jackman toured together, but when White established the Boston Royal Giants in 1932, Jackman headed up the Philadelphia Giants and toured New Brunswick and Cape Breton for a series against the Broadway Stars, and against town teams along the way.

Traveling throughout the Maritimes, White and the Giants kept an eye out for local Black players who might be interested in touring with the club for a couple of weeks and filling in when required. In interwar Truro and Yarmouth, Blacks and Whites often played together on local diamonds. The Truro Sheiks, a Black club that became a mainstay of the local sporting scene for decades, often had White players in their lineup, while Yarmouth's Gateways occasionally had Black players in their regular batting order. In addition, Yarmouth fielded an all-Black team that played a regular schedule in the Yarmouth town league in the 1930s, a precursor of the predominantly Black Yarmouth Novies of the postwar era. In New Glasgow, the Coloured Wonders began playing White teams as a member of the Pictou County League in 1932, and young Black stars like slugging catcher Freeman Paris, second baseman Ernest Dorrington, and outfielder Alvin McLean were given the chance to play on New Glasgow's all-White town team a couple of years later. After a game in Truro in June 1935 involving what the *Halifax Herald* called "a mixture of white and coloured boys" – most likely the Sheiks – White spoke highly of Gordon Maxwell and center fielder Bob Mentis. A former high-school track star and hockey player who some thought was the finest player in the country outside the NHL, Mentis agreed to accompany the Giants as they completed their tour of the province that year. So did Morton "Bucky" Berry, a young pitcher-outfielder from Yarmouth who joined the Giants for six games in 1937, going 6-for-25 at the plate and sparkling defensively.[6]

White's Royal Giants played more than 100 games in the Maritimes between 1932 and their final tour in 1939, often incorporating clowning routines to attract large crowds. Well-known performer King Tut, whose real name was Richard King, took the field with a glove twice normal size and a hat with an oversized brim; George "Whitey" Michaels delighted fans catching balls between his legs and behind his back; squeaky-voiced Stormy Faulk pestered umpires and visiting players with his constant chatter and spontaneous comedy; and White sat behind the plate in a rocking chair while throwing baserunners out at second. Occasionally local players were put off by the clowning. "Comedy would put off my pitching," Liverpool pitcher Laurie Thorburn claimed. White would "hold the bat, and instead of tryin' to hit with it … would just point it towards the ball. It looked like he was trying to show me up. Once, I threw a close ball to him to see what he was doin', and I split his finger right in two."[7] White missed most of the month in the Royals 1936 tour as a result.

Thorburn's comments aside, the talented Royal Giants were highly respected by ballplayers and fans alike. Busky Johnson was the club's slick-fielding second baseman, and Blacky McKnight, an outfielder with prodigious power, played alongside speedy center fielder Vince Coleman. William "Babe" Robinson, who replaced Bill Jackman as the club's pitching ace, could throw sharp breaking curveballs until his arm fell off. During the 1935 tour, for example, Robinson pitched a complete-game victory over the regional champion St. Stephen club early in the day, hopped in a car for a four-hour trip to Cape Breton, and then defeated a team from the Cape Breton Colliery League that evening. The Giants roster would at times include shortstop Mapp, outfielders Barry and Stevens, and third baseman James.

Local clubs respected the talents of White and his teammates, having learned much from them about the game over the years. In turn, White found the St. Stephen Kiwanis, Liverpool Larrupers, and Yarmouth Gateways worthy opponents. In the early '30s, the Giants would often spend a week or so along Nova Scotia's South Shore, schooling local players in the finer points of the game. In a game against Danny Seaman's Liverpool club in August of 1935, Seaman scored the winning run in the bottom of the ninth by kicking the ball out of White's hand as White attempted to tag him. "We wanted to help you," White said after the game, "but not to have you beat us with our own tactics."[8] The *Halifax Herald* on May 19, 1936, announced the impending return of the Royal Giants, and upcoming games against Halifax, Liverpool, and the Yarmouth Gateways. The article testified to their mentorship, and pointed out how the visitors "helped open fans' and players' eyes to snappy ball."[9] The Yarmouth Gateways "learned a new bag of tricks that helped them in the playoffs" on their way to capturing the 1935 Maritime championship.[10] The year before, St. Stephen had split two-game series with both the Royal Giants and Jackman's Philadelphia Colored Giants. By the time of the Royal Giants' final tour in 1939, a number of clubs could play them on equal terms. In their final game of that tour, they were held in check by the region's premier left-hander, Cecil Brownell, losing 5-3 to St. Stephen on their way back to Boston. In the early 1950s the Liverpool Larrupers would honor White and the Royal Giants' contribution to baseball in the province. White appeared in uniform and made a couple of plate appearances that day.

World War II brought different opportunities for Black players playing on Army and Navy teams around the region, in the newly formed Halifax Defense League (HDL) and in military leagues in Britain, where Canadians and Americans sometimes competed against each other. One of the starriest players in the HDL was Manny McIntyre, a native of Devon, New Brunswick, who hit .385 as the league's all-star shortstop, and was voted the "most popular player" in 1944 while playing with Halifax Shipyards.[11] In 1945, while playing for Trois-Rivières of the Quebec Provincial League, McIntyre came to the attention of the New York Cuban Giants and appeared in a season-ending exhibition game with Negro Leaguers at Yankee Stadium. Despite their interest in Manny, he chose to stay in Canada to play, even after being contacted a second time by the same Negro League club when their Minnie Miñoso

Manny McIntyre of the Middleton Cardinals, 1946 Nova Scotia Senior Championship finalists. (Courtesy daughter Marlene McIntyre, Canadiac, Quebec).

signed a contract with the Chicago White Sox. In addition to McIntyre, Fred Thomas from Windsor, Ontario – one of Canada's finest athletes in the first half of the twentieth century – played outstanding ball for Halifax Air Force in 1944. Cape Bretoner Charlie Pyle, a speedy outfielder and, like Thomas, a multisport athlete, had a sensational year in the Canadian Army England Baseball League in 1945, finishing second with a .432 batting average. Pyle also competed in track and field, boxing, and softball, and was voted the best all-around athlete in the Canadian Army that year. Pyle's fellow Cape Bretoner Oscar Seale was equally accomplished, finishing third in the import-laden Cape Breton Colliery League in 1949 with a .350 average. Seale was also an excellent softball player, at one point turning down an offer to tour with Eddie Feigner's King and His Court four-man team.[12]

McIntyre and Thomas contributed as well to what historian Jules Tygiel called "baseball's great experiment," the gradual desegregation of baseball

that followed Jackie Robinson's breaking of the color bar. When McIntyre signed a contract with Sherbrooke of the Class-C Border League in June 1946, he became the first Black Canadian to play in Organized Baseball after World War II. Two years later Thomas signed a Cleveland Indians contract, and broke the color bar in the Eastern League. Given their ability in other sports, neither was particularly interested in concentrating on pro baseball careers. McIntyre was a member of the first all-Black line in professional hockey, and even played in Europe for hotelier Charles Ritz's Paris Racing Club, while Thomas played for the Harlem Globetrotters in basketball, and with the Toronto Argonauts of the Canadian Football league. In the summers both continued to play semipro ball in Quebec, Ontario, and the Maritimes.

In the late 1940s and into the '50s, a number of other Black players flirted with baseball in the summers while concentrating on professional hockey careers. Art Dorrington made history in 1950 when he became the first Black hockey player to sign an NHL contract, with the New York Rangers organization, but despite five productive years in the Eastern Hockey League he was never given a chance to play in the NHL. Dorrington was an excellent baseball player as well, breaking in with his hometown Truro Bearcats as a teenager in 1948 at a time when baseball in the region was turning increasingly to imported players. Playing with Saint John of the New Brunswick League in 1949, the speedy outfielder hit .296, outperforming many of the American players who would later play in the major leagues. After the 1950-51 hockey season, the Boston Braves convinced him to give pro baseball a try, and assigned him to their Wellsville affiliate in the PONY (Pennsylvania-Ontario-New York) League. He showed some power, hitting three home runs in 43 at-bats, but the hockey season had taken its toll, and he ended up in the hospital with pneumonia. After his hockey career ended in 1957, Dorrington took up baseball once more, playing for Hall of Famer Pop Lloyd's Hap Farley All-Stars in Atlantic City, a successor of the Johnson All-Stars owned by Enoch "Nucky" Johnson, a real-life character made famous by the HBO *Boardwalk Empire* series.[13]

Two other players of that era, Truro's Stan "Chook" Maxwell and Fredericton's Willie O'Ree, had professional baseball skills but eventually chose to concentrate on their hockey careers. As a 19-year-old, Maxwell broke into the import-laden H&D League with the Truro Bearcats, leading the club with a .283 average, finishing ahead of future major leaguer Grover "Deacon" Jones and two First Team All-Americans from the University of Michigan, Ken Tippery and Bruce Haynam. (Along with Maxwell and Jones, a dozen or so Black players played in the Maritimes during the '50s, including future major leaguers Don "Chook" Eaddy and Dave Ricketts.) Braves scout Jeff Jones tried unsuccessfully to sign both Eaddy and Ricketts. For Chook a requirement of playing winter ball in the Caribbean was a deal-breaker because it interfered with his pro hockey aspirations. That same year another young Black player, Halifax Citadels second baseman Billy Carter, finished second on the club in batting, behind Zeke Bella and ahead of double-play partner Tommy Carroll, both of whom went on to play in the majors for the Yankees.[14]

At about the same time, teenager Willie O'Ree was playing baseball in Fredericton, and accepted an invitation to spring training with the Braves in Waycross, Georgia, in 1956. Appalled by the racist environment in the South, Willie decided at that point to concentrate on hockey, and became the first Black player in the NHL, with the Boston Bruins in 1958. Another Truro native, Johnny Mentis, turned down offers to play baseball in the States, but became a well-known figure in Quebec baseball and hockey in the 1960s, making history as the first Black hockey player to play against the Russians. Author Merritt Clifton, who wrote a history of the Quebec Provincial League, featured Johnny as one of the top five performers of the '50s and '60s in Quebec baseball. According to Clifton, Mentis, in a career that spanned over a dozen years, still holds the highest career batting average of any player in the Provincial League, with more than 1,000 at-bats.[15] Johnny's brothers Burton, Ray, and Bob "Cook" Mentis were fine players as well. Burton played with a predominantly Black team in Halifax, the Vaughan Furriers, who captured the Maritime Junior championship in 1962, and starred in senior ball after that.[16]

In the changing racial environment after that, all-Black teams in the Maritimes were a rarity; Black players played instead on senior-league clubs throughout the region. A few, such as Curtis Falls and Curt Coward, played briefly in the minor leagues. By this point, however, other sports – hockey, football, and softball in particular – offered more attractive professional opportunities. Outfielder Ken Walcott grew up playing baseball in Cape Breton, starred in senior ball for a number of summers, and was eventually selected by Baseball Nova Scotia on its all-star "team of the century" in 2005. Walcott ended up playing three years in the Canadian Football League rather than pursuing a baseball career. In addition, Mark Smith, who had a tryout with the Kansas City Royals in 1982, became one of the world's finest softball pitchers, and a five-time all-world selection at the ISC world championship as a member of Team Canada.

NOTES

1   Quoted in Roger Nason, "Early Black Baseball Teams in Fredericton: A Sign of Community Identity, 1889-1906." *Active History*, February 22, 2021. See also, Colin D. Howell, *Northern Sandlots: A Social History of Maritime Baseball* (Toronto: University of Toronto Press, 1995), 179-80, 274.

2   George Fosty and Darril Fosty, "Colored Hockey League," *Canadian Encyclopedia*. https://thecanadi-anencyclopedia.ca/en/article/coloured-hockey-league (accessed October 12, 2021).

3   Roger Nason, "A Lost Chapter in the History of Black Baseball in New Brunswick," *Active History*, January 25, 2021; Howell, 179.

4   *Halifax Herald*, June 7, 1922: 9.

5   Greg Mercer, "How an East Coast all-Black Baseball Team Brought Pride to Their Neighbourhoods," *Globe and Mail*, February 27, 2021.

6   Howell, 171-6.

7   Quoted in Robert Ashe, *Even the Babe Came to Play: Small-Town Baseball in the Dirty 30s* (Halifax: Nimbus, 1991), 119.

8   Quoted in Burton Russell, *Nova Scotia Baseball Heroics* (Kentville: self-published, 1993), 30.

9   *Halifax Herald*, May 19, 1936: 10.

10   *Halifax Herald*, May 19, 1936: 10.

11   John Lutz, "Pioneer on the Diamond, Ace on the Ice: Manny McIntyre," in Arif Khadid and Keith Elman, *In the Shadow of Obscurity: Toiling in a Reluctant Society* (Los Angeles: ENH Publishing, 2020), 196.

12   Colin Howell, "Black Bases/Black Ice: The Multi-Sport Careers of Canadian Black Athletes and the Struggle for Social Justice," paper presented at the *Telling the Stories of Race and Sports in Canada* Symposium at the University of Windsor in 2018. Paper here: https://scholar.uwindsor.ca/cgi/viewcontent.cgi?article=1015&context=racesportsymposium.

13   Telephone interview with Art Dorrington, March 20, 2012.

14   Interview with Darrell Maxwell, Truro, August 8, 2017; telephone interview with Grover "Deacon" Jones, March 24, 2021.

15   Merritt Clifton, *Disorganized Baseball: The Provincial League from LaRoque to les Expos* (Brigham, Quebec: self-published, 1982), 7-18, 20; interview with John Mentis, Truro, August 8, 2017.

16   Frank Mitchell, *The Boys of '62. Transcending the Racial Divide* (Halifax: New World Publishing, 2008), 139-141. Other team members included Denny Clyke, Dave Downey, Cecil Jackson, Sonny Parker, Ernie Symons, and Jim Tasco.

BOB EMSLIE

By Larry Gerlach

Robert Daniel Kean Emslie, the least-known famous umpire in baseball history, made his earthly debut on January 27, 1859, in Guelph, Ontario, the fourth son and seventh of eight children born to Alexander and Mary Graye,[1] immigrants from Aberdeenshire, Scotland. (Emslie is a Scottish habitational surname meaning "woodland clearing.") With his last breath on April 26, 1943, a lifelong love affair with baseball that began at age 6 as a batboy came to an end, and with it a career by any standard one of the most extraordinary in baseball history. He had spent 54 of his 84 years, the years 1882 through 1935, in professional baseball, six as a player and 49 as an umpire,[2] 46 in the major leagues, calling 'em for 35 seasons then serving 11 years as umpire supervisor. Solid in stature at 5-feet-11 and 180 pounds, Emslie was a gifted athlete, excelling in sports requiring very different skills: major-league baseball pitcher, international champion in trap-shooting and curling, and late in life an accomplished golfer and bowler.

Bob was not to the manor born, his father a tailor, but he was raised in the hotbed of Canadian baseball, as a youth caught up in the diamond exploits of championship teams, first the Guelph Maple Leafs, then the Tecumsehs after moving to London in 1868.[3] He started playing amateur ball in the outfield but, impressed by Fred Goldsmith's "skew ball" (i.e. curveball), took to the box. In 1879 he began pitching for pay with the Harriston Brown Stockings, employed as head clerk of the leading hotel in town, and paid $1.50 to $1.75 a game.[4] In 1881 he joined the St. Thomas Atlantics, and while he was barnstorming with the team through Eastern American states in 1882, his sharp breaking curveball so impressed the Camden Merritt of the Interstate Association that they tendered his first professional contract, $150 a month. When the Merritt folded in July 1883, Emslie reached the major leagues with Baltimore of the American Association. His devastating curveball portending a brilliant career, the right-hander in 1884 started and finished 50 games for the sixth-place Orioles, winning 17 of his first 21 games, and ending the season 32-17 with one tie. Posting a 2.75 ERA in 455⅓ innings, he struck out 264 while walking only 88. His major-league career ended abruptly the next year in August due to a shoulder injury, probably a SLAP tear,[5] that began in 1884 and worsened while he was pitching in New Orleans during the winter of 1885. He later recalled, "I suddenly felt a stinging sensation in my shoulder. This thing went on for some time, until no matter what kind of a ball I threw, it gave me great pain, and then I knew my arm was dead."[6] Although that season's 3-14 record and 4.71 ERA reduced his major-league career record to a mediocre 44-44 and 3.19 ERA, 362 strikeouts against 165 walks evidenced his once-promising career.

Comeback efforts in the minors, with Toronto of the International League in 1886 and Savannah of the Southern Association in 1887, failed, but his baseball career inadvertently resumed on June 30, 1887, when he was summoned from the stands to call a game in Toronto after the scheduled umpire fell ill. Admitting "it was purely a matter of accident how I came to follow umpiring as a means of livelihood,"[7] he umpired with the International League for the rest of that season and the next two, advancing in 1890 to the majors with the American Association. He began the 1891 season in the Western Association, then returned to the majors in August with the National League, where he remained for 45 years. By then a proven career umpire, in 1893 he married Helena Ward, with whom he had two children, Helen Elizabeth ("Kitty") in 1895 and Robert John ("Jack") in 1900.

Toiling during the three most contentious and difficult decades umpires ever faced, from the violent, umpiring-baiting 1890s through the Deadball Era, Emslie survived injury from thrown and batted balls, physical and verbal assaults from players and fans, and criticism in the press to become the respected, even revered, titular "dean of umpires." He was the acknowledged master of the rule book, fellow arbiter Cy Rigler declaring that Emslie "knows more about the baseball rules than all the other National League umpires together."[8]

Bob performed the common aspects of umpiring in an uncommon way, being respected by players and managers alike for his temperament, style in handling disputes, and ability to "run" the games in an efficient and orderly manner. Of his

work in the turbulent 1890s, Jacob Morse of the *Boston Herald* asserted: "Undoubtedly he has got to be the best umpire who ever handled a game. Umpires there have been who have been as good in the mere minutiae of the game, but none to equal him when it comes to discipline, tact, personal habits, temperance, reliability and ability."[9] Christy Mathewson agreed, regarding Emslie as "one of the finest umpires that ever broke into the League," "the sort of umpire who rules by the bond of good fellowship rather than by the voice of authority."[10] Reflecting upon his career, Emslie said: "I always got along very well with the players and I don't think I ever had an enemy in the game."[11]

Emslie understood that kicking was part of the game: "Of course it is inevitable that players will protest when a decision is given that seems to them erroneous. Umpires make mistakes the same as other people and it is only natural that there should be a protest if the player gets the small end of a decision, but I will put him out of the game just as soon as I feel that he is talking back too much or uses language which he should not use."[12] His first ejection came on July 21, 1892, the Browns' Jack Crooks; his second came two years later when he tossed the New York Giants' Jack Doyle and fined him $5 for "a series of foul names unfit for publication."[13] On May 19 at the Polo Grounds, he had the distinction of giving viciously vituperative John McGraw his first ejection as Giants manager for "raucously expressing his disagreement."[14] Being a former player, Emslie understood the competitive spirit, so typically each season he recorded the fewest fines and ejections on the staff. While the number of his ejections increased from 1901 to 1910, during his career Emslie tossed players far less frequently (once every 26 games) than did his National League contemporaries.[15]

Players so respected Emslie for his ability and integrity that they would come to his aid in time of need. In an 1899 game, when irate Brooklyn fans jumped onto the field and mobbed him after he had called Tom Daly out at home plate in a 2-1 loss to Boston, Daly and Bill Dahlen shielded him from the crowd with their bats.[16] And in 1907, when fans at the Polo Grounds poured onto the field bent on assault, Giants pitcher Joe McGinnity ran from the dugout, and threw an arm around Bob, "occasionally warding off a stray wallop that some angry fan aimed at the umpire's head" until police arrived to restore order.[17]

Team owners also appreciated his long and distinguished service. In recognition of his 25 years of service, the league in August 1916 honored him with "Emslie Day" in Brooklyn, the ceremonies replete with tributes and gifts, including from league President John Tener 25 double-eagle gold coins worth $20 each, and a diamond stickpin from his fellow umpires.[18]

He called his last game on October 2, 1924, leaving the field with numerous major-league umpiring records. At 65 years and 8 months the oldest ever to umpire a game, he had worked the most seasons, 35, and the most games, 4,231, and achieved numerous "firsts": the first umpire to work four decades, to call 2,000, 3,000, and 4,000 games, to be given a celebratory "day," and to be appointed staff supervisor. In 1935 he retired with three service milestones: 45 consecutive years with one league, 46 years in the majors, and 54 in professional baseball – all longer than anyone else in history. With Bill Klem, he still holds the record for the fastest game in baseball history, 51 minutes on September 28, 1919, and until 1969 he had worked the most no-hitters, eight, in the National League.

He had also achieved two personal distinctions: the first Canadian full-time major-league umpire, and the first and only major leaguer to wear a toupee during his career. It has been said that Emslie's hair loss was due to the stress of umpiring during the tumultuous 1890s, but it actually began in 1885 in Baltimore, and was caused by genetics. Vanity was not the only

Bob Emslie, National League umpire and newlywed in 1893. (Canadian Baseball Hall of Fame and Museum)

reason for donning a toupee. It was commonplace for men in the late nineteenth century to regard hair loss as a sign of decreased manliness, and with masculinity accentuated among athletes, it was understandable for an authority figure like an umpire to cover baldness. Although never, as has often been claimed, being nicknamed Wig, he was extremely sensitive about baldness, brooking no references to his hairpiece. He took "a good deal" from Jack Doyle until Doyle suggested Emslie get "a hair restorer," a comment that resulted in Doyle's being escorted from the grounds by a policeman.[19] And when John McGraw shouted in a voice loud enough to be heard by spectators that Emslie should get a box of hairpins to fasten his toupee, the umpire, embarrassed by and irate at "one of the most tragic, brutal cases of 'show up' he had ever experienced," ejected the Giants manager for five days and hit him with a sizable fine.[20]

Unfortunately, Bob Emslie is most famously (or infamously) remembered for his role (or nonrole) in the game between the New York Giants and Chicago Cubs at the Polo Grounds on

September 23, 1908, the so-called "Merkle Boner" game, unfairly criticized for failing to notice that the Giants' Fred Merkle failed to reach second base after the apparent game-winning hit. Emslie, who said he "had to fall to the ground to keep [the batted] ball from hitting me," had properly been looking to see if the batter-runner reached first base, as that concluded the play. Watching to see if Merkle touched second was the home-plate umpire's duty, so Hank O'Day properly made the call that resulted in a tie game, replayed at the end of the season for the first time in major-league history.[21]

Because of the Merkle incident, John McGraw dubbed Emslie "Blind Bob." Emslie, an accomplished trapshooter, took offense. Several stories circulated as to how he demonstrated his visual acuity to the Giants manager. One version is that he showed up one afternoon during a Giants practice with a rifle – not to shoot the Giants manager, but to demonstrate his eyesight. After placing a dime on the pitcher's rubber, he retreated behind home plate, took aim, and sent the coin "spinning into the outfield." Another version says he put the dime on a matchbox on second base. On another occasion, he reportedly challenged McGraw to a contest – shooting at apples set on second base. McGraw declined, sarcastically quipping "Maybe you can see apples, but you can't see baseballs."[22]

Statistically, Emslie is firmly entrenched in the major-league record book with career totals that will likely never be surpassed. He is tied for fourth in number of seasons, 35, with five who umpired on four-man crews,[23] and 16th with Al Barlick in games umpired with 4,231,[24] the most by an umpire working only on two-man crews, and the most by a former major-league player. He also ranks fourth in home-plate games worked, 2,356,[25] remarkable inasmuch as he spent 15 years umpiring only the bases.

More indicative than statistics of Emslie's prominence as an umpire are the views of contemporaries who had first-hand knowledge of his umpiring. Honus Wagner ranked Emslie and Bill Klem "the ideal umpires" during his 20-year Hall of Fame career, 1897-1917, regarding Emslie "the greatest of all the umpires on base decisions."[26] Hall of Fame umpire Bill McGowan agreed, calling Emslie "the greatest base umpire of all time," and thought Bill Klem and Emslie "the best umpiring team the game ever knew – Klem at the plate, Emslie on the bases."[27] Hall of Fame umpire Billy Evans considered Emslie "one of the greatest umpires the game ever produced."[28] Sportswriters, too, thought him "one of the greatest umpires of all time."[29] The first edition of *Who's Who in Major League Baseball* said of Emslie: "Whenever old-time fans get together and start chattering about diamond immortals you'll hear them paying tribute to Bob Emslie, who was one of the greatest of them all in the days of Hurst, O'Loughlin, Sheridan, O'Day and Tommy Connolly."[30]

Famous in his day, Bob Emslie faded into historical obscurity owing to the lone omission in his long and distinguished career: He never umpired a World Series. He had umpired three Temple Cup series, baseball's postseason showcase games in the 1890s, but beginning in 1905, the onset of hyperopia (farsightedness) led to increasing criticism of his calling pitches, and from 1910 to the end of his career he essentially umpired only the bases.[31] Glasses would have corrected the problem, but it then was an unspoken rule that umpires not don spectacles, as it would be taken as an indication of deficient eyesight; the eyeglass-ceiling for umpires was not broken until 1956.

Immediately upon Emslie's death, sportswriters and ex-National League President John Heydler called for his enshrinement in the National Baseball Hall of Fame in Cooperstown. Only players were then deemed eligible for election, but in 1946 the Hall announced its Honor Rolls of Baseball, recognizing the significant contributions to the game of those precluded from official induction. Bob Emslie was one of 11 umpires selected.[32] Beginning with Bill Klem and Tommy Connolly in 1953, 10 umpires have been inducted into the Hall, Emslie's career statistics equal to or greater than most.[33]

Interred next to his wife in Section 92 of the mausoleum in St. Thomas West Cemetery, Bob Emslie eventually, if posthumously, achieved baseball immortality, when he was elected in 1986 to the Canadian Baseball Hall of Fame, and in 2004 to the Guelph Sports Hall of Fame as a player and umpire. And he is one of only three umpires for whom a baseball facility has been named.[34] The lone survivor, Emslie Field in St. Thomas's Pinafore Park, is a fitting living memorial to the achievements and contributions to baseball of Robert D. Emslie.

NOTES

1   Graye, the traditional Scottish spelling, was subsequently rendered Gray.

2   In 1887 he both played his last game and umpired his first game.

3   David L. Bernard, "The Guelph Maple Leafs: A Cultural Indicator of Southern Ontario," *Ontario History*, vol. 84, no. 3 (September 1992), 1-23; Brian Martin, *The Tecumsehs of the International Association: Canada's First Major League Baseball Champions* (Jefferson, North Carolina: McFarland, 2015).

4   *New York Sun*, July 28, 1918; *New York Times*, April 29, 1943.

5   SLAP (Superior Labrum Anterior and Posterior) tears, labral tears of the cartilage where the humerus bone joins the scapula shoulder blade to stabilize the shoulder joint, are common in forceful movements of the arm above shoulder level, such as overhand pitching.

6   *The Sporting News*, February 1, 1896.

7   Robert D. Emslie, "Ramblings of an Umpire," *Baseball Magazine* (November, 1908): 18.

8   *Boston Globe*, August 17, 1920. See also the *Wilmington Evening Journal*, August 2, 1920, and *Vancouver Sun*, August 22, 1920.

9   Undated 1897 *Boston Herald* article, Robert Emslie Collection, Elgin County Museum, St. Thomas, Ontario; *Baltimore Sun*, October 2, 1897.

10 Christy Mathewson, *Pitching in a Pinch* (New York: Putnam's, 1912), 175.

11 Unidentified newspaper article, Emslie Collection.

12 Emslie, "Ramblings," 18.

13 *St. Louis Globe-Democrat*, July 22, 1892; *Sporting Life*, June 23, 1894.

14 *New York Sun*, May 20, 1903; Lou Hernández, *Manager of Giants: The Tactics, Temper and True Record of John McGraw* (Jefferson, North Carolina: McFarland, 2018), 33.

15 Bill Klem 346, Cy Rigler 272, Jack Sheridan 264, Tommy Connolly 261, Hank O'Day 238, and Jim Johnstone 208. Indeed, Deadball Era umpires, including Emslie, constituted 10 of the 12 with the most ejections. David W. Smith, Table 5, https://www.retrosheet.org/Research/SmithD/EjectionsThroughTheYears.pdf.

16 *Brooklyn Daily Eagle, Brooklyn Citizen, Brooklyn Daily Times,* and *Brooklyn Times Union; New York Times, New York Tribune, New York Sun, New York World; Boston Globe;* September 8 and 9; *The Sporting News*, September 9; *Sporting Life*, September 16, 1899.

17 *New York World*, May 21-22; *New York Times, Chicago Tribune, Boston Globe,* and *Washington Post*, May 22, 1907.

18 *New York Times* and *New York Tribune*, August 10 and 13, 1916; *Brooklyn Daily Eagle* and *Boston Globe*, August 13, 1916.

19 *Baltimore Sun,* and *Washington Evening Star,* July 30, 1897.

20 *New York Tribune*, May 26; *Syracuse Post-Standard*, May 27, 1908; Allen Sangree, "As the Umpire Sees Them," *Collier's*, Volume 41 (September 19, 1908): 23; William Patten, and Joseph Walker McSpadden, eds., *The Book of Baseball: The National Game from the Earliest Days* (New York: P.F. Collier & Son, 1911), 110.

21 David W. Anderson, *More Than Merkle: A History of the Best and Most Exciting Baseball Season in Human History* (Lincoln: University of Nebraska Press, 2000), *New York Times*, September 24-25; *New York Tribune, Chicago Tribune*, September 24 and 27; *New York Tribune*, October 3; *New York Evening World*, October 5; and *Sporting Life*, October 17, 1908. For various historians' views on the game, see the special Merkle edition of the SABR Deadball Era Committee newsletter, "The Inside Game," vol. 8, no. 4 (September 23, 2008), at https://sabr.org/research/deadball-era-research-committee-newsletters/.

22 Raymond Schuessler, "You Can't Kill the Umpire," *The American Legion Magazine* (April 1976): 26; James M. Kahn, *The Umpire Story* (New York: G.P. Putnam's Sons, 1953), 39.

23 He trails Joe West, 44 seasons (through 2021), and Bill Klem and Bruce Froemming, 37 seasons.

24 Retrosheet.org's listing of 4,230 games omits Emslie's game on August 5, 1921.

25 Retrosheet's 2,357 includes him at the plate on April 17, 1917, but the *Cincinnati Enquirer* on April 18 specifically reports him calling plays at first base.

26 *Washington Evening Star*, December 24, 1923; John B. Kennedy, "The Flying Dutchman," *Collier's*, vol. 85, no. 15 (April 12, 1930): 81.

27 *The Sporting News* and the *Wilmington News Journal*, March 17; *Wilmington Morning News*, April 13, 1954.

28 *Boston Globe*, March 6, 1915.

29 *Buffalo Morning Express*, January 11, 1914; *Pittsburgh Gazette*, January 28, 1924.

30 Harold "Speed" Johnson, comp., *Who's Who in Major League Baseball* (Chicago: Buxton Publishing, 1933), 448-449.

31 From 1910 to 1924, he worked the plate only 11 times, thrice in 1913 and 1918, and none in eight of those seasons.

32 Five managers, 11 executives, 12 sportswriters, and 11 umpires were chosen. The other umpires selected were Bill Klem, Tommy Connolly, Bill Dinneen, Billy Evans, John Gaffney, Tim Hurst, "Honest John" Kelly, Francis "Silk" O'Loughlin, Tom Lynch, and Jack Sheridan.

33 His 35 seasons as a regular member of the staff is second only to Klem's 37, and at least a decade longer than four other enshrinees. That he umpired more games than five members of the Hall is the more noteworthy as he worked fully half of his seasons, 1890-1908, as a single umpire, the others on two-man crews.

34 The baseball field at the University of Kansas was named after Ernie Quigley, National League umpire from 1913 through 1938, who also briefly served (1944-1950) as the school's athletics director. John Ducey Park in Edmonton, Alberta, honors an Edmonton baseball executive who had previously umpired amateur and minor league ball between 1931 and 1945. Money has since trumped tradition, both facilities having been renamed in honor of financial donors.

ALFRED HENRY SPINK

By Bill Pruden

The irony is clear to anyone who gives it even the slightest thought. At the time that baseball was entering the public consciousness in the United States, emerging as the national pastime, one of the central figures in that development was a Canadian-born entrepreneur and sportsman, Alfred H. Spink. As a sportswriter and unflagging baseball booster, Spink not only helped embed the game in the American psyche, but he also created and developed the newspaper, *The Sporting News*, that would eventually, and deservedly, earn the title the "Bible of Baseball."[1]

Alfred H. Spink was born on August 25, 1852 (some sources say 1853 or 1854), in Quebec City, Canada.[2] He was the third of four sons and one of the eight children born to William and Frances Anne (Snaith) Spink.[3,4] William served many years as a records clerk in Quebec's legislative assembly.[5] After his death in February of 1867, the family emigrated south from their native Canada, presumably in search of better employment opportunities in post-bellum America. Settling on the west side of Chicago, the growing boys, all one-time cricket enthusiasts, quickly adapted to the developing game of baseball, one well on its way to being crowned America's national pastime.[6] Indeed, once they were old enough, the

Spink boys joined the roster of one of the Windy City's most prominent amateur teams, the Mutuals (some sources credit the brothers with being central figures in the team's creation),[7] named for a famous squad in New York City whose major financial backer was the infamous New York political leader Boss Tweed.[8]

With their father dying not long before the family moved to the United States, the boys had to help with family responsibilities. The oldest, William, known as Billy, did a stint as a telegraph operator before eventually going into journalism. Alfred too went in that direction as a way to stay involved with the game that had captured the older boys' interest upon their arrival in the United States.[9] In 1875 Alfred left Chicago and moved south to follow Billy, who was then working for the *St. Louis Globe-Democrat*.[10] According to Al, Billy was a trailblazer, persuading the paper's editor to add sports coverage to its offerings. While Billy was initially a virtual one-man sports bureau, it was apparently a natural fit, since in Al's view his older brother was "the best all around sporting writer of the day, if not the best all around sporting editor that ever lived."[11]

While Al joined his pioneering brother Billy in St. Louis, he initially worked for the

Globe-Democrat's rival, the *St. Louis Post*. However, just about the time Al started working there, newspaper mogul Joseph Pulitzer merged the *Post* with the *Globe-Democrat*. Not long afterward, Al left the paper, eventually serving as sports editor of first the *Missouri Republican* and then the *St. Louis Chronicle*.[12]

While Spink's work as a journalist was generally focused on sports, as a young reporter he displayed an adventurous streak that was nowhere better illustrated than in his foray into Grenada, Mississippi, in 1878, in the midst of a yellow fever epidemic. Taking leave from the *Globe-Democrat* to serve as special correspondent for the *New York Herald*, Spink recounted the veritable decimation of the town of Grenada. He wrote of a town so paralyzed with fear that no one would even venture to retrieve the body of one who was a victim of the disease ravaging both the bodies of countless inhabitants and the psyches of those physically untouched. He told of seeing bodies being taken directly from the site of their death to the cemetery, so as to reduce possible contact with the dead body and the disease. So fearful was the community, and so contagious was the disease believed to be, that Spink reported that had he actually entered the town of Grenada, he would have been unable to enter any of the towns down the road. It was a time of fear and anxiety, a reality brought home by the fact that upon the outbreak of the disease Grenada was a community boasting a population of 2,500. However, once the fever arrived all but about 250 Whites fled the town; almost all of these were affected, with over 125 dying. It was devastating. Spink noted that the fever did not discriminate, for of the almost 80 Blacks who were hit by the disease, about half of them died as well.[13]

That experience revealed a different side of Spink, whose reporting on the human tragedy exhibited an impressive empathy, as well as an ability to make the larger issues come alive through his depiction of the many individuals who

suffered. His report of burning his own clothes and personal effects as he left Grenada brought home both the personal nature of the plague but also the extent of its impact: after speaking of the conditions that were "simply beyond description," he made clear that he knew he was one of the lucky survivors.[14] Fortunately, such ventures were aberrations for the young man who had grown up with a cricket bat in his hand, but had easily transferred that experience into a passion for the game of baseball; in spite of a few detours by the sometimes mercurial Spink, baseball remained a central part of his life until his death in 1928.

Both Al and Billy used their positions as sports editors to boost the fortunes of the city of St. Louis and its professional baseball teams. This was a particularly important undertaking in the aftermath of a widespread gambling scandal in 1877 that led the leaders of the city's National League entry, the Brown Stockings, to withdraw from the league.[15] Their efforts were rewarded in 1880 when they persuaded Chris Von der Ahe, a German immigrant saloonkeeper often credited with forging the bond between beer and baseball, to sponsor a new team.[16]

Having appealed to his vanity, convincing him that his involvement would lead to local prominence and fame, in the fall of 1880 the Spinks got Von der Ahe to assume the role of president of the newly formed Sportsman's Park Club and Association. Al Spink was selected as secretary. Backed by the infusion of funds that Von der Ahe's involvement brought to the enterprise, the association quickly set about renovating Sportsman's Park. At the same time, under the auspices of the St. Louis Baseball Association, Al, his brother William, and Ned Cuthbert were organizing the latest version of the St. Louis Browns, a team that would play in Sportsman's Park – where Von der Ahe had the concession rights. Playing an independent schedule intended to revive interest in the game in St. Louis, the team was a resounding success. By the end of the summer the new St. Louis Browns were taking on all challengers, and the large crowds made Von der Ahe a lot of money. Indeed, so successful was the whole enterprise that at year's end, the savvy German immigrant, having come to the realization that "baseball was an excellent adjunct to his grocery and saloon business," effectively bought the team, incorporating it into the Sportsman's Park Club and Association.[17]

Next came the creation of a league for the team to play in. After discussions and negotiations in the fall of 1881, a six-team American Association of Base Ball Clubs was formed. The six cities were St. Louis, Louisville, Cincinnati, Pittsburgh, Philadelphia, and Baltimore. While the established National League, part of whose mission was to fight the evils of both drinking and gambling, dismissed the new group as the "Beer and Whiskey Circuit," they also quickly realized that the new association represented a very real competitor, and no team was more successful than the Browns.[18]

Over the next few years baseball underwent a renaissance in St. Louis. Fueled by Von der Ahe's funds and Spink's public relations know-how and baseball acumen, the team thrived. While officially the Association secretary, Spink performed a number of roles with the Browns, including serving as both the secretary and press agent for the new franchise. He is generally credited with helping assemble the team that won four straight American Association pennants beginning in 1885.[19] While his fingerprints may have been all over the roster, Spink was only there to see the first pennant; he left the club after the 1885 season, determined to start a weekly newspaper that would report exclusively on sports. Even there, his support for the local teams never flagged. Indeed, he later came to personally loathe Von der Ahe, a sentiment stemming in part from his disappointment over the fact that, having done so much to boost the fortunes of both the city itself and its baseball community, Von

der Ahe had in Spink's opinion squandered the accumulated good will, and let the city down.[20]

Why exactly Spink decided to found *The Sporting News* remains unclear. Some have pointed to a conversation he had with fellow St. Louis reporter (and later publishing powerhouse) Joseph Pulitzer, who reportedly told Spink, "Given a good business manager and an editor who can really write, any newspaper should fast become a good paying institution."[21] But whatever the reason, in typical fashion, Spink turned his considerable energies to creating a paper that would soon be recognized as a leader in the field.

The first edition of *The Sporting News*, an eight-page offering, was available to the public on St. Patrick's Day, March 17, 1886, at a price of 5 cents, with those who were optimistic about its survival able to secure a yearlong subscription for $2.[22] At the time, the nation boasted just one other sports-only offering, *Sporting Life*, based in Philadelphia. While recognizing the competition, the publicist in Spink did not wait long before boasting that *The Sporting News* had the highest circulation of any sports-only paper west of the City of Brotherly Love.[23] Despite its reputation as a sports-only publication, in the early going the paper in fact reflected both Spink's varied interests and his desire to broaden the paper's circulation, seeking in particular to appeal to what sport historian John R. Betts termed the "'barroom fraternity,' gentlemen of leisure interested in politics, theatre, and sports."[24] While baseball coverage was the centerpiece, columns entitled "The Wheel," "The Gun," "The Stage," "The Ring," and "The Turf" provided readers with news about an array of other activities, including rowing, horse racing, hunting and fishing, bicycle racing, boxing, theater, and even billiards.[25] In fact, while baseball was the original focus, it was only after his younger brother Charles had assumed full control of the paper that it focused exclusively on baseball.[26]

The Sporting News was an immediate success, but the multiplicity of tasks involved in running the paper soon taxed even Al Spink's considerable energies. Consequently, recognizing both his own weakness and the wisdom of Pulitzer's advice, he persuaded his younger brother Charles to give up the homesteading venture he had been pursuing in South Dakota to join him in St. Louis and assume the position of business manager at the princely sum of $50 a week.[27] It was, at least initially, a perfect pairing. The passion for the game that his younger brother lacked was more than made up for by a business acumen that was manifested in countless ways, and quickly helped turn the paper into a baseball centerpiece. Between securing advertising and expanding circulation by distributing each edition to all parts of the country – and sending the unsold copies to news dealers as samples – he raised the profile of the paper, and helped further expand awareness of the game it served. To further aid in that effort, Charles persuaded a number of minor leagues to name *The Sporting News* their "official organ," a designation that helped secure the young paper's place in the baseball establishment.[28]

Al, meanwhile, continued to handle the editorial side, making the paper must reading for an increasingly sports-hungry public. But things changed in 1890 when *The Sporting News*, after first breaking the story about the player revolt, then came out in support of the Players' League, a single-season effort intended to help the players wrest control of the professional game from the owners.[29] When the ill-fated plan went awry and the league collapsed, *The Sporting News*, its relations with the baseball establishment consequently strained, suffered as well. His interest in the paper waning, Al turned control of the paper over to Charles, leaving it to him to stop the publication's slide.[30]

Al then turned his energies to one of his other passions, theater. He was determined to write and produce a play that he intended to bring to a national audience. The venture represented a drastic change of focus, but he poured both his energies and his assets into the theatrical production, and in 1891 began work on what would become a three-act play, *The Derby Winner*.

A romantic comedy, the show was a tale of a cash-poor character named Milt West who was determined to race his mare, Missouri Girl, in the St. Louis Derby, all in an effort to make enough money to pay for his approaching wedding. However, when his fiancée, Alice, gets wind of his "relationship" with the Missouri girl, things take a turn for the worst, and the effort to undo the damage only exacerbates things. In the end, Missouri Girl wins the race, giving Milt the funds he needs for the wedding, and he is finally able to convince Alice that she is his one and only love. But the path to happiness is one fraught with drama. So too was the production. For while the story was comparatively straightforward, if not trite, the showmanship and the staging of a spectacular that included a cast of 42 humans, as well as a number of horses (animals who "ran" the derby on a treadmill onstage), made for a singular and extravagant viewing experience, as well as a costly production. And of course, such a venture was not without its risks; the horses, in particular, were often a problem.[31] The play itself debuted on August 25, 1894, at the St. Louis Grand Opera House. Befitting Spink's earlier career in journalism and public relations, the premiere was accompanied by no small amount of fanfare.[32]

After an enthusiastic response in St. Louis, Spink decided to take the show on the road, subsequently playing in Baltimore, Chicago, Cincinnati, Kansas City, Lawrence (Kansas), Louisville, Nashville, Washington, and Wheeling, while also doing repeat shows in St. Louis.[33] In March of 1896, Spink sold the rights to *The Derby Winner* to a St. Louis sportswriter and one-time secretary, business manager and part-owner of the St. Louis Browns, George Munson, who had left baseball to manage the show during its travels.[34] Despite

Press Power: Sid Mercer of the *New York Journal*, Al Spink of *The Sporting News*, and G.W. Axelson of the *Chicago Herald*. (Photograph by Charles Martin Conlon of the *Chicago Herald*)

numerous good reviews, as well as advertisements for the show that claimed that *The Derby Winner* was the "most successful racing and comedy drama ever staged with a race track as its theme" (which it may have been), it was subsequently revealed that in fact Spink lost almost a quarter of a million dollars over the course of the effort.[35] It proved to be a devastating financial disaster for Spink: Not only was he forced to return to the newspaper world, but he also had to sell the shares of *The Sporting News* that he had put up for collateral for the show, thus ceding control of his creation to his brother.[36]

Indeed, in the aftermath of the financial setback that *The Derby Winner* represented, Spink sought comfort and refuge in a return to the newspaper world, and specifically *The Sporting News*. However, between the altered business relationship with his brother and his dismay at the continuing struggles the paper was experiencing in the aftermath of its misguided

support of the Players' League, the situation soon proved untenable. Al derisively termed the paper "The Sporting Death," and while he put in a short stint helping his brother revive the venture and reverse the decline in revenue and advertising, the experience marked the beginning of a deep family rift.[37] It got so bad that Al sued his brother in early 1913, claiming that he was owed considerable funds based on an agreement signed in 1895 to divide the profits earned in the succeeding 15 years.[38] The suit never went to trial, but it only exacerbated the already gaping filial breach, one that would only be repaired in April 1914 when Charles was on his deathbed.

The brothers, who together had built and developed a journalistic institution that had done much both for the game and for St. Louis's reputation as the country's leading baseball city, were able to reconcile in a tearful deathbed reunion. And whatever the nature of his grievance, all seemed to have been forgotten when Al accompanied the report of Charles's death in the next edition of *The Sporting News* with a piece headlined "An Elder Brother's Tribute" that lauded Charles's skillful efforts and business acumen.[39] In that same familial vein, when Charles's son John George Taylor Spink, who went by J.G. Taylor Spink, succeeded his father as publisher, Al offered strong support. Indeed, in 1925 when Taylor wrote Al seeking his thoughts on the state of the paper, Al's comments said much about how he viewed his long-ago creation. He opened the three-page letter declaring, "I feared that the one paper I was so proud of would fall from the fine level he (Charles) had established for it," before offering a detailed mix of analysis, constructive criticism, and praise for the paper, as well as for the efforts of his nephew.[40] Indeed, the aging Al closed with some fatherly advice: "Take sunshine to your office each day and bring it home with you at night. Make those who work for you love and respect you and bring your children up in the same way. Do those things, dear boy, and many happy days are in store for you." He signed the letter, "Dad."[41]

In fact, that response was reflective of an important aspect of his life. Alfred H. Spink was also a family man. He was married twice, his first wife dying only two years after they were married.[42] He also had four children, three sons and a daughter. One of those children, William, was at the center of an incident that once left Spink on the brink of death. While at work at his office on New Year's Eve 1907, Spink, at the time the president of the *St. Louis World* Publishing Company and editor of the *St. Louis World* newspaper, the publication he had started just a few years before, heard a quarrel outside his office. He emerged to find his son engaged in a scuffle with one Victor D. Grow, a printer and sometime employee of the paper, who had apparently come to the *World's* office to pick up a check for some back wages. Spink later said that when he entered the room, Grow was standing in front of William, aiming a revolver at the younger man. Spink then rushed forward intending to disarm Grow, but Grow quickly changed direction and, with the men separated by about four feet, Grow fired twice, hitting the 53-year-old in the side. The bullet entered, according to one report, at the ninth rib and apparently lodged in the abdominal cavity. While Grow surrendered quickly to police, Spink was rushed to the hospital. The bullet could not be found initially, and doctors were pessimistic about his prospects, but after a full day's hospitalization they began to predict a full recovery. After a few weeks in the hospital, Spink was released, whereupon he took a trip west to regain his health.[43] Later that year, with final preparations for Grow's trial underway, Spink urged prosecutors to drop the charges. Saying he believed that Grow "was not in his right mind when he fired the shot," Spink asked for mercy, a request prosecutors were initially reluctant to grant, but ultimately did, ending the dramatic chapter in the editor's life.[44]

In 1910 Al Spink published the book *The National Game*, an effort that, paired with his earlier founding of *The Sporting News*, cemented his status as a central contributor to the literary and historical record of baseball. The book included biographical profiles and a trove of statistical information, as well as illustrations, all of which combined to provide readers with a comprehensive picture of the many people whose efforts on and off the field had shaped the game's early history. It also revealed Spink's deep commitment to the game, as well as his vision for the sport that he had helped shepherd to a place at the forefront of the American sports consciousness. Indeed, his view of the game was evident in his dedication, in which he shined a spotlight on the people who, for Spink, made baseball special, writing, "I dedicate this book to the professional base ball players of America, to the silent army, to the force that is on the field to-day and to the legions that are to follow in years to come."[45] He added, "I want this book to live forever, so that the names of those who helped to build up and make base ball the greatest of outdoor sports may never be forgotten."[46]

The comprehensive volume, a work that foreshadowed the cottage industry that is the baseball-book business, was well received upon publication. The *New York Times* observed that it had "great autobiographical value" as well as "many pages of valuable statistics, which greatly enhance its value." Praising its "vast amount of research work," it called the book the "most complete book of reference that has ever been written on the game of baseball." The *Times* also noted that the book had been given the official endorsement of the American League at its annual meeting.[47] The *St. Louis Globe-Democrat* also praised the effort, asserting that it was "nothing more nor less than a history of baseball, containing a story of most of the happenings of the game since it was first played up to the present time." Terming it "the only standard work of the kind ever published," it observed that it "promise[d] to become a permanent fixture in every well-regulated library."[48]

Upon its rerelease as part of the Southern Illinois University Press's Writing Baseball series, the book was hailed as "the first important history of baseball, predating Albert G. Spalding's better-known *America's National Game* by a year. As noble as Spink's goal of having the book live forever may have been, the book was in fact out of print from 1911 until its rerelease in 2000. Upon that rerelease, Writing Baseball series editor Richard Peterson noted that in contrast to the competing volume published by Spalding in 1911, a work that told "the story of the moral triumph of the courageous and honest magnate over greedy and crooked players," Spink's effort "celebrates the accomplishments of the 'great players who helped bring the game into the prominence it now enjoys.'"[49]

In December 1914 the *St. Louis Globe-Democrat* reported that Spink had taken a job with a San Francisco paper, leaving behind the place he had called home for almost five decades.[50] But while he may have been officially tied to San Francisco, in fact in the years after his brother's death he appears to have thrived as a freelancer, a prolific and broadly based writer on the full array of sports that had captivated him throughout his long, if occasionally interrupted, journalism career. Indeed, his byline appeared in papers from coast to coast, and north and south, on subjects ranging from reflections on baseball to reports on the current state of boxing. He reported and offered commentary, both of the moment and with a historical perspective that was both learned and personal. And even if much of the country was unaware of his Canadian roots (one article that noted his longtime relationship with Charles Comiskey stated that Spink had been born in Chicago, but had moved to St. Louis as his journalism career was getting under way),[51] he did not forget his native Canada; his articles were just as likely to appear in the *Winnipeg Tribune*

or the *Saskatoon Daily Star* as they were in the *Buffalo Times*.[52] A favorite was the *Reno Gazette-Journal*, which not only included his regular reports on boxing but also featured his column, "The Sportsman's Corner."[53] He had a similar forum in the *Pittsburgh Post-Gazette*, which hosted "Al Spink's Column."[54] As well, the *Salt Lake Tribune*, the *Birmingham* (Alabama) *News* – where he was listed as one of their "news sports experts" – and the *Mount Carmel* (Pennsylvania) *Item* were among those publications that regularly featured Spink's work.[55] From a nostalgic look back to 1919 and the first time the White Sox and the Reds had battled for a championship, to a hard-line discussion of what should happen to the Black Sox who emerged from that World Series, to a more whimsical look at heavyweight champion Jack Dempsey's short-lived theatrical career, the stories flowed.[56] To the delight of readers everywhere, Spink offered a wide range of articles that reflected his writing and reporting skills and his insatiable curiosity, not to mention the wealth of knowledge and perspective he had gained over the course of over five decades in the newspaper business. In addition, in 1921, he published a three-volume series entitled *Spink Sport Stories: 1000 Big and Little Ones*, a collection that included a wide range of stories from Al's decades in the sports world.[57]

Meanwhile, Spink's reverence for the game and its history led to his helping found an organization in Chicago, the Old Timers' Baseball Association, for which he served as secretary. Begun in 1919, it sought to "revive the baseball spirit of the day gone by and especially to celebrate the fiftieth anniversary of the organization of the Chicago White Stockings as a professional team."[58] The group was a fitting reflection of Spink's love of the game as well as the esteem in which he held the game's pioneers, a feeling he had made clear in his book, *The National Game*. After his death in May of 1928, Association members were well represented among the attendees at his funeral.[59]

Spink's wife, Bertha, died on November 5, 1926, and the reports of her death indicated that the aging baseball writer was himself ill and at home.[60] Consequently, Spink's death on May 27, 1928, in Oak Park, Illinois, outside Chicago, was not a total surprise, but it was nevertheless one widely recognized by the baseball world.[61] Indeed, befitting his stature in the baseball community, the eulogy at his funeral was delivered by no less a luminary than Commissioner Kenesaw Mountain Landis.[62]

With *The National Game* and *The Sporting News*, not to mention his extensive and wide-ranging journalistic efforts, Spink left behind a written legacy he could be proud of. In an interesting twist of fate, however, very soon after his death, his words made news in another area, when it was revealed that he had left behind a potentially explosive affidavit. In the document, which had been embargoed and authorized for release only after his death, Spink shared information arguably exonerating radical labor leader Tom Mooney from the Preparedness Day parade bombing of 1916, for which Mooney was then serving an extended prison sentence in San Quentin Penitentiary.[63] While the Federation of Labor voted to use the new evidence to seek Mooney's release, their hopes were ultimately dashed, and it was not until January of 1939 that Mooney was released and pardoned by California Governor Culbert Olson. The pardon brought an end to a case that had been a high-profile cause célèbre for some of the nation's most prominent liberal and radical forces, who had asserted that Mooney had been framed.[64]

Over the course of a full life, Alfred H. Spink was a journalist, an entrepreneur, a publicist, a businessman, and a sportsman, one whose involvement in baseball represented a way to manifest all those traits while also reflecting a view of the game that would only be fully realized decades later. While a quixotic and sometimes mercurial individual, Al Spink nevertheless left an indelible impact on the game of baseball. No one can deny the importance of *The Sporting News* to the growth of the national pastime, not to mention its role as the chronicler of a game whose history is captured in the words and numbers that the paper so faithfully shared with its readers over the years. Similarly, his book *The National Game* represents one of the earliest efforts at illuminating the game's history, serving as both an example and an inspiration for generations to come. In all of these efforts, Spink showed himself to be a visionary, although one with a short attention span who laid out his vision before leaving it to others to implement. The many shifts and short term "careers" he enjoyed reflected this multifaceted approach to life. Indeed, while *The Sporting News*, *The National Game*, and his years as a sportswriter tend to dominate perceptions of Spink's relationship with and influence on the game, his years with the St. Louis Browns before he left to found *The Sporting News* are no less noteworthy, while also providing context for his journalism and writing efforts. In the end, over the course of a lifetime in and around the game, Alfred H. Spink impacted in no small way both how the sport developed and the way in which it was perceived and embraced by the American people. No small legacy for a Canadian-born immigrant who traded in his cricket bat for a baseball one when he was not yet in his teens.

NOTES

1   Steven P. Gietschier, "Leading Off: The First Years of the Sporting News Archives," *Provenance, Journal of the Society of Georgia Archivists*, Volume 7, No. 1, January 1989: 42.

2   Mark Cooper, "Alfred Henry Spink," in Frederick Ivor-Campbell, Robert L. Tiemann, and Mark Rucker, eds., *Baseball's First Stars* (Cleveland: Society for American Baseball Research, 1996), 156; "Alfred Henry 'Al' Spink, Sr." Find a Grave; https://www.findagrave.com/memorial/83037142/alfred-henry-spink. Spink's baptismal certificate gives the 1852 date.

3   Steven P. Gietschier, Foreword, in Alfred H. Spink, *The National Game*, Second Edition (Carbondale and Edwardsville: Southern Illinois University Press, 2000), lxiii.

4   An interesting family tie is that between the Spinks and longtime baseball historian Ernest J. "Ernie" Lanigan. One of Al Spink's sisters, Frances Elizabeth, married George Thomas Lanigan. Their son Ernest was born in 1873 in Chicago.

5   The 1866 Quebec city directory lists William as a member of the legislative assembly, although his official title was clerk of routine and records.

6   Steven P. Gietschier, Foreword, lxiii.

7   Mark Cooper, "Alfred Henry Spink."

8   Gietschier, Foreword, lxiii.

9   Gietschier, Foreword, lxiii.

10 Gietschier, Foreword, lxiii.

11 Gietschier, Foreword, lxiii.

12 Gietschier, Foreword, lxiii.

13 "Ghastly Grenada," *Minneapolis Star Tribune,* September 5, 1878.

14 "Latest News: The Yellow Fever Still Rages with Unabated Fatality," *Nebraska State Journal* (Lincoln), September 3, 1878.

15 Chris Von der Ahe (1851–1913), *Missouri Encyclopedia*; https://missouriencyclopedia.org/people/von-der-ahe-chris.

16 J. Thomas Hetrick, *Chris Von der Ahe and the St. Louis Browns* (Clifton, Virginia: Pocol Press, 1999), 5.

17 Hetrick, 5-8.

18 Hetrick, 9.

19 Gietschier, Foreword, lxiv.

20 Hetrick, 287.

21 Lowell Reidenbaugh, "Introduction," *The Sporting News: The First Hundred Years 1886-1986* (St. Louis: The Sporting News, 1985).

22 Steve Gietschier, "The Sporting News," SABR BioProject, https://sabr.org/bioproj/topic/the-sporting-news/.

23 Lowell Reidenbaugh, "A Lucky Day Back in 1886," *The Sporting News: The First Hundred Years 1886-1986,* 14.

24 Steven P. Gietschier, "Leading Off: The First Years of the Sporting News Archives."

25 Lowell Reidenbaugh, *The Sporting News The First Hundred Years 1886-1986,* 15.

26 "A History of The Sporting News[,] the Oldest Sports Publication in the U.S.," collectinggoldmagazines.com; https://collectinggoldmagazines.com/magazines/sporting-news/.

27 Gietschier, Foreword, lxiv.

28 Gietschier, Foreword, lxiv.

29 "A History of The Sporting News."

30 Gietschier, Foreword, lxiv.

31 "Alfred Spink's 'The Derby Winner,'" Ahead by Three, https://aheadbythree.wordpress.com/2016/11/20/alfred-spinks-the-derby-winner/. Accessed July 7, 2021.

32 "Alfred Spink's 'The Derby Winner.'"

33 "Alfred Spink's 'The Derby Winner.'"

34 "Alfred Spink's 'The Derby Winner.'"

35 "Alfred Spink's 'The Derby Winner.'"

36 Gietschier, Foreword, lxiv.

37 Cooper, 156.

38 "Al H. Spink Sues His Brother for an Accounting," *St. Louis Globe-Democrat*, January 14, 1913.

39 Lowell Reidenbaugh, Introduction, *The Sporting News The First Hundred Years 1886-1986* (St. Louis: The Sporting News, 1985).

40 Reidenbaugh, Introduction.

41 Reidenbaugh, Introduction.

42 "Alfred Henry 'Al' Spink Sr." Find a Grave.

43 "Printer Saved from Going to Jail by the Editor Whom He Shot," *Buffalo Times*, November 15, 1908.

44 "Spink's Plea Saves Printer Who Shot Him," *St. Louis Post-Dispatch*, November 9, 1908.

45 Alfred H. Spink, Dedication, *The National Game*, Second Edition.

46 Alfred H. Spink, Dedication.

47 "'The National Game' by A.H. Spink," *New York Times*, December 19, 1910.

48 "Al Spink Publishes History of Baseball," *St. Louis Globe-Democrat*, October 13, 1910.

49   "Rare Baseball History Back in Print for First Time Since 1911," press release, Southern Illinois University Press, April 3, 2000.

50   "Al Spink Accepts Position on Paper in San Francisco," *St. Louis Globe-Democrat*, December 2, 1914.

51   G.W. Axelson, "'Commy' the Grand Old Roman," *Salt Lake Tribune*, October 26, 1919.

52   Al Spink, "John McGraw Not Likely to Realize His Baseball Dream," *Winnipeg Tribune*, December 16, 1919; Al Spink, "More Stories of the 'Lucky Dutchman,'" *Buffalo Times*, July 13, 1918.

53   Al Spink, "Lavigne's Career in Ring Recalled," *Reno Gazette-Journal*, January 28, 1924; "The Sportsman's Corner Conducted by Al Spink," *Reno Gazette-Journal*, January 19, 1919.

54   "Al Spink's Column," *Pittsburgh Post-Gazette*, December 21, 1922.

55   Al Spink, "Perils and Thrills Attended Travel of Old-Time Ball Clubs," *Salt Lake Tribune*, January 2, 1920; "News Sports Experts," *Birmingham News*, August 14, 1920; Al Spink, "Sacrifice Hitting Help to the Giants," *Mount Carmel* (Pennsylvania) *Item*, July 17, 1919.

56   Al Spink, "Romance Is Added to Coming Meeting of the White Sox and Cinci," *Saskatoon Daily Star*, September 13, 1919; Al Spink, "Al Spink Says Guilty Should Be Blacklisted," *Birmingham News*, January 21, 1921; "Theatrical Life Palls on Jack Dempsey," *Mount Carmel Item*, October 6, 1919.

57   Gietschier, Foreword, lxiv-lxv.

58   "Baseball Fans of '69 Make Plans for 'Golden' Dinner," *Chicago Tribune*, October 26, 1919.

59   "Old Time Players," *Cincinnati Enquirer*, May 30, 1928.

60   "Mrs. Al Spink, Wife of Sports Writer, Dies," *Los Angeles Times*, November 6, 1926.

61   Mark Cooper, "Alfred Henry Spink," 156.

62   Gietschier, Foreword, lxv.

63   "Dead to Mooney's Aid," *Kansas City Star*, June 4, 1928.

64   "Tom Mooney," Spartacus Educational; https://spartacus-educational.com/USAmooney.htm.

THE ST. THOMAS ATLANTICS' 1882 US TOUR

By Larry Gerlach

With the rapid spread in popularity of baseball across North America after the Civil War, St. Thomas, Ontario, was among the many burgeoning communities to use the game as a prominent civic community and promotional enterprise. The seat of Elgin County grew slowly until the arrival of the Canadian Southern and the Great Western railroads in 1872,[1] thereafter becoming a major railroad hub, its location near the northern edge of Lake Erie halfway between Detroit and Buffalo providing inexpensive, fast linkage with major Northern American cities.[2] Upon being designated a city in 1881 with a population of 10,000, St. Thomas and its business and civic boosters sought to enhance its reputation by fielding a competitive team in the intercity barnstorming world of Ontario baseball.

Since its first organized team in 1868, St. Thomas had fielded nines made up of local players, but in 1881 hired William "Bill" Watkins, player-manager of the 1880 Canadian champion Guelph Maple Leafs, to import players for a team pretentiously named the Atlantics after the Brooklyn Atlantics, the dominant US team of the 1860s.[3] The strategy paid off immediately, St. Thomas in August 1881 defeating Guelph to win the Ontario championship, the equivalent of being the champions of Canada.[4]

In March 1882 the club's board of directors, headed by President Elijah Moore, a founder of the St. Thomas Street Railway, allocated $100 for formal playing grounds behind the Horton market, conveniently located a half-block north of Talbot, the town's main thoroughfare.[5] But then, heady with grandiose visions, they decided instead to build a playing facility worthy of a championship team near the Great Western "Air Line" railroad station at a cost, including fencing and a grandstand, "in the neighborhood of $700." To fund construction and cover team expenses, the club innovatively reorganized as a joint stock company, issuing $1,000 worth of shares, 30 percent coming from team members.[6] The directors also deviated from tradition by outfitting the team in gray Halifax tweed uniforms accented by red stockings and belts, instead of traditional flannel jerseys and woolen pants.[7] Meanwhile, player-manager Watkins wasted no time recruiting "a first class nine," signing by early April seven players, including Bob Emslie, former star of the Harriston Brown Stockings, as the team's pitcher.[8]

After a couple of games against the London Tecumsehs, a 2-2 tie and a 5-4 loss in 10 innings, the Atlantics tested their mettle against major-league competition on May 24 against the National League's Detroit team. Agreeing at the last minute to replace the Cleveland Blues, and having arrived late in Detroit that morning from Chicago, the Wolverines took a special train to St. Thomas, dressed for the game en route, and raced to the ballpark. Despite their harried rush, they disappointed the more than 1,600 who flocked to the ballpark by thoroughly outclassing the home team, 6-1. Emslie gave up only six hits, but George Derby flummoxed Atlantic batters, allowing only one hit and striking out 13.[9]

Struggling with only modest success, winning three games but dropping two more games to London, 20-3 and 13-3, the Atlantics regrouped, added players, and went on a winning streak.[10] Returning to the diamond in late June, they won three straight, besting London 4-3, Hamilton 13-3, and Guelph 7-4. Following a 7-6 loss to the Tecumsehs on July 4,[11] the Atlantics went on the road for six games in six consecutive days from July 9 to 14, outscoring opponents 84-42 in defeating the Guelph Maple Leafs 9-8, the Bowmanville Royal Oaks 19-0, the Cobourg Mutuals 14-9, the Port Hope Dauntless 19-9, the Maple Leafs again 21-14, and concluding with a 2-2 tie against the Hamilton Standards.[12] Back home, they beat London 18-9 on July 15, then coasted to two victories over Hamilton on July 20 and 21, 10-1 and 14-7.[13]

Riding high, the Atlantics now faced a scheduling, and therefore financial, problem. The semiprofessional independent team depended on raising money by barnstorming, traveling from town to town to play games for a share of gate receipts; they now had difficulty scheduling games, London and Hamilton being the only towns having the wherewithal to field competitive teams. So Watkins decided to seek more and better competition south of the border in New York, where there were many semipro and professional teams eager for games.

Early on Sunday morning, July 23, the Atlantics boarded a train for games against Rochester, Syracuse, and Auburn. The tour began auspiciously on July 24. With no advance promotion, only a "small audience" was on hand to see the Atlantics, described as "a champion professional team," give a 15-4 shellacking to the Rochesters, whose pitchers "failed to arrive."[14] Their success was short-lived, as they dropped three straight games, to Rochester the next day 8-7 in 10 innings, then Syracuse 6-2 and Auburn 4-3.[15]

Having reached the end of scheduled tour, and exhausted from playing four games in a row, the Atlantics were ready to go home. Emslie, as did his teammates, expected that the trip would last about a week, and accordingly had his uniform hastily "done up in newspapers" instead of luggage, and had packed only "one shirt and one pair of socks."[16] But Watkins, hoping for a lucrative grand tour, had sent inquiries to other American clubs. The result was a grueling barnstorming tour of 36 days over five weeks, featuring 26 games in New York, New Jersey, and Pennsylvania.

Personal connections had made arranging games in Ontario easy, but scheduling contests on the road was more complicated. As the trip progressed, Watkins, given suggestions and contact information from each host club, telegraphed ahead, hoping to find teams whose schedules could accommodate a game or two for a share of gate receipts sufficient to cover travel, accommodation, and per diem expenses, plus enough to pay each player.

Rejuvenated and excited about playing American teams, the Atlantics ran off a string of eight straight victories in upstate New York: Auburn 15-3 and 14-5, Oswego 17-0 and 14-3, Syracuse 3-2 and 11-7, and Binghamton 2-0 and 10-2.[17] Emboldened by success on the diamond, they then headed to New York City for a date with the Metropolitans, namesake of the current National League club, en route playing two games in Newark, New Jersey, winning 5-2 and losing 9-8.[18]

It is easy to imagine what went on in the minds of the small-town lads as they gaped at the awe-inspiring urban scene as they ferried across the maritime-clogged Hudson River to Manhattan on Wednesday, August 9, then wended their way uptown through the teeming streets of the largest metropolis in North America, population just over a million, by far the largest city anyone on the team had ever seen.[19] (The population of Toronto in 1880 was 86,000.) Jaws dropped even further when they entered the Polo Grounds, located at 110th Street and Fifth Avenue, across from the northwest corner of Frederick Law Olmsted's vast Central Park. An expansive elliptical field originally built to accommodate the sport of polo, it had been reconfigured for baseball in 1880 as the home grounds of the Metropolitans.

Managed by Jim Mutrie, the Metropolitans, eventual champions of the League Alliance, were a top-flight independent professional squad, major league in all but name.[20] (In 1883 the Mets would join the major-league American Association, finishing fourth in the eight-team league.) The Atlantics knew they faced a formidable challenge in taking on a team whose roster included two native-born Canadians, both future major leaguers, John "Jack" Doyle from Halifax, Nova Scotia, and James "Tip" O'Neill from Springfield, Ontario.[21] Although blanked 5-0, the Atlantics acquitted themselves well. Their batting was "very weak," as they produced only two hits (O'Neill hitless), but they were complimented on having "a good battery" and received "well deserved" applause for "sharp fielding" and making "quite an interesting fight of it."[22]

Both teams regarded the rematch on August 10 as an exhibition game. The Mets, in order to rest their regular pitchers and catcher for the next day's League game against Cleveland, used a battery from the amateur Olympic Club of Manhattan; the Atlantics responded in kind, moving Emslie to center field, with Frank Beck pitching.[23] The Canadians got off to a good start,

scoring three runs in the top of the first, only to have the Mets plate eight in the bottom of the inning. Emslie then returned to pitch, holding the Mets to four runs the rest of the game, not giving up more than one hit in an inning. The Atlantics, with six extra-base hits including two home runs, outhit the Mets 15 to 10, but came out losers, 15-5.[24] Despite suffering two defeats, they left New York satisfied with having given a top-flight professional ballclub a good tussle.

On the way to Philadelphia to take on another top Alliance club, the Atlantics stopped in Camden for a two-game set with the Merritt of the Interstate Association, New Jersey's best professional squad. The arrival of the Canadians created great enthusiasm, the games being reported on the front page of both the *Camden Post* and the *Camden Courier*. For the game on Friday, August 11, advertised as "Jersey vs. Canada," some 1,000 fans showed up at City Hall Park to see the home team's 5-2 victory over the "Canucks," the first time that term had been applied to the Atlantics. While Beck pitched a good game, giving up six hits while striking out six, the Atlantics again had trouble with professional pitchers, collecting only two hits themselves. The local papers praised the visitors, "a fine-looking set of men," for "playing excellently in the field, making some beautiful stops and catches," albeit "throwing rather wildly," thinking "no club has created a better impression on the Merritt's ground than they."[25] The following day, the Atlantics reversed the result, defeating the Merritt 6-4, the offense finally erupting for nine hits, including a home run over the right-field fence by London native Tony Friend. They were praised as "a very gentlemanly set of men" who, in the "one or two instances decisions were against them smiled pleasantly." Emslie pitched "very effectively," giving up but four hits and striking out 10, his sharp breaking curveball so impressing the Merritt management that after the game they signed him to his first professional contract, to commence after the Atlantics tour.[26]

After six straight games, the Atlantics rested on Sunday, August 13, leisurely crossing the Delaware River into Philadelphia, then catching a train heading northwest 60 miles to Reading, the shipping center for anthracite coal, there to play two games with another Interstate Association team, the Active. The local newspaper noted the novel appearance of a Canadian club with sizable advertisements and front-page reports of both games. On August 14, the Atlantics beat the Actives 8-5; the next day about 1,500 saw the hometown team, behind their first-string pitcher, who yielded but five hits, return the favor, downing the visitors 6-0.[27]

The Atlantics returned to Philadelphia, a bustling seaport of 850,000 on the Delaware River. That America's second largest city was also its most historic – the home of Benjamin Franklin, the site of Independence Hall, where the Declaration of Independence was adopted in 1776 and the Federal Constitution drafted in 1787, and the capital of the nation between 1790 and 1800 – may or may not have been of interest to the Canadian visitors, but the appearance of the first "foreign" team was much anticipated. The newspapers had printed accounts (with box score) of the earlier Atlantics games with Camden and Reading, noting that the Canadians' "pitcher, catcher and third baseman are spoken of as more than ordinarily expert."[28] The Atlantics' opponent was not the major-league Philadelphia Athletics of the American Association managed by George "Jumbo" Latham, late of the London Tecumsehs, but rather the Philadelphia Phillies of the League Alliance, the games likely having been arranged while the Atlantics were in New York playing the Mets. (Major-league quality like the Mets, the Phillies would join the National League in 1883 as the Quakers.)

Philadelphia in Greek means "City of Brotherly Love," but the locals proved ungracious hosts at Recreation Park on August 16, handing their guests a 7-4 beating. Emslie walked five but allowed only four hits, the Inquirer reporting that the "heavy batsmen of the home nine were completely outwitted" by his "very peculiar and puzzling delivery," Philadelphia probably not scoring a run were it not for eight Atlantic fielding errors. Assessing the talent level of "the championship baseball nine of Canada," the local papers thought the "fine, muscular set of young men" had given "evidence of careful training, but [that they] lack the experience necessary to cope successfully against such a nine as their opponents." In particular, Atlantics batters, striking out 11 times, "showed themselves to lack experience against curve pitching." Observing that the tour of the United States had been made "by management with the hope of reviving interest in base ball in Canada and also to induce American clubs to cross the border," the assessment concluded: "If the Canadians stay in this country any length of time they will undoubtedly show a great improvement in their batting and fielding"; and that "all they need to cope successfully with their American cousins is more experience against curve pitches and better coaching."[29]

The next day, Philadelphia scored twice in the second inning to post a 2-0 victory. Emslie continued to baffle Philadelphia batters with his "puzzling curves," again yielding only four hits, and received better fielding support, the Atlantics countering five errors with three double plays, and Billy Hunter in right field making "two marvelous fly-catches, taking both on a full run and jump." The Canadians could muster just three hits, but thanks to three errors filled the bases in the ninth, then failed to score when Stapleton[30] struck out to end the inning and the game.[31]

Unhappy about dropping two in Philadelphia, but buoyed by better performance in the second game, the Atlantics headed across New Jersey to Atlantic City, a popular ocean beach resort town.[32] It was not a pleasant stay. On August 18 and 19, they lost two games, 8-1 and 2-1, games pitched respectively by Beck and Emslie, against

Ferguson "Fergy" Malone's Atlantic City nine, self-proclaimed champions of the Garden State.[33]

Undoubtedly tired after playing six days in a row, dispirited by five consecutive defeats, and weary of a trip that had extended far beyond initial expectations, the Atlantics finally headed for home. On the way they stopped again in Reading, dropping the rubber game of the series 18-3, and Syracuse, losing 9-5 to the Stars, another League Alliance team, finally arriving back in St. Thomas on Sunday, August 27.[34] It had been a remarkable journey, the players benefiting from the cultural experience, developing camaraderie with teammates, and honing their baseball skills competing against more experienced American teams.

There were only a few days' rest for the weary. On August 29 the Atlantics hosted Port Huron, Michigan, five of whose players, including pitcher Bill Mountjoy, were members of the recently disbanded London Tecumsehs. The Atlantics committed 10 errors, Hunter at first and Watkins at third responsible for three apiece. Emslie yielded but one run through six innings, but in the bottom of the sixth "severely" sprained an ankle while running the bases. Although "practically disabled," he returned to the box for the seventh, whereupon the Hurons scored six runs, and added two more in the eighth to win 9-3. The next day the teams played in London, the Atlantics defeating Port Huron 20-7.[35] And finally, on September 2 they defeated Hamilton 8-6.[36]

Producing "a heap of fame but a paucity of cash,"[37] the glorious tour of 1882 had an inglorious ending, the team disbanding after the Port Huron series. Jim Tray jumped to Port Huron, as did Bill Watkins, who in 1879 had moved to Port Huron; in 1883 he would lead his hometown club to the Michigan State League championship.[38] Charles "Chub" Collins, Jay Faatz, and Billy Hunter also left to play minor-league ball in the United States, each eventually reaching the majors. Emslie, too, departed on September 4 for more baseball with the Camden Merritt. If his recollection of the trip late in life was mistaken in several respects, he was correct in that it was "a lucky trip for me," as it serendipitously led to his first professional contract and eventual appearance in the major leagues.[39]

With the disbanding of the Atlantics, baseball left St. Thomas, not returning in professional form until the 1896 Saints of the Canadian League. Whatever the case, the 1882 St. Thomas Atlantics warrant a prominent place in Canadian – and baseball – history. Cobbled together piecemeal on the road, their peregrination of 26 games in 35 days in three states was by far the most extensive in terms of time and games ever undertaken by a Canadian team, and among the longest taken by North American clubs.[40] Although road and game weariness, combined with higher caliber competition, resulted in their losing 11 of the final 13 games, including the last seven in a row, the Atlantics did win 12 games against far more experienced and skilled opponents, including two major-league-caliber teams. In the process "the champion club of Canada" brought inestimable pride and notoriety to St. Thomas, while introducing Americans to the growing proficiency of baseball north of the border.

NOTES

1   Ron Brown, *The Lake Erie Shore: Ontario's Forgotten South Coast* (Toronto: Dundurn Press, 2009); *St. Thomas: 100 Years a City, 1881-1981* (St. Thomas, Ontario: St. Thomas Centennial Committee, 1981). See also https://www.stthomas.ca/visiting_us/a_brief_history_of_st_thomas.

2   St. Thomas today remains a railroad city, hosting the North American Railway Hall of Fame in the restored Canada Southern Station, as well as the Elgin County Railway Museum: "The Railway History of St. Thomas," https://stthomaspubliclibrary.ca/wp-content/uploads/2018/04/The-Railway-History-of-St-Thomas-Slideshow.pdf.

3   Born in Brantford, Ontario, in 1858, Watkins subsequently became Canada's most successful manager, piloting numerous minor-league clubs and five major-league teams – Indianapolis Hoosiers in 1884, Detroit Wolverines in 1885-1888 (World Series champions in 1887), Kansas City Cowboys in 1888, St. Louis Browns in 1893, and Pittsburgh Pirates in 1898-1899. See Brian Martin, "The Winning Ways of William Watkins," Centre for Canadian Baseball Research, http://baseballresearch.ca/wp-content/uploads/2018/03/Martin17.pdf, and Bill Lamb's essay in this volume.

4   *St. Thomas Times*, August 11, 1881.

5   *Statutes of the Province of Ontario* (Toronto: John Notman, 1878), 216-220. Until electrified in 1898, the streetcars conveyed passengers in horse-drawn cars. Horton market, in its original location, still serves the community as a farmer's market.

6   *St. Thomas Times*, March 28, April 4, and 6, 1882.

7   *St. Thomas Times*, April 25, 1882.

8   The other players then under contract were E. Faatz and H. Faatz of St. Thomas, and Londoners T. Friend, Wm. Hunter, J. Queen (or possibly Quinn), and J. Smith.

9   *Detroit Free Press*, May 25, 1882; *St. Thomas Times*, May 25, 1882.

10 *St. Thomas Times*, June 8, 1882; *New York Clipper*, June 27, 1882.

11 *St. Thomas Times*, June 27, 1882.

12 *St. Thomas Times*, August 29, 1882.

13 *St. Thomas Times*, July 18 and 23, 1882.

14 The trip began with the following Atlantics lineup: Billy Hunter 2B, Bill Watkins 3B, Bob Emslie P, Jim Tray C, Jay Faatz LF, Tony Friend CF, Charles "Chub" Collins 1B, Snider RF, and Quinn SS. Beck and Hunter were the backup pitcher and catcher respectively, with Stapleton utility.

15 *Rochester Democrat and Chronicle*, July 23, 25 to 28, 1882.

16 Robert D. Emslie, "Ramblings of an Umpire," *Baseball Magazine*, November 1908: 18. In his Memoir (p. 1), Emslie said the trip began on May 24 and ended June 30; he was off two months on either end.

17 *St. Thomas Times*, August 1, 3, and 8, 1882.

18 *St. Thomas Times*, August 10, 1882.

19 Edwin G. Burrows and Mike Wallace, *Greater Gotham: A History of New York City to 1898* (New York: Oxford University Press, 1999); Esther Crain, *The Golden Age in New York, 1870-1910* (New York: Black Dog & Leventhal, 2016); John Duffy, *History of Public Health in New York City, 1866-1966* (New York: Russell Sage Foundation, 1974).

20 In 1882 the Metropolitans won the League Alliance title with a 20-12 record, their season total being 101-57-3. For Mutrie, see Peter Mancuso, "Jim Mutrie," at https://sabr.org/bioproj/person/jim-mutrie/. For the League Alliance, see Brock Helander, "The League Alliance," at https://sabr.org/bioproj/topic/the-league-alliance/.

21 Doyle pitched three games for the St. Louis Browns in 1882, while O'Neill in 10 major-league seasons was a record-setting slugger, leading the St. Louis Browns to four pennants and a World Series victory in 1886. See Dennis Thiessen, *Tip O'Neill and the St. Louis Browns of 1887* (Jefferson, North Carolina: McFarland, 2019).

22 *New York Times*, *New York Sun*, and *Brooklyn Daily Eagle*, August 10, 1882.

23 Beck, whose real name was Frank Hengstebeck, later pitched in the major leagues, in the American Association and the Union Association in 1884.

24 *New York Times*, *New York Sun*, and *Brooklyn Daily Eagle*, August 10, 1882.

25 *Camden Post* and *Camden Daily Courier*, August 12, 1882.

26 *Camden Post* and *Camden Daily Courier*, August 14, 1882.

27 *Reading Times*, August 15-16, 1882.

28 *Philadelphia Times*, August 16, 1882.

29 *Philadelphia Inquirer* and *Philadelphia Times*, August 17, 1882.

30 Stapleton is Guelph-born Edward Jones Stapleton.

31 *Philadelphia Inquirer* and *Philadelphia Times*, August 18, 1882.

32 Nelson Johnson, *Boardwalk Empire: The Birth, High Times, and Corruption of Atlantic City* (Medford, New Jersey: Medford Press, 2010).

33 *Philadelphia Times*, August 19-20, 1882, and *St. Thomas Times*, August 22, 1882.

34 *Reading Times*, August 22; *Philadelphia Times* and *Wilmington News Journal*, August 26; *St. Thomas Times*, August 29, 1882.

35 *Port Huron Daily Times*, August 31, 1882.

36 *Detroit Free Press*, September 5, 1882; *New York Clipper*, September 9, 1882.

37 *St. Thomas Times-Journal*, April 26, 1943.

38 *St. Thomas Times*, September 7, 1882; *Sporting Life*, January 13, 1886.

39 Emslie, Memoir, Elgin County Museum and "Ramblings," 18. He erroneously said the team lost only eight games, that New York and Philadelphia were National League teams, and that his last game for the Atlantics was July 1, Dominion Day, against Detroit, a 5-3 loss. He also claimed to have been the team's only pitcher; he was, at the start of the tour, but as the trip progressed, he played at least three games in right field while Beck pitched. His memory was also faulty in identifying sites of games: "We played in Harrisburg, Pottsville, Pottstown, Redding [*sic*], Binghamton, Elizabethtown, Troy, Albany, Poughkeepsie, Wilmington, Chester and other cities." Binghamton and Reading were the only named towns in which the Atlantics played, although they may have passed through or near the other places, with the exception of Wilmington, Delaware. He was probably confused about timing, as with Camden in 1883 he did play in Harrisburg, Pottsville, Reading, and Wilmington. The errors were invariably repeated as in the *New York Times* obituary, April 27, 1943, and in *St. Thomas: 100 Years a City, 1881-1981*, 98-99.

40 The Brooklyn Excelsiors initiated touring in 1860, traveling through upstate New York to play six games in towns from Albany to Buffalo. In 1869 the Cincinnati Red Stockings from mid-September to mid-October hopped the new transcontinental railroad to play 12 games between St. Louis and San Francisco. And in July and August, 1874, Albert Spalding led members of the Boston Red Stockings and Philadelphia Athletics of the National Association on a 15-game tour of England and Ireland. Several American teams subsequently undertook touring, but not as extensively as did the Atlantics.

EARLY BATTERIES FROM
THE GREAT WHITE NORTH

By David Matchett

On September 6, 1993, Denis Boucher pitched his first game for the Montréal Expos in front of 40,000 hometown fans. The lead story was that he was the first player born in Montréal to suit up for the Expos[1] but it was also noted that Boucher and Joe Siddall, born in Windsor, Ontario, formed an all-Canadian battery. The rarity of the latter event was acknowledged but complete information was not available about other Canadian pitcher-catcher combos.[2] The gap in the historical record inspired this search to identify the earliest major-league games that had a Canadian pitcher throw to a Canadian catcher.

WHAT IS A CANADIAN?

According to the Canadian Citizenship Act, a person is Canadian if they were born in Canada, they became a citizen through the naturalization process, or they were born outside Canada and one of their parents was a Canadian citizen at the time of their birth.

Every major leaguer with a Canadian birthplace is included in this analysis even if they emigrated at a young age. Ongoing research can revise biographical information, so Baseball-Reference, a regularly updated online database, was the primary source to confirm places of birth.

Family histories about naturalized citizens or foreign-born players with Canadian parents are harder to find than places of birth. This usually requires anecdotal evidence that doesn't have a centralized and searchable database, so it is acknowledged that the list may be incomplete, and that new Canadian players in these two categories may be found in the future. Players of this sort have been identified but, at the time of this writing, no nineteenth-century foreign-born Canadians have been found to have participated in a Canadian battery.[3]

Another issue is the definition of Canada, which was created by the British North America Act on July 1, 1867, with additional territory added through 1947. This creates a concern because every Canadian major leaguer who debuted before 1890 was born before Canada existed.[4] This paper assumes that anyone born somewhere that later became part of Canada is Canadian, even if they were born before Confederation.

WHICH LEAGUES ARE MAJOR LEAGUES?

Today there is a clear distinction between the 30 major-league clubs and the minor leagues, but over the years there have been several rival organizations that warrant inclusion, so it is important to define which ones are to be considered. The Special Baseball Records Committee of 1968-1969 convened by Commissioner William Eckert ruled on a number of points, including a decision about which leagues to define as major leagues. In addition to the National League (1876 to the present) the other major leagues of the nineteenth century were the American Association (1882 to 1891), the Union Association (1884), and the Players' League (1890). All other leagues have been excluded.[5]

METHODOLOGY

A year-by-year list of the major-league careers of all Canadian players who either pitched or caught was sorted to find teams that had both a Canadian pitcher and catcher in the same season. Box scores from those team seasons were then reviewed to find games with a Canadian battery. What follows is a review of every nineteenth-century major-league team that had innings pitched and games caught by Canadians. Unless otherwise noted, all biographical and statistical data and all team schedules and results were found at Baseball-Reference, and all sorting of this data was done through Stathead Baseball. This was last confirmed between October 4 and 7, 2021.

THE FIRST CANADIAN MAJOR-LEAGUE PITCHERS AND CATCHERS

Through the 2021 season, 257 players born in Canada had appeared in the major leagues; 134 pitched and 38 caught. Eighteen of these catchers played in the nineteenth century, but they collectively donned the tools of ignorance for a total of only 212 games, about 4 percent of all of the major-league games caught by Canadians. Twenty of their countrymen pitched in a total of 438 games in this period, only 3 percent of the Canadian hurlers' overall total.[6] Despite this dearth of opportunities, the first all-Canadian batteries played in the nineteenth century.

The first Canadian to pitch in the major leagues was Edward Sylvester "The Only" Nolan (Trenton, Ontario), with Indianapolis of the National League in 1878, and the first catcher was William B. "Bill" Phillips (Saint John, New Brunswick), with Cleveland of the National League in 1879. Nolan and Phillips were teammates with Cleveland in 1881, but Phillips played only first base that season so they never formed a battery. The first Canadian battery followed a couple of years later.

1883 NEW YORK GOTHAMS (NATIONAL LEAGUE) – TODAY'S SAN FRANCISCO GIANTS

The 1883 New York Gothams were the first team to have a Canadian at each of the battery positions. James "Tip" O'Neill (Springfield, Ontario) is better known as an outfielder, but he began his big-league career that season as a pitcher with a 5-12 record and an ERA worse than the league average. Catcher John Humphries (North Gower, Ontario) played two major-league seasons, the first of which was the 1883 campaign.

This was New York's first season in the National League, but the Gothams were far from being a typical expansion team. Hall of Famers Mickey Welch and John Montgomery Ward pitched over 80 percent of the team's innings, with O'Neill taking most of the rest, including 19 starts. Another Hall of Famer, Buck Ewing, was the regular catcher; he started behind the plate for all but five of the team's first 45 games, with manager John Clapp as his backup. Humphries

The 1884 New York Gothams, featuring catcher Jack Humphries (front row, far right). Humphries' improbable journey took him from the hamlet of North Gower, outside Ottawa, to Cornell for Latin and Greek, then to New York, to catch Mickey Welch and Tip O'Neill. (David McDonald)

was finishing his studies at Cornell and didn't make his debut with New York until July 7.

O'Neill and Humphries were the starting battery on July 13 in a complete-game 6-3 loss in Buffalo. All of Buffalo's runs were unearned due to nine New York errors, including two apiece by O'Neill and Humphries; the overall poor defensive showing was compounded by Humphries' two passed balls and a wild pitch by O'Neill. Humphries was shut out at the plate but O'Neill foretold his future hitting prowess by contributing a double.

O'Neill and Humphries were not the first to represent a nation with an international battery. Irishmen Curry Foley (Milltown) and Sleeper Sullivan (born in Ireland, city unknown) accomplished that with Buffalo of the National League in 1881, and Sullivan caught countryman Tony Mullane (Cork) with St. Louis of the American Association earlier in 1883. But O'Neill and Humphries formed the first Canadian-born major-league battery.

O'Neill's next start was a 10-1 loss in Cleveland on July 18. Humphries began the game in right field and Ewing was the starting catcher, but was injured during the game and he and Humphries swapped positions.[7] Bill Phillips was Cleveland's first baseman and in the eighth inning he became the first Canadian-born batter to face a Canadian battery, delivering a single to drive home his team's last run.[8]

O'Neill started again on July 28 in a 4-2 loss at Detroit, as he and Humphries were batterymates for the third time. George Wood (Pownal, Prince Edward Island) was the Wolverines' leadoff hitter; he had a single in four at-bats as the second Canadian to bat against a Canadian battery. He was the last to do so for over a century.[9]

O'Neill didn't pitch again until September 5. Humphries caught for him that day, but it was an exhibition match against a team from Staten Island, so it is excluded from their major-league totals. They had one last regular-season game together on September 8 in Philadelphia. New

York fell behind 3-0 after two innings before tallying 13 runs in the third frame and cruising to a 16-6 victory. O'Neill went the distance for the win but, as noted in the *Times* (Philadelphia), the battery had a rough day:

"O'Neil [sic] pitched for the visitors and was terribly wild. Six of the home nine reached first base on called balls and he made six wild pitches, besides breaking his catcher up. Dorgan came in to catch in the second inning…"[10]

Humphries was sufficiently "broken up" to not catch again for three weeks, and O'Neill's next start, his last of the season, was with Mike Dorgan as his catcher. The game on September 8 was therefore the last of four in which O'Neill and Humphries formed a Canadian battery.

Humphries began the 1884 season with Washington of the American Association, then returned to the Gothams for the last two months of the schedule after the Nationals folded. He spent the following three seasons with minor-league teams in Syracuse, Toronto, and Rochester before ending his professional playing career and devoting most of the rest of his life to being a teacher. O'Neill also switched leagues for 1884. He pitched better, going 11-4 with a 2.68 ERA for St. Louis of the American Association, and he raised his OPS by 268 points while playing most of his games in left field. He never pitched after 1884, but became a hitting star of the Association, winning the Triple Crown in 1887. He remains one of the greatest Canadian-born major leaguers, and an annual award presented by the Canadian Baseball Hall of Fame is named in his honor.[11]

1884 PHILADELPHIA QUAKERS (NATIONAL LEAGUE) – TODAY'S PHILLIES

The 1884 season saw the inauguration of the single-year Union Association and an expansion of the American Association. The number of major-league teams doubled, allowing over 300 players to make their debuts, including 20 Canadians. Two of the Canadian rookies played with Philadelphia.

Jonah William "Joe" Knight (Port Stanley, Ontario) pitched in six games with a 2-4 record and a 5.47 ERA. His debut was a 9-0 loss at home to Buffalo on May 16, and his last game with the club was on June 25. He finished the year with Muskegon of the Northwestern League, then became an outfielder and returned to the majors in 1890 with Cincinnati of the National League. He played professionally until 1899.

Finding a reliable catcher was a season-long problem for Philadelphia, which employed 13 players at the position, a major-league record to this day.[12] One of the backstops was Onesime Eugene "Gene" Vadeboncoeur (Louiseville, Québec), who played in four games between July 11 and July 22. His professional career lasted until 1888 but these games were the extent of his big-league experience.

Vadeboncoeur's first game with Philadelphia was 16 days after Knight's last, so although the 1884 Quakers had both a Canadian pitcher and a Canadian catcher, the two of them never had the opportunity to form a battery.

1884 CHICAGO WHITE STOCKINGS (NATIONAL LEAGUE) – TODAY'S CUBS

Another Canadian rookie in 1884 was Joseph E. "Joe" Brown (born in Canada, city unknown). Brown started the season with Fort Wayne of the Northwestern League and ran up a record of 15-21 with a 1.72 ERA while pitching over 300 innings. He accumulated those impressive totals by mid-August, then signed with the White Stockings, for whom he made his debut on August 16 in a 13-9 victory over New York.

The White Stockings also had a Canadian who caught one game in 1884, but it can be stated with full certainty that the team didn't have a Canadian battery because the catcher was Joe

Brown. After pitching a complete-game loss on August 20, Brown was Chicago's starting catcher the next day. According to *Sporting Life*, "Brown's catching was inferior and manager Cap Anson relieved him in the fifth inning."[13]

Brown never caught again, but he was the starting pitcher in another four games, he had one relief appearance, and he also made eight starts in right field. He finished the season with a 4-2 record, pitched four times for Baltimore of the American Association in 1885, and played professionally until 1887. He died the following year.

1885 DETROIT WOLVERINES (NATIONAL LEAGUE) – FRANCHISE FOLDED AFTER THE 1888 SEASON

Nineteenth-century pitchers were expected to go the distance, and those with Detroit were no exception, completing all but three of their starts in 1885. One of the team's rare relief appearances was by outfielder George Wood, who was noted earlier for batting against Tip O'Neill and John Humphries.

One of Wood's teammates that year was Jeremiah S. "Jerry" Moore (Windsor, Ontario). Moore debuted with the short-lived Altoona team of the Union Association in 1884, and after the franchise folded spent a couple of months playing in the Northwestern League before finishing the season with Cleveland of the National League. He joined the Wolverines in 1885, playing six regular-season games for them, all at catcher.

Wood played his usual left field through a spring barnstorming tour, but on April 13. 1885, he was given a pitching assignment in Louisville. He lost 8-0 with Moore catching but, since this was a preseason exhibition game, it doesn't count in the search for major-league Canadian batteries.

Wood was back in left field once the regular season began, including the game played on May 22

when Detroit's starting pitcher was Frank Meinke. Meinke had pitched 31 complete games for Detroit in 1884, but this was his only outing of 1885. With Boston ahead 12-0 in the sixth inning, he was relieved and switched positions with Wood, who pitched the rest of the game with his countryman Moore behind the plate.[14] This was Wood's lone appearance in the box in 1885, but it was enough for him and Moore to form the second Canadian-born battery. It was the only game in which they did this, but it was sufficient to brand Wood as the sole player to ever pitch in a Canadian-born battery and bat against another one.[15]

Moore caught his last major-league game on May 28, then finished the season in the Canadian League. He continued to play in various minor leagues through 1888 and died at age 35 in 1890. Wood's big-league career lasted until 1892, and he played professionally until 1896. Even though he retired more than 120 years ago, Wood is still in the top 10 for Canadians in many career batting statistics,[16] and as recently as 2013 he was the Canadian leader for games played in left field.[17] Wood was inducted into the Canadian Baseball Hall of Fame in 2011.

1885 BUFFALO BISONS (NATIONAL LEAGUE) – FRANCHISE FOLDED AFTER THE 1885 SEASON

Arthur Albert "Art" Irwin and John Irwin (both born in Toronto, Ontario) were the first of five sets of Canadian-born brothers to play in the major leagues, and the first to be teammates.[18] The second pair in each category was Peter Burke "Pete" Wood and Frederick Llewellyn "Fred" Wood (both born in Dundas, Ontario).

The Wood brothers (no relation to the aforementioned George Wood) began the 1885 season playing for the Hamilton Clippers in the inaugural campaign of the Canadian League. Both were released after objecting to the benching of their teammate and brother Jeff,[19] soon signing on with the league rival Primroses team, also of Hamilton. Their stays were short-lived.

After only two games with the Primroses, Pete Wood was engaged by Buffalo, replacing future Hall of Famer Pud Galvin in the rotation. He played his first big-league game on July 15 at the tender age of 18 years and 164 days; he remains the youngest Canadian-born player in major-league history.[20] He pitched 24 times over the last three months of the season with a record of 8-15 in almost 200 innings.

After leaving the Clippers, brother Fred played a few games for the Primroses, then moved to the league's Toronto franchise before being released in late August. He rejoined the Primroses and wrapped up his Canadian League season in September. Concurrently, Buffalo's roster was being decimated by the transfer of most of its top players to Detroit, so manager Jack Chapman was looking for warm bodies to ride out the last few weeks of the season. Fred had appeared in a dozen games for Detroit in 1884 under Chapman, and that connection, plus a brother in the starting rotation, led him to make the move southeast to Buffalo.

The Wood brothers formed a battery on September 28 in an exhibition game in Hamilton won by their old Clippers team,[21] then, on September 30, they formed the major leagues' third all-Canadian battery in a 5-3 loss at home to Boston, Pete going the distance and Fred catching and contributing a single. The score was tied until Boston recorded two unearned runs in the eighth inning to take the game that the local press dubbed "[b]y far the best general playing that the local team has done since it was bereft of the 'Big Four.'"[22] Buffalo played another six games that season, but the September 30 match was the last of the year for each of the Wood brothers.

Apart from three games in 1889, the stint in Buffalo was Pete's only major-league experience, but he also appeared in over 100 games in various minor leagues between 1885 and 1890. He

studied medicine after retiring as a professional baseball player, living in Ontario and Montana, and spent his last years in Chicago, where he died in 1923. The game on September 30 was the final one of Fred's major-league career, although he returned to Buffalo in 1886 to join the city's new entry in the International League. His playing career lasted another few years, after which he became a dentist and practiced until his death in 1935 in London, Ontario.

Although the Wood brothers were teammates for only one major-league game, that game gave them a spot on the list of Canadian-born batteries, and they were the last of their compatriots to be the starting battery of a major-league game until Denis Boucher and Joe Siddall repeated the feat with the Montréal Expos 108 years later.

1898 LOUISVILLE COLONELS (NATIONAL LEAGUE) – FRANCHISE FOLDED AFTER THE 1899 SEASON

The Wood brothers' game kicked off a decade with few Canadian-born pitchers or catchers in the big leagues. Between 1886 and 1896 only three Canadians caught (11 games total)[23] and just nine pitched (25 games),[24] and no major-league team had a player at each position in the same season. That started to change in 1897 when William J. "Bill" Magee (born in New Brunswick, city unknown) pitched 23 times for Louisville.

The Louisville franchise was a perennial doormat of the National League, and the Colonels entered 1898 with a string of five seasons finishing either last or next to last. That season didn't start much better, and their catching corps was one of the problems. Bill Wilson was the regular, backed up by Charlie Dexter, but the former couldn't hit and the latter was better suited to the outfield; as a result, the team acquired the contract of Abraham Conrad "Cooney" Snyder (Chinguacousy, Ontario) from league rival Washington. Snyder played his first game on May 19, starting 17 times over the next month.

Pitching was also a concern. Bert Cunningham was the team's ace, but the rest of the rotation was subpar. Magee was a swingman, getting only three spot starts and one relief appearance in the season's first 25 games before Snyder joined the team.

New York visited Louisville on Monday, May 23, and they pounced on starter Pete Dowling for nine early runs before Dowling was replaced by Magee. Snyder was catching, and for the last four innings the Colonels had the major leagues' fourth Canadian-born battery. The *Louisville Courier-Journal* noted, "… Magee, who succeeded Dowling, did little better on account of his wildness."[25] Magee gave up six walks in his short outing and Snyder committed a passed ball, although he did contribute a single in four plate appearances. New York won 12-4.

Snyder caught roughly every second game for the next three weeks, but Magee didn't get off the bench until a relief appearance on June 14 when Snyder had the day off. Magee's next game was a start in the opener of a doubleheader on June 19, but Snyder caught only the nightcap.

By mid-June Dexter had moved to right field, Wilson had worn out his welcome with an OPS+ of 32, and Snyder was even worse, so Louisville acquired the contracts of catchers Doc Powers and Malachi Kittridge. Starting June 22, Kittridge caught 86 of the team's last 98 games, and Snyder was out of a job. He was released before the month was over and joined the Toronto entry in the Eastern League.

Magee was the starting pitcher the day of Kittridge's first game with Louisville and he tossed a complete-game shutout, earning a spot in the rotation for the rest of the season. This was only his eighth appearance, but by the time the schedule was complete he had pitched almost 300 innings with a record of 16-15.

Snyder had one more year of organized ball, with Reading of the Atlantic League in 1899, then he retired at age 26. Magee split the 1899 season among three major-league teams, then played two full seasons in the Eastern League before he got a late-season call-up to the big leagues in 1901. Despite having won 16 games in 1898 at age 22, Magee after that season compiled a major league record of only 9-24, and he was finished as a ballplayer by 1906.

SUMMARY

Snyder was the last Canadian catcher until John Bannerman "Larry" McLean (Fredericton, New Brunswick) in 1903, so Louisville had the last Canadian battery of the nineteenth century. The era had four all-Canadian batteries appear in a total of seven games:

1883	New York (NL), 4 games Tip O'Neill (P) and John Humphries (C)
1885	Detroit (NL), 1 game George Wood (P) and Jerry Moore (C)
1885	Buffalo (NL), 1 game Pete Wood (P) and Fred Wood (C)
1898	Louisville (NL), 1 game Bill Magee (P) and Cooney Snyder (C)

The New York games on July 13 and 28 and September 8, 1883, and the Buffalo game in 1885 each had a starting Canadian battery. In the New York game of July 18, 1883, O'Neill started but Humphries entered the game as a replacement catcher. The Detroit and Louisville games each involved a starting catcher and a relief pitcher. The lone win was in the fourth New York game.

POSTSCRIPT

The Deadball Era featured five of the seven most prolific Canadian-born catchers. They accumulated over half of all of the major-league games caught by their countrymen,[26] but a lack of pitchers resulted in only two more Canadian-born batteries by 1920:

1908   Cleveland (AL), 1 game
         Jack Graney (P) and J.J. Clarke (C)

1918   New York (NL), 1 game
         Bob Steele (P) and George Gibson (C)

After this period there were very few Canadian-born catchers until the start of the twenty-first century, and there were only two more batteries in the next 87 seasons:

1955   Kansas City (AL), 1 game
         Ozzie Van Brabant (P) and
         Eric MacKenzie (C)

1993   Montréal (NL), 2 games
         Denis Boucher (P) and Joe Siddall (C)

The Negro Leagues from 1920 to 1948 are now recognized as major leagues; they were considered in this review but, based on current records, no Canadian-born player ever caught a game in these leagues. As a result, there are no Negro League batteries to add to the list.

Canadian batteries have become more common in recent years, mainly because of the careers of catchers Russell Martin (East York, Ontario) and George Kottaras (Scarborough, Ontario), and how teams are now employing expanded bullpens, opening up many more opportunities for Canadian pitchers:

2006   Los Angeles (NL), 1 game
         Eric Gagné (P) and Russell Martin (C)

2008   NL All-Star Team, 1 game
         Ryan Dempster (P) and Russell Martin (C)

2010-12 Milwaukee (NL), 32 games
         John Axford (P) and George Kottaras (C)

2013   Pittsburgh (NL), 1 game
         Chris Leroux (P) and Russell Martin (C)

2014   Cleveland (AL), 4 games
         John Axford (P) and George Kottaras (C)

2014   Pittsburgh (NL), 9 games
         John Axford (P) and Russell Martin (C)

2015   Toronto (AL), 1 game
         Andrew Albers (P) and Russell Martin (C)

2015   Toronto (AL), 10 games
         Jeff Francis (P) and Russell Martin (C)

2018   Toronto (AL), 28 games
         John Axford (P) and Russell Martin (C)

This review included postseason and All-Star games. The 2008 midseason classic is the only one to have a Canadian battery, and there has never been a Canadian-born battery in a playoff game.[27]

There have been a total of 99 major-league games with Canadian-born batterymates; Axford/Martin accounted for 37 of them and Axford/Kottaras 36. John Axford (Simcoe, Ontario) pitched 73 of these games and Martin caught 51 of the total.

If the definition of Canadian is expanded to include players born abroad to Canadian parents, or those who moved to Canada at a young age, then four other batteries can be included:

1908-09   Cincinnati (NL), 26 games
           Jean Dubuc * (P) and Larry McLean (C)

1913   Detroit (AL), 2 games
           Jean Dubuc * (P) and Henri Rondeau * (C)

1915   Pittsburgh (FL), 12 games
           George Leclair * (P) and Yip Owens (C)

1918   Pittsburgh (NL), 2 games
           Bob Steele (P) and Jimmy Archer ** (C)

* Born in the United States to Canadian-born parents.
** Born in Ireland, raised in Canada.

This part of the list is likely to grow as more research is done and biographies are written about players who had Canadian ties other than their place of birth.

No Canadian-born catcher has appeared in the major leagues since Russell Martin's last game on September 28, 2019. A possible future Canadian battery is pitcher Cal Quantrill (Port Hope, Ontario) and catcher Noah "Bo" Naylor (Mississauga, Ontario) with the Cleveland Guardians in 2022. Quantrill is already established as a pitcher for the team, while Naylor is a top prospect who played for Double-A Akron in 2021.[28]

NOTES

1. The Montréal Expos played from 1969 through 2004, and in that time 16 Canadian-born players wore their uniform. Three were born in Québec: Claude Raymond (St. Jean, 45 kilometers southeast of Montréal) from 1969 to 1971, Denis Boucher (Montréal) from 1993 to 1994, and Derek Aucoin (Lachine, a suburb about 15 kilometers west of downtown Montréal) in 1996.

2. "Expos Story," *Montréal Gazette*, Tuesday, September 7, 1993: F3. The article was not attributed but it was likely written by either Michael Farber or Jeff Blair: "Prior to the arrival of Joe Siddall from Windsor, there have been five Canadian catchers in the big leagues in this century. The roster: Nig Clarke, Amherstburg, Ont. (nine years between 1905 and 1920), George (Moon) Gibson, London (1905-18), Frank (Yip) Owens, Toronto, (1905, 1909 [*sic*]), Joe (Stubby) Erautt, Vibank, Sask (1950-51), Eric MacKenzie, Glendon, Alta. (1955). Nig, Moon, Yip, Stubby. Perhaps the Expos rookie should be called Joe "L" Siddall. 'Amherstburg is about 20 miles from Windsor,' Siddall said. 'You heard it here first. Windsor, Cradle of Canadian Catchers.'"

   Note: This article failed to mention Larry McLean (Fredericton, New Brunswick), Art McGovern (Saint John, New Brunswick), Tom Daly (Saint John, New Brunswick), Ed Wingo (Ste. Anne de Bellevue, Québec), and Jim Lawrence (Hamilton, Ontario), all Canadian-born players who also preceded Siddall as major-league catchers in the twentieth century. It also excludes Owens' two seasons in the Federal League in 1914 and 1915.

3. One nineteenth-century pitcher who was considered in this analysis was Leon Viau. Viau was born in Corinth, Vermont, to a French-Canadian father. Little is known about Viau's heritage but the French name and proximity of his birthplace to the border were enough to at least infer some Canadian roots. Viau pitched for four major-league teams between 1888 and 1892, and was twice a 20-game winner. His teammates included Canadians Joe Knight (Port Stanley, Ontario – 1890 Cincinnati, 127 games in left field), Pat Lyons (Belleville, Ontario – 1890 Cleveland, 11 games at second base), and Spud Johnson (born in Canada, city unknown – 1891 Cleveland, 79 games in right field and one game at first base) but since none of them was a catcher, Viau never had an opportunity to form an all-Canadian battery.

4. Forty-three Canadian-born major leaguers played at least one game between 1876 and 1889, and 42 of them were born before July 1, 1867. The exception is Ed Springer (Oil Springs, Ontario), whose birthdate is listed as simply "1867," so there is a chance that he was born after Confederation. Phil Routcliffe (Frontenac, Ontario), who played one game in 1890, was born on October 24, 1870, and is the first Canadian major leaguer with a confirmed birthdate after Confederation.

5. Some resources consider the National Association (1871 to 1875) to be a major league. Through its five-year history only two Canadian-born players appeared in the league: Bob Addy (Port Hope, Ontario – 1871 and 1873 to 1875) and Tom Smith (Guelph, Ontario – 1875). They were never teammates and neither one pitched or caught so the National Association didn't have any Canadian batteries. The other major leagues – the American League (1901 to present), the Federal League (1914 to 1915), and the recognized Negro Leagues (1920 to 1948) – didn't operate in the nineteenth century and were therefore excluded from this analysis.

6. Stathead Baseball was used to identify Canadian-born major leaguers. The Batting Player Season Finder found 250 players who played between 1876 and 2021, and the Player Pitching Season & Career Finder found another seven who pitched in the DH era, played for only American League teams, and never played in an interleague game in which pitchers batted [Ryan Braun (Kitchener, Ontario), Barry Cort (Toronto, Ontario), Steve Green (Greenfield Park, Québec), Peter Hoy (Brockville, Ontario), Trystan Magnuson (Vancouver, British Columbia), Chris Mears (Ottawa, Ontario), and Dustin Molleken (Regina, Saskatchewan)]. The two Stathead searches were merged to get the total of 257, and that list was filtered to find pitchers and catchers. The 134 pitchers completed a total of 41,601 innings in 13,130 appearances. The 20 pitchers who played in the nineteenth century appeared in 438 games (3.34% of the total) comprising 3,483 innings (8.40%). The total games caught by all Canadian-born major leaguers is 5,048, 55% of which was accumulated by Russell Martin (East York, Ontario – 1,579 games) and George Gibson (London, Ontario – 1,194). The 212 games caught by the 18 pre-1900 catchers represent 4.20% of the total.

7. "Out and In-Door Sports," *Cleveland Plain Dealer*, Thursday, July 19, 1883: 4: "Ewing's hands were so battered that in the eighth inning he went to right field and Humphries went behind the bat."

8. The timing of the position switch between Ewing and Humphries is key to determining if Bill Phillips came to the plate while Humphries was catching O'Neill. The most comprehensive report of the game action can be found in the *Cleveland Leader* and, based on its description plus a few details gleaned from other publications, the top of the eighth inning can be summarized as follows:

   Fatty Briody was retired on a fly ball to right field.

   Fred Dunlap hit a double to left field, then stole third.

   Pete Hotaling hit a single to center, scoring Dunlap, then advanced to second on a wild pitch.

   Jack Glasscock singled to right to score Hotaling, stole second, and went to third on a passed ball.

The result of Tom York's at-bat was not recorded in any of the publications that were reviewed, but he made it safely to first base. Glasscock didn't score and York didn't walk or get a hit, so the most likely scenario is that he reached on one of New York's errors, and Glasscock was unable to advance on the play.

Bill Phillips singled to left to score Glasscock, and moved up a base when New York's second baseman committed an error on the throw back in from the outfield.

York was put out at third base for the second out of the inning, but the details of the play have not been found. This could have been a continuation of the play after Phillips's hit, or York could have been picked off or caught stealing home during the subsequent at-bat.

Mike Muldoon ended the inning by hitting a fly ball to center field.

The game summary in the *Cleveland Leader*, Thursday, July 19, 1883: 3, noted that Ewing caught Briody's fly to start the inning, and that he threw the ball that second baseman Dasher Troy muffed after Phillips's single, which means that Humphries had to have been the backstop as the inning began, confirming Phillips's at-bat against the Canadian battery.

9   The next Canadian-born batter to face a Canadian-born battery was Justin Morneau (New Westminster, British Columbia) of the Minnesota Twins against the Milwaukee Brewers' pitcher John Axford (Simcoe, Ontario) and catcher George Kottaras (Scarborough, Ontario) on May 23, 2010. Joey Votto (Toronto, Ontario) of the Cincinnati Reds confronted the same battery on June 26, 2012, and, after Axford and Kottaras had moved to Cleveland, they engaged Michael Saunders (Victoria, British Columbia) of the Seattle Mariners on June 29, 2014. In all three cases Axford struck out his countryman. The list is longer if the definition of Canadian is expanded to include foreign-born players with Canadian-born parents. Examples include Canadian-born George Gibson having 17 plate appearances against US-born Jean Dubuc and his Canadian-born catcher Larry McLean in 1908 and 1909, and US-born Freddie Freeman batting twice against Canadian-born Jeff Francis (Vancouver, British Columbia) and Russell Martin on April 19, 2015.

10   "The League Games," *Philadelphia Times,* September 9, 1883: 2.

11   The James "Tip" O'Neill Award is presented annually by the Canadian Baseball Hall of Fame to the Canadian player judged to have excelled in individual achievement and team contribution while adhering to baseball's highest ideals. More information can be found at the Hall's website at http://baseballhalloffame.ca/museum/awards/.

12   The next highest total is 11 catchers for Indianapolis (AA) in 1884, and five other teams are tied for third place with 10 catchers. All of these teams played in the nineteenth century. Ten teams have employed nine catchers in a season, including the 2021 Chicago Cubs. The most recent team before that was the 1914 Pittsburgh Pirates.

13   "Providence vs. Chicago," *Sporting Life*, August 27, 1884: 5.

14   *Sporting Life*, May 27, 1885: 7.

15   The Postscript of this paper summarizes the 99 major-league games with a Canadian-born battery; with the exception of George Wood, none of the pitchers batted against another Canadian-born battery.

16   Wood ranks first among all Canadian-born major leaguers in triples, third in runs scored, fourth in hits, fifth in at-bats, sixth in plate appearances and stolen bases, eighth in doubles, and ninth in games played and runs batted in.

17   Wood was the leader until Jason Bay passed him during the 2013 season, 121 years after Wood's last major-league game.

18   Jim Shearon, *Over the Fence Is Out* (Kanata, Ontario: Malin Head Press, 2009), 245. Under the title "Canadian Brothers in the Major Leagues," the author lists the following five sets of Canadian-born brothers in the major leagues:

Arthur and John Irwin (Toronto, Ontario)

Fred and Pete Wood (Dundas, Ontario)

Gene (Milton, Nova Scotia) and Russ Ford (Brandon, Manitoba)

Rob (East York, Ontario) and Rich Butler (Toronto, Ontario)

Jeff and Jordan Zimmerman (Kelowna, British Columbia)

Arthur Irwin played in the major leagues from 1880 until 1894, appearing in a total of 1,010 games. His brother John played professionally from 1882 until 1899 but most of his career was spent in the minor leagues. John appeared in one major-league game in 1882 when he played first base for Worcester (National League) with Arthur at shortstop. They were teammates again in 1889 with Washington (National League), where they played together 52 times at third base (John) and shortstop (Arthur) between July 29 and the end of the season. Arthur was the manager of Boston (American Association) in 1891 and he got into a handful of games, one of which was with John, on May 31. That was the last game to have Canadian siblings as teammates, but the Zimmerman brothers got into one game as opponents on July 2, 1999, when Jeff pitched the eighth inning for the Texas Rangers and Jordan faced one batter in the ninth inning for the Seattle Mariners.

19 In each of their first 12 games the Clippers had at least one Wood brother (Pete, Fred, or Jeff) in the starting lineup, with three of the games featuring all three. Fred Wood played in eight of the Clippers' first 12 games, including five as the team's catcher. On June 24, Jerry Moore was catcher. Once he joined the Clippers, Moore caught more than 60 percent of the team's games over the rest of the season. One catcher who participated in a major-league Canadian battery (Moore) therefore replaced another one (Fred Wood) for the Hamilton Clippers of the Canadian League in 1885.

20 Pete Wood is the only Canadian to make his debut at age 18, and one of only four Canadian-born teenagers to play in the major leagues.

21 "Ball Games Yesterday," *Buffalo Morning Express*, September 29, 1885: 2.

22 "Boston 5, Buffalo 3," *Buffalo Morning Express*, October 1, 1885: 2.

23 Pop Smith (Digby, Nova Scotia) caught one game for Pittsburgh (American Association) in 1886, Fred Lake (Cornwallis, Nova Scotia) caught four games for Boston (National League) in 1891, Kid Summers (Toronto, Ontario) caught one game for St. Louis (NL) in 1893, and Lake caught five times for Louisville (NL) in 1894.

24 Nine pitchers appeared in 10 seasons (two for George Wood), pitching in a total of 25 games.

25 "New York Took the First Game," *Louisville Courier-Journal,* May 24, 1898: 6.

26 The main Canadian Deadball Era catchers were George Gibson (1,194 games caught), Larry McLean (761), J.J. Clarke (Amherstburg, Ontario – 462), Yip Owens (Toronto, Ontario – 215), and Tom Daly (144). These five players caught a total of 2,776 games, 55 percent of the 5,048 games caught by all Canadian-born major-league catchers. The other two catchers in the top seven are Russell Martin (1,579) and George Kottaras (246); no other Canadian-born player has caught more than 75 major-league games. Irish-born Canadian Jimmy Archer also played in the Deadball Era and he caught 736 games. This period could be named the Golden Age of Canadian catchers.

27 John Axford and George Kottaras both played for Milwaukee in the 2011 postseason, but were not in a game at the same time and didn't form a battery. No other postseason roster included both a Canadian-born pitcher and catcher.

28 Quantrill and Naylor both appeared in Cleveland spring-training games on February 28 and March 10, 2021, but Naylor entered each game after Quantrill had left, so they have yet to form a battery, even in a preseason exhibition game.

BILL WATKINS

By Bill Lamb

Prominent in the baseball circles of his time but now forgotten, Bill Watkins spent more than 30 years as a player, manager, front-office executive, and team owner of various major- and high minor-league franchises. His playing career short-circuited by a near fatal beaning in 1884, Watkins thereafter assumed the manager's post for the Detroit Wolverines and within three years transformed that National League doormat into the baseball world champions of 1887. During his heyday, however, Watkins was most often associated with Indianapolis, serving no fewer than eight baseball organizations established in the Indiana capital. Finally leaving the diamond scene in the early 1920s, Watkins, a Canadian by birth, spent his remaining years as the leading citizen of Marysville, Michigan, a suburban Great Lakes community that Watkins himself helped to found.

The long and productive life of William Harton Thomas Watkins began in Brantford, Ontario, on May 5, 1858.[1] Bill was the second of five children born to John Luke Harton Watkins (1824-1915), a farmer turned prosperous dry-goods merchant, and his wife, the former Eliza Jane Tyler (1834-1868).[2] Both parents were Canadian, descended of Irish Protestant stock.

Bill's youth was unsettled by the untimely death of his mother in 1868. He was then sent to the rural enclave of Erin to be raised by his maternal grandparents.[3] Bright and with mechanical aptitude, Watkins was educated at local prep schools and then spent a year at Upper Canada College, a prestigious postgraduate school in Toronto. During his school years, Watkins was introduced to baseball, his interest in the game developing as he began his working life as an apprentice in a novelty-machine manufacturing plant. Thereafter, he was employed by a Canadian branch of the Ingles-Corliss Engine Works.[4] Watkins emigrated in 1879, taking up residence in Port Huron, Michigan, the Great Lakes city that he would call home for the next 40 years.[5]

Demonstrating leadership qualities from an early age, Watkins began his baseball career in 1880 as the youthful playing manager of the Maple Leafs of Guelph, Ontario, a nearby semipro nine.[6] The following year, he moved up a competitive notch, steering the St. Thomas Atlantics, one of Canada's top semipro clubs. Thereafter, Watkins took command of his new hometown's side, piloting the Port Huron club to the Michigan State League championship in 1882 and 1883. The following year, Watkins entered the professional ranks, taking the post of second baseman-manager of Bay City in the minor Northwestern League. Watkins had his latest team in pennant contention (37-14, .725) when financial difficulties precipitated the dissolution of the Bay City franchise in early July 1884. Despite posting only a .234 batting average, Watkins had caught the eye of those in charge of even faster competition, preserving his career in baseball.

With three professional operations – National League, American Association, and Union Association – all claiming major-league status, the 1884 season supplied ample employment opportunities for unattached ballplayers, even those with only marginal playing ability. Bill Watkins, now 26, was among their number. In late July, he signed a contract to play for the woeful Indianapolis Hoosiers of the 12-club American Association. Then a lean 5-feet-10 and 156 pounds, the right-handed Watkins[7] was immediately inserted into the Hoosier lineup at third base and went 1-for-4 in his August 1 major-league debut, a 7-6 loss to Columbus. Ten days later, the rookie infielder was given charge of Indianapolis fortunes, replacing Jim Gifford at the helm of the 25-60, 11th-place team. Once in charge, Watkins switched himself to second base and "played [his] position nicely."[8] He also began to show some pop at the plate, going 9-for-24 (.375) over a six-game stretch. On August 26, however, an errant first-inning fastball by Cincinnati fireballer Gus Shallix effectively ended the playing career, and almost took the life, of Bill Watkins. Struck squarely in the head by the pitch, Watkins spent the next several days in and out of a coma before recovering.[9] On September 11 Watkins was able to place himself back in the Hoosiers lineup, going 2-for-4 at the plate while handling six chances cleanly at second base. But it soon became obvious that he was not the player he had been before the beaning. In his last 12 games, Watkins went 3-for-37 (.081) with the bat and played erratically in the field. And by season's end, Watkins had benched himself. The

Hoosiers joined their skipper in the performance tailspin, losing their last 13 games in a row and finalizing Watkins' managerial log at a dismal 4-18 (.182) for the next-to-last-place Indianapolis club. That fall, the American Association dropped the Indianapolis franchise.

Like the defunct Hoosiers, Bill Watkins never played another major-league game. In his 133 lifetime plate appearances, he had batted an anemic .205, with only four extra-base hits. In the field, he had been no better, posting a substandard .878 fielding percentage between second, third, and two games at shortstop. But if Watkins' ballplaying career was behind him at an early age, two lifelong endeavors beckoned. On November 6, 1884, Watkins married Edna Buzzard, the daughter of a Port Huron sea captain. The marriage would endure for the next 52 years, but apparently without children. Three months after marrying, Watkins commenced his tenure as a full-time baseball executive, joining Ted Sullivan, Tom Loftus, and George Tebeau in organizing the Western League, a new minor-league circuit composed of teams located in six midsized Midwestern cities. Watkins himself took command of the league's Indianapolis entry, a team which retained the Hoosiers nickname but otherwise bore little resemblance to its hapless AA predecessors. This new Indianapolis nine quickly took a commanding lead in the inaugural WL pennant chase. Then on July 6, 1885, the first-place (27-4) Hoosiers franchise failed financially, precipitating the immediate demise of the new league. Shortly thereafter, the assets of the Indianapolis franchise, including the contracts of manager Watkins and star outfielder Sam Thompson, were purchased by the Detroit Wolverines of the National League.

With Detroit (7-31) hopelessly out of pennant contention, Watkins replaced Charlie Morton as Wolverines manager. In keeping with nineteenth-century norms, on-field decisions – batting order, defensive alignment, in-game stratagems, and the like – remained the province

Manager William Watkins with his 1887 National League Champion Detroit Wolverines. (National Baseball Hall of Fame and Museum, Cooperstown, New York)

of Wolverines team captain and center fielder Ned Hanlon. Watkins served as a one-man front office, attending to administrative chores like player acquisition, traveling/hotel accommodations, collection of gate receipts, and the scheduling of exhibition games, an important revenue source for the financially shaky Detroit franchise. Watkins, something of a martinet as a younger man, also attended to team discipline, doling out $10 fines for shoddy play in the field and leveling more substantial penalties for late-night carousing, a common player pastime that Watkins could not abide. Under his regime, the Wolverines made progress, finishing the 1885 campaign at 41-67 and positioned for advancement in league standings.

The 1886 season would prove an eventful one for Bill Watkins. The previous winter,

pharmaceutical manufacturer/sportsman Frederick K. Stearns had assumed the presidency of the Detroit club and was determined to transform the Wolverines into a championship nine. To that end, Stearns purchased the defunct Buffalo franchise, and with it the contracts of the club's famed Big Four: Dan Brouthers, Deacon White, Hardy Richardson, and Jack Rowe. Once in uniform, the group elevated Detroit into an immediate pennant contender. Then at midseason, Watkins came to terms with crack second baseman Fred Dunlap, late of the St. Louis Maroons – the first in a series of events that would earn Watkins the enmity of Mound City partisans.[10] Paced by the offense supplied by Brouthers (.370), Richardson (.351), and Sam Thompson (.310), and with Lady Baldwin and Pretzels Getzien combining for 72 wins from the pitcher's box, the Wolverines' record skyrocketed to 87-36 (.707). But that sterling performance was good only for second place, three games to the rear of the NL pennant-winning Chicago White Stockings of Cap Anson/King Kelly/John Clarkson fame.

During the offseason, controversy arose from Watkins' attendance at the American Association winter meeting, a gathering focused on the crisis created by the jump of the Pittsburgh club to the National League. When quizzed about Detroit's intentions, Watkins played it coy, neither confirming nor denying Detroit's interest in transferring to the AA. Thereafter, following long-distance consultation with Stearns, Watkins announced that the NL had granted the concessions sought by Detroit and withdrew himself from the AA conclave. This proved too much for *The Sporting News*, still angry over the Dunlap signing and other suspected Watkins designs against the hometown Maroons. In a pair of December 1886 editorials, *TSN* blistered *Windy Hawfulgall Watkins* as a "peddler of franchises" and "an ill-mannered boor" intent upon undermining the good standing of the St. Louis club in NL councils.[11] But while Al Spink and company were denouncing Watkins, the Maroons franchise was being targeted for acquisition by a different menace, a consortium of Indianapolis businessmen headed by department store magnate John T. Brush. Early in 1887, control of the NL St. Louis club was acquired by the Brush group and transferred to Indianapolis for the coming season.

The Wolverines got off quickly in 1887, winning 18 of their first 20 games and assuming the lead in NL standings. Notwithstanding that, there was dissension in the Detroit clubhouse, with the disciplinary measures of manager Watkins being a sore point. Particularly resented was his tendency to fine lesser lights like catcher Fatty Briody and pitcher Stump Weidman for infractions that went unpunished when committed by team stars.[12] He even got into arguments with opposition players. Near season end, it was

reported that Indianapolis field captain Jack Glasscock had to be restrained by teammates from "wiping the thoroughfare" with Watkins.[13]

The 1887 season would prove the highlight of the Detroit Wolverines' existence, and of Bill Watkins' tenure as a major-league executive. After a six-week spring-training sojourn in Macon, Georgia,[14] the Wolverines got off fast in the pennant chase and were never headed, the team dynamic improved by the voluntary withdrawal of the caustic-tongued Watkins from the Wolverines bench during games. Although tensions remained between Watkins and his charges, it mattered little in the end. With Sam Thompson (.372, with a NL-leading 166 RBIs) ably supported by Brouthers, Richardson, White, and Rowe, all of whom hit over .300, and a five-man pitching staff led by 29-game winner Getzien, the Wolverines captured the pennant with a handsome 79-45 (.637) log. Detroit then attained the title of baseball world champions, defeating the AA-standard-bearing St. Louis Browns in a 15-game series, played to conclusion in 10 different cities before ever-smaller galleries.[15] But even a world championship title could not cure the financial ills of the Detroit franchise. With its population then under 150,000, Detroit proved unable to draw large crowds at home. NL owners, led by Eastern team magnates still smarting from Stearns' absorption of the Buffalo franchise, then reneged on away-game gate receipt concessions accorded Detroit a year earlier. Unable to balance a payroll loaded with stars, the Wolverines slipped into red ink.

Nor was Bill Watkins a happy man. Club President Stearns's failure to mention Watkins' name in a lengthy banquet tribute to the world champions had bruised the manager's feelings.[16] Then Watkins got into a nasty public dust-up with the revered Deacon White. The specifics of the dispute are murky but its nature can probably be inferred from the mea culpa that Detroit club directors extracted from Watkins: "Some of the statements made in the public press, alleged by [White] to have been made by me, I have never authorized. Other things I have said thoughtlessly, but with no malicious intent toward White. They were made on the spur of the moment and without consideration of their consequences or of the effects the remarks would have upon his feelings. ... Realizing now that I have undoubtedly wounded his personal feeling by public expression, I now take occasion to repair the damage as far as possible."[17] This opaque non-apology did little to mollify White. Nor did it repair the strained relations that now existed between Watkins and his employers. With restive charges underperforming on the field and feeling besieged on all sides, Watkins resigned as Detroit manager in late August 1888, leaving the Wolverines (49-44, .527) in the middle of the NL pack. Replaced at the helm by club secretary Bob Leadley, Watkins had posted an excellent 249-161 (.607) log, with a recent world baseball championship to his credit, during his term as Wolverines overseer. The Detroit Wolverines would soon exit the scene as well. His ambitions satisfied by the 1887 championship, the wealthy Stearns had thereafter relinquished control of the club to fellow directors. They, in turn, proved unable to bear the burden of financing a nonprofitable major-league baseball operation. Accordingly, those now in charge sold off the club's star players and disbanded the Detroit franchise at the close of the 1888 season.

After leaving Detroit, Bill Watkins did not remain unemployed indefinitely. On September 7, 1888, he assumed the post of manager of the Kansas City Cowboys, the American Association cellar dwellers. As in Detroit, manager Watkins' duties were mainly in the front office, not on the bench. But lacking the fiscal resources once supplied by Stearns, Watkins was unable to turn club fortunes around. The following season, the Cowboys finished a noncompetitive (55-82, .401) seventh place in AA standings and the franchise was dissolved shortly thereafter. Watkins began

the ensuing season on the sidelines, but in late June assumed command of the last-place and financially troubled St. Paul Apostles of the Western Association.[18] But the Apostles were a lost cause, with a playing roster so threadbare that Watkins even had to place himself occasionally in the lineup.[19] At season end, 37-84, .306 St. Paul was securely ensconced in the circuit cellar, 43 games behind the pennant-winning Kansas City Blues.

Watkins returned to St. Paul in 1891, but with the club anchored in last place at 17-34, the franchise was shifted to Duluth, Minnesota, in early June. Two months later, the club disbanded. By then Watkins had been supplanted as manager by Jay Anderson. Thereafter, Watkins spent at least part of the 1892 season as manager of the Rochester Flour Cities of the Eastern League. The following year, he resurfaced in the majors, becoming the latest in the parade of baseball men installed as manager of the once-proud St. Louis Browns by volatile owner Chris Von Der Ahe. Watkins, however, had no more success at the Browns helm than his most immediate predecessors and was dismissed after a 10th-place (57-75, .432) St. Louis finish in a National League now swollen to 12 teams.

In 1894 the Watkins odyssey continued as he became manager of the Sioux City Cornhuskers, an entry in the latest version of the Western League. With a lineup jammed with .300+ hitters and a pitching staff headed by 35-game winner Bert Cunningham, the 74-52, .587 Cornhuskers captured the WL pennant for manager Watkins. The following season, the Cornhuskers were removed to St. Paul by incoming club owner Charles Comiskey. But Watkins did not accompany the team. Rather, he signed on as manager of a Western League rival, the Indianapolis Hoosiers, a move that in time placed Watkins in the middle of a skirmish between the two executive giants of turn-of-the-century baseball: Ban Johnson and John T. Brush.

Originally a Cincinnati sportswriter, Johnson had assumed the presidency of the Western League upon its re-formation in October 1893. Able and energetic, Johnson soon transformed the new circuit into a premier minor league. Throughout its early existence, however, the Western League was nagged by the problem of competitive imbalance, a situation largely attributable to the maneuvers of Brush, the owner of the WL's Indianapolis Hoosiers. By now, Brush was also president and majority owner of the National League Cincinnati Reds,[20] whose roster Brush manipulated ruthlessly to Indianapolis advantage, fortifying the Hoosiers lineup for crucial games against WL rivals with Reds players, at times optioned to Indianapolis for no more than a weekend and then recalled to Cincinnati. With big-league ringers at his disposal, Watkins managed Indianapolis to Western League pennants in 1895 and 1897, while his 1896 nine finished a solid second. By 1898, the complaints of fellow club owners had precipitated enactment of a prohibition against simultaneous ownership of a major- and minor-league baseball team, forcing Brush to relinquish (at least on paper) control of the Indianapolis club. By then, however, Bill Watkins had moved on, returning to the majors as pilot of the NL Pittsburgh Pirates.

In Pittsburgh, as elsewhere – with the notable exception of Detroit – Watkins was well liked, age and experience having greatly moderated his once-biting tongue, as reflected in the more frequent appearance of the semi-affectionate nickname *Watty* in newsprint.[21] But sadly for Watkins, he got to Pittsburgh too soon, his installation as manager predating the arrival of Honus Wagner, Tommy Leach, Deacon Phillippe, Sam Leever, and the other stalwarts who would shortly make the Pirates the class of the National League. Saddled with mediocrities, Watkins guided the Pirates to an eighth place (72-76) finish in 1898. The next season the Pirates started 8-15, and Watkins resigned. Although his

baseball career would continue for another two decades, Bill Watkins' days as a major-league manager were now over. In five different locales, Indianapolis (1884: 4-18), Detroit (1885-1888: 249-161), Kansas City (1888-1889: 63-99), St. Louis (1893: 57-75), and Pittsburgh (1898-1899: 79-91), Watkins-led clubs had posted a 452-444 (.504) regular-season log, while taking 10 of the 15 postseason games that gave Detroit the 1887 world championship.

In 1900 Watkins returned to Indianapolis, where he resumed command of the Hoosiers, now a member of the American League, the new moniker bestowed on the Western League by Ban Johnson in anticipation of declaring his circuit a major league in 1901. A prudent conservator of his own resources, Watkins now had the financial wherewithal to assume majority ownership of the Indianapolis club as well.[22] That season, owner-manager Watkins led the Hoosiers to a third-place (71-64, .526) finish in the AL of 1900. In the ensuing offseason, Watkins became embroiled in a new and far more momentous clash between Ban Johnson and John T. Brush – the battle over the establishment of a new major league in baseball.

Johnson had made no secret of his ambitions for the American League, and NL magnates had played right into his hands. After the 1899 season the senior circuit had contracted from 12 clubs to eight, freeing up major-league-quality venues like Washington, Baltimore, and Cleveland for settlement by the American. At the end of 1900, Johnson moved right in, jettisoning Indianapolis (as well as Buffalo, Kansas City, and Minneapolis) from his circuit in the process. Meanwhile, NL club owners, preoccupied with squabbling among themselves, were slow to respond. Belatedly in January 1901, NL leaders, led by Brush and encouraged editorially by *Sporting Life* founder Francis C. Richter, engineered the revival of the old American Association, now defunct for a decade. To be stocked with surplus NL players,

AA franchises would be established in Chicago, Philadelphia, Boston, Baltimore, Washington, Milwaukee, and Detroit, while incorporating the Indianapolis team just abandoned by Johnson's circuit.

In short order, Indianapolis owner/president/manager William H.T. Watkins emerged as AA spokesman and interim chairman/league president. "The AA is not a dream," proclaimed Watkins. "It is an absolute fact. We have the cities and we have the financial backing of reputable and responsible businessmen in every one of them."[23] Despite cheerful weekly progress reports published by *Sporting Life*, the new AA never got off the drawing board, quickly undermined by NL owners like John I. Rogers of Philadelphia and Boston's Arthur Soden, who wanted neither an American League nor an American Association rival in his city. With Brush and Watkins the target of most public finger-pointing, the AA revival was stillborn, its passing noted sadly by Richter in mid-March.[24]

These developments left Bill Watkins the owner of a professional baseball team with no league to play in. Scrambling, Watkins secured a berth for Indianapolis in the Western Association, a second-tier minor league. The caliber of WA play proved unacceptable to Indianapolis fans, only 400 of whom would attend a typical Hoosiers game. In mid-July, Watkins sold the club to new owners who removed the franchise to obscure Matthews, Indiana, to complete the season. But a brighter baseball future for Watkins and Indianapolis was on the horizon. In November 1901, an Indianapolis club newly assembled by Watkins joined one-time major-league cities like Louisville, Milwaukee, Kansas City, Columbus, and Toledo, plus St. Paul and Minneapolis, to form the independent minor-league American Association, destined to become one of baseball's most stable professional circuits.[25]

Laced with major-league-quality material like outfielder George Hogreiver (a league-leading 124 runs scored) and pitchers Win Kellum (25-10), Jack Sutthoff (24-13), and Frank Killen (16-6), Watkins, fully exercising the duties now commonly associated with being a baseball team manager (in addition to being club owner and president), guided the Indianapolis Indians to the maiden AA pennant, its 96-45 (.681) season mark good for a two-game margin over Louisville.[26] The following season, however, Indianapolis dropped to fourth place (78-61, .561) and placed dead last in home attendance (88,000) among AA clubs. In early 1905, Watkins resigned as Indianapolis club president/manager to take over the reins of AA rival Minneapolis. But after a disappointing campaign leading the Millers, Watkins sold the Minneapolis franchise to former St. Paul manager Mike Kelley for a reported $25,000 in December.

But Bill Watkins was far from through with baseball. In 1906, he reacquired the Indianapolis franchise, reinstalling himself as the Indians president and manager. This time, however, on-field success eluded him as a field skipper. With Indianapolis headed for last place, Watkins resigned as manager, tapping first baseman Charlie Carr to preside over the club's 53-96 (.356) finish. For the next five years, Watkins confined himself to front-office duties for the Indians, reveling in the 1908 pennant brought in by manager Carr behind the exploits of future major-league standouts Rube Marquard and Donie Bush. Thereafter, disputes with front-office subordinates gradually soured Watkins on Indians baseball. On May 23, 1912, now approaching his 54th birthday, Watkins resigned as Indianapolis club president and sold the team, returning home to Port Huron to tend to his farm and business interests.[27] But not for long.

In February 1914 Watkins returned to Indianapolis to assume the post of business manager for the renegade Federal League Hoosiers, the eighth and final time that Watkins would serve a professional baseball organization seated in the Indiana capital. "I am glad to get back into harness and particularly glad to return to Indianapolis," Bill declared upon signing on.[28] The Federal League crown captured by the 1914 Indianapolis club was the sixth pennant winner that Bill Watkins would be associated with. It was also his last. Watkins resigned his position with the organization when the Indianapolis franchise was acquired by oil tycoon Harry Sinclair and transferred to Newark for the 1915 season. Once again Watkins returned to Port Huron to attend to his interests there, his 30-year involvement in professional baseball seemingly at its end.

Back home, Watkins immersed himself in local business affairs, serving in executive positions at various Port Huron banks, land development companies, and manufacturing concerns, and as president of the Port Huron Chamber of Commerce. A naturalized American citizen since 1897, Watkins was also active in civic matters, particularly after taking up residence in Marysville, a fledgling nearby community that he helped to establish.[29] In 1919 Watkins served as the first president of the village of Marysville, and thereafter chaired the committee that upgraded Maryville's municipal status to that of a city. Simultaneously, Watkins maintained his interest in baseball. He declined an offer to return as Indianapolis Indians manager in 1918,[30] but took keen interest in the local game. He was a financial backer of the Port Huron Saints of the Class-B Michigan-Ontario League, and served as club president in 1921-1922. In appreciation of his support, Saints home games and those of the local high school were played at a downtown Port Huron field named in Watkins' honor.

Watkins remained a leading citizen of his new home town, even at an advancing age. He served on the Marysville Board of Education for 10 years and was elected justice of the peace in November 1933. In early 1937 Watkins' health began to fail. Hospitalized for a month in Port Huron, he died there of diabetes complications on June 9, 1937, age 79. Following services at Grace Episcopal Church, Watkins was interred at Lakeside Cemetery in Port Huron. Without children, he was survived by wife Edna and sisters Lily Shilton and Ella Crisp.

In the ensuing years, Bill Watkins slowly faded from collective consciousness. Watkins Field was razed in the early 1940s and area residents who knew him personally steadily passed away. Decades later, however, the research of baseball historian Marc Okkonen brought the Watkins legacy back to local attention. And in October 2008, long deceased William H.T. Watkins was inducted into the Port Huron Sports Hall of Fame,[31] a modest but apt testimonial to a bygone but well-spent life.

SOURCES

The biographical details provided above are drawn primarily from material furnished the writer by Reference Librarian Barbara Kirk of the St. Clair (Michigan) County Library system and Local History Librarian Denise Kirk of the Brantford (Ontario) Public Library. Other sources included the Bill Watkins file at the Giamatti Research Center, National Baseball Hall of Fame and Museum, Cooperstown, New York; US Census data and other Watkins family info accessed via Ancestry.com; and certain of the newspaper articles cited in the endnotes. Stats have been taken from Baseball-Reference.

NOTES

1   Beginning with the 1951 first edition of the baseball encyclopedia of Turkin & Thompson to the present, modern reference works have erroneously listed our subject's birth name as William Henry Watkins. Efforts to correct Bill Watkins' biographical data were ongoing at the time this essay was revised. William Harton Thomas Watkins took his middle name from his grandmother Barbara Mary Jane Harton Watkins (1774-1847), an immigrant to Canada and the daughter of Anglo-Irishman Daniel Harton of County Offaly.

2   Bill's siblings were sisters Lily (Sarah Barbara Eliza, born 1855), Ella (Mary Ellen Louise, 1860), and Anne (1862). Youngest sister Lizzie (1865) did not survive infancy.

3   John L.H. Watkins promptly remarried, taking Ann Hoyle as his second wife in 1869. Why son Bill remained thereafter in the care of his grandparents is unknown.

4   Per the Watkins obituary published in the *Port Huron* (Michigan) *Times Herald,* June 10, 1937: 1.

5   Port Huron and nearby Michigan communities are separated from Ontario, Canada, by the St. Clair River.

6   Per "Death Strikes Out Veteran of Baseball," *Port Huron Times Herald,* June 10, 1937: 1-2.

7   Current authority such as Baseball-Reference and Retrosheet designate Watkins a righty batter, with his throwing arm listed as unknown. By the mid-1880s, however, left-handed second basemen had become a rarity.

8   The appraisal offered in *Sporting Life,* August 20, 1884: 4.

9   In obituaries and post-mortem remembrance it was claimed that the Shallix beaning caused Watkins' hair to turn white virtually overnight. See e.g., "Necrology," *The Sporting News,* June 17, 1937: 2; Edgar G. Brands, "Beanball Turned Watkins' Hair White," *The Sporting News,* July 8, 1937: 4. This piece of Watkins folklore, however, is belied by post-beaning photographs, all of which show the auburn-headed Watkins with darkish hair and mustache until he was well into middle age.

10   *Sporting News* founder Al Spink was convinced that Watkins had tried to break up the hometown Maroons, an offense that Watkins later compounded via an unintentional snub of Spink at a meeting of St. Louis club supporters. Spink retaliated with an uncomplimentary editorial. See *The Sporting News,* December 18, 1886: 2.

11   See *TSN* editorial blasts published December 11 and 18, 1886.

12   In reaction to the Briody and Weidman sanctions it was reported that "dissention is rife throughout the [Detroit] club, but Watkins does not have the guts to fine the more prominent malcontents," as per an unidentified July 21, 1887, news item contained in the Bill Watkins file at the Giamatti Research Center at the National Baseball Hall of Fame.

13   See "Glasscock and Watkins," *The Sporting News,* September 3, 1887: 1.

14   The Macon trip admits Watkins into that legion of claimants upon the title of initiator of baseball spring training in the South.

15   Game 14 in Chicago drew only 378 paying spectators.

16   As subsequently revealed in "The Detroit Row," *Chicago Tribune,* March 19, 1888: 3.

17   "Manager Watkins Amende [*sic*] Honorable," *Washington Post,* March 19, 1888: 1.

18   As revealed in "Now in New Hands," *St. Paul Globe,* June 28, 1890: 5.

19   On August 12, 1890, Watkins played an errorless right field but went 0-for-3 at the plate in an 8-1 loss to Lincoln. It was the first regular-season game played by the now 32-year-old since the 1884 season.

20   Over Brush's vigorous objection, the National League had liquidated this weak Indianapolis franchise in early 1890 as a preemptive measure in the coming battle with the newly-arrived Players' League. Brush, however, retained his seat on the NL owners' council and was promised the next available franchise which, in 1891, turned out to be Cincinnati.

21   See e.g., "Watkins Goes to Pittsburg," *Indianapolis Journal,* November 14, 1897: 9; "Sporting Gossip," *Sioux City* (Iowa) *Journal,* November 27, 1898: 2; "'Watty' Don't Buy," *Duluth* (Minnesota) *News-Tribune,* October 27, 1899: 2.

22   Watkins' minority partner in Indianapolis club ownership was local businessman Charles F. Ruschaupt, although sentiment lingered that the two men were no more than a front for the club's true owner, their friend John T. Brush. In time, however, the bona fides of the Watkins-Ruschaupt partnership became evident.

23   "New Baseball Factor," *Washington Post,* January 15, 1901: 8.

24   See *Sporting Life,* March 9 and 16, 1901. For more detail on Watkins' role in the aborted attempt to revive the American Association, see Bill Lamb, "Thrice Stillborn: Turn-of-the-Century Attempts to Revive the Once-Major League American Association," *Base Ball 11: New Research on the Early Game* (Jefferson, North Carolina: McFarland, 2019), 156-161.

25   The American Association played the 1902 season as an independent organization outside the provisions of the National Agreement. The AA was admitted to Organized Baseball the following year, and remained in continuous operation as a top-echelon minor league through the 1962 season. Watkins' partner in the new Indianapolis venture was again Charles F. Ruschaupt, the firm of Watkins & Ruschaupt being listed as "proprietors of the Indianapolis Base Ball Club" in Indianapolis city directories, 1901-1905.

26 More than a century later, baseball historians Bill Weiss and Marshall Wright rated the 1902 Indianapolis Indians 27th in their ranking of the top 100 teams in minor-league baseball history, at http://www.mib.com /history/top100. jsp?idx=27.

27 Baseball-Reference's inclusion of our Bill Watkins among the five managers of the 1911 Huntsville (Alabama) Westerns of the Class D Southeastern League is erroneous. Among other places, Watkins' retention of his post in Indianapolis during the 1911 season is attested by correspondence contained in the Garry Herrmann file at the Giamatti Research Center. Various 1911 letters to Herrmann bear the Watkins signature on stationery with the letterhead: "W.H. Watkins, President, Indianapolis Athletic Association," the corporate name of the Indianapolis Indians franchise.

28 Per "'Watty' Comes to Terms," *Indianapolis Star,* February 1914: 1.

29 According to Watkins' obituary in the *Port Huron Times Herald,* June 10, 1937: 1-2.

30 See "Refuses to Come Back," *Washington Post,* February 21, 1918: 8.

31 Per "Former Area Resident 'Very Worthy of Honor,'" *Port Huron Times Herald,* October 24, 2008: 11.

TIP O'NEILL:
A SEASON OF FIRSTS

By Dennis Thiessen

Tip O'Neill was inducted into Canada's Sports Hall of Fame in 1994. The opening sentence in the Hall's online tribute reads: "James Edward 'Tip' O'Neill was a sensational hitter who slugged his way to the top of the American baseball ranks during the 1880s."[1] O'Neill was the most valuable batsman on the St. Louis Browns,[2] champions of the American Association for four years in a row (1885–1888) and world champions in 1885 and 1886.[3] During the 1886 world championship, O'Neill was the leading batsman in the six-game series, hitting .400, with four extra-base hits (two home runs and two triples). O'Neill was at his best when he batted for average and power, a combination that was on full display in his record-breaking season of 1887.

Baseball historian David Nemec describes O'Neill's extraordinary batting achievements of 1887 as "perhaps the most dominant offensive season in history,"[4] a dominance that, in an earlier book, he defines in terms of leading in the most batting categories.[5] In this season of soaring achievements, O'Neill enthralled fans throughout the American Association with his multihit games, numerous hitting streaks, timely extra-base hits, and run-producing prowess.[6] In this season of firsts, O'Neill not only ranked first in most batting categories but also did so with marks that set major-league records.

The following three sections illustrate some of O'Neill's record-breaking performances in batting for average, batting for power, and batting for both average and power.

BATTING FOR AVERAGE

Tip O'Neill is best known for his batting championship in 1887, a season in which he hit .492. This percentage was the highest single-season batting average ever achieved in the American Association since its inaugural season in 1882, and better than any National League average since its inception in 1876. In subsequent years O'Neill's .492 mark appeared in most record books as the highest average in two lists, among those batters who were the single-season league leaders in batting average, and among those who hit .400 or higher.[7] From 1969 onward, however, most sources cite O'Neill's 1887 average as .435, which relegates his average to second-best on the all-time list of single-season batting champions, behind Hugh Duffy's 1894 record of .440.[8]

Between 1888 and 1968, record-keepers were uncertain about how best to treat the controversial

Two initiatives resulted in the revision of O'Neill's average and the loss of his standing as the batsman with the all-time single-season record for the highest batting average. In 1968 the Special Baseball Records Committee developed a code of rules governing record-keeping procedures, one of which stated that "bases on balls shall always be treated as neither a time at bat nor a hit for a batter."[11] Coinciding with this decision, Information Concepts Incorporated (ICI) completed the most thorough study ever conducted into the batting statistics of nineteenth-century players.[12] Following the decision of the Special Baseball Records Committee, ICI did not count walks as hits or times at bat. Accordingly, ICI recalculated O'Neill's average to .435[13] and in 1969 this revised average was reported in the "Big Mac."[14]

In 2001 O'Neill's average was part of another revision, this time based on the resuscitation of the walk-as-a-hit rule. Jerome Holtzman, Major League Baseball's official historian, turned back the clock with his declaration: "If a walk was a hit in 1887 it should stand as a hit forevermore."[15] Based on the statistics on hits, bases on balls, and times at bat determined by ICI in the late 1960s, O'Neill's average was adjusted to .485,[16] returning him to the top of the list with the best all-time single-season batting average. However, despite Holtzman's ruling, most record books and online databases, with the exception of *Total Baseball*,[17] continued to report batting records based on the normalized code introduced by the Special Baseball Records Committee, which for the 1887 season meant a walk would not be counted as a hit or a time at bat. Consequently, O'Neill's batting average continued to be listed in most sources as .435.

Mindful of this traditionalist-revisionist debate about O'Neill's changing 1887 batting average, the National Baseball Hall of Fame and Museum in Cooperstown, New York, displays a poster entitled, "Highest Batting Average in a Season Since 1876." It features a photo of Hugh

James E. O'Neill, Champion Batsman of the American Association. The 1888 *Reach Guide* was the first to publish a photograph, rather than a drawing or sketch, of the champion batsman in the American Association. (National Baseball Hall of Fame Library, Cooperstown, New York)

change made in one of the scoring rules for the 1887 season: a batter was assigned a hit and a time at bat for a base on balls.[9] Most record books added a note indicating that O'Neill's batting average occurred in a season in which bases on balls counted as hits. Others were more critical of O'Neill's record, and sought to discredit the season and any other record made in 1887.[10] Those who chose to honor the scoring rules of the day (traditionalists), albeit qualified with an asterisk, stood in tension with those who wanted to ensure that, to the greatest extent possible, the calculation of batting records in every season is based on the same scoring rules (revisionists). This debate came to a head in the late 1960s.

Duffy and his .440 average in bold print. In the bottom half of the poster, there is an 18-line statement that suggests how O'Neill can also be considered for the highest single-season batting average:

For record books that regard the National League's first year (1876) as the start of major league play, Boston's Hugh Duffy is generally cited for holding the mark for highest single-season batting average: .440 in 1894. But another player from baseball's early days has a legitimate claim to the title. In 1887, baseball implemented two rules which lasted just one season: a walk counted as both a base hit and at bat (today it counts for neither), and a strikeout occurred after *four* [italics in original], not three, strikes. At season's end, more than a dozen players posted batting averages above .400, with Tip O'Neill leading the way with a .485 mark. While one cannot retroactively "correct" for the advantage batters gained for the extra strike, most modern-day statisticians have accounted for the unusual walk rule. In so doing, O'Neill's mark has been retroactively dropped to .435.[18]

In sum, on at least two occasions, O'Neill's officially declared batting average was the all-time single-season record in the major leagues: in 1887 when Wheeler Wyckoff, the secretary and president of the American Association, confirmed that O'Neill was the batting champion of the Association with an average of .492, and again in 2001, when Jerome Holtzman endorsed his recalculated average of .485, adding in parentheses, "still the record."[19] In those sources that list the progression of records over the years, O'Neill's revisionist average of .435 appears as the single-season record in the major leagues between 1887 and 1893, with Duffy's .440 average as the record from 1894 onward.[20]

The following two sections describe some of O'Neill's power records and average-plus-power records, marks that are not explicitly entangled in this traditionalist-revisionist debate.

BATTING FOR POWER

O'Neill was a line-drive hitter who most times made solid contact, driving the ball with considerable force to all fields. Although he was taller and heavier than many of the major-league players in the 1880s,[21] Tip used a wagon-tongue bat that was smaller than those preferred by most other batsmen.[22] O'Neill seemed to appreciate the importance of bat speed, something he could more effectively control and quickly generate with a smaller bat. As the season unfolded, O'Neill was variously applauded for his power with such appellations as the "champion slugger"[23] or "the hardest hitter in the profession."[24]

In 1887 O'Neill led the American Association with 52 doubles, 19 triples, and 14 home runs. His total of 85 extra-base hits established a new single-season Association record for long hits,[25] which became the new major-league record as well. Hugh Duffy tied O'Neill, getting 85 long hits in 1894. In 1920 Babe Ruth's 99 long hits eclipsed their record. Nonetheless, O'Neill is the only player in major-league history ever to lead the league in a single season in all three extra-base-hit categories.

Across the season, two out of every five hits by O'Neill were doubles, triples, or home runs. Occasionally, he delighted fans with power surges, periods when he drove out long hits game after game with even greater frequency than usual. Such was the case between August 24 and September 5 when he set a record of 12 consecutive games with one or more extra-base hits. During this streak, O'Neill hit .596. Of his 34 hits, 21 were long hits: 14 doubles, 5 triples, and 2 home runs.[26] O'Neill scored or batted in 53 of the 135 runs scored by the Browns, who won 11 of the 12 games played during his extra-base-hit surge.

In 1927 Paul Waner broke O'Neill's mark when he recorded one or more extra-base hits in 14 consecutive games. Chipper Jones tied Waner's 14-game long-hit streak in 2006. Tip O'Neill and Rogers Hornsby (1928) are tied for the second-longest streak of extra-base hits.[27]

BATTING FOR BOTH AVERAGE AND POWER

The 12-game long-hit streak also illustrates O'Neill's capacity to bat for average and for power, a talent he demonstrated with comparable impact at other points in the season. For example, during a stretch of seven games as part of the Browns' early-season 15-game winning streak, O'Neill hit .727, with 14 of 24 hits going for extra bases: seven doubles, three triples, and four home runs. In this historic week, he also hit for the cycle twice, in a six-hit outburst in a game against Cleveland on April 30 and in a five-hit performance in a game against Louisville five games later.[28]

In a season-long milestone of batting for average and for power, O'Neill won the Triple Crown. To win this honor, Tip led the American Association in hitting safely (Batting Average), in driving the ball for distance (Home Runs), and in producing runs (Runs Batted In).[29] In addition to the three batting categories that constitute the Triple Crown, O'Neill headed the AA list in eight other categories, extending his dominance to 11 of the following 12 batting categories:[30]

H	S	D	T	HR	RBI
225	X	52	19	14	123
LH	TB	OB	SLG	OPS	BA
85	357	.490	.691	1.180	.435

H-Hits; S-Singles; D-Doubles; T-Triples; HR-Home Runs; RBI-Runs Batted In; LH-Long Hits; TB-Total Bases; OB-On-Base Percentage; SLG-Slugging Percentage; OPS-On-Base plus Slugging Percentage; BA-Batting Average; X-indicates that O'Neill did not lead the AA in singles

Though O'Neill faced pitchers under the same conditions and rules as all other major-league batsmen, he fared much better than his peers on almost every measure.[31] Of the 11 batting categories in which he led, O'Neill broke

the American Association record in 10 categories (all except triples). Nine of these stand as single-season records in the 10-year history of the Association.[32] Eight of O'Neill's 10 AA records both exceeded previous NL marks[33] and endured as major-league records for the era (1876-1892).[34] With most records in the major leagues, "records are made to be broken," the old adage goes. Seven of the single-season major-league records O'Neill established in 1887 were broken in the next era (1893-—1900) and one in 1920.[35] However, a more recent adage, namely, some "records will never be broken,"[36] also applies. O'Neill is the only batsman who, in a single season, not only led in the most batting categories but also set the most records in these categories.

In the 1876-1892 era, three other batsmen[37] had a season of firsts similar to that of O'Neill: in 1876, Ross Barnes led in 10 categories, in the NL only (all except Home Runs, Runs Batted In);[38] in 1883, Dan Brouthers was first ranked in nine categories (all except Singles, Doubles, Home Runs) in both the NL and the major leagues; and in 1884, Fred Dunlap finished at the top of eight categories (all except Singles, Doubles, Triples, Runs Batted In) in the Union Association, seven of which were also first-ranked in the major leagues.[39] In this era, O'Neill has the all-time single-season league record for leading in 11 batting categories while Brouthers holds the all-time single-season record for leading in nine batting categories in the major leagues. In the number of league-plus-major-league rankings, O'Neill's 19 firsts (11 in the AA plus 8 in the major leagues) edges Brouthers' 18 firsts (nine in the NL plus nine in the major leagues) in the total number of batting categories in which they respectively led.

On the number of records established in the 12 categories, O'Neill broke a total of 18 records, 10 in the AA (all except Singles, Triples) and eight in the major leagues (all except Singles, Triples, Home Runs, Runs Batted In), a sum that was well ahead of those achieved by Barnes, Dunlap, and Brouthers. Both Barnes and Dunlap were in the inaugural seasons of the NL and UA respectively, and thus, in the categories in which they led (10 for Barnes, 8 for Dunlap), they established the first league records. Dunlap also set four records in the major leagues for a total of 12 records in both the UA and major leagues. Brouthers set eight new marks in the same four categories in both the NL and in the major leagues.[40]

Tables 1 and 2 compare O'Neill's rankings and records to six batsmen[41] who, in subsequent eras (1893-2020), were single-season leaders in 10 or more categories.[42] Table 1 reveals that in 1901 Nap Lajoie tied O'Neill's record of leading the league in 11 batting categories. The last column also shows that Lajoie in 1901, Honus Wagner in 1908, and Ty Cobb in 1911 tied O'Neill's record of leading in the combined total of 19 batting categories.

As noted above, and also reflected in the final column of Table 2, O'Neill set single-season records in 18 of the 19 batting categories in which he led, 10 in the AA and eight in the major leagues. Nap Lajoie was in the initial season of the American League and, therefore, his leading marks became the first AL records in these 11 batting categories; none were major-league records. The only other batsmen to set records in the 10 batting categories in which they led were Cobb, with five records in the American League in 1911, and Rogers Hornsby, with four records in the National League in 1922. In this group of champion batsmen, O'Neill is the only one whose marks established both league and major-league records. In short, when it comes to breaking records, O'Neill is ahead of these elite hitters by a significant margin, both in the number of single-season records he broke in the major leagues, and in the total number of records he established in both the AA and the major leagues.

TABLE 1: 1893-2020
SINGLE-SEASON LEADERS IN 10 OR MORE BATTING CATEGORIES

Name LG-YR	H	S	D	T	HR	RBI	LH	TB	OB	SLG	OPS	BA	Total LG-M
O'Neill AA-1887	225 ML	X	52 ML	19 X	14 X	123 X	85 ML	357 ML	.490 ML	.691 ML	1.180 ML	.435 ML	19 11-8
Lajoie AL-1901	232 ML	156 X	48 ML	X	14 X	125 X	76 ML	350 ML	.463 ML	.643 ML	1.106 ML	.426 ML	19 11-8
Wagner NL-1908	201 ML	X	39 ML	19 X	X	109 ML	68 ML	308 ML	.415 ML	.542 ML	.957 ML	.354 ML	19 10-9
Cobb AL-1911	248 ML	168 ML	47 ML	24 X	X	127 ML	79 ML	367 ML	X	.620 ML	1.086 ML	.419 ML	19 10-9
Hornsby NL-1922	250 ML	X	46 X	X	42 ML	152 X	102 ML	450 ML	.459 X	.722 ML	1.181 ML	.401 X	16 10-6
Klein NL-1933	223 ML	X	44 X	X	28 X	120 X	79 X	365 X	.422 X	.602 X	1.025 X	.368 ML	12 10-2
Musial NL-1948	230 ML	X	46 ML	18 ML	X	131	103 ML	429 ML	.450 X	.702 ML	1.152 ML	.376 ML	18 10-8

TIP O'NEILL: RECORD-BREAKING BATSMAN

In this remarkable season at the plate, O'Neill had numerous record-breaking performances, which, along with his various extraordinary feats, defined the tapestry of his batting supremacy in 1887. Whether one accepts the .492 batting average officially recognized in 1887, his revised and widely acknowledged average of .435 in 1969, or his recalculated but largely ignored average of .485 in 2001, O'Neill either held the record for the highest single-season batting average for six years at .435 (since 1894, he is second on the all-time list) or still holds the all-time single-season record at .485 or .492. Most of his other records are not in dispute. For example, O'Neill's record for consecutive games with one or more long hits lasted 40 years. He is still the only player ever to lead in doubles, triples, and home runs in a single season.

Though not records as such, O'Neill's two cycles in a span of five games and his Triple Crown are both relatively uncommon and noteworthy feats.

As to the extent to which O'Neill had the "most dominant offensive season in history," to reiterate Nemec's claim, O'Neill compares favorably to the premier batsmen in both his era and in subsequent eras in the number of batting categories in which he led in the same season. O'Neill set the all-time single-season record for both his league and the major leagues, leading in 11 of 12 batting categories. Nap Lajoie tied his mark in 1901. What sets O'Neill apart from Hall of Famer Dan Brouthers,[43] Ross Barnes, and Fred Dunlap, his three closest competitors in the 1876-1892 era, and from the six Hall of Famers[44] in the eras after 1892 listed in Tables 1 and 2, is the aggregate number of single-season batting records O'Neill established in both the AA and the major leagues. O'Neill's total of 18 records (10 in the

TABLE 2: 1893-2020
SINGLE-SEASON RECORDS IN BATTING CATEGORIES

Name LG-YR	H	S	D	T	HR	RBI	LH	TB	OB	SLG	OPS	BA	Total LG-ML
O'Neill AA-1887	AA ML	X	AA ML	X	AA X	AA X	AA ML	AA ML	AA ML	AA ML	AA ML	AA ML	18 10-8
Lajoie AL-1901	AL X	AL X	AL X	X	AL X	AL X	AL X	AL X	AL X	AL X	AL X	AL X	11 11-0
Wagner NL-1908	X	X	X	X	X	X	X	X	X	X	X	X	0
Cobb AL-1911	AL X	AL X	X	X	X	AL X	AL X	AL	X	X	X	X	5 5-0
Hornsby NL-1922	X	X	X	X	NL X	X	NL X	NL X	X X	NL X	X	X	4 4-0
Klein NL-1933	X	X	X	X	X	X	X	X	X	X	X	X	0
Musial NL-1948	X	X	X	X	X	X	X	X	X	X	X	X	0

AA-American Association; AL-American League; NL-National League; LG-League; ML-major leagues.
NOTE: A single "X" in a cell indicates that the batsman did not lead (Table 1) or set a record (Table 2) in both the league and the major leagues. An "X" placed below a leading number or percentage (Table 1) or below a league abbreviation (Table 2) indicates that the batsman did not lead in the category (Table 1) or set a record (Table 2) in the major leagues. "ML" in a cell and placed below either a leading number or percentage (Table 1) or below a league abbreviation (Table 2) indicates that the batsman led in the category (Table 1) or set a record in the category (Table 2) in the major leagues.

AA plus eight in the major leagues) is unmatched by these batsmen. O'Neill was "first ever" in that he broke the existing records in all but one of the batting categories in which he was first ranked. In record-breaking feats, O'Neill is first among a small but distinguished group of batsmen, each of whom also had his own "season of firsts."

In honor of O'Neill's incredible 1887 season and outstanding career, the Canadian Baseball Hall of Fame and Museum created the James "Tip" O'Neill Award, which since 1984 is "presented annually to the Canadian player judged to have excelled in individual achievement and team contribution while adhering to baseball ideals."[45] The award is a fitting legacy for Tip O'Neill, the record-breaking batsman, whose standard of excellence and fair play on and off the field provides an exemplar for the many outstanding Canadian players who followed in his footsteps.

ACKNOWLEDGMENT

This article is based on research conducted for the author's book on Tip O'Neill, *Tip O'Neill and the St. Louis Browns of 1887* (Jefferson, North Carolina: McFarland, 2019). The title of this article is an adaptation of the title of Chapter 16, in the book.

JAMES O'NEIL
Champion Base Ball Batter

In 1888, W.S. Kimball & Co's cigarettes released the series "Champions of Games and Sports." The series featured four baseball players: catcher, pitcher, batter, and fielder. O'Neill was included in the collection to represent the "Champion Base Ball Batter." (Author's collection)

NOTES

1   Tip O'Neill is one of seven major-league players induced into Canada's Sports Hall of Fame. He is the first of two position players to receive this honor. Larry Walker, the second position player, was inducted in 2007. The other five major-league inductees are pitchers: Phil Marchildon (1976), Fergie Jenkins (1987), Ron Taylor (1993), John Hiller (1999), and Claude Raymond (2005). See "Honoured Members." Accessed on April 1, 2021 at https://sportshall.ca/hall-of-famers. Tip O'Neill was also one of three baseball players inducted into the first class of the Canadian Baseball Hall of Fame in 1983. The other two players were Phil Marchildon and George Selkirk. See "Inductees." Accessed April 1, 2021 at http://baseballhalloffame.ca/museum/awards.

2   O'Neill's major-league career spanned 10 years, seven with the St. Louis Browns (1884-1889, 1891), and one year each with the New York Gothams, NL (1883), the Chicago Pirates, Players' League (1890), and the Cincinnati Reds, NL (1892).

3   St. Louis tied the Chicago White Stockings (NL) for the world championship in 1885, each winning three games with one game ending in a draw. The Browns beat the same Chicago team in 1886, winning four games and losing two for the outright world championship.

4   David Nemec, ed., "O'Neill, James Edward 'Tip,'" in *Major League Baseball Profiles, 1871-1900. Volume 1.* (Lincoln: University of Nebraska Press, 2011), 589.

5   Nemec also described O'Neill as the "runaway leader in just about every batting department." David Nemec, in *The Beer and Whisky League: The Illustrated History of the American Association – Baseball's Renegade Major League* (Guilford, Connecticut: Lyons, 2004), 128.

6   In 1887 O'Neill played 124 games, missing 12 games due to injuries. He had 69 games with two or more hits, 34 games with three or more hits, 14 games with four or more hits, and four games with five or more hits. He had a 25-game hitting streak and a 22-game hitting streak (7 games at the end of the 1887 season and 15 games at the start of the 1888 season). He is one of only two players to get a hit in nine consecutive times at bat, twice in the same season. Of his 225 hits, 85 (or 38 percent) went for extra bases. In run production, O'Neill scored or drove in 60 runs that tied or put the Browns ahead, and 19 that proved to be the winning runs. O'Neill scored 167 runs, a major-league single-season record at the time; it currently ranks fourth all-time, tied with Lou Gehrig. For a more detailed account of O'Neill's batting accomplishments in 1887, see "Appendix B: Tip O'Neill – Single-Season Batting Records and Feats in 1887," in Thiessen, *Tip O'Neill and the St. Louis Browns of 1887*, 183-188.

7   *Sporting Life's Official Baseball Guide 1891* (Philadelphia: Sporting Life, 1891) and Hy Turkin and S.C. Thompson, *The Official Encyclopedia of Baseball, Jubilee Edition* (New York: A.S. Barnes and Company, 1951), 240, 532, 542, 552.

8   "Leaders: Single-Season Leaders & Records for Batting Averages." Accessed on April 11, 2021, from https://www.baseball-reference.com/leaders/batting_avg_season.shtml.

9   There was also controversy over a second rule change which required four strikes for a strikeout. The four-strike rule and the base-on-balls-as-a-hit rule were discontinued after one season.

10 Two of the publications that both denigrated the 1887 season for the two rule changes and challenged the credibility of O'Neill's record were: John Ward, "1887, the Black Sheep of Baseball Records," *Baseball Magazine* 15, 2, 1915: 67-74, and F.C. Lane, "One Batting Championship That Never Was Deserved," *Baseball Magazine*, 30, 6, 1923: 547-48, 575.

11 *The Baseball Encyclopedia: The Complete and Official Record of Major League Baseball* (Toronto: The Macmillan Company, 1969), 2328.

12 Baseball's records prior to 1920 were inconsistent, incomplete, or, in some cases, unavailable, often lost or destroyed as the American Association and other leagues folded. Information Concepts Incorporated (ICI) set out "to build a databank of major league baseball's existing statistics." *The Baseball Encyclopedia: The Complete and Official Record of Major League Baseball*, 5.

13 ICI reported the following batting statistics for O'Neill in 1887: At-Bats - 517; Runs - 167; Hits - 225; Doubles - 52; Triples - 19; Home Runs - 14; Bases on Balls - 50; Stolen Bases - 30; Batting Average - .435; Slugging Percentage -. 691 in *The Baseball Encyclopedia: The Complete and Official Record of Major League Baseball*, 1310. The ICI statistics are available through the National Baseball Hall of Fame Library. "American Association, I.C.I. Statistics, 1887: Batting and Fielding Record, O'Neill" (Cooperstown, New York: National Baseball Hall of Fame Library, Microfilmed, 2002).

14 "Big Mac" became the nickname of the following 2,348-page encyclopedia *The Baseball Encyclopedia: The Complete and Official Record of Major League Baseball*. For an account of ICI's research project and the development of *The Baseball Encyclopedia*, see "Big Mac," in Alan Schwartz, *The Numbers Game: Baseball's Lifelong Fascination with Statistics* (New York: Thomas Dunne Books, 2004), 92-109.

15 Jerome Holtzman, "An Important Change to the Official Record of Major League Baseball." Accessed on May 13, 2017, from https://ourgame.mlblogs.com/why-is-the-national-association-not-a-major-league-and-other-issues-7507e1683b66.

16 Based on the statistics generated by ICI, *The Baseball Encyclopedia: The Complete and Official Record of Major League Baseball* reported that O'Neill had 517 times at bat, 225 hits, and 50 bases on balls. Walks were no longer counted as hits or times at bat. O'Neill's batting average was revised to .435 (225 hits divided by 517 times at bat). Following Holtzman's declaration in 2001, O'Neill's 50 walks were again counted as hits and times at bat and included in the recalculation of his batting average to .485 (225 hits + 50 walks divided by 517 + 50 times at bat).

17 In *Total Baseball*, O'Neill's .485 batting average appears in the historical profile of "1887," the "Players Register," in second place on the "Batting Average" list in "The All-Time Leaders - Single Season" (Levi Meyerle is first with an average of .492 in 1871), and the leader in "Batting Average" in "The Annual Record - 1887 American Association." John Thorn, Pete Palmer, and Michael Gershman, *Total Baseball: The Ultimate Baseball Encyclopedia, Seventh Edition* (Kingston, New York: TOTAL SPORT Media Publishing, 2001), 551-52, 1066, 2065, 2326; and John Thorn, Phil Birnbaum, and Bill Deane, *Total Baseball: The Ultimate Baseball Encyclopedia, 8th Edition* (Toronto: SPORT CLASSIC Books, 2004), 38, 1512, 2438, 2459, 2485.

18 The author took a photograph of the poster during a visit to the National Baseball Hall of Fame and Museum in Cooperstown, New York, on July 22, 2011.

19 Jerome Holtzman, "An Important Change to the Official Record of Major League Baseball."

20 "Leaders: Progressive Leaders & Records for Batting Averages." Accessed on March 27, 2021, from https://www.baseball-reference.com/leaders/batting_avg_progress.shtml.

21 In 1887, O'Neill was 6-feet-1-inch tall and weighed 187 pounds.

22 O'Neill's bat probably weighed around 30 ounces, was 30-32 inches long and no more than 2¼ inches in diameter (below 2½ inches, the maximum allowed). A wagon tongue bat was made out of ash from the spokes or tongue of wagon wheels on horse-drawn carriages. See Stuart Miller, *Good Wood: The Story of the Baseball Bat* (Chicago: ACTA, 2011), 113.

23 "Bunched Hits," *St. Louis Sunday Sayings,* May 15, 1887: 8.

24 "Local Hits," *The Sporting News,* August 13, 1887: 5.

25 In the 1880s, the expression "long hits" was used to describe extra-base hits (doubles, triples, home runs). "The Long Hitters," *St. Louis Republican,* August 12, 1887: 6.

26 In six of the 12 contests, O'Neill slugged more than one long hit. For example, he had three doubles on August 24 and a double and two triples on August 30.

27 Lyle Spatz, ed., *The SABR Baseball List and Record Book: Baseball's Most Fascinating Records and Unusual Statistics* (New York: Scribner, 2007), 149.

28 A cycle is a single-game example of hitting for average and power. Four players have hit for the cycle three times: John Reilly (1883-2, 1890), Babe Herman (1931-2, 1933), Bob Meusel (1921, 1922, 1928), and Adrian Beltre (2008, 2012, 2015). In 1887 O'Neill tied Reilly for the most cycles in a career and for the fastest two cycles, both completing the feat in a five-game span. For a further discussion of O'Neill's cycles, see "Two Cycles" in Thiessen, *Tip O'Neill and the St. Louis Browns of 1887,* 75-78.

29 O'Neill is one of only 15 players to win the Triple Crown. Paul Hines (1878) and O'Neill (1887) are the only players who achieved this feat in the nineteenth century. For the full list of Triple Crown winners, see https://www.baseball-reference.com/awards/triple_crowns.shtml.

30 In the two tables in this section, I include those batting categories that explicitly and directly represent what happens when a player hits the ball, which, in the scoring rules of 1887, included the following five categories: Hits, Doubles, Triples, Home Runs, and Batting Average. "Scoring," *Reach's Official American Association Base Ball Guide 1887* (Reprinted St. Louis: Horton, 1989), 164. I added two categories that were frequently reported in newspapers in 1887: Single, the one hit that was not a required statistic in 1887, and Long Hits, which simply required the addition of the total number of doubles, triples, and home runs. The other five categories – Total Bases, Runs Batted In, On-Base Percentage, Slugging Percentage, and On-Base Percentage plus Slugging Percentage – each officially approved at different points in the twentieth century – were nonetheless statistics periodically suggested in newspapers and guides by various baseball commentators in the nineteenth century. The 12 batting categories provide a more comprehensive framework for understanding the many facets of how O'Neill combined hitting for average and for power. For batting rankings in the American Association in 1887 in each of the 12 categories, see "Leaders" (Yearly League column). Accessed April 11, 2021 at https://www.baseball-reference.com/leaders.

31 The following statistics are from the 1887 batting records compiled by Baseball Reference at https://www.baseball-reference.com. The table shows how O'Neill's first-ranked marks in 11 of the 12 categories (Tip was sixth in Singles) compare to the second-ranked marks in the AA and the first-ranked marks in the NL:

Batting Category	O'Neill-First Ranked	AA-2nd Ranked Mark-Name	NL-First Ranked Mark-Name
Hits	225	220 - Browning	203 - Thompson
Singles	140 - 6th	165 – Browning - 1st	162 - Ward
Doubles	52	43 - Lyons	36 - Brouthers
Triples	19	19 - 5 others	23 - Thompson
Home Runs	14	10 - Reilly	19 - O'Brien
Runs Batted In	123	118 - Browning	166 - Thompson
Long Hits	85	63 - Lyons	68 - Brouthers
Total Bases	357	299 - Browning	308 - Thompson
On-Base Percentage	.490	.464 - Browning	.426 - Brouthers
Slugging Percentage	.691	.547 - Caruthers	.565 - Thompson
On-Base + Slug	1.180	1.011 - Browning	.988 - Brouthers
Batting Average	.435	.402 - Browning	.372 - Thompson

32 O'Neill's all-time single-season records in the AA include the following: Hits, Doubles, Runs Batted In, Long Hits, Total Bases, On-Base Percentage, Slugging Percentage, On-Base plus Slugging Percentage, and Batting Average.

33 In 1887 O'Neill broke the major-league records in the following batting categories: Hits, Doubles, Long Hits, Total Bases, On-Base Percentage, Slugging Percentage, On-Base plus Slugging Percentage, and Batting Average. These records are also the all-time single-season records in the major leagues in this era (1876-1892).

34 In their introduction to a section on Lifetime and Single-Season Leaders in batting, fielding, and pitching categories, Gary Gillette and Pete Palmer explain the importance of recognizing the leading performances by era: "Some of the lists are divided by time period in order to more clearly highlight the standout performers of each era. Eight significant eras in baseball history have been defined for this purpose – each is distinguished by rule changes, by large changes in the number of leagues or teams, or by other important factors." "The Glory of Their Times: The Lifetime Leaders," in Gary Gillette and Pete Palmer, eds., *The ESPN Baseball Encyclopedia, Fifth Edition* (New York: Sterling, 2008), 1756.

35 The following table shows O'Neill's single-season major-league records in his era (1876-1892) for eight batting categories (first two columns) and, in the third column, the new record, when O'Neill's records were first broken, and by whom. The fourth column lists the current record, when the record was broken, and who holds the record:

Batting Category in which O'Neill Set Records in 1887	O'Neill's Record for Era (1876-92)	New Record (Year-Name)	Current Record (Year-Name)
Hits	225	237 (1894 - Hugh Duffy)	262 (2004 - Ichiro Suzuki)
Doubles	52	55 (1899 - Ed Delahanty)	67 (1931 - Earl Webb)
Long Hits	85	99 (1920 - Babe Ruth)	119 (1921 - Babe Ruth)
Total Bases	357	374 (1894 - Hugh Duffy)	457 (1921 - Babe Ruth)
On-Base	.490	.521 (1894 - Billy Hamilton)	.609 (2004 - Barry Bonds)
Slugging	.691	.696 (1894 - Sam Thompson)	.863 (2001 - Barry Bonds)
OPS	1.180	1.196 (1894 - Hugh Duffy)	1.422 (2004 - Barry Bonds)
Batting Average	.435	.440 (1894 - Hugh Duffy)	.440 (1894 - Hugh Duffy)

36 Numerous observers have compiled lists of records that they believe "will stand the test of time." For one example, see Matthew Cohen, "The Top 25 Sports Records That Will Never Be Broken," April, 2012. Accessed on April 11, 2021 at https://bleacherreport.com/articles/1151636-the-top-20-sports-records-that-will-never-be-broken.

37 Other batsmen in this era (1876-1892) who led in six or more batting categories in one season include: Deacon White (8 - 1877), Paul Hines (6 - 1878), Cap Anson (7 - 1881), Pete Browning (6 - 1885), Sam Thompson (6 - 1887), Jimmy Ryan (6 - 1888), and John Reilly (6 - 1888).

38 Barnes is not credited with any firsts in the major leagues because the NL was the only officially recognized major league in 1876.

39 There is no information available on Runs Batted In for UA batsmen.

40 With only one major league in 1876, Barnes is credited with only 10 records in the NL. Dunlap set major-league records in Hits, Total Bases, Slugging Percentage, and On-Base plus Slugging Percentage. Brouthers set both NL and major-league records in Hits, Runs Batted in, Long Hits, and Total Bases.

41 In Table 1, this article relies on baseball-reference.com for the batting statistics for O'Neill and the other six batsmen.

42 Two of the batters listed in Tables 1 and 2 also led in 10 batting categories in another season, Ty Cobb in 1917 and Rogers Hornsby in 1921. Those who led their respective leagues in nine categories: Nap Lajoie (1904), Cy Seymour (1905), Ty Cobb (1909), Heinie Zimmerman (1912), Rogers Hornsby (1920), Joe Medwick (1937), Stan Musial (1943, 1946), and Carl Yastrzemski (1967).

43 Dan Brouthers was inducted into the National Baseball Hall of Fame in 1945. Ross Barnes and Fred Dunlap are not in the Hall of Fame.

44 The six batsmen highlighted in Tables 1 and 2 were also inducted into the National Baseball Hall of Fame in the following years: Ty Cobb (1936), Honus Wagner (1936), Nap Lajoie (1937), Rogers Hornsby (1942), Stan Musial (1969), and Chuck Klein (1980).

45 Since its inception, Larry Walker has won the James "Tip" O'Neill award nine times, three times with the Montréal Expos, five times with the Colorado Rockies, and once while in the minor leagues. Joey Votto has won it seven times, each time with the Cincinnati Reds. Two others have won the award three times: Justin Morneau, twice with the Minnesota Twins and once with the Colorado Rockies, and Jason Bay, twice with the Pittsburgh Pirates and once with the Boston Red Sox. "James 'Tip' O'Neill Award," Canadian Baseball Hall of Fame and Museum. Accessed April 3, 2021 at http://baseballhalloffame.ca/museum/awards.

JOE PAGE

By Patrick Carpentier

Long before he died in 1947, Joseph Henry Page was regarded as the Father of Baseball in Canada. Not that he introduced the sport above the 49th Parallel. But he did more than anyone else to popularize it with Canadians, especially those in French-speaking Quebec. In a baseball career spanning 60 years, Page played for countless teams, organized countless leagues, and made countless connections in the baseball world, making him the quintessential Montréal baseball man.

In a 1936 *Sporting News* article, J.L. McGowan wrote that "Joe Page is a hard man to get to know, yet everybody knows him, which makes him something of an enigma."[1] Indeed, little is known about Joe Page's youth besides what is recounted in that article and a few others. Page liked to say that he was from Chicago, where he worked on the railroad, played baseball in his spare time, and was a batboy for Cap Anson's club in 1876. He told that he had played for a semipro team in Michigan, the Hiawathas, where he was a teammate of Tip O'Neill. He is supposed to have later played for Big Rapids in the Northern Michigan League. He then boasted of having been a catcher for Indianapolis of the National League, after which he settled in Montréal.

In reality, Joe Page was born in England on April 19, 1868, in the London suburb of Dalston. His father was a well-known con artist, his mother a well-known pickpocket.[2] The Pages began to feel the wheel of justice turn on them so they emigrated to the United States in 1877. The family settled in Chicago but moved often as the elder Page was always on the lookout for swindle opportunities. The family might have crossed the Pond but it had not turned over a new leaf. Harassed by the authorities, they fled to Boston in 1880. They were back in Chicago by 1884. After years of criminal activities in several states, Page's father was convicted of fraud in Chicago in late 1888. The Page family had left the Windy City and had settled in the Detroit-Windsor area some time before the proceedings. From there, they made their way to Montréal after a heavily covered stabbing incident in February of 1889.[3]

It was during his time in Michigan that young Joe Page's baseball career took off. He did play for the Big Rapids club but not in 1887 as he claimed. His assertion of having played with Tip O'Neill in Michigan in the early 1880s is unfounded, as O'Neill had already reached the majors by that time and Page was barely a teenager. Page being a catcher on the roster of the Indianapolis franchise during its brief stint in the National League is also in serious doubt. Batboy for Cap Anson in 1876? Page and his family were still in England at the time. One thing that is certain is that Page became involved in baseball as soon as he set foot in Montréal in 1889. He played all season for the famed Clipper Base Ball Club, one of the oldest and most successful amateur baseball teams in Montréal.[4]

The following three years would define Page for his entire lifetime. On the business side of things, early in the summer of 1890 Page became the owner of the Turf Exchange, a betting saloon on Victoria Square in Montréal . This move was a natural one; he was now well acquainted with the Montréal sporting scene and had met several of its most important actors. The business allowed him to indulge in his love of baseball without depending exclusively on it to make ends meet.

Joe Page also saw a major change in his personal life. He had been raised in the Church of England, but he soon converted to Catholicism in order to tie the knot with Mary O'Brien, a Montréaler of Irish descent. The wedding took place at St. Patrick's Basilica in downtown Montréal on September 23, 1890. Together they had 10 children but only four survived the couple. The family lived for more than 60 years in the Ste-Cunegonde district of Montréal (now known as Little Burgundy), where many baseball players also lived and played.

The 1890 season also saw Page embark on a significant baseball endeavor. Several sportsmen of the city and many of its best players banded together to form the Montréal Baseball Club, the first overtly professional team in Montréal. Baseball in Montréal had remained amateur since its introduction into the city in 1869, and fans had clamored for professional baseball for a long time.[5] Although Joe Page was not one of the founders of the club, nor one of its directors, his standing was clear. He coached the other players during practice and in early May had a notice published

A 22-year-old Joe Page in the uniform of the Montréal Baseball Club, the first overtly professional team in Montréal. The photo, taken in 1890, was used by Page as a carte de visite that he signed for acquaintances well into his 70s. (Author's collection)

in the *Boston Globe* announcing the creation of the club and its willingness to play against established professional clubs from New England. The notice was clear: Those interested had to reply to him directly.[6] In all likelihood, the founding of the club and Page's marketing in the United States helped attract the attention of baseball magnates in the United States. Later that summer, two International League teams, first Buffalo in June then Hamilton in July, moved to Montréal, although briefly and quite unsuccessfully. It was nonetheless Montréal's first real introduction to Organized Baseball.

The last of Joe Page's life-defining moments came on June 8, 1891, when Montréal liquor commissioners decided not to renew the license of Page's betting saloon. His father, back at his old tricks, used the saloon to find his new fraud victims. The authorities took notice and acted accordingly. Joe Page soon found employment with the Canadian Pacific Railway in 1892. He first worked as a brakeman in the small town of Farnham, about 40 miles southeast of Montréal. He was soon promoted to baggageman at the local station. Farnham had a semipro team that played games against Quebec, Vermont, and upstate New York teams. Page immediately joined the Farnham nine. Within a year, he had become its manager. He remained on and off with the Farnham club until 1897, when he moved back to Montréal. It is to be noted that the revocation of his liquor license was Page's only major run-in with the law. His father, on the other hand, was in and out of Montréal jails for years.

For the 1895 season, Page earned a spot on the newly organized National club of Montréal, which played in the Eastern International League with Plattsburgh, New York, and St. Albans, Vermont. The National was the strongest and most prestigious French Canadian baseball team of the time, and Page was its best player and one of the league's offensive leaders. He played mostly second base, his natural position since his first days in Montréal. That year Page played against Cy Seymour of Plattsburgh and Ed Doheny of St. Albans. Both men reached the majors months later. The following year, Page returned to Farnham as a baseball player and helped the local club join the league in an expansion that also included Hull and Saint-Hyacinthe in Quebec, as well as Malone in upstate New York. Again, Page played against soon-to-be major leaguers: Louis Sockalexis, John Pappalau, and Doc Powers.

His growing influence in Montréal baseball circles now undeniable, Page was instrumental in bringing W.H. Rowe to Montréal in March of 1897. Rowe was well known throughout New England, having managed, among others, Pawtucket of the New England League. He, together with Page, immediately set out to gather local and American players and formed a new Montréal Baseball Club that would play against teams from Quebec and New England.[7] They had, however, set their eyes on a bigger prize. Several Eastern League clubs were struggling financially. It became the two partners' goal to bring one of these clubs to Montréal. Their big break came in July when the Rochester entry lost its ballpark to fire. The two men successfully negotiated a transfer to Montréal. And so, Joe Page helped bring the first incarnation of the Royals to Montréal. This episode proved to be classic Joe Page. Without having any money of his own, he was able find an investor who would bring money to the table to bring one of his projects to fruition.

In the fall of 1897 Joe Page was also busy founding the Montréal Baseball League, which included the best English-speaking amateur teams from Montréal.[8] Page's French-speaking competitors responded by establishing a new league of their own for 1898, the Quebec Provincial League, whose 1940s iteration would become famous in North American minor-league circles. Page's new league wasn't as successful as he had hoped, so he joined the Provincial League and played for several of its semipro clubs between 1898 and 1903.

He played for Saint-Jean in 1899, went back to manage Farnham in 1900 and spent the entire 1901 season umpiring home games for the Royals in the Eastern League. He reconnected with the Provincial League in 1902 with a transfer to the Delorimier club of Montréal. As Page had undergone eye surgery during the winter, everyone thought he would no longer be able to play or manage. So it was a surprise when he ended up with Delorimier. Montréal's French-language daily *La Presse* reported that the Provincial League magnates, once so certain that Page would be out of commission for the year, would now have to deal again "with this cunning man and contend with the new team he just organized."[9]

Page's reputation in the Montréal baseball community was forever set. He was named secretary of the Provincial League in 1903 and the same year started a new club, the Shamrocks, which was admitted into the league. The circuit collapsed before the 1904 season and Page immediately helped create a new semipro loop to replace it, the Eastern Canada League. He was named its secretary while the original Tip O'Neill, who had since moved to Montréal and whose brother had become vice president of the Royals, was named its president.[10] Seizing on a brand-new opportunity, Page tried in 1906 to place a Montréal club in the Northern New York League.[11] When this failed, he founded a new league of his own, the Canadian League, which had semipro teams as far east as Trois-Rivières and Quebec City.[12] Until then, most baseball leagues in the province had their heart in Montréal, with other clubs operating within a short distance from the city. Page's new league was the first to have its clubs spread so far apart and, most importantly, was first to capitalize on the Quebec City market.

The reason why is simple. Joe Page was first and foremost a Canadian Pacific Railway employee, and he wanted to attract new patrons for the railroad's train lines. The Canadian League experience proved a disaster, as travel expenses encroached on club profits. His league folded in 1908 after trying to place a franchise in Montréal. It would not be the last time Page would use baseball to promote the activities of his employer. He had received a promotion in 1902 and had been transferred to the Montréal-St. John, New Brunswick, line as a train baggageman. From then on, he spent less time on the diamond as a player or manager and more as an organizer and promoter. His place of residence was still Montréal but he traveled frequently to New Brunswick. And he was getting older. He was 38 when he last played regularly for the Quebec entry in the Canadian League in 1906.

In 1909 a new league came to life, the Montréal City League. Organized with the help of Page, this semipro league comprised the best teams in the city. Page was at one point its president and umpired league games until the middle of the 1920s. The league was the best and most stable loop in the province for some 20 years, with established local baseball stars. Several of these players even ended up on the roster of minor-league teams, including Oscar Major, who would later play for the Royals and become a Quebec-based scout for the Dodgers. At the same time, Page umpired games for a rival semipro circuit located in the East End of Montréal, the Independent League.

Page took no time to mingle with the baseball community in New Brunswick after his transfer to St. John. By 1905, he was already working to create a league.[13] His project came to fruition in 1911 when he founded the New Brunswick-Maine League with six teams scattered across the province, which of course increased traffic for the CPR. In 1913 the league joined Organized Baseball as a Class-D circuit. From the beginning, the league made good use of established players such as George Winter, pitcher for the Boston American League club between 1901 and 1908, and Bob Ganley, formerly with Washington. Several players in the league would go on to have minor-league careers of their own as well. Some even reached the majors, like Merwin Jacobson and Casey Hageman.[14] When the league folded after the 1913 season, Page attempted to form a new league with clubs in New Brunswick and Nova Scotia, but failed.[15] He also tried to place the St. John club in the New England League for 1915.[16] This also failed.

Page's interests shifted somewhat after his league ceased operation in 1913. His devotion to the CPR slowly began to take more of his time. Always with an eye toward increasing traffic for the railroad, Page started promoting hunting and fishing expeditions in New Brunswick and Nova Scotia, most notably in the pages of *Sporting Life*, for which he had been a Montréal-based correspondent since 1897. In a December 1916 promotional piece, he explained that "in the Summer season, the province of New Brunswick is a happy land, where the sunny hours speed away on the feet of delightful dreams" and reminded readers that the Algonquin Hotel, owned by the CPR, was perfect for the outdoor game player.[17] He was no doubt influenced by George Ham, a former Canadian journalist who was head of the CPR press bureau from 1891 until 1926. Ham was a marketing man himself who promoted the CPR and its use for tourism throughout North America and the world. He was first to recognize the tourism potential of St. Joseph's Oratory in Montréal, and wrote the first biography of its founder, Brother André, who was canonized by the Catholic Church in 2010.

Page had the full support of the railroad in these enterprises as he set out to create new baseball clubs and to promote tourism destinations to sportsmen, making sure that they used the CPR for their travels. For his efforts, Page was rewarded with a promotion in 1922. He was named passenger traffic sports representative, a job created exclusively for him by George Ham. In that capacity, he guided each year several hunting and fishing expeditions that took sports reporters from major US newspapers to the Maritime Provinces and Quebec.

In the fall of 1914, Joe Page was among a group of investors who came close to buying the Royals from longtime owners Sam Lichtenhein and his two partners. The Federal League had made life difficult for the Montréal franchise and its owners decided it was time to quit, especially since their ballpark had burned to the ground that summer and the rebuilding had put them in the red. In the end, the deal fell through and Lichtenhein ended up buying out his two partners. Page later said that his group had offered $35,000 but that the Royals ownership held firmly for $60,000. It was also revealed that Lichtenhein and Page were not best of friends, which might have hindered the deal.[18]

In 1922 Page founded the Eastern Canada League and orchestrated its entrance into Organized Baseball as a Class-B minor league.[19] The league changed its name two years later to the Quebec-Ontario-Vermont League when it welcomed two clubs from Vermont into its ranks. More than anything else, the league was a vehicle for Page's scouting activities. He had been a scout for the Chicago White Sox since at least 1914, and he used his league to gather and develop players for Charles Comiskey. A half-dozen players were signed by the White Sox, but all had undistinguished minor-league careers. Bob Lawrence and Augie Swentor reached the majors but played only one game. Plagued by financial woes and player and fan rowdiness, the league folded after the 1924 season.

Joe Page was always a clever promoter. He was instrumental in arranging the visit of the Chicago White Sox and New York Giants to Montréal and Quebec City in 1924, the first leg of their grand tour of Europe after the World Series. Both teams used the CPR for their travels and sailed from Quebec City to Liverpool on the SS Montroyal of the Canadian Pacific Steamship Line.[20] Two years later, Page was the mastermind of one of Montréal's most famous sporting events as Babe Ruth traveled to the city to play in an exhibition game. More than 3,000 people filled small Guybourg Grounds in the Longue-Pointe district of Montréal to see the Bambino hit no fewer than 36 batting-practice balls into the St. Lawrence River.[21] In 1934 Page again contracted with Ruth and other all-stars as they started their tour of Japan. He helped organize transport for the major-league players. They ended up traveling to the Land of the Rising Sun on the Canadian Pacific's fastest ocean liner, the RMS Empress of Japan. Page was on hand in Vancouver to send the All Americans off.[22]

Page also promoted other sports. As early as 1919, he had attempted to bring the big Dempsey-Willard fight to Montréal, which would have brought heavy traffic to the Canadian Pacific Railway. It went to Toledo instead. In 1923 Page served as an interpreter for a series of bouts held in the Province of Quebec between Jack Johnson and Senegalese fighter Battling Siki. In October 1925 Page was selected as delegate of the New Brunswick Skating Association, and spearheaded the organization's successful bid to host the 1926 World Speedskating Meet in St. John.[23] By the 1930s, Page was into horse racing and acted as a patrol judge at a number of racetracks, most notably at King's Park near Montréal.

He got involved in hockey as well. In 1922 he was one of the directors of the new amateur Quebec Hockey League. Four years later, he helped Quebec City win an entry in the Canadian-American Hockey League. The league later rebranded itself and survives as the American League. Then, in 1926, Page was hired as a scout for the Pittsburgh Pirates of the National Hockey League. The team's coach was fellow Montréaler Odie Cleghorn, who had become acquainted with Page in the early 1910s when Cleghorn played for the Star baseball club of Montréal with his brother Sprague and future Montréal Canadiens coach Cecil Hart. Page also became adviser to team owner James Callahan. Page claimed to have sold Madison Square Garden manager John Hammond on hockey when Hammond was looking for new events to increase the arena's revenues. Hammond was seduced and soon declared after a meeting with Page that "Madison Square Garden will go in for hockey."[24] The New York Americans began play at the Garden on December 15, 1925. Legend or not, Page was sometimes regarded after that as the "Founder of Hockey in the United States."

One of Page's last major and long-lasting accomplishments in baseball was his tireless work to bring high-level professional baseball back to Montréal. In 1923 he was involved in negotiations to transfer the Syracuse Stars of the International League to the city. Branch Rickey's St. Louis Cardinals would have bought the Stars and placed them in Montréal. The deal fell through when no suitable grounds could be secured.[25] Then, in early 1926, Page tried unsuccessfully to secure for a local syndicate the placement of a New England League franchise in Montréal.[26] In November of the same year, Page raised the possibility that Reading of the International League could be cut from the league and replaced by a Montréal club.[27] Again, the fact that Montréal lacked a suitable ballpark came under scrutiny in both instances. Page had two sites in mind for a new ballpark but no money with which to build it.

Undeterred and having learned from recent experiences, Page came up with a new plan in 1927. He first sought potential local investors who were able to not only buy a team, but, most importantly, also able to build a ballpark. Montréal businessman Ernest Savard and his partners were these men. Then, when he learned that George Stallings was looking for potential investors to acquire the Jersey City franchise with the intent of moving it, Page lost no time. He introduced Stallings to his group of Montréal investors and the deal was signed soon after. The transfer was approved. Construction on the ballpark began on the site of a former Provincial League stadium. The Montréal Royals began play on April 18, 1928, in Reading.[28] For the fourth time in almost 40 years, Joe Page was responsible for bringing the International League to Montréal. As usual, Page brought no money to the table, but rather served as matchmaker. He remained close to Royals management until his death.

He later arranged a tour of Western Canada by the Montréal Royals and the Toronto Maple Leafs in September of 1932.[29] Page was also successful in having Montréal selected as host of the National Association convention for 1930 and again in 1936. Both times he entertained baseball writers at resorts in the Laurentian Mountains of Quebec. Page claimed that he had attended every National Association convention since 1901.

Joe Page in 1934 in his capacity as a CPR sports representative. The image was used by Page as a personal introduction to his sports ventures, and given freely to friends and acquaintances. (Author's collection)

Joe Page retired from the Canadian Pacific Railway on July 1, 1937.[30] Although he was best remembered for his sporting activities, Page also left his mark as an innovative railroad employee. He was the holder of several Canadian patents pertaining to railroad operations. These included an improved luggage rack and an improved braking mechanism, among others. Many of these inventions were still in use at the time of his death.

After retiring, Page was less active as a promoter. He attended almost every Royals home game in his reserved box seat. He became the elder statesman of Montréal baseball and a reference for the younger generation of newspapermen. He was quoted often in Montréal, Canadian, and US

newspapers. In the media, he gave advice to managers, analyzed rookies and established players alike, and reminisced about the good old days. Of course, Page was no stranger to the journalistic world. Besides being a correspondent for *Sporting Life*, he was also the editor of the Canadian edition of the *Spalding Guide* from 1910 to the early 1920s. He was sporting editor of the *Montréal Evening News* in the late 1910s and wrote articles for several Montréal and US newspapers during his career. For his journalistic work, he was named an honorary member of the Baseball Writers Association of America. He attended the BBWAA's annual ball from its inception until his death.

Joe Page left a final mark on Quebec and Maritime baseball when he served as National Association liaison in the Quebec Provincial League's effort to join Organized Baseball after several years as an independent, and at times outlaw, league. With his help, the league achieved Class-B classification for the 1940 season.[31] The league collapsed after that season and Page was hired to represent the Quebec and Trois-Rivières franchises in their successful bid to join the Canadian-American League. Both teams would remain in that league through the 1950 season, Quebec winning two pennants and Trois-Rivières one.[32] He had served in a similar capacity in early 1937 when he was asked by the National Association to evaluate the Cape Breton Colliery League's request to join Organized Baseball.[33]

Page's connection to Organized Baseball never faded. His personal friends included players and executives. Commissioner Kenesaw M. Landis, Ban Johnson, and Connie Mack were all acquaintances of his. Page was especially proud of his friendship with Chicago White Sox owner Charles Comiskey, for whom he served as a guide when they ventured together on fishing and hunting trips in Eastern Canada. He knew just about every baseball columnist in North America. And it was common knowledge that he had attended every World Series since 1903. There he could take the pulse of the baseball world and promote either his baseball ventures or the Canadian Pacific Railway. His fall classic attendance record became his claim to fame in the twilight of his life.

Joe Page died in Montréal on April 3, 1947, from complications related to a stroke he had suffered while attending the 1946 World Series.[34] His funeral at St. Patrick's Basilica in downtown Montréal was covered by the press from Montréal and abroad. He was laid to rest in Montréal's Notre-Dame-des-Neiges Cemetery. Hundreds of people, including representatives from the Canadian Pacific Railway, the Montréal Royals, Organized Baseball, and the BBWAA attended. All were there to pay their homage to the man who for more than 60 years seemed to be ever-present within the baseball scene.

NOTES

1   J.L. McGowan, "Joe Page, 'The Man Everybody Knows,' Has Served Nearly 50 Years as Game's No. 1 Booster in Canada," *The Sporting News*, November 26, 1936: 5.

2   "Page Found Guilty," *Montréal Gazette*, June 9, 1892: 2; "The Woman Jackson Must Then be Produced or the Bail Will be Forfeited," *Detroit Free Press*, February 13, 1889: 3.

3   "A Stabbing Affray," *Detroit Free Press*, February 10, 1889: 23.

4   "Clippers Want Opponents," *Montréal Gazette*, June 13, 1889: 8.

5   "A Montréal Nine," *Montréal Gazette*, April 19, 1890: 5.

6   "Canada Taking it Up," *Boston Globe*, May 4, 1890: 8.

7   "Preparing for the Season," *Montréal Gazette*, March 13, 1897: 5.

8   "The Name of the New Baseball Association," *Montréal Gazette*, November 5, 1897: 5.

9   "Joe Page Sera Gérant du Club Delorimier," *La Presse*, April 28, 1902: 3.

10 "Big Name, Little League," *Sporting Life*, March 12, 1904: 5.

11 John B. Taylor, "Independent Northern," *Sporting Life*, March 31, 1906: 15.

12 "Canadian Baseball League," *Montréal Gazette*, April 2, 1906: 4.

13 "For a Provincial League," *St. John Daily Sun*, April 21, 1905: 8.

14 Colin D. Howell, *Northern Sandlots* (Toronto: University of Toronto Press, 1995), 140-145.

15 Joe Page, "A Provincial League," *Sporting Life*, April 11, 1914: 10.

16 "Baseball Chatter," *Meriden* (Connecticut) *Morning Record*, March 13, 1914: 3.

17 Joe Page, "Big Game in New Brunswick," *Sporting Life*, December 23, 1916: 15.

18 Frederick G. Lieb, "Joe Page, Mr. Baseball of Dominion, Dies at 79," *The Sporting News*, April 16, 1947: 27.

19 "Four Clubs Join Baseball League," *Montréal Gazette*, April 3, 1922: 18.

20 "Baseball Players Arrive Tomorrow," *Montréal Gazette*, October 11, 1924: 18.

21 "La Lutte Cesse Faute de Balles," *La Presse*, October 18, 1926: 20.

22 Frederick G. Lieb, "All Japan Ready to Hail Ruth and his Team of Stars," *The Sporting News*, October 18, 1934: 3.

23 "Delegates Nominated," *Montréal Gazette*, October 31, 1925: 18.

24 Frank G. Menke, "Hockey Enthusiast's Idea Tapped Sport Gold Mine," *Carbondale* (Illinois) *Daily Free Press*, December 18, 1929: 6.

25 "Le Marché Serait Conclu," *Le Devoir*, November 9, 1923: 7.

26 "Pro Ball Locally Is Again Mooted," *Montréal Gazette*, February 8, 1926: 13.

27 Hugh Bradley, "Montréal Likely to Supplant Keys in Toole's Circuit," *New York Evening Post*, November 5, 1926: 11.

28 "La Renaissance du Baseball Professionnel à Montréal," *La Patrie*, April 28, 1928: 16.

29 "Royals, Leafs En Route," *Montréal Gazette*, September 22, 1932: 16.

30 "Joe Page Leaving CPR Post July 1st," *Montréal Gazette*, June 22, 1937: 16.

31 Joe Page, "Provincial Loop Shaping Up; Pilots for Five Clubs Named," *The Sporting News*, April 4, 1940: 7.

32 David Pietrusza, *Baseball's Canadian-American League* (Jefferson, North Carolina: McFarland, 2005), 45-47.

33 Chauncey MacQuarrie, "Maritime Loop Turns to O.B. for Salvation," *The Sporting News*, February 11, 1937: 5.

34 "Joe Page Dies in Montréal After a Lengthy Illness," *Montréal Gazette*, April 5, 1947: 16.

MIXED OUTCOMES:
CANADA'S BLACK BASEBALL LEGACY

By William Humber

The London, Ontario, baseball tournament held toward the end of August 1869 featured a special category reserved for "colored" teams from Canada and the United States. Two years after the country's Confederation in 1867, Canadians were still held in high regard for having opened their borders to freed slaves in the pre-Civil War era while still a British colony. Canadian baseball organizers of the tournament might now be seen as attempting in their own clumsy way to find an avenue of entrance for the Black community into mainstream everyday life. It is also possible they were respecting, and possibly even communicating with, London's Black citizens about an opportunity for their own distinct baseball competition, at which they could demonstrate an emerging participation in the game. Most likely, however, the organizers were conforming to the evolving American policy of baseball apartheid. The latter unfortunately appears to be the historic verdict despite limited examples revealing a more open-minded intention.

Potential teams from south of the border could have been made up of either recently emancipated slaves, or free Northern Blacks who had taken up the game. Their Canadian opponents could have been those who had fled into Canada before or during the early stages of the American Civil War. Within Canada, however, there are no known documented examples of escaping Black Americans playing games such as baseball in Canada either before or during the Civil War. The examples from London in 1869, however, argue forcefully that such was likely the case shortly afterward. Other evidence suggests as well that such play was far more extensive within other Black communities throughout Ontario than has previously been known.

Too often the only news concerning London's small Black population in the local *Free Press* was in the legal matters column,[1] such as the case of an elderly Black man who sought redress against juveniles who regularly tormented him. Another sporting item was reported in which "A young colored lad, named William Williams, aged 16, who was employed by a Mr. Benson, as a jockey, at the late London races, skedadaled [*sic*] from here with a racing jacket and cap... ." He was tracked down in Toronto and returned to London for a court hearing,[2] but Mr. Bilton (not Benson as reported the day before), stated that, "from circumstances which since transpired, he did not think the boy meant to be dishonest, and desired his acquittal. His Worship, after giving him some advice, dismissed him." Nor was this the only place where indignities or unresolved issues were witnessed. The *London Free Press*[3] described the scene in a local tavern when the member of a party of laborers in Westminster was challenged because of his bronzed complexion, "and this the floor managers looked upon as a fatal objection to his admission, as they made it a rule not to admit to social relationship persons of undecided color." Nor could the small Black population in London have been unaware of the popular London Amateur Minstrel shows as advertised in the *Free Press*.[4] These shows mocked North America's African-originated population.

There were small successes, however, most often in the privacy of the community's social calendar. One such event was the annual celebration of Emancipation Day on August 1, dating back to 1834 with the passing of the Slavery Abolition Act the year before, ending slavery in the British Empire and accordingly also in Canada. The *Free Press*[5] noted that with the first of August falling on a Sunday, "the event was celebrated yesterday [Monday, August 2] by a grand social gathering at Salter's Grove, Governor's Road. Speeches appropriate to the day were made, and a varied programme of amusements provided. A 'base ball' match formed part." The year before, the *Free Press*[6] had spoiled its generally positive reporting on London's Black community by mocking an evening soirée attracting the *bon ton* of colored life, for which "not one dark spot appeared on the harmonious surface of the proceedings." The paper's decorum improved in 1869.

The breadth of baseball's reach within Black communities in Ontario was described in a list of possible entries for the upcoming tournament in the Special Class (Colored) category.[7] The "Goodwills" of London were to be potentially joined by teams from Hamilton, St. Catharines, and Suspension Bridge. The latter likely referred to the area around the Niagara Falls Suspension Bridge, which stood from 1855 to 1897. It was described as the world's first working railway suspension bridge, and connected the Canadian and American sides of the Niagara River. The tournament's American entrant, the Rialtos of Detroit, was described by a Detroit paper as one of the 'negro base ball clubs of Detroit" who, the paper lamely said, "can show the Londoners some big feets."[8] A day later the paper reported, "The colored base ball club have succeeded in whitewashing the interior of the Detroit & Milwaukee Depot," whatever that might have meant!

Surprisingly, London's best known Black team, the Lincoln Nine, did not register for the tournament. In the preceding weeks the London paper had reported, "The Eagle Base Ball Club of this city played the Lincoln (colored) Club on Wednesday, on the Cricket Square, and beat them by a score of 59 to 26."[9] A few days later the London paper said again, "A return match between the 'Wide Awakes' and Colored Club, yesterday, was won by the former, by 26 to 10 runs."[10] While the latter account did not name the Lincoln Nine, they were the likely team in these games against rival White London squads.

That the Lincoln Nine would appear in an unrelated but notable reference speaks to the team's well-known character. The *Free Press* had reported a case of larceny against a Richard Crystler (described as colored) for taking two horse blankets from his employer.[11] Three days later the accused, now called Dick Chrystler, received a one-month jail sentence. The paper described him as "the champion fly-catcher, though not one of the Lincoln Nine. ..."[12] In the same edition of the paper it was noted that "[a] soiree of the colored persuasion was held last night at the Mechanics' Institute, in aid of the Lincoln base ball club." It is surprising, therefore, that the Nine chose not to participate in the Special Class at the London Base Ball Tournament. Quite possibly they objected to the need to be in a separate category. After all, they had played all-White teams before. Why not continue to do so in the London event? It appears to be a sad example of Londoners demonstrating a willingness to follow American practice in treating all-Black teams as ones they might compete against in one-off barnstorming games but not as members of their leagues, or equal participants in their tournaments, or as players integrated within their mainstream squads.

In reporting the game between the Rialto (colored) club of Detroit and the Goodwills (colored) of London, the paper described it as having a "novel character," and drawing a large attendance. In fairness this might have been a positive way of describing something not seen before: Black players on the baseball diamond. The report said, "From the opening of the match until the close, it was quite evident that the 'Rialtos' were the superior players, and the manner in which they defeated their rivals elicited the hearty applause of the spectators. The nine of the Londoners did not seem to understand the game sufficiently, and made but a poor show against their brethren. Their 'muffing' was of a first-class order."[13] Such a description had been applied to other teams of relatively new players, regardless of racial background, so it was not uniquely condescending. Rain cut short the game in the sixth inning with Detroit apparently ahead 85-20. A few days later, however, a correction was forwarded to the paper: "The first figures [i.e. those for the Rialtos of Detroit] should have read '33,' a very wide difference. The Goodwills are newly organized, and have not had much practice; yet they made a very good stand against their opponents, who have played in company for several years."[14]

Regrettably, no box score was included, and so the names of the Goodwills remain a mystery, at least for now. It is possible, however, that the combination of the concept of "goodwill" with the work of railway porters was the link between the tournament-playing Canadian ballplayers, their profession and their residence in London.

Nor do we know the players on the Lincoln Nine. (Though we know Richard "Dick" Chrystler was not one of them!) In the small interest of correcting this omission, and not even certain any of them were ballplayers, below are London citizens listed five years later in a city directory as col'd for "colored":[15]

Meredith Adams – teamster
Joseph Barrynight – laborer
Wm. L. Berry – barber
Spence Bryan – laborer
Reuben Carney – gardener
James Charles – barber
Henry Chrysler – laborer
Ed Collins – barber
Wm. H. Dick – boot and shoemaker
Willis Diggins – laborer
George Duncan – laborer
Horace Duncan – barber
James Fountain – laborer
James Harris – laborer
Morris Harris – laborer
Benjamin Johnston – laborer
George King – plasterer
Moses Lane – no occupation listed
Christian Lewis – laborer
Samuel Lewis – teamster
Henry Logan – laborer
Daniel McIntyre – wood sawyer
William Moorhead – chimney sweeper
Philip Norris – cooper
David Phenix – laborer
Henry Reid – barber
Stephen Scott – laborer
Thomas Scott – barber/laborer
John Wilson – wood sawyer
Richard Smith – barber
Zachariah Williams – laborer
John Wilson – wood sawyer
William Wilson – barber
Thomas Wingate – plasterer

As well as:

The Second Baptist Church (col'd) -
Rev. Thomas F. Scott, pastor

M.E. [likely Methodist Episcopal] Church
(col'd) – no pastor listed

And finally, apologies to Mrs. Julia Fountain, a laundress, Mrs. Eliza Bartlett (no occupation listed), and other women almost certainly not ball-players in that era, but quite possibly spectators. This discovery of a fully-fledged Black community baseball initiative in London, Ontario, was unfortunately not repeated in the *London Free Press* the next season. Hopefully additional research may uncover more details about this significant aspect of baseball history in North America.

THE REST OF THE STORY

Organized Baseball's apartheid process would define the game's reach into Canada. It was a policy generally supported, rather than challenged, by Canadians, though there were some notable exceptions.

The first significant Black professional, the American John "Bud" Fowler, pitched for the Lynn (Massachusetts) Live Oaks of the International Association against the London Tecumsehs in May 1878.[16] Shamefully, the London players objected to Fowler's involvement, but the game went ahead until the Tecumsehs walked off the field in the eighth inning, ostensibly because of a call at the plate. Unfortunately, some online sources, including some sourced by SABR, downgrade Fowler's accomplishment by not critiquing the somewhat popular characterization of the International Association as a minor league. The Association, however, had its own independent decision-making process. It rejected attempts by the National League to arbitrate its affairs. Its lineups consisted of players who had played in the National Association, or were among the elite of

those on the nearly 50 professional nines of the era, and many who would ultimately be part of the rosters of "recognized" major-league teams. The International Association provided urban spaces regardless of size, geographic location, national identity, and (however briefly) racial background with an opportunity to compete at the game's highest level. It was if anything too far ahead of its time. It failed, as did many other National League rivals in the nineteenth century. Its breadth of city types and even its name would later be associated with the minor-league system, similarities that caused many modern appraisers to deem it as such. The concept of such a major/minor structure did not even exist at the time, however.[17] The International Association's downgrading diminishes Fowler's accomplishment. Historians are in danger of being enablers of the National League's one-time apartheid policy by their continuing willingness to accept the rejection by the League, and ultimately by major-league authorities, of the Association's major-league status, and with it the seminal role of Bud Fowler. Possibly that was the whole point of the League's objection to the International Association equal status in the first place.

The National League's overt racism continued into the 1880s when its next significant rival, the American Association, briefly integrated. The Association's subsequent backtracking would be the final nail in the coffin of Blacks participating in the highest levels of Organized Baseball until 1947. In 2020 Major League Baseball finally admitted its moral culpability, and recognized the statistical accomplishment of twentieth-century Black players in distinct "Negro" leagues.

Bud Fowler was invited to play in Guelph in 1881, but once again members of a Canadian team objected, resulting in his release before he caught on briefly with a team in Petrolia. So this shame knows no borders. Toronto and Hamilton were part of what was an elite minor league, the International Association (not the same league, despite its name, as that in which Bud Fowler had played in 1878), which in 1887 banned any future signing of Black players after Buffalo had played Frank Grant. Continuing this pattern of Canadian subservience to Organized Baseball's apartheid, William Hipple Galloway, a Canadian from Dunnville, Ontario, signed on with a Canadian team, the Woodstock Bains, in the Canadian League of 1899, but was eventually released when a teammate objected. He went on to play for the all-Black Cuban X Giants.

An exception to these ongoing tragedies was Quebec's Provincial League outside the jurisdiction of Organized Baseball in the 1930s. Several Black Americans were employed, though they were left off an all-star team scheduled to play the International League's Montréal Royals when members of that team objected to their presence.[18] In the same decade Chatham's Colored All-Stars, an entire team of Black players, won the Ontario Intermediate B title in 1934 in a competition that was integrated, though outside the purview of Organized Baseball, and not without its moments of racial discord.[19] Likewise, Black barnstorming teams traveling through Canada often enjoyed a largely Jim Crow-free experience on the railways, though they were served by Black Canadian porters for whom this was one of the few "professions" available. Finally, Canadian-born Jimmy Claxton was briefly employed in the Pacific Coast League in 1916 before his racial background resulted in his banishment; he later played for two teams in the East-West League in 1932. As such he is, to date, the only Canadian Negro League player raised to major-league identity as recently recognized by Major League Baseball.[20]

Only with the signing of Jackie Robinson by the Brooklyn Dodgers and his ironic placement with the Montréal Royals of the International League in 1946 did the process of integrating Organized Baseball begin. Literature in French Canada has often depicted the francophone experience in Canada as similar to that of the Black population in the United States.[21] On many levels, this is a false premise. Francophones were neither victims of slavery, as in the United States, nor did they experience its American aftermath in the form of Jim Crow-type legislation; a second-class status felt by many French Canadians may, however, account for Robinson's warm welcome in Montréal throughout the 1946 season. Manny McIntyre,[22] from New Brunswick, would become the first acknowledged Black Canadian signed to an Organized Baseball contract in the modern era, but complete integration would be slow and often frustrating, the last team to integrate being the Boston Red Sox in 1959. With Major League Baseball's decision in 2020 to recognize the various "Negro Leagues" between 1920 and 1948 as major leagues, opportunities have arisen for researching the statistical record of any Black Canadians (in addition to Claxton) who played in those leagues. Still to be accomplished, however, is the belated recognition of the International Association's major-league status, and its challenge to the National League on so many levels, including its signing of Bud Fowler. His major-league identity would help correct a record of National League apartheid too long tolerated within the baseball research community.

NOTES

1   *London Free Press*, April 20, 1869: 3.

2   *London Free Press*, June 19, 1869: 3.

3   *London Free Press*, July 23, 1869: 3.

4   *London Free Press*, August 21, 1869: 2.

5   *London Free Press*, August 3, 1869: 3.

6   *London Free Press*, August 5, 1868: 3.

7   *London Free Press*, August 20, 1869: 3.

8   *Detroit Free Press*, August 26, 1869: 1.

9   *London Free Press*, August 13, 1869: 3.

10 *London Free Press*, August 17, 1869: 3.

11 *London Free Press*, August 16, 1869: 3.

12 *London Free Press*, August 19, 1869: 3.

13 *London Free Press*, August 28, 1869: 3.

14 *London Free Press*, September 1, 1869: 3.

15 London City Directory 1874-5, (Detroit: Polk, Murphy and Co. publishers, 1874). Notably the listing of London citizens as colored was in this American-produced directory. Make of that what you will. Of the two Canadian publications reviewed for this period, neither listed a racial (i.e. colored) identity for anyone. They were the *City of London and County of Middlesex Gazetteer and Directory 1874-75*, published by Irwin and Co. 1874, retrievable at https://www.canadiana.ca/view/oocihm.8_00296_1/5?r=0&s=1, and *McAlpine's London City and County of Middlesex Directory 1875,* published by McAlpine, Everett and Co. retrievable through the Public Archives of Canada at https://central.bac-lac.gc.ca/.item?op=pdf&id=e010780536_p1.

16 May 17, 1878, as reported in the *New York Clipper*, June 1, 1878. Lynn's lineup had Harry Spence, William Lapham, and Patrick Gillespie, three former Guelph Maple Leafs, a team for whom the *London Free Press* (May 17, 1878) used the adjective "old," suggesting that their days of glory were already consigned to the history books.

17 For further analysis of the status of the International Association, see Andrew North's essay "The 1877 International Association Championship Game" in this volume.

18 Dan Ziniuk, "A Shameful Day in the Annals of Canadian Baseball," *Ottawa Citizen*, June 21, 1998. Jackie Robinson's contract signing with the Montréal Royals in 1945 led the *Montréal Standard* newspaper of October 27, 1945, to recall a 1936 incident. Several Montréal Royals players had refused to play an exhibition game against an all-star squad of Quebec Provincial League players as long as the latter had three Black ballplayers in their lineup. They were dropped and the game was played without the three receiving any of the promised gate receipts.

19 The Chatham Coloured All-Stars story is being told through "Breaking the Colour Barrier," a partnership between the Harding family, the University of Windsor's Department of History, the Leddy Library's Centre for Digital Scholarship, and the Chatham Sports Hall of Fame. It was funded by an Ontario Trillium Foundation grant in 2016-2017. For details consult: http://cdigs.uwindsor.ca/BreakingColourBarrier/.

20 Email from Gary Ashwill, who maintains the Seamheads Negro Leagues Database, to David Matchett, April 22, 2021.

21 The most notable of these being *Nègres blancs d'Amérique* (1968) by Pierre Vallières (Montréal: Éditions Parti pris, 1967), which pluralized the racially charged "N word" in its English translated title.

22 http://www.attheplate.com/wcbl/profile_mcintyre_manny.html.

MONTRÉAL ROYALS BEGINNINGS

By Marcel Dugas

When tasked with discussing the first game in the history of the Montréal Royals, one must decide which one of the club's first games he or she believes to be the real one. The conventionally accepted description of the Royals as having been around from 1897 to 1917 and from 1928 to 1960, although not factually wrong, does not tell the whole story. Montréal was represented in the Eastern/International League by five different clubs in a 70-year span. Some were in for the long haul, while others spent so little time in Canada's then largest city that most Montréalers didn't even notice.

Before the beginning of the 1890 season, the International League (which was called alternatively a league or an association) considered Montréal as a possible landing spot for a franchise.[1] The loop ended up playing with six clubs in Ontario, New York, and Michigan. However, one-third of the league's franchises tried to keep from going belly-up by moving to Montréal in a three-week span during that season. In its June 3 edition, the *Gazette* of Montréal announced that the Buffalo team, unable to compete with the Buffalos that had just joined the upstart Players' League, would now call the city home. They chose the Shamrock Club's lacrosse grounds,

located across the street from where the Montréal Forum would be built 3½ decades later, as their home field, and christened the new grounds on June 9.

The team comprised 13 players, including four pitchers and two catchers. They had not been performing in overwhelming fashion, but general manager Bacon spoke very highly of his troops' off-the-field habits: "A sober, steady lot of fellows. Not a boozer among them."[2] Two thousand admirers of baseball, to use the vernacular of the day, attended the very first game of professional baseball played in Montréal, which also happened to be the first installment of the Toronto-Montréal baseball rivalry. The visitors took the day by a score of 11-10. The game was riddled with errors (eight for each club), as was common for baseball in those days.

Of more concern to those who cared about Montréal's status in big-time baseball was a report out of Toronto saying that the club was in town "only as a feeler,"[3] which Bacon denied. However, after a win attended by fewer than a thousand fans in the second game of the series, and then a loss (apparently caused entirely by poor officiating), the *Gazette* ran a headline that read: "They Lose and They Quit. Montréal Drops Another

Game and Drops Out of Town."[4] The team called Grand Rapids, Michigan, home for what was left of the season.

Overall, it was a very challenging season for the International League, which would end up halting its operations in July. When the Hamilton club found itself on the verge of going under in late June, it was undeterred by the failed Montréal experiment of two weeks earlier. On June 23 Canada's largest city had a baseball team again.

This second Montréal aggregation introduced itself to its new fans with a twin bill on Dominion Day. And as fate would have it, the new Montréal team faced the old one. Or at least, what was left of the old one. Grand Rapids had been significantly reinforced; only two of the men who had defended the Montréal colors in June took the field for them. Again, offenses (with a little help from the opposing defenses) ruled the day. The visitors took the morning game 17-10 and the locals earned a split with a 9-4 afternoon decision. Game one drew 800 fans, while game two was attended by somewhere between 600 and over 1,000, depending on which newspaper you choose to believe.[5]

Not even a week later, the team directors were convinced they could not turn a profit, and the latest Montréal club left, not to return. Reporters were not impressed with what the city had been subjected to. "If any one desired to disgust Montréalers with professional baseball they could not have picked out better means to that end than by sending two moribund crews of traveling fakirs to this city and parading them as 'Montréal's ball team.' … Why should Montréal be called upon to father every insolvent aggregation of peripatetic ball-tossers that can find nowhere else willing to take them in?"[6] The sentiment was that those clubs were beneath what the city deserved, and that was the reason fans did not flock to the park. The same newsman, who certainly did not feel any kind of municipal inferiority complex, opined that "the next team that comes along

and desires to represent this city must first show some grounds upon which that honor should be extended to them."[7]

No aggregation of peripatetic ball-tossers tried to earn the honor of representing Montréal for seven years. But when the city did reenter big-time baseball, everything happened at lightning speed. At 5 in the morning of July 16, 1897, fire broke out at the ballpark of the Eastern League's Rochester club. And at 2 P.M., a dispatch from New York announced that the Rochesters were now the Montréals, and that the club would be playing at the Shamrock lacrosse grounds seven days later.[8]

A crowd of about 1,200 ventured to the ballpark despite the threat of rain, a threat that materialized during the fifth inning, causing a 17-minute stoppage in play. Fans were treated to a good game and responded enthusiastically. Work had been done on the playing surface, and men were hard at work building new grandstands as the game went on.[9]

For its first home game, the new Montréal club had drawn Wilkes-Barre, the only team that stood below it in the league standings. Despite that, the locals lost 11-10 even though "that did not count for so much after all, because everybody who saw the game was perfectly satisfied."[10] Reporters believed that this would not be merely a flirtation with professional baseball, as had been those two 1890 episodes, and that the club was there for the long run.

The Royals, as they were intermittently called on a suggestion made by the *Wilkes-Barre Record* a few days into their existence,[11] enjoyed some success. They won an unexpected league title in 1898 under the stewardship of captain, manager, and first baseman Handsome Charley Dooley. However, after the 1902 season, Baltimore was dropped by the American League to make room for what would become the New York Yankees. The Eastern League jumped at the opportunity to add such a proven baseball city, and Montréal, which many of the league's owners considered too distant from the loop's other markets, found itself on the chopping block.[12]

The spring of 1903 brought no Opening Day at the ballpark. But a new iteration of the Royals was on its way. The Worcester, Massachusetts, Eastern League team was in dire straits, and in late July began representing Montréal. However, in one of those quirks of baseball calendars of the past, Montréalers had to wait almost a full month before they saw their team in action.

The team had a dismal record of 29 wins and 66 losses when it arrived at its new home port, a record that was, oddly enough, good for sixth place out of eight in the league standings. Newspapers almost guaranteed defeat for the August 21 home opener as the club faced second-place Jersey City, and the Montréal aggregation did not disappoint, so to speak. With 1,400 fans on hand on a Friday afternoon, the Royals were defeated 7-3.[13] They lost their first four contests at what was now called the Montréal Baseball Grounds, stretching their total losing streak to 12; "there will probably be many more," noted *La Presse* wryly.[14]

That prognosis proved true, not only for the 1903 season but for the remainder of that iteration of the club's existence. Montréal finished in the league's first division only once before being, once again, bumped out of the loop after the 1917 season.[15] And this time, there was no club waiting to fall into Montréal's lap. The city had to wait 11 years before making its way back into the upper echelons of professional baseball.

There was a different feel to the final first game in Royals history, played on May 5, 1928, compared with the previous ones. Montréal had grown a lot, both in area and in population since the beginning of baseball's adventure in the city. The sport was a lot bigger deal than it had been in the past and this new club, the former Jersey City Skeeters team that had just been bought by a local group for $225,000, was playing in a real concrete and steel ballpark instead of a park outfitted with wooden stands, as had the old Royals.[16]

Delorimier Stadium, which the team would occupy until its demise, was filled almost to capacity as longtime New York Yankees hurler Bob Shawkey got the assignment for the Royals. Many among the 22,000 in attendance had received free passes to attend the game, but it was an impressive crowd nonetheless. The locals defeated Reading 7-4, and the comments from the press were overwhelmingly positive. The ballpark was a beautiful and comfortable construction, the sight lines were great, the huge scoreboard (100 feet by 28) was remarkable. The outside of the ballpark was not finished, and the field, after days of uninterrupted rain that had postponed the grand opening, was in terrible shape. But nobody seemed to mind.[17]

This latest version of the club brought a level of stability and success the city had not seen before. It also cemented Montréal's position as a viable market for professional baseball, so that when the Royals ceased operation after the 1960 season the door was left wide open for the arrival of Canada's first major-league team in 1969.

NOTES

1   "In the International, Montréal Replaces Buffalo in the Baseball Struggle," *Gazette*, June 3, 1890: 8.

2   "All Ready for the Game To-Day," *Gazette*, June 9, 1890: 8.

3   "All Ready for the Game To-Day."

4   "They Lose and They Quit. Montréal Drops Another Game and Drops Out of Town," *Gazette*, June 12, 1890: 6.

5   The *Montréal Herald* reported 600, the *Gazette* 1,000, and the *Daily Witness* over 1,000. July 2, 1890.

6   "The Second Orphan Asylum," *Gazette*, July 5, 1890: 8.

7   "The Second Orphan Asylum."

8   "Montréal Is in It. Will Begin the Eastern League Series Next Week," *Gazette*, July 17, 1897: 5.

9   "Victoire des Wilkesbarre," *La Presse*, July 24, 1897: 14.

10   "Good Opening Game. Montréal and Wilkesbarre Play Hot Baseball," *Gazette*, July 24, 1897: 5.

11   "The Royals Defeated," *Wilkes-Barre Record*, July 20, 1897: 3.

12   William Brown, *Baseball's Fabulous Montréal Royals* (Montréal: Robert Davies Publishing, 1996), 13-14.

13   "The Skeeters Won. First Appearance Here of New Baseball Team," *Gazette*, August 22, 1903: 6.

14   "Montréal Débute par une Défaite," *La Presse*, August 22, 1903: 3.

15   Brown, 183.

16   Brown, 26-27.

17   "Le Club Montréal Ouvre Sa Saison Locale par Deux Victoires. De Grandes Foules Voient Montréal Remporter Ses Deux Premières Victoires Locales," *La Patrie*, May 7, 1928 : 10.

PROFESSIONAL BASEBALL COMES TO TORONTO TO STAY:

THE TORONTO BASEBALL CLUB IN THE EASTERN LEAGUE, 1895

By David Siegel

The first game played by the Toronto-based professional baseball team that ultimately became the Maple Leafs took place on April 29, 1895, and marked the beginning of a proud franchise that would play in the International League (and its predecessor) continually for 72 years.

TORONTO OF THE 1890S

During the nineteenth century, Toronto went from being an unincorporated frontier settlement on the harbor between two semi-navigable rivers to attaining full-fledged metropolitan status. At the beginning of this period, it would have been optimistic to say that it had roughly the same status as Newark (later Niagara on the Lake), Kingston, and London (the aspiring capital located on the Thames River). By 1900 Toronto was eclipsed by only Montréal, a rivalry that would continue through the twentieth century.

How did Toronto achieve this metropolitan status? Metropolitan status has been defined as "the dominance of an urban centre over an adjacent area or hinterland."[1] This dominance is economic, political, cultural, and social.

By 1890, Toronto had become the second largest city in Canada. With a population of 181,000, it ranked second to Montréal,[2] and it was continuing to grow rapidly. It had doubled in area in the seven years between 1883 and 1890 by spreading its tentacles north and taking in the outlying suburb of Yorkville and beyond.[3] Its population more than tripled between 1871 and 1895. Some of this came from the added territory, but it was also a product of in-migration from other countries and from within Canada, as well as natural increase.[4]

The city was large enough to develop specialized sectors – the transportation sector on the lakeshore; the financial sector around King and Bay; an emerging but thriving retail sector centered on the new Eaton's and Simpson's stores at Yonge and Queen; and factories located in the east end near the harbor at the mouth of the Don River, and in the west end near the railway lines. The factories provided steady employment to large numbers of men who formed unions, which led to improved wages, better working conditions, and shorter hours of work.[5] This produced an emerging middle class that had the time and money to spend on entertainment like sports.

It was large enough to support several newspapers. They came and went fairly quickly, but some of the names are recognizable today –

Evening Telegram, Evening Star, the *Globe,* and the *Daily Mail and Empire.*[6]

Electric lighting was replacing gaslights, and telephones and telegraph were the modern means of communication. As of 1894, all the previous horse-drawn streetcars were replaced by electric streetcars,[7] making getting around the city much easier and quicker.

Even the blemish on this pristine landscape had a metropolitan tone. Toronto was large enough to attract diverse groups of people who did not always agree on important issues. It became the scene of bitter division based on language, religion, and race. (Race at this point referred to the English and French races.) These fights played out not only in the legislature in clashes over issues like education, but they also found their way onto the streets in the form of bitter confrontation.[8]

SPORT IN THE METROPOLITAN CITY

Looking back at this time, it is difficult to determine the role that sport played in society. There was some interest in baseball, as illustrated by the oft-told story of the 11-year-old boy who was offered the option of paying a fine or going to jail for the grave offense of playing ball in the street.[9] Linda Shapiro suggests that "[b]aseball began in Toronto about 1875 with two semi-professional clubs known as the Dauntless and the Clippers."[10] Louis Cauz argued that cricket was popular because it was a British import, whereas baseball was an interloper from the United States. This meant that "for many years the game was not highly regarded by the better class of Toronto citizens."[11]

There was clearly an emerging interest in sport generally and baseball particularly. This might have been a reflection of the changing work world, as the hardscrabble earlier times were giving way to the luxury of regular, fairly well paid factory employment, while improvements in the streetcar system made it easier to attend games.

As Toronto developed into a metropolitan city with dominance over the hinterland, it was not surprising that this dominance was also exhibited in baseball. Toronto had joined the nearby Canadian cities of Guelph, Hamilton, and London to form a Canadian League in 1885, but this lasted only one year.[12] As the metropolitan city, Toronto needed higher status, so it placed a team in the International League in 1886 (not the same as the later International League), but this team folded part way through the 1890 season – not an unusual circumstance at the time. Toronto was without a professional team from 1890 until it joined the Eastern League in 1895. This franchise played in that league (and its successor International League) until 1967, when the team was moved to Louisville, Kentucky. It was not the major leagues, but it was the highest minor-league level, which put Toronto above most other Canadian cities that flirted with teams in the lower minors, and on the same level as its rival, Montréal, which had a team in the same league from 1928 to 1960.

This was the environment in 1895 when Toronto's new professional team entered the Eastern League.

THE MINOR LEAGUES OF THE 1890S

Chronicling the early years of minor-league baseball is not easy. Neil J. Sullivan summarized the situation well: "During the 1880s and 1890s, minor leagues came and went at a dizzying pace. A few survive to the present day, but most collapsed in futility."[13] William Humber provides an idea of how complicated the terrain looked for Canadian teams.[14] It seems that new teams and leagues emerged and disappeared each season, providing virtually no continuity. It must have been difficult for fans who might develop loyalty to a local team that would disappear after one year.

The Eastern League had functioned since 1884.[15] The hierarchy of minor leagues was not as well defined then as it came to be in later years, but the Eastern League seems to have been the top tier of the minor leagues. It drew players on the way up from the New England and New York State Leagues, and it sometimes lost its better players to the National League. It changed its name to the International League in 1912 and existed under that title until 2020, when Major League Baseball demolished the existing minor-league system.

THE FIGHT FOR THE FRANCHISE

The size and growing population of Toronto made it ripe for a professional baseball franchise. The city had had a franchise before starting in 1885, but it failed in 1890. In 1894 there was discussion of Toronto having a National League franchise, even though the 12-team league was then working toward contraction rather than expansion.

When the Eastern League held its annual meeting in New York City on December 5, 1894, it had some important decisions to make. Several teams had dropped out of the league at the end of the previous season, so there would need to be new teams in the league for the 1895 season.[16]

It seemed a foregone conclusion that Toronto would be awarded a franchise,[17] but it was such an attractive location that there were at least four contenders at the league meeting jockeying for the franchise. All four contenders were represented by experienced managers, but three had no real ties to Toronto. The Toronto proposal was from a group of local capitalists fronted by W.J. Smith, identified as "owner of the grounds," and Chas. Maddock, identified as "keeper of the grounds," with no explanation of that cryptic title.[18] The newspaper stories of the time did not provide much information, but two of the capitalists were identified as Al. De Roy and Peter Ryan (with no

further identification). W.J. Smith was from a family that had significant business operations in the city's east end.[19] Charlie Maddock was well-known in Toronto baseball circles.

The bids were identified with the manager who was fronting the bid. The newspaper descriptions were worded to suggest that the league was deciding among the four managers, without much regard to the financial backing. There was no indication in the newspapers that the suitors presented a business plan or any financial information. The leagues were in heavy competition with one another to attract teams, so it is possible that they did not want to discourage potential new teams by asking too many questions. This could explain why so many teams lasted for only part of a season before folding.

No details of the discussion are available, but the newspaper stories indicate that the three contenders without Toronto ties accepted the inevitable and stepped aside.[20] Toronto had its Eastern League franchise.

For the first three years of its existence, the team played at Riverside Park, just east of the Don River, close to the corner of Queen and Broadview at a small street called Baseball Place which remains as the site of the Riverside Square Condos. The team played here until 1897, when it moved to Hanlan's Point on Toronto Islands.[21]

With the business side of the franchise in place, the next step was to assemble a team.

THE TORONTO BASEBALL CLUB

It was clear that Toronto's 1895 entry in the Eastern League was a brand-new team that did not build on any previously existing team in Toronto. The manager, Charlie Maddock, had a strong connection with baseball in Toronto, but he conducted his search for players in New England and the state of New York. A few Canadian players were given trials with the team, but only one was from Toronto.[22]

The newspapers usually described the Toronto team as the "Toronto Baseball Club" or just "baseball team" in the absence of a clearly defined nickname. Sometimes the newspapers referred to the "Torontos," but it was unclear if this was a nickname that the club espoused or merely journalistic license. For example, there were also references to one of the Boston teams as the "Bostons." Marshall Wright's *The International League*[23] and the Baseball-Reference.com website refer to the 1895 team as the Toronto Canucks, which was a nickname used by an earlier Toronto team. Eventually, the team became known as the Maple Leafs; some sources say this occurred in 1896,[24] 1902, or some other date. Baseball-Reference.com begins using the Maple Leafs appellation with 1899.[25] The research undertaken for this article related to the 1895 team included extensive review of several newspapers, and found that the usual reference to the team was "Toronto Baseball Club," with infrequent use of "Torontos." No newspaper story in 1894 or 1895 was located that used the nickname "Maple Leafs" or "Canucks" to refer to the Toronto team. At the time the Guelph Maple Leafs were being feted as the champions of Canada; having another Maple Leafs would have been confusing.

There was nothing like an expansion draft in those days, so Maddock was on his own to find players. There was never any mention of a coaching staff or any other assistance. Maddock was aided in his search by the fact that the lower minor leagues did not seem to have any equivalent of a proper reserve clause, so he was free to recruit players from the lower minor leagues like the New York State League and the New England League. Of course, elevating all his players from a lower minor league guaranteed that his lineup would be weaker than the mixture of experienced and newer players found on the other teams.

The newspapers carried stories of Maddock traveling around New York and the New England states signing individual players here and there. Supposedly the owners of the club had given him free rein to spend what he needed,[26] but even then he lost some players. However, Maddock was an experienced manager, and by March he had assembled a team.

He described his players as having "first-class reputations in the past, and whose habits for sobriety will compare favourably with any other club in the league." His on-field aspirations seem a bit restrained: "[The] sole aim of my managerial ability [is] to keep Buffalo in the rear, as we have always done in the past."[27]

The league held a meeting in New York City on March 14-16, 1895, to finalize the schedule and handle other league business.[28] Teams would play 112 games. Toronto's first game would be on April 29 at Springfield, Massachusetts, its home opener would be on May 13 against Scranton, and its final game was scheduled for September 14 in Buffalo.[29] At this point, it was made clear that "[t]he Toronto Club will under no circumstances play Sunday games."[30] Of course, if they had played on Sunday it would have been difficult to get to the games with no street cars operating.[31]

Spring training was quite different then. Major-league teams went off to exotic spots like Hot Springs, Arkansas, or Birmingham, Alabama.[32] In the absence of a farm system, the minor leagues were on their own for spring training, and most teams did not have much money. For the Toronto team, spring training consisted of arriving in Elmira, New York, two days before the team's first exhibition game against the local team.[33] There were some hiccups along the way. Maddock picked up the team uniforms in Toronto and headed off to Elmira with some players. However, he was surprised when he was assessed $18 in duty on the uniforms that he carried with him.[34] After two days of practice in Elmira, the team traveled around New York, New Jersey, and Massachusetts playing games. There was a semi-established schedule; sometimes scheduled games disappeared because the team disbanded, but other teams were found.

The team gradually worked its way to Springfield, where it played its first league game on Monday, April 29, 1895.

OPENING DAY LINEUP: TORONTO AT SPRINGFIELD, APRIL 29, 1895

Charlie Maddock, manager, was well known in Toronto baseball circles. He had managed the city's 1890 entry in the International League which ceased operating in the middle of the season.[35] He was described as having a "modest exterior," but being a "stern disciplinarian."[36] He "had been a member of the famous Maple Leafs of Guelph when it claimed the world championship. Maddock had gnarled, twisted fingers as catchers in those days didn't wear gloves."[37]

It is worthwhile to think about Maddock's role as manager. First of all, there is no mention of coaches, trainers, traveling secretaries, or clubhouse attendants. Presumably these duties fell to the manager. As mentioned earlier, Maddock played the role of promoter in making the case for having the franchise awarded to Toronto, then he took on the role of scout when he was beating the bushes to find players, general manager when it was time to sign players, and publicist when he sent telegrams to the local newspapers about his activities. Then there was the earlier cryptic comment about his being "keeper of the grounds." Clearly, the role of manager was different in 1895 from how we think of it today.

Ed or **Ned Crane**, pitcher. Sad story. Ed "Cannonball" Crane was revered early in his career as an incredibly hard thrower. "He was a key factor in three consecutive pennant winners (1887-1889) in Toronto and New York." By the time he found his way back to Toronto in 1895, he had discovered hard liquor, sedatives, and high living, and the "cannonball" sobriquet had been replaced by "fat boy." "He appeared in 29 games, went 7-18, and was released in July." The next year, he was found dead in a hotel room in Rochester, New York, victim of a drug overdose.[38]

Fred Lake, catcher, was born in Nova Scotia, but his family moved to Boston when he was 2 years old. He spent most of his lengthy career in the minor leagues, but he did accumulate 125 at-bats in the majors to get a .232 batting average.[39] He did better than this in Toronto, where he played 96 games and hit .343.[40] He also managed Boston teams in the National and American Leagues.[41]

Charles William "Luke" Lutenberg, first base, was born in Quincy, Illinois, in 1864, turned pro in 1886, and was much traveled, having played in Quincy; Oakland, California; London, Ontario; Macon, Georgia; Mobile, Alabama; Memphis, Tennessee; and Evansville, Indiana.[42] He was in the majors for one year with Louisville in 1894, batting .192.[43] In 1895 he appeared in 105 games for Toronto, batting .312 and hitting 4 home runs.[44] He continued his playing career in the minors for a few more seasons after 1895, but there is some evidence that he was distracted by the fact that his billiard parlor in Quincy was doing so well.[45]

Arthur Sippi, second base, was the manager of the London Alert team when he was recruited to come to Toronto. He was one of the few Canadians on the team. He played in 38 games for Toronto, hitting .235.[46] His name is found in some baseball statistics websites, but there is no evidence that he played professional baseball before or after his short stint in Toronto.

Judson Smith, third base, was born in Green Oak, Michigan, and was well traveled before he arrived in Toronto.[47] In 1895 he was the best hitter on the team, although his precise average is in dispute.[48] However, it is clear that he led the league with 14 home runs.[49] "Smith fashioned a 20-year career in professional baseball that took him to all corners of the continent from Toronto to Los Angeles and seemingly everywhere in between. ... Smith played in well over 2,000 professional games, but only 103 of them were at the major-league level. Smith's career reflected a pattern: He showed enough promise to get separate trials with four different National League teams, but each time was found wanting and returned to the minors." While playing, he studied dentistry at The Ohio State University, and he set up a successful dental practice in Los Angeles when he retired.[50]

Gene DeMontreville, shortstop. His name was also rendered as Demontreville, Demont, or Dermont. He had played 29 games in the Eastern League in 1894, and led all shortstops with a fielding average of .898.[51] In 1895 he played 112 games in Toronto, batting .316 and stealing 40 bases,[52] before moving on to play 12 games for the Washington Senators in the National League. He went on to play parts of eight seasons in the National League, compiling a .303 batting average and stealing 228 bases before finishing his career in the minors. He also managed for three seasons in the minor leagues.[53]

Jack Meara, left field, had a reasonably good year for Toronto in 1895. He played in 70 games and hit .256 with 26 stolen bases.[54] There is no further information about him in the standard baseball databases.

William Millar "Bunk" Congalton, center field, was born in Guelph, Ontario, but was a much-traveled journeyman player. Toronto was his first stop, and it did not go well, as he was released after 13 games with a .186 average.[55] He played in the majors for four years and hit a respectable .292, but he could not stick anywhere because he was so inconsistent.[56] After he retired from baseball, he lived in Cleveland, where he suffered a heart attack while attending a game at Cleveland Stadium, and died several days later.[57]

James Patrick "Doc" Casey, right field. At 5-feet-6 and 157 pounds, he was described as "almost a midget," but a good ballplayer.[58] In 1895 he played in 95 games for Toronto and hit .274.[59]

He played in Toronto for four years, before going on to a 10-year major-league career in which he hit .258.[60] He also served as a player-manager and manager in the minor leagues.

THE GAME

There was some question whether the game would be played because Springfield had experienced a spring flood, but the water receded enough to allow the game to proceed, although there was reference to the field being slippery.

The story in the *Globe* reads like a foretaste of something that Damon Runyon would write 30 years later:

> *Eighteen hundred people saw the Eastern League championship season opened with a rush in this city to-day by the Torontos, the newest members of the league, and the same number of people went home happy at the end of the game after seeing the visitors easily defeated by a score of 13 to 1.*[61]

The box score of the game was reported in several newspapers,[62] but there seems to be nothing like a scorecard or detailed list of all plays. The *Globe* provided some narrative of the major plays. Understandably, there is a precise description of how Toronto scored its lone run, but much less detail about the 13 scored by the Springfield Ponies.[63]

Toronto scored its only run in the bottom of the third inning. (The home team could choose if it wanted to bat first or last, and in the Dead Ball Era, there was an advantage to batting first when the ball was still fresh.)

Ed Crane, the Toronto pitcher, opened the inning with a hit over shortstop, but was forced out on a bunt by Meara. Lutenberg then hit a double that scored Meara. The side was retired without further scoring. There were two additional Toronto hits in the game, including a single by Crane, but no other Toronto player got beyond first base. The Springfield pitcher, Callahan, was obviously effective in giving up only four hits and one walk, but he struck out only two. Callahan also helped himself by hitting a home run.

The Ponies scored their 13 runs on 13 hits, which seems quite economical. However, they were aided by five Toronto errors, which explains the fact that only five of the 13 runs were earned. *The Globe's* correspondent was pretty ruthless about the fielding prowess of certain Toronto players: "Lutenburg made a couple of inexcusable errors at first, which counted high in the score, but the weakest spot in the team is evidently at centre field where Congalton proved slow in judging flies and showed poor judgment in throwing to bases." Crane did not help his own effort by giving up five bases on balls, hitting two batters, and throwing a wild pitch. He struck out only two batters.

Several things stand out about this game from the perspective of a present-day viewer. There were four strikeouts out of 54 total outs. Crane pitched a complete game while giving up 13 runs on 13 hits. There was no such thing as a relief pitcher, so Crane had the honor of pitching a complete game while losing 13-1. Both pitchers started the season with a good batting average. Callahan was 2-for-5 with a home run. Crane was 1-for-3. The time for this 14-run game was 1:55.

WHAT FOLLOWED

The team continued its 12-game road trip, finishing 3-9. It played its first home game on May 13, 1895. Alas, its fortunes were not changed by home cooking. The team lost 2-1 to Scranton before 1,500 fans, "including a large number of ladies." However, attendance was held down by the wintry weather.[64] Attendance could also have been held down by the fact that there did not appear to be any paid advertising in the local newspapers, even though other leagues, even amateur ones, advertised in the papers.

The Toronto Baseball Club finished the season in seventh place in an eight-team league with a record of 43-76.[65] This put the team five games ahead of the other expansion team, Rochester.[66] Maddock was replaced during the season when the team had a record of 14-34. He was succeeded by Jack Chapman, who led the team to a 29-42 record. Chapman was not at the helm for the next season.[67]

The team had an inauspicious start, which is not surprising for an expansion team. However, it was the start of a 72-year run in the Eastern/International League. In an era when leagues seemed to have a revolving door for entering and exiting teams, this was quite an achievement.

ACKNOWLEDGMENTS

The author would like to thank staff at the Brock University library for their assistance in locating newspapers and other material.

SPRINGFIELD 13, TORONTO 1

Springfield	0	0	2	0	4	1	1	5	0	13
Toronto	0	1	0	0	0	0	0	0	0	1

Springfield	AB	R	BH	PO	A	E
Shannon, ss	5	1	1	1	6	0
Donnelly, 3b	5	1	3	2	0	0
Lynch, lf	4	2	1	4	0	0
Sheffler, rf	5	2	2	1	0	0
Gilbert, 1b	6	2	3	9	0	1
Garry, cf	5	2	0	3	0	1
Gunson, c	4	1	1	4	1	0
McDonald, 2b	3	1	0	3	3	0
Callahan, p	5	1	2	0	3	0
Totals	42	13	13	27	13	1

Toronto	AB	R	BH	PO	A	E
Mear, lf	3	1	0	1	0	0
Lutenberg, 1b	4	0	0	9	0	2
Smith, 3b	4	0	0	0	4	2
Lake, c	4	0	1	9	1	0
Demont, ss	4	0	0	2	5	0
Casey, rf	3	0	1	3	0	0
Sippi, 2b	3	0	0	0	0	0
Congalton, cf	3	0	0	0	0	0
Crane, p	3	0	1	0	1	0
Totals	31	1	4	27	16	6

Earned runs: Springfield 5; Toronto—1.
Total bases: Springfield, 20; Toronto—5.
Sacrifice hits: Donnelly, Sheffler.
Stolen bases: Shannon 2; Lynch 2; Sheffler, Gunson.
Two-base hits: Donnelly, Callahan, Lutenberg. Three-base hit: Gunson; Home run: Callahan.
First base on balls: Off Crane 5; off Callahan 1. First base on errors: Springfield 4; Toronto 1.
Left on bases: Springfield 9; Toronto 3.
Struck out: by Crane 2; by Callahan 2. Hit by pitcher: By Crane 2. Wild pitch: Crane.
Time—1:55. Umpires—Snyder and Swartwood.

NOTES

1   *D.C. Masters, The Rise of Toronto: 1850-1890* (Toronto: The University of Toronto Press, 1947), vii.

2   *Census of Canada, 1890-91. Volume I.* Ottawa: Government of Canada. 1893.

3   C.S. Clark, *Of Toronto the Good: The Queen City of Canada as It Is* (Montréal: The Toronto Publishing Company, 1898), 2.

4   *J.M.S. Careless, Toronto to 1918* (Toronto: James Lorimer & Company, Publishers, 1984), 120.

5   Masters, 175-8.

6   Masters, 167-8

7   G.B. deT. Glazebrook, *The History of Toronto* (Toronto: University of Toronto Press, 1971), 178.

8   Glazebrook, 161-8.

9   Clark, 5.

10 Linda Shapiro, ed., *Yesterday's Toronto: 1870-1910* (Toronto: Coles Publishing Company Limited, 1978), 102.

11 Louis Cauz, *Baseball's Back in Town* (Toronto: A Controlled Media Corporation Publication, 1977), 11.

12 Shapiro, 102.

13 Neil J. Sullivan, *The Minors* (New York: St. Martin's Press, 1990), 20.

14 William Humber, *Diamonds of the North: A Concise History of Baseball in Canada* (Toronto: Oxford University Press, 1995), 201-2, 208-9.

15 Sullivan, 20-21.

16 https://www.baseball-reference.com/bullpen/Eastern _League#Ontario (Accessed October 16, 2021).

17 "After Toronto's Franchise," *Toronto Daily Mail*, November

18 "Toronto in the Eastern," *Toronto Daily News*, December 7, 1894: 2.

19 Leslieville Historical Society, "Smith's Grounds: A Lost Riverside Athletic Field," https://leslievillehistory. com/2018/02/01/smiths-grounds-a-lost-riverside-athleticfield/ (Accessed October 17, 2021).

20 "Local Parties Want It," *Toronto Daily Mail*, November 20, 1894: 2; *Toronto Daily Mail*, November 21, 1894: 2; "Toronto in the Eastern," *Toronto Daily News*, December 7, 1894: 2.

21 This came to be known as Sunlight Park, but probably not until after the Toronto Baseball Club had departed. Leslieville Historical Society, "Smith's Grounds: A Lost Riverside Athletic Field," https://leslievillehistory. com/2018/02/01/smiths-grounds-a-lost-riverside-athletic-field/ (Accessed October 17, 2021).

22 *Daily Mail and Empire*, February 14, 1895: 2; *Daily Mail and Empire*, March 29, 1895: 2; *Daily Mail and Empire*, April 1, 1895: 2.

23 Marshall D. Wright, *The International League: Year-by-Year Statistics, 1884-1953* (Jefferson, North Carolina: McFarland & Company, Inc., Publishers, 1998), 74.

24 Wright, 78.

25 https://www.baseball-reference.com/register/team. cgi?id=ba731cc5 (Accessed October 16, 2021).

26 *Daily Mail and Empire*, February 25, 1895: 4; *Daily Mail and Empire*, April 15, 1895: 2.

27 *Daily Mail and Empire*, April 11, 1895: 4, 18.

28 *Daily Mail and Empire*, March 14, 1895: 4; *Daily Mail and Empire*, March 15, 1895: 2; *Daily Mail and Empire*, March 16, 1895: 4.

29 *Daily Mail and Empire*, March 15, 1895: 2.

30 *Daily Mail and Empire*, February 28, 1895: 4.

31 Careless, 183.

32 "SABR Spring Training Database." https://sabr.org/ spring-training-database (Accessed, October 15, 2021).

33 *Daily Mail and Empire*, March 21, 1895: 4; *Daily Mail and Empire*, April 15, 1895: 2.

34 *Daily Mail and Empire*, April 18, 1895: 2; *Daily Mail and Empire*, April 23, 1895: 5.

35 Cauz, 25.

36 *Daily Mail and Empire*, April 15, 1895: 2.

37 Cauz, 23. See also Humber, 28-32.

38 Brian McKenna, "Ed Crane," SABR Biography Project, https://sabr.org/bioproj/person/ed-crane/ (Accessed October 7, 2021).

39 Don Hyslop, "Fred Lake," SABR Biography Project, https://sabr.org/bioproj/person/fred-lake/ (Accessed October 7, 2021); https://www.baseball-reference. com/register/player.fcgi?id=lake--001fre (Accessed October 7, 2021).

40 https://www.baseball-reference.com/register/team. cgi?id=106d86ad (Accessed October 7, 2021).

41 https://www.baseball-reference.com/bullpen/ Fred_Lake (Accessed October 7, 2021).

42 *Daily Mail and Empire*, February 22, 1895: 2.

43 https://www.baseball-reference.com/bullpen/ Luke_Lutenberg (Accessed October 7, 2021).

44 https://www.baseball-reference.com/register/team. cgi?id=106d86ad (Accessed October 7, 2021).

45 https://www.baseball-reference.com/bullpen/ Luke_Lutenberg (Accessed October 7, 2021).

46 https://www.baseball-reference.com/register/team.cgi?id=106d86ad (Accessed October 7, 2021).

47 Terry Bohn, "Jud Smith," SABR Biography Project, https://sabr.org/bioproj/person/jud-smith/ (Accessed October 24, 2021).

48 Wright, 70.

49 Wright, 70.

50 Bohn, "Jud Smith." It is clear that Smith had a lengthy career. Whether the precise number of seasons was 19, 20, or 21 is not clear. https://www.baseball-reference.com/register/player.fcgi?id=smith-001jud (Accessed October 27, 2021).

51 *Daily Mail and Empire*, March 14, 1895: 4. The microfilm was unclear with regard to the fielding average.

52 https://www.baseball-reference.com/register/team.cgi?id=106d86ad (Accessed October 7, 2021).

53 https://www.baseball-reference.com/register/player.fcgi?id=demont001eug (Accessed October 7, 2021).

54 *Daily Mail and Empire*, February 14, 1895: 2; https://www.baseball-reference.com/register/team.cgi?id=106d86ad (Accessed October 7, 2021).

55 https://www.baseball-reference.com/register/team.cgi?id=106d86ad (Accessed October 7, 2021).

56 https://www.baseball-reference.com/bullpen/Bunk_Congalton (Accessed October 7, 2021).

57 Bill Nowlin, "Bunk Congalton," https://sabr.org/bioproj/person/bunk-congalton/ (Accessed October 7, 2021).

58 *Daily Mail and Empire*, February 14, 1895: 2.

59 https://www.baseball-reference.com/register/team.cgi?id=106d86ad (Accessed October 7, 2021).

60 https://www.baseball-reference.com/bullpen/Doc_Casey (Accessed October 7, 2021).

61 *Globe* (Toronto), March 30, 1895: 8. The box score and the description in the following paragraphs come from this article.

62 *Daily Mail and Empire*, April 30, 1895: 2.

63 Newspaper stories referred to the team as the Ponies. Baseball-Reference indicates that the team was called the Maroons in 1895, but it was called the Ponies both before and after 1895. https://www.baseball-reference.com/bullpen/Eastern_League#Ontario (Accessed October 16, 2021.)

64 *Daily Mail and Empire*, May 14, 1895: 4

65 It was reported earlier that the league had a 112-game schedule. There is no explanation of why the Toronto team apparently played 119 games. All the teams in the League played more than 112 games, but the number varied. Toronto played some exhibition games, and it is possible that those games are included in the total. https://www.statscrew.com/minorbaseball/l-IL/y-1895 (Accessed October 18, 2021).

66 https://www.statscrew.com/minorbaseball/standings/l-IL/y-1895 (Accessed October 16, 2021).

67 Cauz, 144.

WILLIAM "HIPPO" GALLOWAY

By Richard Armstrong

When Jackie Robinson debuted with the Montréal Royals on April 18, 1946, he became the first Black player to appear in what was then known as Organized Baseball in nearly 47 years. Canadians feel a special connection to Robinson because of his year spent in Montréal. What many Canadians don't know is that they have a connection to the last Black player in Organized Baseball before Jackie Robinson. That player was Canadian. His name was Hippo Galloway.

William Henry "Hippo" Galloway, a multisport athlete, did not spend long in Organized Baseball. Statistically speaking, his career is a mere footnote in the history of the game. But his career is not a mere footnote; his story is worth telling. Hippo Galloway is believed to be the first Black Canadian to play Organized Baseball, possibly the first Black player in amateur hockey in Ontario, and the last Black player in Organized Baseball before Jackie Robinson broke the color barrier for good.[1]

The story of Hippo's early life is confusing, starting with his parents. There is no record of who his father was. The name of his mother was Julia Sims.[2] Sims was born in Ontario around 1860,[3] and lived in Dunnville for at least two decades. By 1881, Sims was living at the residence of Harriett Galloway. It is not clear why Julia took up residence with Harriett. Documents explain that by the time she did, though, she had a two-year-old son named John.[4] There is no record of his birth, and no record of him, or of Julia, after 1881.

Harriett Galloway had children of her own. Her eldest son, William David Galloway, was born in 1850 and lived in Dunnville right up until his death in 1930. William was the adoptive father of Hippo Galloway.[5] As a child, Hippo lived in the United States, yet there is no record of Julia Sims crossing the border, and no record of her giving birth to another child. Given that Harriett Galloway and Julia Sims were known to each other, it cannot be a coincidence that William adopted Hippo. But the circumstances surrounding the adoption are not known. As such, there is no definitive proof that it was William Henry Galloway, and not John Sims, that William adopted. Whatever the case, William's adopted son moved to Canada in 1888,[6] and, going by the name Willie Galloway, enrolled at Dunnville Public School.[7] The 1891 Canadian Census supports the possibility that Hippo is actually John Sims. For Dunnville, it lists a 12-year-old "Wm. Galloway," born in Ontario.[8] No other document supports this date. Every other government record suggests Hippo was born in the early 1880s, and it is clear that Hippo Galloway came to believe, or at least accept, that he was born on March 24, 1882, in Buffalo, New York.[9] Whether Hippo was born in Ontario in 1879, or in Buffalo in 1882, he was Canadian.

In spite of all of the mysteries surrounding Hippo's early years, one thing is clear: He was a notable athlete. Young Hippo "played all sports with mixed teams as a youth."[10] In 1897 local newspapers recognized him for his feats on the diamond. That year, he played outfield and third base with the highly successful amateur Dunnville B.B.C. Dunnville, an independent club, filled its schedule playing amateur teams from neighboring towns. As one local reporter put it, Hippo "proved to be one of the shining stars of the Dunnvilles."[11] At season's end, the *Dunnville Chronicle* declared the Dunnville B.B.C. "the champion amateurs of Canada," noting that they "are all stars and their colored third baseman, 'Hippo' Galloway, is probably the most popular young fellow in Dunnville."[12] But baseball wasn't his only talent. He also played lacrosse and was a skilled hockey player. Galloway spent the baseball offseason playing hockey with the Dunnville town team.

In 1898 Galloway graduated to baseball's professional ranks. Professional baseball in Dunnville was still in its infancy. Dunnville's professional team, like its amateur team, was independent. It played its games at Jubilee Park, which was built in 1897 by hotelier David Price. The team rostered only a few local players, including Galloway; the rest of the roster was rounded out by imported professionals.[13]

The Dunnville nine opened its season at Brantford. Galloway played the outfield and smacked a double. Dunnville walked away 5-3 winners.[14] Dunnville next took the field for its home opener, and the team secured another victory. In the eighth, Galloway hit an RBI single, stole second,

advanced to third on a hit, and scored on an outfield fly.[15] As the season progressed, and Dunnville continued to pile up wins, Galloway established himself as its most notable position player. He deftly moved between center field, third base, and shortstop. Against Buffalo on May 20, he hit his first home run. Meanwhile, he threatened to steal any time he was on base. On June 24 he and his squad met their match. That day, the club traveled to Chatham and lost 1-0. The story of the game was actually the Chatham pitcher, future Hall of Famer Rube Waddell. Waddell held Dunnville hitless, striking out 17 batters. When asked what Waddell was throwing that baffled the Dunnville club so badly, Galloway replied, "Man, don't ask me, only time I saw the ball was when the catcher was throwing it back!"[16] Despite the fact that the team excelled on the field, about halfway through the season Dunnville found itself in financial peril. While ownership had done a good job of fielding a competitive team, the lack of local talent hurt them at the gate. Local papers explained that fans had stayed away "because more local players were not on the nine."[17] One by one, teams that Dunnville had competed against poached its players. At the end of June, Galloway and three of his Dunnville teammates left town to join the Woodstock Bains. On July 22 the *Dunnville Chronicle* printed an obituary for the ballclub, which had officially ceased operations.[18]

The Woodstock Bains were a semipro team that played in the independent three-team Brantford and Woodstock Baseball League. Galloway made his debut with the Bains on July 1, playing third base in both games of a doubleheader. Facing the Page Fence Giants, Woodstock lost both contests. Hippo's defense was shaky, but he was quick to put those losses behind him. In the very next game, Galloway went 2-for-4 and stole three bases. A few games later, he went 3-for-5 with three putouts and three assists at third base. On July 23 he hit his first home run with the Bains, leading the team to a 7-3 victory.

The Bains were so dominant that they secured the league championship on August 13, with more than a month left on the schedule. A local cigar store displayed the team's championship trophy in its window. The cup attracted such a crowd that the local police chief ordered the trophy removed. The shop owner refused, and the trophy remained on display for all to see.[19] The Bains spent the rest of the summer playing out their league schedule and picking up exhibition games. On October 1 the Bains closed their season against Hays & Co., a rival Woodstock semipro team. The Hays lineup boasted future major leaguers Bunk Congalton and Alex "Dooney" Hardy, but it wasn't enough. The Bains claimed the unofficial city championship with an easy 17-8 victory. Galloway went 1-for-5 in the contest, with two stolen bases and a run scored.[20]

After the baseball season, Galloway remained in Woodstock and played for the Woodstock entry in the newly formed Central Ontario Hockey Association, a subsidiary of the Ontario Hockey Association. He debuted in Hamilton on January 20, likely becoming the first Black player in the OHA.[21] Another Black player, Charlie Lightfoot, played for Stratford in the Big Four Hockey League, another subsidiary of the OHA, in 1899, but it appears that he debuted after Galloway. In his first game, Galloway scored one goal in a losing effort. Not much else is known of his hockey exploits in 1899, and while Woodstock was considered "one of the fastest teams in Western Ontario," Paris won the league.[22]

In April Galloway re-signed with the Bains. The team opened its season on May 6 against the Stratford Poets of the Canadian League. In 1899 the Canadian League was designated a Class-D League in Organized Baseball. In the opener, Galloway went 3-for-4 with two runs and two stolen bases, but also committed two errors that resulted in runs for the Poets. Stratford won, 8-6. Woodstock's next game came against London's Knox Club, with future Pittsburgh Pirates ironman George Gibson. Galloway went 2-for-4 in the 11-2 victory, as the "Bains were immeasurably superior to their opponents."[23] On June 9 the Bains played an exhibition game against the famed Cuban Giants, defeating them 11-5. Galloway went 3-for-5 with two runs scored. Accompanying news of Woodstock's victory came an announcement that the Stratford Poets had resigned from the Canadian League, and that the Bains had agreed to fill the vacancy.[24]

On June 12 the Bains traveled to London to make their Canadian League debut. As reported by the *Woodstock Daily Sentinel*, "Very few had hopes for a victory" for the Bains. London was the fastest team in the league, and the defending pennant winners.[25] Regardless of the matchup, the game became historically significant well before the battle ended. When Galloway assumed his position at third base in the bottom of the first, he became the first Black Canadian to play in Organized Baseball. Galloway fielded a clean game, recording two putouts and an assist. He struck out in his first at-bat in the top of the second, but in the top of the fourth, he recorded his first Canadian League hit and Woodstock's first run batted in when he "brought Busse in by a beautiful drive to the right garden."[26] That run made the score 6-1 in favor of London, which defeated Woodstock 8-3. Woodstock's luck was no better the next day, and the Cockneys defeated them 14-6. Galloway went 0-for-4 at the plate, but for the second game in a row he earned the crowd's appreciation: "Galloway made a brilliant catch of a high hot liner by Mohler in the fourth inning that won applause."[27] Woodstock followed up its two defeats in London with two defeats in Chatham (future Hall of Famer Sam Crawford played left field for Chatham), and a loss to St. Thomas. The St. Thomas game was especially tough for Galloway. He made three errors and faced taunts from the crowd.[28] The next day, the Woodstock Bains released him. Whether this action was influenced by his .150 batting average

William Galloway, back row center, with the Woodstock City team, 1899. (Canadian Baseball Hall of Fame and Museum)

(3-for-20 in five games), or by claims that certain players on the Hamilton roster were unwilling to play against him[29] is unclear.

What is clear is that Hippo Galloway was still in demand. News of his release included a reporter's plea to keep him in Woodstock: "An effort should be made to keep 'Hippo' in town, as our hockey team need his services."[30] The pleas were answered. He signed with the Woodstock City Team (formerly Hays & Co.), despite offers from Dunnville and the Cuban Giants.[31] Galloway made an immediate splash with the City Team. In his debut, he batted fourth, ahead of future major leaguer Ernie "Curly" Ross. Hippo played first base, and went 4-for-5, with two runs and four

stolen bases in a lopsided 16-6 victory. Galloway played out the season with the City Team. Local newspapers did not provide much coverage for the City Team, surely owing to a preference to cover Woodstock's Canadian League team instead. Newspapers did provide coverage when the City Team squared off against the Bains. In three such games, Galloway showed off his versatility, playing first base, left field, shortstop, and center field. But the Bains were dominant and won every game.

After the baseball season, Hippo planned to lace up his skates again with Woodstock's hockey team. However, there was a complication. The five games Galloway played with the professional

Bains in June made him a professional, and thus ineligible to play in the Central Ontario Hockey Association. In December he applied to be reinstated,[32] but the Canadian Amateur Athletic Union denied his request.[33] Hippo appealed the decision, but his appeal was denied.[34] Galloway was left with nowhere to play hockey in 1900.

In the spring of 1900, Galloway joined the Cuban X-Giants, an independent colored team. The team spent the summer playing games all over the United States and Canada. Galloway appears to have made his debut on May 14 against the Meriden Silverites of the Connecticut State League. The Meriden lineup included five players who would eventually reach the major leagues, as well as Eugene Mack, the younger brother of baseball legend Connie Mack. Galloway went 3-for-5, but Meriden won, scoring a run in the bottom of the ninth to walk off an 11-10 winner.[35] The X-Giants had a reputation for playing an aggressive style of baseball – well suited to his skills. He was a serviceable third baseman for the X-Giants, and a reliable singles and doubles hitter, with the occasional triple or home run. His speed allowed him to wreak havoc in multiple facets of the game. Galloway remained with the X-Giants until mid-August, but there is no record of him again until he resurfaced in January of 1902, working as a bellhop at the Genesee Hotel in Buffalo.[36]

It's likely about this time that he met his future wife, Hamilton-born Gladys Dancey.[37] Hippo and Gladys eventually married, but not before Hippo spent a few more summers traveling with the Cuban Giants. In August of 1903, the Giants matched up with the Mountain Athletic Club in Fleischmanns, New York, for a three-game series. MAC won the first game, 3-1. Hippo played second base and scored the Giants' only run. The Giants won the second game, 6-3, and the outcome of the third game is not known.[38] In 2020 the Mountain Athletic Club Grounds at Fleischmanns Park was added to the US National Register of Historic Places.[39] In September, in a game in North Adams, Massachusetts, Galloway made headlines for showing his less serious side: "A play which is only seen in the funny sections of Sunday papers was made by Sattersfield and Galloway. The former is about four feet extreme height and the latter overtops him a couple of feet. Sattersfield set himself to catch a high pop fly off Mackey in the sixth and was in the very act of catching the ball when Galloway who had stolen up behind him interposed his hands and made the out. There was no make believe in Sattersfield's disgust and astonishment."[40] Galloway went 3-for-6 and scored two runs, but the game ended tied 8-8. After the 1904 season, he returned to Woodstock and reported that the team had played 169 games, losing only 31 with four ties.[41]

In the offseason, Galloway returned to hockey. He joined the Wingham Club of the Northern Hockey League.[42] He led Wingham to the league championship, winning a best-of-three series final over Harriston. The team celebrated its victory at the Hotel National with speeches and live music. Galloway was called forward, "read a well-worded address," and was presented with a "handsome gold watch on behalf of the sports of Wingham." Surprised by the gesture, Galloway "thanked those who had been so thoughtful in his welfare, stating that he had enjoyed his stay in town and would be back again in October."[43] He kept his word. In early October, he returned to Wingham after a summer of making headlines for his strong defensive play with the Cuban Giants. He took a job at the local foundry.[44] In November, the Wingham hockey club held a concert as a preseason fundraiser. Galloway was just one of the acts, but performed multiple guitar solos. The benefit raised approximately $40.[45] Once again Wingham defeated Harriston in the finals to claim the championship.[46] That victory marked the end of Hippo Galloway's hockey career. After one more summer playing with the Cuban Giants, his baseball career also came to an end.

In 1908 an Industrial Institute opened in Woodstock. Galloway was hired as a laborer.[47] Hippo and Gladys lived in Woodstock with their young family until at least March of 1914.[48] By 1921 they had moved to Hamilton, where he took a job as a machinist.[49] From Hamilton, Hippo, Gladys, and their seven children relocated to Buffalo, New York, where he was employed as a tinsmith.[50] He remained in Buffalo until he died on February 17, 1943, at the age of 60.[51]

On November 16, 2021, William "Hippo" Galloway was inducted into the Canadian Baseball Hall of Fame in recognition of having been the first Black Canadian to play in Organized Baseball.[52]

NOTES

1 Gary Cieradkowski, *The League of Outsider Baseball* (New York: Touchstone, 2015), 178.

2 "World War II Draft Registration Cards, 1942" digital image, The National Archives (https://www.ancestry.com,accessed November 12, 2021), draft registration card for William H. Galloway, Birth Date: March 24, 1882; Serial Number U353.

3 1861 Canadian Census.

4 1881 Canadian Census.

5 "William D. Galloway," *Dunnville Chronicle*, November 21, 1930: 3.

6 1911 Canadian Census.

7 "Dunnville Public School," *Dunnville Gazette*, January 6, 1888: 1.

8 1891 Canadian Census.

9 "World War II Draft Registration Cards, 1942".

10 William Humber, *Diamonds of the North: A Concise History of Baseball in Canada* (Toronto: Oxford University Press, 1995), 144.

11 "Again Victorious," *Dunnville Gazette*, August 13, 1897: 1.

12 "Another Victory," *Dunnville Gazette*, September 3, 1897: 1.

13 Cheryl MacDonald, *Grand Heritage: A History of Dunnville and the Townships of Canborough, Dunn, Moulton, Sherbrooke and South Cayuga* (Altona, Manitoba: Friesen Printers, 1992), 403.

14 "Won One and Lost One," *Dunnville Chronicle*, May 6, 1898: 1.

15 "Bains And 19th Centurys – Two More Scalps Taken by the Dunnville Baseball Braves," *Dunnville Chronicle*, May 13, 1898: 1.

16 MacDonald, 404.

17 "Obituary," *Dunnville Chronicle*, July 22, 1898: 1.

18 "Obituary."

19 "Bains Have Won the Cup," *Woodstock Daily Sentinel-Review*, August 15, 1898: 5.

20 "Bains Win the Town Championship by a Score of 17 Runs to 8," *Woodstock Daily Sentinel-Review*, October 3, 1898: 5.

21 "An Unsatisfactory Ending," *Woodstock Daily Sentinel-Review*, January 21, 1899: 1.

22 "Nationals Tie Woodstock," *Toronto Globe*, March 17, 1899: 10.

23 "One Won, the Other Lost," *Woodstock Daily Sentinel-Review*, May 15, 1899: 5.

24 "Bains Are in the Canadian at Last," *Woodstock Daily Sentinel-Review*, June 10, 1899: 5.

25 "Bains Made Their Debut," *Woodstock Daily Sentinel-Review*, June 13, 1899: 5

26 "Bains Made Their Debut."

27 "Woodstock Lost One More," *Woodstock Daily Sentinel-Review*, June 14, 1899: 5.

28 Humber, 144.

29 Humber, 144.

30 "Changes in the Bain Club," *Woodstock Daily Sentinel-Review*, June 18, 1899: 5.

31 "Sporting Notes," *Woodstock Daily Sentinel-Review*, June 23, 1899: 5.

32 "Athletics," *Ottawa Citizen*, December 20, 1899: 6.

33 "Championships for Ottawa," *Toronto Globe*, January 11, 1900: 10.

34 "Sporting Notes," *Woodstock Daily Sentinel-Review*, January 31, 1900: 5.

35 "Meriden Defeats the Cuban Giants," *Meriden (Connecticut) Record-Journal*, May 15, 1900: 2.

36 "'Hippo' with Cuban Giants," *Toronto Daily Star*, January 10, 1902: 8.

37 1901 Canadian Census.

38 Collin Miller, "Cuban Giants Go to Bats with Mountain A.C. at Fleischmann's – August 10-12, 1903," Mountain Athletic Club Vintage Base Ball, accessed November 12, 2021, https://www.macvintagebaseball.org/post/cuban-giants_fleischmanns-mac-1903.

39 Max Lang, "Mountain Athletic Club at Fleischmanns Park Gains Historic Designation," *Oneonta* (New York) *Daily Star*, accessed November 12, 2021, https://www.the-dailystar.com/sports/local_sports/mountain-athletic-club-at-fleischmanns-park-gains-historic-designation/article_8da500f0-f098-5882-9ff4-dfb52c77d273.html?fbclid=IwAR1O61nXttgMg3h2dE-hSDT8G-do8NZ-ZUf_5-GwaiTR0JdDnI9P_RcX4Dkc.

40 "Sensational Ball," *North Adams* (Massachusetts) *Transcript*, September 21, 1903: 2.

41 "'Hippo' Galloway Home," *Toronto Daily Star*, October 21, 1904: 10.

42 "Puckerings," *Toronto Globe*, December 20, 1904: 9.

43 "Hockey Club Banquetted," *Wingham Advance*, March 23, 1905: 1.

44 "Personals," *Wingham Advance*, October 5, 1905: 1.

45 "Hockey Club Concert," *Wingham Advance*, November 23, 1905: 1.

46 "Wingham Holds the Trophy," *Wingham Times*, March 22, 1906: 1.

47 "College for Pupils of African Blood," *Woodstock Daily Sentinel-Review*, May 26, 1908: 1.

48 "World War II Draft Registration Cards, 1942."

49 1921 Canadian Census.

50 1925 New York State Census.

51 "Births," digital image, The National Archives (https://www.ancestry.com, accessed November 12, 2021), Birth Registration for Ida Norene Galloway, Birth Date: March 26, 1914; Serial Number 044166.

52 Canadian Baseball Hall of Fame, "William Hipple Galloway," accessed November 12, 2021, https://baseballhalloffame.ca/hall-of-famer/william-hipple-galloway/.

PART II:
THE TWENTIETH CENTURY

For much of the twentieth century, baseball in Canada was influenced by two dominant themes. The earlier of these, unfortunately, was war. Because Canada's involvement in both of the Great Wars was more direct, and longer lasting, than that of the United States, the impact of war was felt more acutely by the general populace. In the United States, baseball's role diminished somewhat during the wars, as schedules were shortened and rosters weakened through the use of replacement players of lesser ability. In Canada, however, the game played an increased role in the war effort, particularly overseas. Leaders of the Canadian Expeditionary Force in Europe viewed baseball as a means of teaching the values of discipline and sacrifice, as well as promoting physical and mental fitness. The game's popularity led to the formation of a league based in Britain. When Canadian soldiers returned to Europe in 1939, play resumed at a higher level, as baseball was again used as a means of alleviating boredom. Canadian involvement in the Second World War even extended to the use of Toronto's Maple Leaf Stadium as a temporary base for the Norwegian Army Air Force!

World War II brought about two more pertinent developments. In Chicago, Phil Wrigley formed the All-American Girls' Professional Baseball League in 1943. Rosters of the league's Upper Midwest franchises would soon be populated by scores of Canadian players, most of them from the southern portions of the nearby prairie provinces of Alberta, Saskatchewan, and Manitoba. And then there were the Vancouver Asahi, the tremendously popular (and successful) masters of baseball's finer points of play for decades along the West Coast. Pearl Harbor transformed their story, originally an uplifting one, into one of the more regrettable episodes in the nation's history.

The second major influence was the spread of Black baseball. The independent barnstorming teams from the United States expanded their horizons northward, recognizing the opportunities represented by the untapped territory. Chappie Johnson's All-Stars toured Quebec in the 1920s and '30s, but it was the prairie provinces that were the biggest beneficiaries of the touring talent. The town of Indian Head, in southern Saskatchewan, hosted an annual tournament that attracted top teams from all over North America, offering significant prize money. Teams like the Broadview Buffaloes featured the sort of fully-integrated roster that would not become common in the major leagues until some 25 or 30 years later. Leagues were formed across Canada, welcoming Black players who were looking for alternative employment following the decline of the Negro Leagues, or who simply preferred the more relaxed racial attitudes. The ManDak and Quebec Provincial Leagues in particular developed a reputation as "safe haven" leagues after the Second World War.

Canadian-based leagues came and went throughout the century. There were numerous incarnations of both the Canadian League and the Quebec Provincial League. Both the Montréal Royals and the Toronto Maple Leafs ceased operation after lengthy stints in the International

League, but their loss was assuaged by the arrival of major-league baseball with the Montréal Expos in 1969 under the ownership of distiller Charles Bronfman.

Influential and noteworthy figures were numerous. Ed Pinnance, from the First Nation reserve at Walpole Island, Ontario, became the first full-blooded Native American to pitch in a regular-season major-league game when he debuted with the Philadelphia Athletics in 1903. Martin Leo Boutilier, from the coal-mining community of Lingan on Cape Breton Island, Nova Scotia, became, as Brother Matthias, guardian and mentor for a precocious Baltimore youngster named George Herman Ruth. Joseph Lannin left his Lac-Beauport, Quebec, home for Boston (on foot all the way, according to unverifiable legend) to become a wealthy hotelier, and the owner of the Boston Red Sox responsible for the signing of that same Babe Ruth to his first major-league contract. Lannin died under mysterious circumstances, falling from a window in one of his own hotels. And Montréaler Allan Roth parlayed his passion for statistics into a job with the Brooklyn and Los Angeles Dodgers, and later NBC Sports. Roth was one of the most important in a line of pioneering predecessors to Bill James and the rise of the use of analytics in baseball.

Finally, longtime SABR members will remember the contributions of researcher Al Kermisch. His "From a Researcher's Notebook," a miscellany of unrelated items of historical interest, was a regular feature in the *Baseball Research Journal*, often at the end. Our book closes with a Canadian equivalent to his Notebook.

ED PINNANCE

By Martin Healy Jr.

At the turn of the twentieth century, Native American baseball players found themselves becoming integrated into the professional ranks of baseball. Charles Albert "Chief" Bender, a member of the White Earth Band of Chippewa, became a Hall of Fame pitcher for Connie Mack's Philadelphia Athletics. Louis LeRoy of Stockbridge-Munsee, the boy with the "ten thousand dollar arm,"[1] went on to star with the St. Paul Saints of the American Association, after brief stints with the New York Yankees and Boston Red Sox. And perhaps most famously, due to his all-around athletic prowess, Jim Thorpe of the Sac and Fox played in the big leagues for the New York Giants, Cincinnati Reds, and Boston Braves. These three players were among a long list of First Nations players who proved their worth in baseball during the Deadball Era. They were all born in the United States. But the first full-blooded Native American to appear in a regular-season game in the major leagues was a member of the Chippewa tribe born in Canada. His name was Edward Pinnance.[2]

On September 22, 1880, Elijah Edward Pinnance, the first son of John and Martha Pinnance, came into the world at Walpole Island, Ontario, Canada. Walpole Island is a First Nation reserve located 25 miles north of the town of Chatham, Ontario. (Chatham is the birthplace of Hall of Famer Ferguson Jenkins.)

As a young child, Pinnance demonstrated great skill in athletics and excelled at traditional Native games. When he became of school age, Edward enrolled at the Shinkwat Indian Residential School in Sault Ste. Marie, Ontario. There, he was introduced to baseball and quickly became a star player for the school.[3] The first accounts of Pinnance playing in fast company came in 1902 when he suited up for New Baltimore, a club in a local amateur league in Michigan. New Baltimore is on the American side of the St. Clair River, a mere 19 miles from Ed's birthplace. He played great ball in the amateur league, earning recognition from the Detroit Tigers. The *Detroit Free Press* wrote, "Phenoms for the Tigers are being dug up in Michigan one a day. The latest heard from is one Pinnance, a Walpole Island Indian wonder, who has been instructed to report for trial on Thursday."[4] There are no reports of Pinnance ever attending a tryout with the Tigers, but his splendid pitching for New Baltimore put him on the baseball map.

Pinnance did not end up playing with the Tigers. Instead he enrolled at the Michigan

Agricultural College, today's Michigan State University. A pitcher, he helped MAC beat up on rival teams like the University of Michigan, Detroit College, and Depauw University in 1903. In a change of pace for the college men, MAC scheduled a game with the top nine from Walpole Island. In what must have been an exciting game for Pinnance, he got to play against his fellow Chippewa tribesmen. He likely knew his opponents. Pinnance retreated from the pitching box to play third base in the game. He went 2-for-5 at the plate in a 10-4 victory. The *Detroit Free Press* subheadline stated, "Walpole Redskins Trimmed Neatly by M.A.C."[5] As the school season ended, Pinnance easily found a baseball job with the Mount Clemens club of the Great Lakes River League. Nicknamed the Lawyers, Pinnance and his teammates laid down the law on all comers throughout the summer. In a late-season game, he pitched an 8-0 shutout against the Myrtles of Detroit. In this game he got his lucky break. Philadelphia Athletics superstar Harry Davis was in Mount Clemens to take advantage of the town's famous hot springs. He decided to take in a baseball match. Pinnance caught the eye of Davis, who recommended him to his boss, Connie Mack. Mack summoned the young Canadian to the City of Brotherly Love at once.

Before Pinnance could meet up with Mack's big-league club, the Athletics' leader rescinded his original order and instructed him to report to Lebanon, New Hampshire, for seasoning with that town's nine. Pinnance hopped on a train from Michigan to New Hampshire armed with a "suit case made from the skin of a large elk he killed himself with a bow and arrow."[6] His stay in Lebanon did not last long. On September 6, 1903, in his first game with the small-town club, he made it through only three innings. In the fourth frame, the big Native Canadian was hit by a pitch, which forced him to retire from the match. Notwithstanding the severity of the injury, Mack

soon recalled Pinnance from the Lebanon independent nine.

Just a few days later, on September 14, Pinnance made his big-league debut at American League Park, home of the Washington Senators. "In the eighth Manager Mack trotted out the Indian, Pinnance, from the wilds of Michigan, and his first endeavors against the professionals cannot be said to have been a success," commented a *Washington Evening Star* columnist, who was wrong.[7] Edward Pinnance did not hail from the wilds of Michigan and, more to the point, he did not pitch poorly. Pinnance allowed only one run in two innings of work in his debut, and finished a 13-1 victory for his club. Hardly unsuccessful. The paper did relent later in the article and gave him a break: "He is only a youngster and very green, but he will do to farm out next season."[8]

On the lighter side of the diamond, the young pitcher earned a moniker from the Washington fans upon his arrival to big-league soil. "As soon as Pinnance stepped on the rubber he was christened 'Peanuts' by the bleacherites, and this nickname will probably stick with him for all time."[9] In his book *Over The Fence Is Out!*, baseball historian Jim Shearon explained the occasion further: "At the start of the eighth inning, the public address announcer stepped in front of the grandstand to call out, 'Pinnance now pitching for Philadelphia.' The bleacher crowd, straining to catch his name, couldn't quite hear. 'What's his name?' a man asked his neighbor. 'Peanuts, I think' was the answer."[10] Pinnance's teammates overheard the fans and adopted the moniker with glee. Days later, Pinnance was asked about his nickname, "Why should that name annoy me? I'll be roasted more or less, and from what I've been able to observe, the roasting process vastly improves the peanut."[11]

Pinnance stood 6-feet-1 and is listed as weighing 180 pounds. He threw right-handed and batted left-handed. On September 17, Philadelphia sportswriter Charles Dryden noted: "He has a low raise curve, said to equal [Joe] McGinnity's famous 'Old Sol,' and other effective slants and shoots. But the youngster lacks even a minor league experience. Mack thinks one season in a strong independent team would fix Mr. Pinnance about right."[12]

Despite not being in the pennant race, Connie Mack didn't use Pinnance down the stretch. His next appearance for the tall lanky manager came on the final day of the American League season. Donning his brand-new Athletics uniform, he pitched with excellence during his first career start. "In the five innings that Pinnance was in the box the Clevelanders made but three hits and scored one run," noted the *Philadelphia Inquirer*.[13] Unfortunately for Pinnance, manager Mack wanted to take a look at another rookie, Jim Fairbank. Fairbank proceeded to give up six runs to conclude the game, and the A's lost their season finale, 7-5. Although Pinnance failed to earn his first career victory, he did not fail in impressing his manager. Mack appointed him to pitch in the city series against the National League's Phillies. Another good performance there secured Pinnance an invitation to 1904 Athletics spring training in Spartanburg, South Carolina. A syndicated article picked up by the *Palatine Enterprise* suggested that Mack's 1904 squad would change its name to Indians, as the skipper signed three Natives to his roster: Chief Bender, Lou Bruce, and Ed Pinnance.[14] The name change never happened.

Spring training began well for Pinnance. Mack played him with the regulars and he had two strong performances in intrasquad games. The *Philadelphia Inquirer* spoke of the skipper's confidence: "Manager Mack is satisfied that Pinnance is possessed of the material of which great

The 1904 Philadelphia Athletics, from the Sporting Boiler Supplement set. Ed Pinnance is top row, third from right. (oldcardboard.com)

pitchers are made, and that it is only a matter of a little time when he will demonstrate his ability to be classed among the crackerjacks of the profession."[15] Then Pinnance's pitching started to deteriorate. He lost a game he should have easily won against the Princeton University Tigers. The *Inquirer* noted, "Pinnance did not show good form to-day, having no control and lack of his usual speed."[16] His troubles continued in a preseason series against the Phillies. Despite the Athletics' taking the series from the Phillies, the games that Pinnance pitched resulted in losses. The manager had no choice but to send him out for polishing. He ordered the young recruit to the Wilmington Peaches of the Tri-State League.

Tri-State League rivals were not happy that Wilmington received a player contracted to a major-league team. The Camden team filed an official complaint to the league president. Before any word came from the president, manager Mack put out his own statement: "Pinnance is a member of the Wilmington club. He has been signed by Manager Frysinger, of that club, for the season of 1904. … I do not care to get mixed up in any Tri-State arguments, but this much is certain, Pinnance belongs to Wilmington."[17] After Mack spoke, Pinnance's appointment to the Peaches became official. He started well and in just his third start with his new club, "Pinnance of Wilmington Pitched a Remarkable Game."[18] The Lancaster team came to Wilmington and was beaten badly by the Peaches. Pinnance pitched a one-hitter in the 6-0 victory. "Pinnance was responsible for the calamity that befell the lads from the land of sauerkraut and onions [Lancaster had a large German population]. But thirty-one men faced him during the game and of that number but one hit the ball safely," the local paper observed.[19] In spite of his great pitching for Wilmington, the game of July 3 was his last with the team. He spent the remainder of the 1904 season as a vagabond baseball player. He pitched for Federalsburg of the Maryland Amateur League and Nashua of the New England League. In August he settled in to play for Amsterdam-Gloversville-Johnstown of the New York State League. He played well with the aptly nicknamed Hyphens, earning himself a contract with the team for 1905, a contract which he signed in mid-March.

By mid-May of 1905, Pinnance grew out of favor with manager Earl Howard. Not worried about future retaliation, Howard released Pinnance to the league-rival Troy Trojans. Pinnance joined fellow Canadians Alex Hardy and Abbie Johnson on the Trojan squad. His season highlight came at a game in Scranton, Pennsylvania, in mid-July: "Pinnance's Pitching Was More Than the Locals Could Solve With Success."[20] Pinnance pitched brilliantly in a 4-0 shutout of the Scranton Miners. For the following season Pinnance stayed in the New York State League but jumped to the Albany Senators. Late in the 1906 season, manager Mike Doherty inserted Pinnance to pitch against Scranton. The Miners batted the Canadian hurler hard, tallying 13 hits off him. Scranton won the game, 4-3 in 10 innings. Perhaps because Pinnance usually handled Scranton with relative ease, upon the defeat the *Scranton Truth* pelted Doherty and Pinnance with seemingly retaliatory, culturally insensitive slander. "[Doherty] uncaged his noble red skin, Hiawatha Strongheart Pinnance, but Poor Lo has been seen on parade here so often this summer that he was no more novelty than the average Indian who attends the park. The act fell flat. The red man carried neither tomahawk nor scalping knife, and caused no more uneasiness or shakes in the local camp than his wooden relative in the cigar business."[21] Pinnance was not oblivious to the callous chants he often heard, and stood stoic against them. Nonetheless, he left the New York State League at the end of 1906 and never returned.

In 1907 Pinnance returned home and played in the Southern Michigan League. He became a top contributor for the Bay City team. In September, for reasons unknown, he was transferred to the Flint Vehicles. His continued excellence with the Vehicles garnered him interest from around the nation. At the end of the 1907 campaign, manager Judge McCredie of the Portland Beavers drafted Pinnance as an insurance measure for the 1908 Pacific Coast League season. He made the team out of spring training but was not on the top rung of the ladder for McCredie's pitching staff. His first appearance for Portland came in a relief role during the team's fourth game of the season. Despite the team's 11-2 loss to the San Francisco Seals, the reviews were shining. "Pinnance was the only Beaver who showed any class at all. He worked during the last three spasms and the best the Seals did was a pair of hits," observed a sportswriter.[22] Pinnance struck out five batters. McCredie's Beavers lost their first seven games of the season. A Portland reporter wondered, "Why doesn't Mac send Pinnance in to pitch the first ball over? The Indian might scalp the Seals."[23] McCredie relented in his trepidation about using Pinnance, and allowed his new pitcher to make a start. The move paid off.[24] Pinnance threw a complete-game 5-0 shutout against San Francisco in his debut start in the Pacific Coast League. He allowed just five hits. "The Indian was a life saver," said a San Francisco sportswriter. "The way he twisted that ball around the necks of the Seals caused [San Francisco manager] Danny Long to throw at least fourteen fits. ... The red man struck the ball right over the plate all the time and put plenty of smoke behind it."[25]

Pinnance quickly became a fan favorite. He also earned praise, not just around Oregon, but across the country. Papers from Los Angeles to Wilkes-Barre to Brooklyn spoke of Pinnance's superlative pitching with the Beavers. The former Connie Mack student seemed destined to finally prove his worth after years of toiling in the minors. The *Oregon Daily Journal* of Portland wrote of Pinnance: "Of all the new ones McCredie has sprung on the San Francisco public this time,

Pinnance, the Indian, looks the best. After that game he pitched last Saturday afternoon against the Seals he was voted all the candy by every one who saw him work. The way he twisted that ball around the neck of every hard hitter on the local lineup was awful for the admirers of the home team to stick around and look upon, and the steadiness that he displayed all the way through made the multitude sit up and take notice. The redskin has the most peculiar line of benders that any man has thrown from a box in this city for a long time. The curves seem to approach in a threatening sort of manner and then they break sharply at the plate. As Pinnance tosses every one of them with practically the same motion, none of the local batters ever could get jerry to his system."[26] But just as the accolades began to roll in, Pinnance found himself with the ultimate dilemma. Back home in Canada, the government began to allocate reservation lands to Natives. Pinnance, who was entitled to 160 acres of land in the Walpole Island area, "explained to McCredie that unless he is on hand when the allotment is made he will not get his farm."[27] The Portland bench boss reluctantly let his top pitcher go.

On June 12 Pinnance left for the East with every intention of returning to Portland to finish the PCL season after attending to his business matters in Canada. Pinnance never journeyed back to the West Coast, instead preferring to stay home and play for the local club in St. Clair, Michigan.

Pinnance received a telegram that asked him to return to Portland for the 1909 season. Perhaps because of his abrupt departure and failure to return, he found himself demoted to the city's number-two club, the Portland Colts of the Northwestern League. Judge McCredie of the PCL Beavers released his top pitcher from the first half of 1908 to manager Pearl Casey, who felt so confident of a pennant win for his Colts that he placed an order for a new flagpole before the season even started. Manager McCredie reserved the right to recall any of the Colts during the season, including Pinnance, whose play did not justify a call-up to the Beavers. He finished 1909 with 15 victories and 18 losses, and the team finished in fourth place in a six-team league. Pinnance fell out of favor with the management and fans of the West Coast leagues. His career seemed destined to return East.

Flint, Michigan, ended up being Pinnance's new baseball home. He found comfort in the Michigan League, but his pitching skill became needed elsewhere. The Native Canadian journeyed to the Midwest to play for the Davenport Prodigals of the Illinois-Indiana-Iowa (Three-I) League. Pinnance had a terrible go with the Davenport club and in midsummer the local paper sarcastically praised a win: "The unusual happened again yesterday. Pinnance won a game

and pitched an average grade of good ball in doing so at that."[28] He won just five games in 1910. In 1911 Pinnance returned to the Michigan League to play for Bay City, the last stop in his professional baseball career. He continued to pitch in local exhibitions, but never returned to the form of his early career.

Edward Pinnance's son Parker later described his father's departure from baseball. "Dad finally quit baseball when he became a diabetic. He would not stay on his diet given by his doctor and manager. He liked his food and you know what a diabetic diet is like."[29] After he retired, Pinnance worked as a marine contractor. He built docks and seawalls on Lake St. Clair and the St. Clair River. He also worked as a blacksmith. His time on earth ended on December 14, 1944, after he suffered a heart attack at home on Walpole Island.

NOTES

1   Jeffery Powers-Beck, *The American Indian Integration of Baseball* (Lincoln: University of Nebraska Press, 2009), 188.

2   Robert Peyton Wiggins, *Chief Bender* (Jefferson, North Carolina: McFarland, 2010), 49.

3   Clipping file, National Baseball Hall of Fame, Cooperstown, New York.

4   "Local Baseball Talk," *Detroit Free Press*, August 26, 1902: 10.

5   "Scalped Indians," *Detroit Free Press*, May 31, 1903: 9.

6   "Gossip of the Diamond," *Topeka State Journal*, September 9, 1903: 2.

7   "Sports of All Sorts," *Washington Evening Star,* September 15, 1903: 9.

8   "Sports of All Sorts."

9   "Sports of All Sorts."

10   Jim Shearon, *Over the Fence Is Out!* (Ottawa, Ontario: Malin Head, 2009), 86.

11   Charles Dryden, "Athletics Must Win Nine Games to Beat Out Spiders," *Philadelphia North American*, September 17, 1903: 5.

12   Dryden, "Athletics Must Win Nine Games to Beat Out Spiders."

13   "Cleveland Takes the Final Game," *Philadelphia Inquirer*, September 30, 1903: 10.

14   "Odds & Ends of Sport," *Palatine Enterprise*, October 17, 1903: 3.

15   "Athletics Will Be Stronger Than They Were Last Year," *Philadelphia Inquirer*, April 3, 1904: 36.

16   "Princeton Puts Athletics Away," *Philadelphia Inquirer*, April 2, 1904: 10.

17   "Tri-State Troubles," *York* (Pennsylvania) *Dispatch,* May 13, 1904: 5. The newspaper article actually read: "I do not case to get mixed up in any Tri-State arguments ..." but we have changed that to reflect what we believe was the intended wording.

18   "Lancaster Had One Hit," *Lancaster* (Pennsylvania) *New Era*, May 20, 1904: 2.

19   "Lancaster Got But One Hit Off Pinnance," *Wilmington* (Delaware) *Evening Journal,* May 20, 1904: 7.

20   "Troy Gave Us White Wash Coat," *Scranton Truth*, July 20, 1905: 8.

21   "Locals Win Again in Ten Innings," *Scranton Truth,* September 8, 1906: 9.

22   "Seals Pound Beaver Curve Artist," *San Francisco Call*, April 8, 1908: 9.

23   "Squeeze Plays," *Oregon Daily Journal*, April 11, 1908: 12.

24   "Beavers Break Seven Day Hoodoo by Indian's Good Work," *San Francisco Call*, April 12, 1908: 46.

25   "Beavers Break Seven Day Hoodoo by Indian's Good Work."

26   "Pinnance Looks Best of Beavers," *Oregon Daily Journal*, April 19, 1908: 36.

27   "Indian Twirler Released by Portland," *San Francisco Examiner*, June 12, 1908: 11.

28   "Pinnance Wins a Game," *Quad-City Times* (Davenport, Iowa) August 12, 1910: 6.

29   Clipping file, National Baseball Hall of Fame, Cooperstown, New York.

BOB BROWN

By Tom Hawthorn

Bob Brown figured more money was to be made in baseball as an owner than as a player.

After leading the Aberdeen Black Cats to a pennant in 1907, the catcher-manager sought to leave the coastal sawmill town in Washington state by trying to purchase the baseball club in Vancouver, British Columbia. The Canadian city, a terminus for the transcontinental railroad, was booming as a port. Brown figured prospects were bright for success on the field and in the ledger book. When his offer was rejected by the Vancouver owners, he returned to Aberdeen and a year later bought a quarter-interest in the Spokane club for $1 on top of his $2,300 salary as manager.

Sales at the Spokane box office were brisk in 1909, as Brown led the team to 100 wins while a land boom in Idaho and the Alaska-Yukon-Panama Exposition in Seattle lured to the city in Eastern Washington many "excursionists with time on their hands and money in their pockets."[1] The club turned a $10,000 profit, a quarter of those dividends going to Brown. After failing to buy the club, he sold his quarter-share back to majority partner Joseph Cohn for $2,500. Flush with money, he tried again to purchase the struggling Vancouver club.

Brown realized the franchise was in trouble when the league had to pay the cost of the team's return home from a series in Spokane. Creditors were pressing team owner A.R. Dickson, a grain merchant. Brown set up a secret offseason meeting with two of the club's directors, renting a lavish suite at the old Hotel Vancouver, which he then had stocked with fine whiskey and a box of first-class cigars. He walked away with an option to buy after handing over a check for just $500. He later returned to the city with the league president in tow to complete the deal, which included 14 players and a three-year lease on Recreation Park.

"This is the first club I ever owned in my life," Brown told a reporter as he boarded a train back to Seattle after buying the team, "and don't you make any mistake about it, I am going to get a team that will be strictly in the running for the pennant."[2]

The British Columbia port city had a population of 100,000, a fourfold increase over the past decade, and held great promise as a sports mecca. Brown was not the only aspiring sports tycoon with eyes on the city. The Patrick brothers – Lester and Frank – were soon to open a 10,000-seat hockey arena. "I liked this town first time I saw it," Brown wrote in 1957. "Figured it had a real future, industrially, and in baseball, too."[3]

Brown was not yet 34, a wiry, scrapping ballplayer who had spent time as a cowboy. He did not smile for photographs, preferring instead to glower. A Seattle newspaper once wrote in evaluating his baseball skills: "He can't bat; he can't field much; he is only an ordinary thrower – but he is a mighty good ballplayer. Bob is always in shape and he is always popping with pepper."[4] Unlike many in the sport, he was college-educated. As a manager, he was known for a hot temper. "Ball players weren't made to be molly-coddled like prima donnas," he said.[5] He baited umpires. As an owner, he was a tough negotiator, pinching pennies on player salaries. He was also shrewd, as we have seen, parlaying $1 into a franchise ownership in just one year.

Brown kept baseball alive in Vancouver through the Spanish flu pandemic, the Depression, and both world wars, and on into the television era. As early as 1917, *The Sporting News* was hailing him in large type as "Vancouver's Connie Mack."[6] As with Mack in Philadelphia, or John McGraw in New York, or Clark Griffith in Washington, DC, the summer game in Vancouver was entirely associated with Brown, who was known as Mr. Baseball. Only in the hockey world did the likes of Conn Smythe in Toronto or the Molson family in Montréal have so strong an association between a city and the owner of a franchise in a major sport.

Brown brought the great Babe Ruth to town, introduced night ball to Canada, and carved a ballpark out of forest with his bare hands (and the occasional stick of dynamite). That same Athletic Park would twice burn to the ground and twice be rebuilt. Brown played host to lacrosse, soccer, and football, though baseball always occupied the most dates. He built an adjacent gymnasium to add indoor sports to his calendar, and he formed the Vancouver Athletic Club to compete in various events. When professional baseball lapsed in the

city, he nurtured a competitive semiprofessional city league. His Athletic Park junior clubbers, restricted to 1,200 members, who were known as the baseball kindergarten, were granted free entry to the park, turning children into lifelong patrons.

When the 1910 season opened, Brown was owner, manager, and starting shortstop of the Vancouver Beavers. The club finished second, and the report on the Northwestern League for *Spalding's Official Base Ball Guide* saw in Brown a budding tycoon. "Vancouver probably cleaned up the biggest roll on the season through the sales of pitcher Harry Gardner to Pittsburgh, third baseman (Dick) Breen to Cincinnati, (Cy) Swain to Washington and the drafting of another outfielder, (Bill) Brinker, by the Chicago White Sox," Roscoe Fawcett reported. "Vancouver's profits were close to $3,500, Spokane's $1,500, Seattle's $1,000 and Tacoma's minus several hundred."[7]

Despite a successful campaign, Brown suffered a nervous breakdown after the season and a brother escorted him to Long Beach, California, where a doctor helped his recuperation.[8] For a tough guy, Brown spent a lot of time in the hospital. In fact, he would meet his second wife, a nurse, while recovering from an ailment.

Robert Paul Brown was born in Scranton, Pennsylvania, on July 5, 1876, the day after American centennial celebrations in his birthplace included picnics, parades fronted by colorful banners, and religious services held in churches bedecked with floral arrangements. The city was a mining and railroad center that attracted immigrants by the thousands, including his parents, the former Julia Ann Manley and Anthony Brown, who were from County Mayo, Ireland, which suffered dreadfully during the Great Famine. Robert was the ninth of 10 children born to the Roman Catholic family.

His father worked as a laborer in the anthracite coal mines at a time of declining wages and labor unrest. Scranton was roiled by a bloody general strike shortly after the boy's first birthday, and the Browns relocated nearby to Dunmore before moving to Sherman, Iowa, north of the state capital in Des Moines. Anthony Brown's occupation in Sherman was written in shorthand by an enumerator in 1880 as "working on RR sect," or a worker on a section of a railroad, known as a gandy dancer. In time, the family settled for good in Blencoe, on the state's western border with Nebraska, where Anthony Brown operated the only hotel in the community. On New Year's Eve in 1890, when Bob Brown was 14, a dance was held in Blencoe. So many people from Monona County attended that the hotel turned away patrons, which proved a blessing, as the barn burned to the ground that night and 17 horses were killed. The cause of the fire was unknown, though arson was suspected. "It seems almost a miracle that the fire was confined to the one building," the *Sioux City Journal* reported, "as the wind was blowing briskly toward buildings not over twenty feet distant."[9]

In his youth, Brown traveled the dusty summer roads of Iowa, racing horses and playing town ball at dots on the map along the railroads. "I was a bit of a jockey, too, in those days," Brown told a newspaper in 1930. "Guess I rode 1,000 races in the tank towns for my elder brother, who was the family horse fancier. They were ponies, you know, but they could step, and we used to race down the main street of most of the towns we made. Played baseball, too, from one town to another."[10]

At 17, Brown entered St. Joseph's College (now known as Loras College) at Dubuque. After two years, he continued his education at Notre Dame University in South Bend, Indiana, where he wore wing-collar shirts and a serious expression on his face. He also began parting his oiled hair in the middle, a country boy seeking to adopt a sophisticated appearance.

Each summer during his university schooling, Brown returned to Iowa to play summer ball and organize a local football team. On campus, he won letters in both baseball and football.

Teammates called him "Red Robert" or "Red" Brown. He earned a reputation as a pugnacious and relentless halfback despite a smallish, 5-foot-9, 150-pound frame. (Military documents gave his height as 5-feet-6.) His playing coach, H.G. Hadden, stood eight inches taller and 90 pounds heavier. Training included boxing, wrestling, and cross-country runs, as well as scrimmages and lectures on tactics. "In those days we had three downs to make 5 yards, and if we'd find ourselves just a couple of feet short, the other backs used to pick me up and toss me right over the line," Brown reminisced years later.[11] He scored a touchdown in a 32-0 whipping of the College of Physicians and Surgeons, and scored two majors in an 18-0 defeat of the Chicago Cycling Club.

Fifty players attended the start of baseball training camp on February 1, 1896, trying to win a varsity spot for what would be the team's third season. By mid-March, half had been cut, but Brown survived to win a spot in right field. In 1898 a bout of dizziness, including fainting spells, led him to seek recovery in the fresh air of Miles City, Montana. A decision to forgo tobacco seemed to repair his health. As a result, he never again smoked or pinched a wad between his cheek and gum.

After recuperating, Brown worked on the range before volunteering to fight in the Spanish-American War on May 13, 1898. The occupation he provided on enlistment papers was "cowboy." Though he would later recall his eagerness to fight in Cuba, he spent most of the war as a private at a dusty camp in Georgia with Troop I, 3rd US Volunteer Cavalry. The *Vancouver Sun's* archives once included a biographical form Brown filled in by hand in the spring of 1955. Under the entry for honors under military service, Brown wrote: "was returned on furlough to enlisted base Miles City Montana account typhoid malaria."[12] He was mustered out in September, returning to Indiana to finish his schooling at Notre Dame.

Football teammate Albert J. "Wild Bill" Galen, who had been born on a Montana ranch and would be a future state attorney general and Montana Supreme Court justice, found Brown a $125-a-month job with baseball's Helena Senators, whose Montana State League rivals included the Anaconda Serpents, Butte Smoke Eaters, and Great Falls Indians. The Senators had only a dozen players: one for each fielding position and four pitchers. One of his teammates was Joe Tinker, an infielder of great promise. Brown was an outfielder and backup catcher, breaking every finger on both hands in the days when pitchers could legally throw spitballs, mudballs, and shineballs (daubed with polish from baseball shoes). The breaks were set with splints jury-rigged from a cigar box. When asked for distinguishing features on citizenship documents, he offered "crooked little finger on right hand," bent, undoubtedly, by a baseball.

Baseball offered men an escape from lives of toil down on the farm, or down in the mine, or on the factory floor. These rough-hewn men did not easily give up a day job in the sunshine. "Salaries? Well, I won't say we just played for the principle of the thing, but none of us fussed much about the money, there not being much to fuss with anyway," Brown said in 1956. "A couple of hundred dollars per month was a pretty good average in those days, and $1.50 per day looked pretty good for eating money on the road."[13]

Nor was the diamond a place for milquetoasts. Fights were not unknown, on or off the field. "I had a pretty reckless mouth," Brown admitted, "and a hot temper."[14] The Helena club folded with the rest of the league after the season. When ex-league President W.M. Lucas started up a Pacific Northwest League on the coast, Brown and Tinker joined a Portland club known as the Webfooters. "Joe Tinker hit .322 that year, which was real good hitting then," Brown said. "I managed .245, but I was never a hitter. Couldn't hit much, but I guess I was never accused of lack

of life. Had the reputation of being pretty rough out on the field."[15] Brown's memory was faulty – Tinker hit .290 and Brown hit .215 – but his scouting report was otherwise accurate.

Brown knew that if he were to stay in baseball, he'd be better off trying to do so as a manager or owner. He lost a competition to become the playing manager at Portland to teammate Sammy Vigneux, so instead Brown helped form a team in Pendleton, Oregon, in an unaffiliated league. (His friend Tinker signed after the 1901 season with the Chicago Cubs before being immortalized by Franklin Pierce Adams in a bit of doggerel about the double-play combination "Tinker to Evers to Chance.") Brown quit the Class-D Pendleton team at midseason to play for a new club at Helena, but the club would not complete its second full season. It was while he was with Pendleton that he made his first visit to Vancouver in 1902, when the city's population was barely over 26,000.

In 1903 Brown moved to Aberdeen, where he became a partner in the Brown-Elmore Shoe Company. His name was associated with the store for more than a half-century, long after he sold his interest. In 1904 he played for and managed the Aberdeen Pippins of the Southwest Washington League, piloted the team in 1905, then became manager of the local Grays Harbor Lumbermen in the Northwestern League in 1906.

On October 11, 1905, Brown married Eula Agnes Jameson, who, at 19, was a decade younger than the groom. A well-regarded musician, she performed in amateur theatrics in Aberdeen, Washington. She was the daughter of an accountant who served as mayor of nearby Montesano. She renounced her Protestant faith to marry the baseball man in a Catholic ceremony. Their childless union ended in an uncontested divorce less than four years later on grounds of "incompatibility of temper."[16]

As a playing manager, Brown led the Aberdeen Black Cats to a pennant in 1907, a season during which he had his share of playing time. "Manager 'Red' Brown, who is something of an all-round ball player, came in from the outfield to cover shortstop and when both his catchers were injured went behind the bat regularly and the team continued to win games," *The Sporting News* reported.[17] In the fall of 1908, the same newspaper covered Brown's negotiations for an interest in the Spokane team. The headline read: "Aspires to be a magnate."[18] He signed a two-year contract to manage the Spokane Indians and bought, for $1, a quarter-interest in the club, which he parlayed just a year later into ownership of the Vancouver franchise.

For 1911, Brown concentrated on the front office, while Kitty Brashear led the club to a 103-win season and the Northwestern League pennant. Brown turned down a $35,000 offer for the club from a San Francisco syndicate. He had greater ambitions.

The Beavers played at Recreation Park, a small stadium at Homer and Smythe Streets on the downtown peninsula owned by the Canadian Pacific Railway and leased by city businessmen, to whom he paid rent. When he found out that the park was to be closed for more profitable use as warehousing, Brown bought the bleachers for $500. He covered the cost by forcing the local lacrosse team to share the proceeds of bleacher-ticket sales from their big series against the Eastern champions. Then he began felling trees and blasting stumps in the forest at a 400-by-500-foot site leased from the CPR for 25 years.[19]

The site on the south shore of False Creek overlooked an escarpment with train tracks below. A wooden grandstand was built around home plate, which was at the corner of West Fifth Avenue and Hemlock Street. Brown's Athletic Park, which opened in 1913, was home to rugby, soccer, and lacrosse matches, as well as political and religious rallies. In 1941 it was the site of the first professional football game in British Columbia.

Bob Brown, wearing a Rotary Club insignia around his neck, speaks with Vancouver Mayor L.D. Taylor (right) prior to the Home Opener at Athletic Park in Vancouver on April 20, 1915. The mayor threw out the opening pitch. (British Columbia Sports Hall of Fame)

Most importantly, Athletic Park was the home of Vancouver baseball for 38 years. Several future major leaguers played in the wooden bandbox, among them spitballer Charlie Schmutz (whose name sounded like what he did to the ball) and Dutch Ruether, who later starred for the Cincinnati Reds in the infamous 1919 World Series. Even 47-year-old right-hander "Iron Man" Joe McGinnity took to the mound at the park on his way to closing out a Hall of Fame career.

Athletic Park helped put Vancouver on baseball's map. Barnstorming teams of major-league all-stars would play games in the city, stopping on their way to exhibition series in Japan. One traveling troupe that played in a downpour in 1934 included Babe Ruth, Lou Gehrig, and four other future Hall of Famers. Gehrig played first base in galoshes while holding an umbrella in his throwing hand.

The ballpark lured such itinerant entertainers as the Bloomer Girls, the Chicago American

A dapper Bob Brown surveys his domain from the wooden steps of Athletic Park. The 5' 9" Brown was a dandy of sorts, wearing vests until the 1950s, long after they had gone out of style. (David Eskenazi Collection)

Giants, and the House of David, a team sponsored by a religious sect whose members wore unshorn hair. Players took the field with beards down to their bellies. On July 3, 1931, a game billed as the first to be played at night in Canada and west of the Mississippi was played at the park. The light fixtures cost $8,000.

The local professional minor leagues faltered after the First World War, not to be revived until the late 1930s. Brown launched the semi-pro Senior City League at his park, with teams sponsored by a local clothier, a distiller, and a transport company. Arrows, Home Gas, Arnold & Quigley, and others had their devoted fans, as did the Asahi, a team of Japanese Canadians that won respect for their clever style of baseball.

Norm "Bananas" Trasolini, Billy Adshead, Johnny Nestman, and Coleman "Coley" Hall became Vancouver household names, as did

pitcher Ernie Kershaw, a teacher known as "The Professor," "The Master Mathematician," and "The Slinging Schoolmaster." Kershaw later pitched for the Vancouver Capilanos, who made their home at the ballpark, renamed Capilano Stadium, from 1939 until 1951, at which point they moved to a new ballpark of the same name in the lee of Little Mountain.

The old ballpark was knocked down to make way for an on-ramp for the Granville Street Bridge, a rich history literally overshadowed by concrete and blacktop. Brown had to twice rebuild his old wooden stadium, in 1926 and 1945. "His ball parks kept burning down on him," sportswriter Clancy Loranger said.[20] That he kept baseball on the entertainment calendar in a sometimes indifferent city was proof both of his tenacity and his penny-pinching. "He could squeeze a nickel as well as anybody," recalled sports reporter Jim Kearney, "and he had to."[21]

To put it simply, Bob Brown was cheap. He sort of obeyed a league dictate that the umpire be given a dozen balls at the start of each game. Brown's daily supply included six fresh balls – and six scuffed balls. He encouraged street urchins to retrieve fouls that flew out of the park. The reward for their shagging? Free admission for what remained of the game.

Still, Brown could be a soft touch. In 1928 he bought a train ticket to Eastern Canada for a frail-looking schoolboy who wished to compete at the Olympic trials as a sprinter. It proved money well spent when Percy Williams later returned from Amsterdam with two Olympic Gold medals. Brown was 77 when he became president of the Western International League in 1953. His single year as boss is notable for his hiring of an up-and-coming umpire by the name of Emmett Ashford, who went on to become in 1966 the first African American to officiate in the major leagues.

Brown went into semiretirement at the end of the season, having spent more than a half-century in baseball. He returned to action to lobby for Vancouver as a new home for the Oakland Oaks. A Pacific Coast League franchise had long been his dream. During the Second World War, he had gone to Sacramento with satchels of cash to try to purchase the team. Instead, local interests managed to raise enough money to keep the club in California. Brown subsequently always referred to his failure as the great disappointment of his life.

The Oaks moved to Vancouver and became the Mounties for the 1956 season. Brown was made public-relations director for the inaugural season. He was also put in charge of a youth program. He insisted plenty of youngsters in British Columbia could make careers in professional baseball, even though the province had graduated only a handful of talents in the past. It would take many years before his prediction came true, and homegrown talents like Larry Walker, Jason Bay, and Jeff Francis put the province on baseball's map.

Brown died on June 21, 1962, of ventricular fibrillation, an irregular heartbeat. He was survived by the former Sarah Jean Campion, a nurse whom he had married in 1933. He passed five days short of their 29th wedding anniversary. They had no children. He was buried at Ocean View Cemetery in Burnaby, just east of Vancouver.

The *Vancouver Sun* greeted his death with the headline: "City Loses Mr. Baseball."[22] The *Province* replied: "Local baseball will not forget Bob Brown."[23] The Mounties folded after the 1962 season, and pro baseball disappeared from Vancouver for two seasons, as though in mourning for the man they called Mr. Baseball.

For so important a sporting figure in Canada's third-largest city, Brown and his legacy have been little celebrated. He was posthumously named an inaugural inductee into the British Columbia Sports Hall of Fame (1966), and he was named to the Canadian Baseball Hall of Fame at St. Marys, Ontario, in 1989. Among the few honors he received in his lifetime was being the first named to the Vancouver Baseball Hall of Fame in 1960. The hall consists of a plaque inside Nat Bailey Stadium, as the second Capilano Stadium was renamed in 1978. The Nat, as it is known, is named after the founder of the White Spot restaurant chain who owned the Mounties for several years. Bailey got his start as a restaurateur and baseball entrepreneur in the 1920s by flogging peanuts and hot dogs at Brown's Athletic Park. He was called Caruso Nat for his singalong vendor's pitch delivered in a high tenor: "A loaf of bread, a pound of meat, and all the mustard you can eat!"[24]

A street leading to the park is known as Clancy Loranger Way, a worthy tribute to the indefatigable baseball writer who chronicled the sport for decades. Before his death, Loranger promoted the idea of placing a plaque in honor of Brown in center field, like at Yankee Stadium. As of 2022 it remained just an idea. The city in which he spent more than a half-century promoting baseball has no permanent memorial to its greatest baseball citizen.

In 2008 the Vancouver Canadians minor-league team unveiled a new mascot, a 6-foot-8 plush character called Bob Brown Bear, who is popular with children. He is cuddly and huggable, two attributes not usually associated with his real-life namesake.

NOTES

1   J. Newton Colver, "Took Spokane Money to Make Real Ball Town out of Vancouver," *Spokane* (Washington) *Spokesman-Review,* July 29, 1912: 30.

2   "Five Spokane Players to Wear Vancouver uniform," *Vancouver Daily Province,* January 15, 1910: 10.

3   Bob Brown, "A Little Bit High and Mighty at 25," *BC Magazine, The Province,* July 6, 1957: 4.

4   "Personals," *Notre Dame Scholastic*, May 21, 1910: 526.

5   Brown, "A Little Bit High and Mighty at 25."

6   A.P. Garvey, "Not All the Macks Are in the Majors," *The Sporting News*, March 8, 1917: 5.

7   Roscoe Fawcett, "Northwestern League," *Spalding's Official Athletic Library Baseball Guide,* March 1911 (New York: American Sports Publishing Co., 1911), 317.

8   "Bob Brown Suffers Nervous Breakdown in Vancouver," *Spokane Chronicle,* December 31, 1910: 14.

9   "Barn Burned at Blencoe," *Sioux City* (Iowa) *Journal*, January 2, 1891: 1.

10 Andy Lytle, "Baseball Days: Chapter II," *Vancouver Sun*, March 6, 1930: 15.

11 John Mackie, "This Day in History: June 21, 1962," *Vancouver Sun*, June 21, 2013: 2.

12 Tom Hawthorn, "'I Was Never Accused of Lack of Life,'" in Mark Armour, ed., *Rain Check: Baseball in the Pacific Northwest* (Cleveland: SABR, 2006), 28.

13 Eric Whitehead, "Fanfare" [column], *The Province*, July 5, 1956: 13.

14 Bob Brown, "It's a Great Old Life, by Jingo!," *BC Magazine, The Province*, June 29, 1957: 3.

15 Brown, "It's a Great Old Life, by Jingo!"

16 "Mrs. Robert Brown Secures Divorce," *Tacoma Daily Ledger,* February 7, 1909: 22.

17 Hawthorn.

18 "Aspires to Be a Magnate," *The Sporting News*, October 29, 1908: 8.

19 "Brown Gets New Baseball Park," *Spokane Chronicle,* June 13, 1912: 9.

20 Hawthorn.

21 Hawthorn.

22 Dick Beddoes, "City Loses Mr. Baseball," *Vancouver Sun*, June 22, 1962: 21.

23 Clancy Loranger, "Local Baseball Will Not Forget Bob Brown," *The Province*, June 23, 1962: 17.

24 "Bleacher Briefs," *Daily Province*, June 13, 1925: 23.

BROTHER MATTHIAS

By Brian "Chip" Martin

Shortly before he died, baseball superstar Babe Ruth publicly credited a man who was born on Cape Breton Island with making him the ballplayer and man he had become. He did it in writing. Not once, but twice. In his 1948 autobiography, the third and final telling of his life story, George Herman Ruth was effusive about Martin Leo Boutilier, a man who taught him at St. Mary's Industrial Training School in Baltimore. "It was at St. Mary's that I met and learned to love the greatest man I've ever known," Ruth said of the teacher he knew as Brother Matthias. "He was the father I needed."[1] Ruth admitted he'd been a "bad kid," listed as incorrigible, when he was sent to the reform school and orphanage just west of Baltimore at the age of 7.

On the same day Ruth died, his second tribute to Matthias appeared in an inspirational publication called *Guideposts Magazine*, founded by Christian preacher Norman Vincent Peale, author of the best-selling book *The Power of Positive Thinking*. In the *Guideposts* article attributed to Ruth, billed as his "last message," he repeated that he had been "a bad kid," and that Matthias had turned his life around and had introduced him to baseball. He called the 6-foot-6 Nova Scotian "the greatest man I have ever known."

Ruth said Matthias detected natural talent in the troubled boy, and taught him how to throw, catch, and hit properly. "I would watch him bug-eyed," Ruth said of seeing his mentor drive a ball 350 feet with a bat in his right hand in the St. Mary's schoolyard.[2]

Ironically, although Ruth himself credited Matthias with making him a ballplayer, the press acclaimed another Catholic brother for discovering and coaching the baseball phenom and getting him into professional baseball. And like many things in baseball, the true story was eclipsed by another that became embedded in the lore of the sport. Consequently, the story of the quiet Canadian, Brother Matthias, and his contribution to baseball history are not well known, and deserves to be shared.

Martin Leo Boutilier was born in 1872 in the coal-mining community of Lingan, near the tip of Cape Breton Island, not far from New Waterford, the eighth of 10 children born to Joseph Boutilier and Mary Ann Howley. Two of their sons had died as infants. Joseph Boutilier, variously listed as an engineer or machinist, maintained and repaired equipment in the mine at Lingan, and on seagoing vessels. Because of difficult economic conditions in the Maritimes, some other members of the

Boutilier family had moved to Boston. As the mine in Lingan began to play out, Joseph began to explore employment options elsewhere because he had so many mouths to feed. He first tried Halifax, a bustling seaport of 68,000, but by the late 1870s a lingering recession limited prospects there, so he took his family farther south to Boston, a city of 362,839, late in 1880.[3] The family settled in East Boston, not far from today's Logan Airport, where many expatriate Canadians had taken up residence. Son Martin had just turned 9 years of age.

The Boutilier family settled into a city that was crazy about baseball. They may have been familiar with the game back in Lingan, but it's doubtful they had much exposure to it in the hardscrabble mining community where spare time was rare. With seven boys ranging in age from 6 to 22, the family had nearly enough to field their own team in their new home. Residents of East Boston had been playing the game since as early as 1843, and immigrants considered it an important part of becoming American. The streets of working-class Boston were often filled with men and children playing games to the delight of spectators who cheered them on from front porches and windows. The Boston Red Stockings were charter members of the first professional baseball league, the National Association, founded in 1871; they placed second that first season and were league champions from 1872 to 1875. Boston was a strong franchise and became a founding member of the National League in 1876, capturing the pennant of the new league in 1877, 1878, and 1883. It was clear baseball had a firm grip on America's fifth largest city.

Aside from their love of baseball in their adopted city, Martin and his older brother Thomas were more spiritually inclined than other members of their family. Thomas was attracted to the Brothers of Charity, a Belgium-based Catholic order that operated the House of the Guardian Angel, an orphanage and training school, in Boston. Thomas was sent for training at the Brothers of Charity in Montréal, but his inability to speak French proved to be an obstacle and he returned to Boston.[4]

Back home, Thomas connected with the Congregation of the Brothers of St. Francis Xavier (known as the Xaverians), another Belgium-based order that had its American headquarters in Louisville, Kentucky, and whose operating language was English. The Xaverians (pronounced za-VAIR-ians) focused their work on education and moral guidance for youth. They are laymen who take the same vows of obedience, poverty, and chastity as priests, but cannot conduct Mass or bestow sacramental privileges. Thomas Boutilier discovered that during his sojourn in Canada, younger brother Martin had become involved with the Xaverians in about 1890.

The Xaverians had begun operating a new school in East Boston where Martin likely first encountered them. By 1891, he signed an "agreement of membership" and became an apprentice with the order. By the time his training was completed four years later, he had been assigned the name Brother Matthias, as was the custom of the Xaverians. Thomas also joined the order and became Brother Amandus. During their training, the Boutilier brothers were sent to Xaverian-operated Catholic schools in Baltimore – Amandus to Mount St. Joseph College and Matthias to St. Mary's Industrial Training School.[5] The schools were not far from each other, but Mount St. Joseph was a more traditional high school with tuition and board and a focus on academics, while boys at St. Mary's were often sent there by the courts, were known as "inmates" and were trained to work in the trades. St. Mary's was a combination training school, orphanage, and detention facility for which permission was required to leave the premises.

Brother Matthias was better educated than his older brother and took up teaching at St. Mary's, while Amandus performed administrative duties at Mount St. Joseph. Somewhere along the line in Xaverian paperwork, an "i" was dropped from the spelling of the Boutilier name to become Boutlier. Matthias, likely because of his size, became head disciplinarian at St. Mary's, which sometimes housed as many as 800 boys. He could bring order to an unruly scene simply by showing up and quietly making his presence known. To his colleagues, he was known as Big Matt, but to the boys, he was known as The Boss. Matthias was also one of the baseball coaches at the school, which sometimes fielded 40 or more teams in a season. Baseball was king at St. Mary's, which had two fields, one for the older boys and another for the younger ones. It was to St. Mary's that a youngster would come, just as Matthias was settling into a life in the service of God. The boy changed the life of the big Xaverian who saw something special in him, trained him in the finer points of baseball, and helped him transform the game.

George Herman Ruth was born in Baltimore on February 6, 1895, in the Ridgely's Delight neighborhood, immediately west of Camden Yards. He was the first child born to George and Katie Ruth, who had eight children, but only George Jr. and his sister Mary survived past infancy. George Sr. and his brother John operated a lightning-rod business established by their father, but in 1901 George left the business to operate a bar downtown on West Camden Street, and his family moved in above it. The premises were in a gritty working-class area, and young George soon found himself getting into trouble while his parents worked long hours in their saloon. Strains became evident in their marriage, aggravated by too much alcohol consumption. Meanwhile, George Jr. was becoming a street kid, tossing stolen eggs and tomatoes at the heavy vehicles on their way to and from the Baltimore docks. A lefty, young Ruth developed an accurate arm and also joined his pals in rudimentary games of baseball on the busy city streets. Sometimes Ruth and his fellow troublemakers were caught

and whipped for their misdeeds by truck drivers, and they received beatings from shopkeepers, he recalled in a 1928 autobiography, ghost-written by sportswriter Ford Frick.[6]

In 1902 George Ruth, at the urging of a police officer friend, placed his 7-year-old son at St. Mary's Industrial Training School, to which courts sent many youngsters in a bid to deter them from a life of crime. "I was listed as an incorrigible, and I guess I was," Ruth admitted in his 1948 autobiography.[7] Not long afterward, either in the classroom or on the ball field, the youngster met Matthias, the man who became a surrogate father of sorts. In the classroom, Matthias encouraged the young lefty to write with his right hand, in flowing script. On the ball field, Matthias noticed abundant raw talent and took extra time with the newcomer, drilling him in proper fielding and hitting techniques. Ruth became a catcher, but the school had no gloves suitable for lefties, so he was forced to catch with a glove on his left hand, then quickly flip off the glove and throw the ball with the same hand. It was cumbersome, but young Ruth became adept at it. And when he ridiculed a pitcher he was catching one day, coach Matthias made him take over the pitching duties himself. It was a fateful move that soon began attracting attention to the young hurler. Ruth played on school teams with older boys, winning the school championship in 1912. During his nearly 12 years at the school, Ruth off the field became a skilled shirt-maker in the school's tailoring shop, which also made uniforms for the St. Mary's baseball teams.

Baseball and young George Ruth were meant for each other. And Brother Matthias cultivated and channeled the raw talent of the loudmouthed, good-natured kid to whom he took a shine. One of Ruth's pals, Fats Leisman, figured Ruth was a baseball prodigy who didn't really need much direction. "My personal opinion is that the Babe was born to play ball," Leisman later wrote.[8] For his part, Ruth disagreed. He said this about his mentor and coach:

Brother Matthias had the right idea about training a baseball club. He made every boy on the team play every position in the game, including the bench. A kid might pitch a game one day and find himself behind the bat the next or perhaps out in the sun-field. You see Brother Matthias' idea was to fit a boy to jump in in any emergency and make good. So whatever I have at the bat or on the mound or in the outfield or even on the bases, I owe directly to Brother Matthias.[9]

Ruth was in awe of Brother Matthias and copied many of his techniques. The big man swung with an uppercut at a time when level swings were in vogue to smash line drives during the Deadball Era. But Matthias could easily loft a ball over the outfield fence with his powerful swing. His young protégé developed his own long swing and powerful uppercut. Matthias, a big man, ran around the bases with surprisingly small steps and was rather pigeon-toed. There is no shortage of film showing Ruth scampering around the bases with similar footwork during his long career. The form of Matthias was unorthodox, but effective. By copying much of what he saw in Matthias, young Ruth went on to revolutionize the game of baseball, especially with his bat. "I think I was born as a hitter the first day I ever saw him hit a baseball," the home-run king said of Matthias in his 1948 autobiography.[10]

Ruth's baseball exploits, particularly the effectiveness of his pitching, began attracting attention in the Baltimore baseball community during his years at St. Mary's. In his annual report for 1913, Brother Paul, the school superintendent, proudly reported: "One boy created a sensation by his excellent work."[11] He wasn't talking about academics. The boy was Ruth; the "work" was baseball. A player at Mount St. Joseph, which fielded highly competitive teams, was among those who took note. He suggested to Brother Gilbert, his ball coach and an administrator at the school, that he see the young hurler for St. Mary's.

Gilbert did so, and was impressed with what he saw. Gilbert, an extrovert, unlike the retiring and rather shy Matthias, had many connections in the baseball community, and was friends with Jack Dunn, owner of the Baltimore Orioles of the Eastern and then International Leagues. Gilbert often alerted Dunn to local talent, and Dunn, a former major-league pitcher, was always on the lookout for young pitchers he could develop.

There are several versions of the story about how Dunn learned about Ruth, most involving a tip or introduction by Brother Gilbert. In his 1948 autobiography, Ruth said that during February of 1914, shortly after his 19th birthday, he was throwing a baseball around the still-frozen yard at St. Mary's, when he was approached by Brothers Matthias, Gilbert, and Paul, and the Orioles owner. Gilbert introduced him to Dunn, who asked the startled Ruth if he'd like to sign with the Orioles.[12] Dunn offered to become his legal guardian and pay him $600 for the 1914 season. Babe accepted.

Brother Gilbert had many friends among sportswriters, some of whom promulgated the story that Gilbert not only tipped Dunn to Ruth, but that he had also coached him. In a seven-part series in the *Boston Globe* published in 1923, in which Brother Matthias is barely mentioned, Gilbert's credentials were described this way by the editors: "No other one man, except the Babe himself, knows more about his life than does Brother Gilbert."[13] Gilbert was soon enshrined by sportswriters as the discoverer of Ruth. For his part, the modest Matthias made no protest. He and his surrogate son knew the truth, and felt there was no need to upset Gilbert's applecart. Gilbert, a popular after-dinner speaker, delivered more than 1,000 speeches in his lifetime, many of them discussing his time with Babe Ruth. When he died in 1947, Gilbert was working on his memoirs in which Ruth loomed large. At the time, sportswriters were still hailing him as the one responsible for The Babe.

George Herman Ruth Jr., now 19, was quickly dubbed "Babe" when he appeared at spring-training camp for the Orioles in Fayetteville, North Carolina. "Look at Dunnie and his new babe," one of the older players said at one point, while another took pity on him when Dunn bawled him out for something, saying: "You're just a Babe in the woods."[14] Another story was that Dunn was impressed with a home run Ruth belted at Fayetteville and reportedly said: "This baby will not get away from me."[15] The name stuck. To Matthias, however, he was always "George."

Babe Ruth did well with the Orioles, but Jack Dunn faced unexpected competition in 1914 from the Baltimore Terrapins of the new Federal League, and was strapped for money. In July he sold his "baby" to the Boston Red Sox along with two other players. Babe would earn $650 a month in Boston, up from $500 in Baltimore. As a tailor, for which he'd been trained at St. Mary's, he would have earned about $60 a month. Ruth was unhappy, however, at leaving Baltimore, his home, and Brothers Matthias, Paul, Gilbert, and others. Fortified with the acquisitions from Dunn in Baltimore, the Red Sox were making a run for the American League pennant; by August, however, the Philadelphia Athletics had an insurmountable lead, and Boston owner J.J. Lannin decided to send Ruth down to the Providence Grays of the International League for more playing time and experience. The Grays, purchased by the Canadian-born Lannin from the Detroit Tigers, were a sort of farm team for the Red Sox. Babe retained his Red Sox salary but was unhappy at the move, which he viewed as a demotion. He was in Providence for six weeks, helping the team to the International League pennant. Along the way, he belted his first home run in a professional game, on September 5 in Toronto against the Maple Leafs. Mythmakers insist the ball sailed over the bleachers at Maple Leaf Park on Hanlan's Point island into Lake Ontario,

but contemporaneous press accounts made no such claim of the ball getting wet that day.[16]

Babe returned to Boston and helped the Red Sox win three World Series in the next four years. In 1920 he was famously sold to the New York Yankees. There, he quit pitching so that he could wield his mighty bat in every game. He stayed in touch with Brother Matthias and St. Mary's, and often brought fellow players with him when he returned to the school for visits. In 1919 a fire heavily damaged St. Mary's, and Babe pitched in to help fundraising efforts, persuading the Yankees to let the St. Mary's band accompany the team on a road trip, and to pass the hat to rebuild the school that Babe considered his real home.[17] As his fame grew and he transformed the game with his home runs and made the Yankees a formidable powerhouse, Babe continued to stay in contact with Brother Matthias, and sent him tickets for some games. Babe's late-night extracurricular activities with drink and the ladies often got Ruth into trouble with team brass, who occasionally called upon Matthias to counsel their star.

Matthias visited New York to see Babe play in 1922 or 1923, and was surprised when Ruth announced that he was buying Matthias a brand-new Cadillac as a thank-you for everything he had done.[18] The big brother was astounded at Babe's generosity. Because of his vow of poverty, Matthias had the luxury car registered in the name of St. Mary's, which gave him exclusive use of it. Always the teacher, Matthias used it as an educational tool at times, showing the boys rudimentary auto mechanics. He also ferried around young passengers to various concerts and other events. One night during the summer of 1927, while returning home from an out-of-town event, the Cadillac stalled on some railway tracks and was demolished when struck by a train.[19] Luckily, Matthias and the boys escaped unscathed. When Babe heard about the incident, he promptly bought Matthias another Cadillac.[20]

Babe Ruth greets a Civil War veteran under the approving gaze of his mentor in life and baseball, Brother Matthias. (Erin Casey)

By 1926 Babe was constantly womanizing and had separated from his first wife, Helen. He considered divorce, but Matthias talked him out of it. Ruth recorded 47 home runs that year, bouncing back after a poor 1925 season, but his off-field activities produced grief for Yankees general manager Ed Barrow and on-field manager Miller Huggins. The team assigned a private eye to follow their star, whose late-night antics continued unabated. In June the Yankees made a road trip that included Chicago, a city whose delights Babe always sampled in large dollops. Team management called upon Brother Matthias to come to Chicago and speak to Ruth about

their star's behavior, hoping the Xaverian could yet again provide fatherly advice and modify Ruth's behavior.

The city was hopping when the Yankees arrived in town. The 28th International Eucharistic Congress was being held for Catholics around the world, the first time the event had been held in the United States. The Yankees found an invitation for Matthias to attend the congress, and asked him to speak to Babe while both were in town. One evening Matthias came to the Prado Hotel, where the Yankees were staying, and occupied a chair in the hotel lobby from which he could watch the elevator. Ruth soon appeared, apparently ready for a wild night on the town, but he spotted Matthias and the two men greeted each other warmly. Matthias said he was in town for the religious congress and to see Ruth play the White Sox. He said he wanted to take his former pupil out to dinner and to chat. His plans for the night dashed, Ruth agreed and the pair stayed out until 11 p.m. as Matthias sternly advised Ruth to clean up his act because many people were concerned for him. He likely reminded the Babe that he had been encouraged to live a God-centered life as a young man at St. Mary's, not a hedonistic lifestyle filled with women and booze. What kind of role model was George for young men like those still at St. Mary's? Babe was letting down the boys at his old school who idolized him. The sobering talk left the prodigal son promising to do better. Ruth biographer Marshall Smelser called this a "turning point" in Ruth's behavior. "Certainly he no longer after that time had the reputation for hell-raising that he had before."[21]

It was in that second Cadillac that Matthias himself got into trouble. He was seen driving the big car while repeatedly visiting a much younger woman during 1931, and concerned neighbors reported him to the Catholic Archdiocese of Baltimore. Matthias was 58 at the time, the woman 23. He denied any improper relationship when his activities were investigated by church officials. Matthias could have been expelled from the Xaverians for violating his oath of chastity, leaving him penniless as he approached the age of 60. Instead, the church reprimanded him and transferred Matthias to a Xaverian-operated school in Danvers, Massachusetts, noting: "If Brother Matthias had been more amenable to discipline over a period of years, his scandalous actions might have been avoided."[22] He'd been head disciplinarian at St. Mary's, yet his own conduct had fallen short of what was expected of him. In 1942 he celebrated 50 years with the Xaverian order while living in retirement at St. Joseph's Juniorate in Peabody, Massachusetts. Two years later, Matthias was found dead in his room at the age of 70. He is buried at the Xaverian cemetery in Danvers. It is not known how much he was able to see his surrogate son after his move to Massachusetts.

In his only known interview with the press, the unheralded Matthias told a reporter in 1935 that Babe was one of a kind: "There never was a better boy at St. Mary's School in Baltimore than 'George.' I was there 38 years and there were better ball players, but never a better boy."[23] The affection of the surrogate father was clear. And Babe returned the sentiments publicly in print shortly before his own death in 1948.

SOURCES

The author has also written a full book on Brother Matthias. See Brian Martin, *The Man Who Made Babe Ruth: Brother Matthias of St. Mary's School* (Jefferson, North Carolina: McFarland, 2020).

NOTES

1   Babe Ruth, as told to Bob Considine, *The Babe Ruth Story* (New York: E.P. Dutton & Co., 1948), 13, 18.

2   Babe Ruth, "The Kids Can't Take It if We Don't Give It!," *Guideposts Magazine*, October 1948: 1-2, 23-24, accessed February 10, 2018, http://baberuthcentral.com/remembering-the-babe-/babe-ruths-public-statement.

3   The move of the Boutilier family to Halifax was recorded by Cape Breton researcher Virginia MacDonald in the November 24, 2007, edition of the *Cape Breton Post*. Her grandfather was born in Lingan in 1871 and her father, Bernard, was a machinist/engineer. The 1881 Census of Canada recorded the Boutiliers as still living in Lingan. Descendants of the Cape Breton Boutiliers, Jean Mor and Francis McGillivary, confirmed to the author that the move to Halifax came about this time.

4   Brother Amandus Dossier CCFX, 6/03 #318, of the Xaverian Brothers, University of Notre Dame Archives, South Bend, Indiana.

5   Brother Matthias Dossier, CCFX 6/04 #329, of the Xaverian Brothers, University of Notre Dame Archives, South Bend, Indiana.

6   Babe Ruth, *Babe Ruth's Own Book of Baseball* (New York: G.P. Putnam's Sons, 1928), 3-4.

7   Babe Ruth, to Considine, *The Babe Ruth Story*, 12.

8   Lou Leisman, *I Was with Babe Ruth at St. Mary's* (Aberdeen, Maryland: self-published, 1956), 21.

9   Babe Ruth, *Playing the Game: My Early Years in Baseball* (Mineola, New York: Dover Publications, 2011), 6.

10 Babe Ruth, *The Babe Ruth Story*, 15.

11 Marshall Smelser, *The Life That Ruth Built: A Biography* (Lincoln: University of Nebraska Press, 1975), 31.

12 Babe Ruth, *The Babe Ruth Story*, 20.

13 Brother Gilbert, C.F.X., "Babe Ruth's Great First Home Run – Brother Gilbert Discovers Him," *Boston Sunday Globe*, October 14, 1928: 20.

14 Babe Ruth, *The Babe Ruth Story*, 25-26.

15 "Babe Ruth 'A Natural' Even as Oriole Rookie," *Baltimore Sun*, August 17, 1948: 15.

16 Leonard Levin, "Baseball. Arrival of Ruth Turned Grays' Skies to Blue/81 Years Ago, the Bambino Led Providence to the International League Pennant," *Providence Journal*, August 14, 1995: B4. Levin quotes from *Journal* sportswriter Bill Perrin, who wrote about Ruth's blast that sailed "over the right field fence." No Toronto paper reported that the ball made it into the lake that day.

17 Babe Ruth, *The Babe Ruth Story*, 132.

18 Some reports say the year was 1925 or 1926, but an early 1924 report in the *Baltimore Sun* mentions Matthias taking St. Mary's boys to a theatrical performance "in an automobile given the latter by 'Babe' Ruth, the baseball player." Date of the article is March 17, 1924, "White House Talk Explained by Lang," on page 4.

19 "Auto Presented by Babe Ruth to St. Mary's Smashed by Train," *Baltimore Sun*, August 17, 1927: 22.

20 Babe Ruth, *The Babe Ruth Story*, 107.

21 Smelser, 239.

22 Matthias Dossier, University of Notre Dame Archives.

23 Thomas Sheehan, "Brother Matthias Talks of 'George,'" *Boston Evening Transcript*, February 28, 1935: 6.

FRANK SHAUGHNESSY:
THE OTTAWA YEARS

By David McDonald

For Frank Shaughnessy, a lanky, copper-haired outfielder from small-town Illinois, the 1905 season was a crash course in the uncertainties of dead-ball era baseball. On April 17, a week and a half past his 22nd birthday, the former Notre Dame all-round athletic star had his first sip of big-league coffee, playing right field for the Senators in a game in Washington against the Highlanders of New York. He went 0-for-3 with a hit-by-pitch.

"It wasn't easy in those days, believe me," Shaughnessy said. "Regulars would actually chase a rookie with a bat if he attempted to take a turn hitting. A regular held his job until somebody drove him out, and every youngster was regarded as a menace."[1] Shag, as he was called,[2] got into another game four days later, hitting a bases-loaded triple off future Hall of Famer Jack Chesbro. But the game – and Shag's hit – were washed out before becoming official. The very next day Washington shipped him out, to the Montgomery Senators of the Southern Association.

Shaughnessy hated Alabama – the heat, the mosquitoes, the very real prospect of contracting yellow fever. He dropped 20 pounds, played poorly, and after seven games he was released, whereupon he packed his glove and spikes and headed north to Pennsylvania to play for Coatesville of the "outlaw" Tri-State League.[3] After a few games there he ventured even further north to join the Montpelier-Barre Intercities, a.k.a. Hyphens, of the even more outlaw Northern League.[4] It was already Shag's fourth club of the year, and it was only June.

Frank Shaughnessy was born into a railroading family in Amboy, Illinois, about 100 miles west of Chicago, in 1883, the seventh child of parents from Limerick, Ireland. His father, Patrick, had emigrated to Canada as a boy. After an unsuccessful stint at farming near Montréal, he moved to the United States at the age of 25. Patrick held various positions during a 35-year career with the Illinois Central Railroad, including coal shed foreman and watchman. Two of his sons, William and John, also worked for the Illinois Central. Youngest son Frank was determined not to.

Smart, ambitious, and perpetually in motion, Shaughnessy worked in a pharmacy while attending high school. "I got up at six to open the drug store at seven, then ran three or four miles to school," he recalled. "At noon I hurried back to the store to give the boss time for lunch, got my lunch at home about two blocks away, and dashed back to school. When school let out, I ran again to be at the store by 4 P.M. I got a half-hour off for supper, and, at 10 P.M., I could walk home. It's no wonder I always could run fast – I had to!"[5]

Shaughnessy could also play baseball, which earned him a partial scholarship to study pharmacy at Indiana's Notre Dame College, at the time "little more than a farm, and the nuns made our meals and washed our clothes."[6] Shag also excelled at track, and especially at football.[7] In 1904 he captained the Fighting Irish.

"It seems like I can't remember a time when I wasn't working hard," he said in later years. "While at Notre Dame, I also ran the campus newspaper, a confectionery concession and was the correspondent for several Chicago newspapers."[8] Using the *nom de guerre* "Shannon" to protect his collegiate athletic eligibility, Shag spent his summers playing professional baseball in outposts like Sioux City, Iowa, and Cairo, Illinois. In the spring of 1904 he finished his pharmacy degree and immediately began working toward another in law. It was after football season that fall that he came out as a professional athlete, signing with the Washington Senators.

FRANK AND KITTY

Shaughnessy's glory days as a multisport star at Notre Dame were now behind him. His life had become a blur of steam trains, low-rent boarding houses, and cheap hotels. The only constant was the nagging worry that one's current club – or even the whole league it was part of – might not survive the season, that the next paycheck might not materialize, that the opportunities to forge a career in the snakes-and-ladders, musical-chairs world of dead-ball era baseball might dry up.

The Northern, a colorful but financially shaky circuit based in Vermont and northern New York, was, in those days, the game's answer to the witness protection program: a sanctuary for contract jumpers, collegians playing under

assumed names, and those on the lam from Organized Baseball for a variety of legal, financial, and philosophical reasons.

Certainly, the caliber of play in the Northern was a lot better than one might have expected of a four-team circuit[9] on the fringes of the American baseball map. The Hyphens' pitching staff that season featured Shaughnessy's former Notre Dame teammate Ed Reulbach (playing under the name Sheldon), who would go on to lead the National League in winning percentage three straight years, and Colby Jack Coombs, who would lead the American League in wins in 1910 and 1911. The third baseman on the team was Eddie Grant, who had a 10-year major-league career before being killed in France's Argonne Forest in 1918.

The Northern was also the only integrated league in baseball – if the presence of a lone Black player, former Harvard baseball and football star William Clarence Matthews, counts as integrated. Matthews, putting up excellent numbers in Burlington, Vermont, was rumored to be headed for the National League's Boston Beaneaters, whose manager, Fred Tenney, was eager to have him. When that opportunity failed to materialize, Matthews abandoned baseball and embarked on a prominent legal and civil rights career.

Baseball aside, the Northern League turned out to be the most eventful stop on Shaughnessy's lengthy baseball odyssey. It was during this time he attended some sort of Roman Catholic function in Ogdensburg, New York, where the president of the Northern League introduced him to a young woman named Katherine Quinn, called Kitty. She was the convent-educated daughter of an Ottawa hotelier, Michael Quinn.[10] That brief encounter might go a long way to explaining Shaughnessy's decision to sign a $140-a-month contract to play for a Northern League expansion franchise in Ottawa the following summer. The manager of the new club – quickly branded the Outlaws – was Shag's former Hyphens field boss, Arthur Daley. The Outlaws played their home games at the University of Ottawa's Varsity Oval, where they drew respectable crowds of 1,000-1,500.

Once again the quality of play in the Northern was surprisingly fast. The Rutland team boasted future Hall of Fame second baseman Eddie Collins and right-hander Dick Rudolph, a 26-game winner for the Boston Braves in 1914. Burlington featured third baseman Larry Gardner, who would play 17 years in the American League. One of Shag's Ottawa teammates, playing under the alias C.R. Ray, was Ray Demmitt, who had a seven-year career in the American League.

Shaughnessy acquitted himself well in this company, finishing with a .297 batting average and a league-leading five homers. He also proved a fan favorite. "Shaughnessy is the idol of the small boy and incidentally the ladies also," said the *Ottawa Journal*. "His appearance at bat is always the signal for an outburst of applause and kindly advice to slam it over the fence again or to murder the umpire when he calls a strike."[11]

Despite its blaze of talent the cross-border Northern League proved no more durable than its 1905 iteration. Plattsburgh folded in midseason, then Rutland. On August 20, with the league down to three teams and the club nearly $6,000 in debt, the Outlaws, too, surrendered. Shaughnessy, manager Daley, and several more Outlaws had to sue to try to collect their final pay. It would not be the last time Shag would sit in a Canadian courtroom on a baseball matter.

While the league withered around him, Frank's romance with Kitty blossomed. But with several weeks of summer left, Shaughnessy reluctantly hopped the train back to Indiana to try to squeeze a few more games and a few more dollars out of the remains of the season. He joined the South Bend Greens of the Class-B Central League, where he was said to have hit "the ball like a fiend,"[12] batting .333 in 18 games. That fall — it was an era of distinct sporting seasons —

Shaughnessy launched a backup career, coaching football at Welsh Neck Academy, a Baptist high school in Hartsville, South Carolina.

Frank and Kitty exchanged a lot of letters in those years. Shag spent the spring and fall of 1907 in South Carolina, where he coached baseball and football at Clemson Agricultural College. In the summer it was San Francisco, where he played left field for the San Francisco Seals of the Pacific Coast League. In 1908, after again coaching baseball at Clemson, Shag returned to Washington to join the D.C. entry in a wannabe third major circuit, the Union League. Sportswriters soon dubbed it the Onion League, "because it was cheap and smelled bad."[13] The Onion survived two months before landing on the baseball compost heap. Shaughnessy, though, landed on his

Kitty Shaughnessy, ca. 1908, the person responsible for Shaughnessy's move to Canada. (Courtesy Honora Shaughnessy)

feet – Connie Mack immediately signed him to play for his Philadelphia Athletics.

In his first game, in St. Louis on June 8, he went 3-for-4 against the Browns' oddball future Hall of Famer Rube Waddell. But Shag's big-league dream lasted all of two weeks. "I thought I had a good chance with the A's," he recalled years later. "I was hitting .321 [sic – it was actually .310 on a team with a .223 batting average] after eight games and feeling pretty proud of myself. Then one cold day in Chicago, I had to make a hard throw to the plate and something snapped in my arm. I couldn't throw overhanded for a year..."[14]

Mack promptly shipped Shag and his wounded wing to Reading, Pennsylvania, of the Tri-State League, now a Class-B circuit under the umbrella of Organized Baseball, for a player to be named later. That player turned out to be a young third baseman named Frank "Home Run" Baker,

who went on to a Hall of Fame career. "That was a pretty good deal for the Athletics, I would say," said Shaughnessy, adding, in faux-self-deprecating style, "I guess I wasn't much of a player."[15] That fall 25-year-old Frank Shaughnessy, vagabond baseball player and football coach, married 20-year-old Kitty Quinn at St. Brigid's, the English Roman Catholic church serving Ottawa's Lower Town neighborhood.

A TEAM OF ONE'S OWN

In 1909 Shaughnessy bought his release from Reading so that he could take a job playing for – and, for the first time in his baseball career, managing – the Roanoke Tigers, a.k.a. Highlanders, of the Class-C Virginia League. He was the youngest manager in Organized Baseball. It was an auspicious debut. Shag batted .285 with

This cheery-looking bunch is the Washington entry in the short-lived Union League, a.k.a. Onion League, in 1908. Shaughnessy is in the middle row, second from left. Washington's Toronto-born manager Arthur Irwin is the gentleman with the cookie duster moustache and the derby hat. Shag played well enough in Washington to be picked up by Connie Mack's Philadelphia Athletics when the league folded in June of 1908. (*Washington Times*, April 18, 1908)

a league-leading five home runs and guided his team to the pennant. It was a nailbiter of a finish – which would become something of a Shaughnessy managerial trademark – with the Tigers nipping the Norfolk Tars by just a half-game and .003 percentage points.

The Shaughnessys stayed put in Roanoke for another two years. The prospect of not having to pack up and move must have been appealing, especially with the arrival of their first two boys. (The family would eventually total nine children– eight boys and a girl.) It was also an opportunity for the indefatigable Shaughnessy to add to his gridiron résumé, as coach of the freshman squad at Washington and Lee College in nearby Lexington, Virginia, and to try his hand at a number of business sidelines. In Roanoke he bought into a couple of cigar stores, a garage, and an automobile agency, one of the first in the country.[16] He

also found time to pass the Virginia bar exam and hang out a shingle, although, according to legendary Montréal sportswriter Dink Carroll, Shag lacked the patience to build up a practice. As *Maclean's* magazine once said, "Indoors irks this man."[17]

On the surface Roanoke appeared a good fit for the Shaughnessys. But Kitty missed her family in Ottawa, and, equally, as a devout Roman Catholic, she never felt entirely comfortable in the Protestant South. Although the anti-Catholic KKK was between waves of activity during this period, Virginia was still the heart of Klan country. So Shaughnessy began to formulate a plan, one that would accommodate both his wife's desire to raise a family in a more hospitable environment and his own to assert some measure of control over a perennially precarious baseball career. During his third and final year in Roanoke, he kept an

The 27-year-old Shaughnessy made his managerial debut with the Roanoke Tigers in 1910, leading his team to the Virginia League pennant. (J. Harry Kidd, Roanoke, Virginia)

eye on the fortunes of an upstart Class-D circuit operating in Western Ontario.

Consisting of teams from London, Hamilton, Brantford, St. Thomas, Guelph, and Berlin, the grandiosely named Canadian League had a moderately successful first season in 1911. Despite the failure of the Northern League in Ottawa, Shaughnessy felt the capital might be a good fit for this new loop. "Well, this always looked like one good ball town to me, and I am surprised you haven't entered some league before this," he had told an Ottawa reporter during a 1910 visit.[18] The city in fact was reportedly the only one of its size in Canada or the United States that did not have professional baseball. Shag decided he would be the one to fix that. And so after the 1911 season, the Shaughnessys packed their bags, bundled up their baby boys, and boarded a northbound train, destination: Canada.

In Ottawa, Shaughnessy found a couple of partners among members of the fourth estate. They were Tommy Gorman, the 25-year-old Olympic lacrosse gold medalist turned "sporting editor" of the *Citizen*, and Malcolm Brice, 36, sporting editor of the *Free Press*. Publicity for the venture was not going to be a problem. Nor was money. A good chunk of the financial backing for the team came from Frank Ahearn,[19] son of wealthy inventor and entrepreneur Thomas "Electricity" Ahearn, known as "the Edison of Canada." The senior Ahearn was the principal owner of the Ottawa Electric Railway Company.

In December 1911 the Canadian League awarded a franchise to the Ottawa Baseball Club, Frank Shaughnessy, president (as well as part-owner, manager, and center fielder). The Peterboro (now spelled Peterborough) White Caps were also added for the 1912 season, making the Canadian an eight-team league and bumping it up, by virtue of the total population it represented – more than 300,000 – to Class C. Despite its elevated status, the league was hardly big business. In 1912 you could have bought the entire defending-champion Berlin club for $2,500. Team salaries – exclusive of the manager's – were capped at $1,500 a month, although most teams played fast and loose with that notion.

TWO-TIMER

If building a team from scratch wasn't challenging enough, two weeks after Ottawa landed its franchise came the revelation that the boss of the Senators was something of a baseball bigamist. Apparently, Shag had already signed a contract to play for and manage the Fort Wayne Railroaders of the 12-team, Class-B Central League. He might have gambled on Fort Wayne owner Claude H. Varnell not standing in the way of his new Ottawa venture, that Varnell would find someone else to conduct the Railroaders. He was soon disabused of that notion. "Shaughnessey [*sic*] will manage the Fort Wayne team unless he dies or gives up baseball," Varnell responded.[20]

Undeterred, Shag persisted in his game of contractual chicken and spent the winter and spring months laying the groundwork for his Ottawa team's debut. The first order of business was to negotiate a deal to play home games at Lansdowne Park. (Upgrades included the removal of a pesky fire hydrant in center field.) Season-ticket prices for 54 home games were set at $25 for grandstand seating and $15 for the bleachers. Advance, single-game tickets – 25 cents for general admission, 50 cents in the grandstand – would be sold through J.L. Rochester's Drug Store on Sparks Street. The Senators also put out a call for men to supply "peanuts, cigars, chocolate and chewing gum"[21] to the anticipated throngs at Lansdowne, where the team would play Monday through Saturday.

Sunday was another matter. No one played Sunday baseball in true-blue Ontario. A number of sites on the lawless Quebec side offered to host the Senators on the Sabbath, but Shaughnessy eventually bowed to unspecified pressures and shoved Sunday ball to a back burner. "Ottawas Have Yielded to Wishes of Better Element," a *Citizen* headline said, without feeling the need to specify who exactly this better element was.[22]

But Shaughnessy's most crucial task was to fill the Senators' spiffy new maroon, black, and white uniforms with 14 capable bodies. As minor-league managers did in those days, he took out a few help-wanted ads in the sporting press. The response was encouraging. "Now that Ottawa is on the ball map, letters are coming in like answers to a patent medicine ad," said the *Journal*.[23] "Fast Men Coming Here from All Parts of United States," said the *Citizen*.[24] But by the end of March it had become abundantly clear that Varnell had no intention of divorcing his two-timing manager. Reluctantly Shaughnessy said goodbye to his family and left for Indiana, leaving veteran second baseman Louis Cook, a University of Illinois engineering grad, in charge.

Dampening the considerable excitement surrounding the baseball season in Ottawa was the news of an unfolding maritime disaster in the North Atlantic. In one of the great Dewey-Defeats-Truman headlines of all time, the *Journal* reported: "White Star Liner 'Titanic,' Largest Vessel Afloat, Crashes into Iceberg; 1300 Passengers Are Safe."[25] Among the casualties was Charles Melville Hays, the driving force behind Ottawa's landmark Château Laurier, which opened a few days after the great ship went down.

Shaughnessy meanwhile was determined to make the best of his exile in Indiana by adroitly managing both ends of his predicament. Without kiboshing Fort Wayne's chances in the Central League, he funneled a handful of reject Railroaders north to round out the Ottawa roster. Without this injection of talent it's safe to say the Senators would not have challenged for the Canadian League pennant in their inaugural season.

Weeks earlier Shaughnessy had chosen Thursday, May 16 – Ascension Day and therefore a civil service half-holiday – for the Senators'

home debut. The city welcomed their 14 young Americans – there were no homebrews on the roster – with a civic luncheon, free tickets to the 1,500-seat Russell Theatre, a visit to the big horse show, and guest privileges at the YMCA. A flag in team colors flew over Sparks Street, a block from Parliament Hill. "Everyone is talking baseball," said the *Citizen*.[26]

OPENING DAY

For the opener the Senators had arranged with the Ottawa Electric Railway Co. to lay on specially decorated streetcars. There would be a parade of automobiles, the band of the Governor General's Foot Guards would play, a number of MPs would attend, Mayor Charles Hopewell would throw out the first pitch, and the *Citizen* would post out-of-town scores on big boards in front of the grandstand. Six thousand "fans" (still written with quotation marks in 1912) were expected.

But on Ascension Day the rain came down. And kept coming down into the weekend. Finally, on Saturday afternoon, "Jupiter Pluvius," a.k.a. "Jup. Pluvius" or, simply, "Jup. P." – the sports pages' soggy euphemism for rain – let up long enough for the Senators to take the field against the defending champion Berlin Busy Bees (formerly Green Sox). Almost 7,000 fans, the biggest crowd in Lansdowne history save for the Central Canada Fair, jammed the park to watch the locals trounce the Berliners 7-1. In a bold marketing move, the Senators allowed 30 or 40 automobiles to park down the right-field line.

When it came to cars, the Senators were miles ahead of the pack. Before the advent of drive-in restaurants, movies, and even drive-in gas stations, the club, with an eye on the city's ballooning automobile population (400 and counting in the spring of 1912) offered drive-in baseball – likely a first anywhere – at Lansdowne Park. Ticket-holders could chug right into the stadium and take in a ballgame without ever having to leave the comfort of their own flivvers. Shaughnessy, stuck in Fort Wayne, got to see none of this.

By mid-July, thanks mainly to their strong pitching, the Senators were solidly in first place. After an Opening Day loss to the Saints in St. Thomas, one of the Senators' Fort Wayne loaners, right-hander Joe McManus, won 14 straight before finally dropping a 6-5 decision to Hamilton on July 16. After the game he confessed he'd been feeling poorly for a couple of days. A week later it was revealed that he had suffered "a light attack"[27] of typhus, a common summer occurrence in Canadian cities of the day. McManus dropped 35 pounds from his 180-pound frame and was done for the season.

Even without him, the Senators kept winning. And on August 17, 1912, 4,500 fans – including about 60 motorists – packed Lansdowne to see the Senators clinch their first Canadian League championship. Second baseman Jimmy Louden scored the pennant-clinching run in a 2-1 win over the London Tecumsehs by beating out an infield hit, stealing second and third, and scoring on a wild throw. "Ottawa has gone baseball mad as the result of the team's success," said the *Citizen*.[28] Another Fort Wayne castoff, lefty Frank "Cubby" Kubat, was the winning pitcher.

The Canadian League schedule ended on Labor Day with Ottawa nine games ahead of second-place Brantford. The *Journal*'s baseball writer typed this classic expression of postseason *tristesse*: "Louis Cook's Senators have nearly all left town, the pennant will be purchased by the league, labelled 'Ottawa' and sent up by parcel post, and the season is ended so far as the city is concerned."[29]

With the Canadian flag in the bag, Shaughnessy summoned Kubat (12-7) back to Fort Wayne, where the resurgent Railroaders, a last-place club as recently as July 1, were now in a tight pennant race with the Youngstown Steelmen. Kubat won a couple of key contests down the

stretch, and the Railroaders finished on top by 2½ games. Shag, for his part, batted .304 and stole 34 bases. When it was all over, he sent a businesslike telegram to Kitty back in Ottawa: "Ft Wayne won the pennant. Had a hard battle we play Cleveland Wednesday at Ft Wayne expect to get home Friday phone Brice about pennant. Frank."[30] Somehow Shag had managed to parlay his divided loyalties into pennants for two teams in two countries in the same year.

Despite a shriveling Canadian economy, a soggy spring, a typhus outbreak, and a pennant race devoid of suspense, the Senators made about $1,000 on the season. Shaughnessy declared the Canadian the most successful minor league on the continent. Although at least 18 circuits across North America had lost teams or folded outright that summer, most observers expressed optimism about the future of the game in the capital. "This is sure a great ball town," said right-hander Fred Herbert (16-9).[31] "It is quite evident," said the *Citizen*, "that baseball has come to stay."[32]

After the season, Shaughnessy touched down in Ottawa just long enough to announce that he would not, as expected, be taking charge of the Roughriders football club. Instead he packed his whistle and reported to McGill University in Montréal, where he became the first professional coach in Canadian collegiate football. It was a move that led to Shaughnessy's third sporting championship of the year – a Yates Cup[33] win for his Redmen over the University of Toronto.

The title earned Shaughnessy a $500 bonus. And at a time when there was little, if anything, to choose between the collegiate and the pro game, it also earned his squad an opportunity to challenge for what was then formally known as the Earl Grey Football Cup. The coach declined, insisting instead that his players concentrate on preparing for upcoming exams. Shag coached at McGill for 19 seasons, during which time he helped define and refine the Canadian game.[34]

Now Shaughnessy, as a jock of all trades with a growing family, needed something to bridge the icy gap between football and baseball seasons. Although he knew next to nothing about hockey, he took on the job of coaching and managing Frank Ahearn's Ottawa Stewartons senior amateur club in the Interprovincial Union. "I told them I didn't know anything about the game and, in fact, hadn't even seen hockey, aside from kids playing in the neighborhood rinks," said Shaughnessy. "They insisted I knew how to handle men and organize sports, and that's what they were interested in..."[35] It was here that his string of sporting championships came to an abrupt end.

A BRAND-NEW SUIT

Shaughnessy might have continued his cross-border juggling act in 1913. He actually liked Fort Wayne – he even liked the club's owner, Claude Varnell – and he really liked the idea of owning a club in one league and pulling in a good salary in another. Kitty, however, wanted him home, and this time Varnell agreed to release him for a reported $750 – a ransom deemed "a small fortune" by the *Citizen*.[36]

For spring training in 1913, Shag assembled more than 30 returning and prospective Senators in balmy Fort Wayne, where, should he have a position or two to fill, he had ready access to any surplus Railroaders. "It is the hardest thing in the world to rebuild a ball team shot to pieces in the major league draft. But fortunately we will have a small army of players to choose from," said Shaughnessy, adding, "There are thousands of glittering stars in the bushes and we may be fortunate to pick up maybe one or two of them."[37]

Among the no-shows at the start of training camp was Jimmy Louden, the promising young infielder who had single-handedly manufactured the run that won the 1912 pennant. Louden, who in civilian life was actually a University of Illinois electrical engineering student named

George Kempf, was laid up due to complications from surgery to remove a facial tumor, allegedly the consequence of his having been struck by a pitched ball two years previously. Now word came from Chicago that Louden/Kempf had died. The cause of death was reported as "tuberculosis of the jaw."[38] There were rumors he'd been engaged to an Ottawa girl. He was just 21.

A subdued Ottawa team opened the 1913 season on May 8 in Brantford, where every store and factory in the city shut down for the day to allow their employees to take in the game. The Senators lost 8-7.

In the meantime, preparations were underway for the Senators' home opener. A Sparks Street tailor, A.J. Curry, announced that he would present a $30 suit to the first Senator to hit a home run at Lansdowne Park. Curry's offer seemed pretty generous, until you consider that Ottawa had failed to hit a single homer at home during its entire first season. Said one writer: "Any man to get credit for a four play wallop at the local ball yard [has] to sock the ball a quarter of a mile, more or less, and complete the circuit at a Ty Cobb clip"[39] – which is exactly what Frank Shaughnessy did in his first game back in his adopted city since the demise of the Outlaws in 1906.

On Thursday, May 16, 1913, much of the federal government shut down at 1 P.M. so civil servants could get out to the ballpark in time to see Colonel Sam Hughes, the eccentric minister of militia and defense, throw out the first pitch. But mostly it was to witness Frank Shaughnessy's debut as a Senator. As he stepped to the plate in the fourth inning, the game was halted so local MP Dr. Jerry Chabot could present Shag with a floral horseshoe wishing the team "Good Luck 1913." After the interruption the pumped-up skipper drove the first pitch he saw over the head of the Brantford right fielder. The ball bounded up a slope and skipped toward the cattle barns near the Rideau Canal. Shag scored standing up. He finished the day with the Senators' first-ever home-field homer, a single, a double – and a new suit.

In 1913 baseball was the hottest sporting ticket in the country. A record 24 Canadian cities fielded professional teams, and even in Ottawa, which had long been a lacrosse town in the summer, baseball was king. On Saturdays and holidays most clubs played morning and afternoon contests (no lights, no night ball) and charged separate admissions for each. On Saturday, May 24, for instance, the Senators drew several thousand fans for a morning game against Brantford and another 6,000 in the afternoon. This included the trendy occupants of 52 on-field automobiles – about 10 percent of the cars in the entire city.[40] "Some of the most fashionable people in the city are regular patrons of the Ottawa ball club," noted the *Citizen*.[41]

But the play of the defending champs was mediocre at best. In a game in St. Thomas, an increasingly short-tempered Shaughnessy charged in from center field to ream out the umpire, who happened to be an old nemesis of his from the Virginia League. During their discussion Shag bumped the ump. He was tossed and fined $5 on the spot. When he protested, the umpire upped it to $10. For once the skipper went quietly, apart from complaining afterward that the umps were out to "get him."[42]

The Senators closed out May by dropping seven straight, which prompted Shag to blow up his club. He suspended one player, made some trades, and re-signed some of the previous season's Senators who had failed to stick at higher levels. By mid-July, despite Shag's hot hitting – after 33 games he was hitting .427 – the revamped Senators

Shaughnessy (middle, second row) guided the 1913 Ottawa Senators to their second straight Canadian League title, nosing out the London Tecumsehs by a single game. First baseman "Cozy" Dolan (top row, third from left) led the Senators with a .358 batting average. (Alfred Pittaway of Pittaway & Jarvis Photographers, Ottawa)

were still mired in fifth place. In St. Thomas an even testier Shag was charged by police after a run-in with a spectator, a hotel proprietor from Port Stanley, Ontario, named Joseph Coffey, for using abusive language with ladies present.

On the Senators' next Western trip, Shag finally had his day in court. Senators and Saints alike packed the courtroom to hear the Virginia barrister argue his case. It was, said the *Citizen*, a "burlesque" of a trial.[43] Witnesses testified that Coffey had called Shag "a big stiff," and that Shag had retaliated by calling Coffey "a grey-headed old loafer."[44] Apparently, "loafer" trumped "stiff" in the insult arsenal of the day, and the judge, amid much hooting from the players, fined Shaughnessy $10.

"BIG, BOWLEGGED AND DOMINEERING"

A far bigger offense than Shag's vocabulary, some said, was his Simon Legree management style – "more like McGraw's than Mack's," as one baseball writer put it.[45] It is a constant thread through his time in the Canadian League and, before that, in Fort Wayne and Roanoke. Described by the *Hamilton Herald* as "the big, bowlegged and domineering pilot of the Ottawas," Shag was said to hand his men a raise one minute and a "blue envelope" (i.e., a pink slip) the next.[46] "Shaughnessy's methods are unpopular at times with the fans and with his players, but," the *London Advertiser* conceded, "he gets results..."[47] "All credit must be given to Shag," said the *London Free Press*, "for he not only drives his players, never overlooks an opening, but he makes mediocre performers live wires."[48]

One player who responded particularly favorably to Shaughnessy's alleged heavy-handed style was Edgar "Lefty" Rogers, an Arkansas native acquired from Fort Wayne for $300. In Ottawa, Rogers created a buzz by virtue of being chauffeured to Lansdowne on game days by

an attractive redhead in a white roadster – and even more of a buzz for what he did when he got there. Rogers had started as a pitcher but had been converted into an outfielder because of his lively bat. The Senators insisted on using him in both capacities. Behind Shaughnessy's hitting, returning right-hander Erwin Renfer's pitching, and a double-duty performance by Rogers, the fifth-place Senators took off.

On an early July homestand they won nine of nine to move into second place. On July 30 the Senators beat the Busy Bees 9-5 in Berlin to kick off another winning streak, this one of 13 games. On the August civic holiday they took two from Brantford to finally move into first place. Renfer's win three days later was his 17th straight, and 20th of the season.[49]

The Senators continued to play winning ball for the final month, but they were unable to shake off the London Tecumsehs, under player-manager Rube Deneau, one of the few Canadian-born Canadian Leaguers.[50] But whenever the Senators absolutely needed a win – as they did going into the final game of the 1913 season, having lost three straight to London and another to Peterboro – Shag brought Rogers in from left field to pitch. And so on Labor Day afternoon, with the Canadian League pennant on the line, Lefty took the mound before 7,000 fans at Lansdowne Park and tamed the White Caps, 14-2.

The win enabled the Senators to snatch their second straight flag, this time by a single game over London.[51] When Shaughnessy was presented with the obligatory floral wreath to mark the victory, he immediately hung it around his pitcher's neck. For the season, Rogers, the Senators' big-game player, won 13 of 17 decisions and recorded a .336 batting average. Senators first baseman and longtime Shag loyalist Frank "Cozy" Dolan[52] also had a big year, batting .358, third best in the league. Center fielder Shaughnessy had a .340 average – eighth best – along with 37 stolen bases and two home runs. That performance, combined with his refuse-to-lose management style, may have made him the most valuable Senator in 1913.

In the fall Shaughnessy returned to McGill and bossed his Redmen to another Canadian intercollegiate title. And again, this time citing professionalism in the Interprovincial Rugby Football Union, they declined to go to the Grey Cup, eventually won by the Hamilton Tigers.

A NATIONAL PASTIME

By 1914, as historian Alan Metcalfe[53] argues, baseball was Canada's *de facto* national pastime. No other sport was growing as quickly – or as widely. In the summer of 1914 there were 19 Canadian-based professional teams spread across five minor-league circuits. The Canadian League was proving to be one of the more solid baseball ventures on the continent. In 1914 even the economically borderline Hamilton club was valued at $8,000, a far cry from the $2,500 asking price for the Berlin franchise three years earlier. Shaughnessy's investment in the Senators looked promising. But baseball, along with everything else, was about to be severely tested by events in Europe.

For the new season two of the Canadian League's smaller centers, Berlin and Guelph, were replaced by Toronto and Erie, Pennsylvania. With its larger population base, the Canadian moved up to Class B, which in those days was three rungs below the major leagues.

Meanwhile Shaughnessy faced the annual challenge of all minor-league managers of the day, namely, the scramble to piece together a club mostly of rejects from higher classifications. While the Senators trained in Chatham, Ontario, the skipper made his annual cross-border spring shopping trip. This time he came back with a couple of raw pitchers and a catcher/singer/dancer named Eddie "Bowery" Wager, whose true ambition, it turned out, was to be a vaudeville star. When it became apparent Wager could hit the high notes better than the curveball, Shag was quick to give him the hook.

Shaughnessy had considerably more luck with a catcher turned pitcher, previously with the Windsor team of the Class-D Border League, with just 16 mound appearances at any level under his belt and a tabloid headline for a name. He was Urban Shocker, born Urbain Jacques Shockcor in Cleveland in 1890. In Ottawa everyone called him Herbie. Herbie Shocker would be the best player the Canadian League ever produced.

For their May 14 home opener the Senators hosted Canadian baseball legend Knotty Lee's fledgling Toronto Beavers in front of 4,500 fans. "Clergymen, politicians, rail road magnates, civil servants, office boys, school children and people of every description were amongst the excited assembly that sat through two hours of rapid fire baseball," reported the *Citizen*.[54] Royalty, too.

The governor general, Prince Arthur, Duke of Connaught, and his 28-year-old daughter, Princess Patricia, of Light Infantry fame, watched the game from the royal limo, with the Ottawa bullpen corps of Shocker and Wager hanging around trying to explain what was happening on the field. It was decided to install a vice-regal box for next time.

Three days later the Senators, no longer willing to sacrifice potentially lucrative Sunday dates to the wishes of the capital's "better element," played their first-ever game in Hull, Quebec, just across the Ottawa River. Leading up to the 3 P.M. first pitch, special streetcars departed the Château Laurier every two minutes. More than 5,000 fans eventually squeezed into Dupuis Park, capacity 4,500. The overflow sat on the grass in front of the grandstand, and cars parked two deep down the left-field line. Toronto won 6-5.

While Sunday ball was a big hit with fans on both sides of the river, a watchdog group called the Lord's Day Alliance decided to challenge its legality under federal legislation that, in essence, outlawed having fun in public on Sundays. The case charging Shaughnessy, partner Malcolm Brice, several Senators players, and the management of the London club with "conducting a certain performance on the Lord's Day for gain,"[55] would kick around Hull Police Court for more than a year.

Finally on August 6, 1915, Judge Goyette rendered his decision. More concerned with protecting provincial rights than advancing professional sport, Goyette ruled that the federal Lord's Day Act could not be used to deprive Quebecers of the rights and liberties they enjoyed prior to its passage in March 1907. Sunday ball, he noted, had been a fixture of Quebec life for 30 years, and, since provincial law did not expressly prohibit such activity, the federal legislation was not applicable. Case dismissed, with costs. The long battle for Sunday ball had been won, at least in Quebec. It was soon eclipsed by a real war.

On Saturday, June 27, 1914, the Senators celebrated the raising of the 1913 pennant with a 3-2 win over Hamilton at Lansdowne Park, Shaughnessy again belting the Senators' first home-field homer of the season to win the game in the bottom of the ninth. Shag's heroics were reported on page 8 of the *Citizen*. Buried on page 12 next to an item headlined "Conservative M.L.A. Is Sued for Poker Debt," was a dispatch from Sarajevo: "Austrian Heir Apparent and Wife Meet Death at Hands of Young Serb Student/May Seriously Affect European Peace."[56] It's unlikely many baseball fans paid much attention to Balkan affairs, and the season continued pretty much as normal.

SPIT AND POLISH

By mid-July Shaughnessy had come to the inescapable conclusion that his sputtering team simply didn't have the goods to catch archrival London, managed by former major-league pitcher and offseason dentist Carl "Doc" Reisling.[57] But

Shag, being Shag, was not about to roll over. "London's lead is big,"– it had, in fact, grown to eight games – "but there's plenty of time, and I'm confident I can overtake them," he declared.[58] He told the press he was willing to spend $5,000 if that's what it took to turn his club around.

Skipping a series in Hamilton, Shaughnessy set off, checkbook in hand, on a scouting expedition to Michigan. In Adrian he caught up with Jack Mitchell,[59] a hotshot 19-year-old shortstop whom the Senators had faced in a spring-training game. Shag went all in. The $1,000 he coughed up for Mitchell was reportedly the most ever paid for an infielder by a Class-B club. But, as one writer later noted, "This change put reverse English on the playing of the champions, and they inaugurated a winning streak seldom seen in organized baseball."[60] Mitchell more than justified his hefty price tag. He not only solidified Ottawa's infield defense, he finished the season with a gaudy .344 batting average.

Shaughnessy made another key midseason adjustment. Novice pitcher Herbie Shocker had struggled to find a reliable breaking pitch. Shag suggested he experiment with a spitball. The day after Mitchell's July 18 debut, Shocker unveiled his spitter in a Sunday game in Hull. He won, and pretty soon scouts from higher leagues were salivating over him. Thanks to the miracle of slippery elm, Shocker was on his way to becoming the pitcher who eventually won 187 games for the Yankees and the St. Louis Browns, before a fatal heart ailment ended his career – and his life – at age 37.[61]

With seven weeks to go in the season, the "Shagmen," as the papers often called them, languished 8½ games behind London. But with Shocker and Mitchell leading the way, they went on a tear. On the August civic holiday the Senators took two one-run, extra-inning games from Hamilton. Shocker got the win in the second game with eight strikeouts in a three-inning relief stint. The gap with London now stood at

4½. Excitement over the improved play of the Senators was run over the following day by the real-world news that Canada had joined Britain in declaring war on Germany. Attendance cooled as the war heated up, but the Canadian League schedule proceeded without a hiccup. And the Senators kept on winning.

Mitchell continued his hot hitting down the stretch, and Shocker dominated, winning four games in a single week in August. On August 18 Ottawa beat Brantford 8-3 at Lansdowne to close to within half a game of the Tecumsehs. For this game the players had a new reminder of the gathering storm beyond baseball – soldiers camped around the edges of the outfield. "Hits into volunteers went for two bases only," said one game report.[62] The war had become a ground rule.

Shaughnessy responded by declaring the Senators' August 20 match with St. Thomas a "Booster Day," with all gate receipts save for the visiting team's $75 guarantee going to the Hospital Ship Committee, headed by Lady Borden, wife of the prime minister. Both teams wore red crosses on their sleeves. The game dragged on for 11 innings and ended in a stalemate.

With a week and a half to go, the Senators traveled to London for a crucial series. They took three of four games to finally overtake the Tecumsehs after a chase of 57 days. "[T]he always-fighting 'Shag' never gave up and his stick-to-itiveness has resulted in him again topping the clubs and putting him on the road to the championship," said the *Hamilton Herald*. "He's a fighter, and it's the fighter who wins."[63]

LET'S PLAY THREE!

But it wasn't over yet, and the battle again came down to the final day of the season. Following a remarkable 40-13 run, the Senators had claimed a precarious hold on first place with a record of 75-45 (.625). London, plagued by an inordinate number of rainouts, ties, and the illegality of Sunday ball in Ontario, sat at 69-43 (.616), two games but only .009 percentage points behind. What happened next was one of the most bizarre finishes ever.

Both clubs were scheduled to play a pair at home on Labor Day, the Senators against the sixth-place Peterboro White Caps, the Tecumsehs against the fifth-place St. Thomas Saints. A sweep would give Ottawa the pennant no matter what London did. That much was obvious. But beyond that, especially with a cold, low-pressure system blanketing the province from Western Ontario to the national capital, things got cloudy.

An Ottawa split and a London sweep, to consider one possibility, would hand the flag to Ottawa by the slimmest margin in baseball history, .6229 to .6228. On the other hand, a pair of Ottawa losses, coupled with a pair of London wins, would create a virtual tie atop the standings, but hand the pennant to the Tecumsehs on the basis of superior winning percentage, .623 to .615. The picture got even hazier if the dodgy weather were to wipe out one or both games in either city. And even more so when London manager Doc Reisling hatched a plan to play *three* games against the Saints on Labor Day, the extra contest ostensibly a makeup for an earlier rainout.[64] A third game would provide Reisling with an extra piece in this most intricate of pennant endgames. If the Tecumsehs won three (.626) and the Senators were completely rained out (.625) or lost at least once (.620), London would squeak by.

In London the weather lifted in the morning, and the Tecumsehs beat the Saints 4-1 to move to within a game and a half of the leaders. In Ottawa the showers eased enough to permit the Senators to take the field against the White Caps. But in the second inning the skies opened up and the tarps rolled out again. Finally in early afternoon the rain in the capital subsided. Shaughnessy, knowing he had to win at least one game to guarantee the pennant, sent his groundskeeper out for a 20-gallon can of gasoline. It was sloshed over the soggy infield, and someone tossed a match in to burn off some of the damp. When the smoke cleared the umpire gave the go-ahead, and Shaughnessy's prize discovery, Herbie Shocker, took the mound on one day's rest in search of his 20th win of the season. Shocker delivered, and the Senators won 6-2.

Now, with Ottawa's victory in Game 1, three things would have to happen for London to prevail. The rain would have to hold off in both cities, the Tecumsehs would have to beat the Saints for a second and a third time, and Peterboro ace Louis Schettler (20-12) would have to shut down the Senators in Game 2 in Ottawa. In the end, all three conditions were met: no rain, London victories in Games 2 and 3, and Schettler's continued mastery of the Senators – and yet Doc Reisling's gambit failed. What happened was this: After a couple of chilly and scoreless innings in Ottawa, Shaughnessy and Peterboro manager Curley Blount huddled, after which they persuaded the umpire to call the game on account of the cold. That snuffed any hopes of London catching Ottawa.

"In view ... of the fact that Frank Shaughnessy and his Senators have come from behind within four weeks and have overhauled London's ten game lead, no one will dispute them the honours," said the *Citizen*.[65] Well, not exactly *no one*. "Probably the Cold Was in Shaughnessy's Feet," said the *London Advertiser*. "Maybe it was too cold to play ball and maybe it wasn't, but, at any rate, it is a peculiar fact that the cold was not noticed until after the second game had been started."[66]

The *London Free Press* concurred, complaining about the appearance of "fix up baseball" in Ottawa. The cancellation of Game 2, they surmised, came only "upon the discovery of what a loss to Peterboro in the second game meant."[67] The *London Advertiser* nonetheless paid Shaughnessy grudging respect, which was the type of respect he typically received: "Shag is a foxy boy and if you want to win any pennants from him

you have to sit up nights and dope out a fancy line of stunts to get ahead of him."[68]

Whether the cancellation of the second game was due to Shaughnessy's cunning or simply to a confluence of cold weather and dumb luck is not known, although it is difficult to imagine that the skipper wasn't fully aware of all the permutations and combinations on that day, and catching a telegraphic whiff of a third game in London, decided to quit while he was ahead. Regardless, Shaughnessy and the jubilant Senators adjourned to a hotel to get warm and celebrate. The Shagmen had won 42 of their final 55 games to grab a third straight pennant for Ottawa. For London it marked the second straight season with no cigar – the Tecumsehs' cumulative margin of defeat, .006 percentage points.

Shaughnessy himself had another strong season in 1914. In 119 games he batted .289 with 37 stolen bases and a team-leading six homers, half of them coming in a May 31 game at Dupuis Park, when he blasted three over the short left-field fence. But perhaps his most significant contribution to Ottawa's success was his indomitable personality. "The continued success of this shrewd Irishman smashes all idea of luck," said one baseball writer. "That commodity might land him a winner once, but when success is spoiled on success there is something in the man himself above ordinary."[69]

Organized Baseball, on the other hand, did not have a good season. The editor of *Sporting Life* designated it "the universal wreck of the minor leagues."[70] 43 minor leagues started the year; 36 finished in some form or other. Organized Baseball, involved in a territorial war with the upstart Federal League, had spread itself perilously thin. Too many clubs made too little economic sense, especially in the second year of a North American economic recession. Erie, for example. Erie, in the words of *Sporting Life's* London correspondent, "did not draw as much as a soap spieler at a hobos' picnic."[71] And then there was the exploding war in Europe.

Despite the nailbiter of a pennant race and a Canadian League monopoly on Sunday ball, attendance at Senators games reportedly took a 40 percent attendance hit over the final month of the season, and the club reported a $2,700 loss. Shag's gamble on baseball in the capital was starting to look a little less sure.

In the fall of 1914, Shaughnessy again coached at McGill. Over the winter he made his debut as "business manager" of the other Ottawa Senators, those of the National Hockey Association, the forerunner of the NHL. Shaughnessy courted local football and hockey star Eddie Gerard by plopping $400 cash on his desk and telling him he could walk out with it if he signed a contract on the spot. Gerard did and scored in his first game, a 4-3 win over Quebec. That spring Shag came close to adding his name to the Stanley Cup, but the NHA-champion Senators dropped the final to the Pacific Coast Hockey League Vancouver Millionaires.

TO SHREDS

In 1910, the peak year for minor-league baseball until after the Second World War, there were 50 leagues in operation. By the spring of 1915, the number was down to 32, only 23 of which staggered through the season. A no-frills, bargain-basement, six-team, Class-C Canadian League was one of them. So stripped down were the teams that star pitcher Herbie Shocker was assigned to prepare the diamond for the Senators' abbreviated spring training in Chatham.

But few paid much attention to the petty concerns of baseball. In the spring of 1915 Prime Minister Robert Borden was contemplating conscription. Young Canadians were being gassed at Ypres. On May 7 a German U-boat torpedoed the Cunard liner *Lusitania* off the coast of Ireland; 1,193 passengers and crew were killed, including 128 Americans.

Shaughnessy knew nothing about hockey when he settled in Ottawa in 1912, but two years later he was the business manager of the 1914-15 National Hockey Association champion Ottawa Senators. (George T. Wadds, Photographer, Ottawa).

The Senators, hobbled by injuries and hampered by a barebones roster, got off to their usual sluggish start. By the King's Birthday holiday, June 4, they were mired in fifth place, and for the rest of the month they hovered around .500. But in July they took off. They played at a .705 clip for the rest of the way, leaving 1915 pretenders Hamilton and Guelph in the dust. The season played itself out without much excitement, the Senators eventually stretching their lead to 12½ games over the wilted Maple Leafs of Guelph. "...Ottawa had the championship clinched so early this year that the enthusiasm fell to shreds," said the *Citizen*.[72] Attendance dropped by half.

Shaughnessy had yet another strong season at the plate. He batted .295 with three homers and 30 stolen bases in 101 games. He had now finished no worse than third in all seven years of his managerial career, winning five flags in three different leagues. His teams had played .597 baseball during that span. Shocker, meanwhile, tossed 303 innings and won 19 games. He was snapped up by the Yankees, who paid Ottawa a $750 draft fee.

In an attempt to further bolster the team's bottom line, Shaughnessy arranged a series of well-attended matches in Ottawa against a couple of barnstorming Black teams, the Cuban Giants (actually out of Buffalo, New York) and the Havana Red Sox (from Watertown, New York). The Senators held the Giants to five runs over the course of a five-game sweep, and then took three of four from "Havana."

That fall Shaughnessy coached football at McGill, but also moonlighted with the Ottawa Roughriders of the Interprovincial Rugby Football Union (the "Big Four"). In the winter he again acted as "business manager" of the hockey Senators, who would finish second in the NHA, well back of the Montréal Canadiens.

His baseball future, however, remained uncertain. The rumors and the speculation – about the Senators, about Shaughnessy, about the future of minor-league baseball itself – swirled all fall and winter: Shag would manage Toronto in the International League. Or maybe a team in the upstart Federal League. The Senators would replace Richmond in the International League. Or they would join the New York State League. Or maybe there would be another iteration of the Canadian League, which might or might not include Ottawa.

FROZEN IN TIME

On Valentine's Day 1916, the Parliament Buildings burned down. It would serve as an apt metaphor for Ottawa baseball that season.

In March St. Thomas resigned from the Canadian League. The remaining clubs debated the wisdom of carrying on, but the discussion ended when a new battalion, the 207th, moved into Lansdowne Park in April. There was now no place for the perennial champion Senators to play. And with that, the team and the league suspended operations for 1916. It never resumed. The Senators' peerless record – four seasons, four pennants – remains frozen in time. "People will feel lost without league baseball in Ottawa and Hull this year," mourned the *Citizen*. "About July 1 fans will

begin to sigh for the good old days when London and Ottawa fought it out in a neck and neck race for the Canadian League pennant."[73]

Shaughnessy, as always in need of a summer job, returned to Pennsylvania to manage the Warren Warriors of the split-season, eight-team, Class-D Interstate League. (He was reportedly Warren's second choice, after the notorious Hal Chase, who joined the Cincinnati Reds instead.) Six Senators stalwarts, including first baseman Cozy Dolan, shortstop Frank Smykal, and right-hander Louis Peterson, joined Shag in Pennsylvania.[74] Someone else could worry about the financial viability of a minor-league baseball team for a change. As it turned out, there would be lots to worry about.

It didn't take long for Shaughnessy's "ugly temper"[75] to make an appearance. In early June, during a game in Olean, New York, he launched an X-rated tirade at the umpire (hint: It did *not* include the phrase "grey-headed old loafer"), after which he flung his bat into the crowd. For Shag it marked a reprise of a bat-tossing incident in his days as a Roanoke Tiger. Fortunately for all concerned, no one was injured in either incident, but newspapers in other league cities were not impressed. "We believe there are a large number of good sportsmen in Warren who would blush for shame at the 'rank stuff' pulled here by their manager," the *Ridgway Record* chastised. "If he tries it again he will be arrested."[76]

With a population distracted by preparations for the war in Europe and by an actual war with Mexico, attendance in the Interstate was down by half. On August 3 Warren, some $800 in debt and owing players two weeks' salary, became the second of three league clubs to fold in less than a month. The *Wellsville Reporter* speculated that Shaughnessy would return to Canada to raise a company of athletes to fight in the war. Instead Shag signed with the first-place Bradford Drillers, but as a player only. Then, a few weeks later, he moved over to the also-ran Wellsville Rainmakers as playing manager. In an uncertain, no-fixed-address kind of season, Shag still recorded a .301 batting average and stole 19 bases in 76 games. But for the first time since 1911, he failed to win a pennant.

Back home in Ottawa in early September, Shaughnessy set about arranging a pair of exhibition games for Lansdowne Park, pitting future Hall of Famer Tris Speaker and his "All-Americans" barnstorming squad against the "International All-stars," a team consisting mostly of Montréal Royals and managed by the Royals' Dan Howley. On October 6 both Shaughnessy and Howley played in the field against the American Leaguers. Shag had a hit off the Detroit Tigers' Jean Dubuc, but the Internationals lost 6-2.

After a couple of games in Montréal – Shaughnessy played in one of them – the teams returned to Ottawa for a Thanksgiving Monday exhibition game. The game marked a homecoming for prize Senators grad Herbie Shocker, who had split the season between the Yankees of the American League and the Maple Leafs of the International, where he'd gone 15-3 with a 1.31 ERA. Facing the likes of Speaker, the American League batting champ, ill-fated Cleveland shortstop Ray Chapman, and future Black Sox first baseman Chick Gandil, Shocker scattered nine hits and beat eventual 223-game winner George "Hooks" Dauss of the Detroit Tigers, 3-2.

SIBERIA

For Shaughnessy it would not be fall without football. But with collegiate ball on hold for the year, the autumn of 1916 found him coaching the 207th Battalion team to the championship of the military's Overseas Football League. He also continued as business manager of the hockey Senators, even swinging a deal to pry future Hall of Famer Cy Denneny away from Toronto. But in November Shaughnessy, now 33 and the father of four boys, decided to sign up.

On his Officer's Declaration form he gave his profession as "attorney and athletic director,"[77] and he agreed to be vaccinated. His medical sheet lists him at 6-feet-1½-inches and 195 pounds, with "excellent physical development."[78] Said the Citizen: "Frank has worn baseball and football togs for so many years that he had no difficulty in adapting himself to the King's uniform."[79]

At first Shaughnessy's military career was not all that different from his civilian one. He coached and played baseball, coached football and even coached hockey. ("... Frank's advice is invariably brief, but to the point, viz: 'Get the goals and then lay back on the defense.'")[80] But Shaughnessy's real value to the military was his extensive web of contacts in the sporting world. After all, who better to take on the Hun than an army of elite young athletes? He was soon placed in charge of recruiting in Ottawa for the 207th Battalion, and in typical Shag style he out-recruited all the other recruiters. "In his short-term as re-inforcing officer, Lieut. Shaughnessy established a record for recruiting as he secured over a hundred men."[81] "Before the current call is exhausted ... the Capital will be without ninety per cent of its leading athletes, and unless the war ends shortly, it will be difficult for the various local clubs to carry on successfully," said the Citizen. "The list of Ottawa athletes who have given up their lives for the Empire is a glorious one and, apparently, the majority of those now rallying to the colors are eager to sign up, that they may perpetuate the glory of those who have gone before them."[82] Dulce et decorum est.

Shag spent part of 1918 in a familiar working environment. In early summer his battery was quartered at Lansdowne Park, a fairly short walk from his home in Ottawa's Glebe neighborhood. Summer evenings his men played baseball. In September 1918 Shaughnessy transferred to the Ammunition Column, 35th Battery, Canadian Expeditionary Force (Siberia). The big show in Europe had only a few weeks left to run, but

Canada was still involved in – and in command of – a confused and half-hearted Allied campaign to support the White Russian Army against the Bolsheviks in Russia's Far East. Shag had experienced a number of baseball Siberias during his career, but never before the real thing. And now, at the peak of the Spanish flu pandemic, he found himself in New Westminster, British Columbia, preparing to embark on a slow boat to Vladivostok.

On November 28, 17 days after the war ended on the Western Front, Shag and his mates finally sailed from Vancouver on the "remount ship" *S.S. War Charger*. They carried a cargo of 500 or 600 horses – half of them on deck – and a load of 16- and 18-pound artillery shells below. "I think they picked me because I was as big as a horse," Shag said.[83] They wallowed 500 miles in 23 days until, in danger of running out of coal, they were ordered to turn back. The ship docked in Vancouver on December 4, no doubt to the widespread relief of most of its passengers. "The funniest thing that happened to me was that I was sentenced to Siberia – and never got there," said Shag.[84] On January 21, 1919, Lieut. Frank Shaughnessy left the army by "reason of General Demobilization"[85] and returned home to Ottawa.

THE INTERNATIONAL

Shaughnessy resumed his McGill position, which had expanded to include responsibility for all outdoor sports at the university. But, as always, he would need a baseball gig to see him through the summer. "I worked hard because I liked it," he said, "and if I needed a better reason, I had a big family and had something of a grocery bill every week."[86]

Shag pursued a number of leads, including the possible formation of an all-Canadian league that would incorporate the Ontario clubs from the Michigan-Ontario League, along with Ottawa and Montréal. "If the new league is formed, I will take either the Montréal or Ottawa franchises, or

at least will take a financial interest in them...," he said. "There is no doubt in my mind that an all-Canadian league would be a howling success."[87] But his fellow magnates did not share his conviction, and the league he envisioned failed to get off the ground.

There was also talk of relocating an International League franchise to Ottawa. But nothing panned out on that front either. Shaughnessy, with considerable reluctance, accepted an offer to play for and manage the Hamilton Tigers of the Class-B Michigan-Ontario League. Now 36 and returning after a two-season layoff, Shag nonetheless put up one of the best offensive seasons of his long career, batting .313 with a .412 on-base percentage in 109 games. But his Tigers, featuring several former Senators, came up just short. They finished second, three games back of the Saginaw Aces.[88]

Shaughnessy seemed to be growing weary of the peripatetic baseball life and the burdens of leadership. In August he went as far as announcing his intention to retire as both player and manager at season's end. "Managing a baseball team is far from being what it may seem to the average fan in the bleachers," he told the *Citizen*. "The player who has nothing to do but play his position each game, and whose worries end with the game each day, has an easy time; but the manager has just as many worries off the field as on. I will make a desperate effort to win the pennant this year, but win or lose I am not going to attempt to fill the role of manager any more."[89]

And yet in the fall of 1919 Shaughnessy was rumored to have the inside track on replacing Canadian Baseball Hall of Famer George "Mooney" Gibson as manager of the Toronto Maple Leafs. That didn't happen either. And so, in 1920, he returned to Hamilton as player-manager of the Tigers. His team again finished second, this time 14½ games behind the runaway London Tecumsehs. It was the same old fiery Frank, though. In late May he was arrested for getting into a fight in Flint. His offensive production, however, declined dramatically – a .262 batting average with 16 stolen bases in 93 games. It was his swan song as a regular or semi-regular player.

During the 1920-21 offseason, Shaughnessy continued his struggle to bring high-level baseball back to either Ottawa or Montréal. There was talk of Shag and Knotty Lee acquiring the Syracuse or Akron franchise in the International League and moving it north of the border. There were also reports of the pair trying to add some Canadian content to the New York State League. If they landed a baseball franchise for Ottawa, Shag and his rapidly expanding family – seventh son Peter would be born in 1921 – would stay put. In the event of a team for Montréal, he would relocate his family there. But in the end the Shaughnessy-Lee duo could not make a business case for either city.

A BRISK NORTH WIND

In 1921 the Shaughnessys decamped with their seven boys to Montréal, with the half-baked idea of Frank selling insurance to supplement his McGill income. The Shaughnessy era in Ottawa was over.

Predictably, Shag's insurance career lasted about as long as his half-hearted attempt to practice law in Roanoke. "In fact," *The Sporting News* noted, "every time Shag decided to 'settle down,' baseball sounded a recall."[90] In midseason 1921 he took over as manager of the chronically second-division Syracuse Stars of the International League. It was a position he would hold until the 1925 season, when he was fired after a 9-28 start. More significantly the Syracuse gig marked the beginning of a 40-year relationship with the circuit.

In 1932 Charles Trudeau and his partners hired Shaughnessy as general manager of the Montréal Royals. While with the Royals, Shag successfully pushed for what came to be known as the Shaughnessy playoff system, a postseason

series widely credited with saving minor-league baseball from extinction during the Depression. In 1936 he was appointed president of the International, and for the next 24 years he served as a passionate defender of the interests of minor-league baseball. Said the *New York Times*: "He's as big as all outdoors and as hearty as a brisk north wind."[91]

Among the highlights of his tenure was the Royals' 1945 signing of Jackie Robinson. Shaughnessy, caught flatfooted by the historic breakthrough, nevertheless endorsed integration "as long as any fellow's the right type and can make good and can get along with other players."[92] As for Robinson being that fellow, Shag professed no doubts: "He's the best player in minor league ball. He's also the smartest."[93] We might wonder whether during this time Shaughnessy ever thought of his old Northern League opponent, William Matthews, and the four decades of racial hypocrisy since he had been touted as a sure-fire major-league talent.

Shag finally retired in 1960, at the age of 77. Over his career, which spanned more than half a century, he had established himself as one of the most influential personalities in baseball – or, as Montréal sportswriter Tim Burke said, "one of the most extraordinary figures in the history of sport."[94]

Kitty Shaughnessy, whose homesickness led to the creation of the Ottawa Senators, died in 1958 in Montréal, a week after the Shaughnessys' 50th wedding anniversary. Frank died on May 15, 1969, also in Montréal, at the age of 86. He was among the first inductees into the Canadian Baseball Hall of Fame, in 1983.

"I remember him as kind and big and gruff," his granddaughter Honora Shaughnessy told me. "He would always have a TV and one or two portable radios going at the same time, listening to various games. I remember my father always called him 'Sir.'"[95]

NOTES

1   Joe King and Cy Kritzer, "Shaughnessy," *The Sporting News,* December 14, 1960: 16.

2   After two unrelated Shaughnessys who preceded him to Notre Dame, both nicknamed "Shag."

3   An "outlaw," or independent, league is one that is not part of the National Agreement and therefore beyond the jurisdiction of Organized Baseball.

4   Not to be confused with another circuit called the Northern League, which operated in Manitoba, North Dakota, and Minnesota during this period.

5   Joe King and Cy Kritzer, "Diamond Ace, Gridiron Star and Executive," *The Sporting News,* December 14, 1960: 10.

6   From "The Man Has Better Things to Do Than Talk About Himself," unattributed 1968 newspaper clipping. Courtesy Honora Shaughnessy.

7   He was the starting right end on the undefeated 1903 team that outscored its opponents 291-0 over nine games.

8   David Pietrusza, *Minor Miracles: The Legend and Lure of Minor League Baseball* (Lanham, Maryland: Taylor Trade Publishing, 1995), 119.

9   Soon to be a two-team league, as Montpelier-Barre and Burlington were the only teams to survive the season.

10   Quinn was the proprietor of Revere House, 475-479 Sussex Drive, Ottawa, until selling out in 1912.

11   "Notes of Sport," *Ottawa Journal,* July 13, 1906: 2.

12   "Greens Take One of the Doubleheader," *Wheeling News Register,* September 2, 1906: 6.

13   Jerry Kuntz, *Baseball Fiends and Flying Machines: The Many Lives and Outrageous Times of George and Alfred Lawson,* (Jefferson, North Carolina: McFarland Publishing, 2009), 126.

14   Pietrusza, 120.

15   Pietrusza, 120.

16   The dealership sold – or at least attempted to sell – the Virginian, a short-lived make built in Richmond.

17   Frederick Edwards, "Old-Fashioned Father," *Maclean's,* October 1, 1934: 15.

18   "'Home Run' Shaughnessy Pays Ottawa a Visit," unattributed 1910 newspaper clipping. Courtesy Honora Shaughnessy.

19   Ahearn became part-owner of the hockey Senators, 1920/21-1933/34. He was selected to the Hockey Hall of Fame as a builder in 1962.

20   "News Notes," *Sporting Life,* February 24, 1912: 15.

21   "Arranging for Sunday Baseball Games," *Ottawa Journal,* April 2, 1912: 9.

22   "No Sunday Ball to Be Played Here in Canadian League," *Ottawa Citizen,* April 23, 1912: 8.

23   "Ottawa Ball Club Sign Up a Star Catcher," *Ottawa Journal,* March 2, 1912: 5.

24   "Ottawa's Now Certain of Draper, Deal Was Closed Yesterday," *Ottawa Citizen,* April 2, 1912: 8.

25   *Ottawa Journal,* April 15, 1912: 1.

26   "Rousing Reception Now Assured for Members of Ottawa Ball Club," *Ottawa Citizen,* May 9, 1912: 8.

27   "Expect McManus to Recover Quickly," *Ottawa Journal,* July 26, 1912: 5.

28   "Canadian League Pennant Comes to Ottawa, Senators Took Doubleheader from London," *Ottawa Citizen,* August 19, 1912: 8.

29   "Watch the Race," *Ottawa Journal,* September 4, 1912: 4.

30   Telegram from Frank to Kitty Shaughnessy, September 2, 1912. Courtesy Honora Shaughnessy.

31   "Ottawa Baseball Team Disbands, Kind Words for Local Friends," *Ottawa Citizen,* September 4, 1912: 8.

32   "Ottawa Didn't Play Yesterday, All Games Off Because of Rain," *Ottawa Citizen,* August 20, 1912: 9.

33   The oldest active football trophy in North America, dating back to 1898.

34   "He is credited with having more to do with changing Canadian football, by introduction of American football tactics, than any other man." King and Kritzer, "Shaughnessy." "It was largely through his campaigning that the Canadian game adopted the forward pass, 12-man teams and the direct snap from center. ..." Marven Moss, "Frank 'Shag' Shaughnessy Is Still Rolling in High Gear Despite His Age, Leading Battle for Minor Clubs," *Sherbrooke Daily Record,* January 11, 1958: 8.

35   King and Kritzer, "Shaughnessy."

36   "Ottawas Get Frank Shaughnessy as Manager for Next Season," *Ottawa Citizen,* January 17, 1913: 9.

37   "Ottawa and Brantford Teams Open Local Season Month from Today," *Ottawa Citizen,* April 15, 1913: 8. The Senators lost three key players to higher classifications in the 1912 draft: shortstop Artie Schwind (Boston Braves) and pitchers Fred Herbert and Frank Kubat (Toronto Maple Leafs).

38   "George A. Kempf Dead," *Chicago Inter Ocean,* 16 April 16, 1913: 14.

39   "Ottawa and Brantford Teams Open Local Season Month from Today," *Ottawa Citizen,* Apr. 24, 1913: 8.

40   Later in 1913, Shaughnessy, as he had done in Roanoke, bought into an Ottawa automobile dealership.

41   "Great Pitching Duel Expected at Lansdowne Park Today," *Ottawa Citizen,* May 17, 1913: 8.

42 "Darkness Ended Thrilling Game, Ottawa & St. Thomas Play Tie 1-1," *Ottawa Citizen*, May 21, 1913: 8.

43 "Shaughnessy Hailed to Court at St. Thomas," *Ottawa Citizen*, July 9, 1913: 8.

44 "Shaughnessy Hailed to Court at St. Thomas."

45 "Shaughnessy May Become Big League Manager," *Ottawa Citizen*, August 12, 1915: 8.

46 "'Shag' Deserves Credit," *Hamilton Herald*, August 29, 1914: 9.

47 Bert Perry, "Looks Like Fourth Straight Pennant for Ottawa Club," *London Advertiser*, August 4, 1915: 8.

48 Bill Rhodes, *London Free Press,* undated 1915 clipping. Courtesy Honora Shaughnessy.

49 Renfer finished with 21 wins and was drafted by the Detroit Tigers in the fall of 1913. After a four-week layoff, he started – and lost – a game against the Washington Senators. That was the extent of his major-league career.

50 Deneau was born in Amherstburg, Ontario, in 1879, and played 10 years in the minors.

51 Ottawa, at 66-39, finished .008 ahead of London, 64-39.

52 In the offseason Dolan served as trainer of whatever football or hockey club Shaughnessy happened to be coaching at the time.

53 Alan Metcalfe, *Canada Learns to Play: The Emergence of Organized Sport in Canada, 1807-1914* (Toronto: McClelland and Stewart, 1987).

54 "Toronto Broke Ottawa's Winning Streak in First Game of Canadian League Season, Bullock's Error Paved Way for Defeat," *Ottawa Citizen*, May 15, 1914: 8.

55 "Ottawa and London Baseball Clubs Summoned for Sunday Ball in Hull," *Ottawa Citizen,* August 10, 1914: 1.

56 *Ottawa Citizen*, June 29, 1914: 12.

57 Reisling and Shaughnessy had both played for Coatesville/Shamokin in the Tri-State League in 1905.

58 "Ottawas Have Chance to Make Fresh Start Against St. Thomas Team This Afternoon," *Ottawa Citizen*, July 16, 1914: 8.

59 Mitchell (born Kmieciak) would be called Johnny Mitchell during a five-year major-league career, 1921-25.

60 "Champs. Caught London after Stern Chase of 57 Days," unattributed newspaper clipping, 1914. Courtesy Honora Shaughnessy.

61 Shocker would be the last legal spitballer on the Yankees after the pitch was outlawed in 1920. In 1921 he tied for the major-league lead in wins with 27. He died in September 1928, two weeks shy of his 38th birthday.

62 "Ottawas Scored 8 Runs in Two Innings and Easily Disposed of Brantford; Del Chase No Puzzle for Senators," *Ottawa Citizen*, August 19, 1914: 8.

63 "'Shag' Deserves Credit: Hamilton Papers Comment on Baseball Struggle," *Ottawa Citizen*, August 29, 1914: 9.

64 Tripleheaders in Organized Baseball were extremely rare, but not unprecedented. By this time there had already been two at the major-league level. On September 1, 1890, the Brooklyn Bridegrooms beat the Pittsburgh Alleghenies three times on their way to the NL title. On September 7, 1896, the pennant-bound Baltimore Orioles swept a Labor Day tripleheader from the Louisville Colonels.

65 "Canadian Ball League Pennant Comes to Ottawa; Champions Downed Peterboro and Won Flag Again," *Ottawa Citizen*, September 8, 1914: 8.

66 *London Advertiser*, September 8, 1914: 7.

67 "London Downs Saints Three Times but Loses Pennant," *London Free Press*, September 8, 1914.

68 "Probably the Cold Was in Shaughnessy's Feet," *London Advertiser*, September 8, 1914: 7.

69 Unattributed clipping from summer 1915. Courtesy Honora Shaughnessy.

70 M.H. Sexton, "By the Editor of 'Sporting Life'," *Sporting Life,* December 12, 1914: 13.

71 J. Harry Fowler, "The Canadian League," *Sporting Life*, November 21, 1914: 19.

72 "Hard to Prove Ottawa Broke Limits," *Ottawa Citizen*, September 22, 1915: 9.

73 "Baseball Men Making Ready for Opening," *Ottawa Citizen*, April 3, 1916: 7.

74 Contemporary Ottawa newspapers all spelled Peterson's first name as Louis.

75 "Olean Beat Warren," *Jamestown* (New York) *Journal*, June 7, 1916: 14.

76 "League Notes," *Jamestown Journal*, June 8, 1916: 14.

77 Officers' Declaration Paper, Canadian Over-Seas Expeditionary Force, December 22, 1916.

78 Medical History Sheet, February 17, 1917.

79 "Shag in New Role," *Ottawa Citizen*, December 21, 1916: 8.

80 "Shag in New Role."

81 "Ottawa Athletes to Kingston School," *Ottawa Citizen*, January 15, 1917: 8.

82 "Many More Ottawa Athletes Called in First Draft under New Military Service Law," *Ottawa Citizen*, May 6, 1918: 8.

83 John Kieran, "Under Two Flags," *New York Times,* January 23, 1941: 27.

84 Kieran.

85 Canadian Expeditionary Force Certificate of Service, March 4, 1920.

86 Joe King and Cy Kritzer, "Shag, as a Farm Manager, Polished Rickey's Kid Stars," *The Sporting News,* December 14, 1960: 26.

87 "Shaughnessy Is Planning for New Baseball League," *Ottawa Citizen*, August 4, 1919: 8.

88 Some sources say the team finished 3½ games back.

89 "Shaughnessy Is Planning for New Baseball League."

90 King and Kritzer, "Shag, as a Farm Manager, Polished Rickey's Kid Stars."

91 Kieran.

92 "Montréal Signing Negro Ace a Headache for Chandler," *Bergen* (New Jersey) *Record*, October 24, 1945: 19.

93 Sam Blackman, Tim Bourret, and Dabo Swinney, *If These Walls Could Talk: Stories from the Clemson Tigers Sideline, Locker Room, and Press Box* (Chicago: Triumph Books, 2016).

94 Tim Burke, "Shaughnessy Clan Full of Rich History," *Montréal Gazette*, June 15, 1982: B-5.

95 Honora Shaughnessy, telephone interview with author, August 6, 2002.

ERNIE QUIGLEY:
ARBITER EXTRAORDINAIRE

By Larry Gerlach

Before the age of television, umpires worked in anonymity, only a handful of dominant personalities gaining widespread recognition. Among the virtually unknown arbiters is Ernest Cosmos Quigley, an outstanding and influential umpire who also was the greatest sports official in history. Indicative of how overlooked he has been is the fact that even a fairly comprehensive listing of Canadian-born major-league players, coaches, managers, and umpires, the latter including arbiters Jim McKean and Paul Runge, omits Quigley.[1]

For 31 years, 1913-1944, "Quig" served the National League with distinction as a field umpire, supervisor of officials, and public relations director. And for 26 of those years, he not only umpired major-league baseball, but also gained national prominence officiating major-college football and basketball, in all some 250 games a year. (It was then possible to combine major-league umpiring with officiating other sports because college schedules were more seasonal and limited in number—typically eight football and 18 basketball games in the 1920s.) In over 40 years of officiating, Quigley estimated working some 5,400 baseball, 1,500 basketball, and 400 football games logging 100,000 miles a year in coast-to-coast travel.[2] When baseball commissioner

Kenesaw Mountain Landis wondered how his wife liked her husband being gone 325 nights a year, Quigley quipped: "Mrs. Quigley likes it fine. We're constantly getting reacquainted."[3]

Ernie was born on March 22, 1880, in Newcastle, New Brunswick, Canada, to Lawrence B. Quigley, an Irish immigrant, and Mary J. (Weir) Quigley, of Saint John, New Brunswick. His father, a salesman, sought greater opportunities by moving the family to Concordia, Kansas, in the 1880s. Quigley was an all-around athlete at the University of Kansas, but baseball was his favorite sport. He turned professional in 1905 as a shortstop with Topeka in the newly formed Class-C Western Association. His professional career, which included occasional stints as a manager, took an abrupt turn in 1910 when, sidelined by a broken hand, he agreed to replace an umpire who had quit the Class C Wisconsin-Illinois League. Quigley was a natural: Three years later he reached the major leagues.

A National League umpire for 26 years, he umpired 3,351 games, the seventh most in major-league history at the time. His career highlight was umpiring 38 games in six World Series including the infamous 1919 "Black Sox" series between Chicago and Cincinnati in which he worked home plate in Games Three and Seven. Shocked to learn that eight White Sox players had thrown the Series, Quigley said he "never saw a team try harder to win, and that they were beaten on the square by the superior strength of the Reds."[4] He was also behind the plate on June 1, 1923, when the New York Giants beat Philadelphia 22-8, setting a modern league record by scoring in all nine innings. He achieved another distinction when he and Charley Rigler in 1920 became the first National League umpires ever to "hold out" for more money before eventually signing their contracts.

Quigley experienced the physical dangers of umpiring home plate. On July 11, 1923, he was hospitalized for several days after being knocked unconscious by a foul ball to the left temple in the first game of a doubleheader. Cy Pfirman had to work the second game alone, making Quigley indirectly responsible for the last major-league game officiated by a single umpire.[5] In 1934 another foul ball hit him on the jaw; temporarily unable to speak, he had to communicate for days with pencil and paper. And in August 1934 he was overcome with heat exhaustion after the first game of a doubleheader in Philadelphia.

Sometimes Quigley just had a bad day. One such occurred while umpiring behind home plate in the 1935 World Series. In the fourth inning, while racing toward the Detroit dugout to track a foul popup, he "slipped in a puddle and was like to bust his neck falling into the Tigers dugout."[6] Another unfortunate occurrence came after a game at Wrigley Field in 1933, when Quigley suddenly collapsed unconscious in the umpire's dressing room. Taken to a hospital, he had not suffered a stroke as feared, but instead had been severely shocked after backing into an exposed electrical wire while exiting the shower. Contrary to doctor's orders, he returned to the diamond the next day.

As with all umpires, Quigley's decisions occasionally prompted arguments from players and managers as well as boos and even barrages of pop bottles from fans. On balance, however, he reportedly had good relations with players and managers owing to his diplomatic posture, decisiveness in upholding decisions, and total command of the rulebook. Casey Stengel thought him "a splendid man who knew all the rules."[7]

He repeatedly demonstrated knowledge of the most intricate applications of both playing and scoring rules and adamantly refused to tolerate verbal abuse. Instead of debating decisions, Quigley turned challengers away by sternly asking: "Now just what was it you said?" Continuing the discussion resulted in ejection from the game. He lost control once, early in his career on July 22, 1915, when he punched Johnny Evers, claiming that the Boston second baseman had stepped on his foot during an argument. Umpire and player were each fined $100.

Quigley enjoyed universal respect for his demeanor as well as his umpiring ability. At a time when players and managers like John McGraw were openly combative and profoundly profane, some umpires retaliated in kind with vulgarities and insults. Not Quigley, who had taught history, English, mathematics, and physical education at St. Mary's College in Kansas. Fred Lieb, the most prominent baseball writer of his day, who covered baseball for three New York City newspapers from 1909 to 1934, recalled that Quigley was "strictly high class" and "spoke with the diction and proficiency of a college professor." When McGraw once shouted, "Don't put on any airs with me," Quig replied: "One doesn't put on airs by speaking good English." To a player's uncomplimentary comment, he once responded: "Sarcasm, sir, is the weapon of the weak-minded." He enjoyed the respect of adversaries. He regarded Boston's Tony Boeckel, with whom he had numerous run-ins, as "the most pestiferous player in uniform," but when a serious illness sent Quigley to the hospital, Boeckel sent flowers.[8]

Quigley's contributions to umpiring extended abroad. After the 1928 season, the second most senior National League umpire to Bill Klem spent three months on an instructional mission to Japan with three recently retired ballplayers, including Ty Cobb. Treated "like royalty," he traveled throughout the country umpiring ball-games, lecturing, and conducting clinics, and even establishing schools for baseball umpires and basketball referees.

When Quigley retired at the end of the 1936 season, National League President Ford Frick appointed him the league's supervisor of umpires. (The administrative appointment theoretically ended Quigley's on-field duties, but he returned to the diamond as a replacement umpire for several games in April and May 1937 and again in July and September 1938.) His duties as umpire-in-chief were to supervise the current

umpire staff, review complaints of their decisions and performances, adjudicate fines levied for confrontations with umpires, and interpret rules for Frick and the teams. In this capacity Quigley's legendary knowledge of the rules was put to good use. Asked by Frick to facilitate the creation of a uniform code for both the major and minor leagues, he called senior circuit umpires to a three-day meeting to review "every word of every rule," posing questions about the formal rules as well as unusual situations and vague applications. The undisputed authority on baseball rules, he routinely received inquiries about interpretations from across the country and from as far away as Australia and Japan.

In December 1940 Ford Frick designated Quigley the league's first full-time director of public relations, a position he held until July 1944. The reassignment was both political and

Game One of the 1921 World Series at New York. Umpires (left to right) Cy Rigler (home plate), Ernie Quigley (2nd base), George Moriarty (1st base), and Ollie Chill (3rd base). This was one of 38 Series games to be umpired by Quigley. (Canadian Baseball Hall of Fame and Museum)

practical. The National League's Bill Klem, the most famous and respected major-league umpire, had retired in November 1940. When Tommy Connolly, Klem's famous counterpart in the American League, retired in 1931, he became major-league baseball's first umpire supervisor, so the National League followed suit by appointing Klem, "the King of Umpires," to the like position. Because Quigley had served concurrently as the voice of the league and umpire supervisor, the expansion of his public relations functions was apt. And in recognition of his skill in identifying new talent, he continued to be in charge of scouting for new umpires.

Ever the ambassador for sports, Quigley taught from 1938 to 1940 a summer-school course at Columbia University. To facilitate instruction on baseball rules in his course on Techniques and Mechanics of Umpiring, he invented Magnetic Baseball, a magnetized "blackboard" featuring the outline of a baseball diamond. By using a series of colored magnetized rings to represent players and umpires, he was able quickly and clearly to diagram positioning on various plays.[9] In the early 1940s, Quigley joined with fellow National League umpire Charlie Moran, a former football player and coach, to publish "educational" pamphlets on "All phases of Foot Ball, Basket Ball and Base Ball."

No less significant was his public persona: The highly visible, personable, and outgoing Ernie Quigley did much to put a "human face" on umpires, thereby countering the conventional negative attitudes toward baseball's men in blue serge suits. It was commonplace for baseball players to endorse a variety of commercial products, but Quigley was the first sports official known to do so, pictured and identified as the umpire supervisor in a newspaper advertisement: "We solved the timing problems of baseball when we adopted Longines Watches for the use of all umpires."[10]

Sensitive to verbal abuse from fans and press coverage that called attention to controversies, umpires typically were reticent and inconspicuous off the field. Quigley, however, relished the spotlight. He eagerly made a well-publicized appearance on a WEAF radio sports interview program in New York explaining how umpires dealt with difficult and unexpected situations, and regularly joined civic leaders at a variety of celebratory community affairs ranging from the annual Brooklyn Dodgers Knot-Hole Club fete to a joint Sportsmanship Brotherhood-New York City Baseball Federation dinner honoring Connie Mack, the 78-year-old owner-manager of the Philadelphia Athletics.[11] And he occasionally returned to the field as a celebrity umpire, as for the annual Army-Navy Day game at West Point and benefit games between teams from two New York military bases.[12] Perhaps his most effective outreach activity was the thrice-weekly evening radio program he hosted on station WIBW in Topeka for 17 years, from the late 1920s to the mid-1940s, talking about sports in general but mostly baseball, answering questions from listeners.

Although overshadowed in the minds of fans and historians by some of his more flamboyant contemporary National League umpires, Quigley's on-field reputation and administrative contributions following retirement testify to a long, distinguished, and influential career as a major-league umpire. In 1960, looking back over a half-century of covering baseball, Fred Lieb in his weekly column for The Sporting News, declared: "It is doubtful if any man ever had the rules of baseball, football and basketball at his finger tips as did Quigley. Unless it was Bill Klem, no National League umpire of his day commanded as much respect as did Quigley."[13]

The baseball diamond provided Quigley with his greatest officiating success, but football and basketball brought even more widespread recognition. For 40 years, 1904 to 1943, Quigley worked college football games, for most of his career serving as the referee, the head crew official.

(He missed two seasons: 1928 because of the baseball trip to Japan and 1938 due to a severe ankle injury in September that kept him on crutches until the start of the 1939 baseball season.) He thought refereeing football was easier than umpiring baseball in one fundamental respect: Football players "usually vent their enthusiasm on their adversaries instead of taking it out on the officials."[14] Quigley was in demand for "big games" across the country including three Rose Bowls, and as with baseball, his command of football's rulebook was unrivaled; after retiring from the gridiron, he served as the ranking member of the NCAA Football Rules Committee from 1946 to 1954.

Quigley refereed college basketball from 1906 to 1942, rising to the top of basketball officialdom in the United States. In addition to a full slate of regional college games each year, he was selected to work premier national contests and officiated more national tournaments than any other referee. He was the second referee to be enshrined in the National Basketball Hall of Fame. Departing from the customary staid demeanor of sports officials, Quigley became the first flamboyant, "colorful" official, famous for exaggerated verbal and physical gestures as well an unorthodox behavior. To Quigley, the whistle was merely a device to announce a referee's presence.

His trademark call became world renown. Upon detecting a violation, Quigley pointed an accusing finger at the offending player and in a stentorian voice shouted: "YOU can't D-O-O-O that!" – a call invariably echoed by the spectators. His trademark call was so well known that in 1945 he received in Lawrence, Kansas, a letter from Europe addressed only as "You Can't Do That! U.S.A."[15]

His officiating career finally over, Quigley returned in 1944 to his alma mater, the University of Kansas, as the athletic director. He promptly retired the department's debt and launched a major resurgence in its athletics program by reinstituting five sports canceled during World War II and hiring superb coaches who elevated football, basketball, and track to championship levels. After he retired in 1950, the school's first baseball field, built in 1958, was named Quigley Field in his honor.

Ernest C. Quigley underwent extensive cancer surgery in September 1958, and finally succumbed to the disease on December 10, 1960, aged 81. He is interred in Mount Calvary Cemetery in Lawrence. Perhaps the best epitaph for the one-of-a-kind official came from his alma mater's student newspaper: "The most famous man in the field of sports."[16]

NOTES

1   William Humber, *Cheering for the Home Team: The Story of Baseball in Canada* (Erin, Ontario: Boston Mills Press, 1983), 149.

2   This essay is extracted with revisions from my comprehensive account of Quigley's career. See Larry R. Gerlach, "Ernie Quigley: An Official for All Seasons," *Kansas History* vol. 33, no. 4 (Winter 2010-2011): 218-239.

3   Gerlach.

4   *The Sporting News,* October 7, 1920.

5   John Schwartz, "From One Ump to Two," *SABR Baseball Research Journal 2001*: 85-86.

6   *Chicago Daily News* and *New York World Telegram*, October 7, 1935.

7   Joseph Vecchione, ed., *The New York Times Book of Sports Legends (*New York: Simon & Schuster, 1992), 332.

8   *The Sporting News*, July 29, 1915; *New York Times*, January 9, 1927, December 5, 1929, and December 11, 1960.

9   "Magnetic Baseball á la Quigley," August 1941 press release, Ernie Quigley File, National Baseball Library, Cooperstown, New York. See also *New York Times*, July 30, August 3, and August 11, 1941; *Topeka Capital*, August 3, 1941.

10 *New York Times,* July 4, 1937; unidentified newspaper advertisement, September 29, 1940, Quigley File, National Baseball Library.

11 *New York Times,* July 31 and August 1, 1937; April 13 and 15, 1940; October 4, 1941.

12 *New York Times,* June 1 and 13, 1941.

13 *The Sporting News*, December 21, 1960.

14 *Sporting Life*, December 12, 1914.

15 University of Kansas Sports Bureau News Release, August 2, 1945. Ernest C. Quigley Collection, Spencer Research Library, University of Kansas, Lawrence, Kansas.

16 *University Daily Kansan*, December 12, 1960.

JOSEPH J. LANNIN

By Bill Nowlin

Joseph J. Lannin owned the Boston Red Sox for less than four full years, but in that short span, the team won two world championships in the back-to-back years 1915 and 1916.

A native of the Province of Quebec, he came to the United States at a very young age – the story says he was orphaned and walked all the way to Boston. He became a remarkably successful businessman. This Canadian from rural Quebec became the team owner responsible for bringing Babe Ruth to the Red Sox. Lannin departed life plunging from the ninth story of a hotel he owned in Brooklyn, New York.

Lannin was a dedicated baseball fan. When he first made a splash in the Boston newspapers, it was with his purchase of a significant share of the Red Sox, announced in the newspapers of December 1, 1913. He did at the time own a portion of Boston's other major-league ballclub, the National League's Boston Braves. He had tried to buy the Braves outright but that offer had been declined.[1]

John I. Taylor of the Red Sox had sold half of the club on September 15, 1911, to James McAleer, manager of the Washington Senators, and Robert McRoy, who was secretary to American League President Ban Johnson. It was, say

Boston Red Sox owner Joseph J. Lannin (Public domain)

Red Sox historians Glenn Stout and Richard A. Johnson, "no secret that McAleer was only the front man in the deal. Most of the money was Johnson's."[2]

For his part, Taylor became vice president but was not actively engaged in running the ballclub. His eyes were on real estate and he used the income from the sale to help fund his Fenway Realty Company, which purchased the land on which he built Fenway Park in time to open on April 20, 1912. That very year, the Red Sox won the World Series.

During 1913, however, there was competition brewing in the form of the Federal League – which did indeed "raid the rosters" of both established major leagues and fielded teams in both 1914 and 1915. As it became clear that the Federal League was becoming a reality, and a threat, Ban Johnson moved to bring in someone else – someone he perceived as more pliable, but someone who had money, too. He turned to Lannin and his Lannin Realty Company, which purchased the shares owned by McAleer and McRoy. The *Boston Globe* noted, "The change in ownership has the sanction of Pres. Johnson of the American League, who had a prominent part in the negotiations, which will be closed at an early date."[3]

Lannin couldn't own 50 percent of the Red Sox and retain a minority stake in the Braves. Braves owner James E. Gaffney declared, "Lannin will sell his stock in my club and will resign from the board of directors." He said he was sorry to see Lannin leave, that he thought he was the "right man" to take over from McAleer et. al., adding that he "has plenty of money and is a baseball fan of the 33rd degree."[4]

The *Globe* story added about Lannin, "Mr. Lannin is a large real estate owner in New York, as well as in this city. He owns Arborway Court, Jamaica Plain, and many large apartment houses in Greater Boston. Mr. Lannin is a baseball enthusiast."[5]

At the time, Lannin was a resident of Hyde Park, New York. He had only become a member of the five-person board of directors of the National League ballclub in November.[6] The *Boston Herald* characterized him as a "Boston man" in its headline on its front-page story about his buying into the Red Sox, but noted him as "of Boston and New York." The forced sale of the Red Sox stock was said to be "the direct outcome of the 'royal rooters' episode of the world's series of 1912."[7]

The amount Lannin invested was reported as $220,000 for half of the shares of the Red Sox, acquiring those held by McAleer, McRoy, and Garland "Jake" Stahl. General Charles H. Taylor and his son John I. Taylor had sold the shares to McAleer et al. for $170,000 in the winter of 1911-12. The Red Sox beat the New York Giants to win the 1912 World Series and were said to have turned a profit of $400,000. However, management had blundered badly before Game Seven. The long-standing booster club, the Royal Rooters, paraded onto the field prepared to take the several hundred seats that had always been reserved for them, only to learn that "in a huge miscalculation, team treasurer Robert McRoy made the Rooters' tickets available to the general public."[8] The Rooters pretty much boycotted the final game of the Series, leaving the park only half-full; with the Series tied at three wins each, attendance for the clinching game dropped from 32,694 to just 17,034. Boston Mayor John "Honey Fitz" Fitzgerald was an active Rooter and had gone with the group to the games in New York. He called for McRoy to be removed from his position.[9]

The Taylors wanted to buy back the shares they had previously sold and become 100 percent owners of the ballclub, but Ban Johnson steered the sale to Lannin.[10]

Joseph John Lannin was born in Lac-Beauport, a town about 15 miles north of Quebec City. Officially known as Saint-Dunstan-du-Lac-Beauport, the town was a municipalité de paroisse in the region Le Jacques Cartier; it was renamed simply as Lac-Beauport in 1989.

His father, John, was a farmer, born in Skull, County Cork, Ireland, in 1814, who had emigrated to Canada. John had lost his first wife and mother of four at St. Dunstan in 1846 and married Catherine Evers, likewise an Irish immigrant, in 1847.

Catherine was mother to nine more children, one of whom died in infancy. Joseph was the next-to-last child to join the Lannin family. He was born at Lac Beauport on April 23, 1866.

John Lannin died on September 6, 1869.[11] Though it is unclear from records consulted, the family perhaps continued to farm. Joseph was only three years old at the time of his father's death. His half-sisters, Mary and Ann, and half-brother, William, were all in their mid-20s or early 30s, and his older brother, Thomas, was 16.

Catherine Lannin remarried in 1874, but died on December 1, 1880. Joseph was orphaned at age 14. He took a job working as a bellhop at the St. Louis hotel in Quebec and came to know some of the clients who used the hotel.[12] He then made his way to Boston. His great-grandson researched the journey as best he could and says, "J.J. walked many segments during his route to Boston, taking odd jobs along the way to rest and earn money, and it is believed that he also rode some trains along the fur route during his journey."[13] A profile in the *Boston Globe* said he "knew several Boston men who went to Quebec and Montréal to buy fur garments, and when he came to Boston [in September 1881] it was to begin as office boy in a store to which he was recommended by one of these friends."[14]

Lannin soon found another position, working as a bellhop at Boston's Parker House for a year, and then the new Adams House.[15] He was apparently a diligent worker, and personable, and worked his way up to head bellboy and was then put in charge of one of the watches. He became a waiter, and then headwaiter. One of the men he had gotten to know over a couple of years told him of a position at the new Charlesgate Hotel and he became steward and "in a short time he became manager."[16]

Lannin became a naturalized United States citizen on October 19, 1887. The formal paperwork said he had arrived in Boston "on or about the third day of September in 1881." He was, the document stated, "an Alien and a free white

person." He was working in a cigar business at the time. In signing the form, he forswore "any allegiance and fidelity to every foreign Prince, State, Potentate, and Sovereignty whatsoever – more especially to Victoria, Queen of the United Kingdom and Ireland, who subject he had heretofore been."[17]

Lannin had married Hannah J. Furlong in Boston on November 29, 1890. He was listed as a waiter at the time; she was a milliner, hailing from Montréal.

He was ambitious, and even at a young age made an early investment in real estate in the Forest Hills section of Boston, as well as beginning to take a two-year course in business at a local business school, studying in his spare time.

He was apparently also proficient in playing lacrosse, playing with the championship South Boston Lacrosse Club, and became a fan of baseball.[18]

After four years at the Charlesgate, Lannin came to learn of an opportunity out of state and leased a hotel at Lakewood, New Jersey, and then the Garden City Hotel on New York's Long Island; the *Globe* article said he was "backed by friends who had great confidence in his ability." He became proprietor of the hotel at Garden City, and was also brought into ownership of the Great Northern Hotel in New York. The former bellhop had now "entered the road toward wealth."[19] He came to own a couple of apartment buildings in Forest Hills and had a number of other real estate investments in New York.

An 1889 article in the *Philadelphia Inquirer* suggested some of the circles into which Lannin had entered, citing him as a partner with Willard D. Rockefeller in New Jersey's Allenhurst Inn.[20]

In 1903 the *Boston Herald* showed him opening the Summit Spring Hotel resort in Poland, Maine.[21]

Lannin was very interested in competitive checkers as well as lacrosse and baseball, and in 1905 greeted a group of 10 British checkers masters who had come to New York on their way to Boston for an international match.[22]

He maintained his legal residence in Boston, at least through the time of the 1910 census.[23]

It 1912 Lannin purchased a number of shares in Boston's National League club, the Braves. Team vice president C. James Connelly had known him "since almost the first day he put in an appearance as a bellboy at the Adams House." Connelly said Lannin "was popular with everyone from his first day on the job ... and as a youngster showed the same care for detail and thoroughness in everything he did that since has served to bring him so great a success in his chosen calling."[24]

The naming of Lannin as president of the Boston Red Sox was formalized on December 24, 1913, at the team's offices in downtown Boston.[25]

Lannin said he had been asked, "Why did I wish to be the president of a baseball club?" He simply said, with a laugh, "Well, because I was such a darned fan."[26] He later said, "I have wanted to own a baseball club ever since I was a bellboy in Boston, I used to sneak into the games then every chance I got, and if one of the players let me carry his bat I was the happiest little Irish kid in all Boston."[27]

In 1914 the Red Sox finished in second place in the American League. They had been world champions in 1912, then dropped to fourth place with a record of 79-71 in 1913, finishing 15½ games behind the Philadelphia Athletics.

The shares of the Braves that Lannin had owned were placed with Gaffney and before year's end were sold to C.J. Connelly.

The Federal League launched as a third major league and fielded competitive teams in both 1914 and 1915, inducing a number of players to jump their contracts with American League and National League clubs, while driving up salaries for the better players because of the entry of a third competitor.[28] Lannin professed not to be worried about the Federal League and foresaw a stronger season for the Red Sox in 1914.[29] Rather,

Joseph J. Lannin, December, 1913 (Bain News Service, courtesy of the Library of Congress)

there was some talk that the Red Sox were so well supplied with talented ballplayers that they might let a couple of them go to the New York Yankees.[30]

On March 6 Tris Speaker signed a two-year deal with the Red Sox for what was thought to be $18,000 a year — more than had ever been paid any player to that date. He reportedly had turned down an offer for $60,000 from the Federal League. Lannin declared, "Baseball is an exciting sport for a new beginner. We had to give Speaker the money, but he is worth it."[31] Speaker's signing resulted in enthusiastic support from Boston baseball backers.[32]

Lannin joined the team for 1914 spring training in Hot Springs, Arkansas. On May 11 at Hot Springs, he announced another two-year deal, this one for left-hander Ray Collins.[33] Both Collins and Speaker excelled for the Red Sox in 1914.

On May 14 Lannin bought all the common stock shares that the Taylors owned and became the sole owner of the Red Sox.[34] Though he had many real estate ventures in New York, Lannin still reportedly had "something like a thousand tenants in the apartment houses he owns in Boston" and he "presented each rent payer with a season pass to the games played by the Red Sox."[35]

Lannin was said not to smoke, drink, or chew tobacco, and he said he wasn't one for sequestering himself in a box seat at a game. "I should say not. I like to get out among the real fans and hear what the supporters of the game think about my team. Some days I go out in the bleachers and sit among those who know all the players by their first names."[36]

He enthused about how thrilled he had been to see the Red Sox win the World Series in 1912 and how disappointed he had been to see them fall as badly as they had in 1913. At the end of July 1914, he said, "I have been traveling with the Red Sox all season and I have enjoyed it immensely. I like to fraternize with the players, with whom it is a pleasure to talk over the games after they are played. Any real baseball fan probably would like to know his favorite players personally, and I always remember than I am as much a fan as anybody."[37] He said he had never – and would never – interfere with his manager.

On July 14 it was announced that Lannin had purchased the contracts of two pitchers named Ruth and Shore from Baltimore's International League ballclub, as well as a catcher named Ben Egan, for a price he said was more than $25,000.[38]

At the end of the month, he purchased the International League's Providence Grays baseball team as well as its grounds, not for his own sake but in order to help the fight against the Federal League.[39]

On August 4 Lannin offered the Boston Braves free use of Fenway Park for Saturday games and on holidays.[40] (The South End Grounds, where the Braves played, had half the capacity of Fenway Park.) After August 11, the Braves played every one of their remaining 27 home games at Fenway Park. and they played all the home games of the 1914 World Series in Fenway Park. Brand-new Braves Field opened in April 1915.[41]

Catcher Bill Carrigan was player-manager of the Red Sox; he had taken over from Jake Stahl midway through the 1913 season. The 1914 team struggled in the first half of the season, often in the second division, but on July 22 reached second place and never relinquished that position. Ray Collins and Dutch Leonard were the team's best pitchers. Leading the team in all three categories, center fielder Tris Speaker had a .338 batting average, four home runs, and 90 runs batted in. His 287 total bases led the league. At the last game of the season, Lannin announced that he had signed Carrigan to a new contract covering the 1915 and 1916 seasons.[42]

The Red Sox had improved to 91-62, but the Philadelphia Athletics won 99 games. The Boston Braves won the National League pennant, having gone in two years from last place in 1912 to the pennant. The so-called Miracle Braves won the World Series from the Athletics.[43]

After the season was over, the Federal League made overtures toward peace but Lannin – now a significant force in American League circles – wasn't having any of it.[44] That was his public stance, but he was later said to have held talks behind the scenes in a number of clandestine meetings.[45] The story was later dubbed a "yarn."[46]

In a post-Christmas message, Lannin wrote an article for the *Boston Herald* predicting that the Red Sox would win the pennant in 1915.[47]

The Federal League kicked off 1915 with a lawsuit against Lannin and the other magnates of the two more established leagues. Lannin said it appeared that the upstart league was upset because some of its players were wanting to jump back to the American and National Leagues. In a public pronouncement on being served papers to appear in court, he voiced an argument that began, "Baseball is not commerce. ..." The argument perhaps foreshadowed the US Supreme Court ruling in *Federal Baseball Club v. National League, 259 US 200* (1922) that granted baseball an exemption from antitrust law.[48] Lannin worried that the "millions of dollars" being spent in the fight with the Federal League might result in it sometime costing as much as $2 to see a major-league baseball game.[49]

As the 1915 season began, Lannin selected the location at Fenway Park from which the Braves could fly their two pennants – the National League and World Championship flags.[50] The team played all its home games at Fenway Park until August 18, when the new Braves Field opened its gates and hosted its first Braves game.

Lannin was optimistic before the 1915 season began, but expressed concern that all the nice things being said about the Red Sox might result in the players becoming "too sure of winning" and undercut their play on the field.[51]

On March 4 Lannin boarded the train at Boston's South Station and headed for spring training again in Hot Springs. Once more he traveled with

the team throughout the season, though not to every game. Interestingly, a "movie man" traveled with the Red Sox filming the team. A news story explained, "Lannin will use the pictures in movie theaters in and around Boston during the winter. They will illustrate baseball talks. The pictures will show the Sox on every American league playing field."[52]

The Red Sox had perhaps the highest payroll in baseball, as the team featured a number of standout players. It had no 20-game winner on the pitching staff but had five starters who each won 15 or more games and a team ERA of 2.39. Rube Foster was 19-8. The two pitchers Lannin had purchased from Baltimore excelled – Ernie Shore was 19-8 and Babe Ruth was 18-8. Dutch Leonard and Smoky Joe Wood each won 15. There was a more balanced offense, too. Speaker once more led in batting average (.322), but Duffy Lewis drove in 76 runs, seven more than Speaker.

Baseball magnates at Fenway Park, Boston: Joseph J. Lannin, Byron Bancroft Johnson, John Kinley Tener, and August (Garry) Herrmann. World Series Game Two, October 9, 1916. (George Grantham Bain Collection, courtesy of Library of Congress)

"Nuf Ced" McGreevy's season pass to Fenway Park for the 1916 Boston Red Sox season. (Michael T. "Nuf Ced" McGreevy Collection, Boston Public Library)

And the leading home-run hitter on the team was its 20-year-old pitcher, Ruth.

It wasn't as though it was smooth sailing all year. Dutch Leonard was suspended for a couple of months for undermining the authority of Bill Carrigan.[53] There were personnel changes; Lannin purchased the contract of Jack Barry in July. The team finished May in fourth place, but finished June in second. The Red Sox attained first place on July 19 and – save for August 19-20 – remained there for the remainder of the season. It was a tight race and they finished with 101 wins, just one more than the Detroit Tigers.[54]

On September 22 Braves President Gaffney extended the same courtesy that Lannin had previously provided to the Braves: the use of Braves Field for any World Series games, should the Red Sox win the pennant.[55] There was a brief brouhaha when there was word that the NL champion Philadelphia Phillies might not set aside 400 seats for Boston's Royal Rooters. Lannin declared that he might not permit the Red Sox to play in the World Series if the team's most fervent fans were denied attendance.[56]

The Red Sox lost the first game of the Series but then won the next four, every one of the wins by just one run. Games Two, Three, and Four were all 2-1 wins. Rube Foster was 2-0. Babe Ruth never pitched. His only appearance was in Game One, when he pinch-hit for Shore and grounded out to first base unassisted.

A planned transcontinental postseason tour that would have taken both teams to California was canceled by Lannin when the Phillies said they needed instead to go to a banquet in Philadelphia.[57]

By mid-December, Lannin had re-signed all but two of the 1915 ballclub for the coming season.[58] He was one of three American League owners on the committee to try to work out terms of a "peace agreement" with the collapsing Federal League.[59]

The contracts Lannin sent out for 1916 contained, in a number of instances, what were characterized as "radical reductions in salaries."[60] With the demise of the Federal League, there was not the competition there had been to drive up salaries as had been the case in 1914 and 1915. Bill Carrigan was fairly clear: "The boys will receive remuneration more in conformity with their worth before the war [with the Federal League began] than with that which has prevailed during the past two years."[61] Several signed right away.

Lannin announced a reduction in ticket prices, the top rate dropping from $1.50 to $1.00.[62] He sold the Providence Grays.[63] There were some comings and goings, but the notable uncertainty at Hot Springs was the status of Tris Speaker. There were already tensions on the ballclub between Protestants (like Speaker, Wood, and Gardner) and Catholics (like Duffy Lewis and Carrigan). Lannin reportedly offered Speaker only half of the salary he'd been paid in the

Season pass to the 1916 Boston Red Sox season. (Michael T. "Nuf Ced" McGreevy Collection, Boston Public Library)

two prior years.[64] Speaker held out, and Lannin traded him to the Cleveland Indians, getting Sad Sam Jones, Fred Thomas, and $55,000 in cash.[65] Stout and Johnson assert that Ban Johnson had an interest in building up the Cleveland club and that there was "some evidence Lannin was coerced into making the trade, for soon relations between the two cooled dramatically."[66]

Joe Wood refused to take a pay cut and sat out the whole season, despite the personal involvement of Lannin in talks. There were even reports that Wood had offered Lannin $10,000 to let him out of his contract.[67] In February 1917, Wood's contract was sold to Cleveland.

The 1916 Red Sox won the pennant again and won the World Series again, too. They won 10 fewer regular-season games than in 1915, but topped the White Sox by two games and the Tigers by four. They started the season well, struggled in May and June and even opened July in fifth place, but then righted their ship with a 20-10 month of July, closing the month in first place. They held steady through the end of the season.

Speaker was gone.[68] Larry Gardner's .308 average placed him first on the team, as did his 62 RBIs. Three players each hit three home runs, enough to lead the team: Tillie Walker, Del Gainer, and Babe Ruth. Not one Red Sox player homered at Fenway Park all season long.

Ruth led the pitchers both in wins (he was 23-12) and ERA (1.75). Dutch Leonard and Carl Mays each won 18. Shore won 16 and Foster 14.

It was again a five-game World Series, this time beating the Brooklyn Robins. For the third year in a row, a Boston baseball team won the World Series – playing in a ballpark that was not their home park. The Red Sox, once again, played Series home games at Braves Field.[69]

Shore was 2-0 in the Series, with Ruth and Leonard each winning a game. Gardner's six RBIs were triple those of any teammate. He hit the only two home runs for Boston. Ruth was 0-for-5, still without a hit in his postseason career. He drove in one run with a groundout in the third inning of Game Two, the only run of the game until a walk, sacrifice, and Del Gainer's single won the 2-1 game in the bottom of the 14th inning, a complete-game win for Ruth.[70]

The business of baseball was definitely not as enjoyable for Lannin as it had been. He had also begun to clash with Ban Johnson. Just a couple of years later, the *Atlanta Constitution* wrote that a clever businessman like Lannin "could not understand why the league owners permitted Ban Johnson to pursue the tactics of a czar." Lannin became restless. "Several clashes with Johnson were the potent factor that drove Lannin to look for a way out of the national game."[71] Perhaps he may have only served Ban Johnson's purposes for a period of time, becoming less pliable once McAleer and McRoy were gone and the Federal League threat was over. In any event, Mike Lynch writes, "Despite the success, Lannin wanted out. He was tiring of Johnson's meddlesome ways, and his health was beginning to fail."[72]

Less than three weeks after winning back-to-back World Series, Lannin sold the team. He had "tired of [Ban] Johnson's constant interference. … Not even a world championship offset Lannin's growing dismay. … He realized that the rules for doing business were different if your name was Mack or Comiskey. Besides, Lannin had heart trouble."[73] It is possible that doctors urged him to give up his interests in baseball. He told the newspapers, "I am too much of a fan to own a ball club."[74]

Lannin acted quickly. "Before Johnson could interfere and attempt to bring in an owner of his liking, Lannin sold the Red Sox to Harry Frazee and Hugh Ward, both of whom had made their fortunes in the theater."[75] The price was a reported $675,000. Frederick G. Lieb wrote, "Lannin caught Ban quite unawares in selling the valuable property to Frazee and Ward, and that Joe made the sale to the theatrical men knowing it would pique Johnson."[76] It was said that Lannin had made a paper profit of $400,000 on the sale.[77] The sale included the grounds at Fenway Park.

Lannin still owned a controlling interest in the Buffalo Bisons, but expected to sell that, too.

Manager Bill Carrigan announced his retirement to Lewiston, Maine.

Part of the Frazee/Ward purchase was by a secured note for $262,000 to be paid later, and in 1919 the payments stopped. Lannin had to initiate legal proceedings in 1920 against the new owners. A court order was obtained to force them to sell Fenway Park and give the money to Lannin.[78] Matters were, however, worked out.[79] In August, he said he was going to get out of baseball altogether, selling off or breaking up his ballclub in Buffalo.[80]

In October 1920 Lannin sold the Buffalo team, saying he was leaving baseball "with regret" because he needed the time to attend to his "numerous hotel interests." The *New York Times* averred that "Mr. Lannin was one of the big factors in the successful rebuilding of the International League, following the disastrous war with the Federal League. He furnished considerable capital to keep the league moving in the lean years following the settlement of the baseball war."[81]

When Frazee sold the Red Sox to a new ownership group in July 1923, there were several who remembered the success the club had enjoyed under Lannin and hoped that new ownership could restore the team to some of its former glory. As it turns out, the new group was seriously undercapitalized, particularly so following the unexpected death in 1927 of its principal financier, Palmer Winslow. The Robert Quinn group held on for nearly a decade before selling to Tom Yawkey in early 1933.[82]

Lannin did stay active in competitive checkers tournaments.[83] In 1924 he made headlines with his ongoing ownership of the Salisbury Country Club in Garden City, Long Island, replete with four 18-hole golf courses on over 900 acres.[84] He appeared from time to time, hosting a social event in Garden City or appearing at a ballgame in Boston. Lannin also owned The Balsams, a resort hotel in Dixville Notch, New Hampshire.

The year 1927 opened with a controversy when Frank Navin, owner of the Detroit Tigers, expressed resentment concerning games back in 1916, charging that Lannin had given bonuses to pitchers on other teams who beat the White Sox, and that a number of beanballs had been thrown at Tigers players in 1917.[85]

One of Lannin's properties was Roosevelt Airfield on Long Island, the field from which Charles Lindbergh took off on May 20, 1927, for his famous trans-Atlantic flight as the first aviator to fly solo and nonstop across the Atlantic Ocean. Lindbergh had spent the night before at the Garden City Hotel owned by Lannin, who watched the pilot take off on his 33-hour flight to Paris.

A couple of transactions made the news in the first part of 1928. Lannin sold the Roosevelt Field runway; the land was to be made into a polo field.[86] And in April he purchased the Granada Hotel, a 364-room hotel in Brooklyn, for $2,500,000.[87]

A few weeks later, Lannin was dead.

On May 15, he had either fallen, jumped, or was pushed out of a ninth-story window at the Granada. He had died instantly, landing on the two-story roof of a restaurant that extended off the hotel. The New York State certificate of death reports that his skull and chest were crushed. He was 62 years old. The medical examiner's ruling was that he had fallen.

Friends said he had suffered a series of heart attacks and that – even though there was reportedly no one present in the room at the time – he had been "seized with a sudden attack and fell over a balcony of the window as he sought air."[88] That word was conveyed by his family and lawyer, disputing the notion of suicide. His attorney said, "He was worth seven to eight million dollars. He had no business nor family troubles."[89] A police detective and the assistant medical examiner, however, told the *New York Times* that he "fell or jumped."

The idea that he had accidentally fallen was compromised by the fact that the window was "a narrow French one" with an aperture of only 15 inches. One pane opened inward and one outward. Dr. Auerbach, the assistant medical examiner, said, as worded by the newspaper, that "it was difficult to see how a man of the size of Mr. Lannin could have gone through the window without turning sideways and squeezing the body through."[90] The window sill was about three feet from the floor.[91]

Lannin had reportedly been in Room 915 to inspect plaster work that was being done at the hotel, and he had been attentive to the refurbishing of the newly purchased hotel, driving over just that morning from his residence at the Garden City Hotel. He had been in good spirits, his family said. He had asked his chauffeur to wait for him at the entrance and 15 minutes later a woman on the fifth floor saw him falling past her window.[92]

He was survived by his wife, Hannah, and their children, Paul and Dorothy.

Lannin is interred at the Cemetery of the Holy Rood in Garden City.

After his death, some came forth with stories of his generosity. The priest who gave the eulogy at his funeral, Rev. Francis J. Healey, reportedly recounted a story from a church service a few years earlier requesting assistance for a family that was having difficult times. Lannin went up to the priest afterward and said he wanted to help the family, but that it had to be completely confidential. "By the next morning, a truck load of food and clothing from the Garden City Hotel was delivered to the family in need." The eulogy ended with Father Healey saying, "J.J. Lannin had respect for all people living their lives by their own honest convictions."[93]

Another tale of generosity is told by Chris Parillo, the grandson of Louis and Carmella Parillo. Carmella's father, Felice Eanaccone, had emigrated from Italy to the United States in 1906. Over time, he purchased some pieces of property in Westbury, Long Island. One such parcel was on Post Avenue, and the Parillos built a small shoe-repair shop on a portion of the land. Lannin was buying up land in order to build another luxury hotel and Eanaccone sold his parcel without realizing that it would mean the shop would have to close. "My grandmother paid a visit to Mr. Lannin at the Garden City Hotel, and basically pled her case. Mr. Lannin was well within his rights to just shoo her out of the office. Instead, he asked two questions: 'How much do you think your building is worth?' and 'How much do you think you need for a down payment on another piece of property?'"

"He could have just asked her to leave, but he was a rags-to-riches guy. An immigrant. He came up from nothing. I think he said to himself, 'I'm not going to deprive these people of their little piece of the American dream.' He cut her a check. With that check, they were able to put a down payment on another piece of property up the street and build their own building, Louis Parillo Shoes."[94]

Parillo's own father inherited the store and Chris vividly recalled growing up in the shop that provided his family's livelihood. "After he died, my grandparents put flowers on his grave once a week. I was born in 1968 and I remember as a little kid going to Holy Rood with my grandmother. My grandfather Louis Parillo died in 1963. He's buried in the same row that Mr. Lannin's buried.

She would visit him and then she would visit Mr. Lannin. She lived until she was 96. She would go every week. I was 4 or 5. Forty-plus years later, she was still doing that."[95]

J.J. Lannin had never forgotten his ties to his native land. As his great-grandson tells it, "Once he got established in Boston, he would send about $20 a month to Canada and one of his sisters was instructed to get nickels or whatever and distribute them to kids on the street, so they could go to a movie or a ballgame. He did that every single month throughout his life."[96]

Other properties Lannin owned included the Great Northern Hotel and the Grenoble Hotel in New York City, and a winter home in Tarpon Springs, Florida. Just two weeks after his death, the Grenoble was sold by his estate. In August, Paul Lannin began to arrange the sale of the Lannin Realty Company's holdings.

Later in 1928, the annual checkers tournament in Boston became the Joseph J. Lannin Memorial Tournament.[97]

Son Paul Lannin became a lyricist and musical composer of note. The year after his father's death, he initiated a golf tournament in his father's honor.[98] He roomed at the famous Lambs Club at 130 West 44th St. when he was composing and arranging music with the likes of Ira Gershwin and Vincent Youmans. One of his musicals, *Two Little Girls in Blue*, ran on Broadway; he also took the show to London. Other Broadway shows included a musical comedy, *For Goodness' Sake*, starring Adele and Fred Astaire, *The Whichness of the Whatness of the Whereness of the Who*, and the *Ziegfeld Follies*.[99]

Dorothy Lannin's grandson Christopher Tunstall has taken on her role as family historian, a mantle passed down through his mother and father.

Joseph J. Lannin was named to the Canadian Baseball Hall of Fame in 2004; it was Tunstall who delivered the acceptance speech.

In April/May of 2012, Christopher Tunstall recreated the 410-mile walk that young Joseph Lannin took from Lac-Beauport, Quebec, to Boston in 1880. He hadn't needed to stop and take up work along the way as Lannin had, but the journey took him 26 days, following as best he could the routes used by the traders of the late nineteenth century. "It was still pretty rugged," he recalled. "Being able to make my journey and walk in my great-grandfather's footsteps was a tremendous spiritual journey for me."[100]

NOTES

1 "Red Sox President Got His Start as Bell-Boy," *Boston Herald*, December 2, 1913: 7.

2 Glenn Stout and Richard A. Johnson, *Red Sox Century* (Boston: Houghton Mifflin, 2000), 71. It was widely understood that the stock in the names of McAleer and McRoy was actually held by Ban Johnson and Charles Comiskey. For information on the sale, see "To Get Half Interest," *Washington Post*, September 13, 1911: 8. In 1919 Johnson admitted as much in court testimony. See "Johnson Admits He Once Owned Portion of Boston Red Sox," *Chicago Tribune*, September 12, 1919: 17.

3 "McAleer and McRoy Are Out," *Boston Globe*, December 1, 1913: 1.

4 "McAleer and McRoy Are Out."

5 "McAleer and McRoy Are Out."

6 "Braves' Park Will Be Greatly Enlarged," *Boston Herald*, November 22, 1913: 9.

7 "Boston Man Likely to Control Red Sox Team," *Boston Herald*, December 1, 1913: 1.

8 *Red Sox Century*, 88.

9 Lawrence J. Sweeney, "Royal Rooters an Angry Lot," *Boston Globe*, October 16, 1912: 6.

10 For more details on the actual sale to Lannin, see "Ban Johnson Swings Big Deal for Boston Red Sox," *Washington Evening Star,* December 1, 1913: 16.

11 Catherine Lannin is found in the 1871 census of Canada at St. Dunstan, indeed listed as an Irish immigrant but already widowed. The census indicated that she was unable to read or write. No occupation is indicated, but she lived with eight children: Thomas (20), Bridget (18), Margaret (14), John (12), Sarah (9), Ellen (6), Joseph (4), and Patrick (2).

12 Harvey T. Woodruff, "Joseph J. Lannin, Canadian 'Bell Hop,' Who Became Baseball Magnate," *Chicago Tribune*, January 11, 1914: B3.

13 Christopher Tunstall, email to author, February 2, 2021.

14 "Joe Lannin a Bostonian," *Boston Globe*, December 14, 1913: 37. The notion, on Wikipedia, that "Penniless, he had remarkably made his way from Lac-Beauport to Boston on foot" seems fanciful and unlikely.

15 Woodruff; "Joe Lannin a Bostonian."

16 "Joe Lannin a Bostonian."

17 The original document is available on Ancestry.com. https://www.ancestrylibrary.com/imageviewer/collections/2361/images/007327479_00042?tree-id=&personid=&hintid=&queryId=36845d8024f7493966b503b2ad59a2fe&usePUB=true&_phs-rc=yoG301&_phstart=successSource&usePUB-Js=true&pId=2084530

18 Woodruff.

19 "Joe Lannin a Bostonian." One can find any number of advertisements for the Garden City Hotel in New York newspapers such as the *New York Daily News* and *New York Tribune* listing "Joseph J. Lannin, Prop." See, for instance, the section of "Summer Resorts" on page 12 of the April 21, 1902, *New York Daily News.*

20 "Up-Jersey Resorts," *Philadelphia Inquirer*, May 28, 1899: 6. The following year, another New Jersey resort – the Essex-and-Sussex Hotel, situated on 500 acres at Spring Beach Lake – announced that Lannin had leased the hotel for a number of years. Lannin, the newspaper said, "by his past connection with the best-known resorts of the country, is well-known to the traveling public." See "Essex-and-Sussex," *Philadelphia Inquirer*, June 17, 1900: 11.

21 "Fine New Maine Resort," *Boston Herald*, June 26, 1903: 10.

22 "British Checker Masters Arrive," *Boston Herald*, March 13, 1905: 3. Articles as late as 1911 show his ongoing involvement with checkers.

23 The 1913 *Boston Herald* article agreed. "Red Sox President Got His Start as Bell-Boy,"

24 "Joe Lannin a Bostonian."

25 "Lannin Is Now Sox President," *Boston Herald*, December 25, 1913: 7.

26 Arthur Constantine, "A City Without Its Baseball Team Is Not on the Map," *Boston Herald*, December 28, 1913: 37. The title of the article was a quotation from Lannin. The article explores at some length Lannin's comments on baseball at the time of his ascension to leadership.

27 "Lannin Refuses to Sit in Box at Ball Games," *Wilmington* (Delaware) *Evening Journal*, July 28, 1914: 11.

28 Former ballplayer and now veteran sportswriter Tim Murnane discussed some of the competition, taking a pro-management tack. See T.H. Murnane, "The Magnate Has More Consideration for the Men He Gathers Around Him Than the Players Have for the Man Who Takes All the Chances," *Boston Globe*, March 1, 1914: 37.

29 T.H. Murnane, "Federal a Two-Club League," *Boston Globe*, January 11, 1914: 111.

30 "Yankees to Get Boston Players," *New York Times*, January 29, 1914: 7.

31 T.H. Murnane, "Speaker Stays with Red Sox," *Boston Globe*, March 7, 1914: 4. There was reportedly a bonus paid Speaker as well.

32 "Flowers at Lannin's Plate," *Boston Globe*, March 8, 1914: 15.

33 "Ray Collins Signs Two Years Red Sox Contact," *Boston Herald*, March 12, 1914: 6.

34 "Pays Big Price," *Washington Evening Star,* July 19, 1914: 57. "Lannin Sole Owner of Red Sox," *New York Times,* May 15, 1914: 13. The Taylors retained ownership of Fenway Realty, as well as some preferred shares. In 1916 Paul J. Lannin served as vice president of the Red Sox and Thomas W. Lannin as business manager. See "New Red Sox Officers," *Washington Post,* May 15, 1914: 9. All told, the cost of his purchasing the team was said to be $600,000. Thomas Lannin died in 1934. "Thomas W. Lannin," *New York Times,* December 15, 1934: 13.

35 "Base Ball Briefs," *Washington Evening Star,* May 29, 1914: 15.

36 "Lannin Refuses to Sit in Box at Ball Games." Knowing the players' first names was not as simple as it might sound because newspaper sportswriters generally did not use them.

37 "Joseph J. Lannin in Game for Pleasure," *Washington Times,* August 1, 1914: 12. Lannin added, "I didn't buy the Red Sox with the idea of making big profits, although some persons may not believe me. I love baseball, and I believe that after thirty years of hard labor as a business man I am entitled to some amusement. If the club breaks even this year or loses some money I will feel satisfied, for I am trying to build up the team so that Boston fans will soon be able to boast of another world's championship."

38 "Timely Baseball Bits," *Hartford Courant,* July 14, 1914: 17.

39 "Lannin Has Courage," *Springfield* (Massachusetts) *Union,* July 31, 1914: 18. See "Lannin and Baker 'Fan' Moguls; Both Are Type of 'New School,'" *Washington Post,* October 11, 1915: 8.

40 "Just Another Victory for 'Pride of East Orange,'" *Newark Evening Star,* August 5, 1914: 13.

41 Bill Nowlin and Bob Brady, eds., *Braves Field – Memorable Moments at Boston's Lost Diamond* (Phoenix: SABR, 2015).

42 T.H. Murnane, "Bill Carrigan for 1915-1916," *Boston Globe,* October 2, 1914: 7.

43 Bill Nowlin, ed., *The Miracle Braves of 1914: Boston's Original Worst-to-First World Series Champions* (Phoenix: SABR, 2014).

44 Bozeman Bulger, "Red Sox Owner to Oppose All Plans for Peace," *St. Louis Post-Dispatch,* October 20, 1914: 17.

45 "Lannin Friend of Dove of Peace," *Detroit Times,* November 3, 1914: 6.

46 "Lannin Is Opposed to Granting Peace," *Boston Herald,* November 5, 1914: 7.

47 "Red Sox – 'Red Sox Should Win the 1915 Pennant in the American League Race,'" *Boston Herald,* December 27, 1914: 14.

48 For a discussion of the exemption, see Joseph J. McMahon Jr., "A History and Analysis of Baseball's Three Antitrust Exemptions," Villanova University, 1995, at: https://digitalcommons.law.villanova.edu/cgi/viewcontent.cgi?article=1264&context=mslj.

49 "Lannin Predicts $2 Baseball if Feds Keep On," *Boston Journal,* February 12, 1915: 1. Ticket prices at the time began at 25 cents and ranged up to $1.50 for a box seat.

50 T.H. Murnane, "Fenway Park Entire Season," *Boston Globe,* January 21, 1915: 7.

51 "Jackson, of Naps, to Join Yankees," *Philadelphia Inquirer,* February 2, 1915: 12. We note that Joe Jackson did not become a New York Yankee. In August 1915 he was traded to the Chicago White Sox.

52 "Movie Man Travels with Red Sox Club," *Salt Lake Telegram,* July 25, 1915: 12.

53 Melville E. Webb Jr., "Red Sox Berth Is No Joy Ride," *Boston Globe,* May 29, 1915: 4.

54 The Red Sox finished 101-50 and the Tigers were 100-54. The Red Sox had played four games that ended in a tie.

55 "Braves' Field to Be Loaned to the Red Sox," *San Francisco Chronicle,* September 23, 1915: 9. The deal was the same – free use, with reimbursement only for actual expenses.

56 "May Refuse to Let Sox Play," *Boston Herald,* October 2, 1915: 6. The issue was satisfactorily resolved. See Lawrence J. Sweeney, "400 Seats for Royal Rooters," *Boston Globe,* October 3, 1915: 16.

57 "Phillies Blamed for Tour Fizzle," *New York Times,* October 16, 1915: 12.

58 T.H. Murnane, "Players the Big Problem," *Boston Globe,* December 16, 1915: 7.

59 "Details of Plan to Be Worked Out," *Springfield* (Massachusetts) *Union,* December 16, 1915: 18. Lannin took ill at the meeting in Chicago but completed his committee work before a slow recovery. See "Training Card of Champion Red Sox to Be Rearranged," *Providence Evening Bulletin,* December 28, 1815: 14.

60 "Lannin Cuts Players' Pay in Contract for 1916," *Chicago Tribune,* January 9, 1916: B2.

61 He said, as one might expect, that he thought his employer's offers were fair. He expected that everyone on the team would return. James C. O'Leary, "Thinks Sox Will All Sign," *Boston Globe,* January 6, 1916: 7.

62 T.H. Murnane, "Fenway Park Prices Reduced," *Boston Globe,* January 20, 1916: 7.

63 "Providence Grays Bought by Draper," *Hartford Courant,* January 25, 1916: 16.

64 This meant his proposed salary would be cut from $18,000 to $9.000. One justification was that his average had declined for three consecutive years – from .383 to .363 to .338, and then to .322 in 1915). After he was traded to Cleveland, he led both leagues in 1916 with a .386 average.

65 One detailed account of the trade was Melville Webb's: "Speaker Cost Cleveland More Than $50,000," *Boston Globe,* April; 9, 1916: 1. The trade was a shock to the players on the team, who thought Carrigan was kidding

them when he first broke the news. Webb was present when Carrigan told the team and wrote that "[n]o aeroplane bomb could have startled" the team more.

66   Stout and Johnson, *Red Sox Century*, 110.

67   Melville E. Webb Jr., "Wood Declines to Sign with Red Sox," *Boston Globe*, July 28, 1916: 7.

68   Lannin had been "sound in his judgment of the team," said a *Boston Globe* subordinate headline. See "Speakerless Red Sox Triumph," *Boston Globe*, October 3, 1916: 7.

69   Games One, Two, and Five were played at Braves Field, with attendance averaging 42,370.

70   The lone run Ruth gave up was a first-inning inside-the-park home run by Hy Myers in the first inning. Attendance was 47,373.

71   "Disgusted by Ban, Lannin to Retire from Great Game," *Atlanta Constitution*, August 16, 1919: 13. The decision to leave baseball was not taken for at least a few months. T.H. Murnane offered words of praise for Lannin's leadership. See "Nearly Ready for the World's Series," *Boston Globe*, October 1, 1916: 16. Lannin was, of course, "elated" that the Red Sox won the pennant. See "Lannin Praises Red Sox Spirit," *Boston Globe*, October 2, 1916: 7.

72   Lynch, 41.

73   Stout and Johnson, *Red Sox Century*, 115. Lannin said that owning the ballclub was interfering with his health, citing his heart condition. See "Champion Boston Red Sox Are Sold," *New York Times*, November 2, 1916: 14. A few days later, Lannin added, "Running a ballclub is not all pleasure, and I felt that I would enjoy the game that I am so fond of more as a spectator." See T.H. Murnane, "Lannin Says He Is Out for Good," *Boston Globe*, November 5, 1916: 16.

74   John J. Hallahan, "Champion Red Sox Club Sold to Frazee and Ward," *Boston Herald*, November 2, 1916: 1.

75   Michael T. Lynch Jr., *Harry Frazee, Ban Johnson, and the Feud That Nearly Destroyed the American League* (Jefferson, North Carolina: McFarland 2008), 40-41. Lannin had sold the Newark, New Jersey, ballclub a few days earlier.

76   Frederick G. Lieb, *The Boston Red Sox* (Carbondale: Southern Illinois University Press, 2003), 155. Lieb's book was originally published in 1947 by G.P. Putnam's Sons.

77   Frederick G. Lieb, 155.

78   "Fenway Park to Go Under Hammer," *Hartford Courant*, February 10, 1920: 10.

79   John J. Hallahan, "Red Sox Not Sold, Peace with Lannin," *Boston Globe*, March 4, 1920: 8. Frazee sold the ballclub in 1923.

80   "Lannin Threatens to Quit the Game," *Washington Post*, August 22, 1920: 18.81 "New Owners for Bisons," *New York Times*, October 29, 1920: 22.

82   See in particular Chapter 2 in Bill Nowlin, *Tom Yawkey – Patriarch of the Boston Red Sox* (Lincoln: University of Nebraska Press, 2018). For the sale to the Quinn group, see "Red Sox Are Sold for Over Million," *New York Times*, July 12, 1923: 15.

83   The February 24, 1925, *Boston Globe* had a photograph on page 21 of a considerable number of men – almost all wearing hats despite being indoors – at the New American House in Boston, competing in the Joseph J. Lannin Tourney.

84   "This Club Has Four 18-Hole Courses," *Boston Globe*, June 1, 1924: 40.

85   "Navin Attacks Lannin, Ex-Owner of Red Sox," *Boston Globe*, January 3, 1927: 1. Lannin emphatically denied he had ever given such bonuses; he also pointed out that he had not owned the team in 1917. See James C. O'Leary, "Navin's Story Brings Denial from Lannin," *Boston Globe*, January 3, 1927: 9.

86   "Famous Airplane Runway to Give Way to Great Polo Field," *Boston Globe*, March 24, 1928: 9.

87   "Lannin Buys Granada, Big Hotel in Brooklyn," *Boston Globe*, April 3, 1928: 23.

88   "Ninth-Story Drop Kills J.J. Lannin," *Boston Globe*, May 16, 1928: 1.

89   "Ninth-Story Drop Kills J.J. Lannin."

90   "J.J. Lannin Killed by Fall at Hotel," *New York Times*, May 16, 1928: 16.

91   "Lannin Plunges to Death at Granada," *Brooklyn Daily Eagle*, May 15, 1928: 1.

92   "J.J. Lannin Killed by Fall at Hotel."

93   Author interview with Christopher Tunstall on December 3, 2020.

94   Author interview with Chris Parillo on December 15, 2020.

95   Parillo interview. The shop that was built in 1927 was ultimately sold in 1998, more than 70 years later.

96   Tunstall interview.

97   "Checkers Today for Lannin Memorial," *Boston Globe*, November 12, 1928: 19.

98   Ralph Trost, "Lannin Memorial Pros' Last Northern Chance for Gold and Glory," *Brooklyn Daily Eagle*, October 15, 1929: 31; Ralph Trost, "Pros Will Have Course in Best Condition for Lannin Memorial," *Brooklyn Daily Eagle*, August 3, 1931: 18. Paul Lannin died on September 8, 1953.

99   Email communication from Christopher Tunstall on December 20, 2020.

100 Tunstall interview.

TORONTO MAPLE LEAFS PLAY THEIR FIRST GAME IN DOUBLE-A INTERNATIONAL LEAGUE

APRIL 19, 1912: JERSEY CITY 2, TORONTO 1, AT WEST SIDE PARK, JERSEY CITY, NEW JERSEY

By Warren Campbell

The 1912 season was the first for the newly named International League. The eight-team league, formerly known as the Eastern League, the six-team Pacific Coast League, and the eight-team American Association had just been accorded Double-A status, representing the top level of minor-league professional baseball at the time.

The Toronto Maple Leafs held their spring training in Macon, Georgia, before making their way north to begin the season in New Jersey. They were scheduled to play the Jersey City Skeeters, who had completed their training camp in Bermuda.[1]

Opening Day of the inaugural International League season for all of its teams was scheduled to be April 18, but rain delayed the Maple Leafs-Skeeters game until the next day. The teams were able to get their seasons going on April 19 at West Side Park in Jersey City, which was still feeling the effects of the poor mid-April weather. "Fans braved the chill air," reported the New York Tribune.[2] The game-time temperature of 46 degrees Fahrenheit (8 degrees Celsius) was noticeably cooler than that of a normal mid-April day in New Jersey (61 degrees Fahrenheit or 16 degrees Celsius).[3]

The headlines in newspapers were still fresh with accounts from the British passenger liner RMS Titanic, which had sunk six days earlier, and the arrival on the 19th of the RMS Carpathia seven miles (11 kilometers) away at Pier 59 in New York City with 705 survivors from the doomed ocean liner.[4] Even with the poor conditions and significant distractions, 5,000 rooters came out to see the home-team Jersey City Skeeters (they were named after the mosquito infestation next to West Side Park)[5] face the heavily favored Toronto Maple Leafs, led by manager Joe Kelley, former player-manager of the National League's Boston Doves and Cincinnati Reds.

The game was of such importance that Toronto City Alderman (and future mayor) Charles Maguire, and the lieutenant governor of the Province of Ontario, John Gibson, came to attend the game. Also in attendance was International League President Ed Barrow, former manager of the Maple Leafs.[6]

The mayor of Jersey City, Henry Otto Wittpenn, threw out the ceremonial first ball with much fanfare. He also put out a fire when an overzealous Skeeters fan threw a lighted match onto the field, setting the decorations on fire.

Mayor Wittpenn reacted quickly, jumping over the railing to extinguish the flames.[7]

Manager Kelley, a 1971 Cooperstown Hall of Fame Veterans Committee inductee, had put together an exciting Maple Leafs roster during the offseason, and the league's westernmost team was expected to challenge for the inaugural title.

The poor conditions undoubtedly played a part, as the batters generally struggled against starting pitchers Art Mueller of Toronto and the Skeeters' Marty McHale. Mueller, one of the Maple Leafs' top four starters, had won 17 games for the team the previous year. Right-hander McHale, getting the Opening Day call for the Skeeters, had pitched six games over the previous two seasons for the American League's Boston Red Sox. Each pitcher was effective, scattering six hits throughout the game.

Toronto was first to get on the board. The second batter to face McHale, former St. Louis Cardinals center fielder Al Shaw, hit his first International League home run to deep center field over the head of Cuke Barrows, a one-time Chicago White Sox prospect. Jersey City responded in the bottom of the first when the third batter, Barrows, drew the first of four bases on balls ceded by Mueller. The fourth hitter, veteran Pep Deininger, hit a ball to right field. The throw from right fielder Jack Dalton sailed over the head of third baseman Bill Bradley, a former longtime Cleveland Indian, allowing Barrows to score.

The Skeeters scored what proved to be the winning run on the bottom of the sixth when Barrows once again reached base on a walk from Mueller. Groundouts by Deininger and George

Wheeler moved Barrows to third. The youngest player in the game, 19-year-old Hal Janvrin, who would go on to play nearly 800 games with the Red Sox, Cardinals, Senators, and Robins, then walked.[8] That brought up shortstop Roxey Roach, who hit a line drive past Maple Leafs shortstop Ed Holly, and Barrows scored. This provided all the runs that McHale would need on this day.

The Maple Leafs had chances in the later innings, as both Shaw (eighth inning) and left fielder Benny Meyer (ninth) hit doubles, but both were left stranded. The 2-1 loss in their first game was disappointing for Kelley and the rest of the Maple Leafs players, who felt this was a game they should have won. A couple of key errors and a lack of timely hitting proved their undoing.

Not playing for Toronto that day was the regular left fielder, Toronto-born Bill O'Hara, who had previously accumulated 380 major league at-bats. The 30-year-old O'Hara was not in the Opening Day lineup as he had looked slow during the spring in Macon. He did find a regular spot with the team shortly thereafter, hitting .304 for the 1912 season. O'Hara died in Jersey City in 1931.

Joe Kelley's Maple Leafs rebounded from this opening defeat to finish the season with a 91-62 record, winning the pennant by five games over the three-time defending Eastern League champion Rochester Hustlers.[9] This was the first of eight International League championships for the Toronto Maple Leafs, one of the most successful teams in the league's history. The franchise was sold and moved to Louisville after the 1967 season.

NOTES

1 *Brooklyn Standard Union*, April 19, 1912: 14. Jersey City's having trained in Bermuda was unusual in that it was only the second team to hold spring training outside the United States. The Chicago White Sox had trained in Mexico five years earlier. See also "Crack of Bat Against Ball," *Boston Globe*, January 29, 1912: 7.

2 "Jersey City Victorious," *New York Tribune*, April 20, 1912: 10.

3 National Centers for Environmental Information report, National Oceanic and Atmospheric Administration Order # 2837844.

4 "*RMS Titanic*: Arrival of the *Carpathia* to New York": https://www.youtube.com/watch?v=dOFpwNPJkcs.

5 "News of Sport: Baseball," *Toronto Globe*, April 20, 1912: 26.

6 "News of Sport: Baseball."

7 "News of Sport: Baseball."

8 Janvrin later became one of the few to pinch-hit for Babe Ruth, doing so twice in August of 1916. Mike Emeigh, email, January 15, 2022.

9 https://www.baseball-reference.com/bullpen/1912_International_League_season.

The Maple Leafs drop the 1912 International League season opener to the Jersey City Skeeters, 2-1. (New York Tribune)

THE VANCOUVER ASAHI

By Tom Hawthorn

A curving pitch appears in slow motion from a hurler not in focus. The voice-over is somber, an older man, remembering. "We were born in Canada," says Kaye Kaminishi. "We spoke English." On screen, a batter pushes a bunt toward the first-base line. The image changes. A young man out for a walk is deliberately bumped in the shoulder by a larger man. "On the streets, we weren't welcome," Kaminishi says, as the scene returns to the baseball diamond, "but on the field we were the Asahi, Vancouver's champions." The video concludes with Kaminishi, a slight, aged man, sitting on a bench wearing the uniform of his Vancouver baseball team, the name spilling in glorious red, Coca-Cola script across the chest, a rising sun on the sleeve.

Kaminishi and his Asahi baseball teammates were among the 22,000 Japanese Canadians interned during the Second World War. The players continued to play baseball in the camps, and brought the game with them as they dispersed across Canada after the war. The release of the Heritage Minute for broadcast in February 2019[1] cemented the team's place in Canadian history. The Asahi, whose story was ignored for decades by a disinterested Canadian public, were being celebrated for their achievements as a team of Japanese Canadian players. They were also being acknowledged for having endured the unfairness of discrimination and the cruelty of having been forced into internment.

The team's story was given further official imprimatur two months later when Canada Post released a commemorative postage stamp celebrating the team. The round stamp featured an image of a baseball with a 1940 team photograph, as well as the team logo, imposed on it. A teenaged Kaminishi appears in the photo. He was born in 1922, and was aged 97 when the stamp was issued.

Japan's 1941 attack on Pearl Harbor led to war. Months later, the Canadian government declared that all those of Japanese ancestry, including those born in Canada, must register as enemy aliens. Property was seized, much of it later sold without permission and at a great loss.

When the order came to abandon his home, Ken Kutsukake, the team's starting catcher in its final year, carefully reduced 31 years of living into a single suitcase. He packed for life in an internment camp: Clothes. Family photos. Baseball shoes. Shin guards. Catcher's mask. Catcher's glove. The baseball equipment was a reminder. They could seize his home, deny him a livelihood, compromise his freedom, but no one was ever going to stop him from playing the game he loved.

They played baseball in the camps, and eventually held a tournament among teams in British Columbia's Slocan Valley, with the Lemon Creek All-Stars, featuring several ex-Asahi players and coached by former pitcher Ty Suga, emerging victorious. Kaminishi, who was interned near Lillooet, British Columbia, played on a team of internees who challenged local amateurs. In his one permitted suitcase, he packed his Asahi uniform and pants, as well as his purple Asahi team sweater. Along with Naggie Nishihara's team jacket, in the possession of the Canadian Baseball Hall of Fame, these four items are believed to be the only remnants of uniforms left from a team that existed for 27 years.

The aspirations of the Japanese Canadian community in Vancouver were expressed through the play of the Asahi. The team was a symbol of the community's struggle for equality and respect. Away from the baseball diamond, people of Japanese ancestry, even those born in Canada, were barred from citizenship and the possibility of working as teachers, doctors, lawyers, or accountants. On the baseball diamond, they could compete as equals.

Smaller physically than their opponents, the Asahi adopted a style of play that came to be known as Brain Ball, in which they relied on "small ball" tactics to produce runs – bunting to get on base, judiciously using sacrifice bunting, and basestealing on offense; and superior pitching and fielding on defense. So precise was the work of Asahi batters, it was said they could bunt with a chopstick. In one memorable game in 1927, the Asahi failed to get a hit off a local pitcher named Lefty Delcourt, yet won the game, 3-1, remarkably scoring two runs on a squeeze play without an error when Roy Yamamura sped all the way home from second base.

For residents of Little Tokyo, or Japantown, as the neighborhood surrounding their home

Ty Suga, 1926 (Nikkei National Museum 2010-26-13)

diamond at Vancouver's Powell Street Grounds was known, the Asahi were gods in flannel. "We were the toast of the town," Kutsukake said in 2003. "To be an Asahi player meant lots to a lot of people."[2]

Their style of play and success on the field gained them a following among Caucasian fans as well, though the team heard plenty of racial insults over the seasons. Vancouver's daily newspapers lazily invoked ugly racial stereotypes and other demeaning descriptions in writing about the players. (A notable exception was the reportage of Clancy Loranger, who started as a sportswriter at the *Vancouver News-Herald* before moving to the *Vancouver Daily Province*, where he covered what would be the Asahi's final game at the end of the 1941 season.) Amateur and semipro baseball in Vancouver was a rough-and-tumble affair in the first half of the twentieth century, and the Asahi took part in their share of dust-ups and brawls, even though they had been instructed to ignore racial slurs, and to not argue with umpires.

The Asahi Baseball Club was formed in 1914, after a visit by a touring Japanese university team fired up local interest in the game. Four years earlier, a Vancouver Nippon Baseball Club had been formed. That team was organized in the wake of a race riot, when residents of Little Tokyo beat back a White mob chanting, "A White Canada!" and "Down with Japs!" The mob torched businesses in nearby Chinatown, and only a desperate defense, including throwing rocks from rooftops, prevented the same destruction happening to their neighborhood.

Asahi, meaning "morning sun," was a name also used earlier by a local youth group, some of whom came to play for the baseball team. In time the Nippon club collapsed, and the better players were absorbed by the Asahi, which also organized teams for younger players (Athletics, Beavers, Clovers) as a feeder system.

In 1918 the Asahi played against three other teams (Hanburys, Empress Manufacturing Co., and Rose & Howard) stocked with local White athletes in the International League, a grand name for one of several amateur commercial leagues in the city. Over the seasons, the Asahi would move between commercial leagues, and some seasons competed in the City Senior League, the top circuit in the early 1930s when Vancouver lacked a professional team. The Asahi also competed against town teams along the British Columbia coast, and headed south to play other clubs with players of Japanese ancestry along the American coast. In 1921 the Asahi president, Dr. Henry Masataro Nomura, led an Asahi all-star team on a tour of Japan, bolstering the roster with three White players from rival teams.

The Asahi claimed championships in the International League (1919), the Terminal League (1926, 1930, 1932, and 1933), and the Burrard League (1938-40). In 1938 they claimed the Burrard title before sweeping Merritt-Gordon, the Commercial League champion, in three games to claim an interleague city title. That same year they also won the Pacific Northwest title over the Seattle Nippons to claim the coast's Japanese baseball crown, a title they held for five consecutive seasons before the outbreak of war in Asia.

The Little Tokyo neighborhood included baths, barbers, bakeries, diners, greengrocers, haberdashers, dry-goods stores, ice cream parlors, and silkware merchants catering to a Japanese Canadian clientele without the snubs to be had in the city's main shopping district a few streets to the west. At the heart of the community was the baseball diamond, which had four rows of wooden bleachers hugging the corner of Dunleavy Avenue and Powell Street. Chicken wire protected spectators from foul balls. The field itself was merciless, a rock-hard pan pitted with stones.

Midge Ayukawa remembered her father, Kenji Ishii, a carpenter, wandering past the Powell Street Grounds, empty lunchpail in hand, dawdling on his way home for supper, hoping to catch a couple of innings of action. "Life was awful, it was so tough," she recalled. "But at the baseball game he was no longer a hard-working, harassed father. He was like a little boy. He didn't have much money. He didn't drink and he never gambled. Going to see the Asahi was about his only luxury."[3]

Fans in the team's early years cheered on such stars as Tom Matoba and Junji "King of Bunting" Ito, as well as the brothers Yo Horii, Mickey, and Eddie Kitagawa. In the 1920s, manager Harry Miyasaki, the first baseman for the 1919 championship team, built the foundations of the culture for which the team would be remembered. He recruited catcher Reggie Yasui and Roy Yamamura, a wicked fielder and fearless baserunner, from the Yamato team, which was based in the city's Kitsilano neighborhood. Their contemporary was left-handed pitcher Kenichi Suga, nicknamed Ty after Ty Cobb, the best pitcher in club history. The trio was at the heart of the Asahi dynasty of the 1930s.

The great Yamamura, known as the Dancing Shortstop in his playing days, served as the Asahi manager in what would be the club's final four seasons. He was a harsh taskmaster. "If you can't stop by glove," he instructed infielders, "stop by chest."[4] One of the more interesting characters on the squad was Satoshi "Sally" Nakamura, a second baseman born in Vancouver who preferred comedy and singing to baseball. In 1940 he left for Japan, where he would have a long career as a

movie and television actor under the name Tetsu "Teddy" Nakamura, appearing in such postwar B-movies as *Oriental Evil*, *Attack Squadron!*, and the monster movie *Mothra*.

The championship teams of the 1930s relied on the likes of sure-handed left fielder Frank Shiraishi, pitcher Naggie Nishihara, infielder George Shishido, and pitcher-outfielder Kaz Suga, who had the team's top batting average for the final five seasons, including a Burrard League-leading .490 in 1939.

One of the highlights of the era was a series of exhibition games at Con Jones Park against the

Triple Crown Winners: Champions of three different leagues for 1938. (Nikkei National Museum 2010-30-1-3-15 ab)

touring Tokyo Giants. The Terminal League All-Stars included the Asahi's Yamamura at short. Although the Asahi picked a few star White players from the commercial leagues to bolster their roster, they still fell 9-2 to 18-year-old right-handed phenom Eiji Sawamura, who struck out 15. The previous year, the kid hurler, while still in high school, struck out Charlie Gehringer, Babe Ruth, Lou Gehrig, and Jimmie Foxx in succession during an exhibition game against barnstorming major leaguers in Tokyo. Sawamura was killed during the war when his troopship was sunk by an American submarine.

After games, players and fans retreated to Sumiyoshi, a diner with a long counter at 392 Powell Street, just behind home plate. The café was owned by the family of utility infielder Masao (Ken) Shimada. That property, along with private homes and personal possessions, was seized by authorities after the federal government ordered anyone of Japanese ancestry away from the coast. Families were split up. The internees were assigned to ghost towns in the British Columbia interior, where they were forced to live in unsanitary and primitive shacks. Even after the end of the war, the internees were not allowed to return to the coast. They were encouraged to move to war-torn Japan, a country many had never even visited. The restrictions were not lifted until 1949, four years after the war's end.

Some former players headed to Eastern Canada to rebuild their lives. They brought with them baseball. Ty Suga's Montréal Nisei team won the city championship in 1949. His kid brother, Kiyoshi, who had been secretary and official scorer for the Asahi, played catcher. Kaz Suga, another brother, spent two seasons with St. Jean of the independent Quebec Provincial League before helping the St. Jerome Lions win the Laurentide League with timely playoff hitting, despite having missed six weeks of the 1953 season after needing 20 stitches in a knee torn while stealing a base.

Ken Kutsukake played amateur baseball briefly before becoming a manager of teams playing out of Christie Pits in Toronto. In 1956, his Honest Ed's Nisei team won the city's senior championship. Ed Mirvish, the team's delighted sponsor, feted them with a banquet, and presented each player a commemorative wristwatch. In 1979 Yamamura received a plaque and a wristwatch for his service as Mr. Ump in the 24th annual Toronto Star Peewee Baseball Tournament at the Canadian National Exhibition.

Thirty-one years passed from the final game in 1941 before the Asahi diaspora had a chance to reunite. Some 300 former players and fans gathered at the Japanese Canadian Cultural Centre in Toronto on October 8, 1972. A first attempt to establish an all-time roster of Asahi players, based on memory and newspaper clips, counted 70 athletes. Most of the documents that would have helped in the task were, of course, lost or destroyed during the war.

An indefatigable campaign by Pat (née Kawajiri) Adachi, who celebrated her 101st birthday in 2021, promoted interest in the forgotten story of the Asahi. In 1992 she self-published a scrapbook about the team's history, and two years later she appeared at a festival at the old Powell Street Grounds, known today as Oppenheimer Park, with several former players, including Mickey Terakita, Katsukake, and, wearing his old uniform, Kaminishi. The Adachi book became a starting point for anyone seeking to tell the Asahi story. In 2003 Jari Osborne's National Film Board documentary *Sleeping Tigers* included archival photographs and interviews with surviving players.

That same year, the Asahi as a team were inducted into the Canadian Baseball Hall of Fame. By that time, only 10 former players were still alive, a roster that shortened with every passing year.

By September 18, 2021, the 80th anniversary of the Asahi's final game, an 8-5 Burrard

League playoff loss against a team sponsored by the Angelus Hotel, only Kaminishi remained. As a voice-over by the author Joy Kagawa states in the Heritage Minute, "The team never played another game."[5]

SOURCES

In addition to the sources cited in the Notes, the author consulted:

www.attheplate.com

Adachi, Pat. *Asahi: A Legend in Baseball* (Etobicoke, Ontario: Coromex Printing and Publishing, 1992).

Hotchkiss, Ron. *Diamond Gods of the Morning Sun: The Vancouver Asahi Baseball Story* (Victoria, British Columbia: Friesen Press, 2013).

National Film Board of Canada. *Sleeping Tigers: The Asahi Baseball Story*. Documentary, 50:00. www.nfb.ca/film/sleeping_tigers_the_asahi_baseball_story/.

NOTES

1   Heritage Canada. "Heritage Minutes: Vancouver Asahi." February 19, 2019. Educational video, 1:01. www.youtube.com/watch?v=wBv-MYAf9P0.

2   Tom Hawthorn, "Sun Rises Again for B.C. Ballplayers," *Globe and Mail* (Toronto), June 27, 2003: A1.

3   Tom Hawthorn, "Rising Sun Shone," *Province* (Vancouver), October 21, 1994: A59.

4   "Rising Sun Shone."

5   Heritage Canada.

BATTED BALLS AND BAYONETS:
BASEBALL AND THE CANADIAN EXPEDITIONARY FORCE 1914–1918

By Stephen Dame

Bill Humber, Canada's foremost baseball historian, has long made the case for baseball's distinction as Canada's earliest "national game." Before indoor rinks and reliable refrigeration, hockey had yet to freeze itself into the collective Canadian consciousness. "If you were to peruse the Canadian newspapers and magazines at the time of Confederation," he once wrote, "one thing would strike you. There's no mention of hockey!"[1] Yet, since at least the 1830s and probably long before, Canadians had been playing baseball. Bruce Kidd noted that baseball was played "by significant numbers all across Canada," and was the only game "which drew players and spectators from all classes."[2] When the British Empire put out the call to arms in 1914, more than 60,000 Canadian men signed up within the first few weeks. Even though nearly 70 percent of those citizen soldiers were British-born,[3] they had already adopted the ways of their new land, including its love of baseball. During the period immediately before the war "baseball was the game of import in Canada – not the British game of cricket nor the Native Canadian game of Lacrosse."[4]

As the volunteers of the Canadian Expeditionary Force suited up and shipped out, they packed their gloves and bats and took their national game with them to war. A total of approximately 600,000 Canadian men entered into military service and baseball proved to be an important part of the First World War experience for many.[5] Canadian commanders were not at first convinced that baseball could provide more than just distraction for soldiers at the front. When the first Canadian recruits arrived on the Salisbury Plain in 1914, they were tasked with drills, exercise and discipline. The men bridged the gap between Civvy Street and enlisted life by playing baseball whenever they could.

Canadian officers generally regarded the game as a pursuit that had cathartic qualities, promoted physical and mental fitness, unit cohesion, and sacrifice, and could involve a large number of players simultaneously.[6] They discounted, however, the emotional attachment many soldiers had to the game. One member of the 58th Battery Canadian Field Artillery noted that overseeing the training ground, "one can almost picture himself back in Canada watching a lot of kids on the sand lots working out to be big leaguers."[7]

Sentimentality aside, sport provided many practical lessons. Sport is often a blunt and honest teacher. Could baseball, with its cruel propensity for failure, prepare soldiers for the agonizing crucible ahead? Craig Greenham, a professor at Wilfrid Laurier University, attempted to explain why baseball seemed well suited to serve as a training ground for war:

"The game provided a chance to cultivate leadership in pressure situations. Baseball allowed for individual responsibility within the framework of a larger cooperative effort as each player/soldier was accountable for his place in the field as well as his turn at the plate. It showed the honour in sacrifice when a batter bunted a ball, giving himself up in the process, to move a runner along the base paths in the name of teamwork and victory. The game encouraged discipline for players who were only to swing at good pitches, but rewarded calculated risks, such as a base runner advancing from first base to third base if the right fielder was known to have a weak arm. Baseball showed its participants how to hold onto an advantage, yet never surrender when behind. Like war itself, baseball had no clock. For both, events continued until finished."[8]

By the spring of 1915 the Canadians were spread across England and on the verge of action in Flanders. In order to maintain fighting efficiency, military commanders developed a system in which units rotated regularly between front line, reserve, and rest areas.[9] The time between the trenches was a boon for baseballers. Suddenly it was possible to schedule games, and even plan for regular league matches. The Canadian training center at Shorncliffe and the nearby soldier-billeting town of Folkestone soon had a calendar of games for home and away.

Word of wartime baseball spread across the ocean quite quickly. Letters from the front spoke of sandlot games and triumphs on the diamond. Propaganda posters featured military men bettering their soccer, boxing and baseball skills. Even recruiting officers sold potential soldiers on opportunities for nonlethal competition while in khaki. Recruiters spoke of sport days in the military camps during their enlistment rally speeches and assured that there would be plenty of opportunity to play games like baseball for all those who signed up to serve their country.[10] Private Nurse, a wounded veteran, joked with a Toronto recruiting rally that "we've got a lot of baseball over there and we need pitchers."[11] The audience may have laughed, but Nurse and his government understood the use of baseball as a powerful recruiting tool.

Once overseas, Canadian soldiers held the military to its promise. The Canadian Army Fields Comforts Commission was established to provide soldiers with whatever luxuries the military deemed permissible. From cigarettes to socks, the CFCC was tasked with soliciting requests from soldiers and communicating those desires back to Canada. The commission published a magazine in which soldiers could request items and express their thanks for things received. The frequency with which baseball equipment was requested by the men in 1915 demonstrated that baseball was already the most popular sport among the Canadian Forces.[12] The Shorncliffe base was the first unofficial home of organized Canadian baseball overseas. Locals jokingly referred to the area as a suburb of Toronto. Canadians became a part of local culture. Researchers discovered that local jargon changed to reflect "Canadianisms," with people saying "sure" when asked questions instead of "yes."[13] One soldier wrote that at Shorncliffe, amid all the uncertainty of war, one thing was always certain: "baseball takes over in the evenings."[14] Baseball was so often showcased before curious English crowds that Canadian soldiers during the Great War were likened to Union and Rebel troops during the US Civil War: "agents of expansion"[15] who spread the knowledge and popularity of baseball as they traveled far and wide playing the game.

As the war expanded, more men arrived from Canada. The CFCC was having trouble keeping up with the demand for baseball. They went so far as to put a stop to further sock and wool donations and specifically requested more baseball equipment. Though much was donated, it still wasn't enough to meet demand. So the CFCC took it upon itself to finance the soldiers' ball field recreation. At Folkestone, not far from the Shorncliffe base, a Patriotic Tea Room was opened to sell drinks and delicacies to the locals. The proceeds went toward purchasing baseballs, bats, and ball gloves. It argues well for baseball as Canada's national game that no such tea rooms were established to secure goalie pads or lacrosse sticks. Baseball was top of mind.

Word of the Canadians and their baseball madness spread beyond the pages of the CFCC magazine. The *Globe and Mail* and *New York Times* ran stories of sports behind the lines. In May of 1915, Ban Johnson, president of the American League, wired Toronto Mayor Tommy Church and offered to send a "big assortment of baseball paraphernalia" for distribution among the Canadian Forces in France.[16] Infamous Minister of Militia Sam Hughes, viewed as an unstable megalomaniac by many, simply a maniac by others,[17] was notified of the offer and accepted. Hughes, a supporter of enlisted baseball, received 720 baseballs, 50 bats, 6 sets of catcher equipment, 6 sets of uniforms, and an unknown number of baseball gloves.[18] Johnson's generosity was widely reported and he basked in the positive press. "The American League club owners and players will cheerfully make this contribution," he told the *New York Times*.[19] Days later, the *Times* reported that AL players would also sign souvenir baseballs for shipment to the Canadian troops. The gestures were perhaps not entirely altruistic. Professor Greenham argued that Ban Johnson saw the Canadian soldiers' embrace of the *American* game as a furtherance of the earlier Spalding tours, which once sought to popularize baseball around the world. The Canadians' showcasing of the game was another step toward "exhibiting

and spreading baseball as authentic American culture … transform(ing) the sport into a global phenomenon."[20]

By the midsummer of 1915, the Canadian troops training in England and fighting in Flanders were so identified with baseball that they began to garner challenges from civilian teams. A group of expatriate United States citizens living and working in London began to formally petition the Canadian command for "friendlies." Jack Norworth, a comedian and the co-writer of "Take Me Out to the Ball Game," was the honorary sponsor and organizer of these men who called themselves the London Americans. A game between "Team Canada" (staff and convalescent soldiers from the Epsom military hospital) and "Team USA" (London Americans) took place in June during a military sports festival at Stamford Bridge.[21] The enlisted Canadian men defeated the American civilians 10-6. The second game of the series saw the London Americans beat Team Canada 9-7. It was the Canadians, however, who took the rubber match, 15-6. By the fall of 1915, the hallowed green of Lord's Cricket Ground was playing host to these international baseball friendlies. This time, a group of soldiers from Shorncliffe wore the title of Team Canada. They beat the London Americans 14-4.

Sam Hughes threw out the first pitch before a team of Canadians from Epsom convincingly defeated a team of "touring American all-stars."[22] In Canada, the minister of the overseas forces, Edward Kemp, authorized financial support for the event, including travel costs for soldiers to attend. The players were winning, the government was paying and perception among the soldiers placed baseball at the top of their recreational pursuits. Besides, Canadian soldiers playing baseball at Lord's Cricket Ground was, to quote one expert, "a very big deal."[23] It was clear by the end of the first informal military baseball season that a more formally organized league structure, with full government support, would flourish in 1916.

The first formal league was encouraged by the Canadian government but financed and organized by the YMCA. Military hospitals and bases at Orpington, Buxton, Covington, and Epsom were among the first sites for structured league games. Hospitals would field multiple teams and be represented by staff and convalescent soldiers at various positions. This caused their lineups to be more fluid as men were discharged, transferred, or newly arrived. Other teams were formed out of army divisions, their games scheduled around rotations to and from the front lines. These teams, the Fighting 18th, the Queen's Own Rifles or the Engineering Training Corps, to name a few, kept and fostered a more permanent lineup of skilled players. J.G. Lee, an American baseball entrepreneur who had tried to create a British Baseball League before the war, jumped at the opportunity to give the Canadian soldiers a league of their own.

Lee negotiated with the Canadian government while also taking control of the London Americans. He created what was a de facto professional baseball league which featured Canadian soldiers being paid by their government and American ex-pats for whom he would foot the bill. Lee was careful to point out that all proceeds from tickets sold to view games in his league would be donated to causes associated with wounded soldiers. Yet, he hoped the enlisted Canadians would help build a baseball culture in Britain and Europe that he could then exploit for profit after the war. Lee's Military Baseball League would stage games at the Canadian military hospitals at Taplow, Epsom, Bearwood, and Bushy Park. He also secured the Arsenal football grounds as a neutral location for games.

By 1917, the number of baseball games being played throughout the Canadian Expeditionary

Canadian soldiers play baseball against their American allies at Lord's Cricket Ground in London during the First World War. (Library and Archives Canada)

Force created a momentum for the sport that could not be stopped.[24] Two baseball leagues were in operation concurrently in Britain. J.G. Lee's league was renamed the Military Hospital Baseball League. Lee organized over 150 games that year, an impressive feat given the other training, recuperative, administrative, and even combat duties expected of his players. The MHBL hosted games at its five original sites, including the Arsenal grounds, while also adding a diamond at Uxbridge. The second league, called the United Kingdom Hospitals and Units league, featured sponsors such as Massey-Harris and the Astor family. The UKHU featured 13 teams playing a schedule of games stretched over the summer months. The Canadian hospitals at Epsom and Taplow played in both leagues simultaneously. The staff, officers, and soldiers at both sites had long considered themselves to be the elite of CEF baseball. During the early organization of Canadian all-star teams, drawn together to face American squads, men from these two locations dominated the lineups.

The leagues structure of 1917 would give the cocksure soldiers of Epsom and Taplow a chance to finally prove their worth. By September, the Epsom team found itself at the top of the MHBL standings and among the top teams in the UKHU. They played and conquered the hospital team at Whitley, which featured Lou Grove as a pitcher. Grove, a standout with the Toronto Maple Leafs baseball club when he signed up for service, was billed as the "best pitcher in the world."[25] With these achievements secured, the boys at Epsom declared themselves champions of the Canadian Overseas Forces in England.

On September 1, 1917, Epsom was invited to play against the Canadian Forestry Corps. The Corps consisted of Canadian bushmen and lumberjacks who had been massed in Europe to fell trees and cut the lumber needed for rail lines, gun stocks, corduroy roads, and other wooden necessities of war. The Royal Family donated Windsor Great Park to the Corps for the duration of the conflict. There, literally in the shadow of Windsor Castle, they lived, trained, and played baseball. The men of the Corps were tough, competitive troops. Epsom had its own reputation to protect. The game, witnessed by Princess Mary, was said to have been a combative, hard-fought affair. The Corps beat Epsom 1-0. Her Royal Highness, so impressed with what she had seen, invited members of her family along to enjoy the Corps' next contest. So, on September 7, the vaunted "Forestry Game" was played. The Forestry Corps beat Orpington Hospital 2-1. But it was the peanut gallery that stole the show. Thousands of spectators packed the grounds. In attendance was again Princess Mary. Beside her sat Princess Helena Victoria, General McDougall, Lady Perley, wife of the high commissioner for Canada, and in specially covered seats near the Canadian dugout: the King and Queen of the British Empire. King George informed General McDougall that he had enjoyed the game and had been impressed with the enthusiasm the Canadians exhibited.[26] The soldiers were undoubtedly honored to play before their Head of State and the man for whom they rallied to "King and Country." Yet, it was Princess Patricia, known then as the prettiest of the royal family, whom soldiers clamored to glimpse at during the ballgame. Patricia was already iconic in Canada. She had lived in Ottawa while her father was governor general. By 1917 she not only adorned the name of a military regiment based in Edmonton, but was also pictured on the one dollar bill. Patricia "truly enjoyed baseball more than any other royal with the exception of the king."[27] She volunteered at the Canadian hospital at Orpington and regularly attended baseball games there.

A photo of what became known as "The Forestry Game," held in the collection of Library and Archives Canada and colorized by the Vimy Foundation for its 2018 book *They Fought in Colour*,[28] clearly shows Charlie Kelly, a Black man, at bat for the Forestry side. It stands as evidence that desegregated baseball was taking place in the Canadian Expeditionary Force in 1917.

Special occasions and holidays warranted highly touted baseball games. On July 1, 1917, Canada marked 50 years since its political confederation. Celebrations at home were subdued due to the war. In fact, a national celebration of Dominion Day, as July 1 was then called, wouldn't occur in Ottawa until 1927, when the country marked its diamond jubilee. Overseas, however, the event was commemorated with baseball games. Special Dominion Day games were played at Cliveden and Ramsgate. The anniversary was also marked on two separate July occasions with international matches at Lord's Cricket Grounds. A July 2 crowd of 10,000 saw the Canadian Pay Records team (billed as Team Canada) defeat the London Americans (billed as Team USA) by a score of 7-3. On July 28 Canada (Taplow hospital) defeated Team USA (London Americans) 12-3. The Canadian successes on the diamond, the soldiers' appetite for baseball as their primary form of recreation, and the arrival of American troops with whom to compete, forced the government's hand in the fall of 1917. By January of 1918, the Canadian government had stopped outsourcing their troops' baseball fix. The Canadian Military Athletic Association was formed. From that point onward, baseball was a fully funded and officially organized and sanctioned division of the Dominion government and its war effort.

Professor Greenham provides the most succinct and eloquent description of the CMAA:

"The Canadian Military Athletic Association stated that its mandate was to inaugurate athletics and competition between Canadian units in Great Britain, as well as standardize athletic contests of all kinds. Baseball, boxing, soccer and athletics were overseen by the CMAA. All the local games were reported to the national office, which not only recorded outcomes but appointed umpires. The national office also provided prizes and arranged intra-area playoff matches which would crown a national champion."[29]

The CMAA was financed via a one-pound sterling fee collected quarterly from each unit. The more formal recognition of the CMAA system gave teams like Epsom the opportunity to back up their bluster. Epsom had long claimed to be the best baseball team on offer, and now they would have a chance to prove it. The CMAA season began with exhibition games between Canadian and American all-star teams in Swansea and Reading. Over 10,000 people witnessed each game. When the regular season began in May 1918, the CMAA boasted 14 teams playing 250 scheduled games at six locations. Both the Arsenal grounds and the stadium at Stamford Bridge hosted games. Some league teams, like the 2nd Canadian division, played so many additional challenge and exhibition matches that they claimed to have played 300 baseball games in May alone. Baseball was being played significantly more than any other sport.[30] By the time the season ended, Epsom did indeed find itself in the championship final. Epsom was then beaten by the Canadian Engineers Training Corps. The engineers took the title via an unknown score before a large, mixed crowd of soldiers and curious locals. The engineers took their Canadian title into battle against the American champs, the US Regimental 9. In what can be considered the first military World Series, the Canadian side won, 8-2. Film footage of the game survives on YouTube.[31]

The arrival of the United States on the side of the Triple Entente radically altered the trajectory of both the war and its ancillary baseball games. Many major leaguers volunteered, among them Branch Rickey, Christy Mathewson, and Ty Cobb. These men were asked to join teams but all demurred for fear of the "slacker" label. The summer of 1918, with the Doughboys now playing baseball in uniform, saw an ever greater presence of organized leagues for soldiers. Canadian and American troops played in the CMMA baseball league, a Southeast Military Bases League, and even a league organized around Paris once it became safe enough to do so. But no organization ever came so close to supplanting major-league baseball as the center of the baseball world than the Anglo-American Baseball League.

The AABL was the brainchild of American entrepreneurs Howard Booker and W.A. Parsons, and ballplayer Arlie Latham. Recognizing the Canadians as pioneers and missionaries of the sport during the early days of the war, they saw the potential for a professional league in Britain. With American and Canadian troops arriving by the literal boatload, major leaguers like Hugh Miller and Mike McNally willing to play, and names like Rickey, Mathewson, and Cobb creating a baseball buzz behind the lines, the infield soil had never been so fertile. The AABL created two divisions, Canadian and American, and scheduled at least 150 games to be played at seven sites with two teams sharing use of the Arsenal grounds. The Canadian division consisted of the hospital teams at Epsom and Sunningdale and administrative teams from the pay and records offices. The American division featured teams from the US Navy, US Army, Hounslow barracks, and Northolt aviation camp. The arrival of overwhelming numbers of American players ended the Canadian dominance of First World War baseball. Only Epsom sported a winning record at the end of the AABL season. The US Army team claimed the championship, but it was their July 4, 1918, match against Navy that dominates American lore. The match was held at Stamford Bridge before 38,000 spectators. The crowd included a man who had been introduced to the game by the play of hard-scrabble Canadians: King George V.

Aside from league play in Britain, Canadians played baseball informally in France, Belgium, both sides of Ireland, Wales, Scotland, and even Salonika, Greece. Future Canadian Prime Minister Lester B. Pearson played games for the Bramshott team in England, recalling his home run there as one of his most enduring Great War memories.[32] Wherever the Canadians were stationed, they played baseball. The soldiers themselves believed that top-class baseball had been transferred[33] from Flatbush and the Bronx to Flanders and Bovington. The Canadian Expeditionary Force played baseball at close to 90 international points of interest, over 50 of which were home to organized league or government sponsored games. These CEF baseball locations are pinpointed on an interactive digital map created by the author. The map may be accessed at www.hipmuseum.com/greatwarbaseball.

The high point for Canadian baseball during the First World War occurred on July 1, 1918, in Tincques, France. There, the Canadian Corps organized a sports day. The Corps was in its glory, Vimy and Hill 70 had been won, and the Canadians would soon be in the midst of the fabled "Last 100 Days" victories over Germany. Morale was high. The end of the war seemed near. A reported 70,000 people packed a specially constructed stadium to watch the championships of many track and field events. The baseball final was the main event. It was scheduled last, after tea, for 4:15 P.M. in the large stadium. The soccer final, scheduled for the same time, was held in a small field without grandstands. The baseball game was reportedly a classic, as tight, low-scoring affairs were considered the best type of baseball at the time. The 7th Engineer Battalion, consisting of Vimy veterans from various provinces, defeated the 1st Divisional Ammunition Column, an Ontario regiment that once included John McCrae, author of the famed war memorial poem "In Flanders Fields," by a score of 3-2 in 11 innings. Prime Minister Robert Borden and Lieutenant General Arthur Currie watched the game in person. Famed Indigenous athlete and soldier Tom Longboat had won the eight-mile running race earlier in the day, and may have been among those soldiers watching the game.

The placement of baseball in the schedule of events supports the idea that the game was valued as the top form of recreation by the soldiers and officers who played it. Canadian men loved their national game. The commanders who encouraged baseball play had come to recognize it as not only valuable physical activity, but also as a comfort against the horrors of war, a powerful tool against idleness and boredom and a reminder of more peaceful times back home. Baseball had come to be seen as an essential part of Canadian military life during the Great War.

The official expression of the Government of Canada's support for baseball was first seen in the December 1917 *Guide to Military Sports*

and Recreation Training. The *Guide* specified that baseball was a game well suited to building better soldiers. It encouraged soldiers and officers to play together. The government authors of the guide rationalized sport in military terms. They praised its incorporation of muscular Christian ideals. They claimed that the participation of officers would ensure that baseball matches took place with "the true sporting spirit" and would thereby encourage esprit de corps through the promotion of self-sacrifice.[34] The volume of games in the thousands per year, the organization of official leagues, the funding of tournaments, stadiums, and transportation coupled with the presence at matches of generals, ministers, the prime minister and His Majesty, all attest to the status afforded Canadian baseball during the conflict.

The 7th Canadian Engineer Battalion, champions of military baseball. July, 1918. (Library and Archives Canada.)

The greatest endorsement of the game may be its consistent reference within regimental diaries. The diaries were permanent records of daily wartime experience. Entries were written by a commanding officer, usually at the end of a day if circumstances permitted. Two of the diaries survived intact and are now digitized. They provide us with the best glimpse into the soldiers' perspective on baseball. They reveal also that games, particularly if the pennant was on the line, were fiercely waged. Baseball still mattered to these troops. The game's significance did not diminish during wartime.[35]

The diary of the Toronto-based Queen's Own Rifles mentions 68 different baseball games played throughout Flanders. Baseball is mentioned more than any other sport and is third only to references of battle and training. The diary details a game which was played at Bois de Froissart, France, during the preparations for the attack on Hill 70. The diary notes that soldiers were looking forward to the game, largely due to the fact that it was an "officers vs. men" affair. The men won, by a score of 26-3.[36] After a multi-sentence entry about a baseball game, the diary then states simply, "the German offensive continues." The diary of the 18th Battalion, a group of soldiers from Western Ontario, contains a typical sketch of boys at play when it is interrupted by the reality of war. During a game played behind the lines, a stray bullet from a nearby rifle range found its way onto the diamond. A military transport driver named Mills was hit and killed. The diary records that "owing to a very unfortunate incident [the team] went right off their game and lost." The diary scribe goes on to say "this accident naturally spoiled the game."[37]

When the war ended, the Canadian government faced two major problems: the lack of discipline from men who were less willing to submit to military drill, and the long period of time it took to transport these men home. Such idle men could of course be pacified with baseball. Matchups were organized and a 1919 Inter-Allied Games, quasi-Olympics featuring baseball, was held for impatient soldiers still stuck in Europe. When it was finally time to go home, Canadian soldiers were discharged near Kinmel Park close to the River Dee. The Kinmel Park Canadian Athletic Association organized a series of baseball games. Men passing through Kinmel were encouraged to play one last game before heading home. Canada's First World War baseball story, which began on the Salisbury Plain in 1914, ended at Kinmel Park in 1919. For many Canadians, their last act as a soldier was stepping up to the plate in a military baseball game.

For many of the rank-and-file, baseball was vital to their Great War experience. "From the moment our men get out of the trenches," remarked Lieutenant Coningsby Dawson, "they begin to play baseball."[38] For enlisted men, the game eased the burden of homesickness, because it allowed them to recall the pleasanter circumstances of normal existence.[39] For officers, the game provided a wholesome and worthwhile alternative to the unsavory temptations that awaited idle soldiers.

Many officers saw the physical, mental, and emotional benefits that the game brought their troops and incorporated it into their routines, even using it as a recruitment tool.[40] As the casualty lists lengthened, fewer Canadians saw war as a game.[41] Baseball was the necessary salve for men being introduced to the horrors of the First World War. Baseball's ability to recall Canada, home, and peace comforted men while its expressions gave them a vocabulary with which to express and suppress their experiences at the front. Canadians played other sports, but none so often as baseball.[42]

The presence of the game at hospitals and convalescent homes cannot be overlooked. Baseball served a purpose during the war. An American pitcher, soldier Leon Vannais, wrote home to his mother in Hartford, Connecticut. Commenting on a game between his US squad and Canadian soldiers, Vannais touched upon the higher calling for Great War ballplayers:

"The side lines were as noisy as the bleachers of home – the cheers will be for our opponents (the Canadians) and the jeers will be for us; yet we're happier that way for the fans are the wounded. Mother, you can't conceive of how wonderful they are! Bright blue suits, bright red ties, clean white bandages, many slings, numerous crutches; if it were not for the faces, one would weep to look at them. But one has no desire to feel sad except in a sub-conscious way. The cheerfulness of the wounded men is contagious. They sit there – their eyes sparkling with mirth and interest – their shouts full of the old familiar rooting expressions made wonderfully fresh and greatly supplemented by their witty mixing in of the new slang of war. No wonder we don't mind who they cheered for, it's enough that we're able to give them an afternoon of real sport."[43]

If the clichés about Canada and the First World War are true, if this was indeed Canada's "coming of age" and "baptism by fire," then it must be noted that she came of age playing her national game: baseball.

ACKNOWLEDGMENTS

The author wishes to thank Andrew Horrall, Craig Greenham, and Jim Leeke for their incredible and invaluable resources. All three men were also very kind to put up with, and respond to, pestering digital correspondences. This project stands on the significant foundation they laid.

NOTES

1 William Humber, "What Was Early Canadian Hockey and What Does It Owe to Others?" Research paper, Seneca College, 2017: 1.

2 Bruce Kidd, *The Struggle for Canadian Sport* (Toronto: University of Toronto Press, 2017), 24.

3 Chris Sharpe, "Enlistment in the Canadian Expeditionary Force," *Canadian Military History* 24, no. 2 (2015): 19.

4 Craig Greenham, "On the Battlefront," *American Review of Canadian Studies* 42, no.1 (March 2012): 3.

5 Greenham: 1.

6 Greenham: 2.

7 Andrew Horrall, "'Keep-A-Fighting! Play the Game!' Baseball and the Canadian Forces During the First World War," *Canadian Military History* 10, no.2 (2001): 4

8 Greenham: 4.

9 Horrall: 4.

10 Greenham: 4.

11 Horrall: 4.

12 Horrall: 5.

13 Mark MacKinnon, "We'll Take Care of Your Boys Forever," *Globe and Mail,* April 17, 2015: F1.

14 Anonymous Correspondent, "Work and Play Well Mixed," *Tank Tatler,* October 1918: 12.

15 Greenham: 5.

16 Horrall: 4.

17 Tim Cook, *Warlords: Borden, Mackenzie King, and Canada's World Wars* (Toronto: Penguin Group, 2013), 37.

18 Jim Leeke, *Nine Innings for the King* (Jefferson, North Carolina: McFarland & Company, 2015), 16.

19 Leeke, 16.

20 Craig Greenham, "On the Battlefront," *American Review of Canadian Studies* 42, no.1 (March 2012): 6.

21 Leeke, *Nine Innings for the King,* 16.

22 Horrall: 5.

23 Leeke, 16.

24 Horrall: 6.

25 Horrall: 8.

26 Leeke, 24.

27 Leeke, 54.

28 The Vimy Foundation, *They Fought in Colour* (Toronto: Dundurn Press, 2018).

29 Greenham: 10.

30 Horrall: 10.

31 "Americans v. Canadians – Baseball (1916-1918)," Youtube.com, last modified April 13, 2014, https://www.youtube.com/watch?v=r84a8yYxWhE.

32 Lester B. Pearson, *Memoirs of the Right Honourable Lester Pearson. Vol 1.* 1972 Page 40

33 Horrall: 8.

34 Horrall: 8.

35 Greenham: 13.

36 "Queen's Own Rifles Museum," World War I resources, last modified June 30, 2019, https://qormuseum.org/.

37 "Canadian Great War Project," Private John Cushnie collection, last modified January 10, 2013, http://www.canadiangreatwarproject.com/transcripts/cushnie191806.asp.

38 Greenham: 1.

39 Greenham: 10.

40 Greenham: 10.

41 Horrall: 5.

42 Horrall: 12.

43 Leeke, 23.

PUNCHING ABOVE ITS WEIGHT: THE QUEBEC PROVINCIAL LEAGUE

By Christian Trudeau

George Gmelch, then playing for the Drummondville Royals, recalled a 1968 incident after a bad call by an umpire: "Some Drummondville fans went to the parking lot and let the air out of the tires of the umpire's car. When the umps came out, some fans were still there. They cursed the umps and beat on the hood of their car. ... It was strange seeing fans get that upset over a fairly unimportant game...I wondered why the fans cared more about the outcome of the game than we did."[1]

Intensity was a feature of various incarnations of the Quebec Provincial League in the 1920-70 period, the product of a mix of civic pride and heavy gambling. It led to many such ugly incidents as the one described above, mostly involving umpires. However, it also allowed the league to punch far above its weight, with a level of play significantly above that of leagues with comparable population bases. This intense desire to win, fueled by the rivalries among the cities in the geographically compact league, meant that the teams were always on the lookout for the player who would give them the edge. At various times in its existence, the Provincial League raided New England colleges, encouraged players in neighboring leagues to jump their contracts,

opened its doors and its checkbooks for Mexican League jumpers banned by the major leagues, and provided opportunity to Negro League veterans or Latin American youngsters.

Unsurprisingly, the league's relationship with Organized Baseball was rocky, as it gained and lost official sanction. This passion led to incredible highs – the St. Louis Cardinals were outbid by Drummondville for Sal Maglie's services – but also to inevitable lows. Passion and reason do not mix well, and huge amounts of money were burned in the process. Baseball fans, at least those gambling in moderation, came out ahead as they were able to witness players who should have been playing at a higher level elsewhere.

The first serious attempt to organize a baseball league in Quebec that rose above the level of semipro came during the early 1920s, as Montréal had been without a professional league after the Royals' departure from the International League after the 1917 season. Organized and presided over by Joe Page,[2] the Eastern Canada League was a four-team Class-B league that operated in 1922-23. In its original season, it had teams in Montréal, Trois-Rivières, and Ottawa.[3] The next year, Quebec City was added to the league, while the Ottawa team, struggling to find a suitable park, played all but three home games in Montréal. With Trois-Rivières limping to the finish line in 1923 and quitting for 1924, the league responded by expanding, adding teams in Rutland and Montpelier, Vermont, and reorganizing the Ottawa team, creating the Quebec-Ontario-Vermont league. Unsurprisingly, travel expenses killed the two American teams in midseason, and the league itself at the end of the 1924 season. The league provided a decent level of play, as Del Bissonette, Fred Frankhouse, and Bill Hunnefield, for example, graduated to decent major-league careers. The league is however best remembered for having hosted African American Charlie Culver for six games in 1922,[4] and for incessant fights between players, umpires, and fans.[5]

Following the demise of Page's league, more local leagues emerged, and it wasn't until 1936 that a league with a schedule of more than a dozen games was established. This new Provincial League,[6] outside of the structure of Organized Baseball, had teams in Montréal, Drummondville, Granby, Sorel, and Sherbrooke, as well as the Black Panthers, a travel team of African American players. The addition of Sherbrooke, then the fifth largest city in Quebec, was a major boost to the league. Located near the US border, it had until then played almost exclusively in leagues with teams in Vermont and New Hampshire.

Pushed by a desire to get an edge on its rivals, Granby added to its roster African Americans Fred Wilson in 1935 and Ormond Sampson in 1936. The league quickly rose from a local circuit to one of the top leagues outside of Organized Baseball; by 1939 it was playing a 72-game schedule, and had moved out of Montréal[7] to the east, adding solid franchises in Quebec City, Trois-Rivières, and St. Hyacinthe. The Black Panthers struggled in 1937 and were replaced thereafter, no longer fitting with the league's new and loftier ambitions. By 1939, state-of-the-art twin ballparks had been built in Trois-Rivières and Quebec City, with

both of them still in use today. Granby and Sherbrooke also were equipped for night baseball. The league was compact, allowing for travel by car and for the famous home-and-home doubleheaders played each Sunday, a practice that continued throughout the existence of the league.

On the field, the league quickly replaced New England college players with veteran minor leaguers, raiding the nearby Canadian-American and Cape Breton Colliery Leagues. Two players stood out in 1938: Pete Gray with Trois-Rivières and Paul Calvert with Sherbrooke. Trois-Rivières signed Gray sight-unseen, and were shocked to see when he showed up that he had only one arm. He was given a chance and was an immediate sensation, attracting large crowds throughout the league. Gray, an outfielder, would famously play with the St. Louis Browns in 1945.[8] Calvert, a Montréal native, became arguably the best prospect ever to come out of Quebec. Armed with a blazing fastball, he rose to fame in 1938, leading the league in strikeouts before refusing an offer from the Yankees, pitching a few games for the Royals, and obtaining a tryout with the New York Giants. Arm issues robbed Calvert of his fastball the following offseason, although he still went on to pitch in 109 major-league games. In 1939 Trois-Rivières opened its checkbook to sign accomplished minor-league stars Dutch Prather, Harlin Pool, Moose Clabaugh, and By Speece. While it was expected that Trois-Rivières had thereby bought the championship, the team barely edged Quebec City for the pennant, before bowing to the same team in the playoff finals. Led by manager Del Bissonette and local star Roland Gladu, Quebec City overcame the loss of three of its pitchers just before the playoffs started.

Being outside Organized Baseball, the teams had little recourse against players who bailed on their contracts; almost all teams were affected by this problem or by players holding out for more money.[9] This inability to enforce contracts, combined with out-of-control expenses resulting

Quebec Provincial League All-Star Game of July 19, 1939. Representatives of Sherbrooke, St. Hyacinthe, Drummondville and Granby. Top Row: Harry Winston, Ted Veach, Ward Sheldon, Art O'Donnell, Vince Barton, Howard Moss, Jim Castiglia, Ray Coté, Keith Drisko, Mike Pociask, Leo Marion, Larry Fisher. Bottom Row: Glenn Larsen, Bob Swan, Joe Cicero, Jerry Levey, Tom Hammond, John Ayvazian, Chris Shearer, John Huxtable, Fletcher Heath, Jim Irving. (Collection of Alexandre Pratt)

in alleged financial losses of $50,000,[10] led the league to seek admission into Organized Baseball in 1940.

Discussions with the National Association of Professional Baseball Leagues continued for most of the offseason, in part because of the hostility of the Montréal Royals. It wasn't until February that the league was admitted into Organized Baseball, as a Class-B league. The Sorel team would not make the jump. It had made enemies both within and outside the league by signing Bill Powley from Ottawa of the Canadian-American League after rosters had been set for the 1939 playoffs, and then having him use the name of a different player.[11] It is not clear whether Sorel refused to play by the rules of Organized Baseball, or whether the club was not invited back by the league. Knowing that Drummondville was its weak link, the league explored many different replacement options, but was constrained by the proximity of existing teams, with potential teams in Hull (now Gatineau) and Lachine (on the island of Montréal) respectively blocked by the Ottawa and Montréal clubs. Unwilling to go on with an uneven number of teams, the league confirmed Drummondville as the sixth team in mid-March.

Drummondville's return was so late in being announced that the league had already allowed other teams to poach the Drummondville 1939 roster (as well as that of Sorel). The team was terrible, and with attendance further affected by a major strike in a local textile mill, Drummondville folded in early July. At the end of the month, with payroll due and about 1,000 soldiers about to leave town for training, Sherbrooke followed. The remaining four teams continued for a final month of regular-season play, with all of them moving to the postseason. Predictably, fans had a hard time feeling engaged, especially with the unending stream of bad news coming from Europe, as Germany took control of most of Western Europe. Bad weather also played a part. St. Hyacinthe, which had won the pennant, saw big playoff games postponed over Labor Day weekend. Unable to sustain more financial losses, it forfeited its semifinal series to Trois-Rivières, which went on to edge Granby in the finals.

League President Jean Barette resigned after the season, loudly questioning the business acumen of French-Canadians in the process.[12] Attempts were made to continue for 1941, but when teams willing to round out the league could not be found, Quebec City and Trois-Rivières jumped to the Canadian-American League, with Quebec City inheriting the rights to Granby players, and Trois-Rivières to the St. Hyacinthe roster.

With the war raging, only low-level local leagues continued their activities, and even the Canadian-American League suspended play after the 1942 season. In 1946, with renewed optimism Quebec City and Trois-Rivières returned to the Can-Am League, while Granby and Sherbrooke joined the Class-C Border League. That was the season in which Jackie Robinson debuted in Montréal, and soon Trois-Rivières and Sherbrooke joined the very short list of integrated teams. As a farm club of the Brooklyn Dodgers, Trois-Rivières welcomed Roy Partlow and Johnny Wright, while Sherbrooke signed Manny McIntyre, an Atlantic Canada two-sport star known primarily for his hockey skills. On the field and in the ledger books, the Border League experience was a failure, with Sherbrooke folding in August and Granby opting out of the league after the season.

In 1947, Sherbrooke and Granby returned to a revamped Provincial League, in which they joined old rivals Drummondville and St. Hyacinthe, along with newcomers St. Jean and Farnham.[13] The league started as a typical semipro league, one that could give a chance to a talented but raw player like NHL legend Maurice Richard, who played for Drummondville. But a number of factors quickly contributed to pushing the level of play to unprecedented heights over the next few seasons.

First, local players who had starred in the 1938-40 Provincial League were able to advance their careers during the war. Roland Gladu and Jean-Pierre Roy (who debuted with Trois-Rivières in 1940) both starred with the Montréal Royals and reached the majors during the war. They were joined there by Stan Bréard, too young to have played in the Provincial League previously. Paul Martin, hard-hitting outfielder for

Trois-Rivières, didn't reach the majors but played in the high minors. The network of contacts they had collected, including those in the Cuban winter leagues, would soon come in handy.

Second, returning servicemen provided a sudden surplus of skilled players. Taking advantage of this situation, millionaire Jorge Pasquel offered high salaries to attract major-league players to his Mexican League. Facing a five-year suspension from Organized Baseball, only about 18 players ended up signing, including Gladu. The jumpers were viewed as toxic, and some others, like Roy, Bréard, and Paul Calvert, were suspended for playing with them in the offseason in Cuban winter leagues.

Third, the United States League, and its Pittsburgh Crawfords in particular, had adopted Quebec as a second home in 1945 and 1946, playing many league games in the province. As the league collapsed after the 1946 season, Farnham signed four of its players, although none of them stars. By 1948, with integration decimating the Negro Leagues, Farnham was able to recruit Joe Atkins and brothers Dave and Willie Pope. Nap Gulley, Clarence Bruce, Tom Parker, Buddy Armour, and Len Hooker followed the next year.

Jean-Pierre Roy was the first local star to come back to the Provincial League in 1947, winning 12 games for St. Jean, the eventual champion. Gladu and Bréard returned to Mexico but as their promised money became tougher to obtain, they went looking for new options for 1948. Gladu signed as manager for Sherbrooke, and Paul Martin with St. Hyacinthe, while Roy returned to St. Jean. The result was a scramble for the freely available talent, as Provincial League owners convinced themselves to pay ever-increasing salaries.

Roy brought to St. Jean jumper Bobby Estalella, who had hit .298 and .299 for the Philadelphia A's in 1944 and 1945, and Negro League stars Buzz Clarkson and Terris McDuffie, who had also played in Mexico. Estalella (.374-24-95) and Clarkson (.408-31-75) terrorized Provincial

League pitchers all season, while Roy and McDuffie each won 19 games. In Sherbrooke, Gladu built a team of Latin American stars, starting with the Cuban Adrian Zabala, who had pitched with the New York Giants in 1945. He led the pitching staff with 18 wins, providing Sherbrooke with a great one-two punch with Paul Calvert, who went 11-1. On offense, Cuban Claro Duany (.365-27-90) and Puerto Rican Francisco "Pancho" Coimbre (.312-8-66) helped Gladu (.368-11-78) lead the team to the pennant. In the 1948 playoff finals, they met Paul Martin's St. Hyacinthe team. Martin (.356-16-74) did not have the same level of contacts as did Roy and Gladu, but he brought in two veteran hitters he had met in the Southern Association, Gene Nance (.335-14-91) and Connie Creeden (.430-8-71). The best-of-nine series went to the limit and was decided in a see-saw game that, in keeping with the character of the league, included a brawl involving players, umpires, and part of the crowd. Cuban second baseman Jorge Torres' walk-off single gave Sherbrooke a 10-9 win.

Drummondville was a nonfactor in 1948, but signed Stan Bréard late in the season. Bréard brought with him outfielder Danny Gardella, one of the biggest names among the jumpers, who had hit 18 home runs for the 1945 New York Giants. If it was too late to change tides for 1948, it was a sign of what was to come for 1949.

With the Mexican League jumpers fighting Organized Baseball in court and running out of options – they were reduced to barnstorming and taking odd jobs – most of them accepted offers from the Provincial League. Drummondville named Bréard manager, brought back Gardella, and added pitchers Sal Maglie (only five major-league wins to that point, but with 114 left in his arm) and Max Lanier (who had been 40-21 with a 2.22 ERA with the Cardinals from 1943 to 1946), as well as first baseman Roy Zimmerman, who had hit 32 home runs for Newark and five more with the Giants in 1945. Defending champion Sherbrooke countered with pitchers Fred Martin (briefly with the 1946 Cardinals) and Harry Feldman (23 wins for the '44-45 Giants) joining Zabala. St. Jean named catcher Red Hayworth (146 games with the Browns in 1944-45) as manager, replacing the reinstated Jean-Pierre Roy. Hayworth added pitcher Alex Carrasquel (50 wins over seven seasons with the Washington Senators) and second baseman Lou Klein, who had received down-ballot MVP votes as a rookie with the 1943 Cardinals before the war derailed his career.

Bréard also brought to Drummondville two top prospects from Puerto Rico, outfielder Vic Power and pitcher Roberto Vargas, and added veteran Negro League catcher Quincy Trouppe,

The 1949 Drummondville Cubs, Quebec Provincial League champions. Left to right: Gerry Cotnoir, Roy Zimmerman, Roger Bréard, Quincy Trouppe, Len Hooker, Sal Maglie, Conrado Perez, Roberto Vargas, Joe Promowicz (Prom), Joe Tuminelli, Danny Gardella, Stan Bréard, Vic Power, Ernie Sawyer. (Collection of Daniel Papillon)

whom he had met in the winter leagues. Gladu had most of his team back in Sherbrooke, but had added Silvio Garcia, one of the top Cuban players, who had been a candidate to break the color barrier a few years before. St. Jean started the season with three star Negro Leaguers in its rotation, with Chet Brewer (who had been a member of the legendary Kansas City Monarchs) and John "Neck" Stanley (a mainstay for the New York Black Yankees) joining Terris McDuffie. In the outfield, Quincy Barbee replaced Buzz Clarkson. Granby stuck mostly to its strategy of rostering veteran minor leaguers, although it added Tex Shirley, a regular rotation member for the St. Louis Browns in 1945-46. St. Hyacinthe followed the same strategy, its big acquisitions being Walter Brown (who had spent the 1947 season in the Browns' bullpen), and shortstop Charley Brewster (who had played for four major-league teams from 1943-46, mostly with the Phillies).

As playing with the jumpers could result in suspension, some players used an alias to play in the Provincial League. Ebba St. Claire's experience is typical. Convinced that he had no future in the Pirates organization, the catcher signed with Sherbrooke, but played as Eddie Thomas. Sherbrooke newspapers revealed St. Claire's use of an alias, and provided great details on his minor-league stops, making it easy, at least with today's tools, to identify St. Claire.[14] Given the intense competition between teams, it was not unusual for a newspaper to reveal the identity of a rival team's hidden player.

Not surprisingly, the league attracted a lot of attention. On June 1, *The Sporting News* ran a nearly full-page article on the league, stating that Lanier would be paid $10,000 for the season. Drummondville team owners came up with $6,000, with the rest coming from the local business community to ensure that he would not sign with a rival. League President Albert Molini claimed he was aware that the bonanza wouldn't last forever, and that the league would be seeking

entry into Organized Baseball in the next year or two.[15] Not shying away from the publicity, Molini later declared that any of his teams could easily defeat International League teams. He also said that teams had an $8,000 to $10,000 monthly payroll, with stars averaging $6,000 to $7,000 for the season.[16] Molini also claimed an average of 2,500 fans per game, a number in line with the reported attendances, which rarely dropped below 1,000 and peaked at over 4,000, above capacity.

On the morning of June 6, 1949, as Drummondville sat comfortably at the top of the standings with a 16-3 record, the bubble burst. News that Commissioner Happy Chandler had reinstated the jumpers without condition struck the Provincial League. Jumpers would simply need to write to the commissioner to obtain automatic reinstatement, before obtaining a 30-day grace period during which they could not be released or reassigned to the minors. Molini was initially defiant: "I believe this is the best thing that could have happened. Those that want to leave now can, but I doubt there will be many. Most are satisfied with their lot, and their teams are having great seasons." While players vowed not to abandon their lawsuits, they listened to offers. Lou Klein (St. Jean) was the first to leave, on June 13, pinch-hitting for the Cardinals three days later. Lanier (8-1 in Drummondville) bargained for three weeks before joining Klein in St. Louis. Soon afterward, Alex Carrasquel returned to the White Sox, while Sherbrooke lost Adrian Zabala (Giants), Fred Martin (Cardinals), and Harry Feldman (San Francisco in the PCL).

If some left in a hurry, others lingered. Zabala, who had spent a year and a half in Sherbrooke, agreed to a going-away start, which turned out to be his best of the season, a 10-inning two-hitter to beat Drummondville 1-0. Others with a limited future in Organized Baseball gladly stayed in Quebec. Sal Maglie was not in this situation. He drew interest from the New York Giants but eventually decided to stay in Drummondville, where he was rumored to have received $15,000 for the season, in addition to a furnished house.[17]

Drummondville, which had a record of 27-10 when Lanier left, cooled down considerably, but still won the 1949 pennant easily with a 63-34 record, led by Maglie (18-9), Gardella (.283-15-59), Zimmerman (.247-22-79), and Power (.345-9-54). The club also bought Tex Shirley (13-3) from Granby for the stretch run. Granby had a surprising second-place finish, led by New Brunswick native Bud Kimball (.314-21-88), but without Shirley, they bowed in the first round to Farnham. Defending champion Sherbrooke had plenty of offense in Gladu (.305-19-81), Duany (.290-22-99), and Garcia (.315-4-76), but after they lost their three jumpers, their pitching staff could not keep up and they were eliminated by St. Jean.[18]

St. Jean had lost Carrasquel and Negro League stars Chet Brewer and John Stanley during the 1949 season, but was led by McDuffie (12-10) and minor-league veteran Leonard Bobeck (15-10) on the mound, and Barbee (.342-26-86) at the plate. It was not enough against the red-hot Farnham team, which eliminated St. Jean in seven games. Meanwhile, Drummondville needed the maximum nine games to dispatch sixth-place St. Hyacinthe in the other semifinal.

Farnham had finished only in fifth place in the regular season, but had a talented team led by former Negro Leaguers Buddy Armour (.348-8-67), Dave Pope (.293-22-87), Joe Atkins (.253-21-71), and Willie Pope (12-10), as well as veteran minor leaguer Vern Thoele (.305-3-27). For the second series in a row, Drummondville needed the full length of the best-of-nine series. In the ultimate game, Armour homered off Maglie, and Willie Pope kept Drummondville off the scoreboard for six innings before imploding in the seventh, as the Cubs won 5-1. Maglie struck out 10, winning his third game of the finals. Drummondville ended up champions as expected, but the difficult path it took to get there raised suspicions of game fixing. Molini did not silence these rumors when he decried in *The Sporting News* the report that $20,000 had been gambled on a semifinal game involving Maglie.[19] We can assume at least as much was gambled on the final game.

As the season wrapped up, attention turned toward joining Organized Baseball. The league argued that its high caliber of play warranted Class-B status. Given that the combined population of its cities was less than 250,000, the league was granted Class-C status. The payroll in a Class-C league was a more manageable $3,400 per month.[20]

While the jumpers were gone, Provincial League teams still were trying hard to win. With no team being affiliated, rosters were filled with veterans, including many who had starred in 1949. Sherbrooke, still managed by Gladu, was the dominant team in 1950 and 1951, losing in the last game of the 1950 finals and winning it all the next year. Silvio Garcia was the star player, winning the Triple Crown in 1950 (.365-21-116). His Cuban compatriot Claro Duany skipped the 1950 season but came back to hit .337-23-84 in 1951. Gladu also added veteran Negro League pitchers Ray Brown and Max Manning. Manning spent only a few weeks in Sherbrooke, but Brown married a local woman and spent many years in Quebec. Brown, who had been the star pitcher of the Homestead Grays, was elected to Cooperstown in 2006. The St. Jean team that stopped them in 1950 was built around young Puerto Ricans Carlos Bernier (.335-15-39) and Ruben Gomez (14-4) and Negro League veterans Barbee (.284-11-35) and Ernest Burke (15-3).

In the early 1950s, many young African Americans and Latin Americans passed through the league on their way to the major leagues. Vic Power, who returned to Drummondville in 1950 (.334-14-105) was sold to the Yankees for $7,000. Other future major leaguers include Julio Becquer (Drummondville, 1952), Ed Charles (Quebec, 1952), Connie Johnson (St. Hyacinthe, 1951),

Humberto Robinson (various teams, 1951-52), and Valmy Thomas (St. Jean, 1951). The quartet of Bob Trice (16-3), Al Pinkston (triple crown winner with a .360-30-121 line), Hector Lopez (.329-8-75), and Joe Taylor (.308-25-112) led St. Hyacinthe to the pennant in 1952.

Farnham became the first team in Organized Baseball to hire an African American manager, Sam Bankhead, in 1951. The team, composed mostly of former Negro Leaguers, including Josh Gibson Jr., was competitive in the first half, but a lack of depth and resources sank it later. Other former Negro Leaguers who sojourned in the Provincial League in that era include Bill Cash (Granby, 1951), Alphonso Gerard (Trois-Rivières, Granby, 1951-52), Everett Marcell (Farnham, 1950-51), Roy Partlow (Granby, 1950-51), Joe Scott (Farnham, St. Hyacinthe, 1950-51), and Archie Ware (Farnham, 1951).

Major changes quickly swept through the league. Quebec and Trois-Rivières moved from the Canadian-American League to the Provincial League in 1951. The same night that Sherbrooke won the 1951 championship, its ballpark burned to the ground, and the team was forced to skip the 1952 season.[21] The smallest town in the league, Farnham, could no longer compete and quit, shrinking the league to six teams for 1952. Quebec, which had been a successful affiliate of the Boston Braves, brought a new mentality, and soon all teams were affiliated. The focus quickly changed: Productive but older players, like locals Gladu, Bréard, and Paul Martin, as well as former Negro Leaguers like Ray Brown, Quincy Barbee, and Ernest Burke, were pushed to local independent leagues.

When Sherbrooke rejoined in 1953, it was affiliated with the Cleveland Indians, and fielded an all-White team with an average age of 21.7 years. Even though Sherbrooke won the pennant, it attracted barely half of its 1951 attendance total. Sherbrooke's time as the dominant team was over, as the Quebec Braves, managed by seven-time

major-league All-Star George McQuinn until 1954, were the playoff champion every year from 1952 to 1955.

After the excitement of hosting major-league-caliber players for so many years, the transition to a farm league understandably was not a crowd-pleaser. Some young local players, like future major leaguer Georges Maranda, were popular, but they were few and far between. There was financial fatigue, especially after years of deficits, and while Thetford Mines was added to the league in 1953, Granby and St. Hyacinthe gave up after the season. Drummondville followed after the 1954 season, replaced in 1955 by Burlington, Vermont. As had been the case for the Eastern Canada League 25 years earlier, expanding into Vermont was not a good omen. After losing its affiliation, Sherbrooke quit after the 1955 season. When Trois-Rivières and St. Jean still had not committed to a return in April 1956, the league disbanded.

In these final three years, the Provincial League was a much more typical farm league, the most interesting future major leaguers in that final era in Organized Baseball being Gary Bell and Bobby Locke (Sherbrooke, 1954), Dick Brown (Sherbrooke, 1955), Lou Johnson (St. Jean, 1955), Don Nottebart (Quebec, 1954), and Dan Osinski (Sherbrooke, 1953).

Baseball returned to its local roots in the following years, but by the mid-1960s a strong Provincial League reemerged, in pretty much the same cities.[22] Foreign players were initially limited, but that limit was soon lifted and replaced by a salary cap. When that cap was routinely ignored, it too was scrapped, and from 1968 to 1970 the only restriction imposed was that no player could be signed who had played at Double A or above in the past two years. The league attracted players recently cut from the minor leagues, like George Gmelch cited in the introduction; many young Latin Americans looking for a second chance, like Pepe Frias and Fernando Gonzalez, who would make it to the big leagues; and a few former major leaguers, like Felix Mantilla.

Once again, the intense competition between the teams led to ballooning deficits, and only five teams completed the 1970 season. With the Expos debuting in 1969, the baseball landscape was changing in the province. Quebec and Trois-Rivières jumped to the Double-A Eastern League for 1971, becoming affiliates of the Expos and Reds respectively, and killing the Provincial League in the process. Sherbrooke and Thetford Mines would follow in subsequent seasons. The Eastern League adventure lasted until 1977, the last time affiliated minor-league baseball was played in Quebec.

Overall, the Provincial League, through most of its incarnations, refused to accept being a typical Class-C league, as it should have been given the population of its members. The result was a constant cycle between relevance and irrelevance. The high points have been less frequent since, with various senior leagues coming and going, and none approaching the heights of the Provincial League. A few more recent events have evoked memories of the glory days. Independent pro baseball did return to Quebec City (1999) and Trois-Rivières (2012), in the twin stadiums built in 1938, witnesses of much of the Provincial League history. In 2002 the World Junior Championships were held in Sherbrooke, with Yulieski Gurriel and his Cuban teammates winning gold, on the same spot where Silvio Garcia and Claro Duany had celebrated the 1951 Provincial League championship.[23]

ACKNOWLEDGMENTS

Heidi Jacobs and Patrick Carpentier provided useful comments on early drafts. My work on the Provincial League builds on that of Bill Young and Merritt Clifton.

SOURCES

In addition to Baseball-Reference and *The Sporting News* Player Contract Cards database, many Quebec newspapers were consulted (available on the website of the Bibliothèque et Archives Nationales du Québec). Gary Fink's database of Negro Leaguers in the minor leagues in the first decade of integration was also useful. Other sources include:

Clifton, Merritt. *Disorganized Baseball: The Provincial League, from LaRoque to Les Expos,* mimeo, 1982.

Paradis, Jean-Marc. *100 Ans de Baseball à Trois-Rivières,* 1989.

NOTES

1   George Gmelch, *Playing with Tigers* (Lincoln: University of Nebraska Press, 2016), 235-36.

2   See Patrick Carpentier, "Joe Page," SABR BioProject, https://sabr.org/bioproj/person/joe-page-2/.

3   The fourth team in 1923 was in Valleyfield, close to Montréal, where it played many local games. It moved in midseason to Cap-de-la-Madeleine, next to Trois-Rivières, after being bought by the local paper mill.

4   Christian Trudeau, "24 Years Before Jackie Robinson, Charlie Culver Broke Barriers in Montréal," *Baseball Research Journal*, Spring 2020.

5   The Montréal teams claimed that umpires were intimidated while working in Trois-Rivières in 1922, and briefly refused to return there in 1923 when something was thrown at their manager. Trois-Rivières similarly claimed in 1923 that Montréal won the second-half pennant after umpires were intimidated in a game in Quebec City. The 1922 incident also caught the attention of legendary columnist Ring Lardner. See "Kill the Umpire," a Bell syndicate column appearing in Ron Rapoport, ed., *The Lost Journalism of Ring Lardner* (Lincoln: University of Nebraska Press, 2017).

6   Early leagues that used the same name existed as early as 1898, and reemerged periodically.

7   The Montréal Royals returned to the International League in 1928, and their relationship with the Provincial League was not always smooth. While a few exhibition games were organized and a few players were signed out of the league, the Royals also opposed the entry of the league into Organized Baseball and vetoed the addition of a team on the Montréal island.

8   Gray also came back to Trois-Rivières in 1942, this time in the Class-C Canadian-American League.

9   Of course, the playoffs coincided with the start of World War II, which might also have been a factor.

10 "Dans le Monde Sportif par Oscar Major," *Le Samedi,* October 28, 1939: 8.

11 Powley played in the Provincial League as Allen McElreath, the name of a contemporary player who had nothing do to with the Provincial League and split his 1939 season between the Southern Association and the South Atlantic League. Powley later claimed that his huge salary was paid in part by P.J.A. Cardin, the federal public works minister from Sorel. See "Between Ourselves," *Bridgeport Post,* August 29, 1948: 35.

12 "Jean Barrette Abandonne la Ligue Provinciale," *Le Droit,* October 22, 1940: 10.

13 The league also had teams in Lachine and Acton Vale, but both folded midway through the season, as the caliber of the league quickly improved.

14 "Sherbrooke Aura un Fort Receveur en Al Thomas," *La Tribune,* April 21, 1949: 18.

15 "Lanier to Get $10,000 This Year at Drummondville, City of 30,000," *The Sporting News,* June 1, 1949: 32.

16 "Molini Dit Que les Clubs de Son Circuit Peuvent Battre Ceux de l'Internationale," *La Tribune,* June 4, 1949: 21.

17 Maglie claims he was not in good enough pitching shape in 1949 to stick with the Giants, and he preferred to return in 1950. He is the only jumper who made a lasting major-league impact after 1949. See "Maglie Relates His Story," *The Sporting News,* May 2, 1951: 34.

18 Among the players hired by Sherbrooke to replace the jumpers was Blackie Schwamb, less than a year removed from pitching with the St. Louis Browns. He asked for a few days of leave in August and never returned. A few months later he was arrested and later found guilty of a murder in California. See Eric Stone, *Wrong Side of the Wall: The Life of Blackie Schwamb, the Greatest Prison Baseball Player of All Time* (Guilford, Connecticut: The Lyons Press, 2005).

19 "Canadian Chief Raps Gambling," *The Sporting News,* September 28, 1949: 30.

20 "Les Athlétiques de Sherbrooke Ont de Bonnes Chances de Faire de Nouveau Partie de la Provinciale," *Le Courrier de St-Hyacinthe,* December 30, 1949: 4.

21 Bill Young, "The Day Sherbrooke Baseball Died," *Sherbrooke Record,* September 19, 2006: 7.

22 In 1969, for instance, Sherbrooke, Drummondville, Granby, Trois-Rivières, Québec, and Thetford Mines, all veterans of the 1950s Class-C league, were joined by Plessisville and Lachine.

23 On a personal note, as a volunteer for the event, I was asked to dig into the history of baseball in Sherbrooke to prepare radio spots, which is how I developed an interest in Quebec baseball histaory.

EARL "FLAT" CHASE

By Heidi LM Jacobs

Earl "Flat" Chase (1913 – 1954) was skilled as a batter, pitcher, catcher, and any field position he was asked to play. Chase was nicknamed Flat for his running style, and his skills on the field and charismatic athleticism earned him a reputation as one of the most exciting players to watch in Southwestern Ontario in the 1930s, '40s, and '50s. He is perhaps best known for outpitching Phil Marchildon in the 1934 Ontario Baseball Amateur Association championship series and thus helping his team, the Chatham Coloured All-Stars, defeat Penetanguishene. The Chatham Coloured All-Stars were the first Black team to win this provincial series.

Chase was born on August 16, 1913, in North Buxton, Ontario, a community founded in 1849 by and for Black settlers, many of whom were former slaves. Chase was one of nine children born to George Chase, a laborer, and Elva Gambril. His siblings were Arthur, Viola, Lloyd, Harold, Edith, Richard, Ileen, and Ione. Early in his life, Earl moved with his family to Windsor, Ontario, across the river from Detroit. The Chases lived in the McDougall Street corridor, the center of Windsor's traditional Black neighborhood and business district. The Chases' house was on Mercer Street, which was the eastern edge of Wigle Park, the geographic and social heart of the McDougall Street corridor. The park offered a range of social and recreational facilities, including a baseball diamond.

Chase spent most of his days playing baseball, honing his skills, watching and then competing against the many teams that visited from the Windsor-Essex and Chatham-Kent regions, as well as from Detroit. Chase's eldest son, Earl Jr., reflected that his father "grew up in the park across the street."[1] The McDougall Street corridor was less than five miles from downtown Detroit, and the Windsor newspapers of the 1930s document a steady flow of regional Black baseball teams into Wigle Park.[2] These teams included the Saginaw Michigan Colored Baseballers (1930), the Ecorse Colored Giants (1930 and 1936), the Hamtramck Colored Stars (1931), the Philadelphia Colored Giants (1931), the Wolverine Colored Stars (1933), Quinn's Colored Stars of Detroit (1935 and 1939), and the Detroit Colored Stars (1936), among others. It has proved difficult to locate formal documentation about these teams, but it is highly probable that they were not part of formal leagues, but rather informally organized pickup teams with crossover players playing exhibition games against teams around the area.[3]

Around the age of 15, Chase started playing for church league teams in both Windsor and Detroit. While there appears to be no extant record of these games, it is safe to assume that in playing for church teams in Detroit, Chase was regularly playing with and against a wide range of Black baseball players, some of whom likely played on more formalized Negro Leagues teams in and around Detroit. It is also likely that playing with and against such teams in Detroit helped push the young Chase's innate skills to the next level.

In 1933 the Windsor newspapers document Chase playing for the Windsor Stars, along with another future Chatham Coloured All-Star, Ferguson Jenkins Sr.[4] It may have been through playing for the Stars at Wigle Park that Chase and Jenkins got to know Wilfred "Boomer" Harding and his brother Len Harding from Chatham.[5] It's not surprising that in 1933, when the All-Stars were looking for talent to round out their team for the Chatham City League playoffs, they sought out Chase.

A story in the August 24, 1933, *Chatham Daily News* describes how "Chase[,] a hurler from Windsor who has been working in the Riverside league," had signed on to play with the All-Stars.[6] The All-Stars would go on to win the Chatham City League's Wanless Trophy that year, and Chase's contributions on the mound were a large part of the team's success. Describing the final game of the series, the *Chatham Daily News* writes, "It was simply a case of too much Chase, who worked on the mound in both games."[7] Chase would stay in Chatham for the rest of his life, playing for a number of teams in and around Chatham.

The All-Stars' home field, Stirling Park, was not unlike Wigle Park in that it was located in the heart of Chatham's predominantly Black neighbourhood. Like the McDougall Street area, the East End has a long-standing tradition of baseball. Most of the Black teams prior to the 1930s were informal teams like the Chatham Giants from the 1920s, who played some league games but also pickup and exhibition games at church homecomings and other weekend events. In 1932 a group of young players from the East End formed a team that, with the assistance of Archie Stirling, a neighborhood business owner and local baseball advocate, would be formally recognized in 1933 as the Stars and later be known as the Chatham Coloured All-Stars. Most of the players grew up in the East End and lived within a few blocks of the ball diamond, and hundreds of residents would turn out to watch baseball on summer evenings and weekends.

The crowd who showed up for the All-Stars' season opener on May 17, 1934, would have seen that Chase's 1933 playoff performance was not a fluke but rather indicative of the career he would have in Chatham. Playing second base for the first four innings and then pitching the final three innings, Chase is listed in the box score as getting one run and one hit. In the second inning, Chase turned a 4-3 double play, "nipping what appeared to be a start of a rally in the bud."[8] Of his pitching, *Chatham Daily News* sportswriter Jack Calder commented, "Chase went to the mound in the last three frames and effectively checked any intentions the Duns might have had to fatten their batting averages by allowing only one hit."[9] This one article hints at why Chase would go on to become a Chatham legend: He was a formidable pitcher, fielder, and hitter.

As the 1934 season progressed, Chase showed Chatham fans just what kind of a powerhouse he would become, and the local newspaper recounted the details of his on-field skills. On June 12, Calder wrote:

"With Chase hurling three-hit ball over the abbreviated route, the Stars took advantage of seven errors made by the opposition and seven hits allowed by Belanger to win going away. Chase himself led in the hitting attack with two

doubles and a single in four times at bat, while his battery mate, Washington, accounted for two of his team's other hits. Belanger and Depew worked on the mound for the Braggs and turned in good games but the free-swinging bats of Chase and Washington led to their defeat."[10]

In this game and the game on June 20, Chase's contributions were as both an intimidating pitcher and a strong batter: "Chase worked the entire game [against] the Duns and allowed only seven hits while striking out ten. Wright and Thompson opposed him, the former being chased after two and two-thirds innings. Boomer Harding and Chase each accounted for three of the Stars' safe blows."[11] It is difficult to ascertain precisely how many games Chase's pitching won for the All-Stars since stats for ERA, wins, saves, and losses were not recorded. One thing that is certain, however, is that much of the success of the 1934 team was reliant upon Chase's ability to pitch hard throughout the games, his unstoppable bat, and his competitive spirit.

Throughout the 1934 season, Chase would be described in phrases such as the "smoke-ball artist of the Chatham Nine"[12] and "the speed ball demon."[13] By September of 1934, Jack Calder of the *Chatham Daily News* would call Chase the "mainstay of the All-Stars' pitching staff" and "one of the hardest hitters in amateur ball."[14] Teammate Boomer Harding commented on Chase at the plate. He

"… could hit a ball low and he could hit it high … there's no weak spot. He could hit the ball where it was pitched. If they thought, well, we'll pitch him outside, he'd hit it hard, he'd hit it out of the park, in left field just as easy as in Stirling which was small. But he'd still hit it further out of the park than a right hand batter would hit it out. So he was strong in any field and he'd hit it like it was pitched."[15]

Chase not only awed spectators with his skills, he was also entertaining to watch as this notice in the *Chatham Daily News* reveals: "Flat Chase does something of a rumba every time he goes to bat, not quite the same as Dick Porter's classical toe dance. Chase's little act should have been set to the music of Ferde Grofé's 'Grand Canyon Suite.' It's good but there's something weird about it. But how Chase can leather that apple. He is the hardest hitter in amateur baseball in this part of the province. That's covering some territory."[16] For the rest of his life and beyond, his skills as a player would be talked about with superlatives and awe.

On the field, the All-Stars were challenged by some strong opponents, and they became known for fast, exciting, and occasionally aggressive play. Boomer Harding's son Blake offered this description of the team: "And when it got nasty, they were just as nasty and aggressive and tough as anybody else out there. And if you wanted to play to hurt one of them … they gave what they got."[17] Off the field, the team also met challenges. The farther the team got from Chatham, the more they encountered hostile crowds and difficulties finding restaurants and hotels that would serve and house them. In the 1934 final series in and against Penetanguishene, the team could not find accommodations in town and had to stay in a neighboring town. In Canada discrimination based on race was not as fully codified as it was in the United States, but it was still deeply pervasive.

Sometimes the All-Stars' athleticism, skill, and exciting style of play would win over hostile crowds. Other times having a Black team beat the local team led to events that the players remembered in vivid detail for the rest of their lives. In 1980 Kingsley Terrell, longtime teammate of Chase, recalled how

"… there was never a place that we played baseball that we couldn't go back and play again, except one place and that was in West Lorne. We beat West Lorne and they run us out, they

run us out of the town. They had clubs, and hoes, and rakes, and everything else. We got everything all packed up before the game was over because we knew there was something going to happen anyways. So, we just got the game over. When that last man was out we all got in the cars and took off and we never went back. And we couldn't go back to play ball there no more.[18]

In 1984 fellow All-Star Ross Talbot shared his memories of West Lorne: "One time in West Lorne we caused a small riot. … Boomer was going home and knocked down their catcher and people snatched boards off the fence, but we came out of that all right."[19] "As for heckling," Talbot reflected, "we just had to take it. … At that time we had to live with it."[20] In the same interview Talbot recalled playing in Strathroy: "They wrote on the sidewalks, 'the n___s are coming' and the 'black clouds are moving in,'" Talbot said, a tear coming to his eye.[21] "That was the worst thing we ever came across." An interview with Ferguson Jenkins Sr. suggests that Chase specifically was targeted in some of the things written and drawn on the sidewalks.[22] In their interviews with the *Breaking the Colour Barrier* project,[23] however, Earl Chase Jr. and Horace Chase said their father never really talked about those memories. Instead, they said, his love for the game always won out over whatever threats or hostilities he encountered.[24]

Chase, Boomer and Len Harding, Guoy Ladd, and Kingsley Terrell formed a core group of players who stayed with the Chatham Coloured All-Stars until they disbanded in 1939. Chatham fielded a competitive team for the remainder of the 1930s but they never won another OBAA championship. The All-Stars made it to the OBAA finals in 1939 but withdrew when conflicts regarding payment of expenses and location of the final games could not be resolved. Although the print record is vague about these controversies, oral histories have suggested there were racial undertones to the unfair travel expectations put on the All-Stars, and the lack of proper compensation for expenses. When the 1940 baseball season began, World War II was underway and several All-Stars had enlisted to serve.

Chase remained in Chatham during the war. By this time, he and his wife, Julia (Black) Chase, whom he married in November 1934, had four children, Earl Jr., Horace, Marilyn, and Gladys. Chase worked for the City of Chatham's sanitation department and eventually was hired in a supervisory role. Work and family were a priority for Chase, but so was baseball. As Horace Chase recalled, "most of the time my dad actually played ball, tell you the truth. His love of the game was phenomenal because that was his sport. In fact, when all four of us children was born he wasn't there for the birth, he was playing ball. That's how much he played."[25] The Chases were a baseball family, Horace commented: "We weren't what you'd call a much outside baseball family. We liked our baseball."[26] Chase "didn't get into soccer or hockey, golf or any of those things. I think because my dad was used to working, and times were tough. And like I say, having four young kids with mouths to feed. I think that was his only thing, was to play ball. Live to play ball, eat, sleep, and enjoy life."[27] The centrality of baseball is a recurrent theme in Chase's sons' descriptions of their father's life.

As was the case when he lived in Windsor, Chase played baseball for a range of community and regional teams, playing whenever and wherever he could. In 1938 and 1939 Chase appears to have played with the London Majors, a predominantly White team in the Intercounty Baseball League, as well as with the Chatham Coloured All-Stars. In 1944 Chase was a key part of the London Majors' winning the Canadian Sandlot Congress Championship. In 1943-1945, there are records of Chase playing for the Chatham Arcades, who won the OBA Intermediate Championship in 1944. In 1946 a number of former All-Stars reunited to play for the Taylor A-Cs.

There were enough All-Stars on the team that the *Chatham Daily News*'s sports page had a headline that said, "Chatham Coloured Stars Return Under New Name."[28] From 1947 until his death in 1954, he also played with the Chatham Shermans and Chatham Hadleys. Very little formal documentation from those leagues exists today but the Chase family scrapbook documents his career, with notes and mostly undated clippings. In the scrapbook, it suggests that Chase's batting average ranged from .447 while playing for the Shermans in 1947 to .525 in the City League to .786 partway through an Industrial Baseball League season. My own calculations for all the games Chase played in 1934 have him batting .488 in 127 at-bats.[29] No statistics were kept for his pitching.

In the absence of official statistics, much of what we know of Chase comes from newspapers and oral histories. One of the recurrent stories of Chase is that over the course of his career he would hold the record for hitting the longest home-run balls in Sarnia, Strathroy, Aylmer, Welland, Milton, and Chatham. Whether these are official records or not, those who saw Chase play are unwavering in their description of him as a fierce competitor. All-Stars scorekeeper Orville Wright commented, "Flat hit one in Chatham I don't think they've found yet. It cleared the center field fence at Stirling Park, [it] went over the trees and a house on Park Street, cleared the road and the houses on the other side and landed in a back yard on Wellington Street."[30] In 1980, King Terrell described Chase's skills in this way:

"He could run. He was a power hitter. He could hit home runs just about as easy as the rest of us could hit singles and doubles and triples. Because at Stirling Park it didn't seem like it took him very much of a swing to get a double over [by] the right field fence, or a homerun over the centerfield fence. He was a spray-hitter. That means that you can hit a ball in any park over the field.

Earl 'Flat' Chase, ca. 1947-1954. (Archives and Special Collections, Leddy Library, University of Windsor)

Nine times out of ten if he hit a ball south, the ball would be going direct over right field because he was a power hitter. A spray-hitter means that you can spray a ball in the outfield. Because that's when you don't know where it's going to go. He was one of those kinds of guys: you didn't know where the ball was going to go. It's the same as his pitching. Because lots of times, Donise would ask him for a fast ball and he's liable to throw him a curve. And ask him for a curve and he's liable to throw you a fast ball, which I know all about – his fast balls and his curves – because he darn near killed three of us in one night."[31]

Virtually every retrospective of the All-Stars' 1934 victory features commentary like that about the legend of Flat Chase.

With all the talk about Chase's undeniable talent, the question is always whether he could have played major-league baseball. While we will never know if Chase thought he could have played in the major leagues, everyone who saw him play was convinced he could have had there not been a color barrier. Teammate Don Washington told the *Chatham Daily News* that "Chase should have been a big league pitcher"[32] and King Terrell told an interviewer, "Flat Chase, he could've been in the big leagues. There was not a better second baseman around than he was. And he was a good pitcher. God-all knows that there was nobody around in the country that could hit a ball any better or any further than he could."[33] Archie Stirling – frequently referred to as Chatham's Mr. Baseball – wrote in 1960: "Today if Flat Chase were as good as he was when he first came to Chatham, the Detroit team would pay him thirty thousand dollars to sign with them."[34] Whether Chase could have made it to the big leagues is, of course, conjecture. Nevertheless, it is imperative that we consider the impact of the color barrier on the careers, lives, and legacies of players like Earl "Flat" Chase, and on the ways in which Canadian baseball history is written.

NOTES

1   "Interview With Earl Chase Jr. and Shyla Chase," *Breaking the Colour Barrier: Wilfred "Boomer" Harding & the Chatham Coloured All-Stars,* http://cdigs.uwindsor.ca/BreakingColourBarrier/items/show/722; "Interview with Horace Chase," *Breaking the Colour Barrier: Wilfred "Boomer" Harding & the Chatham Coloured All-Stars,* http://cdigs.uwindsor.ca/BreakingColourBarrier/items/show/725.

2   I am grateful for Linda Bunn's research assistance in locating these notices in the Windsor-Essex County newspapers.

3   The mention of these teams in the Windsor papers might help further what is known about the rich and active Black baseball tradition in the Detroit area in the 1930s, and offer new avenues of inquiry into the ways in which the influence of Negro League baseball may have moved into Canada.

4   Ferguson Jenkins Sr.'s son is Hall of Famer Ferguson Jenkins Jr.

5   Box scores from the Windsor newspapers show the Hardings and other Chatham players competing at Wigle Park against each other.

6   "R.G. Funs and Stars Will Open Championship Series," *Chatham Daily News*, August 24, 1933: 13.

7   "Stars Win Wanless Trophy in Two Straight Games," *Chatham Daily News*, October 10, 1933: 8.

8   Jack Calder, "1934 Inaugural Indicates Real Battle for Honors," *Chatham Daily News*, May 18, 1934: 11.

9   Calder, "1934 Inaugural Indicates Real Battle for Honors."

10 Jack Calder, "Braggs Defeated in City Baseball Games Last Night," *Chatham Daily News*, June 12, 1934: 11.

11 Jack Calder, "Duns Defeated in a Hard Fought Game Last Evening," *Chatham Daily News*, June 21, 1934, section 2: 5.

12 Jack Calder, "Chase to Be on Hill for Chathamites," *Chatham Daily News*, July 20, 1934: 11.

13 Jack Calder, "Sarnia Red Sox Beaten at Home in OBAA Contest," *Chatham Daily News*, September 10, 1934: 8.

14 Jack Calder, "Stars Begin OBAA Playdowns Thursday," *Chatham Daily News*, September 5, 1934: 11.

15 Dan Kelly, "Interview with Wilfred Boomer Harding," *Breaking the Colour Barrier: Wilfred "Boomer" Harding & the Chatham Coloured All-Stars,* http://cdigs.uwindsor.ca/BreakingColourBarrier/items/show/719. Accessed July 15, 2021.

16 Jack Calder, "Stars Will Draw Them," *Chatham Daily News*, September 12, 1934: 11.

17 "Interview With Blake and Pat Harding (Part 1)," *Breaking the Colour Barrier: Wilfred "Boomer" Harding & the Chatham Coloured All-Stars,* http://cdigs.uwindsor.ca/BreakingColourBarrier/items/show/716.

18 Interview with Kingsley Terrell by Wanda Milburn, Multicultural History Society of Ontario, August 6, 1980.

19 Bill Reddick, "From the Bullpen: Chatham Colored All-Stars," *Chatham Daily News*, October 4, 1984: 9.

20 Reddick.

21 Reddick.

22 Interview with Ferguson Jenkins Sr. by Vivian Chavez and Wanda Milburn, Multicultural History Society of Ontario, October 3, 1980.

23 Breaking the Colour Barrier: Wilfred "Boomer" Harding & the Chatham Coloured All-Stars is a website that tells the story of the Chatham Coloured All-Stars. It features oral histories with players' families, newspaper clippings from the 1934 season, player biographies, and curricular resources for K-12 teachers. *Breaking the Colour Barrier* is a partnership between the Harding family, the University of Windsor's Department of History, the Leddy Library's Centre for Digital Scholarship, and the Chatham Sports Hall of Fame. It was generously funded by an Ontario Trillium Foundation grant in 2016-2017.

24 "Interview with Earl Chase Jr. and Shyla Chase."

25 "Interview With Horace Chase," *Breaking the Colour Barrier: Wilfred "Boomer" Harding & the Chatham Coloured All-Stars,* http://cdigs.uwindsor.ca/BreakingColourBarrier/items/show/725.

26 "Interview with Horace Chase."

27 "Interview with Horace Chase."

28 Doug Scurr, *Chatham Daily News*, June 12, 1946, np.

29 Elsewhere, Chase's average has been listed as .525 for 1934 but the source for this figure isn't clear. My calculations are based on every game for which I could find a box score in 1934, including exhibition games, various league games, and playoff games.

30 "Chatham's First Champs Played the Game for Fun," *London Free Press*, October 20, 1967, np.

31 Interview with Kingsley Terrell.

32 Bill Reddick, "'34 Champions Denied Opportunity in Pro Ball," *Chatham Daily News*, October 10, 1984: 9.

33 Interview with Kingsley Terrell.

34 Archie Stirling, "A Brief History of Baseball," in "Official Program: Chatham's Victoria Day (1960), *Breaking the Colour Barrier: Wilfred "Boomer" Harding & the Chatham Coloured All-Stars,* http://cdigs.uwindsor.ca/BreakingColourBarrier/items/show/957.

THE QUEBEC ADVENTURES OF CHAPPIE JOHNSON'S ALL-STARS

By Christian Trudeau

The reception that Jackie Robinson received in Montréal is well known. A few years later, the Provincial League became a prime destination for Negro League veterans. Many factors can explain how that came to be, but a neglected factor is the presence, almost a generation earlier, of Chappie Johnson and his African American team. For a decade starting in 1927 he held an almost constant presence in Quebec. For more than four years, Johnson based his team in the province, before supplying players to different teams. He brought in tremendous athletes, playing everywhere in Southern Quebec. While his team remained 100 percent African American, some of his players integrated local teams. A few incidents occurred over the years, but the experience was largely positive: Their name was synonymous with victory, and 15 years after their departure there were still signs of their presence in the Quebec vocabulary. After briefly describing the baseball scene when Chappie first set foot in Quebec, this article will describe his adventures in Quebec, before listing the players stolen from Chappie by local teams, and concluding with the cultural impact of his presence.

CHAPPIE JOHNSON BEFORE 1925

Born in 1877 in Ohio, George "Chappie" Johnson had a two-decade career as a player for various African American teams, building a reputation as an excellent defensive catcher. He notably played with Rube Foster, Sol White, Pete Hill, Joe Williams, and Pop Lloyd, all inducted into Cooperstown. Already in his 40s when the Negro Leagues were born, Chappie moved to inferior circuits, where he acted as manager and team owner. His first mention in Quebec newspapers came in 1925, when he managed a team sporting his name, the Chappies, based in Schenectady, New York. They visited Sherbrooke for a three-game series.[1] They won 12-2 and 8-2 against the local team, with the third game rained out.[2] Newspapers did not hesitate to claim that this was the best team ever seen in town, at least as good as the Boston Braves,[3] who had been seen twice previously in the Eastern Townships capital, in 1920 and 1923.[4]

QUEBEC BASEBALL IN THE 1920S

With the Royals having left Montréal after the 1917 season, the province had no pro team for part of the decade. The Eastern Canada League (1922-23) and the Quebec-Ontario-Vermont League (1924), both Class-B circuits, provided Quebec good baseball, but 1925 saw only strong semipro leagues in Montréal, and some good independent clubs elsewhere in the province, but little formal structure.

The province saw a first wave of visiting African American teams at the end of the 1910s. They were quite popular, returning year after year and attracting large crowds. The Manhattan Giants even spent the 1920 season in the province, renaming themselves the Quebec Royals for the occasion.[5] A few players, like Charlie Culver and Chick Bowden, even decided to move permanently to Quebec, with Culver bending the color line by playing six games in the 1922 Eastern Canada League.[6] The province was thus well aware of African American baseball, and Chappie Johnson was about to push that relationship up a few notches.

1927: RESCUING THE MONTRÉAL CITY LEAGUE

The beginning of July 1927 provided the first news that Chappie Johnson was coming to Montréal: He published an ad challenging the best teams in the province, listing a St. Antoine Street address to contact him.[7]

His timing could not have been better. In 1927 two semipro leagues were battling for attention in Montréal: the City League, older and better established, and the more recent Guybourg League. Two leagues may have been too many for the city, and the St. Henri team of the City League was out of funds. League officials turned to Chappie to fill the vacant spot. Chappie was confident, even though he inherited St. Henri's 3-6 record; he even boasted that attendance would double in a month.[8]

Everything was in place for a success. The show started even before the first pitch, as the

Chappies brought shadowball to Quebec, a common element of the show offered by African American teams consisting of players pretending to hit, field, and throw an invisible ball. On the field, the team was impressive, catcher Duke Lattimore and shortstop Babe Hobson attracting the most attention. Both had short Negro Leagues careers, content instead to stay with Chappie. The team did feature some players with more impressive resumes, although they received less publicity, notably second baseman Frank Forbes, a veteran of good teams of the 1910s, and pitcher Wayne Carr, who alternated between the Chappies and the Eastern Colored League. Chappie seemed to have a close relationship with the Brooklyn Royal Giants in that league, bringing in outfielder Country Brown toward the end of the season. Agustin Parpetty, veteran Cuban hitter at the tail end of his career, was also brought in as reinforcement. Parpetty was inducted into the Cuban Baseball Hall of Fame in 1983.[9] Chappie also had a few interesting prospects, notably Ted Page, who became the regular right fielder on one of the best teams ever, the 1933-34 Pittsburgh Crawfords, with Josh Gibson, Oscar Charleston, Cool Papa Bell, and Satchel Paige as teammates. Another youngster on the Chappies was Dick Seay, a superb defensive second baseman who, a decade later, was part of the Newark Eagles' Million Dollar Infield, next to three players who ended up in Cooperstown: Mule Suttles, Willie Wells, and Ray Dandridge.[10]

All these reinforcements were needed, as the Ahuntsic club proved a tough opponent. Led by Culver, Bowden, and pitcher Rusty Yarnall, who had pitched an inning for the Philadelphia Phillies the previous season, the Ahuntsic team managed to take a few games from the Chappies. This rivalry quickly attracted the large crowds predicted by Chappie, overshadowing the Guybourg League as well as other members of the City League. The two teams met in the finals, splitting the first two games. The deciding game was tied, 3-3, in the ninth inning when Ahuntsic scored four times to win the championship.[11]

A strange episode occurred when the Philadelphia Giants, coming through Montréal, challenged the Chappies for what they dubbed the World Black Championship. The Chappies refused to meet them; it remains unclear whether the teams were unable to agree on profit-sharing or if Chappie thought he had too much to lose from such a challenge.[12]

The season was a success, on the field and in the ledger book. The team's return for 1928 was announced, and both Chappie and star shortstop Babe Hobson even spent the winter in Montréal.[13]

1928: TOO BIG FOR THE CITY LEAGUE

The Montréal baseball scene changed a lot in a year: The Royals were back in the International League in a brand-new Delorimier Stadium in 1928, and the Guybourg League had disbanded. The Chappies, back in town after a monthlong spring training in the US south, were ready for another season in the City League, with pretty much the same roster as in 1927.[14]

Still riding the wave of the interest generated by their rivalry, the Chappies and Ahuntsic announced a seven-game series across the south of the province.[15] Even if it were to obtain permission to use Delorimier Stadium on Sundays when the Royals were on the road, the City League suffered from its top two teams preferring these outside activities. The relationship between the league and the Chappies worsened as the Chappies realized how valuable they were. In early July, the City League, no longer willing and able to accept the team's financial demands, kicked the Chappies out.[16] They then had a 4-1 record. The league soon imploded, with Ahuntsic the only team strong enough to continue operating.

Freed of their league obligations, the Chappies played seemingly everywhere, and against whoever promised a nice paycheck. On August 4 they defeated the Brooklyn Royal Giants and their ace pitcher Dick "Cannonball" Redding by a score of 5-4 in front of 4,000 spectators at Delorimier Stadium.[17] A week later, they played the City League's Beaurivage team in the first game of a doubleheader in which the headliners were the New York Giants, taking advantage of a break in their National League schedule to play against Ahuntsic.[18] The Philadelphia Tigers, a barnstorming African American team, were their opponent in a September series.[19]

The Chappies concluded their season with a splash: On October 14 they faced off against an Ahuntsic club reinforced for the occasion by Babe Ruth and Lou Gehrig. The two Yankees were coming through Montréal as part of a North American tour. While it had been announced that the two stars, just off their World Series triumph, would play against one another, they both ended up with Ahuntsic. The Chappies still fought ferociously, as it took a Gehrig home run in the ninth inning for them to lose, 8-6.[20] Ruth pitched in relief of Charlie Culver, striking out three Chappies. However, The Babe was himself a victim of Chappies pitcher Lefty Dillard.

Chappie may have pushed his demands a bit too far on this occasion. According to newspapers, when he saw the huge crowd he asked for more money. Organizers reluctantly gave him an extra $200, while swearing never to deal with him again.[21]

Perhaps feeling that business would promise to be more difficult in Montréal from that point, Chappie announced that he would operate from Quebec City in 1929.[22] He'd be in charge of a team in the newly founded Provincial League, which, like the Eastern Canada League seven years earlier, would have teams in Ottawa, Montréal, and Cap-de-la-Madeleine. But this time there would be no affiliation with Organized Baseball. Johnson himself headed to Trois-Rivières for the winter, as he had been recruited as manager of a bowling alley.[23]

1929: A PROMISING DEBUT

Chappie arrived in Quebec City in 1929 after promising to round out his team with five or six local players. This number was quickly reduced to two or three, then to zero. Chappie was apparently not against the use of local players, but as he was barnstorming regularly while fulfilling his league obligations, the attraction of his team was the presence of its African American players. Thus, local players would have been bad for business.

The rivalry with Ahuntsic was replaced by one with the Montréal team of the Provincial League, as the two teams pushed each other to excellence. The Montréalers obtained permission to use two (marginal) players of the Montréal Royals, William O'Hara and Ralph Brewer. The Chappies, who had lost their star catcher Duke Lattimore, saw more roster turnover than usual. Veteran Negro Leaguer John Cason replaced Lattimore behind the plate, but his power of attraction with fans was considerably less than that of his predecessor. The new league featured the most complete statistics of the era, revealing that newcomers Johnson Hill (.419 with two home runs in 13 games) and Cleo Smith (.679 with seven doubles and two triples in seven games), two more Negro League veterans, provided solid support for Babe Hobson (.468 with 10 doubles, one triple, and one home run in 19 games). On the mound, the star pitcher was Ed Dudley, who had had a much briefer career in the Negro Leagues, but dominated with a 7-1 record in the Provincial League.[24]

Although the rivalry was good for Montréal and for the Chappies, the two other teams were struggling. The Ottawa franchise was transferred to Quebec City in early July.[25] Thereafter known as Quebec-Lambert, they created a stir by signing Willie Gisentaner, famous Negro Leagues

left-handed pitcher.[26] But rain canceled the game in which he was scheduled to appear, and it seems he did not get another chance with the team. The Quebec-Lambert team, while improved, fell behind the league leaders, so with the Cap-de-la-Madeleine team having folded, the league moved in mid-August directly to a playoff series between the Chappies and Montréal. The Chappies, who went 15-4 in the regular season, prevailed. The rest of the season saw the Chappies alternate between exhibition games and challenges with Montréal.

Among the exhibition visitors were the Brooklyn Tigers, the House of David, and the Brooklyn Royal Giants. The best show, however, was provided by the Havana Red Sox and their pitcher Luis Tiant Sr. For one of the challenges, the Montréal team and its manager, Dave Major, hired one player from the House of David team and two from the Havana Red Sox, as well as Gisentaner as pitcher. The Chappies swept the doubleheader anyway.[27] The only saving grace for the Montréalers was that they were able to beat the Havana Red Sox, to whom the Chappies lost three times.

At season's end, Chappie surprised everybody by announcing that he would be switching allegiance; he signed as manager for the Quebec-Lambert team for 1930.[28]

1930: THE SHOW MUST GO ON

Chappie arrived in Quebec City in the spring of 1930 to work for his new boss, J.A.T. Lambert. Talks were ongoing for the return of the Provincial League, but they were moving very slowly. In early May, with nothing imminent, the Chappies announced that they would operate as an independent team in 1930.[29] Once again, Chappie's decision carried weight, and soon thereafter the league abandoned its project.

The result was a lackluster season. Chappie attracted quite a bit of publicity when he signed a tall left-handed pitcher, Nip Winters, among the best African American pitchers of the 1920s. Stats show a 54-17 record with Hilldale of the Eastern Colored League between 1924 and 1926, with a Negro World Series title in 1925. He also had a 3-0 record with a save in five appearances against major-league teams.[30] Winters, who had played with Chappie before his successes, was having problems with the bottle that were derailing his career. While he was immediately recognized as one of the top pitchers in the province, it was a game in which he hit two home runs that was his most memorable one in Quebec.[31]

Chappie finally fulfilled his promise to add a local player to his team … in a way. The local player was Charlie Culver, the former Negro Leaguer who had been in Quebec for a decade.[32]

The Havana Red Sox returned, and this time the Chappies took two out of three games.[33] It was the African American version of the House of David team that gave them trouble, sweeping the Chappies in late August. Locally, Montréal promoter Jos. Choquette built a team that served as the Chappies' main rival for most of the season, replacing Ahuntsic, which did not survive the collapse of the Provincial League. The teams split a two-game series in September.[34]

The season concluded with the rumor that Chappie had agreed to manage a team in Minneapolis in 1931.[35] For the first time in four years, the Chappies' future was uncertain.

1931: THE END OF THE LINE

With the Minneapolis rumor proven untrue, the Chappies were back in Quebec City in the spring, returning with Napoléon Côté, the promoter with whom they had worked in 1929. The Québec-District League was established, with two local teams, Lévis, across the St. Lawrence River from Quebec City, and the Quebec City Canadiens, and two African American teams, the Chappies and the Mohawk Giants. The schedule

called for 30 games per team, with games played at the Exposition Park.[36]

Early-season returns did not meet expectations, as crowds were disappointing. The Chappies, still led by Babe Hobson and Charlie Culver, lost their supporting cast and struggled on the field. They were swept by the Canadiens, and soon played second fiddle to the Mohawk Giants, led by popular catcher Duke Lattimore.

The Chappies left for one of their barnstorming trips in New England, and when they returned, they were kicked out of the league for having missed three league games.[37] The Chappies had had successes before even with no league to play in, but that was with a successful team. In mid-June in Montréal, they were swept by the House of David.[38] The Québec-District League disbanded in early July.[39] The Chappies, too, disappeared; they left the province, about four years to the day after having set foot in Montréal in 1927.

A BRIEF RETURN IN 1935

Out of the province from 1932 to 1934, the Chappies resurfaced in Quebec in 1935, after quite an evolution on the local baseball scene. A new Provincial League with eight clubs had been established, with teams in Montréal (two), Lachine, Sherbrooke (two), Sorel, Granby, and Drummondville. However, by midseason there was financial trouble, the schedule was suspended, and an invitation was issued to any barnstorming team to visit to face the Provincial League teams. This is how the Chappies returned, to Granby for a game on July 24. Other visitors included the Zulu Cannibal Giants, Japanese All Stars, Cleveland Clowns, and House of David, but the Chappies' particular calling card was nostalgia. Newspapers did not miss the chance to remind their readers of the Chappies' past in the province. It was also revealed that the team was now part of a league in upstate New York, playing against teams from

The 1936 Black Panthers. Charlie Culver is the first on the left, sitting. (Jerry Cohen, Ebbets Field Flannels)

Ogdensburg, Saranac Lake, Watertown, and Carleton. A few players from the Quebec days were still with the team, including Babe Hobson, now behind the plate, and Charlie Culver, who had left Quebec temporarily to follow Chappie.[40] While they shut out Granby in their first game back,[41] the Chappies struggled overall, losing to Sorel, Lachine, and the Montréal Police team (also part of the Provincial League). They concluded their exhibition tour with a loss at Delorimier Stadium against an old rival, Jos. Choquette.[42]

With the finances back under control, the league resumed its activities, and the Chappies left the province again, most likely to finish their season in upstate New York.

THE BLACK PANTHERS

The Provincial League continued its activities in 1936, adding an African American team, the Black Panthers. While Chappie Johnson was not, as far as the author knows, directly linked

to the team, it seems likely, as claimed by Merritt Clifton,[43] that he sent many players to the team. Owned by Jack Wilson of Montréal and Jock Smith of Chicago, the team featured a number of former Chappies, including Charlie Culver as manager. Others were outfielder Ted Waters, who had been with the Chappies intermittently since 1929, and Ernie "Black Bear" Jackson, a light-hitting first baseman known for his fantastic glove, and a Chappie regular since 1927. Famous pitcher Nip Winters, now truly at the end of his career, also returned briefly to Quebec with the Black Panthers.[44] While it's possible that Chappies veterans volunteered to come back to Quebec, it's more likely that Chappie himself had a word in the roster composition.

The Black Panthers were in the middle of the pack in 1936, before collapsing in the round-robin tournament that served as the league playoffs. The 1937 edition of the team employed mostly youngsters, as veterans from the Chappies era were almost nonexistent. They slid to the bottom of the standings in a quickly improving Provincial League, finishing with a 10-50 record.[45] They did not return in 1938. It was the end of an era, the last time a team linked to Chappie Johnson was present in Quebec.

PLAYERS HIRED AWAY FROM CHAPPIE

As soon as he arrived in Quebec, Chappie Johnson had to deal with the possibility that his players would be recruited by local teams. It was a phenomenon with some history, as before Chappie, Charlie Culver, Chick Bowden, Peerless Green, and others had stayed behind after touring in Quebec.

The first mention of such hirings was in the spring of 1928. St. Hyacinthe, a team always looking for the best available players, signed pitcher Wayne Carr and catcher Harry Creek.[46] When the Chappies were kicked out of the City League later that season, six of their players moved temporarily to St. Hyacinthe.[47] The situation was likely encouraged by Chappie, as it prevented his players from leaving the province while he arranged exhibition games that allowed him to pay their salaries.

In 1930 Bedford invested in a strong team to compete in a league with Farnham, Iberville, and Sherbrooke. They hired Ed Dudley, star pitcher of the 1929 Chappies.[48] Their Farnham rivals announced that they had signed star shortstop Babe Hobson,[49] but he only showed up in October.[50] Toward the end of the season, the Québec Canadiens, who battled the Chappies in 1930 and 1931, hired Nestor Lambertus, a Cuban outfielder who had been with the Havana Red Sox but had also played briefly for the Chappies.[51] The next year the Canadiens hired pitcher Spitball Smith from the Mohawk Giants.[52]

In 1935, during the team's brief stay for the Quebec exhibition tour, Chappie loaned Fred "Evil" Wilson to Granby, integrating the Provincial League. Wilson, a gifted but temperamental player, would in the following years spend time in both jail and the Negro Leagues, before coming back to the province with the Verdonnet, a Quebec City team, in 1945. In 1936, after the Black Panthers had been eliminated, Granby picked up Ormand Sampson, a transaction eventually ruled illegal by the league because it had occurred during the playoffs.[53]

A few Black Panthers extended their stay in the province, notably pitcher Al Flemming, who played for various teams up to at least 1952, when he served as player-manager with Lachute.[54]

THE CULTURAL IMPACT OF THE CHAPPIES

The Chappies were in the eyes of the Quebec media for more than four years, and left a mark. Of course, given the era, derogatory terms[55] are often used to describe them. But it was primarily their talent that impressed. Soon a few juvenile teams called themselves the young Chappies. Even the senior hockey team in Thetford Mines took the name for the 1929-30 season. In 1931 a young first baseman, excellent defensively, was said to play "like Jackson from the Chappies," a reference to Ernie "Black Bear" Jackson, a mainstay at first base for the Chappies.[56]

A tribute that does not age well occurred in Lévis in 1931. After a religious celebration young parishioners divided themselves into two groups, the Chappies and the Nationals (for the local team in the Québec-District League). To emphasize the distinction between the two teams, the Chappies played in blackface. In 1933 a similar practice was observed in Pike River, with the second group this time using fake beards to personify the House of David.[57]

Periodically, news brought back memories of the Chappies, even years after their departure. When the United States Negro Leagues played multiple games in Quebec in 1945, many comparisons to the Chappies were made. For instance, in *Le Canada*: "In Montréal, we've always liked seeing black baseball players in action. We still recall the Chappie Johnsons, in particular catcher Lattimore who was marvelling the crowds with his play behind the plate and his bat. If blacks had been admitted in organized baseball, Lattimore would not have been in Montréal for long. That was one, for sure, that was of major league caliber."[58]

In 1951, with the Provincial League now a Class-C league, Sam Bankhead, in charge of the Farnham Pirates, became the first African American manager in Organized Baseball. His team was composed primarily of African American players, leading some newspapers, chief among them *Le Nouvelliste de Trois-Rivières*, to refer to them as the Chappies.[59]

Chappie Johnson died on August 17, 1949, in South Carolina. At least one Quebec newspaper, *Le Nouvelliste de Trois-Rivières*, mentioned his death in the weeks following, recalling the winter he had spent in the town as manager of a bowling alley.[60]

Author John Craig, from Peterborough, Ontario, in 1979 published *Chappie and Me*, a semi-autobiographical novel about a young White player joining the barnstorming Chappies for a few months in 1939, playing in blackface. While the book must not be taken as historically accurate, the Chappies are described as a purely barnstorming team traveling with a portable lighting system, something they never had during their stay in Quebec. The Chappies from the novel tour the US and Canada in the summer before retreating to the Caribbean for the winter. Craig also recalls the Chappies' traveling to the protagonist's town (presumably Peterborough) every summer, something that could have happened from their base in Quebec or upstate New York. The novel contains a brief mention of Quebec, as the protagonist and a few teammates meet a French-Canadian cook at an Illinois fair. The cook recalls having seen them play in Trois-Rivières, a fun coincidence (or not) given the history Chappie had with the city.[61]

The book and later the musical inspired by the novel were mentioned in Quebec media in the 1980s, but without anybody recalling the time Chappie actually spent in the province.

CONCLUSION

It is impossible to know what Chappie Johnson was thinking when he showed up in Quebec. Was it a welcoming land, a nice business opportunity, or a bit of both? In the end, he contributed greatly to the image and reputation of African American baseball in Quebec by offering great exhibitions across the south of the province. As some of his players played in the Negro Leagues, and could have played in the majors, Chappie offered to many of these towns a very high level of baseball, possibly the best ever seen in their town.

The media of Jackie Robinson's era made no connection between Robinson and Chappie Johnson. But there's little doubt that the constant media presence of the Chappies over five summers normalized African American baseball in Quebec. His presence also forced his rivals to innovate to keep up with him, including pushing to integrate. Chappie's role with the Black Panthers is less clear, but that team played a crucial role in the rise of the Provincial League, helping them generate revenues and gain credibility.

Maybe Quebec was only an unexploited land in which Chappie could make an easy buck, without competition. But even if that wasn't his goal, he ended up being a trailblazer.

ACKNOWLEDGMENTS

Gary Fink provided helpful comments on an early draft. Merritt Clifton's research on the Provincial League touched on Chappie Johnson's stay in Quebec, and a conversation with him clarified some details.

SOURCES

Baseball-Reference.com and Seamheads.com were the main references. Many Quebec newspapers were consulted (available on the website of the *Bibliothèque et Archives Nationales du Québec*).

NOTES

1   They came to Sherbrooke as the local team was in financial turmoil. "Players may carry on with baseball here," *Sherbrooke Daily Record*, July 13, 1925: 8.

2   "Statement of Baseball Club; Locals Lost," *Sherbrooke Daily Record*, July 15, 1925: 9; "Schenectady Team Scored Over Locals," *Sherbrooke Daily Record*, July 16, 1925: 9.

3   "Le Sherbrooke a Encore été Défait," *La Tribune de Sherbrooke*, July 16, 1925: 6.

4   The Braves won 21-2 in 1920 and 2-1 in 1923: "Large Crowd Present to See Braves," *Sherbrooke Daily Record*, October 11, 1920: 4; "Boston Braves Won Battle in Ninth Inning," *Sherbrooke Daily Record*, October 8, 1923: 8.

5   "Victoire de l'Athlétique," *La Presse*, May 14, 1920: 6.

6   Christian Trudeau, "24 Years Before Jackie Robinson, Charlie Culver Broke Barriers in Montréal," *Baseball Research Journal*, Spring 2020.

7   "Un Club de Nègres Jouera Ici," *Le Canada*, July 6, 1927: 2. The address is of a convenience store owned by William Henry Parham, a member of the local African American community. See 1927-28 Lovell's Montréal directory.

8   "Nouveau Club dans la Ligue de la Cité," *La Presse*, July 8, 1927: 20.

9   Player lists are obtained from box scores and accounts in Montréal newspapers. Player backgrounds are from Seamheads.

10   Both Page and Seay credit Chappie Johnson for their successful careers, helping them to transition from raw athletes to polished players. See John Holway, *Black Giants* (Xlibris Corporation, 2009).

11   "L'Ahuntsic Est Champion de la Ligue de la Cité," *La Presse*, October 17, 1927: 20.

12   "Les Giants de Philadephie à Guybourg," *La Presse*, September 29, 1927: 24.

13   "Glanures Sportives," *L'Autorité*, October 16, 1927: 4.

14   "Doc Newton Jouera avec le St-Laurent," *La Presse*, March 16, 1928: 23.

15   "L'Ahuntsic et les Chappies à Iberville," *La Presse*, May 23, 1928: 25.

16   "Le Club de Baseball de la Brasserie Frontenac Remplacera les Chappies dans la Ligue de la Cité," *La Presse*, July 5, 1928: 20.

17   "Deux Belles Exhibitions Hier, au Stade," *La Presse*, August 5, 1928: 16.

18   "Les Giants Déclassent l'Ahuntsic," *La Presse*, August 12, 1928: 18.

19   "Quatre Victoires pour les Chappies," *La Presse*, September 10, 1928: 18.

20   More precisely, Ahuntsic was the away team, and Gehrig's home run was at the top of the ninth inning. But the field was then filled with seat cushions from the overexcited crowd. Given the cold weather, the game was not resumed. See "Belle Exhibition de Ruth et Gehrig, Hier au Stade," *La Presse*, October 15, 1928: 10.

21   "20,000 Personnes Acclament Ruth et Gehrig," *La Patrie*, October 15, 1928: 10.

22   "Organisation de la Ligue Provinciale," *La Presse*, October 17, 1928: 20.

23   "Chappie Johnson Gérant de la Salle de Quilles Loranger," *Le Nouvelliste*, October 20, 1928: 6.

24   Stats were published at the end of the season: "Un Bon Debut pour la Ligue Provinciale," *Le Canada*, October 2, 1929: 2.

25   "Nap Côté et un 2ᵉ Club à Québec," *Le Soleil*, July 11, 1929: 16.

26   "Disentaener [*sic*] et Silver avec le Club Lambert Dimanche," *Le Soleil*, July 31, 1929: 14.

27   "Le Québec Chappie Enlève avec Brio Ses Deux Parties d'Hier Contre Montréal," *Le Soleil*, August 26, 1929: 15.

28   "Chappie Johnson avec le Club de J.A.T. Lambert l'An Prochain," *Le Soleil*, October 24, 1929: 17.

29   "De Forts Clubs Viendront Jouer Contre l'Équipe de J.-A.-T. Lambert," *Le Soleil*, May 6, 1930 : 16.

30   Seamheads.com.

31   "Les Chappies Remportent une Double Victoire Sur Les Cuban Stars Hier au Parc de l'Expos," *Le Soleil*, June 9, 1930: 13.

32   "Les Chappies à Montréal," *Le Soleil*, September 12, 1930: 16.

33 "Les Havana Red Sox et les Chappies Partagent un Double Header Hier," *Le Soleil*, August 4, 1930: 12.

34 The Choquette team featured three players from the Montréal Canadiens: Wildor Larochelle, Armand Mondou, and future Hockey Hall of Famer Aurèle Joliat. "Les Chappies à Montréal," *Le Soleil*, September 12, 1930: 16.

35 "Chappie Johnson Demeurera aux États-Unis en 1931, à en Croire la Rumeur," *La Tribune*, December 15, 1930: 6.

36 "Chappies et Canadiens Inaugureront la Saison au Parc de l'Exposition," *Le Soleil*, May 8, 1931: 19.

37 "Les Chappies ont Maintenant Fini Leur Règne à Québec," *Le Soleil*, June 9, 1931: 15.

38 "Deux Victoires pour la Maison de David," *La Presse*, June 22, 1931: 19.

39 "La Ligue Que.-District Suspend Ses Activités," *Le Soleil*, July 3, 1931: 14.

40 "Choquette Reçoit les Chappies au Stade, Dimanche," *La Presse*, August 24, 1935: 34.

41 "Granby shut out by Chappie Johnsons," *Granby Leader-Mail*, July 25, 1935: 8.

42 "Chappies Battus 5-4 par Jos Choquette," *Le Canada*, August 26, 1935: 11.

43 Merritt Clifton, "Quebec Loop Broke Color Line in 1935," *Baseball Research Journal*, 1984.

44 "Alignements des Panthères Noires et du Club Granby," *L'Illustration Nouvelle*, May 1, 1936: 17.

45 Christian Trudeau, "Integration in Quebec: More Than Jackie," Jane Finnan Dorward, ed., *Dominionball: Baseball above the 49th* (Cleveland: SABR, 2005), 85-89.

46 "Deux Joueurs des Chappies avec le Club St.-Hyacinthe," *La Presse*, April 25, 1928: 26.

47 "St. Roch and Magog meet here this evening," *Sherbrooke Daily Record*, July 11, 1928: 7.

48 "Le Club Bedford Aspire au Titre de Champions," *La Presse*, April 24, 1930: 27.

49 "Babe Hobson pour Farnham," *La Tribune*, April 28, 1930: 6.

50 "Le Farnham se Signale," *Le Canada*, October 3, 1930: 3.

51 "En Peu de Mots," *Le Soleil*, August 9, 1930: 7.

52 "Joutes de la Ligue Québec-District Hier et Dimanche – Smith Reste avec le Canadien," *Le Soleil*, May 15, 1931: 21.

53 Merritt Clifton, "Quebec Loop Broke Color Line in 1935," *Baseball Research Journal*, 1984.

54 "Lachute Inaugure le Système d'Éclairage de Son Stadium," *Le Canada*, July 7, 1951: 8.

55 We often find the French translation of "Negro," which sits somewhere in between Negro and the N-word in terms of connotation.

56 "Derby Line Vt Can. Celanese," *Le Soleil*, June 12, 1931: 16.

57 "Pike-River," *Le Canada-Français*, August 31, 1933: 4.

58 "Brown Bombers et les Crawfords au Stade Dimanche," *Le Canada*, July 11, 1945: 8.

59 "Les Royaux: Québec à Nouveau Ce Soir et les 'Chappies' de Farnham Dimanche," *Le Nouvelliste*, June 2, 1951: 11.

60 "Chappie Johnson Décédé à 79 Ans," *Le Nouvelliste*, August 31, 1949: 9.

61 John Craig, *Chappie and Me* (New York: Dodd, Mead, 1979).

THE BROADVIEW BUFFALOES

By Daniel Wyatt and Andrew North

Broadview is a Saskatchewan town of fewer than 1,000 people, 90 miles east of Regina on the southern Canadian Pacific Railroad (CPR) line. It's a seemingly unlikely place to have hosted a powerhouse fully-integrated baseball team during the 1930s, but host such a team it did – the Broadview Buffaloes.

My father, Jack Wyatt, was born in Broadview, as was I. One of my father's acquaintances, a local resident named Chris Edwards, had played third base for the Buffaloes.[1] I was able to interview Edwards, along with a friend of his named Bus Conn,[2] who had been a teammate of his on the Buffaloes. Edwards was able to put me in touch with an elderly Regina woman named Edie Maynard,[3] who, along with her husband, Frank, had operated a Broadview hotel on the CPR line, and had helped to bankroll the team during the 1930s. Mrs. Maynard had acted as the team's treasurer, and still possessed the books from her ownership tenure. One interesting expense item therein was a $1,000 bond that the team had to pay at the international border each year to allow the Black players entry into Canada; the payment was then refundable upon the return of the same players at season's end. What was unusual about this arrangement was the number of players being imported en masse to represent a single team. Prior to 1930, there had been many documented cases of imported African American ringers coming to Canada from the US to play, but these were individuals for the most part. Usually, they were pitchers only, as in the case of the legendary lefty John Donaldson, who had thrown for semipro teams in the Saskatchewan centers of Moose Jaw and Radville in 1925.[4] A single Black pitcher helping an otherwise White team was a common arrangement.

The Buffaloes were a semipro squad. It was typically the Black imports who were paid, while most of the local amateurs (who were still good ballplayers in their own right) were not. The Western Canada baseball landscape was a competitive one in that era. Every town and city wanted to win, and side bets were very common. Senior baseball in Broadview dates from 1934 and 1935, when the town fielded an all-White team called the Red Sox. Independent of any league, they played the lucrative tournament circuit (or as lucrative as prairie baseball during the Great Depression could be). By 1936, still as independents, they took aboard a 21-year-old right-handed pitcher, Gene Bremer,[5] and his catcher, Lionel Decuir. The two Negro League players, and their Shreveport

Acme Giants teammates, had visited Winnipeg in 1935 for an exhibition series against future Hall of Fame pitching great Satchel Paige and his Bismarck Corwin-Churchills, an integrated team from across the border in Bismarck, North Dakota. (The Bismarck team captured the inaugural National Baseball Congress semipro title later that year.)[6]

Between 1936 and 1938, the Broadview roster featured Bremer, Decuir (who later moved to the Kansas City Monarchs), and others from the Negro Leagues, including pitchers Jimmy Miller and George Alexander, power-hitting Sonny Harris, and the versatile Red Boguille. (According to Edie Maynard's records, Bremer was paid $45 a month plus housing expenses his first year in Broadview.) The team's White locals, in addition to Edwards and Conn, included Roy Schappert, Kitchie Bates, Harold Horeak, Mack Sinclair, and Dick Webb. All were decent ballplayers, and well-known in the area.

The Red Sox won three major tournaments in 1936 with their beefed-up lineup. On June 11 they took the Broadview Annual Sports Day Tournament, beating the Moose Jaw Athletics, 5-0.[7] On July 1 they won the Moosomin Dominion Day Tournament by defeating Virden, Manitoba, 9-3. (In the semifinal, the Red Sox had defeated Regina Nationals ace Myron Appell, a fireballer who was one of the province's top pitchers.[8] A month earlier, Appell, from Nebraska, had dominated the visiting Houston Black Buffaloes, striking out 14 in seven innings. The loss was the touring Black Buffaloes' first in 27 games. They fared no better against Appell later in the month, victims of a no-hitter.)[9] And on July 22, Broadview took the four-team Yorkton tournament, beating the host team 8-4 behind Jimmy Miller, after Bremer had pitched Broadview to an 8-2 victory over the Northgate (North Dakota) Yankees in the earlier game.[10] Finally, on July 31, the Red Sox, with Miller again on the mound, made a real name for themselves by downing the famous

House of David, the bearded White barnstormers from Benton Harbor, Michigan, in an exhibition game at Indian Head by a score of 8-5.[11]

In 1937 the Red Sox changed their name to the Buffaloes and joined the elite Saskatchewan Southern League, with the Weyburn Beavers, Notre Dame Hounds, and Moose Jaw Athletics as competition. Weyburn's catcher was 19-year-old Elmer Lach, the future hockey Hall of Famer, and the Moose Jaw team featured brothers Doug and Reg Bentley, also of National Hockey League fame.[12] The Notre Dame team was a group of students from the religious and educational institution located in Wilcox, Saskatchewan, some 30 miles south of Regina.[13] The league's deliberately light schedule allowed plenty of time for exhibition and tournament play.

The Broadview crew, preseason favorites based on their high-powered attack, did not disappoint, winning the pennant easily with an 8-1 record, their only loss early in the season to the young students of Notre Dame. As well, they captured four tournament titles, in Grenfell, La Fleche, Lemberg, and Regina,[14] the last featuring a 17-1 whipping of the local Regina Pilsners. In this prestigious Regina Exhibition Tournament, a six-day affair, shortstop Horeak and catcher Decuir led the Broadview attack, while Winnipeg natives Buck Eaton and John Isaacson handled the bulk of the pitching duties.[15] In another tournament nine days earlier, Broadview had split the prize money with the Northgate Yankees after the two teams had battled to a 7-7 tie in Broadview in a game called because of darkness.

The league opted to skip in-house playoffs after the season, electing instead to compete in the provincials with the northern teams. Broadview, however, was denied any postseason competition when an allegation was made that one of its players had played professionally the year before. This was ironic, in light of the fact that there were professional ringers all over the prairies in any given year. Investigation into a further allegation

The Broadview Buffaloes in front of the Broadview, Saskatchewan, CPR Station, 1937. Back row: Buck Eaton, John Isaacson, Chris Edwards, Dick Webb, Gene Bremer, Mack Sinclair. Front row: Lionel Decuir, Red Boguille, Roy Schappert, Kitchie Bates, Ronnie Bates (manager). (Thora Anderson, Broadview)

revealed that the Buffaloes had also been playing against touring American teams without the proper SABA (Saskatchewan Amateur Baseball Association) permits.[16]

The Saskatchewan Southern League opened its 1938 season with only a single change of membership from the previous season, the Regina Senators replacing the Moose Jaw franchise, which did not reapply for entry. The Senators joined the Weyburn Beavers and Notre Dame Hounds in attempting to dethrone the defending champion and preseason favorite Buffaloes. Hard-hitting Broadview infielder Harold Horeak had moved to the Regina team, while Weyburn still featured 20-year-old Elmer Lach, then primarily an outfielder.[17] The schedule had been expanded somewhat from 1937's deliberately short one, but still featured gaps to accommodate the popular tournament play. When league play finished on July 31, the Buffaloes had won another pennant,

finishing 16-5, their closest pursuers the Regina Senators at 9-9.[18]

By this time, the team was making a name outside Saskatchewan. A July 13, 1938, *Winnipeg Free Press* article reported, "A baseball classic of note is scheduled for Moosomin ball park … when the cream of western senior ball teams meet in the $300 tournament. … Broadview Buffaloes, with colored players from the Southern States, are a mighty machine that is tops in the Saskatchewan Senior League right now."[19] The Buffaloes didn't win that tournament, finishing third, but they did win a number of other tournaments and important exhibition games. In the annual Grenfell Tournament in May, the Buffaloes won a semifinal marathon in 14 innings behind eight shutout innings of relief from hurler Ramie (first name unknown). Lionel Decuir's home run in the seventh inning tied the game, and his second won it in the 14th. The team missed out on the tourney's top money, however, falling in the final to the Dunseith (North Dakota) Acme Giants before a crowd of more than 4,000. They rebounded days later with a 2-1 exhibition victory over the strong Northgate Yankees, first baseman Sonny Harris's final-inning round-tripper providing the winning margin.[20]

A season's highlight was another victory in the annual Broadview Sports Day Tournament on June 16, as they thumped the Northgate Yankees 12-4 in the final behind Red Boguille's eight-hitter. Second baseman Sonny Harris had a double and a triple and scored three runs, while third baseman Don Sherran chipped in a triple and two singles. Broadview had blanked Liberty, 5-0, in the semifinal behind George Alexander's four-hitter. Eight days later, they won a 16-team tournament in Watson, Saskatchewan, by defeating the hometown team 2-0. They next claimed first-place money at the Dominion Day tournament in nearby Norquay. That summer, the Buffaloes beat the powerful Grover Cleveland Alexander House of David team twice, as well as the minor-league San Antonio Missions, also twice, and the colored House of David squad.[21]

The Buffaloes' superiority over the rest of the league's teams, however, proved to be the Southern League's undoing. Before the July 31 end of the regular season, fans had become accustomed to seeing them win, and attendance was falling accordingly. By late July, teams stopped playing their scheduled games, failing to meet their commitments to the league. The lost gate revenue had its expected effect on each team's finances. An assessment of the league's 1938 season suggests that while the league's caliber of play was high, in fact as high as that of any other league in the province, the member teams seemed more interested in their individual agendas than in a commitment to the overall welfare of the circuit.[22]

With the bitter taste of the previous year's postseason still lingering, and expecting similar treatment at the hands of the SABA authorities,

Broadview decided to bow out of the 1938 playoff picture and continue on the tournament and exhibition trail into August, before calling it a season. After three impressive years, two of those in the Southern League, the Broadview Buffaloes disbanded. Their run was over.

Several of the White players left to join other prairie teams. Most of the Blacks returned to the Negro Leagues. Lionel Decuir caught for the Kansas City Monarchs[23] in 1939 and '40, where he had Satchel Paige for a teammate. In 1942 Sonny Harris found his way to the Cincinnati Buckeyes, who moved in midseason to Cleveland. His teammate there, Gene Bremer, was the most successful of the Buffaloes imports. Born in 1915 in New Orleans, Bremer was not a big man at 5-feet-8 and 160 pounds,[24] but he could throw hard, using no windup and featuring a fastball that may have hit the low 90s. He was an excellent hitter as well: According to Baseball-Reference, his career OPS+ of 112 is the highest of any post-1900 pitcher (for at least 75% of their game appearances) with at least 100 plate appearances.

But tragedy struck Bremer, when he suffered a fractured skull in a car accident in late 1942 that killed two of his Cleveland Buckeyes teammates.[25] Taking a year off from baseball in 1943 to recover, Bremer came back and still pitched well. He was a four-time Negro League All-Star,[26] appearing in the years 1940, 1942, 1944, and 1945 in the East-West All-Star Game, the Black equivalent to the White major leagues' All-Star Game. These games were held in Chicago, before crowds as large as 50,000. Bremer was talented enough to play with and against such megastars in these games as Satchel Paige, Jackie Robinson, Josh Gibson, Roy Campanella, Buck Leonard, Cool Papa Bell, Sam Jethroe, Ray Dandridge, and Double Duty Radcliffe. With the Buffaloes, he had already been part of what may have been the first fully-integrated team in Canada in the mid-1930s; he seemed poised to repeat his feat nearly a decade later, when a war-time rumor had Bremer and two teammates, third baseman Parnell Woods and outfielder Sam Jethroe, about to receive tryouts with the American League's Cleveland Indians. But the traffic accident then killed the tryouts, in addition to his two teammates.[27] Had Bremer been signed by the Indians, he might have been a two-time trailblazer, once on each side of the border. Bremer retired as a Buckeye in 1948, and died in 1971 at the age of 54, still a Cleveland resident.[28]

The Broadview Buffaloes had a short but successful existence, dominating their competition in the southern prairies between 1936 and 1938. Their legacy is that they were one of the first fully integrated baseball teams in Canada, if not the first. The composition of their roster was not only rare for its time, but a harbinger of things to come in its similarity to the makeup of major-league rosters of 25 to 30 years later.

SOURCES

My father, Jack Wyatt, and local Broadview residents Chris Edwards, Edie Maynard, Bus Conn, and others were very accommodating to interview requests. A useful biographical reference was Barry Swanton and Jay-Dell Mah's book *Black Baseball Players in Canada*. And of immeasurable help was Mah's outstanding website www.attheplate.com, dedicated primarily to baseball in the Western provinces. Many of his accounts are from local newspaper archives. The site is a treasure trove of information and is recommended unreservedly. – D.W.

NOTES

1   Daniel Wyatt interview with Jack Wyatt, Regina, Saskatchewan, September 1975.

2   Daniel Wyatt interview with Chris Edwards and Bus Conn, Broadview, Saskatchewan, September 1975.

3   Daniel Wyatt interview with Edie Maynard, Regina, Saskatchewan, September 1975.

4   Barry Swanton and Jay-Dell Mah, *Black Baseball Players in Canada* (Jefferson, North Carolina: McFarland, 2009), 59.

5   Different sources suggest different spellings of Bremer's surname. The Seamheads Negro Leagues data base uses Bremer. Swanton and Mah use Bremmer.

6   Swanton and Mah, 32.

7   Jay-Dell Mah, "Western Canada Baseball" website: http://www.attheplate.com/wcbl/1936_1k.html.

8   Jay-Dell Mah, http://www.attheplate.com/wcbl/1936_1k.html.

9   Jay-Dell Mah, http://www.attheplate.com/wcbl/1936_50i.html.

10   Jay-Dell Mah, http://www.attheplate.com/wcbl/1936_1k.html.

11   Jay-Dell Mah, http://www.attheplate.com/wcbl/1936_50i.html.

12   Jay-Dell Mah, http://www.attheplate.com/wcbl/1937_1j.html.

13   Jay-Dell Mah, http://www.attheplate.com/wcbl/1937_50i.html.

14   Jay-Dell Mah, http://www.attheplate.com/wcbl/1937_1k.html.

15   Jay-Dell Mah, http://www.attheplate.com/wcbl/1937_1k.html.

16   Jay-Dell Mah, http://www.attheplate.com/wcbl/1937_50i.html.

17   Jay-Dell Mah, http://www.attheplate.com/wcbl/1938_1j.html.

18   Jay-Dell Mah, http://www.attheplate.com/wcbl/1938_1.html.

19   *Winnipeg Free Press*, July 13, 1938: 15. Accessed July 9, 2021 via https://archives.winnipegfreepress.com/winnipeg-free-press/1938-07-13/page-15/.

20   Jay-Dell Mah, http://www.attheplate.com/wcbl/1938v1k.html.

21   Jay-Dell Mah, http://www.attheplate.com/wcbl/1938_1k.html.

22   Jay-Dell Mah, http://www.attheplate.com/wcbl/1938_50i.html.

23   Swanton and Mah, 58.

24   Swanton and Mah, 32.

25   Swanton and Mah, 32.

26   Swanton and Mah, 32.

27   Swanton and Mah, 32.

28   Swanton and Mah, 32.

A SECOND STRIKE:
BASEBALL AND THE CANADIAN ARMED FORCES DURING WORLD WAR II

by Stephen Dame

Ed Smith was twice a hero during Canada's Second World War. Smith, working at the Canadian Military Headquarters in London, never saw combat action. But on separate occasions, with his squad down to its last breath, he pulled off the improbable and delivered for Canada what seemed impossible victories.

During the final game of a three-game baseball series between Canadian and American military all-stars in 1942, the Canadian home side fell behind by six runs in the seven-inning affair. The Memorial Sports Ground in Red Hill was ringed by curious and supportive locals. They cheered as the Canadians rallied to tie the game, 9-9, in the sixth inning. In the bottom half of the final frame, the score remained tied. The Canadians managed to load the bases with two outs. Anything less than a hit would mean that the game, and the series, would end in an unsatisfying tie. Such a result would please neither King nor Country. Ed Smith, who was also pitching a gem that day, crushed a ball into the gap, clearing the bases. The Canadians won the game, 12-9. The *Surrey Mirror and County Post*, perhaps unfamiliar with the finer points of dramatic baseball writing, noted that "through skillful hitting and pitching, Sgt. Eddie Smith brought the Canadian score to

twelve after the Americans were put out without adding to their total."[1] Smith picked up the win, the walk-off, and the series for his country.

Before shipping out, Smith was a renowned two-way player in Kingston, Ontario. Both he and his father had been standouts for the Kingston Ponies amateur team. He excelled also at football and hockey, and even boxed a little. Smith began his enlisted baseball career by playing games on Cockspur Street in front of the Canadian Military Headquarters in London. That career would reach its pinnacle before tens of thousands at Wembley Stadium. Smith played for nearly every Canadian all-star team assembled during the war.[2]

Three days before D-Day, Canadian and American soldiers gathered for a game at Wembley. Some 18,000 paying spectators watched the Canadian Military Headquarters take on the United States Central Base Section Salons. The US team took a 1-0 lead into the bottom of the final inning. With two outs and the bases loaded, it was again Ed Smith who found himself at the front. This time, Smith fell behind early, taking two strikes from the American pitcher. Smith was known for his power hitting in Kingston, where in his youth he'd served as the Ponies' batboy.

During overseas baseball, Smith had also been recognized as a powerful righty on the mound. In this moment, his bat was all that mattered. Smith carefully watched two close pitches sail by. He judged each correctly with his experienced eyes. The count now stood at 2-and-2. A crowd of that size, witnessing this particular sort of baseball drama, must have been thunderous. British fans, having become better acquainted with the game over the past four years, were experiencing the uniquely intense, cinematic, and anticipatory moments that baseball produces best. Perhaps some bit their nails. Others may have held their breath. Ed Smith choked up, dug in and swung his bat. The Canadian sergeant hit a walk-off grand slam to claim the match for Canada by a score of 4-1. The ball was parked in the left-field bleachers, one of the most dramatic game-winning hits of the entire war.[3]

By the time Ed Smith and his fellow Canadians arrived overseas to contest a second world war, baseball's relationship with the average fighting-age Canadian was significantly different from that of the previous hostilities. Hockey promoters, having pioneered Saturday night broadcasts, relayed by echoing radio affiliates across the country, had successfully turned their game into appointment listening. That broadcast exposure, placing a "Hockey Night" on every calendar in the country, coincided with the increased construction of indoor rinks in cities and small towns in every province and territory. As a result, the interwar years saw hockey usurp baseball to become and remain Canada's national game. Canadians still played baseball as a recreation, but that too was facing new competition. Softball, having gained popularity in North America shortly after the end of the First World War, was viewed as a more accessible and leisurely sport.

Regardless of the type of ball, or its place in the recreational pecking order, baseball still had a place in the hearts of Canadian men and boys. Accordingly, members of the Canadian military brass understood the value of the game, both as a training tool and as a way to occupy the time of idle troops awaiting battle. The first organized Canadian baseball games, after the declaration of war in September of 1939, took place in Sturgeon County, Alberta; Val Cartier, Quebec; Gagetown, New Brunswick; and the other permanent homes of the Canadian Army. On the first Dominion Day of the war, Camp Borden, west of Barrie, Ontario, held a sporting carnival which featured a tug-of-war and baseball game as the main events. These home-front baseball games often pitted the enlisted men against their superior officers. A record of the Camp Borden game does not include a final score, but concludes that the infantrymen demonstrated "a lack of training"[4] both as soldiers and ballplayers.

The first Canadian soldiers arrived "over there" by way of Greenock, Scotland, on December 25, 1939. The early "Phony War" months of the conflict created similar conditions to those that allowed military baseball to flourish during the First World War. A sedentary army needed to do something to pass the time, stay in shape, and maintain its esprit de corps. John Maker, of the Laurier Centre for Military, Strategic and Disarmament Studies, wrote that "because soldiers were forced to 'hurry up and wait,' many for 42 months or more … sports served as an essential tonic to the soldiers who were eagerly awaiting action."[5] Baseball and other games mitigated discipline and morale problems. Lieutenant Erik Peterson stated that "softball was a lifesaver for our troops in England."[6]

The Canadians arriving in Britain during the winter of 1939-40 had an older generation of Britons recalling their sporting escapades from the previous war. It was assumed that Canadian military baseball would again be played. The *Daily Mirror* noted that qualified opponents would be needed, and so "men of the RAF … are to spend their winter evenings studying the rules and tactics of baseball which will be played behind the lines in the spring."[7] British newspapers also reacted with great excitement (and some sarcasm) to the introduction by Canadian troops of a new athletic pursuit. Under the headline "The Canadians Give Us a Brand New Game," *The Illustrated Sporting and Dramatic News* provided detailed instructions on how to play softball, "first cousin to baseball," and pointed out that both soldiers and schoolboys would find the game enjoyable. Softball was presented as a lighter, less serious version of baseball, wherein the pitcher was encouraged to "adopt any attitude he pleases in an attempt to bamboozle the batsman."[8]

As training continued and fighting remained elusive, Canadian soldiers stationed at Aldershot took to holding public exhibitions and clinics for softball-curious locals. "Crowd See Softball for First Time in Their Lives," exclaimed the *Worthing Gazette*. "They came, they saw, they listened, and at the end of the hour and ten minutes, the Canadians were hoping they were beginning to understand the game. The rules are really not so complicated as the Canadians imagine, but to the majority gathered at the Farm Recreation Ground on Saturday, softball needed some explaining."[9]

More than 330,000 Canadian troops passed through Aldershot for training before being deployed across the United Kingdom. From the autumn of 1941 until early 1944 the defense of the UK, and particularly the Sussex coast, was in the hands of the 1st Canadian Army. This was the largest force of British Commonwealth troops ever to be quartered in the UK at one time.[10] Playing baseball, and reeducating the locals on the finer points of the game, was not an uncommon duty for Canadian soldiers. On August 23, 1940, two teams of Canadian soldiers, one representing Montréal and the other Hamilton, played a game at the East Surrey Sports Ground in order to raise money for the building of Spitfire airplanes. The *Mirror and County Post* wrote that "before the game commenced the rules were explained. During its progress spectators found Canadian

soldiers ready with further explanations and descriptions of how in Canada, crowds of 75,000 shower 'pop' bottles on the pitch when disgusted with the umpire."[11] The team of soldiers from Montréal defeated their Hamiltonian rivals by a score of 18-16. The reporter also noted that one of the Canadians "displayed a real baseball cap" and that the crowd found its greatest amusement when the umpire "received a blow on the shin and hopped laboriously, rubbing it for all he was worth."[12]

Two months later in Tadworth, England, a team of Canadian Highlanders played against a team of British Home Guards in a baseball match whose proceeds were donated to the war effort. The *Illustrated Sporting and Dramatic News* provided images of the Highlanders "coaching" their opponents and educating curious locals before the game.[13] Dick Fowler, the Toronto-born Philadelphia Athletics pitcher who would return from service and throw a no-hitter against the St. Louis Browns, was serving with these same Highlanders.[14] Fowler was not present, however, serving entirely in Canada because of chronic sinus issues.

During their down time, Canadian soldiers were permitted to join existing British baseball teams near their various barracks.[15] The DeHavilland Comets, the Standard Telephone and Cable squad, and the Ford Motor Company team all employed the services of one talented amateur ringer named Pete Giovanella from Kirkland Lake, Ontario. The Comets even featured Philadelphia Athletics star Phil Marchildon for a few games. After joining the Royal Canadian Air Force, Marchildon surprised unsuspecting opponents with major-league fastballs before they "could even get the bats off their shoulders."[16] Marchildon was joined in the RCAF by Joe Krakauskas of the Washington Senators and Cleveland Indians, while the Boston Braves' Roland Gladu joined the Canadian army. It appears that both Krakauskas and Gladu played only recreationally. A separate

Midlands Baseball League, an existing federation of British ballclubs representing manufacturing plants, invited visiting armies to field their own sides. The league featured a Canadian Army nine and saw United States military teams join later in the war.[17] The Canadian Army team went all the way to the Midlands World Series before losing the final, 13-0, to a team representing the US Army 10th Replacement Depot.[18]

Back home, as Canadians became accustomed to rations and recruiting posters, a ballpark became home to an entire exiled air force. Maple Leaf Stadium had been built in 1926 along Lake Shore Boulevard in Toronto in order to serve as a mainland home for the previously island-dwelling Toronto Maple Leafs. The ballpark eventually hosted an assortment of wartime fundraising events, from film screenings, to "follies" shows to boxing matches and ballgames.

The center-field wall at Maple Leaf Stadium was separated from Lake Ontario by only about 230 meters of open, undeveloped grassland. The airstrips of the Toronto Flying Club stood another 130 meters across a narrow channel of water on Toronto Island. That open space between the ballpark and the airfield would prove invaluable to a small Scandinavian nation that was about to encounter the blitzkrieg.

After the fall of Norway to the Nazis in June of 1940, General Otto Ruge of the Norwegian Army Air Force ordered the evacuation of as many air force personnel as possible. Ideally, they were to take as many aircraft and materiel as they could to a European location. With the fall of France and Nazi occupation of Norway, this became impossible. No aircraft were smuggled out, but 120 members of the air force escaped to Britain and awaited further instruction. Negotiations between the governments of Canada and Norway concluded on September 7, 1940. The 120 officers and men came to Toronto, made use of the Toronto Flying Club on Toronto Island, and were housed in the open field beyond the center-field wall of Maple

Leaf Stadium. Eventually, 17 buildings were constructed around, and in some cases touching, the outfield walls of the ballpark. The Toronto Flying Club turned over its airport and training aircraft to the Norwegians. The Norwegian airmen lived in the shadow of the ballpark in an area that is still known as "Little Norway."

While stationed near the outfield fence, the Norwegian Army Air Force concocted a plan to acquire aircraft. Norway had purchased combat planes from the United States before the war. The planes had not yet been delivered. Technically, those planes now belonged to the occupying German forces. Yet, the neutral United States covertly sent $20 million worth of those airplanes to the airport next to Maple Leaf Stadium. The planes consisted of Fairchild PT-19 elementary trainers, Curtiss fighters, Douglas attack bombers, and Northrop patrol seaplanes. The Norwegians then launched a "Wings for Norway" fundraising campaign, which included events at Maple Leafs games designed to draw donations from baseball fans. The campaign raised over $400,000.[19]

Eventually, the airmen of Maple Leaf Stadium flew to Iceland, where they patrolled the North Atlantic for the remainder of the war. These same Norwegian fliers then escorted and assisted Canadian troops during the Dieppe raid, the Normandy landings, and the liberation of Holland.[20]

In the European Theater, the Canadian missionaries continued their campaign of baseball reeducation. On May 28, 1941, General Andrew McNaughton, commander-in-chief of the Canadian overseas forces, explained the game of baseball to Princess Mary, the sister of King George VI, and assembled British soldiers during an intrasquad game played between members of the Royal Canadian Corps of Signals at a military hospital near London.[21] Canadian troops "learning of the mediocre success which attended the introduction of baseball into this country, were hopeful that their exhibition games would help to further popularize it."[22] At the Braunton Road Grounds, the game was described as "a development of rounders, with which we were familiar in our youthful days, but it has evolved into a vehicle for the display of astonishing skill of which accurate catching and fielding are prominent features."[23] In August, near Burgess Hill, the Queen's Own Rifles made use of a public address system while they played a game against the 12th Field Regiment. A Major Sutherland served as play-by-play man to "explain the game to spectators and give running commentary of the play."[24]

In between adventures both playing and teaching baseball, soldiers were of course trained in Britain as they awaited deployment to Nazi-occupied Europe. The Canadian government encouraged sport as a way to toughen men for their coming crucible. "Senior officers plan to get them into shape for expected combat in the spring and aren't wasting any time," wrote the *Globe and Mail*. "They're being hardened up physically by calisthenics and baseball."[25] The game continued to be a preferred pastime for soldiers as well as a valuable method of maintaining corps readiness for commanders. "There is a strong and reciprocal historical relationship between sports and the military," wrote John Maker. He explained that softball was among the sports that also helped bridge the cultural divide within the Canadian forces:

> *"In Canada at the beginning of the Second World War, sports positively reflected the nation's cultural desires and pastimes. These patterns were reflected in the army overseas. In the army, some sports were differentiated according to English and French-Canadian cultural preferences … however, troops representing both language groups professed a keen interest in hockey, softball and skating. These sports occupied a space of cultural consensus between English- and French-speaking Canadians overseas and differentiated them both from the British."[26]*

The temporary Canadian annexation of the hallowed grass inside Lord's Cricket Ground literally had headlines screaming. "Egad! Most Extraordinary! What! BASEBALL at Lord's?"[27] bellowed the Associated Press on May 10, 1941. Canadian newspapermen (some of whom had watched soldiers play baseball at Lord's multiple times during the First World War) defeated their still neutral American counterparts using "the sacred sod for a baseball game."[28]

Of course, the United States did not remain neutral for long. With the arrival of American soldiers in Britain in 1942, the number and quality of baseball games being played increased rapidly. The London International Baseball League was created as a recreational league for Canadian and American troops stationed around the British capital. The league provided a way to organize and structure the thousands of soldiers playing informal forms of baseball across Britain. It also provided relief from the inaction and tedium that affected many men as they impatiently awaited the invasion of Europe.

The London International Baseball League consisted of eight military teams, two of which were Canadian. The league staged its championship games at the legendary Stamford Bridge Stadium, home to the Chelsea Football Club. The most competitive teams in the league were the US 660th Engineers, the US 827th Signal Battalion Monarchs, the 1st Canadian General Hospital, and the team representing the Canadian Military Headquarters. The 1st CGH team featured Leo Curtis of Orange, Massachusetts. Curtis, an accomplished semipro pitcher, joined the Canadian Forces at the outbreak of the war and played for 1st CGH during his entire stint in the army.[29] Curtis led his hospital team into the LIBL championship on June 25 and 28, 1943. The Canadian team was swept two games to none by the Signal Monarchs.

With so many North American baseball players in action, a series of international friendlies

The Canadian Military Headquarters team defeated their American opponents before a huge crowd at Wembley Stadium on June 3, 1944. The hero of the day, Ed Smith, is back row, third from the right. (Library and Archives Canada)

was scheduled between Canadian and American baseball teams. Three games in particular were promoted and covered as all-star, all-soldier affairs. These games pitted the best enlisted baseball players against each other in a best-of-three series. Game one was held on July 4, 1942, before 6,000 fans at Selhurst Park in London, home to the Crystal Palace Football Club. The United States Army Air Force all-stars triumphed over the Canadian Army all-stars in a "home run fest,"[30] 19-17. The second game of the series took place on August 3 at Wembley Stadium and featured another crowd of around 6,000 spectators. The Canadian Army Headquarters team defeated the American Army Headquarters squad, 5-3. Lady Clementine Churchill, wife of the British prime minister, was in attendance and met with both teams during a pregame ceremony. The game raised nearly $4,000 for the British Red

Cross. The rubber match for the North American neighbors would take place on August 22 at the Memorial Sports Ground in Red Hill. After falling behind early, the Canadians roared back and won the game and the series on the first of Ed Smith's heroic walk-offs described above.

At least 11 other Canada vs USA all-star baseball games were staged, usually for the purposes of raising charitable or war funds. Though they didn't always garner the attention of the three-game series in 1942, the games continued to be a significant draw across the UK. In the early summer of 1943, the Royal Canadian Air Force was defeated by the United States Army Air Force, 7-2, in Sutton, Surrey. Some 5,000 fans were in attendance.[31] On June 6, 1943, at Hounslow Cricket Ground near London, a "Return Challenge Match" was promoted to assist the British Red Cross and the St. John

Prisoners of War Fund.[32] No score is known. On August 7, 1943, a softball game between the US and Canadian armies served as the preliminary attraction at Wembley Stadium before an advertised "all professional" baseball game between the US Air and Ground Forces. A total of 21,500 paying customers saw both games and supported the Red Cross. It was the largest crowd to see baseball in Britain since the First World War.[33] The Canadian softball team featured Ed Smith of Kingston, Don Price and Pete Giovanella of Kirkland Lake, Al Fleming of Halifax, and transplanted Canadian Leo Curtis of Orange, Massachusetts. The US "pro" baseball teams featured Joe Rundus, formerly of the Brooklyn Dodgers organization, New York Giants farmhand Pete Pavich, Paul Campbell of the Boston Red Sox, Louis Thuman of the Washington Senators, Ralph Ifft of the New York Yankees system, Stan Stuka of the Boston Braves and Philadelphia Phillies organizations, Richard Catalano of the St. Louis Cardinals system, and coach Monte Weaver, a former Washington Senators pitcher.

June 3, 1944, featured the most dramatic Canada vs. USA baseball game, when Ed Smith hit his walk-off grand slam at Wembley Stadium. Smith remained in the Canadian Army after the war and eventually retired to Florida.[34] A few days after the Wembley game, mere hours before the D-Day landings of Operation Overlord, another international friendly was organized south of London in Sevenoaks. The *Chronicle* noted:

> "*A surprise tea, organized by Dr. and Mrs. Spon, was held at the Post Office on Wednesday. Following this, the address by Col. Ponsonby attracted a large crowd to the Green, where they later saw a baseball match between Canadian and American teams. The Canadians won by 5 runs to 2. Capt. Harrington, U.S. Army, provided a running commentary.*"[35]

As the war continued, so too did the great game. Baseball games were staged in Shoreham, England, while Canadian troops prepared for their ill-fated raid on Dieppe. On October 16, 1943, the Cameron Highlanders of Ottawa were observed playing baseball outside Hursley Camp. They were defeated by a team of soldiers from Toronto by a score of 13-3.[36] The Torontonians were observed by members of the Queen's Own Rifles and may have been Conn Smythe's 30th Battery. Smythe, the hockey impresario who had served with the Canadian Army during the First World War, recruited his own group of sportsmen-soldiers while training officers in Toronto. Toronto Argonauts football stars Ted Reeve and Shanty McKenzie joined up to fight and play with Major Smythe. Eventually, the men of the 30th Battery were incorporated into the 7th Toronto Regiment. They were first stationed in Victoria and then later shipped to the UK, where they spent months training and hosting softball games. Smythe's 30th Battery Bombers challenged locals to various sporting events, including baseball and softball, throughout their service in both Europe and the UK. In 1944 they were tasked with taking Caen, France, an action Smythe nearly missed due to a softball injury. In the days after the successful D-Day landings, Smythe organized a softball tournament in Caen. He played third base and claimed, in his autobiography, to have been visited by Winston Churchill after a game.[37]

Elsewhere in the European Theater, baseball found a way. Italy's national baseball program credits the introduction of the game there to the contests played between American and Canadian occupying armies.[38] When soldiers in Italy were moved out in order to join the First Canadian Army in the fight to liberate the Netherlands, they brought baseball along with them. The *Liverpool Daily Post* reported on April 2, 1945, that German resistance had cracked. There was "carnage on the roads as Germans race out of Holland."[39] A reporter embedded with the Canadian forces wrote that "German artillery fire has slackened considerably, and on the west bank of the Rhine, north of Cleve, Canadian soldiers are playing baseball where just days ago German shells were falling."[40] To celebrate the German defeat, the Regina Rifles played softball near Rotterdam against a team of female Canadian Armed Forces personnel calling themselves the "Eager Beavers."[41] After the conclusion of the European war, a Canadian Armed Forces Softball Championship was organized in Utrecht. Some of the same teams that competed in the Canadian Army Baseball League took part. On October 3, 1945, the Queen's Own Rifles defeated 2 Canadian General Reinforcement Unit 3-0 to take the championship.[42] The Canadian Army remained in Holland and Belgium after the war and played a great deal of softball. Gary Bedingfield's *Baseball in World War II Europe* provided details:

> *"On the continent, softball was the main game of Canadian servicemen. The Conn Smythe 30th Battery Bombers in Belgium set all kinds of records with 110 wins in 114 games. The 2nd Canadian Advanced Base Workshop team settled for a draw after 18 scoreless innings against an American service team in Antwerp. Baseball did also occur on the continent in the form of exhibition games. On September 6, 1945, the powerful U.S. Army 29th Infantry Division team defeated the 2nd Canadian Division All-Stars, 5-0, before a crowd of 8,000 at Soesterberg Airfield in Holland. But Canadian servicemen were not limited to bringing baseball to Europe. Wing Commander G.N. Parrish of Listowel, Ontario, introduced the game to India. 'I found a dozen Canadians on the squadron willing to play,' the Simcoe Reformer reported on June 15, 1944, 'and I persuaded even Australians and British crews' to play baseball."[43]*

The merciful end of the war did not mean the end of competitive baseball for Canadian soldiers in Britain. On June 26, 1945, the Canadian Army England Sports Committee of the Auxiliary Services, under the chairmanship of Brigadier J.E. Sager, announced an extensive summer of sports. "For five years we have been conditioning these men for war. Now we've got to condition them in how to live, how to relax and enjoy themselves," explained Sager. "All personnel of the Canadian Army are encouraged to compete."[44] The new Canadian league would feature 14 teams of soldiers, playing between 14 and 16 games each, in various locations around southeastern England during the summer of 1945. The season was kicked off with a special exhibition game played between the 1st Canadian Central Ordinance Depot and a visiting team from the United States Army Air Force. Some 1,500 Canadian and American soldiers watched the game on what was billed as "North American Day" at Peper Harrow in Surrey. The Americans won the game 2-0. On July 13 another visiting team of American airmen challenged the 1st Central Ordinance Depot. En route to their own 2-0 victory, the Canadians turned the only recorded wartime triple play. With the bases loaded in the fourth, American batter Bob Froelich hit a line drive to Canadian third baseman Johnny Sefton. Sefton caught the drive for the first out, stepped on the bag before the runner could scramble back for the second, and then threw to first baseman Tommy Marshall for the third.[45]

For the duration, baseball players were willingly exploited as fundraisers. Teams of soldiers played in aid of "Wings for Victory," a National Savings campaign designed to build warplanes. The campaign was staged in almost every city, town, and village, and baseball became an integral part of the proceedings.[46] Canadian soldiers played baseball in Storrington during March of 1942 in order to drive dollars "towards the aim of £120,000, the cost of a new corvette."[47] An

August 22, 1942, game between Canada and the USA in Surrey was a fundraiser for the "Tanks for Attack" fund.[48]

"Holidays at Home" was a series of fundraising and morale-boosting events staged by communities in Britain. A week of entertainment was held for civilians who due to the war and gasoline rationing were unable to travel or enjoy any kind of vacation.[49] Baseball games were almost always a part of these festivities. On May 22, 1943, a game was played at Giant Axe stadium, home to the Lancaster Football Club. It featured "teams representing the United States and Canada."[50] Local attendees were promised that a Lancaster bomber would also be on hand. Those interested could purchase stamps and then place them on a bomb that would be later dropped on Germany.[51] In 1943 alone, the fundraising efforts of Canadian and American ballplaying soldiers raised an estimated $344,000 (US). Adjusted for inflation, that's over $5.5 million in 2021 Canadian dollars.

The following year, service teams supported the "Salute the Soldier" campaign all over Britain. Canadian, American, and British airmen took part in a softball and baseball exhibition in Darlington on May 26, 1944. Monies raised went toward the Mayor of Darlington's War Fund.[52] When American and Canadian forces left Britain at the end of 1945, their baseball playing had contributed to wartime fundraising in a significant way.[53]

After the disaster at Dieppe, where 3,367 Canadians were killed, wounded, or taken prisoner, Canadian baseball found its way into prisoner-of-war camps. Interviewed from a German POW camp, Toronto soldier Carl Scott was happy to see the arrival of Canadian newspapers in the Young Men's Christian Association aid packages sent from home. Under the headline "He Wanted Baseball News," Scott was quoted politely dismissing the field reporter visiting the camp by saying, "Excuse me while I see how the Leafs are doing."[54] The *Belfast News-Letter* reported that the YMCA had started sending baseball equipment into the POW camps where the Dieppe raiders were being held. The equipment was coming "especially from Canada."[55]

R.P. Hall of the Royal Rifles was imprisoned in Stalag 9C. "He reported the Canadian prisoners there were all of good heart and were playing baseball."[56] Stalags (German slang for prison camps) were a common site for Canadian military baseball during the war. Captured soldiers often played the game under the supervision of their Nazi captors. Private Taylor wrote to his mother from Stalag 4B and told her of his participation in baseball games.[57] The distinction of being the best-known baseball-playing POW belongs to Phil Marchildon. After the conclusion of the 1942 major-league baseball season, Marchildon joined the RCAF and refused an opportunity to stay in Canada, saying he did not want special treatment. Marchildon was assigned to a seven-man Halifax bomber crew. On the crew's 26th mission, they were shot down over northern Germany on August 17, 1944. Marchildon was sent to Stalag Luft III, a prison camp for airmen:

> "Some of the better German Prisoner Of War camps were known to have had multiple leagues operating. In Stalag Luft III, during the peak summer of 1944, there were probably 200 baseball teams active. This is an astonishing number, especially considering that the 1943-44 off-season at Stalag Luft III had been considerably disrupted by the Great Escape."[58]

Marchildon did not speak often or reminisce about his time in a Nazi prison camp. While imprisoned, he was fed a diet of watered-down soup and bread mixed with sawdust. He was liberated by British soldiers on May 2, 1945.[59] He spent nine months in captivity and remains Canadian baseball's greatest war hero. He returned to the majors, but displayed the nightmares and physical ailments that we would today consider symptoms of post traumatic stress disorder.[60]

Between training, action, rest, and relaxation, some Canadians spent more than five years in the UK. Some married, many more had partners, and some 22,000 British children were born to Canadian fathers. As they lived their lives overseas, Canadian soldiers played ball at more than 60 known locations in Britain, from Greenock to Torquay and most bases, parks, and stadiums in between. On the European continent, as Canadian armies pushed forward through Italy and the Netherlands, baseball games were played. Records are scarce of baseball being played in India and Hong Kong, in Merchant Marine shipyards, or on the airfields of the British Commonwealth Air Training Plan. Yet given the overwhelming amount of baseball played by enlisted men in the better documented theaters of war, including in captivity, it is very likely that baseball was played everywhere the Canadians went during the Second World War. Upon returning to Canada, many soldiers spoke fondly of the baseball games they played, and of course, continued watching and playing the game back home.[61]

Nineteen Canadians associated with amateur or semiprofessional baseball lost their lives during the Second World War. They were Don Stewart, Liston Anderson, George Atkinson, Roger Carroll, George Dean, Thornton Doig, Robert Dubeau, Harold German, Herman Jonasson, Arthur Judges, Mike Moroz, Don Norton, Con Radocy, Stan Reid, Don Ross, Basil Smith, Albin Sumara, Charles Weatherby, and Mike Zima.[62]

ACKNOWLEDGMENTS

The author wishes to give special thanks and appreciation to Gary Bedingfield, William Humber, and Andrew North. Mr. Bedingfield's research into the story of Canadian baseball players in wartime, chronicled in his book *Baseball in World War Two Europe*, was an invaluable source for this project. The incredible and rare photographs he unearthed also helped illustrate a presentation of this paper for the Centre for Canadian Baseball Research. This project stands on the shoulders of Mr. Bedingfield's work. Mr. Humber, Canada's pioneering and foremost baseball historian, was incredibly generous with his time, resources, and advice. He personally made me feel welcome in the world of baseball historians and their research. Mr. North, founder of the Centre for Canadian Baseball Research and organizer of its annual history conference, gave me a platform to present my initial research and the confidence and encouragement necessary to continue forward. I am grateful to all three gentlemen.

John Thorn and Jim Leeke, who are two of the very best baseball historians and authors, were also available, supportive, and helpful to me during this project.

NOTES

1 "Canadians Rally to Win Rubber," *Surrey Mirror and County Post*, August 28, 1942: 2.

2 Gary Bedingfield, *Baseball In World War Two Europe* (Charleston, South Carolina: Arcadia Publishing, 1999), 89.

3 Bedingfield, 100.

4 "War Diaries 1940," The Queen's Own Rifles of Canada Regimental Museum and Archive, last modified February 5, 2021, https://qormuseum.org/history/timeline-1925-1949/the-second-world-war/war-diaries-1940/.

5 John Maker, "Sports and War – A Winning Combination," Laurier Centre for Military, Strategic and Disarmament Studies – Wilfrid Laurier University, last modified March 13, 2011, https://canadianmilitaryhistory.ca/sports-and-war-a-winning-combination-by-john-maker/.

6 Bedingfield, 5.

7 "Sports Notes," *Daily Mirror* (London), September 13, 1939: 8.

8 "The Canadians Give Us a Brand New Game," *Illustrated Sporting and Dramatic News* (London), April 12, 1940: 50.

9 "Crowd See Softball for First Time in Their Lives," *Worthing Gazette* (Worthing, Sussex, England), December 17, 1941: 22.

10 "History of Canadians Stationed in the U.K.," Canadian Roots U.K., last modified 2016, http://www.canadian-rootsuk.org/historycanadiansuk.html.

11 "Baseball Match Aids Fund," *Surrey Mirror and County Post* (Reigate, Surrey, England), August 23, 1940: 5.

12 "Baseball Match Aids Fund."

13 "A Baseball Match," *Illustrated Sporting and Dramatic News*, October 25, 1940: 23.

14 William Humber, *Diamonds of the North* (Toronto: Oxford University Press, 1995), 161.

15 Bedingfield, 87.

16 Bedingfield, 88.

17 Bedingfield, 44.

18 Bedingfield, 51.

19 Geoff Ward, "Little Norway," WWII Norge, last modified 2021, https://www.wwiinorge.com/notes/little-norway/.

20 Ward.

21 "Princess Royal Watches Canadian Troops Playing Baseball," *Globe and Mail* (Toronto), May 29, 1941: 13.

22 "New World Baseball in Manchester," *Manchester Evening News* (Manchester, United Kingdom), August 13, 1942: 5.

23 "Savings for Victory," *North Devon Journal* (Barnstable, North Devon, United Kingdom), May 20, 1943: 4.

24 "War Diaries 1941," The Queen's Own Rifles of Canada Regimental Museum and Archive, last modified February 5, 2021, https://qormuseum.org/history/timeline-1925-1949/the-second-world-war/war-diaries-1941/.

25 Ross Munro, "Sports Toughen Canadians for Expected Spring Battle," *Globe and Mail,* March 16, 1941: 22.

26 John Maker, "Sports and War – A Winning Combination," Laurier Centre for Military, Strategic and Disarmament Studies – Wilfrid Laurier University, last modified March 13, 2011, https://canadianmilitaryhistory.ca/sports-and-war-a-winning-combination-by-john-maker/.

27 Eddie Gilmore, "Egad! Most Extraordinary! What! BASEBALL at Lord's?" *Globe and Mail*, May 10, 1941: 16.

28 Gilmore.

29 Bedingfield, 87.

30 Bedingfield, 87.

31 "Sports Shorts From Britain," *Globe and Mail*, August 9, 1943: 16.

32 "Baseball," *Middlesex Chronicle* (Hounslow, London, England), May 22, 1943: 5.

33 Bedingfield, 74.

34 Bedingfield, 89.

35 "A Surprise Tea," *Sevenoaks Chronicle and Kentish Advertiser* (Sevenoaks, Kent, England), June 9, 1944: 9.

36 "War Diaries 1943," The Queen's Own Rifles of Canada Regimental Museum and Archive, last modified February 5, 2021, https://qormuseum.org/history/timeline-1925-1949/the-second-world-war/war-diaries-1943/.

37 Conn Smythe and Scott Young, *Conn Smythe: If You Can't Beat 'Em in the Alley* (Toronto: McClelland & Stewart, 1981).

38 "History of Baseball in Europe," Baseball-Reference.com, last modified September 16, 2014, https://www.baseball-reference.com/bullpen/History_of_baseball_in_Europe.

39 "German Resistance Cracks in the West," *Liverpool Daily Post*, April 2, 1945: 1.

40 "Baseball Now," *Liverpool Daily Post*, April 2, 1945: 1.

41 Humber, 10.

42 Gary Bedingfield, "Canuck Baseball," Baseball in Wartime, last modified April 26, 2008. http://www.baseballinwartime.com/canuck.htm.

43 Bedingfield, "Canuck Baseball."

44 Bedingfield, "Canuck Baseball."

45 Bedingfield, "Canuck Baseball."

46 Bedingfield, 101.

47 "Baseball Match," *Worthing Gazette*, March 11, 1942: 6.

48 "Tanks for Attack," *Surrey Mirror*, August 7, 1942: 2.

49 Bedingfield, 101.

50 "Tomorrow's Parade," *Lancaster Guardian* (Morecambe, Lancashire, England), May 21, 1943: 5.

51 "Tomorrow's Parade."

52 "Darlington Baseball," *Newcastle Journal* (Newcastle upon Tyne, Tyne and Wear, England), May 25, 1944: 3.

53 Bedingfield, 102.

54 Douglas Amaron, "Were Waiting for Us Say Wounded Canucks," *Globe and Mail*, August 22, 1942: 7.

55 "A Pep Talk," *Belfast News-Letter*, June 12, 1942: 3.

56 "Prisoners in Good Heart," *Globe and Mail*, November 29, 1943: 15.

57 "Baseball in Stalag," *Globe and Mail*, October 12, 1944: 4.

58 Daniel Gabriel, "Baseball Behind Barbed Wire," *Elysian Fields Quarterly*, last modified 2002, http://www.efqreview.com/NewFiles/v19n2/books-baseballbarbedwire.html.

59 Kevin Glew, "Remembering Phil Marchildon, Canadian Pitching Ace and War Hero," Canadian Baseball Network, last modified November 11, 2020, https://www.canadianbaseballnetwork.com/canadian-baseball-network-articles/remembering-phil-marchildon-canadian-pitching-ace-and-war-hero.

60 Glew.

61 Kelly Anne Griffin, "From Humble Beginnings to Making History in Montréal," The Discover Blog, last modified March 20, 2018, https://thediscoverblog.com/2018/03/20/from-humble-beginnings-to-making-history-in-Montréal/.

62 Gary Bedingfield, "Baseball's Greatest Sacrifice," Baseball in Wartime, last modified March, 2021, https://www.baseballsgreatestsacrifice.com/table_of_all_players.html.

CANADIAN TEAMS IN THE
PONY LEAGUE PIPELINE TO THE MAJORS

By Allen Tait

The Pennsylvania-Ontario-New York (PONY) League was a Class-D (entry-level) minor league that operated from 1939 through 1956 before becoming the New York-Pennsylvania League. (Ontario no longer hosted any franchises.) The successor league operated from 1957 through 2020, when Major League Baseball restructured the minor-league system. As an entry-level league, its role as a pipeline to the major leagues tends to be overlooked in comparison to the higher-level minor leagues. Several notable individuals began their baseball careers in the PONY League, including two members of the National Baseball Hall of Fame (Warren Spahn and Nellie Fox), an umpire (Larry Napp), several managers (Paul Owens, Danny Ozark, Buck Rodgers, and Jerry Coleman), two members of the original Montréal Expos (Roy Face and Maury Wills), as well as a number of other recognizable names.

This review of the history of the PONY League will focus on the contributions of the Canadian franchises based in Hamilton and London, Ontario. Hamilton, despite a few nickname changes, was an affiliate of the St. Louis Cardinals for the duration of its franchise. London was an affiliate of the Pittsburgh Pirates for its franchise tenure.

HAMILTON RED WINGS
(1939–1942)

The PONY League operated as a six-team league from 1939 through 1941 before expanding to eight teams in 1942. Hamilton made the play-offs with a 61-44 record in the league's inaugural season. George Dockins (15-5) led the team in wins and later had a two-year major-league career. Other players with major-league careers were pitcher George Dagenhard (two games), Don Hurst (seven seasons as an outfielder-first baseman), first baseman Buddy Gremp (113 games), and outfielder Nick Goulish (two seasons).

Hamilton defeated the unaffiliated Batavia Clippers in the opening round of the 1939 playoffs. Four Batavia players, including two Canadians, had subsequent major-league careers: outfielder Whitey Platt (five seasons), shortstop Eddie Turchin (11 games), and Canadian pitchers Dick Fowler (9-11, 4.39) and Frank Colman (8-7 3.18).

Fowler, inducted into the Canadian Baseball Hall of Fame in 1985, compiled a major-league record of 66-79 with a 4.11 ERA over 10 seasons. His lifetime record is somewhat deceiving, as he completed 44 percent of his career starts

(75 of 170) and compiled a 42-30 record from 1947 to 1949 for the Philadelphia Athletics. Playing for noncontending ballclubs combined with arm problems to contribute to his sub-.500 career statistics.

Colman, inducted into the Canadian Baseball Hall of Fame in 1999, later played six seasons as an outfielder-first baseman with the Pittsburgh Pirates and New York Yankees, compiling a lifetime batting average of .228.

Hamilton lost the 1939 finals four games to two to the Brooklyn Dodgers-affiliated Olean Oilers.[1] Olean pitchers Glen Moulder (three seasons) and Vince Shupe (one season), and shortstop Stan Rojek (eight seasons) later played in the majors. The Olean catcher also had a lengthy major-league career, but not as a player. Larry Napp hit .253 with Olean before joining the Batavia Clippers in 1940, batting .183 in his final PONY League season. Napp became an umpire in 1948, and joined the American League umpiring staff in 1951. He umpired until 1974 before becoming an American League supervisor of officials. Napp umpired in the World Series in 1954, 1956 (third base during Don Larsen's perfect game), 1963, and 1969. He also umpired in the All-Star Games in 1953, 1957, 1961, and 1968.[2]

In 1940 Hamilton made the playoffs despite a sub-.500 record and was eliminated in the first round of the playoffs by the Olean Oilers, still a Dodgers affiliate. Hamilton pitchers Mike Clark (two seasons) and Ken Holcombe (six seasons), and shortstop George Genovese (three games) had subsequent major-league careers. Olean second baseman Bill Burich (27 games) was the only Olean player to reach the majors.

In 1941 Hamilton again made the playoffs with a sub-.500 record, this time facing the Jamestown Falcons, a Detroit Tigers affiliate, in round one of the playoffs.[3] The Hamilton roster featured no future major-league players other than holdovers Clark and Genovese. Four Falcons reached

the majors: outfielder Earl Rapp (three seasons), second baseman Greg Mulleavy (79 games), shortstop John O'Neil (46 games), and third baseman Frank Carswell (16 games). Hamilton upset Jamestown three games to two in the series to advance to the finals,[4] where the team lost to the second-place Bradford Bees, a Boston Bees affiliate, four games to one.[5] Bradford pitcher Ben Cardoni (three seasons), third baseman Ducky Detweiler (13 games), and catcher Butch Sutcliffe (four games) had brief major-league careers.

In 1942 Hamilton posted its third consecutive sub-.500 season, this time failing to make the playoffs. Catcher Eddie Yount (six games) and outfielder Otis Davis (one game) later made brief major-league appearances.

Three players of note played for other teams during this era. Warren Spahn compiled a record of 5-4 with an ERA of 2.73 while starting nine games and relieving in three others for the Boston Bees-affiliated Bradford Bees in 1940. Spahn was in the majors by 1942 with the Boston Braves, was in military service from 1943 through 1945, and resumed his Hall of Fame career in 1946. Spahn compiled a record of 363-245 with a 3.09 ERA over his 21-year career.

Jerry Coleman hit .304 as a shortstop in 1942 with the Wellsville Yankees, a New York Yankees affiliate. Coleman had a nine-year career with New York (hitting .263 overall) in addition to serving his country in both World War II and the Korean War. Coleman's post-playing career was in broadcasting, primarily with the San Diego Padres, from 1972 through 1979 and from 1981 through 2013. Coleman managed the Padres in 1980.

Danny Ozark hit .247 as a second baseman in 1942 for the Dodgers affiliate Olean Oilers. Ozark did not make the major leagues as a player, but managed the Philadelphia Phillies from 1973 through 1979 and the San Francisco Giants in 1984. He had a lifetime winning percentage of .533, and his Phillies made three consecutive postseason appearances beginning in 1976. They lost the National League Championship Series each time, in three games to the 1976 Cincinnati Reds, and in four games in both 1977 and 1978 to the Los Angeles Dodgers.

LONDON PIRATES (1940–1941)

London, Ontario, had a franchise affiliated with the Pittsburgh Pirates for the 1940 and 1941 seasons. London made the playoffs in its inaugural season, but was eliminated three games to two in the first round of the playoffs by the 58-48 Batavia Clippers, an unaffiliated team. London catcher Andy Seminick (15 seasons), second baseman Jimmy Jordan (four seasons), and first baseman Vic Barnhart (74 games) later reached the majors. In addition to Larry Napp, Olean third baseman Don Richmond (56 games) and outfielder Walt Chipple (18 games) made brief major-league appearances.

In 1941 London fell to last place with a 47-63 record,[6] and the team folded. Despite the franchise's brief existence, the team did leave a legacy to this day. The team played at Labatt Park, which had opened on May 3, 1877.[7] The London Pirates' vice president for the 1940 season was George "Mooney" Gibson. Gibson, a Canadian, was a former major-league catcher who played 14 seasons between 1905 and 1918 with the Pittsburgh Pirates and New York Giants. He is credited with having played a key role in the installation of lights at Labatt Park to enable night games for the PONY League franchise.[8] The ballpark continues to be used by the Intercounty Baseball League London Majors. The IBL is the top-level baseball league in Canada, having operated for 101 years prior to the COVID-postponed 2020 season.[9] More than 40 IBL players have advanced to major-league baseball or returned to the league after their major-league careers, including Fergie Jenkins, Denny McLain, Chris Speier, and Paul Spoljaric.[10]

1943–1945: THE WAR YEARS

During the war years, the PONY League operated without any Canadian franchises. The league operated with six Western New York teams in 1943 (Batavia, Hornell, Jamestown, Lockport, Olean, and Wellsville), and added two Western Pennsylvania teams (Bradford and Erie) for 1944 and 1945.

Nellie Fox was signed out of high school in 1944 by the Philadelphia Athletics, and assigned to the Tigers-affiliated Jamestown Falcons as an outfielder. During the season, Fox was promoted to the Lancaster Red Roses of the Class-B Inter-State League to play first base. His overall batting average for the season was .309. By 1947, Fox was in the major leagues, appearing in a total of 98 games as a second baseman with the Philadelphia Athletics between 1947 and 1949. Fox was traded in the 1949 offseason to the Chicago White Sox for catcher Joe Tipton. Tipton had a seven-year career with a lifetime batting average of .236, while Fox averaged .288 over his 19-year Hall of Fame career.

HAMILTON CARDINALS (1946 – 1947)

The Hamilton franchise returned to the PONY League as the Cardinals in 1946, missing the playoffs in both 1946 and 1947. Canadian outfielder-first baseman Tom Burgess, from London, Ontario, was one of the leading hitters for the 1946 team (.271/16/65); his season was the start of a career of more than 40 years in professional baseball. Although he spent most of his playing career in the minor leagues, he did appear in 104 major-league games, compiling a .177 batting average. Upon retirement as an active player, Burgess became a minor-league manager beginning in 1969, and served as a major-league coach for the 1977 New York Mets and 1978 Atlanta Braves.[11] Burgess was a minor-league hitting instructor for the Kansas City Royals from 1988 through 1995.[12] After his professional career, Burgess supported Canadian baseball by serving as a coach for the Canadian National Baseball Team that included major-league players Jason Bay and Justin Morneau.[13] He was inducted into the Canadian Baseball Hall of Fame in 1992.

The only other Cardinals from those teams to make major-league appearances were 1946 shortstop Jim Clark (nine games) and 1947 pitcher Ralph Beard (one season).

HAMILTON RED BIRDS (1948)

Hamilton finished third and played the Tigers-affiliated Jamestown Falcons in the opening round of the playoffs,[14] losing the series four games to one.[15] Pitchers Dan Lewandowski (two games) from Hamilton and Milt Jordan (eight games) from Jamestown were the only players to make brief major-league appearances.

HAMILTON CARDINALS (1949–1955)

This seven-year stretch was the franchise's most successful, featuring six playoff appearances, a first-place finish in 1952, and the league championship in 1955.

The 1949 team finished third, led by holdover pitcher Lewandowski and future major-league pitcher Willard Schmidt (seven seasons). Hamilton again met the Tigers-affiliated Jamestown Falcons in round one of the playoffs, this time defeating them four games to one. None of the Jamestown players made the major leagues. Hamilton then lost the league finals, four games to one, to the Bradford Blue Wings, a Philadelphia Phillies affiliate. Two players from the Bradford team made the major leagues: third baseman Dick Young (20 games) and fifth starter (based on number of games started) Roy Face. Face (14-2, 3.32) went on to have a 16-year major-league career,

compiling a lifetime record of 104-95/3.48 with 191 saves. He played his final season with the 1969 expansion Montréal Expos (4-2/3.94, 5 saves).

Hamilton finished third in 1950. The team featured four future major-league players: first baseman Pidge Browne (65 games) and catcher Hal Smith (seven seasons), as well as third baseman Ken Boyer and pitcher Stu Miller. Boyer, primarily a third baseman (.342), also pitched in 21 games for Hamilton (6-8, 4.39). He was the starting third baseman for the St. Louis Cardinals from 1955 through 1965, compiling a batting average of .293 with 255 home runs and 1,001 RBIs over those 11 years. Boyer played four more seasons with the New York Mets, Chicago White Sox, and Los Angeles Dodgers before retiring in 1969. His final career statistics include a .287 average, 282 home runs and 1,141 RBIs. Stu Miller was the ace of the Hamilton staff, starting 27 games and compiling a 16-13 record with a 3.21 ERA. He went on to a 16-year major-league career with the St. Louis Cardinals, Philadelphia Phillies, New York/San Francisco Giants, Baltimore Orioles, and Atlanta Braves, compiling a lifetime record of 105-103 with a 3.24 ERA.

Hamilton was eliminated four games to two by the (then) independent Olean Oilers in round one of the 1950 playoffs.[16] Olean infielder/outfielder Chuck Harmon (four seasons) and infielder Len Schulte (124 games) later appeared in the major leagues.

The 1951 Cardinals, featuring future major-league infielder Wally Shannon (65 games), finished fourth. Hamilton was again eliminated in round one of the playoffs by the independent Olean Oilers, this time four games to three.[17] Olean had two future major leaguers on the team, holdover Harmon and first baseman Paul Owens. Owens had a lengthy career with the Philadelphia Phillies organization despite a relatively late start. His postsecondary education was interrupted by three years of service in the US army during World War II. After the war, Owens completed his postsecondary studies before beginning his baseball career by joining Olean in 1951 at age 27. He led the PONY League in hitting that year with a .407 batting average, including 17 home runs and a league record 38-game hitting streak. In 1952 he played for the Class-B Winston-Salem Cardinals, then left baseball for two years. Owens returned to Organized Baseball in 1955 as player-manager of the still independent Olean. Olean became a farm team of the Phillies in 1956 and Owens began his nearly 50-year career with the Philadelphia organization. After the 1957 season, Owens was promoted to be player-manager for the Class-C Bakersfield Bears. In 1960 he became a scout; he advanced to Phillies farm director in 1965, and eventually to general manager from 1972 until 1983, and manager in the 1972, 1983, and 1984 seasons. He continued to serve the Phillies in various capacities until his death in 2003.

Hamilton finished first in 1952, holdover Pidge Browne leading the offense with a .344 average and 15 home runs. The Cardinals were defeated in the opening playoff round, four games to one, by the Brooklyn-affiliated Hornell Dodgers. While Browne was the only Hamilton player to appear in the majors, Hornell featured two: outfielder John Glenn (32 games) and shortstop Maury Wills. Wills had a 14-year big-league playing career, primarily with the Los Angeles Dodgers. He also played two seasons in Pittsburgh, and was an original Montréal Expo in 1969 before being traded with Manny Mota to the Dodgers for Ron Fairly and Paul Popovich in June 1969. Wills had a lifetime batting average of .281 with 586 stolen bases.

In 1953 Hamilton finished third,[18] this time defeating the Hornell Dodgers in three straight games in the opening playoff round.[19] No player from either team reached the majors. The Cardinals then lost the finals to the first-place Jamestown Falcons, still a Tigers affiliate.[20] The Falcons featured four future major leaguers: pitchers Bob

Shaw (11 seasons) and Ken Rowe (26 games), outfielder Ken Walters (three seasons), and outfielder George Alusik (298 games).

Hamilton missed the playoffs in 1954, finishing tied with the Bradford Phillies for sixth with a 61-65 record. Pitchers Marty Kutyna (four seasons) and Tom Baker (10 games) had brief major-league careers.

The 1955 campaign was a championship season for Hamilton. The team finished the regular season in first place with an 82-43 record, leading the league in runs scored and fewest runs allowed. The top four starters had a combined record of 61-24, led by Gary Geiger (20-7 with a 1.98 ERA). Geiger did make the major leagues in 1958, forging a 12-year career as an outfielder with a lifetime batting average of .246. Reliever Paul Toth (three seasons) also reached the majors. The Hamilton hitting was led by 32-year-old second baseman Ed Lyons, who batted .350 and hit 17 home runs. Lyons was the only Hamilton player with previous major-league experience, having played for the 1947 Washington Senators, batting .154 in 26 at-bats.

Hamilton defeated the fourth-place (68-58) Wellsville Braves, a Milwaukee Braves affiliate, two games to one, in round one of the playoffs.[21] Wellsville was led by future major-league pitcher Don Nottebart (18-11, 2.57). Nottebart had a nine-year major-league career with a record of 36-51/3.65. Wellsville catcher Ron Henry (42 games) later reached the majors, and 38-year-old second baseman Alex Monchak had previous major-league experience, having appeared in 19 games for the Philadelphia Phillies in 1940.

Hamilton then defeated the third-place (69-57) Boston Red Sox-affiliated Corning Red Sox in three straight games in the final to win the PONY League pennant.[22] Corning starter Ken McBride (10-9, 3.81) later fashioned a seven-year major-league career, compiling a 40-50 record with a 3.79 ERA. The only other future major leaguer on the team was Bill Monbouquette. He appeared in only one game for Corning, a start that lasted two innings in which he yielded six hits and three earned runs in a no-decision. Monbouquette went on to have an 11-year major-league career, amassing a 114-112/3.68 record.

Several players of interest began their baseball careers in the PONY League during this era. Don Zimmer played shortstop for the 1950 Hornell Dodgers, hitting .315 with 23 home runs. Zimmer hit .235 in a 12-year major-league career. In his post-playing career Zimmer was both a coach and a manager. His 13-year managerial record was .508 (885-858) with one postseason appearance, his 1989 Chicago Cubs being defeated four games to one in the NLCS by the San Francisco Giants. Frank Lary went 5-2 with a 1.88 ERA for the 1950 Tigers-affiliated Jamestown Falcons; he had a 12-year major-league career with a record of 128-116/3.49. And Bobby Richardson played second base and hit .412 for the 1953 New York Yankees-affiliated Olean Yankees. Richardson played second base for the New York Yankees over a 12-year career and hit .266.

HAMILTON RED WINGS (1956) THE FINAL SEASON

Winning the PONY League title in 1955 did not lead to sustained success for the Hamilton franchise. St. Louis did not renew its affiliation with Hamilton for 1956, so the team was rebranded as the Red Wings and attempted to operate as an independent club. These efforts proved unsuccessful, and the franchise, as did the Yankees-affiliated Bradford Yankees, folded on May 16, 1956. *The Sporting News* summarized the contributing factors in an article in its issue of May 23, 1956.[23] Bad weather in early May hurt the league; 25 of the first 40 scheduled games were postponed. This particularly hurt the finances

of the independent Hamilton Red Wings. The league did consider assuming operation of the franchise. However, the Bradford Yankees were also experiencing financial problems, so both franchises were folded on May 16.

With the demise of the sole Canadian franchise, the league renamed itself the New York-Pennsylvania League beginning in 1957. Although some teams returned to Canada for several seasons (Toronto Blue Jays-affiliated St. Catharines Blue Jays 1986-1995 and St. Catharines Stompers 1996-1999, St. Louis Cardinals-affiliated Hamilton Red Birds 1988-1992, and Pittsburgh Pirates-affiliated Welland Pirates 1989-1994), the PONY League name was not resurrected.

Two players of interest began their playing careers in 1956, the final year of the PONY League. Tommy Davis hit .325 for the Hornell Dodgers, still affiliated with Brooklyn. Davis had an 18-year major-league career, batting .294. And Buck Rodgers hit .235 as a catcher for the Jamestown Falcons, still a Tigers affiliate. Rodgers had a nine-year playing career, hitting .232. His post-playing career included 13 years as a manager, compiling a 784-774 (.503) record. He managed the Montréal Expos for seven seasons (1985 through 1991) to an aggregate record of 520-499 (.510). Rodgers made one postseason managerial appearance, with the Milwaukee Brewers, losing the American League East Division playoff (due to the split season resulting from the 1981 player strike) to the New York Yankees, three games to two.

SOURCES

Data regarding the teams and players is drawn from Baseball-Reference.com, except as noted.

NOTES

1   *The Sporting News*, September 28, 1939: 11.

2   Ray Murray, "Ex-AL Ump Knapp [*sic*] Dies at Age 77," *South Florida Sun-Sentinel*, July 9, 1993.

3   *The Sporting News*, September 4, 1941: 7.

4   *The Sporting News*, September 18, 1941: 11.

5   *The Sporting News*, September 25, 1941: 7. From 1936 to 1941 the Boston National League team was nicknamed Bees.

6   *The Sporting News*, September 4, 1941: 7.

7   Thompson, John (ed.), *Intercounty Baseball League – 100 Years Strong* (2018): 137.

8   Thompson: 137.

9   https://www.theibl.ca.

10 https://www.theibl.ca.

11 https://baseballhalloffame.ca/blog/2009/07/29/tom-burgess.

12 https://baseballhalloffame.ca/blog/2009/07/29/tom-burgess.

13 https://baseballhalloffame.ca/blog/2009/07/29/tom-burgess.

14 *The Sporting News*, September 8, 1948: 36.

15 *The Sporting News*, September 22, 1948: 37.

16 *The Sporting News*, September 20, 1950: 42.

17 *The Sporting News*, September 26, 1951: 36.

18 *The Sporting News*, September 9, 1953: 36.

19 *The Sporting News*, September 23, 1953: 35.

20 *The Sporting News*, September 30, 1953: 54.

21 *The Sporting News*, September 21, 1955: 37.

22 *The Sporting News*, September 21, 1955: 37.

23 "Jean and Carroll Jean Drop Pony League Franchise at Hamilton," *The Sporting News*, May 23, 1956: 37.

CANADIANS IN THE AAGPBL

By Tom Hawthorn

The young women gathered on the grass in Chicago shagged flies and fielded grounders. They played scrub games under the watchful eyes of coaches. Even the practice games were not without incident, as Gladys "Terrie" Davis, a batting star in Toronto's amateur softball leagues, discovered during one at-bat. "I've been playing ball for over 12 years," she told a reporter. "I never had a scratch or a bruise. So what happens? The first time I come to bat here at Wrigley Field, I pop a foul tip. Bang! Down comes the ball right on my eye. Just look at the shiner."[1] Davis, who, the reporter assured his readers, "will have no trouble pounding out homers while looking as petite and feminine as a French mannequin,"[2] covered the injury as best she could with makeup.

In May 1943, as the world was gripped by World War II, young women athletes were lured to Wrigley to try out for a roster spot in a new professional softball circuit. The All-American Girls Softball League (later the All-American Girls Professional Baseball League) was formed in February 1943 by chewing-gum magnate Philip K. Wrigley. With the future of major-league baseball uncertain as players enlisted or were drafted to fight in the war, the new league planned to provide entertainment on the home front.

Scouts fanned out across the continent to evaluate ballplayers in the top women's leagues. The best 280 ballplayers were invited to Chicago for a final test. Some players were worldly, while others were as green as the verdant lawn on which they played. For more than one, Wrigley Field was the destination of their first train trip. They hailed from 17 states and four Canadian provinces. In the end, 60 athletes made the cut in the league's first year. Fourteen of them, including Davis, were from Canada.

The league evolved over the years, switching from underhand pitching to side-arm to overhand. As well, the size of the ball shrank and the distance between bases grew, as the game they played came to more resemble baseball than softball, a change reflected in changes to the league's name. The teams were mostly based in midsized cities in the American Midwest. The league folded in 1954, a victim of poor business decisions and the growing popularity of television, which brought major-league baseball into the living room.

Over the years, the league was forgotten, as the former players returned to more conventional lives as breadwinners and homemakers. Many did not even tell their children about their earlier careers as professional athletes. In 1987 documentary filmmaker Kelly Candaele (pronounced can-*dell*) released *A League of Their Own*, featuring the careers of his Vancouver-born mother (Helen Callaghan) and aunt (Margaret Callaghan). Five years later, Penny Marshall directed a Hollywood movie of the same name starring Madonna, Geena Davis, and Tom Hanks. The movie gave the world the immortal (if debatable) line, "There's no crying in baseball." It also revived interest in the trailblazing women who played professional baseball. Most former players went about everyday lives in obscurity. Many had not even told their children. "I never said a word all those years," said Betty (née Berthiaume) Wicken, who had been recruited out of Regina, Saskatchewan. "Nobody seemed to know about it, it never came up, so I didn't say anything."[3] The movie changed that. The National Baseball Hall of Fame at Cooperstown, New York, opened a permanent exhibit on women in baseball, while the Canadian Baseball Hall of Fame at St. Marys, Ontario, inducted all 68 Canadian women to have been placed on a team roster.

Most of the athletes came from the three Prairie provinces, where competitive women's softball circuits were in full swing. Over the league's history, 28 players came from Saskatchewan, 13 from Manitoba, and 10 from Alberta. Another 10 came from Ontario, where women's softball was well established at lakefront Sunnyside Park in westside Toronto. British Columbia produced six players, while a lone player (Alice Janowski of Sherbrooke) hailed from Quebec.

They were clerks, teachers, stenographers, farm girls, and housewives. At least one (Margaret Callaghan) gave up a factory job building warplanes to play pro ball. They were scouted at their amateur league games and in tournaments played in the United States. Most were unmarried.

They played for teams based in midsized cities in the American Midwest: South Bend, Indiana; Rockford, Illinois; Racine and Kenosha, Wisconsin. Later expansion and franchise moves saw

teams in Milwaukee; Minneapolis; Fort Wayne, Indiana; Chicago, Springfield, and Peoria, Illinois; and Muskegon, Battle Creek, Kalamazoo, and Grand Rapids, Michigan.

They played for teams with such nicknames as Chicks, Comets, Peaches, Daisies, and Belles. Instead of traditional wool flannels, they wore pastel uniforms consisting of a short-sleeved, one-piece, belted, flared tunic with a bodice flap that buttoned on the left side, leaving room for a circular crest on the chest. They suffered scrapes on their exposed legs from sliding on tough dirt infields. There were even beauty instructions provided them on how best to cover such abrasions.

In the early years, the players attended evening classes on posture, etiquette, and deportment at the Helena Rubenstein Beauty School. The players were told to be "neat and presentable in your appearance and dress, be clean and wholesome in appearance, be polite and considerate in your daily contacts, avoid noisy, rough, and raucous talk and actions and be in all respects an All-American girl."[4]

There was to be no smoking or drinking in public, no fraternizing unescorted with men, no uniforms in the stands, no slacks off the field. It could be said their training included the application of makeup, as well as the tag. "We were supposed to play like men," Helen Callaghan once told *People* magazine, "but look like women."[5] The "Lipstick League," as some newspapers called it, promised "beauty at the bat, pulchritude on the pitcher's mound, and glamour in the gardens."[6]

The presence of a team chaperone and the threat of fines for not following the rules of conduct ($5 for a first offense, $10 for a second, suspension for a third) did not prevent young athletes away from home from behaving like young athletes away from home. "We did a lot of short-sheeting," Marge Callaghan (later Maxwell) said. "We'd hide brassieres or slip a rubber snake into a chaperone's bed. We were always sneaking out on dates. How could they keep track of 19 girls at once?"[7]

Canadian players were prominent from the first pitch. In the league's 1943 debut season, the batting title was won by Gladys "Terrie" Davis of Toronto, who hit .332, while the pitching title was claimed by Helen Nicol of the hamlet of Ardley, Alberta, who went 31-8 with an earned-run average of 1.81. (The next season she again won the pitching title, dropping her ERA to 0.93.)

Some won recognition for achievement in a single game, such as Betty (née Petryna) Allen, from a farm near Liberty, Saskatchewan, who recorded 12 assists in a game at third base in 1949.[8]

The players sometimes hailed from families with interesting biographies. Mildred Warwick of Regina was an outstanding third baseman in the league's first two seasons. She left the league after marrying Ken McAuley, a goaltender for the New York Rangers of the National Hockey League. Two of her brothers – Grant, nicknamed Knobby, and Billy – also played for the Rangers. The pair were joined by a third brother, Dick, in winning the world hockey championship with British Columbia's Penticton Vees in 1955. Utility catcher Terry Donahue, of Melaval, Saskatchewan, spent four seasons in the league before settling down in a Chicago suburb while working for an interior design firm. Her longtime roommate was Pat Henschel, another Saskatchewan farmgirl who had cheered on Donahue's exploits on the diamond. Even as social mores changed, the pair insisted they were no more than friends, before coming out to their families in 2009. Their romance was at last shared with the world in the touching documentary *A Secret Love*, which aired on Netflix.

Each of the 68 Canadian women to have played in the All-American League has a story. Here are some of them.

MARY "BONNIE" BAKER

Mary Baker was a store clerk who left Saskatchewan in 1943 to become a professional baseball catcher. Her dark good looks made her a favorite choice when a player was needed for publicity photos. She became the face of the league, posing for *Life* and *Sport* magazines and appearing on television's *What's My Line?* Male reporters dubbed her "Pretty Bonnie Baker," giving the league what its owners most desired, a touch of glamour. Many women have charm. Not so many can also whack a ball. She played in 930 regular-season games with an additional 18 playoff appearances. She was the only player to become a manager, coaching the Kalamazoo Lassies for a season even as she fulfilled her daily fielding duties.

A beauty in front of the lens, she was a pugnacious presence behind the plate. The catcher was a fan favorite for her spirited arguments with umpires. Those debates were often conducted in small sandstorms generated by the stomping of her feet, which soiled the polished shoes of the arbiter. The 5-foot-5, 133-pound fireplug hit only one home run in her nine-season career. She finished with an unimpressive .235 batting average, but she had a discerning eye – striking out just six times in 256 at-bats in her rookie season – and was a threat to score once on base. Baker stole 506 bases in her career, including 94 in 94 games in 1946, when she was named the league's all-star catcher.

Baker spent the first seven years of her career with the South Bend Blue Sox. Her first visit to Bendix Field reminded her of her hometown. "The dust was blowing and it was always very windy, but that didn't hinder me," she once said. "I felt like I was playing in Yankee Stadium."[9]

Mary Geraldine George was born in Regina on July 10, 1919.[10] Her father was a mechanic, and both parents were Hungarian immigrants. Her mother died when she was just 11. She had five brothers and four sisters, all of them athletic. She was blessed with a powerful right throwing arm, once hurling a baseball 343 feet. At age 13 she began playing on softball teams with adult women. In 1938 she joined the Army and Navy Bombers, a team sponsored by a department store in which she worked as a $17-per-week clerk. Under manager Arnold "Kappy" Kaplan, the Bombers won the provincial softball championship in 1940.

Baker (then married) and other Saskatchewan players were scouted by Hubert "Hub" Bishop, a well-known hockey scout who was helping his friend, Johnny Gottselig, find worthy players for the new professional league. Gottselig, who was born in Odessa in the Russian Empire and later moved to Regina, was an NHL left winger known for his stick-handling prowess. He became one of the league's first four original managers, guiding the Racine Belles to the league's first championship.

With her husband serving overseas in the air force, Baker was persuaded by her mother-in-law to accept the invitation to attend the original tryout at Wrigley Field even without gaining her husband's permission. The adventure was a welcome hiatus from wartime doldrums. There was nothing to do on the Prairies with men away during the war "except play ball and chase grasshoppers."[11] Baker was popular with the fans, who once presented her with an automatic washer manufactured in a South Bend factory. "The fans treated us as though we were stars," she recalled. "They took us into their homes and treated us as family."[12]

Her younger sister, Genevieve, known as Gene, played in 15 games as a catcher for Muskegon in 1948. Three years later, she married football player Jim McFaul of the Saskatchewan Roughriders.

Baker was traded to Muskegon in 1950, serving as a playing manager. (The league later barred women from serving as managers.) After taking a

year off to have a baby, Baker returned for a ninth and final season. She hit just .208, and for the only time in her career had more strikeouts (22) than stolen bases (20). Baker returned to her hometown, where she led the Regina Legions softball team to provincial and Western Canadian titles in 1953. The team earned a berth in the World Ladies Softball championship in Toronto, losing a one-game showdown for the Canadian title to Toronto Kalyx. Baker hit .500 in the tournament (8 hits in 16 at-bats) in a losing cause.

A broken ankle suffered in 1958 ended Baker's sandlot days. A noted bowler and curler, she managed the Wheat City Curling Club for 25 years. In 1953 she joined two of her brothers in operating the Hunt Club, a restaurant in a Regina mansion. Late in 1964, Baker was hired as sports director of radio station CKRM. She was introduced as Canada's first woman sportscaster to the all-male reporting corps at a press conference held by the Roughriders to announce the signing of Eagle Keys as head coach. Baker insisted that she be treated as one of the boys.

"I've been on radio and television many times before, but it's always me who was being interviewed," she said. "I've never been the interviewer."[13]

On August 17, 1952, Baker appeared on the popular television program *What's My Line?* in which a panel of celebrities question a mystery guest to determine the guest's occupation. "In the course of your work, do you ever take a part of your costume off?" asked panelist Hal Block. "Yes," she replied, referring to her catcher's equipment, as a live audience howled with laughter. While Block's line of interrogation presumed Baker to be a strip-tease dancer, panelist Dorothy Kilgallen correctly guessed her occupation. "I certainly think Mrs. Baker is an argument for allowing women to play in the big leagues," Kilgallen said.[14]

At Baker's memorial service in 2003, mourners rose after eulogies to observe a seventh-inning stretch during which they sang "Take Me Out to the Ball Game."

HELEN NICOL FOX

The first pitching star of the All-American league was a former Edmonton department-store clerk who made her first trip to the United States to attend the inaugural tryouts at Wrigley Field in Chicago. The right-handed pitcher thrived even as the league's game evolved from softball to baseball, with the ball shrinking, the pitching distance lengthening, and the delivery changing from underhand to side-arm to overhand. She spent 10 seasons in the league. "She had to be very athletic and very committed to the game, especially to make the transition from underhand to overhand, and to do it well," said sports historian Merrie Fidler of Trinidad, California, who has written a history of the league. "She had speed and control. She was outstanding."[15]

Helen Margaret Nicol was born on May 9, 1920, in Ardley, a hamlet in central Alberta about 115 miles north of Calgary. She was the middle child and only daughter born to the former Elizabeth May Dunn and Alexander Nicol, who both immigrated to Canada from Scotland. While attending high school in Calgary, she skated for the Avenue Grills, a hockey team sponsored by a local café, leading the women's city league in goal scoring. She was also a top provincial speed skater, yet it was on the softball diamond that she excelled, being first recruited at age 13 to pitch for a senior women's team. She once struck out 23 batters from the Mannville (Alberta) Merrymakers in a playoff game. Much in demand as a hurler, she threw for the Calgary Chinooks, Edmonton Army and Navy Pats, and the Edmonton Walk-Rites, for whom she won the deciding game of the Western Canadian championships in 1942.

When Nicol was assigned to the Kenosha Comets, her All-American contract offered her a princely $85 per week, considerably more than she made as a clerk. The 5-foot-3, 130-pound pitcher was described by the local newspaper as "a handsome brunette, dark-brown hair, violet-blue eyes, and a most charming personality ... a refreshing outdoor girl."[16] She became an immediate fan favorite in the Wisconsin city. "I have always enjoyed playing softball more than anything else, and dreamed of someday spending an entire summer vacation doing just that," she said. "But to be paid for doing it, and be given such a wonderful trip all the way from Calgary to Kenosha still seems like a page torn from a fairy-tale book."[17]

Nicol recorded an impressive 31-8 record to help the Comets win the league pennant in the inaugural season. She led the league in several pitching categories, including victories, win percentage (.795), earned-run average (1.81), games pitched (47), innings pitched (348), and strikeouts (220). She was named league pitcher of the year.

In the All-American's first all-star game, played under temporary lights at Wrigley Field, Nicol hurled three scoreless innings as Wisconsin defeated a combined Illinois-Indiana team 16-0.

She repeated as pitcher of the year in her sophomore campaign with a 17-11 record and a miserly 0.93 ERA. Fox retired after 10 seasons split between the Comets and the Rockford Peaches. When the circuit ceased operation after the 1954 season, she held career league pitching records for games (313) and innings pitched (2,382), as well as strikeouts (1,076). She was also the career leader in wins (163) and losses (118). The 13 consecutive victories she recorded in 1943 went unmatched.

Nicol stayed in Kenosha, working for Motorola and the American Motors Corporation. She later moved to warmer Arizona, where she won several golf tournaments. On her 101st birthday, she received a video greeting from Rockford Mayor Tom McNamara, who acknowledged her "indelible impact on the city of Rockford and the Rockford Peaches."[18]

MARGARET AND HELEN CALLAGHAN

On a pleasant late May afternoon in 1944, young Helen Callaghan posed along the baseline with her Millerettes teammates at Nicollet Park in Minneapolis. Their opponents, the Rockford Peaches, lined up along the foul line in front of their dugout. The two teams formed a colorful V-for-Victory pattern. The mayor's wife threw out the first pitch and was presented with a bouquet of flowers in return. It was Opening Day for the expansion Millerettes, one of two new teams added for the All-American league's second season.

One of the recruits was 21-year-old Callaghan, a spritely 5-foot-1, 115-pound outfielder with the speed of an Olympic sprinter. Callaghan was a star of Vancouver softball, and had been scouted at the world championship tournament in Detroit the previous summer. She left her family in British Columbia for the adventure of a life on the road, earning $65 weekly to play a game she loved.

On the day of her first game, the front page of the *Minneapolis Morning Tribune* heralded the impending capture of an Axis capital with a banner headline reading: YANKS WITHIN 16 MILES OF ROME. Inside the paper, on page 6 of the May 27, 1944, edition, a smaller headline

The Callaghan sisters, Helen (left) and Margaret. (British Columbia Sports Hall of Fame)

on the sports page reminded readers: "It's Powder Puff Baseball in Nicollet Opener Today."[19]

The Millerettes lost the opener 5-4, though Callaghan, batting second in the order, hit a single and caught a fly ball in right field. Her team, coached by former major-league catcher Bubber Jonnard, struggled on the field and at the gate, spending the last half of the season as an orphan team, playing all its games on the road.

By then, Helen had been joined by her sister Margaret, older by 15 months, who got permission to leave her wartime job as a supervisor at the Boeing plant on Sea Island, south of Vancouver, where bomber midsections and flying boats were built by 7,000 workers. The sisters lived out of suitcases through the end of the summer. The itinerant nature of the job didn't bother Helen, who hit .287 to finish in second place in batting in the league.

The Millerettes were dispersed after the season, with both sisters assigned to a new team based in Fort Wayne. The Daisies had several Canadians on the roster, including Penny O'Brian, known as "Peanuts," an outfielder from Edmonton; Arleene "Johnnie" Johnson, an infielder from Ogema, Saskatchewan; Audrey "Dimples" Haine, a pitcher from Winnipeg; Agnes "Aggie" Zurowski, a pitcher from Regina; Betty Carveth, a pitcher from Edmonton; and Yolande "YoYo" Teillet, a catcher of Métis ancestry from St. Vital, Manitoba, whose grandfather was Louis Riel's younger brother, and whose own brother served as Canada's veterans affairs minister under Prime Minister Lester Pearson.

The team chaperone was Helen Rauner, who had been an executive with the International Harvester Company, while the manager was Bill "Wamby" Wambsganss, who earned a place in baseball lore by making an unassisted triple play in the 1920 World Series.

The Callaghan sisters had different temperaments. Helen was quiet, serious, competitive, while Marge was brassy, chatty, and fun-loving. Helen, a left-handed batter, was a proficient drag bunter, maybe the best in the league at deadening a pitch along the first-base line as she raced for the bag. Marge was a home-run-slugging power hitter who is credited with hitting one of the longest homers in league history.

The sisters grew up in Vancouver's Mount Pleasant neighborhood, where they were the fourth and fifth of six children born to the former Hazel Terryberry, a scavenger's daughter, and Albert Callaghan, a machinist and truck driver. He was Catholic, she Protestant. They were wed in a Baptist ceremony at the bride's parental home. The girls were aged 9 and 8 when their mother died on December 6, 1932. Their father remarried and the former Ann Muirhead delivered three more children to the family.

Marge and Helen played soccer, basketball, lacrosse, softball, and hockey through elementary school and on into their years at King Edward High. Helen was a track star as a sprinter. They became top players on the sandlot at Centre Park, a rickety wood stadium on the northeast corner of Broadway and Fir. (An oddity of the park was an outfield fence that in left-center field jutted back toward home plate to make room for the side yard of a house on West Eighth Avenue.) Both sisters played for the Young Liberals, a club sponsored by the political party. On a tour of Oregon in the summer of 1940, a newspaper heralded the pair as the outstanding "feminine athletes" of Vancouver, describing the 17-year-old Helen as "pretty" and a "handy hitter."[20]

Three years later, their team, by then renamed Mutuals after a new sponsor, won the Western Canadian championship to qualify for the Amateur Softball Association world championship to be held at Detroit. The Mutuals played exhibition games on Vancouver Island to raise funds for the war effort before playing warm-up games as they crossed the Prairies on their way to the Motor

City, where they defeated teams from Moose Jaw, Saskatchewan, and Cleveland before being eliminated by the New Orleans Jax, who went on to win the tournament. Baseball scouts attended the tournament. They were looking for talent to stock a new women's pro league.

Back in Vancouver, the sisters had moved out of the family home to join a third adult sister in sharing rooms in an east-side house. All three worked in the sprawling Boeing Production Plant, which still stands at what is now the South Terminal of Vancouver International Airport. Marge, who wore a kerchief on her head and coveralls like Rosie the Riveter, supervised women who stamped identification numbers on bomber parts, ensuring that they did not damage the fragile sheet metal through eagerness or carelessness. She earned $24 a week for eight hours a day for six days a week. When she finally got permission to leave her war job and join Helen with the Millerettes, she tripled her pay.

The presence of her sister at a game possibly saved Helen's life. She collapsed at home plate during a game in 1946. She was diagnosed with a tubal pregnancy, and when doctors were unable to reach her husband Bob Candaele, whom she had married after the 1945 season, Marge gave permission for the surgery. Helen recovered, only to skip the 1947 season with a successful pregnancy. Helen played five seasons in the league, while Marge lasted eight seasons and played in more than 700 games.

After retiring as a player, Helen dedicated herself to raising a family of five sons, four of them born in Vancouver. She and the league's other pioneering women went back to ordinary lives as teachers, secretaries, and homemakers, their story forgotten for three decades.

Helen's youngest, Casey Candaele, showed an aptitude for baseball. His mother encouraged him to develop his skills. "She would hit ground balls and throw batting practice," he said. "I thought everybody's mom was doing that." She told him she had played pro ball, but he always assumed she meant softball. As he grew older and started being scouted himself, she emphasized the importance of being mentally tough and alert. "You can't have a bad day hustling," he remembers her telling him.[21]

Candaele was signed by the Montréal Expos, and after a few seasons in the minors made his major-league debut in 1986. He was small – listed at 5-feet-9 – but versatile, playing all three outfield positions and three of four in the infield. He hustled, earning the nickname Mighty Mite, and finished fourth in rookie-of-the-year voting in 1987. Montréal fans adopted him as a favorite for his spirited play. He showed a rare display of power in one game at Olympic Stadium, punching the ball into the front-row seat adjacent to the right-field foul pole, just beyond the 330-foot sign down the line, for his first home run. The team replaced the blue outfield seat with a yellow one to jokingly mark the shortest home run in the stadium's history. The only other yellow chair in the outfield was about 200 feet farther away from home plate to mark where Willie Stargell hit the stadium's longest home run.

Even after Candaele made the big leagues, his mother had advice for the young hitter. She disdained the light bat he used, thinner than the one she'd used decades earlier. "What are you using this toothpick for?" she'd ask. "This thing is too small."[22] Whatever Candaele's limitations as a player, he remains forever the only major leaguer whose mother played professional baseball.

NOTES

1 "Rockford Is Entry; Play Opens Saturday," *Belvidere* (Illinois) *Daily Republican,* May 28, 1943: 6.

2 "Rockford Is Entry; Play Opens Saturday."

3 Tom Hawthorn, "The Girls of Summer," *Vancouver* (British Columbia) *Province*, June 28, 1992: A25.

4 "Charm School," All-American Girls Professional Baseball League, www.aagpbl.org/history/charm-school, accessed on March 1, 2022.

5 Tom Hawthorn, "Home Runs and Charm School: Baseball's Girls of Summer," June 12, 2018, The Tyee, https://thetyee.ca/Culture/2018/06/12/Home-Run-Charm-Baseballs-Girls-Summer/, accessed on March 2, 2022.

6 Jayne Miller, "Girls' Softball Loop Favors Beauty, Grace as Essential Factors," *Kenosha* (Wisconsin) *News,* May 28, 1943: 8.

7 Tom Hawthorn, "Diamond Days Gone, She's Still in a League of Her Own," *Globe and Mail* (Toronto), November 7, 2007: S3.

8 "South Bend Takes Third," *Racine* (Wisconsin) *Journal Times,* June 1, 1949: 17.

9 "Field of Dreams," *South Bend* (Indiana) *Tribune,* September 29, 2002: 64.

10 While Baker's birth year is often listed as 1918, the official Province of Saskatchewan online database gives the year as 1919. "Genealogy Index Searches," eHealth Saskatchewan, http://genealogy.ehealthsask.ca/vsgs_srch.aspx, accessed on March 3, 2022.

11 Dawn Walton, "Canadian Ball Star Gave U.S. Someone to Cheer," *Globe and Mail* (Toronto), December 22, 2003: A1.

12 "Field of Dreams."

13 "Woman Sports Director for CKRM in Regina," *Saskatoon* (Saskatchewan) *Star-Phoenix,* January 5, 1965: 13.

14 Seamus McFaul, "Mary 'Bonnie' Baker on *What's My Line?*," YouTube.com, May 21, 2008, www.youtube.com/watch?v=tfXG2--b6ys, accessed on March 1, 2022.

15 Merrie Fidler telephone interview with author, August 23, 2021.

16 Alma Overholt, "Helen Nicol, Canadian 'Chucker,' Gets Results from 'Wrist Ball,'" *Kenosha* (Wisconsin) *News,* June 17, 1943: 8.

17 Overholt.

18 "Mayor Tom McNamara Wishes Rockford Peach Helen Nicol Fox a Happy 101st Birthday," *Rockford Register Star,* www.rrstar.com/videos/sports/2021/05/07/mayor-tom-mcnamara-wishes-rockford-peach-helen-nicol-fox-happy-101st-birthday/4995421001/, accessed on March 3, 2022.

19 United Press, "It's Powder Puff Baseball in Nicollet Opener Today," *Minneapolis Morning Tribune*, May 27, 1944: 6.

20 "Handy Hitter," *Salem* (Oregon) *Statesman Journal,* June 25, 1940: 7.

21 Hawthorn, "Home Runs and Charm School."

22 Hawthorn, "Home Runs and Charm School."

CANADA'S OLIVE LITTLE TOSSES THE FIRST NO-HIT, NO-RUN GAME IN AAGPBL HISTORY

AUGUST 15, 1943:
ROCKFORD PEACHES 2, SOUTH BEND BLUE SOX 0,
AT BENDIX FIELD, SOUTH BEND, INDIANA

By Gary Belleville

Olive Little wasn't particularly interested in joining the All-American Girls Professional Baseball League (AAGPBL) for its inaugural 1943 season – at least initially.[1] She had a good teaching job in Poplar Point, Manitoba, and had been recently married. "Then they offered me twice as much in a week as I had been making in a month teaching," she explained. "How could I say no?"[2] With her husband in the Canadian Army, Little jumped at the chance. Her $100-per-week contract made her one of the highest-paid players in the league.

Although the AAGPBL used baseball rules, it gradually transitioned the pitching style, ball, and field dimensions from softball-like to nearly regulation baseball between 1943 and 1954.[3] Little unleashed her blazing fastball using an underhand delivery of a 12-inch ball that first season. The fledgling league initially positioned the mound 40 feet from home plate and the bases 65 feet apart; the dimensions for regulation softball at the time were 35 and 55 feet, respectively.[4]

Little quickly established herself as the ace of the Rockford Peaches pitching staff. The 26-year-old fireballer wasn't afraid to use a brushback pitch whenever a hitter dug in a little too close to the plate.[5] Her popularity soared in Rockford,

and fans rewarded her first-half efforts by voting her to the Illinois-Indiana All-Star team.[6] The All-Star Game was played under temporary lights at Wrigley Field on July 1 – more than 45 years before the Chicago Cubs played what many mistakenly believed was the first night game at the historic ballpark.[7]

Five weeks after making history at Wrigley, she was fêted by Rockford fans with an "Olive Little Night," and presented with a wristwatch.[8] She responded by tossing a three-hitter against the Racine Belles.

Despite Little's outstanding pitching, Rockford came into its August 15 doubleheader against the South Bend Blue Sox in third place in the second-half standings with a 13-20 record.[9] The Blue Sox boasted a 22-11 mark, giving them a three-game lead over the second-place Kenosha Comets.

The first game of the twin bill, which was seven innings in duration, featured an all-Canadian pitching matchup.[10] Little got the start for the Peaches, while the Blue Sox countered with 21-year-old southpaw Doris "Dodie" Barr. Both hurlers came from small towns in southern Manitoba. Barr grew up in Starbuck, less than 40 miles from Little's hometown of Poplar Point.

The two catchers in this game were also Canadian: South Bend's Lucella MacLean (Lloydminster, Alberta) and Rockford's Helen "Swede" Nelson (Toronto).

MacLean was starting in place of South Bend's star catcher, Mary "Bonnie" Baker (Regina, Saskatchewan), who had broken a finger on her throwing hand three nights earlier and was out for the season. Baker was hurt on a foul tip in the first inning of a doubleheader, yet she played the remainder of the first game and even drove in a run after suffering the injury.[11]

Nelson suited up despite getting knocked out cold the night before in a home-plate collision with 15-year-old phenom Dorothy "Dottie" Schroeder.[12] The slightly built Nelson had to be carried off the field and taken to the clubhouse. The *South Bend Tribune* reported that she "received nothing more serious than a bump on the head."[13]

Rockford manager Eddie Stumpf penciled two more Canadians into his starting lineup: Hard-hitting Gladys "Terrie" Davis (Toronto) played center field,[14] and Mildred Warwick (Regina, Saskatchewan) was stationed at the hot corner.[15]

Barr retired the game's first two batters before Rockford's Irene Ruhnke singled into center field. The next two batters, Davis and Mildred Deegan, walked to load the bases. Betty Jane "Moe" Moczynski followed with a sharp single into left field to give the Peaches an early 2-0 lead.

Little opened the bottom of the first inning by walking Betsy "Sockum" Jochum. The speedy Jochum stole second and went to third on Marge Stefani's groundball out. MacLean followed with a short fly ball that was tracked down by an onrushing Davis, and Jochum had to remain at third. Little escaped the inning unscathed by getting Lois "Flash" Florreich to ground out.[16]

Barr and Little settled into a tight pitchers' duel. Neither hurler allowed another baserunner until the bottom of the fifth, when Little walked Barr to open the frame. Josephine "Jo Jo"

Olive Little tossed the AAGPBL's first no-hit, no-run game on August 15, 1943, against the first-place South Bend Blue Sox. (Midway Village Museum, Rockford, Illinois)

D'Angelo followed with what would have been a single with the bases empty, but Barr thought the ball was going to be caught by the left fielder Moczynski and held up at first. The ball fell in front of Moczynski, who relayed it to Ruhnke for the force play at second. D'Angelo's potential single went as a force play, keeping Little's no-hitter intact. The Rockford hurler surrendered her third (and final) walk of the game to the next batter, Johanna Hargraves, before getting a pair of popups to end the inning.

Neither team had a batter reach base for the remainder of the game. Little retired the Blue Sox in order in the final two innings to secure her no-hit, no-run game and give the Peaches a much-needed 2-0 victory. Despite throwing a two-hitter and retiring the last 19 Rockford batters, Barr was charged with the hard-luck loss. The errorless game was completed in a brisk 60 minutes.

Although Little recorded the first no-hit, no-run game in the history of the AAGPBL, it wasn't the league's first no-hitter. That was thrown on June 10, 1943, in Rockford's 7-2 victory over Kenosha by none other than Olive Little.[17]

Little finished the season with a 21-15 record and a 2.56 ERA. Her ERA ranked third in the league, behind fellow Canadian Helen Nicol (1.81) and Margaret "Sonny" Berger (1.91).[18] Little's eight shutouts tied her with Nicol for the league lead.

Rockford stumbled through the remainder of the 1943 season, finishing in last place in the second-half standings with a 20-34 mark. The Peaches' overall record of 43-65 was also the league's worst.

South Bend was a different team without Baker, the league's top catcher. The Blue Sox went 10-14 from August 13 onward and missed the playoffs. They finished the second half of the season three games behind Kenosha.[19]

Little sat out the 1944 season and gave birth to her first child, Bobbi, on June 3. There were reports in late July that Little would return to the Peaches before the end of the season,[20] but she eventually decided there wasn't enough time to get herself back into playing shape.[21]

Rockford held a second "Olive Little Night" on August 6, 1944, with 3,127 fans coming out to celebrate their former top hurler. The large crowd pushed Rockford's season attendance past its 1943 total with a month still left on the schedule.[22] With Little looking on, the Peaches' new pitching ace, Carolyn "India" Morris, tossed a seven-inning no-hit, no-run game to open the twin bill.[23]

Little returned to action in 1945 better than ever. The flamethrowing right-hander struck out 15 Fort Wayne batters on June 28, and less than two weeks later she tossed a nine-inning no-hit, no-run game against those same Daisies.[24] Four

days after Little's third no-no, the league moved the mound from 40 to 42 feet away from home plate to reduce the number of no-hitters.[25] She finished the season with a 22-11 record and a minuscule 1.68 ERA.

The mighty pitching duo of Morris and Little propelled Rockford to the 1945 pennant with a 67-43 record. That season the league scrapped the split-season setup and instituted the Shaughnessy playoff format.[26] Rockford defeated the third-place Grand Rapids Chicks three games to one in the first round of the playoffs before downing the Daisies four games to one to claim the championship.[27] It was the first of Rockford's four postseason titles in a six-year period.[28]

Little returned in 1946 for one final season, posting a 14-17 record and a 2.51 ERA with the Peaches. She retired from professional baseball after the season and returned to Poplar Point, where she spent the remainder of her life.

She was admitted into the Softball Canada Hall of Fame in 1983; two years later she entered the Manitoba Sports Hall of Fame. Little was inducted posthumously into the Canadian Baseball Hall of Fame in 1998 as a member of the pioneering group of 68 Canadian women who played in the AAGPBL.[29]

Little displayed typical Canadian modesty when she was asked about her professional baseball accomplishments, preferring instead to give much of the credit to her father, Jack Bend, and her sports-mad hometown. "Anybody who had the kind of coaching and encouragement I had could have done what I did," she said. "Maybe more."[30]

SOURCES

In addition to the sources cited in the Notes, the author consulted AAGPBL.org and AncestryLibrary.ca.

NOTES

1   The professional women's circuit was originally known as the All-American Girls Soft Ball League. It was renamed the All-American Girls Base Ball League in midseason 1943. Other titles used by the league included All-American Girls Professional Ball League (1944-45), All-American Girls Base Ball League (again, 1946-50), and American Girls Baseball League (1951-54). The league became known as the All-American Girls Professional Baseball League after the creation of the Players' Association in 1986. William McMahon, Helen Nordquist, and Merrie A. Fidler, "AAGPBL History: The International Girls Baseball League," All-American Girls Professional Baseball League, https://www.aagpbl.org/articles/show/51, accessed March 26, 2021; "League History," All-American Girls Professional Baseball League, https://www.aagpbl.org/history/league-history, accessed March 26, 2021.

2   Canadian Press, "Wartime Women's Baseball League Almost Forgotten," *Toronto Globe and Mail*, May 26, 1983: 22.

3   In 1954, the AAGPBL's final season, the mound was 60 feet from home plate and the bases were 85 feet apart. The pitchers threw overhand that season and used a regulation nine-inch baseball.

4   Anika Orrock, *The Incredible Women of the All-American Girls Professional Baseball League* (San Francisco: Chronicle Books, 2020), 62-63. As of 2021, NCAA softball used a 12-inch ball; the mound was 43 feet from home plate, and the bases were 60 feet apart.

5   Dan Turner, *Heroes, Bums, and Ordinary Men: Profiles in Canadian Baseball* (Toronto: Doubleday Canada, 1988), 262.

6   "Belles to Play Sox Tonight; Name All Star Team Lineup," *Racine* (Wisconsin) *Journal-Times*, June 30, 1943: 10.

7   Merrie A. Fidler and Jim Nitz, "July 1, 1943: All-American Girls Play First Game Under the Lights at Wrigley Field," SABR Games Project, https://sabr.org/gamesproj/game/july-1-1943-all-american-girls-play-first-game-under-the-lights-at-wrigley-field/, accessed March 25, 2021.

8   "Belles Divide Doubleheader with Rockford Team Sunday; Lose Saturday Contest, 8-3," *Racine Journal-Times*, August 9, 1943: 10.

9   "Girls' Softball," *South Bend Tribune*, August 15, 1943: 23.

10   AAGPBL doubleheaders consisted of one seven-inning game and one nine-inning game. The second game of the twin bill on August 15, 1943, was washed out in the top of the fifth inning with Rockford leading South Bend, 4-2. The game was replayed on August 16, which was supposed to have been an offday for both teams.

11   Jim Costin, "Injury Puts Bonnie Baker Out for Year," *South Bend Tribune*, August 13, 1943: 21.

12   Nelson is listed in the *All-American Girls Professional Baseball League Record Book* as being 5-feet-1, 100 pounds. Schroeder is listed at 5-feet-7, 150 pounds, although she may have been smaller at 15 years of age when this game was played. Schroeder scored on the play, extending South Bend's healthy eighth-inning lead to 8-1. Two nights later, Schroeder was called out for interference when she crashed into Rockford shortstop Eileen Burmeister, who was in the process of fielding a groundball. "Doris Barr to Face Comets in Series Opener Tonight," *South Bend Tribune*, August 17, 1943: 12.

13   Jim Costin, "Sox Win, 8-1; Lead by Three Games," *South Bend Tribune*, August 15, 1943: 23. Concussion protocols in professional baseball were still almost 70 years away.

14   Canadian slugger Gladys Davis won the 1943 AAGPBL batting title with a .332 batting average, and she led the league with 155 total bases. No other batter in the league (54-game minimum) hit more than .280. Davis also led Rockford with 4 home runs, 58 RBIs, 116 hits, 52 walks, 10 triples, and 78 runs scored in 349 at-bats.

15   In 1943 seven Canadians played for the Rockford Peaches, and five more suited up for the South Bend Blue Sox. In addition to those previously mentioned, utility player Ethel McCreary (Regina, Saskatchewan) and pitcher Thelma Golden (Toronto) donned a Peaches uniform that season; pitcher Catherine Bennett (Regina) also played for the 1943 Blue Sox. Pitcher Muriel Coben (Saskatoon, Saskatchewan) appeared in games for both Rockford and South Bend that season.

16   Jim Costin, "Little Stops Sox; 2-0, in No-Hitter," *South Bend Tribune*, August 16, 1943: 10.

17   Little's first no-hitter was thrown in only the 14th game in the history of the Rockford Peaches. Shirley Jameson scored both runs for Kenosha. Twice in the game the speedy Jameson walked, stole second, and then stole third. She scored on a wild pitch in the first inning and on an error in the third. Jameson led the league with 126 stolen bases in 1943.

18   Helen Nicol, a native of Ardley, Alberta, won her second consecutive ERA title in 1944 with a 0.93 ERA and tossed a nine-inning no-hit, no-run game on September 4, 1944, against the Racine Belles. She got married and played under the name Helen Nicol Fox beginning in 1945. She pitched for 10 seasons, eventually becoming the Cy Young of the AAGPBL. She is the career leader in wins (163), losses (118), pitching appearances (313), innings pitched (2382), strikeouts (1076), hits allowed (1579), and earned runs (499).

19   The first-place teams from the first and second half qualified for the playoffs in 1943 and 1944. Racine swept Kenosha in the 1943 league championship series.

20 Jim O'Brien, "Sidelines," *Racine Journal-Times*, July 26, 1944: 10.

21 Jim O'Brien, "Sidelines," *Racine Journal-Times*, August 9, 1944: 10.

22 "Morris Pitches No-Hit, No-Run Rockford Win," *Kenosha News*, August 7, 1944: 8.

23 The AAGPBL ball was reduced from 12 to 11½ inches at the start of the 1944 season. The distance between the bases was increased from 65 to 68 feet on July 19, 1944, to reduce the number of stolen bases. Eddie McKenna, "Belles Beat Comets in Series Opener, 5-2," *Kenosha News*, July 20, 1944: 12.

24 "Players Scrap as Rockford Beats Daisies, 2-0," *Racine Journal-Times*, June 29, 1945: 12; "Little Pitches No-Hitter as Rockford Wins, 2-0," *Racine Journal-Times*, July 11, 1945: 10.

25 Jim O'Brien, "Sidelines," *Racine Journal-Times*, July 9, 1945: 10. A record eight no-hitters were thrown in 1945. Doris Barr threw a seven-inning no-hit, no-run game for Racine in the nightcap of a July 1, 1945, doubleheader against Fort Wayne – 13 days before the mound was moved back. Racine won the game, 2-0, and Barr knocked in both runs herself in the top of the seventh. It was the first no-hitter in the history of the Racine Belles.

26 The AAGPBL operated as a six-team circuit in 1945. The top four teams qualified for the playoffs, with the first- and third-place teams squaring off in one of the first-round series and the second- and fourth-place teams meeting in the other series.

27 W.C. Madden, *The All-American Girls Professional Baseball League Record Book* (Jefferson, North Carolina: McFarland & Company, 2000), 100-106.

28 The Rockford Peaches were also AAGPBL playoff champions in 1948, 1949, and 1950.

29 Most of the Canadian players in the AAGPBL were from the provinces of Saskatchewan, Manitoba, and Alberta. A big reason why there were so many Canadians in the league was that the Prairie provinces were scoured for talent by AAGPBL scouts, including Johnny Gottselig. Gottselig, who was from Saskatchewan, played in the NHL for 16 seasons with the Chicago Black Hawks. He had also managed women's softball in Saskatchewan. In addition to being an AAGPBL scout, Gottselig managed the Racine Belles (1943-44), Peoria Red Wings (1946-47), and Kenosha Comets (1949-51). Matt Rothenberg, "A Hockey Hero and the AAGPBL," National Baseball Hall of Fame, https://baseballhall.org/discover-more/stories/short-stops/johnny-gottselig-and-the-all-american-girls-professional-baseball-league, accessed April 7, 2021.

30 "Olive Bend Little (May 7, 1917 - February 2, 1987)," Manitoba Sports Hall of Fame, http://honouredmembers.sportmanitoba.ca/inductee.php?id=63, accessed March 26, 2021.

ROCKFORD.

	AB	R	H	P	A	E
Kamenshek, 1b	3	0	0	10	0	0
Warwick, 3b	3	0	0	0	1	0
Rupnke, 2b	3	1	1	2	0	0
Davis, cf	2	1	0	1	0	0
Deegan, rf	2	0	0	0	0	0
Moczynski, lf	3	0	1	1	1	0
Burmeister, ss	3	0	0	3	5	0
Nelson, c	2	0	0	4	0	0
Little, p	2	0	0	0	0	0
	23	2	2	21	7	0

SOUTH BEND.

	AB	R	H	P	A	E
Jochum, lf	2	0	0	6	0	0
Stefani, 2b	3	0	0	1	2	0
MacLean, c	3	0	0	2	0	0
Florreich, 3b	3	0	0	1	3	0
Barr, p	2	0	0	2	1	0
D'Angelo, cf	3	0	0	1	0	0
Hageman, 1b	1	0	0	7	0	0
Holle, rf	2	0	0	1	0	0
Schroeder, ss	2	0	0	0	2	0
	21	0	0	21	8	0

Rockford .... 200 000 0—2
South Bend .... 000 000 0—0

Runs batted in—Moczynski [2]. Stolen bases—Moczynski, Jochum. Earned runs—Rockford, 2. Left on bases—Rockford, 2; South Bend, 3. Struck out—By Little, 3; by Barr, 1. Bases on balls—Off Little, 3; off Barr, 2. Wild pitch—Barr. Time—One hour. Umpires—Gembler and Green.

MONTRÉAL AND JACKIE ROBINSON

By Marcel Dugas

"To the large group of Louisville fans who came here with their team, it may be a lesson of goodwill among men. That it's the man and not his color, race or creed. They couldn't fail to tell others down South of the 'riots,' the chasing of a Negro – not because of hate but because of love."

– Sam Maltin, *Pittsburgh Courier*,
October 12, 1946.

In books and documentaries on the topic, it's generally misquoted along the lines of "It was the first time in history that a White mob chased a Black man with love, instead of lynching, on its mind." But this is the actual quote from Sam Maltin, the only reporter to describe what happened just outside Montréal's Delorimier Stadium on the evening of October 4, 1946. On that day, Jack Roosevelt "Jackie" Robinson, 27-year-old second baseman of the Triple-A Montréal Royals, was chased down for almost three street blocks by hundreds of delirious Montréal baseball cranks.

They had just seen their Royals clinch the Junior World Series, earning the title of best minor-league team in North America. The crowd had asked – and gotten – curtain calls from team manager Clay Hopper and Curt Davis, the winning pitcher of the sixth and decisive game of the series. But the man they really wanted to cheer was the rookie infielder who had been the talk of the town (and the baseball world) that season, when he became the first Black player to compete in "organized" (a.k.a. White) baseball in the twentieth century.

They cheered and cheered and cheered, and when Robinson agreed to come out of the dressing room to receive the adulation of the fans, he had tears in his eyes. "He could never have imagined that a Black man could be treated that way by white people," opined one reporter.[1]

Montréalers had fallen in love with Jackie Robinson to such an extent that they were not satisfied with a simple postgame tip of the cap. Two hundred fans were crowding the ballpark's hallways after the game to touch him, to wish him well, to shake his hand. Robinson had to channel his football-playing days to find a way out of the building. Outside, another 500 or so baseball-loving Montréalers were waiting for him. He had to run until he could jump into a moving car that took him away from his admirers.[2]

The atmosphere was quite different 346 days earlier when Robinson first set foot in what

A mural in Montréal attests to Jackie Robinson's popularity in the city. (Author's collection)

was then Canada's metropolis. Royals President Hector Racine had touted on October 23, 1945, an announcement that would "revolutionize the baseball world,"[3] which led some to believe that Montréal would be awarded a major-league franchise. The signing of a then almost completely unknown infielder from California felt like a dud to Montréalers. "Local sports fans didn't seem to appreciate how monumental and revolutionary a move the Brooklyn and Montréal ball clubs made … . 'So that's what it is,' they said, obviously let down. 'What's so big about that?,'" wrote veteran reporter Dink Carroll in his column.[4]

If fans did not immediately grasp the magnitude of the moment, newspapermen were quick to point out that that "epoch-making event"[5] constituted "perhaps the biggest news in the history of organized baseball."[6] Although one journalist noted that "when Robinson was presented to sports reporters, only three of them shook his hand while others were indifferent or left the room where the announcement was taking place and that attitude can be considered as being quite revealing."[7]

Two months earlier, Brooklyn Dodgers president and general manager Branch Rickey had sent right-hand man and former Royals manager Clyde Sukeforth to Chicago to watch Robinson in action and bring him back to Brooklyn. After years of patient scouting, Rickey was ready to tap Robinson as the standard-bearer of his "great experiment" of baseball integration. The now famous "I want a man with enough guts not to fight back" meeting between the two concluded with a promise that Jackie would be signed by the Dodgers' top farm team before November 1.[8]

After two years of a rather unsuccessful affiliation with the Pittsburgh Pirates, the Royals joined Brooklyn's chain before the 1939 season. Even though the Dodgers' 21-team farm system included another Triple-A club, the International League's Royals were generally considered to be on top of the heap. Robinson was offered to the Royals, and the national pastime of the United States wound up being integrated by a Canadian club.

Even though on the day of the contract signing, reporters mentioned some of the obstacles Robinson would be facing during the season (hostility from fans, pitchers throwing at his head, being turned away by hotels, etc.), no one seemed to doubt that he would be treated well in Montréal. The city had a long history of having Whites and Blacks on the same ball fields. Montréal had been a frequent stop for African American barnstorming clubs going back to at least 1896.[9] Entire teams of Black players had competed in local and provincial leagues throughout the 1920s and 1930s. But Robinson did not simply receive the support of the fan base on the field. He was thoroughly embraced by the community as a whole.

The months that separated Robinson's first visit to Montréal (for the contract signing) and his first game in town were a whirlwind. He married his longtime fiancée Rachel Isum. He was the subject of all sorts of speculation. Many observers thought he would be out of his depth in Triple-A baseball, if he got to play there at all. Rumors were flying left and right that he might not be allowed to play in the International League.[10]

The new Mrs. Robinson was the only wife allowed to attend spring training in the Royals camp. Branch Rickey must have felt that his pioneering ballplayer would need the emotional support, and he was prescient. Training camp proved to be a nightmare for the Robinsons and

John Wright, a right-handed pitcher from New Orleans and former member of the Homestead Grays, who signed with the club in January.[11]

The Robinsons had a rough time getting from California to Florida. They were bumped from two planes because of the color of their skin, and could not find decent accommodation while they were waiting to be allowed onto another plane. They ended up making a long ride in the overcrowded back of a segregated bus to reach the site of spring training. And the horrible trip was only the beginning.

The Royals held their training camp in Daytona Beach, a city considered to be fairly liberal by the standards of the time. But players first went to the city of Sanford, Florida, for pre-camp. The Robinsons and Wright had barely reached Sanford when they literally had to flee the town, where significant resistance to the idea of integrated competition was building. When asked by Roger Kahn if the African American members of the Royals risked lynching had they stayed in Sanford, Rickey replied, "From reports that reached me, that was not entirely beyond the realm of possibility."[12]

Robinson did not have to fear for his life after being repatriated to Daytona Beach. But he still had to earn a roster spot with the club, in an environment that was rife with distractions. A natural shortstop, he had to learn to play second base, at the same time battling arm issues. He struggled at the plate, assessing his own performance by saying he "specialized in pop flies to shortstop" early that spring.[13] He also turned down a lucrative offer to play in the Mexican League.[14]

The hotel that lodged the Royals did not welcome Black patrons, so the Robinsons lived at a private residence in the African American part of town. Robinson and Wright's presence caused the cancellation of seven exhibition games, and Robinson was pulled from a preseason contest when local police threatened to stop the proceedings if the Royals insisted on having an integrated lineup. Despite all this, and despite the many sleepless nights he endured,[15] Robinson ended up going north with the club.

Before being introduced to his new fans, the Royals second baseman (and his teammates) went on a 12-game, four-city road trip. He integrated Organized Baseball in style on April 18, 1946. He was the undisputed star of Opening Day in Jersey City, going 4-for-5 with a home run, 4 runs batted in, and 4 runs scored, as Montréal crushed the local Giants, 14-1. But while the crowds and the opposing teams in both Jersey City and Newark proved easy to handle, things were quite different in Syracuse and Baltimore. The Maryland city was the league's southernmost, and Robinson must have felt as if he had ventured into the heart of the Old Confederacy. Despite the presence of thousands of African American fans at the ballpark, the level of vitriol to which he was subjected was extraordinary.[16] As for Syracuse, the fans did not cause major trouble. But the Chiefs players rode Robinson harder than any team in the league all season long.[17]

After having experienced all this, the Royals' new number 9 must have felt a great sense of relief when the club's plane touched down at Montréal's Dorval airport on April 30, 1946, on the eve of the home opener. He was also, one would think, glad to realize that he didn't have to win the crowd over. The publicity that surrounded his signing, the trials and tribulations of camp, and the remarkable performance he had given during the first road trip of the season earned him "possibly the nicest ovation ever given to a player in Montréal" on May 1.[18] Robinson even received a bigger hand from the crowd than did his double-play partner Stan Bréard, a young man the Royals had plucked from the local sandlots. The *Pittsburgh Courier*'s Wendell Smith went further, saying that Montréalers gave the rookie an ovation that was heard "throughout the British Empire and most of its dominions beyond the seas."[19]

Robinson did not deliver as memorable a performance in his Montréal debut as he had in Jersey City 13 days earlier. But as soon as the game was over, he was surrounded by loving fans. He eventually left the ballpark through a side door, with the assistance of two police officers. Even Rachel was assailed by admirers, and had to sign program after program.[20] Thirteen games into his Royals career, the Robinsons were, even though the term did not exist back then, rock stars.

Montréalers' support for their new hero manifested itself in many ways. On June 30, after Robinson was roughed up on the basepaths early in game one of a doubleheader by Rochester Red Wing Danny Murtaugh, the crowd turned on the future Pirates manager and did not let up the rest of the day.[21] In August, Baltimore hurler Stanley West, who had thrown inside pitches to Robinson in three straight at-bats, was told by the crowd that he would have to answer for his conduct after the game if he kept this up. West considered the threat serious enough that he threw nothing but outside pitches in Robinson's following plate appearances.[22]

The well-known actor from the Quebec scene Marcel Sabourin reminisced how every little boy in town wanted to be Jackie Robinson during the summer of '46: "His pictures were in our scrapbooks. … Instantaneously, he became our idol."[23] There was such high demand for his autograph that he could never eat a hot meal when he was out on the town.[24] And when he joined members of the Montréal Canadiens for a visit to the city's veterans hospital, he stole the show from the Stanley Cup champions.[25]

Montréalers, Quebecers, Canadians had a role to play in the great experiment of integration, and their conduct was irreproachable. But they were never tested in any significant way. The Royals took first place in the International League in late May and never relinquished that lead. As for Robinson himself, he won the league's batting crown with a .349 mark. He had a .468 on-base percentage and scored 113 runs, both tops in the International League. Even more remarkably, he never went through any prolonged offensive drought. His lowest batting average for any month of the season was .319 in an injury-plagued month of June. His defensive play was stellar, and he kept Royals fans on the edge of their seats with his daring baserunning. Would the support have been as unwavering had the man Wendell Smith called "The Black knight of Pasadena" hit .249 for a last-place club? That's a question that can never be answered. But one thing is certain: Local rooters treated Jackie Robinson wonderfully, and he never gave them any reason not to.

The love affair between the Robinsons and Montréal did not stop at the gates of Delorimier Stadium. The newlyweds settled in the Villeray neighborhood, in the northeastern part of town. Back then, Villeray was overwhelmingly White, French-speaking and Catholic. Yet, the Protestant, Black couple who had no knowledge of French felt welcome as soon as they settled into their apartment. The neighbors took very good care of Rachel, who was pregnant with the couple's first child, when the Royals were on the road. Kids helped her carry groceries, she was given extra rationing coupons, and when a few days went by without her being seen outside, someone would knock on the door to make sure she was all right.[26]

The fact that the Robinsons received regal treatment in Canada should not give anyone an exaggerated sense of nationalistic bravado. Although the contrast was stark with what was happening in the Southern United States, Canada was not an Eldorado for its Black population. The Supreme Court of Canada ruled in 1939 that drinking establishments were within their right not to serve Black customers, thus legalizing racial discrimination.[27] And that joyous scene of Jackie Robinson being chased down the street "not because of hate, but because of love"

happened a month before Viola Desmond was dragged out of a Nova Scotia theater and jailed for having watched a movie from the main floor while being Black.[28]

Jackie Robinson certainly enjoyed the love he received in his temporary home. But given everything he had to deal with, he would have benefited greatly from a little less love and a little more peace and quiet while in Montréal. There was the pressure of succeeding in Triple A. The pressure of making a living for himself, his wife, and their coming child. The rough treatment he received from opponents and fans in some cities. Also, he was never quite accepted by his teammates. A fan ran into Royals in a restaurant that summer and heard the White ballplayers lament that the team's catalyst was taking a job away from a White player.[29]

Also resting on Robinson's shoulders was the gigantic amount of pressure that came with being a standard-bearer for African Americans. "I think Jackie really felt," said Rachel Robinson, "that there would be serious consequences if he didn't succeed and that one of them would be that nobody would try again for a long time."[30] The newspapers of the Black community were also quick to remind Jackie, John Wright, and Roy Partlow, a Negro League pitcher who was signed in May to replace Wright on the Royals roster, that they were not playing only for themselves. Partlow was not happy when the club demoted him to Class-C Trois-Rivières (where he joined Wright). Wendell Smith had some harsh words for the veteran southpaw, calling him "an eccentric 'prima donna' and a problem child of no small means" and reminded him of the "14 million Negroes from coast to coast who are pulling for him to make good in organized baseball."[31]

The pressure, the stress and the hatred almost got the better of Robinson that season. By late August he was pretty much burned out, and a physician told him to take time away from the team and rest. Even though he wrote in his autobiography that he asked back into the lineup after one day for fear of being accused of protecting his lead in the league's batting title race,[32] box scores show us that he missed two games and benefited from a rainout, for a total of three days off. Robinson also told reporters in the spring of 1947 that manager Hopper had asked him to cut his vacation short as the team was slumping. There was no mention of the batting championship at that time.[33]

Those three late-season off days did little to improve Robinson's health. It's a wonder that a man in his condition found a way to excel – and keep his composure – on the field over the course of the three high-stakes, high-pressure, best-of-seven playoff series the team played that year. He was shown a black cat by members of the Syracuse Chiefs during an International League championship series game, but persevered.[34] He was jeered like never before, and two Louisville Colonels

Another downtown mural reflects Robinson's importance to Montréal even today. (Author's collection)

tried to spike him when the Royals traveled to Kentucky to play in the Junior World Series.[35] But he kept on going. When the series shifted to Montréal, local fans booed every single Colonels player, as retribution for the way Robinson had been treated in Louisville.

The Royals' number 9 exacted revenge with his bat and his glove. He walked off the Colonels in Game Four, was instrumental in the Game Five triumph, and before the pandemonium that followed his farewell performance as a Royal, the spotlight shined on him one final time in Game Six. Veteran hurler Curt Davis played with fire for eight innings, but still managed to get to the top of the ninth without having surrendered a run. He quickly found himself in trouble again, with Colonels on first and third and nobody out. Louisville's Al Brancato hit a hot shot to second that Robinson handled beautifully. He stepped on second and threw to first for a rally-killing double play. Montréalers went wild, as they had done so many times during the season. After one final groundout, players and fans alike could let loose and celebrate. The social experiment of baseball's integration hadn't resulted in violence and disorder, as its opponents had forecast for decades. It had produced a winner.

Oddly enough, Robinson's next game at Delorimier Stadium almost resulted in a riot. The Dodgers came to Montréal during the 1948 All-Star break to play the Royals. It had been decided beforehand that Robinson would go to the plate once and sit out the balance of the game to rest his ailing back. But that piece of information had not been disclosed, and the 17,000 fans who had bought tickets, in large part to see Jackie Robinson in action one more time, were livid. So much so that Branch Rickey had to do some damage control. Brooklyn forfeited its part of the gate to set up a new fund to help Montréal-area amateur baseball.[36] The love affair between Robinson and the city was still going strong.

"When fans go to bat for you like that," Robinson said in response to the support he got during game four of the Junior World Series, "you feel it would be easy to play for them forever."[37] In a city in which, more than three-quarters of a century later, you can find so many reminders of his short passage (including a statue and two murals), a lot of fans wish he had.

NOTES

1   Phil Séguin, "Montréal Gagne la Petite Série," *La Patrie*, October 5, 1946: 50.

2   Sam Maltin, "Lesson of Goodwill Among Men, Fans 'Mob' Jackie in Great Tribute to Star," *Pittsburgh Courier*, October 12, 1946: 1, 12.

3   "Le Royal Crée un Précédent dans l'Histoire du Baseball Organisé," *La Presse*, October 24, 1945: 18.

4   Dink Carroll, "Playing the Field," *Montréal Gazette*, October 25, 1945: 16.

5   Dink Carroll, "Royals Set Precedent, Sign First Coloured Ball Player," *Montréal Gazette*, October 24, 1945: 14.

6   "Le Royal Crée un Précédent dans l'Histoire du Baseball Organisé."

7   "Joueur N Mis Sous Contrat par les Royaux," *Le Devoir*, October 24, 1945: 11. The altered word in the title is the French equivalent of the N word.

8   Jules Tygiel, *Baseball's Great Experiment, Jackie Robinson and his Legacy* (New York: Oxford University Press, 2008), 67.

9   "Cuban Giants vs Le National," *La Presse*, July 13, 1896: 2.

10 Tygiel, 91.

11 "John Wright, un Autre Joueur N Est Mis Sous Contrat par les Royaux," *Le Canada*, January 30, 1946: 7. See Note 7.

12 Roger Kahn, *Rickey & Robinson, the True, Untold Story of Integration of Baseball* (Emmaus, Pennsylvania: Rodale, 2014), 200.

13 Kahn, 207.

14 "On Veut Avoir Robinson," *Le Droit*, March 20, 1946: 13.

15 Jackie Robinson, *I Never Had It Made* (New York: HarperCollins Publishers, 1995), 43.

16 Tygiel, 122.

17 Tygiel, 128-129.

18 Charles Mayer, "Avec le Royal et dans l'Internationale," *Le Petit Journal*, May 5, 1946: 47.

19 Wendell Smith, "Jackie Gets Ovation in Home Debut," *Pittsburgh Courier*, May 11, 1946: 12.

20 Camil Desroches, "Carrousel Sportif," *Le Canada*, May 2, 1946: 11.

21 Phil Séguin, "Battu Samedi, Montréal Divise Hier," *La Patrie*, July 1, 1946: 12.

22 Sam Maltin, "Jackie Denies He Will Quit Baseball and Return to School," *Pittsburgh Courier*, August 24, 1946: 17.

23 Marc Robitaille, *Une Vue du Champ Gauche* (Montréal: Les 400 coups, 2003), 174.

24 Sam Maltin, "Royals May Attract Million in 1946," *Pittsburgh Courier*, July 20, 1946: 16.

25 Sam Maltin, "Jackie, Hockey Stars Visit War Veterans," *Pittsburgh Courier*, June 29, 1946: 19.

26 Tygiel, 124.

27 Eric Adams, "The Fred Christie case (Christie v York)," *Canadian Encyclopedia*, April 5, 2018. https://www.thecanadianencyclopedia.ca/en/article/fred-christie-case, accessed July 6, 2021.

28 Russell Bingham and Eli Yarhi, "Viola Desmond," *Canadian Encyclopedia*, January 27, 2013. https://www.thecanadianencyclopedia.ca/en/article/viola-desmond, accessed July 6, 2021.

29 William Brown, *Baseball's Fabulous Montréal Royals* (Montréal: Robert Davies Publishing, 1996), 109.

30 Tygiel, 139.

31 Wendell Smith, "What Happened to Roy Partlow?," *Pittsburgh Courier*, July 20, 1946: 16.

32 Robinson, *I Never Had It Made*, 49.

33 Wendell Smith, "Jackie Almost 'Cracked' Last Year," *Pittsburgh Courier*, March 15, 1947: 16.

34 Sam Lacy, "Didn't Mind It, Balto; Syracuse Worse," October 1, 1946: 20.

35 Sam Lacy, "Robinson Victim of Rebel Boos in Series," October 1, 1946: 20.

36 "Les Dodgers Remettent une Somme de $8,000 au Montréal," *La Presse*, July 21, 1948: 20.

37 Brown, *Baseball's Fabulous Montréal Royals*, 110.

THE HALIFAX AND DISTRICT LEAGUE: POSTWAR BASEBALL IN THE MARITIMES, 1946–1960

By Colin Howell

The Halifax and District (H&D) Baseball League was a postwar offspring of the Second World War when Nova Scotia, and Halifax in particular, served as a major debarkation point for troops on overseas convoys assembled for the Battle of the Atlantic. During the war, many of Canada's best ballplayers, some of whom, like Phil Marchildon and Joe Krakauskas, were major-league regulars, suited up with military clubs in the Halifax Defence League before departing for the "big game" overseas. Swollen by the influx of soldiers and sailors looking for entertainment, crowds filled local parks around the region to watch the best local players compete against those from across the country. RCAF veteran Marchildon, who was later shot down and spent time in a German POW camp before returning to the majors after the war,[1] was a member of an Air Force club that featured playing coach Art Upper, who had played in the Cape Breton Colliery League and with the International League Toronto Maple Leafs. Their Air Force teammates included Windsor, Ontario, native Freddy Thomas, a multisport star and one of Canada's best athletes in the first half of the century, and Manitoba native Les Edwards, who would contribute in many ways to baseball in Canada in

the future. Halifax Navy captured Provincial and Maritime honors in 1942 and 1943; HMCS Cornwallis captured the crown in 1944; and in 1945 the Springhill Fencebusters, one of the region's finest town teams of the interwar years, defeated the best military clubs on their way to the Maritime title.

The H&D League opened play in 1946 as a four-team circuit made up of the Truro Bearcats, the Halifax Arrows,[2] Halifax United Services, and Halifax Shipyards. In the league opener in Halifax, a crowd of 6,474 watched the United Servicemen edge the Shipyards 4-3, while Truro split a doubleheader against the Halifax Arrows.[3] Although the Shipyards would continue as a powerhouse through the late 1940s, it was Truro's Bearcats that were the class of the league (and of the region) in its inaugural season, led by young left-hander Philip "Skit" Ferguson from Reserve Mines, Cape Breton, and second baseman-outfielder Johnny Clark from Westville, Pictou County. Clark, Ferguson, and outfielder Buddy Condy led the parade of stars from the Maritimes in the early years, along with the Seaman brothers – Danny, Garneau, and Ike – who were fixtures with the Liverpool Larrupers for a number of seasons. Danny Seaman had demonstrated his abilities during the war against Marchildon, collecting five hits in 12 at-bats and leading the big leaguer to comment that "Seaman hits the ball too hard and too often to be playing in Nova Scotia."[4] These players along with a number of other locals, veteran players from pro ball in the United States, and young college prospects from south of the border, joined together in a league that by the early 1950s was considered by many to be the most competitive unaffiliated summer league in Eastern North America.

There are three distinct periods in the history of the H&D League. The first of these was the period 1946-50, when the league completed a successful transition from military ball and maintained a healthy balance between local and imported players from the United States. At the time it was part of a network of similar semipro leagues operating elsewhere in the Maritimes, Maine, Quebec, and Vermont. The second period spanned the years from 1951 through 1956, when the most competitive summer leagues in the east, including the Albemarle League in the Carolinas, the Blackstone Industrial League in the mill towns of Maryland, and the highly regarded Vermont-Northern League, all ceased operations, making the H&D League an especially attractive destination for American players from as far south as the Carolinas and as far west as the Great Lakes. (Although the Cape Cod League continued to operate at this time, it restricted itself to players from the Cape Cod region, and did not emerge as the leading summer collegiate league until the 1960s.) The final period, 1957 through 1959, saw the H&D League shrink from a regular six-team operation with teams in Halifax, Dartmouth, Liverpool, Truro, Stellarton, and Kentville, to a four-team league made up largely of American college players considered prospects by major-league organizations. Over its history the H&D League and others in the region graduated dozens of players to the majors, including Dick Gernert, Hal Smith, Charley Lau, Turk Farrell,

Moe Drabowsky, Deacon Jones, Ron Perranoski, Al Spangler, Ty Cline, Dave Stenhouse, Rollie Sheldon, Maritime natives Billy Harris and Vern Handrahan, and many others.

THE EARLY YEARS: 1946-1950

With the transition from a wartime to peacetime economy, baseball in the Maritimes experienced a process of adjustment. As wartime athletes returned to their homes elsewhere in the country, or signed contracts within Organized Baseball, the H&D League and other similar circuits in the region such as the Central League, the Cape Breton Colliery League, various New Brunswick leagues, and the Maine New Brunswick League mixed local players and imported collegians and old pros from the United States. Although there were a few American players on H&D League clubs when the H&D League began play in 1946, the import model took hold over the next couple of years as major-league organizations, especially the Red Sox, Dodgers, Giants, Yankees, and Boston Braves, began to send prospects still in school and veteran players and coaches to provide stability and leadership. Former New York Giant Crip Polli was given the coaching reins in Halifax. A longtime minor leaguer in the Yankees system, Bob Decker, served as a Yankee scout and mentor with Dartmouth. Stuffy McInnis, a member of the Philadelphia Athletics' famed "$100,000 Infield," and then baseball coach at Harvard, looked after Red Sox interests with the Stellarton Albions in 1948 and 1949.[5] And University of New Hampshire coaching legend Hank Swasey was at the helm in Kentville, presiding over Wildcats prospects like Art Ceccarelli, Dick Gernert, and 1949 *Varsity Magazine* college player of the year Jack Kaiser from St. John's University. In 1950 virtually the entire St. John's lineup was playing in the league alongside players from high-profile baseball programs in New England, New York, and Pennsylvania.

The Brooklyn Dodgers were especially active in those early years, sponsoring and supplying players for coach Oakie O'Connor in Edmunston, Ed Pesaresi's Central League Amherst Ramblers, and the H&D League Wildcats. The Dodgers' involvement in baseball in the Maritimes explains why the Brooklyn Junior Dodgers club included Halifax in its Brooklyn-Against-the-World Canadian swing in 1948. Sponsored by the *Brooklyn Daily Eagle* newspaper to compete with the *New York World*'s Hearst Baseball Classic,[6] the Junior Dodgers were led by future major leaguers Billy Loes, Don McMahon, and Joe Pignatano, and other prospects, many of whom ended up playing in the Maritimes. In addition to defeating all-star teams in Washington and Providence, the Baby Dodgers played three games north of the border. After defeating junior teams in Toronto and Montréal, they lost their only game in Halifax by a score of 3-1. Led on the mound by local boy John "Twit" Clarke, Halifax held the visitors to four hits. Dodgers scouting director Mickey McConnell later told a Halifax columnist that he watched the defeat of the Dodgers with mixed feelings "since several of the players who put the lash on the Brooklyns were themselves members of the Brooklyn organization, and had been sent by him to the H&D League."[7] McConnell was particularly impressed with former 1947 Brooklyn star Herbie Rossman, who went 2-for-3 with a stolen base, and Saint John native Joe Breen, who along with a towering home run made two fine running catches in center field.

This was only one of a series of barnstorming tours that testified to the region's growing reputation in American baseball circles. Beginning in 1948, the Birdie Tebbetts All-Stars became regular visitors to the region, bringing a cadre of major-league stars that included Jimmy Piersall, Phil Rizzuto, Johnny Pesky, Vern Stephens, Bobby Thomson, Al Rosen, Sal Maglie, and Mike Garcia, to name but a few. Tebbetts threw in the towel after the 1951 tour because of dwindling crowds, but a similar squad led by Spec Shea carried on in future years. Other barnstorming clubs, among them the Georgia Chain Gang, the New England Hoboes, New York Equitable Life, the Boston Royal Giants, the Cambridge White Elephants, and the bewhiskered House of David also crisscrossed the region. For Haligonians, the three-game series between a combined squad from the Shipyards and Halifax Citadels against two-time US Amateur champion New York Equitable Life was particularly memorable. Local sportswriter Ace Foley's memoir described "the greatest game ever played in my life. ... It went into extra innings, the home team won ... and it had everything including a triple play."[8]

At the end of the decade, the import model was entrenched not only in the H&D League but everywhere in the region. Even small towns like MacAdam on the Maine-New Brunswick border – with 13 Americans on its 1949 roster – were looking south of the border for recruits. There was still room for the better local players, however. In 1950, five of the top 10 qualifiers for the H&D League batting championship were home-brews, and outfielders Buddy Condy and Johnny Clark finished one-two in the batting race. Condy led the league with a .358 average in 260 at-bats, Clark followed at .350, and future major leaguer Zeke Bella finished fifth at .306. Gradually, however, local players would increasingly be pushed aside as clubs turned over roster construction to American coaches and big-league scouts. "It was unfortunate," Johnny Clark observed. "Gradually the average player in the league would be an import rather than local. We may not have been stars, but neither were many of those who came in and took our jobs."[9] In the decade to come, as the league expanded its geographical footprint southward and westward, only the best of the locals were able to crack H&D League lineups.

EXTENDING THE GEOGRAPHICAL FOOTPRINT: 1951–1956

From 1951 through 1956, the H&D League operated as a six-team circuit, with teams in Halifax, Dartmouth, Truro, Kentville, Liverpool, and Stellarton. At the same time, it extended its recruitment reach southward into the Carolinas and westward to the Great Lakes region. The Carolinian connection began in earnest in 1951, when the Stellarton Albions assigned coaching and recruitment duties to Bill Brooks, a graduate of Wake Forest University and a four-year minor-league veteran catcher in the New York Giants organization. Brooks brought north the bulk of the Wake Forest Deacons lineup, including former All-American shortstop Art Hoch, father of PGA tour regular Scott Hoch, and 18-year-old infielder Gair Allie, Arnie Palmer's college roommate and eventual starting shortstop of the Pittsburgh Pirates in 1954. Between them, Brooks and Hoch spent 13 summers in Nova Scotia, developing a pipeline of quality players from Southern colleges, especially Duke, UNC, North Carolina State, and Clemson. An NCAA finalist in the College World Series in 1949, Wake Forest represented the United States at the Pan-American Games in the spring of 1951, just a few weeks before heading north to play as the Albions during the summer.

In addition to its emerging Southern connection, the league continued to attract the top players from colleges in Massachusetts, New York, and Pennsylvania, and later with a number of schools in Michigan. In the four years beginning in 1952, three NCAA championship schools, Holy Cross (1952), the University of Michigan (1953), and Wake Forest (1955), sent their best players to the H&D League. The same was true for tiny Elon College (1954), the smallest school ever to reach the College World Series finals. Fifteen of the players on the Holy Cross Crusader squad, for example, played in the league in the early '50s. According to Crusader Don Prohovich, who played four years in the Maritimes, the H&D League was "the place to play for collegians in the 1950s," and the league began to gain the reputation of being "NCAA North."[10] Prohovich played a number of years in the Chicago White Sox organization after that, topping out at the Triple-A level. It is not surprising that 15 first-team American College Coaches Association All-Americans, the equivalent of today's first-round draft choices, ended up playing in the H&D League, as did a number of second- and third-team selections.[11]

In addition to the league's Southern strategy, coach Ray Fisher of the 1953 NCAA Champion Michigan Wolverines began bringing players to the Maritimes in 1951 as the Vermont-Northern League teetered on the verge of collapse. Fisher coached for two years with the Black's Harbour Brunswicks of the Southern New Brunswick League, bringing first team All-Americans Ken Tippery and Bruce Haynam along, then shifted to Truro of the H&D League in 1954. The Maritime connection to collegiate baseball in Michigan, and with the highly regarded Detroit-Windsor Baseball Federation, had already begun a couple of years earlier, when a number of Windsor players with experience in the wartime Halifax Defence League returned to play with the Middleton Cardinals in the late '40s. Windsorites Jimmy Dumeah, Gerry Davis, Bernie Parent, Paul Oleynik, Nick Nikita, William Symonds, and Chester Conn, and Michigan natives John and Jim Wingo, Al Ware, and Hal Smith arrived in 1949. Another Windsor native, Maurice DeLoof, Midwestern regional scout for the Boston Red Sox and well known for signing future Red Sox Norm Zauchin, Ike Delock, and Dick "The Monster" Radatz, headed to Middleton in 1947 to join the pitching staff and keep tabs on H&D League prospects.

Although Stellarton won three successive championships in the early '50s, led by Allie,

Prince Edward Island native and H&D League alumnus Vern Handrahan with the Kansas City Athletics in 1966. (Prince Edward Island Sports Hall of Fame)

among them Prince Edward Island natives Vern Handrahan, who played parts of two seasons in the majors in the early 1960s, and Don MacLeod, another Charlottetown boy who played four years in the Braves organization, reaching as high as the Double-A Texas League.

In the mid-'50s an ill-conceived "bonus baby" regulation, requiring that signees with bonuses in excess of $4,000 be added to major-league 25-man rosters for two years, had an impact on the league. Because of the regulation, Tommy Gastall, who died tragically in a private plane crash in 1956, Tom Carroll, Art "Red" Swanson, Ralph Lumenti, and Moe Drabowsky all went to the majors directly from the H&D League, without a minor-league stop on the way. Wild Bill Oster, who pitched for the Larrupers in 1953, and Angelo Dagres, who played two years in the New Brunswick-Maine league, also made the jump directly to the majors from the Maritimes. After winning the league batting title in 1955, Dagres was invited to a morning tryout with the Baltimore Orioles, who signed him immediately and inserted him in their starting lineup that same afternoon.[12] This would simply not happen in today's baseball environment.

PLAYING OUT THE STRING: 1957-1959

Despite its reputation for high-quality play, the league faced a number of challenges at the end of the 1950s. An economic slowdown, the coming of television, and the development of new patterns of leisure that accompanied widespread automobile ownership affected attendance across the Maritimes. Already facing losses at the gate, Stellarton and Dartmouth began pushing for a restructuring of the league in 1955, calling unsuccessfully for salary caps and limits to the number of higher-salaried veteran pros that clubs could sign. All six teams operated through the 1956 season, but Halifax was close to folding

Brooks, outfielder Joe Fulghum from Wake Forest, and first team All-American first baseman Billy Werber and catcher Leroy Sires from Duke, other teams in the league sported their own young prospects. Two of Werber's Duke teammates, Halifax's Al Spangler, who went on to a 13-year major league career, and Dave Sime, Silver medalist in the 1960 Olympics 100-meter dash, spent two years in the region. Elsewhere, Braves scout Jeff Jones was instrumental in assembling the Truro club every year, holding tryout camps in New England before the H&D League began its summer schedule. Often assisted by former Brooklyn Dodger Doc Gautreau, whose parents came from New Brunswick and Quebec, Jones signed dozens of players to Braves contracts, that year before the Philadelphia Phillies came to their rescue with an affiliation agreement.[13] Having lost their affiliate in Trois-Rivières when the Provincial League folded, and with manager Lew Krausse already signed to a guaranteed contract, the Phillies shifted their attention eastward. It was only a temporary fix, however. Halifax withdrew from the league in 1957, and Liverpool did as well. The Phillies eventually worked out an affiliation with the Kentville Wildcats and eventually signed a number of players, including future big leaguers Norm Gigon and Lee Elia. Halifax returned to the league for the 1959 season with a team assembled by the Boston Red Sox and managed by career minor leaguer and eventual Washington Senators coach Joe Camacho.

In those final years the H&D League was a shadow of its former self. Although there were still a number of talented players on the field, the league had become a "prospects league" similar to short-season leagues within the Organized Baseball of the early twenty-first century. Nova Scotia native Wilson Parsons, who played eight years in the Yankees organization, mostly at the Triple-A level, had the following remembrance of pitching for Dartmouth as a young flamethrower in 1951 and then again in 1959, when he relied on experience to get H&D Leaguers out: "I think the talent in the H&D League in those early days was superior. You still had some individual stars in '59, but I'm not sure that the depth was there like it was in '51 or '52. It just seemed so easy when I came back. I wasn't trying to show anybody up. It was just what I had learned over the years. … I could hardly break a pane of glass, but there were so many different little things that I could do with the ball to set batters up."[14]

Of the many young players in those waning years who would make their way to baseball's higher echelons, the following players stood out. Ty Cline and Jack Kubiszyn ended up playing together with the Cleveland Indians in the early

'60s. Rollie Sheldon ended up pitching for the New York Yankees in the 1964 World Series. Clemson grad Hal Stowe also had a cup of coffee with New York. Future Chicago Cubs Gordon Massa, Moe Morhardt, Don Eaddy, and Danny Murphy – .280 hitters in their stints in the Maritimes – were among a dozen or so players signed by former Cape Breton Colliery League star Lenny Merullo. Dale Willis, Jim Hannan, John Boozer, Jim Bailey, Bill Spanswick, Ed Connolly, and Ontario native Ken MacKenzie were among the many to end up in the big leagues. Of all the prospects in the latter years of the H&D Leagues, none gained more attention than Danny Murphy. In the June 27, 1960, issue of *Sports Illustrated*, Roy Terrell gave a minute-by-minute review of the day the 17-year-old outfielder-pitcher Murphy was signed to a $100,000 bonus by Merullo. Although he didn't fulfill expectations as an outfielder, Murphy later turned into a solid major-league reliever with the Chicago White Sox.[15] Another two-way player, Manly Johnson of the 1958 Kentville Wildcats, was a power-hitting outfielder and 20-game winner at Double A in the White Sox organization.

EPILOGUE

In a story in *The Sporting News* on June 30, 1962, one-time Yankee pitching ace Johnny Murphy, director of the Red Sox minor-league operations in the '50s, spoke at length about the league's demise. "When I was with Boston we were very much interested in the Nova Scotia league, a fast summer league that got most of the good high school and college boys," said Murphy. Conversations with various people in Nova Scotia suggested that the league needed about $10,000 per year in extra funding to continue operating. If spread out equally among all 16 major-league clubs, this would mean a minor outlay of about $600 per team, a pittance given how liberally bonus money was being spread around. With this in mind, Murphy wrote "all fifteen other clubs telling them that this fine league could be kept going ... [but] I got answers from only six clubs."[16] The result was the collapse of a 15-year experiment still remembered as a high point in the baseball history of the Maritimes.

NOTES

1 Phil Marchildon with Brian Kendall, *Ace. Canada's Pitching Sensation and Wartime Hero* (Toronto: Viking, 1993), 111.

2 The Arrows would eventually move across the harbor to Dartmouth in 1949.

3 Burton Russell, *Seven Decades of Nova Scotia Baseball. 1946-2016* (Kentville: Self-published, 2017), 7.

4 Quoted in Burton Russell, *Nova Scotia Baseball Heroics* (Kentville: Self-published, 1993), 38.

5 *The Sporting News*, December 1, 1948 (page 17) reported on McInnis's summer in Nova Scotia. "I don't believe I ever had any better time in my life," said McInnis. "Those coal mining people were crazy about the game and the players, most of whom were boys who worked in the mine all day. But tired and all and with little previous experience, they did well enough to battle Halifax for the championship." McInnis returned to coach in 1949 as well.

6 Alan Cohen is the acknowledged expert on the Hearst Classic. See his "Baseball Stories" at https://alancohenbaseball.wordpress.com.

7 *Halifax Chronicle Herald*, August 4, 1948: 6.

8 Ace Foley, *The First Fifty Years. The Life and Times of a Sportswriter* (Windsor, Nova Scotia: Lancelot Press, 1970), 24-25.

9 Personal interview with Johnny Clark, Halifax, November 29, 1989.

10 Telephone interview with Don Prohovich, June 16, 1994.

11 American Baseball Coaches Association First Team All-Americans to play in the Maritimes: Bill Werber Jr. (Duke), 1952; Jim O'Neill (Holy Cross), 1952; Fred Flemming (Bowdoin), 1953; Bruce Haynam (Michigan), 1953; Charles Heerlein (St. John's), 1954; Linwood Holt (Wake Forest), 1955; Don Prohovich (Holy Cross), 1956; Marsh McLean (Amherst), 1957; Ken Tippery (Michigan), 1957; Frank Saia (Harvard), 1958; Bob Wedin (Connecticut), 1958; Moe Morhardt (Connecticut), 1958; and Ty Cline (Clemson), 1960.

12 Author interview with Johnny Clark, Halifax, November 29, 1989.

13 Author telephone interview with Don Provohich, June 16, 1994.

14 Author interview with Wilson Parsons, Truro, Nova Scotia, September 1, 1995.

15 Roy Terrell, "The Signing of Danny Murphy," *Sports Illustrated*, June 27, 1960: 32-37.

16 *The Sporting News*, June 30, 1962: 4.

CANADIANS DICK FOWLER, PHIL MARCHILDON WIN BOTH ENDS OF TWIN BILL FOR ATHLETICS

AUGUST 17, 1947 DOUBLEHEADER AT GRIFFITH STADIUM:
PHILADELPHIA ATHLETICS 2, WASHINGTON SENATORS 1 (GAME 1)
PHILADELPHIA ATHLETICS 5, WASHINGTON SENATORS 2 (GAME 2)

By Gary Belleville

It was no coincidence that the Philadelphia Athletics' two best pitchers in the 1940s were from the province of Ontario.[1] There was a simple reason for it: Connie Mack's Athletics had a working agreement with the International League's Toronto Maple Leafs.[2]

In 1937 Toronto began conducting tryout camps in the hopes of uncovering local talent.[3] That first summer they discovered Dick Fowler, a 16-year-old string bean from the Stanley Park neighborhood in Toronto.[4] The next year, they spotted Penetanguishene's Phil Marchildon in a tryout camp in Barrie, Ontario.[5] Thinking that he might be too old to be considered a bona-fide prospect, the 24-year-old Marchildon shaved three years off his age when he signed with the Maple Leafs.[6]

Both pitchers performed well during their minor-league stints with Toronto.[7] Mack, who was looking to improve the American League's worst pitching staff, purchased Marchildon's contract from the Maple Leafs at the end of Toronto's

1940 season. A year later, he made a similar move to acquire Fowler.[8]

Marchildon had an easier time transitioning into the majors, in part because he was more than six years older than Fowler at the time of his call-up. "Penetang Phil" was the most effective hurler on the lowly Athletics in 1941-42, compiling a 27-29 record and a 3.91 ERA. The 21-year-old Fowler struggled with a 4.95 ERA in 1942, his first full season in the majors.

With World War II raging in Europe, Marchildon enlisted in the Royal Canadian Air Force after the 1942 season, while Fowler joined the Canadian Army. Both players sacrificed almost three full seasons of their big-league careers to help in the war effort.

Marchildon completed his training as a tail gunner in England in May of 1944.[9] In August, on his 26th mission, his plane was shot down over the Sea of Denmark and five of his six crewmates perished.[10] He spent nine harrowing months in a German POW camp, losing 40 pounds during the ordeal.[11]

Marchildon was a completely different person after the war. Instead of his usual friendly and outgoing self, he was nervous and guarded.[12] After some reluctance, he was persuaded by Mack to return to the team in early July of 1945.[13] He made three appearances that season, including an August 29 start at Shibe Park on Phil Marchildon Night.[14]

Fowler was nearly deployed to Europe in the fall of 1944, but he remained in Canada on compassionate grounds when doctors diagnosed his infant son with terminal cancer.[15] On August 15, 1945, the day after the announcement of Japan's surrender, Fowler was discharged from the army.[16]

In his first big-league start in almost three years, Fowler became the first Canadian to toss a major-league no-hitter when he defeated the St. Louis Browns, 1-0, on September 9.[17] It served as the launching point for his big-league career. For the rest of the decade, Fowler was Mack's most valuable pitcher.[18]

Fowler and Marchildon were the workhorses of the Philadelphia pitching staff. They pitched decently in 1946, but the Athletics stumbled to a 49-105 record, and the Canadian duo was saddled with 16 losses each.[19]

Career years from Fowler and Marchildon helped Philadelphia improve significantly in 1947.[20] The Athletics came into their doubleheader with Washington on August 17 sitting in fourth place with a respectable 58-54 record. The Senators, headed in the opposite direction, were in seventh place with a 46-60 mark.

Fowler (8-8, 2.77 ERA) got the start in the first game of the twin bill against future Hall of Famer Early Wynn. The 27-year-old Wynn had a 12-11 record and a 3.52 ERA.

The two right-handers went toe-to-toe in a tight pitchers' duel. With the game still scoreless in the bottom of the fifth, Wynn came to the plate with one out and nobody on. After Fowler fell behind 3-and-1 in the count, he grooved a pitch that Wynn clubbed over the right-field wall for his second home run of the season.[21]

The score remained 1-0 until the top of the eighth when Fowler singled to start a two-out rally. After Barney McCosky's double moved Fowler to third base, Eddie Joost doubled sharply over the head of Washington third baseman Eddie Yost to drive in both runners and give the Athletics a 2-1 lead.[22]

Wynn hit for himself with two out in the bottom of the ninth and the tying run on first base. The decision by Senators manager Ossie Bluege to let Wynn bat was hardly surprising, since he had hits in his two previous plate appearances against Fowler. The switch-hitting pitcher had also batted .407 against righties in 1946. Wynn looped a double into right-center field with the runner on first, Jerry Priddy, running on contact. Right fielder George Binks caught the ball on one bounce with his bare hand and relayed the ball to second baseman Pete Suder, who turned and fired a strike to the plate to nail Priddy for the game's final out.[23] Fowler earned the victory and lowered his ERA to 2.67.

The second game of the doubleheader lacked the drama of the opener.[24] Marchildon (14-7, 3.26 ERA) took to the hill for Philadelphia. The 33-year-old right-hander had earned a decision in each of his 13 previous starts, with nine of those outings going into the win column. The Senators countered with 34-year-old southpaw Mickey Haefner. The knuckleballer had a record of 7-9 and a 3.73 ERA. He had been red-hot recently, allowing only three runs in his five previous starts.

Philadelphia opened the scoring on Hank Majeski's fly ball in the second inning.

The Athletics exploded for four more runs in the third on five hits and a walk; the big blast was a double by Suder that knocked in a pair of runs. The offensive outburst sent Haefner for an early shower, breaking his streak of five consecutive

Dick Fowler (left) and Phil Marchildon (right) at Philadelphia Athletics spring training in the late 1940s. (Canadian Baseball Hall of Fame and Museum)

complete games. After 2½ innings, Philadelphia held a comfortable 5-0 lead.

Marchildon breezed through the Washington lineup, retiring the first 17 men in order.

With two out in the sixth inning, his perfect game was snapped when the normally reliable Joost booted a groundball hit by reliever Milo Candini. A frustrated Marchildon kicked the mound and walked the next batter, Yost, before getting out of the inning by retiring Montréal native Sherry Robertson.[25]

Mickey Vernon broke up the no-hitter in the seventh with a one-out triple. He scored when the next batter, Joe Grace, singled.

The Senators added an unearned run in the bottom of the ninth on another fielding error by Joost, but Philadelphia hung on for a 5-2 win.

Marchildon tossed a complete-game four-hitter, earning his 15th win of the season.

Marchildon continued to pitch well for the remainder of the season. Nine days after the Washington doubleheader, he took a perfect game into the bottom of the eighth in Cleveland, only to lose it on a missed strike-three call that should have ended the inning. Marchildon went "ballistic" after the blown call, and he was fortunate that he wasn't ejected.[26] He settled for a 12-inning, complete-game victory and drove in the eventual game-winning run himself. He finished the season with a 19-9 record and a 3.22 ERA.

Fowler quietly put together the best season on the Athletics pitching staff. Six one-run defeats limited his record to a modest 12-11, and in 10 of his 11 losses, Philadelphia scored two runs or less. However, his 2.81 ERA was third best in the American League. Fowler's Adjusted ERA (ERA+) of 136 ranked ahead of Bob Feller's 130 ERA+ and second overall in the junior circuit.[27]

The Canadian pitching pair, who were best friends and roommates on the road,[28] helped Philadelphia to its first winning season since 1933. The Athletics finished with a 78-76 record, an increase of 29 wins over their abysmal 1946 campaign. Despite the marked improvement, they still finished in fifth place. It was their 14th consecutive season in the second division.

Philadelphia's resurgent pitching staff deserved credit for the team's rapid improvement. Yankees coach Chuck Dressen raved about the Athletics hurlers after the 1947 season. "Look at the staff of competent pitchers Connie Mack has!" he exclaimed. "Fowler, Marchildon, [Bill] McCahan and [Joe] Coleman. That's the best pitching staff in baseball."[29]

Marchildon and Fowler's double victory in Washington on August 17 may have been the peak for the duo. Marchildon's post-traumatic-stress issues worsened in 1948, and he was never the same pitcher.[30] He won only nine more games in the majors. Prior to the start of the 1950 season, Marchildon's contract was sold to Buffalo of the International League.

Fowler hurt his pitching shoulder throwing batting practice on the first day of spring training in 1948. The injury plagued him for the remainder of his career.[31] Despite pitching through jaw-clenching pain, Fowler still posted back-to-back 15-win seasons in 1948-49. Three more injury-riddled seasons followed, and he was released by Philadelphia on October 17, 1952.[32]

Marchildon and Fowler were inducted into the Canadian Baseball Hall of Fame in 1983 and 1985, respectively.[33]

SOURCES

In addition to the sources cited in the Notes, the author consulted Baseball-Reference.com and Retrosheet.org.

https://www.baseball-reference.com/boxes/WS1/WS1194708171.shtml

https://www.retrosheet.org/boxesetc/1947/B08171WS11947.htm

https://www.baseball-reference.com/boxes/WS1/WS1194708172.shtml

https://www.retrosheet.org/boxesetc/1947/B08172WS11947.htm

NOTES

1   In the 1940s, Fowler went 59-61 with a 3.65 ERA in 1,052⅔ innings pitched, and Marchildon went 68-75 with a 3.92 ERA in 1,213 innings. Despite missing almost three full seasons because of World War II, they were the only pitchers to toss more than 1,000 innings for the Philadelphia Athletics in the decade.

2   Along with the American Association and Pacific Coast League, the International League was at the highest level of the minor leagues in 1937. It was classified as Double A from 1912 until the introduction of the Triple-A classification in 1946.

3   Gary Belleville, "Dick Fowler," SABR BioProject, https://sabr.org/bioproj/person/dick-fowler/, accessed March 9, 2021. International League President Frank Shaughnessy pushed the Maple Leafs to find local talent in the hopes of increasing their attendance. Shaughnessy even acted as an instructor in Toronto's first "baseball school" at Maple Leaf Stadium in July of 1937. Fowler was discovered at that camp.

4   The Toronto media dubbed Fowler the "Stanley Park string bean" during his time with the Maple Leafs.

5   Phil Marchildon with Brian Kendall, *Ace: Phil Marchildon, Canada's Pitching Sensation and Wartime Hero*, (Toronto: Penguin Books Canada Ltd., 1993), 17.

6   Marchildon and Kendall, 22. Fowler knocked one year off his age when he signed with the Athletics. Reporting an inaccurate birthdate was common during this era. The fans, media, and, most importantly, Connie Mack, were unaware of Fowler and Marchildon's correct birthdates throughout their professional careers.

7   Marchildon went 15-20 with a 3.69 ERA with the Maple Leafs in 1939-40. Fowler went 11-10 with a 3.27 ERA with Toronto in 1940-41. The Maple Leafs finished dead last in the International League standings in all three of those seasons.

8   Fowler won his big-league debut on September 13, 1941, against the Chicago White Sox. He tossed a complete game in a 3-1 victory.

9   Marchildon and Kendall, 114.

10   Marchildon and Kendall, 150-51.

11   Ralph Berger, "Phil Marchildon," SABR BioProject, https://sabr.org/bioproj/person/phil-marchildon/, accessed March 9, 2021.

12   Berger, "Phil Marchildon."

13   Marchildon and Kendall, 152-53.

14   Marchildon suffered a leg injury in his August 29, 1945, start. He tried to pitch four days later and had to be pulled after two innings because of the pain. He was shut down for the rest of the season after that start.

15   Belleville, "Dick Fowler." Fowler's son, Tommy, was expected to live for only five months after the diagnosis. He defied doctors' predictions and lived into his early 40s.

16   Gary Bedingfield, "Dick Fowler," Baseball in Wartime, https://www.baseballinwartime.com/player_biographies/fowler_dick.htm, accessed March 11, 2021.

17   As of the end of the 2020 season, the only other Canadian to throw a major-league no-hitter was James Paxton. He tossed a no-hitter for the Seattle Mariners against the Blue Jays in Toronto on May 8, 2018.

18   From the end of World War II to the end of the 1949 season, Fowler went 52-48 with a 3.45 ERA. Over that same period, Marchildon went 41-44 with a 3.89 ERA.

19   Their Philadelphia teammate Lou Knerr also suffered 16 losses in 1946. As of 2021, it was the only time in major-league history that three pitchers on the same team led the league in losses.

20   Rookie Ferris Fain helped the Athletics' offense immensely in 1947. The addition of shortstop Eddie Joost was a significant boost to the team's defense as well.

21   Art Morrow, "A's Defeat Nats, 2-1, 5-2, Behind Fowler and Marchildon," *Philadelphia Inquirer*, August 18, 1947: 20.

22   Morrow, "A's Defeat Nats, 2-1, 5-2, Behind Fowler and Marchildon."

23   Burton Hawkins, "Nats Face Rough Time in West as Batters Lose All Punch," *Washington Evening Star*, August 18, 1947: 12.

24   Four baserunners were thrown out at home in the first game. In addition to the game-ending play, Philadelphia left fielder Barney McCosky threw out Buddy Lewis at the plate to end the bottom of the third. Washington also threw out two baserunners at home: center fielder Stan Spence threw out George Binks to end the top of the fourth and Eddie Joost for the second out in the top of the seventh.

25   Morrow, "A's Defeat Nats, 2-1, 5-2, Behind Fowler and Marchildon." Robertson had a 10-year major-league career with the Washington Senators and Philadelphia Athletics. He was inducted into the Canadian Baseball Hall of Fame in 2007.

26   Marchildon and Kendall, 193-96. Marchildon threw his glove and vehemently argued the call with umpire Bill McKinley, who was in his first full season in the big leagues. Both Marchildon and catcher Buddy Rosar were later fined $25 each by the American League.

27 Fowler's ERA+ of 136 means that his earned-run average was 36 percent better than league average after adjusting for park effects. Joe Haynes of the Chicago White Sox led the American League in ERA+ (150) and ERA (2.42) in 1947. Feller had the league's second-best ERA (2.68). Both Fowler and Eddie Lopat posted a 2.81 ERA. However, Fowler had a slightly better ERA than Lopat when rounding to three decimal places (2.811 versus 2.814).

28 Jim Shearon, *Canada's Baseball Legends* (Kanata, Ontario: Malin Head Press, 1994), 73. Marchildon and Fowler had known each other for quite some time. They attended spring training together with the Maple Leafs in Avon Park, Florida, in 1939 and 1940.

29 "Dressen Claims Pitching Produced Homers in N.L.," *The Sporting News*, October 8, 1947: 27. Dressen was not exaggerating in his praise for the Philadelphia pitching staff; they led the American League with an ERA+ of 109 in 1947. Unfortunately, injuries derailed the careers of Fowler, McCahan, and Coleman. Marchildon's career was cut short by post-traumatic stress from the war.

30 Berger, "Phil Marchildon."

31 Belleville, "Dick Fowler."

32 Fowler gutted it out for two more pain-filled seasons in 1953 and 1954 with the Triple-A Charleston (West Virginia) Senators.

33 Fowler was inducted posthumously into the Canadian Baseball Hall of Fame. He died of kidney and liver disease in 1972.

ALLAN ROTH

By Andy McCue

Henry Chadwick, baseball's first historian, tried to capture a game in a chart for his newspaper readers. It was called a box score, and as it evolved over the years, it offered the raw material for the statistically minded to analyze, understand, and appreciate the game. There were dozens who followed, from Ernie Lanigan, longtime baseball writer and editor, to fans sitting at their dining room tables with pencils and, maybe, a mechanical calculator.

Allan Roth pushed the analysis of baseball statistics to a new level. He promoted himself into a place those other analysts only aspired to. Roth was the first to be employed full time by a major-league team, "the only zealot lucky enough to work for a major league team and to get to test his theories first hand."[1]

Abraham Roth was born in Montréal on May 10, 1917, the son of Nathan and Rose (Silverheart). Nathan, a tailor, had emigrated from Galicia (which straddles the current Poland/Ukraine border) in 1899 at the age of 15. Rose probably came from Bucavina, an area then part of Romania, but now in Ukraine. She arrived about 1910.[2] Abraham had an older brother, Max, who became a leading Canadian architect, and a younger sister Sylvia.

Nathan worked as a tailor and the family moved around Ontario province before returning to Montréal during Abraham's high school years, when he attended Strathcona Academy, playing all the major sports. He also spent many free hours from ages 13 to 16, compiling statistics for the International League and his home town Montréal Royals. He passed the entrance examination for McGill University, where Max was already studying. Family circumstances, however, prevented paying for a second college student, so Abraham took a job. He worked as a salesman, first of magazines and later of men's ties, suspenders, belts and mufflers.[3]

In July 1940, Abraham married Esther Machlovitch and the following winter, changed his name to Allan. Later that year, he began his pursuit of "the type of work that I wanted to do."[4] From an early age, he had been mathematically oriented, entertaining himself and his family at age three by counting backwards from 100 by twos.[5] In his spare time, he had done both hockey and baseball statistics, developing the breakdowns which would characterize his later work.

In December 1940, Roth wrote to Leland "Larry" MacPhail, president of the Brooklyn Dodgers, seeking an appointment to discuss work as a statistician. He tried again in June and August of the next year. He met MacPhail in the Mount Royal Hotel in Montréal and explained his ideas. MacPhail was, at best, non-committal.[6] But, Roth decided to take the plunge, quit his job in men's clothing and began to compile statistics on professional hockey. In October 1941, Roth showed his work to Frank Calder, president of the National Hockey League, who hired him to be the league's official statistician and to write for the league's publicity sheet. His progress was interrupted three months later, when he was drafted into the Canadian Army.[7]

The Army at least recognized his talents and he was put in charge of all the records and statistics of the unit charged with organizing reinforcement contingents for Canadian Forces in Europe. In January 1944, Roth was discharged due to epilepsy, which was of the petit mal variety, and not likely to affect his work.[8] He began to write sports features for the *Montréal Standard* and to compile statistics for the Montréal Canadiens. But, he kept his focus on the Dodgers because he considered Branch Rickey, MacPhail's successor as Dodger president, the most innovative man in sports.

In April 1944, three months after his military discharge, he wangled a meeting with Rickey at the Dodgers spring training site in Bear Mountain, just north of New York City. It was a disaster, Roth said. The dinner included Mrs. Rickey and was in the main dining room of the Bear Mountain Inn, the premier hotel in the region. Rickey was constantly being interrupted by well-wishers. Roth despaired of making a coherent presentation. Finally, Roth told Rickey he didn't think he was getting a fair shake. Asked what he wanted, Roth responded, "Ten minutes of your undivided attention."[9]

Rickey asked that Roth send Ed Staples, his assistant, a detailed outline of Roth's ideas. The four-page letter contained proposals to track a wide range of statistics. Some of these were

standard, but others, such as where the ball was hit and the count it was hit on, hadn't been compiled regularly. Roth also proposed to break the statistics down into various categories that would reveal tendencies which the front office and the manager could use to win ballgames. Breakdowns such as performance against left-handers and right-handers, in day games versus night games, in the various ballparks, in situations with runners in scoring position, are all mundane to us now. But in Roth's time, they were rarely compiled or used, and never part of the public discussion. The letter was intriguing enough to get a meeting with a still-skeptical Rickey. The conversation turned positive, Roth said, when Rickey asked him about runs batted in. Roth said he didn't think much of runs batted in unless they were correlated with the chances to drive them in, and differentiated again by which base they'd been drive in from. This meshed with Rickey's own beliefs and the conversation flowered. Roth was offered the job.[10]

But, with World War II, and then the U.S. government's fears that returning servicemen would have a hard time finding jobs as military production was cut back, Roth couldn't get a visa until 1947. Even then, Rickey had some difficulty persuading his partners, Walter O'Malley and John Smith, to approve a $5,000 salary.[11]

The Roth era began on Opening Day, April 15, 1947, with the Dodgers hosting the Boston Braves at Ebbets Field. Braves shortstop's Dick Culler's ground out to third base was the first plate appearance to go into Roth's specially designed 17x14 inch sheets. Beginning that day, Roth would record virtually every pitch in a Dodger game for the next 18 seasons. The game itself was only part of his day. He estimated he spent another five hours daily, at a minimum, updating the breakdowns on the Dodgers and their opponents. In the offseason, he would refine the numbers further, seeking longer term trends and finding the outliers. Everyone knew right-handed hitters generally performed more poorly against right-handed pitchers and vice versa. Roth would look for, and find, the left-handed hitter who broke the mold and could provide a manager with an unexpected platoon advantage. He tracked bases advanced, a metric that encompassed baserunning statistics as well as the ability to move runners along with outs. He recorded what happened at each point in the count, what happened in bunting situations and differences between night and day games, home and away games, and in individual stadiums. No other team had access to such analysis at that time.

Unlike contemporary statistical analysts, Roth generally ignored higher mathematics. "The figures concerned in baseball statistical work don't call for integral calculus or even advanced algebra," he said.[12] And he also recognized their limits. "I know perfectly well that baseball cannot be played one hundred percent according to figures, and that the human element is even more important. I realize that certain sets of figures on players and teams will change from time to time, but nevertheless, by a deep and systematic research into the detailed statistics which I have in mind, there is bound to come to light numerous facts which were previously unknown, and which would prove of great value."[13] His records would become voluminous. When the team moved from Brooklyn to Los Angeles a decade later, newspapers reported Roth's data took up more space than the rest of the Dodgers' archives.[14]

In fact, outside of baseball, Roth wasn't much of a numbers guy at all. He didn't do his own taxes.[15] He couldn't remember his phone number.[16] What he would do is record the numbers in myriad detail and then use his true talent, recognizing what the numbers meant, to provide value to his employers. He summed up his philosophy: "Baseball is a game of percentages – I try to find the actual percentage, which is constantly shifting, and apply it to the situation where it will do the most good."[17]

In his first season, for example, Roth used another of his innovations – spray charts showing the location of all of a player's batted balls – to show that Dixie Walker's hits were going to the opposite field more and more frequently. Rickey, following his own dictum that it was better to trade a player a year too early, sent Walker to the Pirates. "The People's Cherce" hit .316 in 1948, but was down to .282 the next year, and became a player-manager in the minors.[18] A year after his Walker revelation, Roth's numbers showed that in 1948, Jackie Robinson drove in a higher percentage of baserunners than any other hitter in the lineup. Manager Burt Shotton moved Robinson, who had barely broken into double digits with 12 homers, into the cleanup spot. He hit only four more home runs in 1949, but drove in 124 and won the National League Most Valuable Player Award.[19]

Roth's major league debut was missed in the tumult surrounding Jackie Robinson's that same day, but reporters soon began to notice the latest addition to the Dodgers' traveling party. By June 1947, *The Sporting News* contained a note that Allen (sic) Roth, a "slide-rule expert," was providing Rickey with numbers to analyze the team.[20] In those days, Roth's numbers were considered proprietary and not made public, adding to the mystery. But he would generate awed publicity – the "flesh-and-blood electronic brain" or "Mechanical Brain Can't Match Roth's" and some fear on the part of players, who saw him as Rickey's hatchet man, especially after the Walker trade.[21]

In looking for meaning in the numbers, Roth's methodology was much like that of Bill James and later members of the Society for American Baseball Research – take a piece of accepted baseball wisdom and analyze whether it was true. "Some fellows have mentioned that batting average increases of ten or 12 points would result from the sacrifice fly rule," Roth said during a 1953 discussion of scoring rules, "The figures on the Dodgers for the last two years don't come anywhere near such figures."[22]

Rickey's departure from the Dodgers after the 1950 season meant changes for Roth. The new owner, Walter O'Malley, was dedicated to the business side of the organization. The new manager, Charlie Dressen, managed by the seat of his pants and, after receiving Roth's work politely, would quickly deposit it in the trash can.[23] The new head baseball man, Buzzie Bavasi, cottoned to Roth slowly.

Roth's working position was moved from a seat behind home plate to the press box. To Roth, the move felt like a demotion, and he felt unappreciated.[24] He quit classifying the pitches because he didn't feel he could do it accurately from his new perspective. O'Malley moved him to the press and public relations operation, a department the new president understood. Roth's tidbits began to appear regularly in the newspaper columns and he was put in charge of a publication called *Press Box Pickups*. Distributed to reporters each game day during the season, the magazine was filled with Roth's statistics as well as promotional material.

He provided extensive statistical sections for the team's yearbooks and media guides.

In 1954, he was moved into the radio booth to feed timely material to the Dodger announcers and quickly struck up a strong friendship with Vin Scully, who was becoming the team's lead announcer. "If you had some question that came to you in the middle of a game, he would reach down into the bag, and next thing you knew you'd have your answer. It was marvelous," said Scully.[25] This partnership had an additional benefit to the team's bottom line – the broadcast sponsors began to pay half Roth's salary.[26] A few years later, Roth's spot in the booth included a link to the press box P.A. system, where his choicer items could be relayed live to reporters. He was always available to reporters looking for statistics to back up an angle or ideas for something to write on a slow day. The Dodger switchboard directed all queries of a statistical nature to Roth's desk, and he settled a great number of bar bets. He even tried to answer queries from long before his

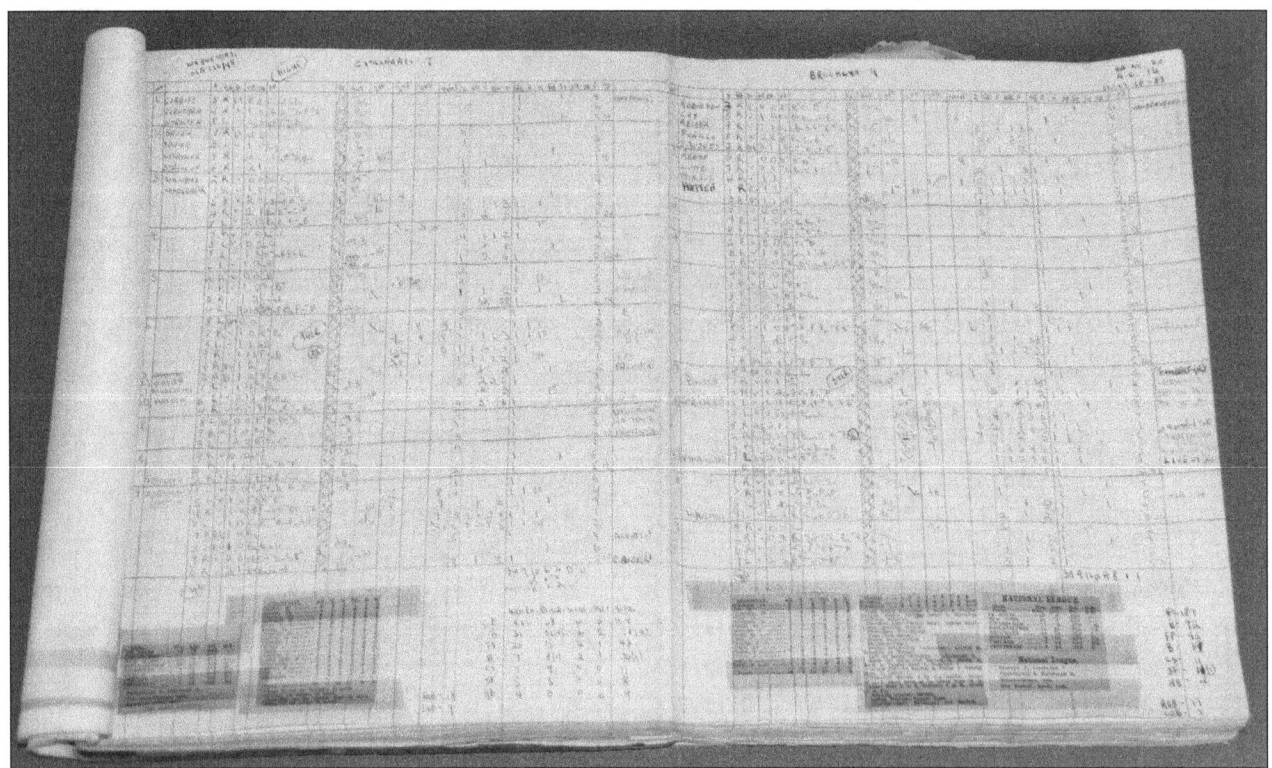

Data collection, 1940s style: The page from Allan Roth's scorebook for May 12, 1948. (Canadian Baseball Hall of Fame and Museum)

Allan Roth with the tools of his trade, 1954. (Wm. C. Greene, courtesy Library of Congress)

time or his statistics, such as why Dodger pitcher Henry Schmidt, who went 22-13 for the 1903 Dodgers at age 30, never pitched in the majors again. Schmidt, a Texas native, had decided he didn't like living in the East and returned his 1904 contract unsigned.[27]

Roth kept up his interest in the more analytical side of his statistical work. As the only full-time team statistician, he became a magnet for others working in the field and an inspiration to many young men who would write him for advice about how they could get into his line of work. He corresponded with Nathan McFadgen, Charles Mercurio, Paul Simpson, Tony Johncola, and others, all researchers with a statistical bent who were self-publishing their findings.

In 1954, Roth's work hit the big time – with a heavy coating of Branch Rickey. *Life Magazine*, one of the largest-circulation magazines in the country, ran an article titled "Goodby [sic] to

Some Old Baseball Ideas." The article said it had been written by Branch Rickey, whose picture graced the first page. Roth's back is visible in the background of that photo, and he is pictured on the article's third page, along with a multipart equation. That equation was clearly Roth's work; Rickey called the equation, "the most disconcerting and at the same time the most constructive thing to come into baseball in my memory." Thirty years later, John Thorn and Pete Palmer, in their seminal book, *The Hidden Game of Baseball*, wrote "Rickey and Roth's fundamental contribution to the advancement of baseball statistics comes from their conceptual revisionism, their willingness to strip the game down to its basic unit, the run, and reconstruct its statistics accordingly."[28]

In many ways, "The Equation" was years ahead of its time. Its first two terms were what we today call on-base percentage and isolated power. It would take the book *Moneyball* half a century later to cement the importance of on-base percentage. The equation, which contained eight different terms, including pieces devoted to run-scoring efficiency, pitching, and fielding, was vastly complicated for contemporary baseball organizations. In his history of baseball analytics, Alan Schwarz summarizes the impact of Roth's equation: "No evidence exists that anyone took it seriously."

While Roth may have felt unappreciated within the Dodger organization, it could not have been completely unexpected. Roth's 1944 letter to Ed Staples outlining the benefits of employing him had suggested exactly the kind of press and public relations work Roth was now performing. More significantly, it is clear the Dodgers didn't see him merely as a producer of press releases and statistical tidbits.

As the 1951 season tottered to a close, the Dodgers felt they had an insurmountable lead – 12 1/2 games on the morning of August 13. So, they detached Roth with scout Andy High for a two-week tour to follow the New York Yankees and Cleveland Indians, the two leading contenders for the American League flag. High would make the traditional scouting report, while Roth would add his statistical insights. These two weeks encompassed the only Dodger games Roth missed from 1947 to 1964. The Dodgers' pennant hopes succumbed to an unbelievable charge by the New York Giants. O'Malley sent Roth a note of thanks.[29]

It wasn't just game statistics where Roth's opinion was sought. That same year, O'Malley sent Roth a pamphlet titled "American Baseball Needs Four Major Leagues" and asked for his opinion of the arguments. The book dealt with questions of population shifts, markets and the structure of major and minor leagues. Roth responded with some mostly statistical comments on the work.[30]

O'Malley turned to Roth again after the 1954 season, and it's clear that he was concerned about Walter Alston, who had just finished his rookie season as the Dodgers' manager. Each year, Roth produced a book which summarized the team's just-ended season. There were only four copies made – for O'Malley, Bavasi, Alston, and Roth. In mid-December 1954, O'Malley queried Roth on when he'd be able to see the report.[31] Roth delivered the report two weeks later, discussing reasons for the Dodgers poorer 1954 performance. He noted some pitching and hitting declines but also suggested Alston wasn't conducting as aggressive a running game as had Dressen.[32] In reply, O'Malley posed additional questions about the number of "hit and run" and "run and hit" plays called, as well as stolen base attempts. "There was a change of managers," O'Malley wrote, "Is there any significance (to that)? Was club direction less enterprising?"[33]

Roth began assuming again more of the role he had played under Rickey. But now his analysis was not going just to Rickey, but to the manager and directly to individual players. On Friday, September 18, 1959, the Dodgers arrived in San Francisco for a key series against the Giants. The team was two games behind the Giants and tied with the Milwaukee Braves. With only eight games left in the season, they need a sweep to have any realistic hope of making the World Series. Friday night's game was rained out and Alston announced that Don Drysdale, who'd been scheduled to start Friday, would pitch the first game Saturday afternoon. Roger Craig would start the Saturday evening game. When Roth saw that Saturday morning, he went to Alston and pointed out that Drysdale's night-game record was substantially better than his daytime performance while Craig showed little difference. Alston switched the pitchers, Los Angeles won both games, and Sunday as well. The Dodgers finished the season in a tie with the Braves, won the tie-breaker playoff and the World Series for an improbable championship.[34]

After the move to Los Angeles, Roth started to attend spring training in Vero Beach, something he hadn't done early in the Brooklyn years.[35] Now he met with each player, along with one of the coaches, and went over their performance the previous year, emphasizing positives as well as negatives and suggesting changes that could improve the player's statistics. Sandy Koufax would credit such sessions in the early 1960s with helping him learn to emphasize first-pitch strikes and taking something off the ball.[36] In the dugout, coach Pete Reiser had a set of Roth's 5x8-inch cards with summaries of player performance keyed to the opposing pitching staff.[37]

Roth also began a campaign that would ultimately result in the creation of the statistic for a reliever's "Saves." In 1951, Roth began to keep track of such situations and began sharing the number with reports several years later.[38] By 1964, pushed by sportswriter Jerome Holtzman, major league publicity directors approved the version of the save that we're familiar with today, although the formula is a bit different from the one devised by Roth.[39]

A few months after the coronation of his invention, Roth was fired by the Dodgers. It was done very quietly. The team made no announcement and it wasn't until reporters asked about Roth's absence from a late-season road trip that the team announced he had resigned because he was tired of all the travel.[40] He may have been tired of the travel, but that wasn't why he was fired. Walter O'Malley hated negative publicity and also had a fear, born in the early years of baseball's integration, that any news of interracial sexual relations could cause an outcry. [41] Bavasi said Roth had developed a relationship with an African-American woman who traveled with him, and then gotten into a screaming match with her in a Philadelphia hotel corridor.[42] Roth's marriage would end in divorce a little over a year later. But he still needed to provide a living for his wife, children, and himself. He began to expand his already extensive freelancing.

Roth's first article in *The Sporting News* had been published in 1946, while he was waiting for his visa to join the Dodgers.[43] There was a long hiatus until the next one, when he got his first byline in 1959.[44] Within weeks of his firing, he was contributing regularly.[45] He revived a monthly column he'd written for *Sport* magazine from 1952 until 1960.[46] He continued to edit the annual *Who's Who in Baseball*, which he'd done since the 1954 issue. He contributed statistical data for *Koufax*, by Sandy Koufax and Ed Linn, and the publisher felt it important enough to be included in advertising for the book.[47] He collaborated with Harold Rosenthal on the spring training magazines from MACO publishing.[48]

In 1966, NBC came calling with its new contract for the Game of the Week, the All-Star Game, and the World Series. The *Sporting News* column disappeared and for the next decade, Roth would sit between Curt Gowdy and Tony Kubek, feeding them the kind of statistical nuggets he'd supplied to Scully for years. A few years later, he moved to ABC to provide the same service. As always, Roth traveled heavy. On his weekly flight from Los Angeles to wherever the broadcast was originating, he was accompanied by several suitcases stuffed with his notebooks, charts and graphs.[49] As he did all his life, his calculations were made with pencil, paper, and often internal calculation.

In the offseason, Roth attended meetings of the Los Angeles chapter of SABR, which was named after him. He'd usually speak, presenting some of his recent findings and answering questions, which often ranged far from his current work.

While spending his time providing statistical nuggets for the broadcasters, Roth continued his exploration of ways teams could use statistics to improve performance. He consulted for 20 major league teams and identified Joe Morgan as the league's most valuable player long before voters did.[50] Harking back to his early talks with Branch Rickey, Roth focused on Morgan's on-base percentage, power, and stolen base success. In a discussion with the San Francisco Giants, he made a case that the tactic of guarding the lines late in games wasn't as effective as believed. The Giants changed their practices.[51]

Ill health forced Roth to retire in the late 1980s and he died of a heart attack in Brotman Hospital in Culver City on March 3, 1992.

Roth was elected to the Canadian Baseball Hall of Fame in 2010. "He was the guy who began it all," said Bill James. "He took statisticians into a brave new world."

NOTES

1   Alan Schwarz. *The Numbers Game: Baseball's Lifelong Fascination with Statistics* (New York: St. Martin's Press, 2004), 55.

2   Immigration and family information courtesy of Alan Greenberg of the Jewish Genealogical Society of Montréal. Much of the material about his youth is contained in biographical handouts produced when Roth was with the Dodgers and included in his papers, which are housed at the Western Reserve Historical Society. Thanks to C. David Stephan and volunteers such as Chuck Carey and Sam James, who preserved the papers after Roth's death. Thanks to Alain Usereau for pointing me to the Genealogical Society.

3   Roth to Edward Staples, Brooklyn Baseball Club, April 4, 1944, Allan Roth papers.

4   Roth to Edward Staples, Brooklyn Baseball Club, April 4, 1944, Allan Roth papers.

5   Schwarz, *The Numbers Game*, 56.

6   L.S. MacPhail to Roth, December 19, 1940 and June 6, 1941. Roth to L.S. MacPhail, Aug. 4, 1941, Roth papers.

7   Roth to Staples.

8   Roth to Staples.

9   Harold C. Burr, "Dull Statistics Alive Under Magic Roth Touch," *Brooklyn Eagle*, January 11, 1953.

10 Burr, and Harold Rosenthal, ed., "The Statistician," in *Baseball is Their Business* (New York: Random House, 1952), 140.

11 Branch Rickey, Memo, April 23, 1947, Branch Rickey papers, Manuscript Division, Library of Congress. Also, Murray Polner, *Branch Rickey* (New York: Atheneum, 1982), 210. Interestingly, in his letter to Staples, Roth had proposed a salary of $30 a week, or $1,560 annually.

12 Rosenthal, ed., *Baseball is Their Business*, 139.

13 Roth to MacPhail, August 4, 1941, Roth papers.

14 *Los Angeles Mirror News*, July 21, 1959; *Los Angeles Times*, August 11, 1963.

15 *New York Times*, February 19, 1961.

16 *Los Angeles Times*, April 14, 1958.

17 *Los Angeles Times*, June 28, 1960.

18 Schwarz, *Numbers Game*, 54-5.

19 Rosenthal, ed., *Baseball is Their Business*, 140.

20 *The Sporting News*, June 4, 1947.

21 *People Today*, July 2, 1952: 28 and *New York Herald-Tribune*, clipping in Allan Roth papers, probably from late 1952. Schwarz, *Numbers Game*, 57.

22 *The Sporting News*, November 25, 1953.

23 Schwarz, *Numbers Game*, 57.

24 Interview, Michael Roth (Allan's son), March 4, 1997.

25 Schwarz, *Numbers Game*, 58.

26 *Los Angeles Mirror News*, July 21, 1959.

27 Richard Goldstein, *Superstars and Screwballs* (New York: Dutton, 1991), 79.

28 John Thorn and Pete Palmer, *The Hidden Game of Baseball* (New York: Doubleday, 1984), 42.

29 O'Malley to Roth, October 30, 1951, Roth papers.

30 Roth to O'Malley, November 1, 1951, Roth papers.

31 O'Malley to Roth, December 14, 1954, Roth papers.

32 Roth to O'Malley, December 28, 1954, Roth papers.

33 O'Malley to Roth, January 7, 1955, multiple handwritten notes, Roth papers.

34 This anecdote is contained in a three-page document in the Roth papers that is clearly a draft of an updated biosheet for Roth after the 1959 season. It is undated, and has the number 1. Centered at the top of the page followed by Roth's name, birthdate, birthplace, and the rest of the material.

35 Rosenthal, ed., *Baseball is Their Business*, 137.

36 Sandy Koufax with Ed Linn, *Koufax* (New York: The Viking Press, 1966), 148 and Jane Leavy, *Sandy Koufax: A Lefty's Legacy* (New York: HarperCollins, 2002), 106.

37 Walter Bingham, "Dodgers in Mufti," *Sports Illustrated*, August 15, 1960: 69.

38 *The Sporting News*, January 30, 1957: 8.

39 *The Sporting News*, December 21, 1963: 10; April 18, 1964: 34; and May 2, 1964: 6.

40 *Los Angeles Herald-Examiner*, September 2 and September 3, 1964. *Los Angeles Times*, September 12, 1964.

41 Frank Graham, Jr., *A Farewell to Heroes* (New York: The Viking Press, 1981), 253.

42 Interview, Buzzie Bavasi, August 30, 1994.

43 *The Sporting News*, January 31, 1946: 15.

44 *The Sporting News*, January 7, 1959: 11.

45 The first appeared October 10, 1964:16 and others appeared sporadically through February 1966.

46 *Los Angeles Times*, February 28, 1965.

47 *The Sporting News*, August 27, 1966: 10.

48 Rosenthal to Roth, September 7, 1964 and December 11, 1964 in Roth papers. From the letters, it's clear even as close a friend as Rosenthal didn't know the real cause of Roth's firing.

49 *The Sporting News*, April 18, 1970: 28.

50 *The Sporting News*, October 25, 1975: 3.

51 *The Sporting News*, January 22, 1971: 42.

INDIAN HEAD AND CANADA'S GREATEST BASEBALL TOURNAMENT, 1947–55

By Max Weder

"Wonder how long it will be before we have baseball in these parts again?" mused the man on Coffee Row as he sipped his java.

He was scanning the sports pages jammed with holiday ball tournaments. There must have been 100 teams within hailing distance of Regina in action.

"You know," he reflected, "I don't know if we want imports. This sort of ball is solid. A little town can muster nine men and compete with city clubs. Start importing pitchers and catchers and long-hitting outfielders and first thing you know the little towns are killed off. They can't keep up with the Joneses and turn to some other sport."

"I'll put in with that," echoed another java-sipper. "Baseball has made its comeback. Let's keep it the way it is. Competition is more important than the calibre of ball."

But did they think baseball would be content to stay as is?

"No," they agreed. "As long as there is money around the south country there will be rich tournaments. Some team will get the idea to bring in a couple of dark horses from the U.S. and that will start it. A dozen others will follow suit. Then baseball tournaments won't be fun any more."

— *"Dave Drybrugh's Sports Byways," Regina Leader-Post,* July 3, 1946.

The musings of the two men in the coffee shop, real or imagined by Dave Dryburgh, proved accurate. The "dark horses" did come. For the next decade, big-money tournaments dominated summer baseball in small towns across the Canadian Prairies, and Indian Head, Saskatchewan, led the way.[1] The "dark horses" did indeed arrive, as Blacks came to play in large numbers. Indian Head itself imported an all-Black team, playing as the Indian Head Rockets. Despite the worries of the men in the coffee shop, baseball was never more popular in Saskatchewan as a result.

Indian Head, a small town with a population of 1,500 in 1947, is located 42 miles east of Regina. The district has historically been a large grain producer, especially with the establishment of the Bell Farm, the first commercial farm in Western Canada.[2] The area was also the site of the Canadian Government's Experimental Farm, whose priorities in its first years were to find and demonstrate adapted cereal crops, vegetables, fruits, shelter trees, and shrubs for prairie settlers. The shelterbelt trees and shrubs were in such high demand that a separate tree nursery was created by the federal government. The railroad brought in a diverse group of immigrants to work from across Canada and Europe. In the early twentieth century, the population of Saskatchewan was 80 percent rural;[3] many workers were required to work the farms, and small towns existed to service those farms. Sport teams were a natural outgrowth, and Indian Head was no different.[4] As in most small towns, baseball was the focus in the summer months.

Baseball grew in popularity from the beginning of the twentieth century, and with that growth came the money tournaments in Saskatchewan,[5] particularly after the Western Canada League folded in 1921. In 1922 Saskatoon held "The Biggest Tournament Ever Offered in Western Canada," with $1,000 in prizes. Somewhat ironically, the tournament was not open to the largest cities of Saskatoon, Regina, and Moose Jaw.[6] And somewhat fittingly, the small town of Conquest (population 250) emerged victorious. However, the Great Depression and World War II led to a substantial decrease in both the number of tournaments and the prize money offered.

The post-war boom saw a return of the money tournaments being held in these small towns. The size and scope of the Indian Head tournament, which was held from 1947 through 1955, led to its being labeled first "Western Canada's Greatest Baseball Tournament," and then "Canada's Greatest Baseball Tournament."[7]

The Indian Head Athletic Association was formed in 1918 as a sports and service organization.[8] While it had operated originally as a service organization for civic matters and other sports in Indian Head, baseball became its main focus. The

Indian Head Rockets sweater crest, 1951. (Indian Head Museum)

Association formed the Rockets as a separately operated division.[9]

Planning began in 1947 for the town's first major tournament.[10] Large money tournaments required the extensive civic involvement of a large number of volunteers. Jimmy Robison was the head of the 14-person committee established to run the tournament. Robison was a noted local sportsman, involved extensively in both curling and baseball, as well as being the mayor of Indian Head.

The field was fixed at 22 teams, and the event was proclaimed boldly as "Western Canada's Greatest Baseball Tournament." Advertisements were placed with radio stations to promote the tournament. The offered prize money was $2,000, with $1,000 going to the winner. In addition to a local response, the call for team entries drew a cross-border one. One newspaper report referred to these American teams as "Three colored teams from California, Minnesota and Texas."[11] These teams were the Ligon All-Stars from Brawley, California, the Broadway Wolverines from Houston, and the Twin City Giants from St. Paul.

Anticipation built for the August tournament.[12] A Regina sports columnist wrote: "Right now most clubs are saving their mound aces for tournaments like those in Yorkton and Indian Head, where more than java and doughnut money is at stake."[13] In the meantime, the Dominion Day tournament in Indian Head drew 10,000 fans, but due to the lack of prize money attracted no teams from outside Saskatchewan in its 13-team open division.

While the focus in the summer was on baseball, hockey was never far from the province's consciousness. In the tournament's opening game on August 7, 1947, the Wilcox Cardinals, featuring NHLer Nick Metz, defeated the Delisle Commandos, with NHL stars Doug and Max Bentley, by a score of 6-1.[14] One of the highlights of this initial tournament was the pitching duel between Bert Shepard of Williston, North Dakota, and the Ligon All-Stars. Shepard was a minor-league pitcher who had lost his leg in World War II. He returned to the major leagues in 1945 as the pitching coach for Washington, and remarkably pitched 5⅓ innings in a game, allowing only one run. He continued his remarkable pitching comeback in the 1947 tournament by losing a 1-0 pitching duel against Ligon.

It was estimated that 15,000 attended the tournament games, with 10,000 to 12,000 on hand for the final, in which the all-Black Ligon All-Stars defeated Wilcox 13-0:

"While an estimated 10,000 rooters jammed around the diamond until there wasn't space for even the circus Thin Man, George Ligon's Colored All-Stars from California, or some other spot south of the snowline, whacked out enough base hits to make Indian Head's enormously successful $2,000 baseball tournament a runaway show on Thursday, tacking a crushing 13-0 setback on Nick Metz and his Wilcox Cardinals in a disappointing final.

"The colored boys were extended only once in romping to four victories that figured out to $250 apiece as they copped first money of $1,000 with something to spare. Only in one game out of four did they yield any runs, making it rather decisive that they were the best ball club on the premises."[15]

The Ligon team proved to be as formidable for the rest of its touring season in Western Canada, winning 81 games and losing only nine.[16]

The tourney was hailed by some in the media as a great success:

"Dig that old baseball glove out of the attic, chum, and start lumbering up behind the barn. The days when a fella could make winter spending money in ball tournaments are on the way back.

"Chances are the walls over at Coffee Row will be plastered with bills announcing $2,000 and $3,000 tournaments next spring. Yorkton revived the diamond game gold trails a couple of years ago. Indian Head topped that this week and the sky's the limit in 1948.

"Set your date early or be locked out."[17]

Newspaper reports did indicate, however, that the overhead was high, with a low estimate of $6,000. This included not only the $2,000 prize money, but $400 for baseballs, lumber for the construction of stands, and wire netting and grading for the three diamonds, in addition to umpire costs.[18]

For the 1948 tournament, the decision was made to expand the total prize money to $3,000. A.R. Beesley of the Associated Screen News was invited to produce newsreel footage of the tournament, and radio station CKRM of Regina was to broadcast the final game.[19] Not surprisingly, tournament costs rose accordingly to $10,000, as 12 new sections of bleachers were added. Attendance increased to 25,000, with a final day turnout of 16,000.

The 1947 champions, the Ligon All-Stars, suffered an early defeat, losing 4-3 in an upset to small-town Rouleau, Saskatchewan. Former Winnipeg Maroon professional Gaylen Shupe[20] led his team to victory. The Manitoba Senior champion Brandon Greys, featuring five Black players in their lineup, captured the tournament prize by defeating a team from Sceptre, Saskatchewan, another small town with a long and storied history of success in baseball.

By 1949 the tournament billed itself as "Canada's Greatest Baseball Tournament." Weather proved capable of wreaking havoc on even the greatest of tournaments, however, as rain washed out two rounds. The Minot Merchants won the tournament, as Brandon was unable to repeat as champion despite the Greys' Winslow Means pitching a seven-inning perfect game in the quarter-finals.

The apparent success of the tournament led to increased local interest in Indian Head's fielding a strong town team itself. It was reported in the newspapers in May 1950 that Rogers Hornsby had lined up players for the Indian Head team at a cost of $6,000 to $7,000 per month.[21] Supportive Indian Head residents advanced $50 each, $5,250 in total, to fund the team. That same month, Luther "Doc" Adams placed an ad in *The Sporting News* looking for players.[22] On May 14, 1950, Robison, Adams, and other members of the Rockets organization headed to the National Baseball Congress meeting in Wichita in search of additional players.[23]

The Wichita newspapers were somewhat bemused by the Canadian delegation:

"Canadians Use Money

"It sounds screwy but they do it up big financially up in central western Canada.

"The five-man delegation here to find baseball talent for their tournament season up in Saskatchewan cites some figures to make us wonder if they use gold mines for club houses up that away.

"Jim Robison, from Indian Head, is after 13 players, and has the finances for it all, and yet Indian Head claims but 1,500 souls.

"A town called Foam Lake, of but 800 population[,] has a tournament coming on which has a guaranteed prize of $3,750 cash.

"The Canadian tournaments last but two days, there are NO lights and NO Sunday ball, unless under a benefit pass-the-hat plan. Daylight extends past 9 P.M. so that a game can be started "after supper" and finished in the daylight. …

"'We have 3,000 out for a tournament session,' the Canadian sponsor said. 'We have a different plan from your tournaments. We play three games at one time on three different diamonds, all within one big enclosure. There is space for hundreds of cars to park and sometimes they go from one game to another.'"[24]

It appears that Hornsby delegated the recruitment task to Mickey Flynn, a well-known figure in Kansas baseball circles, but it was noted that Flynn could not make the trip personally.[25]

In a meeting on May 26, 1950, the Executive Committee of the Rockets approved "the arrangement made by the Scouting Committee to hire a colored team through Wayne Clark."[26] In a letter dated that same day from Jimmy Robison to Mr. Clark, an agreement was concluded with no mention of Hornsby.[27] Mr. Clark was the go-between, but does not seem to have had a high profile in baseball.[28] The letter was addressed subsequently to Big Jim Williams, with his Jacksonville Eagles being the team to head north. The letter required that Williams supply 16 players of Double-A caliber (including five pitchers), a bus, uniforms, and all equipment. Robison also suggested that the team bus lettering be changed to the Indian Head Rockets. He requested that the uniforms be lettered with "Indian Head" on the front, and "Rocket" (singular) on the back with the player's number. This was in fact done with the uniforms. In effect, the Jacksonville Eagles were to become the Indian Head Rockets.

The 1950 Indian Head Rockets and their team bus. Big Jim Williams is at the far left in the back row, and tournament committee head Jimmy Robison (wearing a tie) in the middle of the back row. (Indian Head Museum)

As was true of some of the other earlier touring teams and prairie teams with imports, the Jacksonville Eagles were an all-Black team.[29] Williams himself was a veteran of the Negro Leagues. Monetary considerations were undoubtedly the significant factor in Williams's decision to move the team north. The players were to be paid $200 per month, plus board.[30] It is not clear what portion of any prize winnings from the money tournaments the Rockets players would keep, but it was in addition to their salaries.

Along with other towns on the Canadian prairies, Indian Head was more welcoming to Black players than was much of the United States. The players were billeted in renovated apartments above the Dominion Café, owned by Charlie Koo. They were provided meals, and were not subjected to segregated seating.

They did have a rough time getting to Saskatchewan in the first place. An article in the *Edmonton Bulletin* noted that the team bus broke down 400 miles from Indian Head, with the result that they had to forfeit their first tournament game, in Lloydminster, Alberta.[31] Two days later, the same journalist wrote:

"The all-colored club room [*sic*] Indian Head, performing like some race horses I have known, failed to show. Earlier, the Indian Head people had informed tournament officials that their team had burned out two engines of their bus on the road to Lloydminster.

"But this was so much malarky, according to tourney secretary Joe Schmidt. Somebody was giving somebody the run around, and I have it on good authority that the tournament chieftains weren't running."[32]

It is difficult to imagine a reason why the Rockets would not have shown up, other than engine failure, given the prize money on the line.

The Rockets had better results for the rest of that summer, and won the 1950 tournament with its first prize money of $1,300. They were not able to match the success of the 1947 Ligon All-Stars over the course of the year, but fared quite well, playing 91 games overall against 33 opponents, winning 66 and losing 20, with 5 ties.[33]

The addition of a local team no doubt increased the financial pressure on the organization. A meeting of the Rockets' executive on August 24, 1950, reviewed several issues:

The players' salaries would start June 11 – perhaps indicating that there may have been some disagreement with Big Jim Williams on this.

The team bus had issues, as noted above. The Rockets had apparently advanced $600 to Williams for repairs. The executive agreed to forgo this, but would counterclaim if Williams made any claim for the expenses of running the bus.

Even though the team had been in Indian Head, it was not yet clear who was paying for the players' meals while they were in Indian Head. If Williams insisted on the Rockets paying, the Executive agreed that it would pay $2.00 per day per player.[34]

The loss from the baseball operations in 1950 was $8,775.[35] Because the books of the Rockets are not available, it is unfortunately not possible to determine how the loss arose, whether it was from the operation of the tournament, or from funding the ball team and its travels to other tournaments. The latter is more likely.

The 1951 Rockets featured Chet Brewer, former Negro League star, and Tom Alston, the first Black to play for the St. Louis Cardinals, who had joined the Rockets the previous season. Brewer had been the highest-paid player for Sceptre, making $400 a month there, but left with Prescott at the end of June to play for the Rockets.[36]

The team entered the Western Canada League, as well as continuing to play in money tournaments across the Prairies.[37] They had a successful summer, winning 22 straight games at one point.[38] However, that success could not carry over into their own tournament, as Indian Head lost to the Regina Caps. Canadian Football League star Rollie Miles of the Caps stole second and third in succession in the fifth and eighth innings to lead the upset.[39] Seventeen-year-old Elijah "Pumpsie" Green, playing for the Medicine

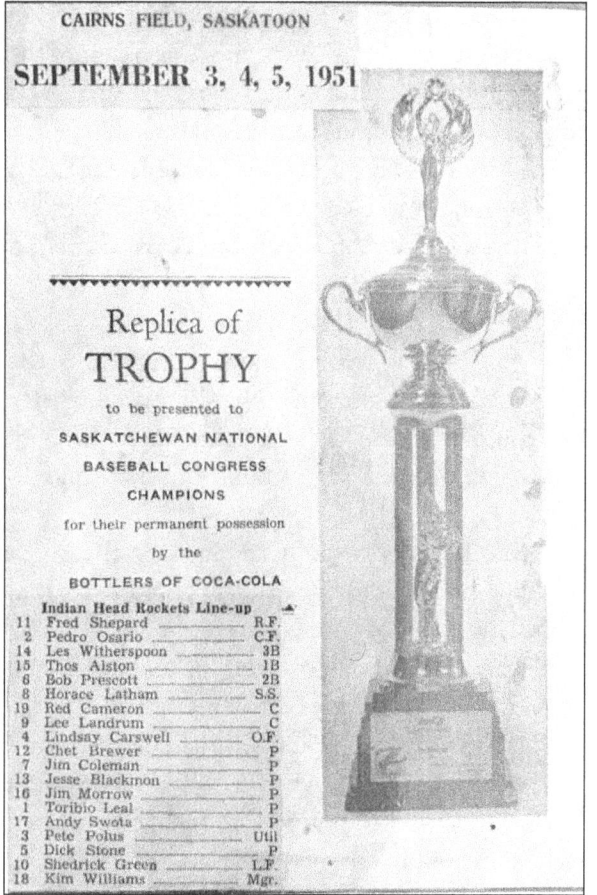

Tournament program from 1951. The Indian Head Rockets roster includes 44-year-old Negro Leagues great Chet Brewer, and 25-year-old Tom Alston, who would later become the first Black player on the St. Louis Cardinals. (Author's collection)

Hat Mohawks, hit three singles and two triples in the semifinal. The Mohawks then defeated the Eston Ramblers in the final game before an estimated final crowd of 11,000, claiming the first-prize money of $1,200.

Despite the large attendance in 1951, and the seeming success of the tournament, financial problems continued. Even with the cash contributions of fans and backers of $4,500 at the start of the season, and a subsequent contribution of $3,000 from the Rockets organization, the financial position remained murky, if not bleak.[40]

The Rockets association started 1952 with a deficit of $3,000.[41] As late as early June of 1952, the Rockets and Big Jim Williams were negotiating the terms of engagement for that summer.

A deal was finally reached under which the team would be strictly on its own, and 10 percent of the receipts would be paid to the town's treasury. As it turned out, Williams and the players were stuck at the Canada-US border with insufficient funds to post bond into Canada. Six of the association's executives put up $50 each to secure the bond for entry.

The Rockets again featured an all-Black team.[42] Pumpsie Green moved over from the Mohawks, as did pitcher Nat Bates, who later became mayor and city councilor in Richmond, California. Bates commented on his time in Indian Head:

"My experience in Canada was the most pleasant, refreshing time in my life. People treated you on the basis of who you were.

"The most offensive thing to us was when people called us darkies. That hurt. It was nothing disrespectful, they just didn't know. After we were there for a while, when we could relate to the community, and they understood us, we started to laugh about it.

"Families invited us into their homes. Girls asked us to dance."[43]

In the 1952 final, the Florida Cubans defeated Baton Rouge, Louisiana, with the Rockets finishing third. The *Indian Head News* noted that the teams "tangled in the first all-colored final in the tournament's six years of life."[44] The tournament experienced its first decline in attendance, drawing 4,000 fewer spectators. Organizers laid the blame on inclement weather:

"Executives of the Rockets and the Canadian Legion, joint sponsors of the tournament, were inclined to place the drop as being due to continued rain and threatening skies before and during the tournament. At that, Indian Head was again held to be 'lucky.' Only one shower held the big tourney up for a few moments."[45]

In April 1953 the Rockets were in danger of dissolving.[46] The club solicited and received the continued support of the local Canadian Legion Branch as co-sponsor of the 1953 tournament. This allowed both the tournament and the Rockets to continue. The local paper noted at a meeting in late May:

"Burial of Indian Head Rockets was deferred Wednesday, due to a lively corpse. The nearly score of young fellows (and not so young) who gathered at the town hall for last rites and dissolution found that the deceased insisted on staying awake at the wake – so the funeral was called off.

"Actually, the assembly felt the Rockets had accomplished a lot of good for the town, the organization was known far and wide, and it was worth while saving."[47]

For the 1953 season, the Indian Head Rockets engaged the services of the Florida Cubans to travel under the Rockets name. Big Jim Williams and most of the 1952 Rockets team moved west to play for Regina. The Rockets were more successful in their tournament this year, winning the final 6-0 over the Saskatoon Gems on July 16. This was the first year that the Indian Head tournament featured night baseball. Despite this new attraction, the stated attendance for the final game was 6,000, a decline from earlier years. Inclement weather was certainly a factor.

In 1954 the prize money was reduced to $5,000 from the previous year's $5,600. It was noted in the local paper that the possibilities were good that the Florida Cubans would return. The club stated it "made a little" and that the deficits that had been run up by Big Jim Williams were no longer occurring.[48] However, minutes of the Indian Head Rockets show that the 1953 tournament had a net loss of $185.80, and that the baseball bank account was $1,449.65.[49] Given the reported loss in the 1950 tournament of $8,750, it is difficult to see how a smaller loss could be incurred given the reduced attendance.

The Rockets entered the Saskatchewan League very late in April 1954, having first negotiated that the Florida Cubans would set up in Indian Head for the summer. A change in the league constitution allowed tournaments to draw on league teams only if a club of their own was in the league.[50]

The *Saskatoon Star Phoenix* noted:

"Tournament play has long been a spoiler of the many attempts to organize a smooth-running league. The people who pay the shot in the hometown were unsatisfied because often a club would shove second-raters into their lineup for a league game and save their strength for a tourney the next day. Country folk didn't bother coming to Saskatoon or any city to watch any ordinary league game when they could visit Indian Head, Prince Albert or some spot and see all the league clubs in an all-out battle for a bundle of cash."[51]

It was the perceived importance of the other teams to the success of the Indian Head tournament that led the Rockets to enter the league, but the exposure of league play also provided financial benefit.

The Kamsack Cyclones won the 1954 tournament before an estimated final crowd of 7,000, claiming a first prize of $1,100. The Rockets finished third. The Cyclones were the youngest team in the tournament, with only two players older than 20. Nineteen-year-old Ted Ellis, with "an ailing back and a great desire to pitch," led them to victory.[52]

While youth was served in 1954, no touring or professional clubs were allowed entry in 1955. The Saskatchewan League had folded. The Western Canada League was formed, but without a team from Indian Head. The absence of a local Indian Head team, accompanied by increasing financial pressure, resulted in a format change for the tournament. Prize money dropped to $4,500, with the top prize dropping to $800. Perhaps fittingly for the last tournament held in Indian Head, the Notre Dame Hounds and the Brandon Cloverleafs played to a 4-4 tie before a crowd of 3,000 when the game was called on account of darkness.

By the mid-1950s, the population of Saskatchewan had shifted such that almost 50 percent of the population was urban.[53] Due to increased mechanization on the farm, fewer workers were required, and the population of many of these towns decreased significantly. The financial pressure on the small towns to field teams, and to travel for tournaments, undoubtedly increased as a result of this shift. The days of the big-money tournament on the Canadian prairies were in the past. However, there is little doubt that Indian Head, and Canada's Greatest Baseball Tournament, left an indelible mark on the history of baseball in Canada.

BIBLIOGRAPHY

Craig, John. *Chappie and Me: An Autobiographical Novel* (New York: Dodd, Mead, 1979).

Ducey, Brant. *The Rajah of Renfrew: The Life and Times of John E. Ducey, Edmonton's "Mr. Baseball"* (University of Alberta Press, 1998).

Hack, Paul, and Dave Shury. *Wheat Province Diamonds* (Regina: Saskatchewan Sports Hall of Fame and Museum, 1987).

Indian Head: History of Indian Head and District (History of Indian Head and District Inc., 1984).

Mah, Jay-Dell, and Barry Swanton. *Black Baseball Players in Canada: A Biographical Dictionary 1881-1960* (Jefferson, North Carolina: McFarland, 2009).

McCabe, Ken. *The History of Sport in Indian Head* (Self-published, about 1980).

Shepard, R. Bruce. *Deemed Unsuitable: Blacks from Oklahoma Move to the Canadian Prairies in Search of Equality in the Early 20th Century Only to Find Racism in their New Home* (Los Angeles: Umbrella Press, 1997).

Stubbs, Lewis St. George. *Shoestring Glory: A Prairie History of Semi-Pro Ball* (Winnipeg, Manitoba: Turnstone Press, 1996). (Note: Despite its title, the author does not mention the Rockets at all.)

Swanton, Barry. *The Mandak League, Haven for Former Negro League Ballplayers, 1950-57* (Jefferson, North Carolina: McFarland, 2006).

SOURCES

Special thanks to the Indian Head Museum for its invaluable assistance. Its collection of Indian Head Rockets baseball documents and ephemera can be searched here: https://memorysask.ca/the-rockets.

Constitution and Bylaws of the Indian Head Rockets, 1947.

Indian Head Rockets Bank Account Book (Indian Head Museum: IHM 2020.0263).

Letter from Steve Niven, Indian Head Baseball Club, to James Dunn, Manitoba Dakota Baseball League, May 12, 1950 (Indian Head Museum: IHM 2020.02).

Letter from Dr. R.C. Morrow, Manitoba Dakota Baseball League, to Steve Niven, Indian Head Baseball Club, May 22, 1950 (Indian Head Museum: IHM 2020.02).

Letter from J.E. Robison to Jim Williams, May 26, 1950 (Indian Head Museum: IHM 2022.0038).

Letter from the Department of National Revenue to Steve Niven, Indian Head Rockets, June 28, 1950 (Indian Head Museum: IHM 2022.0037).

Minutes of the Executive Committee of the Indian Head Rockets (Indian Head Museum: IHM 2020.0272).

Minutes of the Indian Head Athletic Association 1918-1945 (Indian Head Museum: IHM 2020.0260).

Minutes of the Indian Head Rockets 1950-54 (Indian Head Museum: IHM 2020.0262).

Minutes of the Indian Head Rockets 1948-55 (Indian Head Museum: IHM 2020.0265).

NOTES

1   Notable other big-money tournaments were held in Foam Lake, Saskatchewan, and Lacombe and Lloydminster, Alberta.

2   https://bellbarn.ca/bell-farm/history-bell/.

3   "The Population of Saskatchewan," (Government of Saskatchewan, Saskatchewan Health, 2012): 3.

4   Ken McCabe, *The History of Sport in Indian Head.*

5   www.attheplate.com is an invaluable source, compiled by SABR member J.D. Mah, of the history of baseball in Western Canada, and provides much detail on the Indian Head tournaments.

6   Noted by J.D. Mah, http://www.attheplate.com/wcbl/1922_1k.html.

7   Dave Shury, "The Big Tournaments of Indian Head and Foam Lake," *Saskatchewan Historical Baseball Review* (1987): 17-20.

8   Minutes, Indian Head Athletic Association 1918-1945 (Indian Head Museum: IHM 2020:0260).

9   Constitution and Bylaws of the Indian Head Rockets, 1947. The Constitution and Bylaws provided that only men resident in Indian Head and District, and aged between 18 and 40, were eligible to vote and hold office, while men older than 40 could only vote and not be on the executive.

10 The 1946 Dominion Day sports tournament in Indian Head offered $650 in prizes for the harness races, but none stated for the baseball tournament. "Races, Baseball for Indian Head," *Regina* (Saskatchewan) *Leader-Post,* June 19, 1946: 14.

11 "Early Bird," *Regina Leader-Post,* June 7, 1947: 14.

12 "Club Is Ready for Big Crowd," *Regina Leader-Post*, August 1, 1947: 12.

13 "Dave Dryburgh's Sports Byways," *Regina Leader-Post*, July 25, 1947: 16.

14 "Two Regina Teams Stay in Tourney," *Regina Leader-Post*, August 7, 1947: 18.

15 *Regina Leader-Post*, August 8, 1947: 12.

16 http://www.attheplate.com/wcbl/ligon.html.

17 "Dave Dryburgh's Sport Byways," *Regina Leader-Post*, August 9, 1950: 12.

18 "Touring Team Snares Indian Head Cash," *Regina Leader-Post*, August 8, 1950: 12.

19 The search continues to see if this newsreel footage has survived.

20 https://www.baseball-reference.com/register/player.fcgi?id=shupe-001gay.

21 "Indian Head Peps Up," *Regina Leader-Post*, May 6, 1950: 17. Even before any agreement was reached to have players head north, the Rockets applied for league membership in the ManDak League on May 12, 1950. However, time constraints prevented their admittance.

22 "Capable Manager Wanted," *The Sporting News*, May 17, 1950: 48, referred to in Harvey Dryden "About People and Things," *Regina Leader-Post*, May 17, 1950. Adams is an inductee in the Saskatchewan Baseball Hall of Fame.

23 *Regina Leader-Post*, May 20, 1950: 18.

24 Peter Lightner, "The Morning After," *Wichita Eagle*, May 19, 1950: 19.

25 Lightner. It is stated in several newspaper articles that Flynn also played professionally, but there is no listing for him in baseball-reference.com and only articles stating he played semipro ball: for example, "Ballplayers Here Monday," *Hutchinson* (Kansas) *News,* April 12, 1933: 2. Hack and Shury (page 324) suggest that Hornsby met with the delegation, but this does not appear to be the case.

26 Minutes of the Executive Committee, Indian Head Rockets (Indian Head Museum: IHM 2020.0272).

27 Indian Head Museum: IHM 2022:0038.

28 Minutes of the Executive Committee, Indian Head Rockets, (Indian Head Museum: IHM.2020.0272). Mr. Clark was from Milwaukee and does not appear in any baseball-related search for this period.

29 The rosters and many player photos can be seen at http://www.attheplate.com/wcbl/teams_rockets1.html. The Rockets are scheduled for inclusion in the Saskatchewan Baseball Hall of Fame in 2022.

30 Letter from the Department of National Revenue to Steve Niven, Indian Head Rockets, June 28, 1950 (Indian Head Museum: IHM 2022.0038).

31 "Rain Postpones Lloyd Tournament," *Edmonton* (Alberta) *Bulletin*, June 6, 1950: 6. However, it was also suggested the road conditions were the cause: "Rockets Delayed," *Regina Leader-Post*, June 8, 1950: 22.

32 "Lloydminster Ball Tourney in Wind-Up Games Today," *Edmonton Bulletin*, June 8, 1950: 8.

33 "Rockets Hold Ball Meeting", *Regina Leader-Post*, November 7, 1950: 14. This record has not been verified. Hack and Shury (page 324) state that the Rockets record in 1950 was 80 games played, 55 wins, 20 losses and 5 ties.

34 Minutes of the Indian Head Rockets 1950-54, August 24, 1950 (Indian Head Museum: IHM 2020.0262).

35 "Players Go – Debt Remains," *Indian Head News*, September 14, 1951: 1; "8,775 Deficit at Indian Head," *Regina Leader-Post*, November 17, 1950: 24.

36 Telephone interview with George Mahaffy, January 4, 2022.

37 "Rockets First at Foam Lake," *Saskatoon Star Phoenix*, July 12, 1951: 17, winning the first prize money in the $6,000 tournament there.

38 The Rockets did lose in the Western semipro playoffs to Sceptre. "Sceptre Cops Title," *Regina Leader-Post*, September 7, 1951: 16.

39 "Mohawks Supreme at Tournament," *Regina Leader-Post*, July 20, 1951: 18. Miles was in the inaugural season of his 11-year career for the Edmonton Eskimos, and was inducted into the Canadian Football Hall of Fame in 1980.

40 "Players Go – Debt Remains."

41 "Yep, Some Baseball," *Indian Head News*, June 5, 1952: 1.

42 "Rockets Once Ruled Indian Head," *Saskatoon Star Phoenix*, June 9, 2012: E1.

43 "Rockets Once Ruled Indian Head," E2.

44 "Cubans Hit Peak with Tourney First," *Indian Head News*, July 24, 1952: 1.

45 "Cubans Hit Peak with Tourney First."

46 "Seven-Year Life of Rockets Ends," *Indian Head News*, April 30, 1953: 1.

47 "Rockets Not Dead," *Indian Head News*, May 28, 1953: 1.

48 "Cubans Again," *Indian Head News*, December 3, 1953: 1.

49 Minutes of Indian Head Rockets meeting, April 6, 1954.

50 "Surprising Move Brings Rockets Into Ball League," *Saskatoon Star Phoenix*, April 9, 1954: 19.

51 "Power Plays," *Saskatoon Star Phoenix*, March 2, 1954: 12.

52 "Kamsack Youngsters Triumph," *Regina Leader-Post*, July 16, 1954: 22.

53 "The Population of Saskatchewan."

THE TRUE GREATNESS OF
THE MANDAK LEAGUE

By Gary Gillette

On the dust jacket of his book *Small-Town Heroes*, author Hank Davis wrote:

For many baseball fans, a major-league team is a flickering image on a television screen or a story in the newspaper. Real baseball is played in their hometown, in a ballpark that seats 5,000 fans, not 50,000. The players wear uniforms like the ones seen on television, but their names are not household words – unless it happens to be summer and you live in Bluefield, West Virginia; Cedar Rapids, Iowa; or Batavia, New York.[1]

Davis wrote about his 1993 peregrination in the US and Canadian minor leagues. Substitute Brandon, Manitoba, for Bluefield; Minot, North Dakota, for Cedar Rapids; and Bismarck, North Dakota, for Batavia and it would have been just as meet if written in 1950.

According to the 1953 edition of the National Baseball Congress of America's *Official Baseball Annual*, most of its member teams were "town teams" – a recent trend. "Official records show that more than 70 per cent of the clubs in the combined league and tournament program are 'town' teams."[2] The teams that made up the Manitoba-Dakota League of the 1950s followed that trend. The big-market Winnipeg clubs of the first four years were owned by businessmen; the rest of the league was made up of quintessential town teams.[3]

Hundreds of minor-league teams populated the US and Canadian landscapes before 1960 – 446 teams organized into 58 so-called bush leagues in 1950 alone. That is not to mention uncounted numbers of semipro leagues that thrived when baseball was king of the sports world. Yet the modest ManDak League of the Northern Prairies made an impact in its eight years of operation in the 1950s that has outlasted almost all the other leagues of the day.

One subtle tribute to the extent of the Man-Dak's fame is that most fans – and many writers, too – in the twenty-first century believe that the ManDak was a professional minor league and not "just" semipro. Labeling the ManDak as merely semipro borders on insulting. Before the Organized Baseball apocalypse in the late 1950s and 1960s laid waste to most minor leagues and uncounted semipro leagues, semipro ball was the heart of the game in vast stretches of North America – especially in towns too small to support even low-level minor-league clubs. Semipro teams – town teams, factory teams, and teams sponsored by local businesses and civic or fraternal organizations – were the pride of many a small town, large manufactory, or city neighborhood. They were a locus of civic pride as well as an important recreational outlet.

THE FOUNDATION

Often called "senior leagues" to distinguish them from amateur youth leagues, semipro baseball leagues had deep roots in prairie towns and cities both north and south of the 49th parallel in the late 1940s. The new ManDak League grew out of those roots in Manitoba and North Dakota, each of which had integrated baseball traditions of their own during the segregated era.

The ManDak was a noble, if short-lived, experiment made possible by the continuance of racial discrimination against Black ballplayers in the United States even after the American and National Leagues had re-integrated in 1947. It was made possible by a surfeit of available African American talent after baseball's color line was broken because many short-sighted AL and NL owners refused to sign Black players who were supposedly too old or not as good as their favored White players.

Wilmer "Red" Fields was the ace of Homestead's mound corps in 1948 when the Grays won the last Negro World Series.[4] During the 1940s and 1950s Fields played all over Latin America, but he waxed almost poetic in his autobiography about how lovely his time in Canada was in the 1950s:

> There was no comparison between the treatment we received in Canada and the treatment we received in Latin America. In Canada, it was like a home away from home. ... In Latin American countries, everything was business. ... The Canadian people also wanted ballplayers who represented their city and their community off the field as well as on the field. It was a good feeling. The people there accepted my family with so much enthusiasm that our stay there was the finest we ever experienced anywhere but at our home.[5]

Kyle McNary said succinctly in the audiobook edition of his Ted "Double Duty" Radcliffe: 36 Years of Pitching & Catching in the Negro Leagues: "[Negro League] Players went to Canada, where the seasons were short, the pay was good, and minds were liberal."[6]

That opinion was echoed in 2001 by African American player Ron Teasley, a 1950 ManDak All-Star[7] hailing from racially polarized Detroit, which still maintained a substantially segregated public-school system in the 1950s.[8] Barry Swanton, in his excellent and indispensable history The ManDak League: Haven for Former Negro League Ballplayers, 1950–1957, placed Teasley's opinion atop page 1: "Ron Teasley ... stated that in Canada the players were judged by their baseball ability, not by their color."[9]

Teasley reaffirmed that sentiment in a 2018 interview, saying, "[African American ballplayers] found it refreshing and enjoyable to experience a lack of prejudice, both on and off the field, because Canadians were so welcoming."[10]

For eight memorable summers on the Northern Prairie, the ManDak League punched well above its weight in the 1950s.

HOW GOOD WAS THE MANDAK?

"By most accounts, the quality of play in Canada at this time was roughly equal to the high levels of America's minor leagues," wrote Michael Stahl in a 2017 piece entitled "The Secret History of Black Baseball Players in Canada's Great White North" for Salon.com.[11] His opinion concurs with others from the 1950s.

The authoritative publication Dominionball: Baseball Above the 49th reprinted several assessments of the ManDak's level of play[12] from Swanton's book:

"Equal to Class B ball," according to Minot manager Lefty Lefebvre in 1950. When Lefebvre made his evaluation, he hadn't yet seen the Winnipeg Buffaloes, who featured future Hall of Famers Leon Day and Willie Wells, and who would take home the inaugural ManDak championship.

"Between Class A and Class B," according to Minot manager Otto Huber in 1951.

"Pacific Coast League," according to Minot pitcher Al Lyons in 1957. A very marginal former big-league pitcher in the 1940s (6.30 ERA in 100 innings) when he was in his prime in his late 20s, Lyons had previously spent seven years in the PCL, mostly as an outfielder. His 3.08 ERA led the ManDak in 1957 when the league was on its deathbed and when Lyons turned 38.

Swanton's history also included other opinions about the ManDak's quality:[13]

"Many knowledgeable people believe the league was somewhere between Double A and Triple A."

Winnipeg Royals skipper Dee Moore adjudged the ManDak to be "as good as the strongest Class B league in organized ball" in 1953.

Ted Bowles, a scribe who covered the ManDak for the Winnipeg Free Press, *thought the league "rated between Class A and Class B ball" before Winnipeg left the ManDak for the Class C Northern League.*

Jim Adelson, who did radio play-by-play of Minot Mallards games in 1951 and 1952, put the league at "close to Triple-A."

Contemporaneous observers are often better judges, so Lefebvre's, Huber's, Lyons', Moore's, Bowles', and Adelson's opinions carry extra weight. That is especially true because most of them appear not to have inflated their assessments to make their teams and their jobs look more important – as Lyons obviously was doing, based on the enormous gap in his own performance between the majors and the ManDak. Adelson's viewpoint is harder to parse.

The pioneering North Dakota radio-TV sports broadcaster's high estimation of the league's quality is the real outlier. A member of the North Dakota Associated Press Sportscasters and Sportswriters Association Hall of Fame, he spent decades in the Flickertail State covering sports after arriving on the scene at 26 in 1951.[14] It is possible that the young broadcaster had not seen enough of the major leagues or the high minors to be able to make that judgment; it is also possible that he was consciously or unconsciously trying to pump up local pride, and make North Dakota look better to outsiders.

In any case, as with other opinions about the ManDak that place it at the high minor-league level, the evidence just doesn't bear that out. Radcliffe biographer McNary stated, "Some compared the [ManDak] league favorably to Double A or Triple A in the minors." He quotes Winnipeg Elmwood Giants owner Alex Turk's opinion: "The Northern League wasn't close. We would have beaten their All-Star team."[15] Given that the 1946-1962 Northern was only a Class-C league, that's not much to shout about.

Regrettably, evaluating the competitiveness of independent leagues is not straightforward. Independent leagues are defined as not being affiliated with a major-league farm system; they are colloquially called "indy leagues." Most indy leagues are a mix of former professional players and newbies of unknown quality. In the Internet age, it is possible to find background information and even statistics for amateur players in indy leagues, as almost all of them have college playing experience.

In the mid-twentieth century, though, most players in semipro leagues had no pro experience and fewer had collegiate experience. Most were truly *local* heroes: former high-school stars who might have attended a tryout camp run by pro scouts for a big-league club. These camps would gather optimistic young athletes who dreamed of playing in "The Show," but only a tiny percentage would ever sign a professional contract – and those who signed often washed out of pro ball within a year.

The Pirates – who finished last or next to last in the NL in the decade after World War II and were not an organization chockful of talent by any measure – ran just such a three-day tryout camp in Thamesville, Ontario, in August 1947. About 300 hopefuls attended, but only six were reportedly signed by Pittsburgh – very daunting odds.[16] That is especially true because the Bucs' farm system had 19 clubs in 1948, so hundreds of roster slots were available for marginal prospects who probably had no future but who might surprise and pan out.

Of the six who survived the tryout and signed with Pittsburgh, three could be tracked. Two of them appear to have never played in the minor leagues, likely being released by the Pirates before or during spring training in 1948. The third, a high-school pitcher from Windsor named Jim St. Louis, never played in the Pittsburgh farm system but did play four years of Class C or D ball, only one of which was for a big-league farm club.[17]

A clear-eyed look at the upstart league requires painstaking research into the past and future Organized Baseball and Negro League careers of all ManDak players. Although contemporary observers and some who have studied the league's history have commented that the ManDak's quality of play might have been as good as the high minors, rigorous analysis shows that might have

been true only of the strongest ManDak teams, but not of the rest of the clubs.

The only realistic yardstick to measure the quality of the ManDak is the established stratification of the minor leagues in the 1950s. In the 1950s, Organized Baseball essentially operated at six levels below the majors, from Class AAA and AA to Classes A, B, C, and D. (For political reasons, from 1952 to 1957, the Pacific Coast League was classified as "Open," but the PCL was a Triple-A league prior and afterward. The change in nomenclature did not correspond to a meaningful change in quality.)[18]

CRITICAL RELATIONSHIP TO THE NEGRO LEAGUES

The Negro Leagues, by MLB's pronouncement of December 2020 now considered "Major Leagues" between 1920 and 1948,[19] were on life support in the 1950s. The strongest Major Negro League, the Negro National League, had collapsed after 1948 when many White major-league owners realized that Jackie Robinson's stellar performance was not a fluke, and they belatedly undertook the scouting and signing of Black ballplayers.

The Negro American League (NAL), founded in 1937, struggled on after its older sibling died in 1948, but it was hemorrhaging talent at an escalating rate each year.[20] By the late 1950s, the NAL was essentially a loose, low-level barnstorming confederation that merely traded on the NAL's name and history as a marketing strategy.

Baseball historian Scott Simkus did a deep dive into the 1951 NAL in his *Outsider Baseball Bulletin* in 2011 while studying the integration of Organized Baseball five years after Jack Roosevelt Robinson's debut with Triple-A Montréal in 1946. Simkus examined many different angles and concluded that the NAL was not even as good as the typical 1951 Class-C league. However, as he acknowledged, the still prevalent discrimination against Black ballplayers would have had an unquantifiable negative effect.[21]

Using Simkus's data on the percentages of players at each level who would eventually make the major leagues, as well as the percentages of Black players at each level who ultimately reached "The Show," it seems that the NAL was at least Class B and possibly as good as a Class-A league of the day, yet very far below the big leagues.

The waning fortunes of the sole remaining Negro League surely contributed to the health of the ManDak. If the NAL had been thriving, most of the Negro Leaguers who migrated to the ManDak would probably have stayed home, where they had a better chance of being scouted and signed by a major-league organization.

As the 1950s progressed and more of the 16 AL and NL clubs integrated, hundreds of additional Black players were scooped up to play in their farm systems, starving the NAL of young talent – and, by extension, starving the ManDak of good young Black ballplayers. By the mid-1950s, the NAL was probably no better than a run-of-the-mill Class-C league of the day.

METHODOLOGY

For a presentation at the 2019 Canadian Baseball History Conference, I analyzed all regular players in the ManDak's history. A "regular batter" was defined as having 100 or more at-bats in a season. (No walk data was available for the ManDak.) A "regular pitcher" was defined as having made 10 starts or having 10 decisions (wins plus losses) in a season. These criteria produced an average of nine batters and three pitchers per team per year – a reasonable number for a league that played no more than 78 games.

Because all pitchers batted, and starters were expected to throw complete games, and because pitchers sometimes played other positions, a few moundsmen also qualified as batters. The result was an average of 11.8 regulars per team. 243 players qualified as regulars in at least one season. They were individually evaluated to estimate their skill level by examining their pre- and post-ManDak careers in professional baseball, along with how old they were when they played in the ManDak.

Note that player ages referenced in this article are Actuarial Seasonal Ages (ASA), a metric devised by Pete Palmer, legendary baseball historian and analyst and co-editor of *Total Baseball* and *The ESPN Baseball Encyclopedia*. A player's ASA is simply the current season minus his year of birth; it is one-half year older than the commonly used Seasonal Age.[22] (Players whose birth years were unknown were excluded from the calculations.) ASA adopts the actuarial concept that brackets a person's calendar age from six months before their birthday to six months afterward. For example, a person who is 29 years and 7 months old would be considered as 30 years old. This eliminates the problem of having someone 29 years and 364 days old being labeled as 29, when they are obviously much closer to 30.

Examining careers before and after their stay in the ManDak and adjusting for their age and their performance, an equivalent level of OB play was assigned to all 243 ManDak regulars: their Organized Baseball Equivalency (OBEq). Players with no professional experience were assigned to Class E, which didn't exist in the 1950s, but was a designation reserved for semipro leagues in the 1930s and 1940s.[23]

Taking a clear-eyed look at the pedigree of the ManDak regulars, the idea that the league was the equivalent of a high minor league, or that any of its players could have still played well in the majors, becomes merely a romantic notion. OBEq estimates of the players who started most of the games in the ManDak place the league somewhere between a Class-B and a Class-A league. Allowing for discrimination against Black ballplayers in OB that caused some to be placed below their true level of ability, it seems reasonable to evaluate the ManDak as about as good as a typical Class-A minor league of the day.

The career of ManDak star Clifton "Zoonie" McLean is enlightening. The North Dakotan was a standout collegiate player at Minot State University, one of the ManDak's biggest stars, the only player to appear in all eight years of the league's existence,[24] and the shortstop on Barry Swanton's ManDak All-Star Team.[25] His career batting average was .322. McLean reportedly declined an offer from the Philadelphia Athletics to turn pro,[26] yet Otto Huber evaluated McLean as only a Class-A shortstop in 1951 when he was in his prime at 27[27] – a year before he won the ManDak batting title by hitting .369.

Breaking down the ManDak's quality by OBEq ratings of its regulars, it is easy to see that the league could not have been comparable to the high minor leagues of the 1950s. Placing Class A with the higher leagues helps the comparison, but it still leaves almost half of the ManDak's *regular seasons* played by guys who were comparable to Class-B players or worse.

True, some players rated as "Class E" because they had no OB or Negro Leagues experience might have had the potential to play in the minors, but even bumping ManDak star Zoonie McLean up to Class A (per Huber's scouting report) doesn't substantially change things – and McLean clearly stood head and shoulders above the crowd of semipro players that filled out league rosters.

MANDAK OBEq by Regular Seasons		
Zoonie McLean = E		
OBEq	Reg Seasons	Percent
AAA	38	16%
AA	45	19%
A	45	19%
B	47	19%
C	33	14%
D	7	3%
E	28	12%
Total	243	100%
High Minors (AA-AAA)		34%
Low Minors (A-B-C-D plus E)		66%
Upper-level (A-AA-AAA)		53%
Lower-level (B-C-D plus E)		47%

MANDAK OBEq by Regular Seasons		
Zoonie McLean = A		
OBEq	Reg Seasons	Percent
AAA	38	16%
AA	45	19%
A	53	22%
B	47	19%
C	33	14%
D	7	3%
E	20	8%
Total	243	100%
High Minors (AA-AAA)		34%
Low Minors (A-B-C-D plus E)		66%
Upper-level (A-AA-AAA)		56%
Lower-level (B-C-D plus E)		44%

The 1950 ManDak League Champion Winnipeg Buffaloes, featuring four Negro Leaguers: Hall of Famers Willie Wells (front row, fourth from left) and Leon Day (middle, far left), as well as Lyman Bostock (middle, far right) and Butch Davis (front, second from right). Third from right in the front row is John Kennedy, who never played in the Negro Leagues but who would in 1957 become the first African American player on the Philadelphia Phillies. (Jay-Dell Mah Collection, courtesy of Tazena Kennedy)

CONUNDRUM OF THE GREAT NEGRO LEAGUERS

Since 2020, players from the Major Negro Leagues (MNL) are de jure as well as de facto major-league players. However, the ManDak was born two years after the last MNL season in 1948; therefore, unless a Negro Leaguer was still capable of playing a big-league game two years after his last MNL season, he wouldn't have been at a big-league level in the ManDak in 1950, never mind 1955 or later.

The career of a major-league ballplayer is arduous and short, and two years is ample time for their skills to erode unless they are young and still learning. Even the Hall of Famers – who are preternaturally good at their peaks and, therefore have more room to decline over time while still being above-the-bar big-leaguers – will eventually succumb to the irresistible elements of time and age. Often they keep playing long after merely mortal players have hung up their spikes, but that doesn't mean they are nearly as good.

Because so much of the ManDak's fame rests upon the strong shoulders of its cohort of great Black players and other Negro League All-Stars, a closer look is instructive. More than 40 percent of all ManDak regular seasons were logged by former Negro Leaguers.

Wilmer Fields, the well-traveled pitcher and hitter who appeared in the '48 East-West Game, was five years past his All-Star appearance when at age 31 he hit .356 with four homers in 24 games pitching and playing third base for Brandon in 1953. He was called "one of the best players to ever play in the ManDak League,"[28] and played well in Toronto in the Triple-A International League in 1952.

By his own account, Fields received four serious offers from AL or NL clubs to play in their organizations in the late 1940s or early 1950s. Fields said that he turned them all down because he was making as much money or more playing fewer games in the Negro Leagues and Latin America, and because he thought it wouldn't be a good move for his family.[29] While his reasons should be respected, it also means that he did not face the toughest competition in the world in the 1950s after the AL and NL had integrated, so it's hard to say whether he would have topped out at Triple A or been able to thrive under the bright lights in the majors. Regardless, his performance in his brief sojourn in the ManDak indicates he was starring in an inferior league.

Leon Day, who passed through the Bronze Doors in Cooperstown in 1995, was 34 in his first tour of duty in the ManDak in 1950 and 1951. Day pitched well in 40 innings in Triple A in 1951 but was much closer to mediocre in '52, two levels below in the Class-A Eastern League. In 1953, before his return to the ManDak at 38, he wasn't even that effective in a different Class-A league where he was 10 years older than the typical pitcher. At the plate, Day hit .259 with no power in Class AAA and only .279 with little power in Class A. As great as he was in his halcyon days, Day was apparently no longer capable of holding down a regular job in the majors by the 1950s, though he had plenty left in the tank to become a two-way star in the ManDak.

Long-lived Double Duty Radcliffe's stint in the ManDak basically amounted to a cameo. At age 49 in 1951, the durable catcher and pitcher hit .340 in 15 games while going 2-0 on the mound for Elmwood, including hurling a complete game in which he fanned eight batters.[30] Radcliffe also played briefly for Winnipeg in 1952 when he was half a century old! Needless to say, no one could play at that age in the major leagues; Double Duty and his spitter were unapologetically outfoxing players young enough to be his children. Listening to Radcliffe's recollections via McNary, it is easy to hear that the loquacious former star knew he was a man among boys in the ManDak.[31]

Universally loved Hall of Famer Ray Dandridge had torn the cover off the ball in his mid-to-late 30s in Triple-A Minneapolis. He then destroyed ManDak pitching to the tune of a .360 average with 40 extra-basers in only 328 at-bats with Bismarck in 1955 – the year he turned 42.

"Dandy" was tragically deprived of his shot in "The Show," but that was five to seven years earlier and he was probably no better than a good Triple-A player by '55.

Hall of Famer Willard Brown was a decade past his Negro League salad days when he joined the ManDak. The fearsome slugger could still rake, as his .302 BA with 57 extra-base hits in 544 at-bats in 1955 showed – but that was when he was playing *in Double A*. In reality, Brown might have been a good Double-A ballplayer at the end of the line in 1957 – as was the ManDak.

Cooperstown resident Willie "The Devil" Wells played regularly in the ManDak only in its first two seasons. Wells is one of the greatest ballplayers in history – Black or White – as well as one of the least-known of baseball's true titans. Yet the idea that he could play shortstop in a high-level league in his mid-40s is ludicrous. His teammate Frazier "Slow" Robinson provided the key: Wells positioned himself very shallow in the infield to cover for his inadequate arm. Facing big-league hitters, though, that adjustment would have been a disaster, because major leaguers hit the ball much harder than bush-leaguers. Groundballs that major-league shortstops playing deeper would gobble up would have rocketed by Wells for base hits, sending Wells to the bench or to retirement.

Robinson talked about how well the elderly Wells played in the ManDak:

[Wells at 46 years old] was an old man up there in Canada, but he could still play shortstop. And he could still hit; he might have hit around .375 up there [actually, .309 but with little power]. He'd play maybe one or two games a week, but that was because he was managing and playing. It'd look like he wasn't going to throw you out, but he didn't miss throwing out nobody. He played a shallow shortstop because his arm had lost a little something. Sometimes it'd look like he was standing up there by the pitcher, playing shortstop.[32]

The 1950 Carman Cardinals. Gentry Jessup is back row, far right, and Ron Teasley front row, far left. Feisty Carman, population 1,867, was the smallest market in the league. (Jay-Dell Mah Collection, courtesy of Gord Elliott)

Big-league veterans can adapt as they age and their physical skills diminish. A hitter who can no longer get around on a good fastball can "cheat" by starting his swing earlier. A pitcher whose fastball is several MPH slower than in his prime can still get hitters out with pinpoint control, plus breaking stuff, or by changing speeds.

There is a downside to those adjustments, though, even when they are successful. Hitters who cheat on fastballs become very vulnerable to breaking balls and changeups because they've tailored their stroke to the heat and end up too far in front of other pitches. Pitchers who rely on control, crooked pitches, or junk can become predictable. Even if the hitters don't figure out what's coming, these high-mileage arms cannot overpower a hitter when their location is off, their curves flatten out, or they are simply tipping their slow stuff.

Other ManDak stalwarts, both Black and White, have similarly divergent markers.

Roy Weatherly, who forged a 10-year journeyman's career in the White major leagues (811 games, 2781 at-bats, .286 BA but only 98 OPS+), won two ManDak batting titles with gaudy averages of .412 and .371, while also topping the loop in homers once. Last seen in the bigs in 1950 mostly as a pinch-hitter, Weatherly was (to echo broadcast legend Red Barber) "tearin' up the pea patch"[33] four to seven years later in the ManDak.

Thirteen-year National League veteran Ken Heintzelman (319 games, 1502 innings, 3.93 ERA) pitched for one season in the ManDak in 1955 at age 40, posting a 4.50 ERA after playing out the string in Triple A for three years.

"With his arm and his bat, [Marion "Sugar"] Cain was one of the most dominant players of the ManDak League from 1951 to 1957"[34] when 37-43 years old! Indeed, the popular ManDak star fashioned a 62-31 record on the mound in his seven-year sojourn in the ManDak, while batting .319 and whacking 10 round-trippers with the willow. In the years for which there are complete stats available, Cain led the ManDak in ERA twice, strikeouts three times, complete games once, innings once, wins once, and percentage twice. Nevertheless, Cain's Major Negro League career played out much differently. He bounced around in the late 1930s, where limited statistics show him posting a 1-4 record and a painful 8.28 ERA. All things considered, Cain probably peaked at a Double-A level professionally.

ManDak superstar Lomax "Butch" Davis had a similar profile. In three years as a regular, Davis led the loop in steals once and won the batting title twice in his mid-30s with averages of .406 and .454, losing a third title on the final day of the season despite his .369 BA![35] His .341 average with 27 long hits in 67 games with the 1947 NNL Baltimore Elite Giants showed his potential, but he was probably a good Triple-A player when he was scorching ManDak pitching.

A five-time East-West Game selection, Gentry Jessup was a star in both the Major Negro Leagues and the ManDak. However, available data shows a losing career record in the NAL, though an ERA somewhat better than average. With Carman from 1950 to 1952, Jessup was "considered a workhorse"[36] who led the league in wins once while batting .304. Lefty Lefebvre thought Jessup was the best pitcher in the ManDak, but the Minot manager also rated the league as Class B.[37]

Lots of players are literally major leaguers but not good enough to play regularly in the major leagues. They might ride the pine for a while – perhaps even for years – but they are not really *major-league-caliber players*. The major leagues are effectively defined by those who play every day (including rotation starters and closers), not by the substitutes who give them a rest, who collect garbage time during blowouts, or whom the manager is forced to play because of injuries.

Too often, people confuse having been a major-league player at one time or another with being good enough to play in the major leagues *right now* – or, in this case, when they were active in the ManDak. One could become a big-league regular a couple of years in the future, but only

be a Class-A ballplayer in the ManDak, as Jerry Adair showed. On the other side of a ballplayer's typical career arc, one could have been a major-league star six years ago but would be retired if not facing lower-level opposition such as that in the ManDak. Adair would ultimately play 13 years in the American League, nine with the Orioles. He didn't become a regular with Baltimore until 1961, four years after he hit .356 with line-drive power in the ManDak while still in college. Given his age and his subsequent OB minor-league record, he was likely a Class-C player in 1957, certainly no better than Class B.

Finally, there is Ian Lowe, "considered by some to be the best third baseman in the Man-Dak League."[38] He hit .319 in 1950 and tied for the league lead in RBIs with 39, while also managing the powerful Brandon Greys to first-place finishes in 1950 and 1951, and to the playoff championship in '51.[39] Lowe's pro career consisted of 29 games in Class B in 1946, where he hit .223 with zero power. Lowe was later inducted into both the Manitoba Baseball Hall of Fame[40] and the Manitoba Sports Hall of Fame:[41] He is the prototype of a small-town hero, but he was not more than a Class-C ballplayer.

When players who were reserves in the majors step into another league and succeed as regulars, it is obvious that their new league is of lower quality. When marginal big-leaguers dominate another league, it is clear that such a league is of much lower quality.

THE NUT GRAF

The reason that the level of play in the Negro Leagues of the late 1940s and the 1950s is relevant to the ManDak is that the reputation of the ManDak rests in large part upon its importation of former Negro League players – particularly future Hall of Famers Willie Wells Sr., Ray Dandridge, Willard Brown, and Leon Day. Satchel Paige's cameo in the ManDak is oft-touted, but

The lights go on in Carman! On July 6, 1950, Carman unveiled its floodlights at the ballpark. Perhaps visiting Brandon found the improved lighting more helpful, as they defeated the Cardinals 12-5. (Jay-Dell Mah Collection, courtesy of Gord Elliott)

the legendary pitcher was hired solely as an attendance-building gimmick and appeared in just two league games, hurling only three innings in each.[42]

There is no doubt that the careers of this distinguished quartet were at an elite level, even among those memorialized in Cooperstown. A close look, however, tells a somewhat different story. Of the four Hall of Famers, Brown and Dandridge stayed for but a single summer in the ManDak, while Day and Wells lingered on the Northern Prairies for only two years.

More importantly, Brown, Dandridge, and Wells were all 42 years old when they strode onto ManDak diamonds. While younger, Day was no ingénu at 34, and was already a veteran of 10 Major Negro League seasons, as well as having served two years in the US Army in World War II. High-profile Negro League veterans like Double Duty Radcliffe helped burnish the ManDak's reputation, but they didn't play regularly, and thus did not contribute much to the league's level of play.

The rest of the Negro League players who came north were not nearly so accomplished, or else they didn't tarry long in the league. Of 82 other regular ManDak players with Negro League experience, none had been stars aside from the Hall of Famers and Radcliffe. Another four dozen or so former Negro Leaguers also played in the ManDak, either as reserves or for short stints. Of those, only Chet Brewer and Ted Strong were included in Top 100 Black Baseball Players selected by eminent Negro League historian James Riley for the 2008 edition of the *ESPN Baseball Encyclopedia*.[43] Brewer, Radcliffe, and Strong were also the only ones among the Black Baseball stars nominated for consideration for the Hall of Fame in late 2021 by the 42 for 21 Committee poll of more than 100 prominent Negro Leagues scholars and Black Baseball historians.[44] Player-manager Brewer's time on the mound in the ManDak was very brief, as he appeared in only three games for Carman in 1953. Strong played only 23 games for Minot in 1950.

A telling indicator that the ManDak's Negro Leagues' cohort was past its prime is the weighted average age (by season) of former Negro

Leaguers when playing regularly in the ManDak: 33.6 years old (ASA). That is long after the mid- to late-20s peak of most big-leaguers, and it was a whopping 5.6 years older than the ages of other ManDak regulars (almost all of whom were White).

REASONS FOR THE COLLAPSE

After World War II, high-school and college baseball was in decline in the United States as football and basketball came to dominate the prep athletic scene. Though there was a huge postwar surge in minor-league teams, leagues, and attendance in the late 1940s, that quickly collapsed as television began its rapid march to ubiquity in American society. Sitting in front of the family TV set displaced many forms of entertainment – including attending ballgames at the local ballyard.

With the populace staying home, the two major leagues of the day created a lucrative new revenue stream by televising their games. In the early years of baseball on TV, clubs limited their telecasts to local markets, partly due to the cost of transmitting signals via expensive landlines, and partly out of deference to minor-league operators.

The lure of extra lucre soon overcame both constraints, with the American and National Leagues televising games nationwide. Many individual AL and NL clubs followed by expanding their reach, realizing that fans in their hinterlands would rather sit in their living rooms on summer evenings, watching baseball for free on TV. On Saturdays, baseball fans could watch major-league teams for free rather than go out to the ballpark and pay to watch bush-league or semipro ballplayers in the flesh.

In his superb history, Swanton identified the primary reasons for the league's demise as "attendance dwindling and operating costs rising," along with a belief by "many Manitobans" that "Williston and Bismarck [had] exceeded the salary cap."[45] In 2007 a review in the journal *NINE* found that Swanton's "explanation of the ManDak League's demise [was] abrupt" and didn't offer much analysis.[46] Many leagues before and since have struggled with finding competitive balance between not-so-rich clubs and well-off clubs. In the final years of the ManDak, the better-resourced clubs were located in the oil-rich towns of Williston and Bismarck, North Dakota, but there were multiple other reasons for the ManDak's expiration.

As for attendance, the overall trend in baseball was so dire that a league like the ManDak could not avoid being fatally afflicted. Almost 33 million fans attended minor-league games in 1950, the year of the ManDak's birth. By 1957, the year the ManDak died, attendance in the minors had shrunk by 55 percent. Extrapolating those trends to the ManDak's unique niche, it is not difficult to see why the league was doomed.

Other problems inherent in the ManDak's founding placed a continuing strain on league operations and club viability. In the first half of the league's existence, Winnipeg was a member. Its urban area population of 354,069 was more than 10 times the size of the two next-largest markets (Minot at 22,032 and Brandon at 20,598) and almost 200 times the size of Carman's population of 1,867! Disparities between similarly sized Minot and Bismarck (18,640) and Dickinson (7,469) and Williston (7,378) in the second half of the league's lifespan were much more manageable, but the damage had already been done by then with the withdrawal of the Manitoban clubs after 1954.

Even before Williston and Bismarck joined the league in 1954 and 1955, respectively, the ManDak regularly suffered from competition issues:

The Minot Mallards completely dominated the league from 1952 through 1954, finishing first in the regular season and in the playoffs each year. In 1952 Minot was the only team in the league with a winning record, going 8-1 in the playoffs to win the championship in very convincing fashion. In 1954 the Mallards finished 10 games ahead of the runner-up in a 70-game season, then went 8-5 in the playoffs to win its third consecutive ManDak crown.

In 1955 Minot finished third, nine games back, during the regular campaign before winning the first round of the playoffs in six games and then sweeping the final series.

In 1956 Williston finished first by two games in a close race, then went 8-5 in the playoffs to capture its first championship over the defending champion Mallards.

The 1957 season almost didn't happen because finding four viable teams was difficult.[47] Bismarck repeated Williston's feat of finishing first and then winning the championship in a season marked by bad weather and controversy. A protested ruling by the league president resulted in second-place Minot meeting Bismarck in a single-series postseason.

The 1957 championship series gave the struggling league a final big black eye when Minot refused to take the field after Game Three, forfeiting the championship after a dispute about whether the Mallards' home field remained playable following two days of rain.[48]

Another vexing issue for the league was long travel distances; the table below that shows the road mileage from Minot to other league member towns. (Minot was the only town to field a team in all eight ManDak seasons.)

MANDAK LEAGUE MILEAGE

Although these long distances were not insurmountable, the extensive travel placed a burden on team finances. It was no coincidence that, as the league struggled with longer schedules after 1952, the average mileage from Minot to the other ManDak cities decreased substantially, from 236 miles (1950-1953) to 125 miles in 1957.

The table on page 410 shows how ManDak summers varied in terms of number of league games (not including the playoffs), length of schedule, and the average number of official games played per week. Each year had a new wrinkle. In 1950 no league contests were scheduled on Sundays, but teams played numerous tournament and

	Winnipeg	Brandon	Carman	Minot	Williston	Bismarck	Dickinson
Winnipeg	XXX	138	53	304	NA	NA	NA
Brandon	138	XXX	125	168	280	279	NA
Carman	53	125	XXX	236	364	NA	NA
Minot	304	168	236	XXX	125	111	185
Williston	NA	280	364	125	XXX	230	131
Bismarck	NA	279	NA	111	230	XXX	99
Dickinson	NA	NA	NA	185	131	99	XXX

Notes

Winnipeg fielded two teams 1950-1951, including Elmwood club.

NA = Never in the league at the same time.

YEAR	OPEN	CLOSE	DAYS	WEEKS	G	G/WK
1950	5/24/1950	8/28/1950	96	13.7	48.0	3.5
1951	5/21/1951	8/27/1951	98	14.0	64.4	4.6
1952	5/24/1952	8/16/1952	84	12.0	53.5	4.5
1953	5/14/1953	8/31/1953	109	15.6	75.5	4.8
1954	5/24/1954	8/21/1954	89	12.7	70.5	5.5
1955	5/27/1955	8/22/1955	87	12.4	78.0	6.3
1956	5/24/1956	8/31/1956	99	14.1	77.5	5.5
1957	5/31/1957	8/20/1957	81	11.6	71.0	6.1
Key						
OPEN = First regular-season game played by any team						
CLOSE = Last regular-season game played by any team						
G = Average regular-season games played per team						
G/WK = Average official games played per team per week						

other exhibition games that didn't count in the standings. The ManDak's second summer added league games on the Sabbath, upping the games played by more than a third, yet the teams still engaged in plentiful exhibition and tournament play. Tournament play, including four *league-sponsored tournaments*, peaked in 1952.

The 1953 and 1956 seasons saw the ManDak clubs play interlocking schedules with other Western Canada semipro circuits, greatly upping travel friction and costs. The number of official games jumped into the 70s in '53, staying there for the rest of the loop's life. In a sign of things to come, Winnipeg left the league in '54 as struggling Brandon and Carman played some "home games" in the provincial capital – though it didn't forestall their folding for long. In 1955-1956, the ManDak benefited from fewer Negro League veterans. For those two years, it was really the "NDak League" because all four clubs were located in North Dakota. A shaky Brandon team returned to the league in 1957 or the ManDak wouldn't have been able to operate. The Greys ended the season unhappily, protesting the ManDak president's decision to proceed to a shortened playoff schedule without making up all postponed games.

MANDAK SEASONS BY LENGTH AND GAMES

Ultimately, the combined pressure of baseball's sharply declining popularity, especially below the major-league level, and the mismatch of importing Negro League and high-minors players while operating over long distances in tiny markets made the end of the ManDak inevitable. Those 58 minor leagues and 446 teams who had taken the field across the United States and Canada in 1950 had shrunk to 24 circuits and 173 clubs by 1958.

The history of professional baseball in Manitoba and North Dakota before and after the ManDak era demonstrates that, aside from Winnipeg, the area does not have markets large enough to support any but the most tenuous professional franchises. True, the Manitoba-Dakota League was semipro – not professional – but it ambitiously attempted to operate more like a professional league instead of a local or regional semipro circuit. In essence, the ManDak's ambitions were also the seeds of its undoing. The league aspired to a higher level of baseball than its constituent members (teams) and their constituencies (the fans) were able to support. In its final summer, ManDak attendance was less than 1,000 per game for all four clubs.

DÉNOUEMENT

After withdrawing from the ManDak at the end of the 1953 season, Winnipeg joined the Class-C Northern League from 1954 through 1964. In 1963-1964, Winnipeg and the league moved up to Class A. In 1969 the capital of Manitoba hosted a short-season Class-A club that drew barely 500 fans per game. All those teams were in the low minors.

From midseason 1970, when Buffalo's Triple-A team relocated to Winnipeg, through the end of 1971, Winnipeg was an outpost of the Class-AAA International League. In 1971 the Whips were next to last in the IL in attendance, sealing their fate. After they folded, Manitoba would be bereft of professional baseball until the revolutionary new independent Northern League arrived in the mid-1990s.

From 1994 to 2010, the Winnipeg Goldeyes played indy ball in the Northern League, switching to its indy successor, the American Association, in 2011. The Goldeyes are still on the field, though their attendance was only a bit above 1,000 per game in 2021. Pre-pandemic, Winnipeg's attendance had ranged from 3,900 to 5,700 in their Association tenure.

Before the ManDak, Brandon had not hosted a minor-league team for a full season since 1911, and it would not have another until it consummated a three-year fling with the shaky independent Prairie League, beginning in 1995.

Tiny but proud Carman, naturally, never came close to hosting a professional franchise before or after the ManDak.

South of the border, ManDak heavyweight Minot entered the Class-C Northern League in 1958 with a completely new roster as a Cleveland Indians farm club. The revamped Mallards were far from dominant in the pros, playing .500-.550 ball and struggling at the gate for three seasons. In 1962 a new Mallards team took the field for one final summer, finishing last in the loop. Minot also joined the short-lived Prairie League in 1995. That indy league's demise after 1997 brought an end to Minot's professional baseball ventures.

Bismarck also played four years in the old, affiliated Northern League, though the North Dakota state capital waited until 1962 to join the loop. Prior to its ManDak involvement, Bismarck hadn't hosted a pro team since 1923. Its final gasp in pro ball was in the 1995-1996 Prairie League.

Two decades later, in 2017, Bismarck joined the growing trend of former minor-league towns hosting collegiate summer league teams. It has been a member of the Northwoods League since then. Stronger than all other summer collegiate leagues except for the famed Cape Cod League, the Northwoods operates much like a lower-level pro league – except for not paying its players, who thus retain their amateur eligibility.

In 2018 Minot and Dickinson joined the summer collegiate Expedition League, with Brandon following suit a year later. The Expedition is much more fragile and low-budget – and thus more typical – of these summer leagues than is the Northwoods. Average attendance at its games was 459 in 2021 and 611 in 2019,[49] a far cry from the crowds of thousands who lustily cheered the ManDak's heyday.

Dickinson and Williston hosted a minor-league team neither before the ManDak, nor after.

THE LEGACY

The ManDak was truly a *rara avis*, loved by its players and its fans. It is remembered today as a treasure that melded community pride with competitive spirit and good, old-fashioned hardball. Nevertheless, community spirit and love for one's team only goes so far, as former Brooklyn Dodgers fans sorrowfully attest.

The ManDak's place in baseball history – particularly in Canada – is secure. SABR's 2005 history of baseball in Canada featured a statue-like pose of Frazier "Slow" Robinson in his Winnipeg Buffaloes uniform front and center on its cover, superimposed over a red maple leaf and a background map of Canada.[50]

Because of painstaking efforts by such skilled and devoted researchers as Barry Swanton, Jay-Dell Mah, and Gary Fink, the league's legend has grown in the twenty-first century. Major League Baseball's better-late-than-never recognition of the 1920-1948 Negro Leagues as full-fledged major leagues has also given an indirect boost to the little league that could.

For a few brief sunlit summers on the Northern Prairie, the Manitoba-Dakota League was not good – it was *great*. Analysis of the quality of its play does not detract in the slightest from its greatness, which was founded on its enlightened integration of Black players –both on and off the field – and on its rootedness in the community.

With an affectionate nod to English literary "hall of fame" poet Robert Browning, some minor tinkering with two lines from his poem "Andrea del Sarto" nicely sums up the ManDak:

Ah, but a league's reach should exceed its grasp,
Or what's a (baseball) heaven for?

SOURCES

It would be a Herculean task to write accurately about the Manitoba-Dakota League were it not for the painstaking, pioneering, and perspicacious work of Barry Swanton, Jay-Dell Mah, and Gary Fink.

Swanton's *ManDak League: Haven for Former Negro League Ballplayers, 1950-1957* is the irreplaceable guidebook, with its detailed descriptions of each ManDak season, standings, playoffs, and assorted other notable events. *Black Baseball Players in Canada: A Biographical Dictionary, 1881-1960*, which he co-authored with Mah, supplements it beautifully.

Mah's fabulous AtthePlate.com website provides an online encyclopedia of the history of Western Canada baseball with digital reams of information: in particular, detailed game reports and many valuable and precious images. If other states or regions in the United States and Canada had such a website devoted to their nonprofessional baseball history, the game would be much more popular.

Fink's deep dive into the statistics of the ManDak bring the descriptions of the league and its players into sharper focus, as well as making analysis so much easier and better.

Kudos and copious thanks to all three of them. RIP Barry Swanton, who passed at age 83 on October 1, 2021.

James A. Riley's *Biographical Encyclopedia of the Negro Baseball Leagues* remains a landmark in the field and informs so much of the context and judgments about the players and the era. It is literally indispensable. The *Biographical Encyclopedia* is a massive volume (more than 900 pages), and I am fortunate to be in the process of editing the second-edition manuscript, which should be published online later in 2022.

Seamheads.com's authoritative Negro Leagues Database, carefully curated and maintained by Gary Ashwill and Kevin Johnson, provides the best (by far) statistics for Negro League players through 1948. Baseball-Reference.com was used for AL and NL statistics, as well as minor-league statistics. Note that reliable statistics for the Negro American League after 1948 and for other Negro minor leagues are very hard to find.

Historical information on the minor leagues through 2006 was found in the third and final edition of *Baseball America's Encyclopedia of Minor League Baseball*. Additional information about the state of the minor leagues after World War II was found in minor-league expert Bob Hoie's article in John Thorn's, Pete Palmer's, and Michael Gershman's *Total Baseball: The Official Encyclopedia of Major League Baseball*, seventh edition (2001). More recent information on the minor leagues and on collegiate summer leagues was found on Baseball-Reference.com.

The expanded 2020 edition of Larry Lester's magisterial book, *Black Baseball's National Showcase: The East-West All-Star Game, 1933-1962*, was used to verify references to Negro League players' All-Star appearances.

Population data came from Statistics Canada's 1951 Census of Population and from the US 1950 Census via their official websites.

Geographical information, including driving distances, was found on RandMcNally.com.

NOTES

1   Hank Davis, *Small Town Heroes: Images of Minor League Baseball* (Iowa City: University of Iowa Press, 1997).

2   *Official Baseball Annual 1953* (Wichita, Kansas: National Baseball Congress of America), 30.

3   Barry Swanton, *The ManDak League: Haven for Former Negro League Ballplayers, 1950-1957* (Jefferson, North Carolina: McFarland & Co., 2006), 7-8.

4   James A. Riley, *The Biographical Encyclopedia of the Negro Baseball Leagues* (unpublished second edition manuscript), Wilmer Fields entry.

5   Wilmer Fields, *My Life in the Negro Leagues: An Autobiography* (McLean, Virginia: Miniver Press, 2013), 39.

6   Kyle McNary, *Ted "Double Duty" Radcliffe: 36 Years of Pitching & Catching in the Negro Leagues* (McNary Publishing, 1994), Chapter 27, 1951.

7   Barry Swanton and Jay-Dell Mah, *Black Baseball Players in Canada: A Biographical Dictionary, 1881-1960* (Jefferson, North Carolina: McFarland & Co., 2009), 162.

8   Orlin Jones, Detroit historian, telephone interview with author, March 23, 2022.

9   Swanton, 1.

10 Ron Teasley, telephone interview with author, June 21, 2019.

11 Michael Stahl, "The Secret History of Black Baseball Players in Canada's Great White North," Salon.com, April 30, 2017.

12 Jane Finnan Dorward, ed., *Dominionball: Baseball Above the 49th* (Cleveland: Society for American Baseball Research, 2005), 100.

13 Swanton, 63-64.

14 Jim Adelson entry on NDAPSSA.com, accessed March 26, 2022; *Dickinson* (North Dakota) *Press* article, "Legendary ND Sportscaster Jim Adelson Dies at 91," October 1, 2016; "Minot Mallards Memories" pages on AtthePlate.com, accessed March 26, 2022.

15 McNary, Chapter 27, 1951.

16 Email from Dan Kelly of Chatham, Ontario, to Andrew North, March 2, 2022; "Bucs Hold Camp at Thamesville," *Windsor Star*, August 20, 1947; "Pirates Sign Bob Seguin," *Windsor Star*, November 11, 1947.

17 *Sporting News* contract card image for Jim St. Louis, https://digital.la84.org/digital/collection/p17103coll3/id/146268/rec/29, accessed via SABR.org and downloaded March 4, 2022.

18 Author assessment after email correspondence over several years with Dr. Ted Turocy about quality of the "Open"-classification Pacific Coast League in 1950s.

19 "MLB Officially Designates the Negro Leagues as 'Major League,'" December 16, 2020, MLB press release posted on MLB.com, accessed December 16, 2020.

20 Riley, *passim*.

21 Scott Simkus, *Outsider Baseball Bulletin*, Issue Nos. 53-58, June 8-July 13, 2011.

22 Multiple conversations and emails between Pete Palmer and the author dating back to 1992.

23 Robert L. Finch, et al., eds., *The Story of Minor League Baseball* (Columbus, Ohio: National Association of Professional Baseball Leagues, 1952), 38, 45.

24 Swanton, 135.

25 Swanton, 3.

26 Swanton, 3, 135-136.

27 Swanton, 63.

28 Swanton and Mah, 65.

29 Fields, 31-32.

30 Swanton, 24.

31 McNary, Chapter 27, 1951.

32 Frazier "Slow" Robinson, *Catching DREAMS: My Life in the Negro Baseball Leagues* (Syracuse: Syracuse University Press, 1999), 168-169.

33 Paul Dickson, ed., *Baseball's Greatest Quotations, Revised Edition* (New York: Collins, 2008), 42.

34 Swanton and Mah, 43.

35 Swanton, 94.

36 Swanton, 118-119.

37 Swanton, 63.

38 Swanton, 130-131.

39 Swanton, 130-131.

40 https://mbhof.ca/inductees/ian-lowe/, accessed March 2, 2022.

41 http://honouredmembers.sportmanitoba.ca/search.php?criteria_name=lowe&criteria_sport=&criteria_keywords=&criteria_induction, accessed March 2, 2022.

42 Swanton, 146.

43 Gary Gillette and Pete Palmer, eds., *The ESPN Baseball Encyclopedia, Fifth Edition* (New York: Sterling, 2008), 1722-1727.

44 www.42for21.org/results, accessed February 28, 2022.

45 Swanton, 63.

46 John Paul Hill, "The ManDak League: Haven for Former Negro League Ballplayers, 1950-1957 (review)," *NINE: A Journal of Baseball History and Culture* 16, No. 1 (Fall 2007): 142.

47 "Campbells Beaten," *Edmonton Journal*, March 15, 1957: 20.

48 "Bismarck Awarded Mandak [*sic*] Playoffs," *Saskatoon Star-Phoenix*, August 28, 1957: 23.

49 BallparkDigest.com attendance reports for 2019 and 2021. Accessed February 20, 2022.

50 Dorward.

END OF AN ERA:
THE DEMISE OF THE MONTRÉAL ROYALS

By Marcel Dugas

One could make a case that, between 1941 and 1953, the Montréal Royals were the gold standard for minor-league teams in North America. After becoming part of the Brooklyn Dodgers chain in 1939,[1] they followed much the same path as their parent club, going from perpetual also-rans to perennial contenders. In those 13 seasons, they won five league pennants and six Governors' Cups (awarded to the International League's playoff champions), and earned the right to call themselves the best minor-league team on the continent by winning the Junior World Series three times. The team finished in the second division only once during that period, drew great crowds, and – let's not forget – integrated "organized" (a.k.a. White) baseball in 1946.

This golden age was followed by a precipitous fall from grace. On September 7, 1960, less than seven years after the Royals clinched their third Junior World Series title, the team played its final home game in front of 1,016 nostalgic fans.[2]

Many things had changed in those seven years. Television transformed the entertainment habits of Canadians. Delorimier Stadium, the club's home ballpark since 1928, became antiquated. It was located in a residential neighborhood where

parking was scarce, which became more and more of a liability as the 1950s went on.

Most importantly, the baseball world was changing rapidly. Starting in 1953, five Triple-A markets (Milwaukee, Baltimore, Kansas City, San Francisco, and Minneapolis-St. Paul) were elevated to major-league status in rapid succession. Montréal was mentioned as a possible landing spot for a number of major franchises, and for a club in the new Continental Baseball League that Branch Rickey tried to launch. But nothing came to fruition.[3] Minor-league fatigue among baseball fans in the city probably played a role in the club's rapid drop in popularity.

The biggest factor in the Royals' demise, however, may have been when another Triple-A city, although not one to which Montréal could be compared in any way, got its first major-league team. For two decades, Montréal's geographic situation had been instrumental in the club's position as the number-one farm team of the Brooklyn Dodgers. But after 1957, it was apparent that the Los Angeles Dodgers didn't quite know what to do with such a far-flung farm club. After an unexpected Governors' Cup championship in 1958, many of the players who had made that title run possible were taken from Montréal's roster and sent to the Dodgers' other Triple-A affiliates. The Royals dropped to sixth in the standings and eighth in attendance in 1959,[4] and 1960 was even worse.

By the time September 7, 1960, rolled around, many in the press and the fan base had come to terms with the fact that there would be no Royals in 1961. The team was dead last in the standings, 26 games below .500. Tommy Lasorda, the longest-tenured and most recognizable Royal, had left the club in July after almost coming to blows with manager Clay Bryant.[5] Rumors were swirling that the team was losing money, and that the Dodgers had no interest in operating the Royals going forward; the cities of Atlanta and Syracuse were mentioned as landing spots for the franchise.[6,7]

"The game took a backseat to memories of better days" said La Presse of the farewell game.[8] Future Athletic and Yankee right-hander Billy Kunkel toed the rubber as the Buffalo Bisons, who were fighting for their playoff lives, were in town.

The Bisons took the lead with a first-inning tally. The Royals scored two in the sixth, only to see the opposition come back with successive two-run innings in each of the seventh, eighth, and ninth. Veteran Buffalo infielder Bobby Morgan, who had spent three seasons in Montréal during the club's heyday (1948, '49 and '51) clobbered the last home run in the history of Delorimier Stadium, a solo shot in the ninth inning.[9]

Down by five in the bottom of the ninth, the locals tried to mount a comeback and managed to score two runs. But 38-year-old former major leaguer Max Surkont came on in relief and struck out Cuban center fielder Angel Scull for the final out of the final Royals game in Montréal.[10]

In the locker room, players had little to say about the team's situation. They were mostly happy that this dreary season would be over after one final series in Rochester. Manager Bryant told the press he hoped to be back in Montréal next season, although he said the exact opposite four days later.[11] Cuban-born pitcher René Valdés, in his third season wearing Royal blue, took his time before removing his uniform. "If the Royals aren't around next year, I don't know where I'll land. Montréal remains my favorite place," Valdés told reporters.[12]

About 125,000 fans went through the turnstiles in 1960, roughly the numbers the Royals used to draw for the playoffs when things were going well.[13] It came as no surprise when the Dodgers announced, a few days after the conclusion of the season, that they were not picking up the lease on Delorimier Stadium. Their two-decades-long association with the city of Montréal was over.

That didn't mean that the Royals were gone, however. A group of Canadian sportsmen wanted to buy the team and run it as an independent franchise. Some players would be bought from the Dodgers, while others would come to Montréal through a deal with a major-league club. (The Orioles were rumored to be the club in question.) That deal, however, would not make the Canadian Royals, as they were to be called, an Orioles farm team. But the prospective ownership group wanted a better lease on Delorimier Stadium than what the Dodgers had, and the owners of the park were unwilling to budge. An expanded Jarry Park (a baseball stadium) and the current home of the Montréal Alouettes football team, McGill University's Percival-Molson Stadium, were mentioned as possible alternatives. The deal fell through.[14]

The task of saving the Royals went to 77-year-old former team manager and GM Frank Shaughnessy, who had just stepped down after 24 years as president of the International League. After asking $125,000 of other potential suitors, the Dodgers were ready to sell the club to Shaughnessy for $90,000, and were willing to furnish 15 to 16 players for 1961. But again the question of Delorimier Stadium's rent was a problem. There was a $25,000 gap between what Shaughnessy was willing to pay and what the ballpark's owners were asking for.[15] Those efforts also proved fruitless, and the franchise was transferred to Syracuse, New York, in early 1961.

But the Royals were still not dead. The 1960-61 offseason was an eventful one for the International League. In addition to Montréal losing its club, the Miami Marlins moved to San Juan, Puerto Rico. But the new Marlins drew poorly early on. After an Opening Day crowd of 6,600, a grand total of 6,400 attended their next eight games.[16] Given how expensive it was to fly a baseball team to Puerto Rico, the league quickly decided to transfer the club, and Montréal was on the short list to provide a new home for the St. Louis Cardinals' Triple-A affiliate.[17]

The hopes of having the International League back in town were dashed in early May. The new tenants of Delorimier Stadium, the Cantalia club of the Eastern Canada Professional Soccer League, had spent $3,500 to get rid of the dirt infield and the pitching mound. They did not wish to share the building with a baseball team. And contrary to, for example, the National Football League, which had plenty of teams playing in baseball stadiums, the Eastern Canada Professional Soccer League did not allow its members to play on a pitch with a dirt infield.[18] The circuit ceased operations after the 1966 season.

With the only building that could have housed professional baseball being taken out of the equation, the Royals were now officially dead. There was sadness among the diehards, those who were still around for the franchise's final game. But those who believed the city should move on from minor-league baseball thought it was a good thing. "Isn't it better for our city," wrote *Devoir* sportswriter Gérard Gosselin, "to be completely deprived of baseball for a while, so interested parties will open their eyes and prepare a concrete, well planned and adequate gesture toward getting a major league franchise?"[19]

NOTES

1   William Brown, *Baseball's Fabulous Montréal Royals* (Montréal: Robert Davies Publishing, 1996), 55.

2   "Devant Une Vieille Garde de Partisans, Les Royaux ont-ils Présenté Leur Performance d'Adieu aux Montréalais?," *La Presse*, September 8, 1960: 53.

3   Rolland Ricard, "Montréal dans la Ligue Continentale en 1961? Un Sportman Newyorkais Achèterait la Franchise des Royaux," *La Presse*, March 16, 1960: 46.

4   Brown, 171-172.

5   Brown, 176.

6   "Les Dodgers Laissent Tomber le Bail des Royaux," *Le Devoir*, September 14, 1960: 12.

7   Marcel Desjardins, "Si les Propriétaires du Stade Delorimier Faisaient un Geste," *La Presse*, December 5, 1960: 39.

8   "Devant une Vieille Garde de Partisans ..."

9   "Royals Bow to Buffalo in Final," *Montréal Gazette*, September 8, 1960: 30.

10 "Devant une Vieille Garde de Partisans ..."

11 "Clay Bryant ne Désire pas Revenir à Montréal," *La Presse*, September 12, 1960: 37.

12 "Devant une Vieille Garde de Partisans ..."

13 "Les Dodgers Laissent Tomber le Bail des Royaux."

14 Marcel Desjardins, "Choix d'un Gérant Exceptionnel et Entente avec un Certain Club Majeur," *La Presse*, September 15, 1960: 53.

15 "Tentative de Frank Shaughnessy pour Sauver la Cause du Baseball à Montréal," *La Presse*, December 16, 1960: 17, 41.

16 Marcel Desjardins, "À cause de l'Impossibilité d'Obtenir le Stade Delorimier, La Franchise du Club San Juan ne Pourra Être Transférée à Montréal," *La Presse*, May 4, 1961: 42.

17 "Richardson 'Redécouvre' Montréal," *Le Devoir*, May 4, 1961: 11.

18 "À cause de l'Impossibilité d'Obtenir le Stade Delorimier."

19 Gérard Gosselin, "Cavalcade Sportive," *Le Devoir*, December 2, 1960: 14.

TORONTO MAPLE LEAFS' LAST GAME

SEPTEMBER 4, 1967:
SYRACUSE CHIEFS 7, TORONTO MAPLE LEAFS 2
AT MAPLE LEAF STADIUM, TORONTO

By Paul Sinclair

Monday September 4, 1967, the annual Labor Day holiday in Toronto, was a day of many endings. For schoolchildren it was the last day of summer vacation and a day filled with nervousness in anticipation of the new school year and all its concomitant unknowns. Monday evening, the Canadian National Exhibition (CNE) would close its 88th year. The previous night, in Exhibition Stadium, the CNE Grandstand season finished with evangelist Billy Graham delivering a message on faith and hope.

At Maple Leaf Stadium, farther east from the CNE along Lakeshore Boulevard, the Toronto Maple Leafs, the farm team of the Boston Red Sox in the International League, were scheduled to play their final game of the 1967 season. After back-to-back championships in 1965 and 1966, a three-peat was not going to happen in 1967 for this Maple Leafs team. Just one month earlier, the Leafs had been in third place (56-52), and a return to the playoffs looked probable. But the Maple Leafs' season was now destined to end in a sixth-place finish, as the team had won only eight of its previous 30 games. On this sunny Monday afternoon, the Maple Leafs (64-74) hosted the last-place Syracuse Chiefs (62-77).

The Chiefs, the farm team of the New York Yankees, had dominated Toronto during the season. Monday's game was the last of a four-game series over the holiday weekend. The Leafs had won 2-1 in extra innings on Saturday night, while on Sunday afternoon the Chiefs won both games of a doubleheader, 2-1 and 9-8.[1]

Monday also marked the end of the 84th season of the International League. The season was finishing with a tight pennant race as the Richmond Braves and the Rochester Red Wings battled for first place. With the top four teams in the eight-team league qualifying for the playoffs, there would be no postseason games for Toronto and Syracuse. This final game would not impact the standings. For the players, key statistical rankings like batting average, home run, and RBI titles could not be affected. The majority of the players would be heading to their winter homes after the game. Only a select few would continue their season with the parent clubs of Boston and New York as part of the major leagues' September roster expansion.

For the fans of the Toronto Maple Leafs and of baseball in Toronto and across Canada, the significance of the game could not be fully known on that Monday. There was much nervousness about the future of the Toronto franchise, and of professional baseball in Toronto, as declining attendance through the 1960s had continued during the 1967 season.

With the 2:00 P.M. game time approaching and fans going through the turnstiles, the starting pitchers headed to the bullpen to warm up. Starting for the Syracuse Chiefs was Stan Bahnsen. A top prospect in the Yankees organization, Bahnsen was making his 23rd start of the season, and had a record of 8 wins and 11 losses with an ERA of 3.63. He had previous major-league experience as a call-up to the Yankees in 1966, posting a record of 1-1 and an ERA of 3.52. He had failed to make the Yankees roster out of spring training in 1967, but was having a good season with the Chiefs, highlighted by a seven-inning perfect game against Buffalo on July 9.

In the Toronto bullpen, Garry Roggenburk warmed up for his 17th start of the season. Despite a 5-9 record, he had an attractive ERA of 2.45, leading all of Toronto's pitchers with enough qualifying appearances. Roggenburk was finishing his sixth season of professional baseball. During parts of the 1963, 1965, and 1966 seasons, he had played 60 games for the Minnesota Twins, compiling a record of 4-6 with an ERA and WHIP of 3.02 and 1.51 respectively. One year earlier, in September 1966, he had been purchased by the Boston Red Sox and called up to the major leagues. He appeared in one game, facing three batters, giving up a hit and a walk before retiring one hitter. The next spring training, he was assigned to Toronto, for whom he had played the entire 1967 season.

Roggenburk finished his warm-up pitches knowing that he would have to have his best to win his sixth game of the year. He was aware that the Chiefs had dominated the Leafs all season, winning 14 of the 19 games played.[2] He knew he could not rely on the Leafs to score many runs; the Leafs' hitters ranked last in the league in runs and in numerous other key offensive categories.

As had been the case with the weekend's previous games, Toronto manager Eddie Kasko appointed coach Jackie Moore as the acting manager.[3] Across the diamond, Syracuse manager Gary Blaylock was finishing his first season with the Chiefs. The starting lineups were:[4]

SYRACUSE CHIEFS

LF Tom Shopay
2B Matt Galante
SS Jerry Kenney
C Frank Fernandez
1B Ramon Conde
RF Bill Tuttle
CF Ross Moschitto
3B Ron Boyer
P Stan Bahnsen

TORONTO MAPLE LEAFS

SS Al Lehrer
2B Syd O'Brien
CF Al Yates
3B John Ryan
1B Jose Calero
LF Stan Johnson
RF Tony Torchia
C Bob Montgomery
P Garry Roggenburk

Roggenburk started strong against the Chiefs over the first four innings. Working quickly in this last game of the season, he limited Syracuse to two harmless singles. Bahnsen took the mound in the bottom of the first inning fully confident that he would continue his recent success against this weak-hitting Toronto team. The previous Wednesday in Syracuse, he had beaten Toronto 8-1, giving up only three hits. A similarly quick-working Bahnsen continued to dominate over the first four innings, limiting Toronto to four hits. Managing only a lone single in each inning by O'Brien, Johnson, Montgomery, and Ryan, the Leafs failed to put a runner in scoring position.

END OF FOURTH INNING
SYRACUSE 0, TORONTO 0

Roggenburk's string of scoreless innings ended quickly in the fifth, when Bill Tuttle slugged his eighth home run of the year to put Syracuse ahead. The solo home run seemed to rattle Roggenburk, as Ross Moschitto followed with a single. Pitching from the stretch, Roggenburk held Moschitto on first as the eighth-place hitter, Ron Boyer, stepped to the plate. The right-handed-hitting Boyer laced a hit to left field, where Stan Johnson misplayed it, allowing Moschitto to score the Chiefs' second run; Boyer stopped at second base with his sixth double of the season. Boyer was stranded on second as Roggenburk escaped the fifth without surrendering another hit.

In the bottom of the fifth inning, the Leafs went down in order. Bahnsen had retired five consecutive hitters.

END OF FIFTH INNING
SYRACUSE 2, TORONTO 0

With the Leafs hitting so ineffectively, Roggenburk went to the mound to start the sixth inning hoping to shut down the Syracuse hitters as he had done in the first four innings. Luck would not be on his side, however: The Leafs' fielding let him down as it had in the previous inning. The Chiefs' leadoff hitter of the inning, Frank Fernandez, hit a blooper into short center field. Shortstop Al Lehrer gave chase, but the ball was just out of his reach and landed on the outfield grass. Lehrer retrieved the ball and made a poor throw, allowing Fernandez to reach second base. The Chiefs capitalized on Lehrer's 15th error of the season as the next hitter, Ramon Conde, singled, scoring Fernandez, to put the Chiefs ahead

3-0. Conde was stranded on second as Syracuse bats were silenced for the rest of the inning.

Spotted with a lead, Bahnsen again retired the Leafs in order in the bottom of the sixth inning, extending his mastery of the Leafs to eight consecutive hitters.

END OF THE SIXTH INNING
SYRACUSE 3, TORONTO 0

The Chiefs tagged Roggenburk for their second home run of the afternoon in the top of the seventh inning. Tom Shopay, a left-handed hitter, went deep with his ninth home run of the season, extending the Chiefs' lead to 4-0.

The seventh-inning stretch did not raise the Leafs' offense from its slumber. Bahnsen continued his excellent outing by retiring all three hitters, extending his streak of consecutive outs to 11.

END OF THE SEVENTH INNING
SYRACUSE 4, TORONTO 0

Roggenburk's afternoon ended two hitters into the eighth inning. The Chiefs' leading hitter, Jerry Kenney, stroked his second single of the game to start the inning. Frank Fernandez followed with his third hit of the day, moving Kenney to second. Acting manager Jackie Moore headed to the mound to remove Roggenburk and summon the left-handed Billy Rohr from the bullpen. Unless the Leafs mounted an improbable comeback, Roggenburk would take the loss and finish his season 5-10. Roggenburk's disappointing line read seven innings, 10 hits, four runs (two earned), two strikeouts, one walk, and two runners still on . After handing the ball to Moore, Roggenburk humbly exited to the dugout. His 1967 season was over.

The 21-year-old Billy Rohr was making his second relief appearance of the season. Primarily a starter, Rohr had a won-lost record of 3-5 and an

ERA of 3.44. The first hitter he faced was Ramon Conde, who loaded the bases with a single, his second hit of the game. The Chiefs got their fourth consecutive hit of the inning when Bill Tuttle singled, scoring Kenney and Fernandez. Tuttle's second and third RBIs of the game increased his season total to 55. Likely to honor Tuttle's excellent game and his 17 years in professional baseball, Syracuse manager Gary Blaylock sent Tommie Martz to first base to run for him. With congratulations awaiting him from his teammates, Tuttle strode to the Chiefs dugout for the final time as a professional player. His career had come to an end.

Rohr retired Moschitto but then walked Boyer as Syracuse loaded the bases for the second time in the inning. Bahnsen, a poor-hitting pitcher (.143), hit a sacrifice fly to score Conde and extend the Chiefs' lead to 7-0. Rohr retired Shopay to end the inning, but the damage had been done as the Chiefs had scored three more times.

Bahnsen extended his consecutive outs streak to 14 with his fourth consecutive perfect inning. Right-handed-hitting James Russin batted for Rohr with two outs. Russin made the final out, unable to change Toronto's fortunes against Bahnsen.

END OF EIGHTH INNING
SYRACUSE 7, TORONTO 0

Fred Wenz, Toronto's third pitcher, entered the game in the top of the ninth. This was his 44th appearance of the season, all in relief. With a 4-4 record and an ERA of 3.36, Wenz was the final pitcher in Toronto Maple Leafs baseball history. He retired the Chiefs quickly, allowing one hit in his single inning of work.

Bahnsen's streak of 14 consecutive hitters retired ended in the ninth when leadoff hitter Al Lehrer singled. Three outs remained in the game, and in the season, as second baseman Syd O'Brien stepped into the batter's box. Bahnsen's hope for

a shutout vanished as O'Brien drilled his pitch over the fence for a two-run home run. A glimmer of hope for Leafs fans had flickered. The Leafs were now down 7-2 with none out in the bottom of the ninth inning. Were the Leafs going to make a great comeback in the game? If so, would such a comeback foreshadow the franchise's ability to recover from its tenuous ownership and financial situation?

Sadly for Leafs fans, there was no comeback. Bahnsen settled down and retired the side while allowing one more hit. With the final out of the game, the 1967 season of the Toronto Maple Leafs had concluded in disappointing fashion.

FINAL SCORE
SYRACUSE 7, TORONTO 2

Only 802 fans attended Maple Leaf Stadium that last game of the 1967 season. Those fans shared the anxiety concerning the future of the franchise and professional baseball in Toronto. In an article headlined "Leafs Fate Known Within a Week," the *Toronto Daily Star* reported that the sale of the team was imminent and, more worrisomely, that there was "interest from out of town who might move the International League franchise elsewhere."[5]

There would be no comeback for the Toronto franchise. Six weeks after the final game, a transfer to Louisville was approved by the International League directors. After 71 years, the Toronto Maple Leafs, and professional baseball in Toronto, were no more. The September 4, 1967, game against Syracuse would now be forever labeled as the "Toronto Maple Leafs' Last Game."

But the Toronto baseball story was not over. The faith and hope of fans and advocates of baseball in Canada persevered. And, after an absence of more than nine years, professional baseball returned to Toronto with the inaugural game of the Toronto Blue Jays, an American League expansion team. A renovated Exhibition Stadium

TORONTO MAPLE LEAFS
Official Scorecard

15c

1967   TORONTO MAPLE LEAF BASEBALL CLUB   1967

BACK ROW: Jerry Stephenson, Al Yates, Pete Magrini, Gary Roggenburk, Bruce Pfeifer, Dave Vineyard, Bob Myer, Dave Morehead.

MIDDLE ROW: Bill Smith—Trainer, Bob Montgomery, Jim Russin, Bill Rohr, Jose Calero, Jerry Hudgins, George Smith, Fred Wenz, John Thibdeau, Assistant Trainer—Stan Kucway.

FRONT ROW: Dan Rudanovich, John Ryan, Coach—Jack Moore, Manager—Eddie Kasko, Syd O'Brien, Al Lehrer, Tony Torchia, Stan Johnson.

Bat Boys—Paul Carnegie, Nicky Pyhacz.

Celebrate
Canada's Centennial
with The Leafs

A scorecard from the 1967 season of the Toronto Maple Leafs, the team's last of 72 successive years in the International League and its predecessor. (Canadian Baseball Hall of Fame and Museum)

on the Canadian National Exhibition grounds was the home field for the new franchise.

It has been said that the one constant in life is baseball, and that everything connects to everything else. On Opening Day, April 7, 1977, a snowy afternoon, Toronto welcomed the return of professional baseball as the Blue Jays players and coaches stood along the third-base line waiting to be introduced to the fans in the stands and to Canadian baseball fans watching on television. Interestingly, a connection between the "Toronto Maple Leafs' Last Game" and the first

Blue Jays game was established as Jackie Moore, the acting manager of the Leafs in the 1967 finale, was introduced as a coach of the 1977 Blue Jays.

In retrospect, it is perhaps not accurate to describe Monday, September 4, 1967, as a day of endings. Rather, the truth that "every ending is a beginning – we just don't know it at the time" fully applies to the "Toronto Maple Leafs' Last Game," as the emergence of a Toronto major-league baseball team added new chapters to the narrative of professional baseball in Toronto, and in Canada.

NOTES

1   Neil MacCarl, "Leafs Finish Off With Three Losses for Sixth Place," *Toronto Daily Star*, September 5, 1967: 12.

2   Neil MacCarl, "Chiefs Cop Finale, 7-2," *Syracuse Post-Standard*, September 5, 1967: 17.

3   MacCarl, "Leafs Finish Off."

4   MacCarl, "Chiefs Cop Finale, 7-2." See also Phillip Dechman, "Powerless Leafs Bow 7-2 in Final Game of Season," *Toronto Globe and Mail*, September 5, 1967: 33.

5   Neil MacCarl, "Leafs Fate Known Within a Week," *Toronto Daily Star*, September 5, 1967: 12.

CHARLES BRONFMAN

By Maxwell Kates

For 22 years, the name Charles Bronfman was synonymous with major-league baseball in Montréal. As the son of immigrants who made their fortune in the whiskey trade, Charles made a name for himself in his own right. At the age of 37, he raised the funds required to obtain an expansion baseball franchise in the National League. The Expos under Charles's stewardship put an entertaining product on the field in spite of the external forces of baseball economics and national unity politics. His baseball days behind him, he applied his values as a Canadian and as a Jew to improve the lives of others.

The saga of the Bronfmans originated in the town of Otaci, in the region of Bessarabia, in the Russian Empire. In 1880 Yechiel Bronfman married the former Mindel Elman.[1] The Bronfmans were tobacconists, and although they grew quite wealthy, their affluence was no match for the prevailing anti-Semitism throughout the Russian Empire. A wave of pogroms ensued after the assassination of Czar Alexander II in 1881. The Bronfmans felt no choice but to flee, departing with their four children, servants, and personal rabbi for the New World in 1889.[2] The youngest of the four, an infant named Samuel, grew to become the patriarch of the Bronfmans.

Yechiel settled his family first in Wapella, Saskatchewan, and then in Brandon, Manitoba. Mindel delivered four more children, and by 1903 the family had recovered enough of its wealth to purchase the Anglo-American Hotel.[3] Prescient in his business acumen, young Samuel observed that the profits of the hotel were concentrated in the sale of alcoholic beverages. 'Mr. Sam,' as he would become known, soon entered the liquor trade. Meanwhile, in the United States, Congress on October 28, 1919, passed the Volstead Act, which prohibited the sale of alcoholic beverages. Mr. Sam saw an opportunity. He would sell whiskey to American entrepreneurs, but his doing so in Canada made his business perfectly legal. Mr. Sam founded the Distillers Corporation in Montréal in 1924.[4] By 1928, he had accumulated enough capital to purchase Joseph Seagram & Sons.[5] Mr. Sam had married the former Saidye Rosner in 1922; they had four children: Minda, Phyllis, Edgar, and the youngest, Charles Rosner Bronfman, on June 27, 1931.

The Bronfman family lived at 15 Belvedere Road in the Montréal suburb of Westmount.[6] For his education, Charles attended Selwyn House in Montréal and Trinity College School in Port Hope, Ontario. Meanwhile, Mr. Sam's empire continued to expand. According to Charles's memoirs, by 1933, "the Company had 40 percent of the Canadian whisky market."[7] Mr. Sam was the president of the Canadian Jewish Congress from 1939 to 1962, and became an important benefactor to both McGill University and the Israel Museum. These lessons of philanthropy and community activism were not lost on young Charles and his siblings.

After attending McGill University, Charles went to work for Mr. Sam on March 12, 1951.[8] He was appointed to run the Adams whisky label in 1954, and in 1958, "at the grand old age of 27," he was made president of the House of Seagram.[9] In 1961 he married the former Barbara Baerwald; they had two children, Stephen and Ellen.

During the 1950s and '60s, the Seagram's empire expanded its horizons beyond whiskey, entering both the real estate and oil markets. Meanwhile, Mayor Jean Drapeau was concocting his latest *grand projet* for the city of Montréal. During his 30-year tenure as mayor, Drapeau put Montréal on the world stage with Expo 67, Place des Arts, the Metro system, and the 1976 Summer Olympics. Now he was trying to convince Major League Baseball that Canada's largest city should be awarded an expansion team.

Montréal had a storied baseball history as the top farm club for the Brooklyn Dodgers. Charles Bronfman was 15 years old when Jackie Robinson led the Montréal Royals to the Little World Series in 1946. As he told biographer Howard Green, "my mother [maintained] I was crazy about baseball as a kid. ... [I]f she was implying that I played it, that's not the case. I just followed it."[10] The expansion fee for a National League team was $10 million, and Charles offered to put up 10 percent with his own money. His wife, Barbara, questioned his decision to invest: "A million dollars and you just say yes?" "Well," he replied, "it's never going to happen anyway."[11]

"But happen, it did," in the words of Donald Sutherland.[12] Montréal, along with San Diego, was awarded a National League expansion franchise on May 27, 1968. Much like Pierre Trudeau, a fellow Montréaler who was elected Prime Minister in 1968, Charles cited "reason over passion" for his investment in the baseball team. At a time of a burgeoning sovereigntist movement in Quebec in the wake of the Quiet Revolution,[13] Charles envisioned a baseball team as a unifying force, not only in Quebec, but throughout Canada.

The other major investor, Jean-Louis Lévesque, did not share Charles's enthusiasm, and withdrew from the project. Finding a place to play was another ordeal, as the Autostade, home of the football Alouettes, was rejected for baseball. Would the franchise be snapped up by a city like Milwaukee, Buffalo, or Dallas before even taking the field?

"I'd go to see Drapeau, and he would tell me everything was wonderful. And by the way, when I went to see Drapeau, I used to do this. I used to pinch myself and say 'He's a salesman, he's a salesman, he's a salesman. Don't believe him; he's a salesman.' Then I used to see [Lucien] Saulnier, Drapeau's assistant. And Saulnier had two words that were fabulous. They were 'Definitely not.'"[14]

Montréal journalists Russ Taylor and Marcel Desjardins had shown National League President Warren Giles the layout of Jarry Park, a 3,000-seat facility in the north end of the city where home plate faced west, rather than east. Giles was confident that the stadium could be upgraded to meet National League standards by April 14, 1969. Charles eventually put together a consortium supported by Lorne Webster and Hugh Hallward to finance the requisite $10 million investment.[15] Montréal was getting a team, named the Expos after the World's Fair of 1967.

Appointed to oversee the operation were President John McHale, general manager Jim Fanning, and manager Gene Mauch. Fanning remembered the strategy the Expos undertook to build the inaugural roster: "We went for the players who had a name, who could still play, and

Montréal Expos' owner Charles R. Bronfman, wearing his familiar uniform number 83 at spring training, West Palm Beach, Florida, March 1969. (McCord Museum, Montréal)

who had trading value, or they had value, period."[16] The Houston Astros saw sufficient value in the Expos' expansion draft to offer Rusty Staub in a trade for Donn Clendenon and Jesus Alou. Controversy ensued when Clendenon refused to report to manager Harry Walker in Houston. On the eve of the regular season, Commissioner Bowie Kuhn ruled that the trade stood, with the Expos offering Houston Jack Billingham and Skip Guinn as alternate compensation.

Charles remembered the afternoon of April 8, 1969, as Maureen Forrester sang 'O Canada' before the Expos' first game versus the Mets at Shea Stadium: "I remember standing there with tears rolling down my cheeks as 40,000 Americans were standing at attention for our National Anthem. In hockey, yes, Canada was well known but in baseball[?] … suddenly, we were in the big leagues. Canada was in the big leagues, and I had helped make it happen."[17]

The Expos defeated the Mets 11-10 on a trio of home runs, including one by Rusty Staub. 'Le Grand Orange,' as Staub was known, became as legendary in baseball during his three years with the Expos as Jean Béliveau was in hockey. Montréal also won the home opener, an 8-7 victory over the St. Louis Cardinals, with Mack Jones hitting the first major-league home run on Canadian soil.

"The best part of that game," remembered Charles, "was having my mother and father with me. My dad had given me quite a 'what-for' about this whole procedure and then, when he knew that I had put up the money myself, became the biggest and best Expos' fan in Canada," adding that "he couldn't understand why I wasn't up until 2 in the morning listening to baseball games the way he was."[18] Two years after the opener at Jarry Park, in 1971, Mr. Sam died at the age of 82.

The 1969 Montréal Expos finished in last place, as expected, with a record of 52-110. However, they set an expansion record by attracting over 1.2 million fans to Jarry Park. According to Peter C. Newman, the Expos drew red ink in 1969 before turning a profit annually from 1970 through 1975.[19] However, on the field, not once did they breach 79 wins or finish in the first division. It was a frustrating time for Charles as owner of the Expos.

To compound matters, Canada became embroiled in a global energy crisis; in Quebec, the impact was felt even more keenly, as the movement for national sovereignty was gaining momentum. In baseball, it was only a matter of time before the reserve clause would give way to unrestricted free agency for the players. It was amid this economic climate that on December 4, 1974, the Expos felt compelled to trade two of their star players, Ken Singleton and Mike Torrez, to the Baltimore Orioles: "Every club makes lots of little mistakes, but that was a biggie. In the development stage of this club, that set us back two or three years. The fact that in effect, we got nothing for those two fine players. We got Rich Coggins, who was sick, and Dave McNally, who quit. I think we sold Coggins' contract to the Yankees for $100,000, so that's what we got out of Singleton and Torrez."[20]

As the last-place Expos prepared to move from ramshackle Jarry Park to futuristic Olympic Stadium in 1976, baseball finally ushered in a new system of free agency. Charles and the Expos courted Baltimore outfielder Reggie Jackson to play for his former manager Dick Williams in Montréal. George Steinbrenner, meanwhile, could offer Reggie the city of New York and a contending team. In 1977 Jackson was wearing pinstripes and playing in the World Series. He would not be the last blue-chip free agent to spurn an offer to play for the Expos. They also lost Don Sutton to the Houston Astros in 1980.[21]

The Expos knew they had to draw attendance of 1.7 million at the 59,500-seat Olympic Stadium simply to break even, or more than that in order to turn a profit.[22] After failing to reach that figure in both 1977 and 1978, and with the franchise having yet to post a winning season, Charles seriously considered divesting himself of the Expos.[23] Fellow board member Lorne Webster persuaded him to stay. It was a decision Charles would not regret, as la belle époque of the franchise was about to begin.

In the words of Canadian Broadcasting Corporation anchor Knowlton Nash, "after a decade of trying" the 1979 Expos were "considered to be one of the strongest clubs in the game."[24] Led by a collection of young homegrown players, including Gary Carter, Larry Parrish, Steve Rogers, Ellis Valentine, Warren Cromartie, and Andre Dawson, the Expos were complemented by veterans from other organizations like Tony Perez, Bill Lee, and Woodie Fryman. Carter, Parrish, and Rogers represented the Expos at the All-Star Game in Seattle on July 17. At the midway point of the season, the Expos stood 2½ games ahead of the Chicago Cubs with a record of 50-35, the best in the entire National League. "You know,

when you're winning, all of a sudden the world is I think a lot better place to be," said Charles in a 1979 interview. "Last year, we had a disappointing result [of 76-86] with a pretty good team. You try to have a winning team for the good of the city that has other added benefits."[25]

When the 1979 season concluded, the Expos posted a superlative record of 95-65, drawing over 2.1 million fans to Olympic Stadium. Although the team lost the divisional title to the Pittsburgh Pirates, the Expos had cemented themselves for one brief shining moment as Canada's team. As was reported late in the season in one telegram from Ottawa, "no matter what happens, you've given baseball fans across the country a thrilling summer. Bravo."[26] The telegram was signed by Pierre Elliott Trudeau, whose late father Charles-Emile once owned the Montréal Royals.

The Expos and their first pennant race occurred at a time when national unity was at the forefront of the Canadian consciousness. On November 15, 1976, René Lévesque of the Parti Québécois won a majority government on a platform that included a referendum on sovereignty-association. Prior to the election, Charles was quoted in the Montréal Star as vowing "to get out if the PQ wins."[27] Three years later, he was asked to offer his remarks on any link between the success of the Expos and national unity: "This year, there is just a tremendous outflow of goodwill, and everybody is very happy. How that might translate itself politically, I wouldn't have the vaguest idea. I would hope that it would translate itself obviously in a positive way but that's not why we're trying to have a winning team."

Quebec held its referendum in 1980, with 59 percent of the province voting on May 20 to remain in Canada. Meanwhile, with Ron LeFlore added to the lineup, the Expos raced to another stellar season. Despite 81 days in first place, they lost the pennant once again during the final weekend, this time to the Philadelphia Phillies. The disappointment did not stop the Expos from being awarded a lucrative television broadcast deal. Starting in 1981, O'Keefe Ale agreed to sponsor Expos telecasts covering Canada from coast to coast for $35 million over five years.[28]

The broadcast deal proved to be a Pyrrhic victory for the Expos. After a grievance was filed by the Toronto Blue Jays, the Commissioner's Office ruled that the television contract infringed upon the Blue Jays' territorial rights. Expos telecasts would be blacked out in southern Ontario.[29] John McHale mused that "when Montréal became a Quebec-only team, and no longer had the right to compete in Canada, that was a very telling blow to our financial picture."[30] This was the very antithesis to the philosophy behind Charles's involvement with the Expos in the first place.

Notwithstanding the television contract, expectations for the 1981 Expos as baseball's 'Team of the '80s' were high. The team welcomed young players Tim Raines, Tim Wallach, and Jeff Reardon in the early months of the season. However, only two weeks after acquiring Reardon from the Mets, the Expos – and all 25 other teams – were shut down by a players strike on June 12. While the economic losses were significant, $500,000 in the first weekend alone, the positioning of the work stoppage actually helped the Expos in the standings.[31] "We were third in our division when the strike happened," Charles told biographer Howard Green. "Then on August 6, after a settlement was reached, the owners agreed to split the season. Playoff berths were guaranteed for the four teams who were leading their divisions …whichever teams had the best record in the second 'half'… also got playoff berths."[32]

As the team leading the division when the strike began, the Phillies had already clinched a playoff spot. The Expos were leading the Cardinals by 1½ games on the morning of October 3. With the magic number reduced to one, the Expos trailed the Mets 3-2 as rookie Wallace Johnson rapped a triple to drive home two runs. That proved to be the margin of victory as the Expos clinched the division. "In our bar mitzvah year," Charles exclaimed, "the Expos finally came of age.[33]

After defeating the Phillies in a five-game Division Series, Montréal went on to face the Dodgers in the League Championship Series. The series was tied, two wins apiece, on October 19, when Ray Burris faced Fernando Valenzuela at Olympic Stadium. Through eight innings, both teams were limited to one run. Jim Fanning, now the Expos' manager, summoned Steve Rogers to pitch the ninth inning. With two away, Rogers threw a ball to Rick Monday that landed in the center-field bleachers. Charles remembered his reaction. "I wasn't upset. John McHale looked like he was going to croak. I said, 'John, why are you so upset?' He said, 'Charles, this doesn't happen very often. And when it does happen and you don't take advantage, it won't happen again for a while."[34] History would support McHale's clairvoyance, as the franchise did not return to the postseason for as long as it remained in Montréal.

More trouble was on the horizon for the Expos in 1982. Gary Carter, the reigning All-Star Game MVP and face of the franchise, who batted .438 in the NLCS against the Dodgers, was one year away from free agency. Rather than risk losing Carter at the end of the season, the Expos signed him to a contract extension prior to spring training. According to the Washington Post, the contract paid Carter $15 million over eight years.[35] It was a deal Charles regretted from the moment he signed it: "We never won with Gary Carter, and when he was asking for two million dollars a season … [John] McHale and I were furious. Still, we held our noses and did the deal because we felt we had no choice."[36] While the Expos continued to set franchise attendance records in 1982 and 1983, outdrawing the Yankees both years, the large crowds were less than enthused by the third-place performances on the field. A fifth-place finish followed in 1984. Not reaping the desired return on investment on the Carter contract, the

Expos traded him to the Mets on December 10, 1984. "When a team comes that close and doesn't do it," Charles reasoned, "eventually you have to break up the team."[37]

The 'Team of the '80s' was consistent if unspectacular for the latter half of the decade. In 1986, as Gary Carter won his World Series ring with the Mets and *les Canadiens* won yet another Stanley Cup, the Expos drew barely one million fans. Olympic Stadium, its roof finally installed in 1987, had not aged well. While the facility was originally estimated to have cost $124 million, the Canada Broadcasting Corporation reported that the actual cost was $1.5 billion.[38] At a time when revenues were generated in increasingly weak Canadian dollars, escalating salaries were paid in US dollars.

The breaking point took place in 1989. In a stunning role reversal, the Expos traded three pitching prospects, Brian Holman, Gene Harris, and 6-foot-10 Randy Johnson, to the Seattle Mariners for Mark Langston. Initially, the deal was a success, as the left-hander helped to propel the Expos to the top of their division. In the final eight weeks of the season, Langston's impending free-agent status became a distraction as the Expos plummeted from first place to fourth. Finally, in late September, Charles suggested to club investor Hugh Hallward that they meet for dinner at an Italian restaurant instead of going to the game. When they sat down, Charles turned to Hugh and asked, "You know what this means, don't you?"[39] The Expos were for sale.

"I was very bitter," Charles told Danny Gallagher. "I had a Plan A, a Plan B, and a Plan C. Plan A was to sell the team to someone who would [stay] in Montréal; Plan B was to sell to someone who would … keep the team in Montréal for five years; Plan C was to sell to the highest bidder anywhere."[40] On June 14, 1991, the National League announced that the Expos had been sold to a consortium led by former Seagram's executive Claude Brochu for a reported $100 million.[41]

Charles Bronfman was now 60. Now married to his second wife, Andrea, he had reached an age when most people look toward retirement. Charles's mind, however, was headed in a different direction: philanthropy. In 1991 his CRB Foundation pioneered the 'Heritage Minutes,' a series of 60-second films that illustrated pivotal moments in Canadian history. In 1994 Charles and Michael Steinhardt founded Birthright Israel, an educational organization that sponsored free trips to Israel for young Jewish adults. By the time Seagram's had been sold to Vivendi in 2000, Charles and Andrea had relocated to New York. Since 2004, Charles has awarded an annual Charles Bronfman Prize to young humanitarians whose work, grounded in Jewish values, is of universal benefit. Tragedy struck the Bronfman family on January 23, 2006, when Andrea was fatally struck by a passing vehicle in New York.

Charles married Rita Mayo in 2012, and in subsequent years they divided their time among New York, Montréal, and Florida. He is the proud grandfather of six.[42] On June 27, 2021, Charles celebrated his 90th birthday by watching a virtual performance of the 'Concert in Denim.' It was performed by Israel Philharmonic at the Charles Bronfman Auditorium in Tel Aviv. A member of the Order of Canada, he was inducted into the Canadian Baseball Hall of Fame in 1984. In 1992 Charles was honored by the Blue Jays, who invited him to throw out the first pitch before Game Three of the World Series in Toronto. The Expos' Opening Day hero, Mack Jones, was once described as "one man who has not forgotten his roots."[43] That same honor may also be bestowed upon the man who brought the Mayor of Jonesville to Montréal, Charles Rosner Bronfman.

NOTES

1   Peter C. Newman, *Bronfman Dynasty: The Rothschilds of the New World* (Toronto: McLelland and Stewart Limited, 1978), 12.

2   Michael R. Marrus, *Mr. Sam: The Life and Times of Samuel Bronfman* (Toronto: Penguin Books Canada Limited, 1991), 24.

3   Newman, 70.

4   Marrus, 113.

5   Marrus, 130.

6   Charles Bronfman and Howard Green, *Distilled: A Memoir of Family, Seagram, Baseball, and Philanthropy*, (Toronto: Harper Collins Publishers Ltd., 2016), 4.

7   Bronfman, 4.

8   Bronfman, 52.

9   Bronfman, 59.

10 Bronfman, 19.

11 Bronfman, 76.

12 Brian Schecter, ed., *Les Expos, Nos Amours*, English edition (Montréal: TV Labatt, 1989).

13 Rene Durocher, "The Quiet Revolution (Révolution tranquille) was a time of rapid change experienced in Québec during the 1960s." Canadian Encyclopedia article published online July 30, 2013.

14 *Les Expos, Nos Amours.*

15 Danny Gallagher and Bill Young, *Remembering the Montréal Expos* (Toronto: Scoop Press, 2005), 26.

16 *Les Expos, Nos Amours.*

17 *Les Expos, Nos Amours.*

18 *Les Expos, Nos Amours.*

19 Newman, 267.

20 *Les Expos, Nos Amours.*

21 Alain Usereau, *The Expos in Their Prime* (Jefferson, North Carolina: McFarland & Company, 2013), 104.

22 Newman, 268.

23 Gallagher, 27.

24 Mark Phillips, "Win Some, Lose Some," on *News Magazine* (Toronto: The Canadian Broadcasting Corporation, June 1979).

25 "Win Some, Lose Some."

26 Norm King, *1979: The Expos First Great Season* (Toronto: Scoop Press, 2021), 189.

27 Jacques Doucet and Marc Robitaille, *Il était une fois les Expos: Tome 1, les années 1969-1984* (Montréal: Editions Hurtubise Inc., 2009), 282.

28 Usereau, 109.

29 Brodie Snyder, *The Year the Expos Finally Won Something* (Toronto: Check Mark Books, 1981), 163.

30 Usereau, 109-110.

31 Snyder, 160.

32 Bronfman, 95.

33 Jeff Katz, *Split Season: Fernandomania, the Bronx Zoo, and the Strike That Saved Baseball* (New York: Thomas Dunne Books, 2015), 245.

34 *Les Expos, Nos Amours.*

35 Usereau, 153.

36 Bronfman, 97.

37 *Les Expos, Nos Amours.*

38 Bronfman, 92.

39 Bronfman, 101.

40 Gallagher, 28.

41 Jacques Doucet and Marc Robitaille, *Il était une fois les Expos: Tome 2, les années 1985-2004*, (Montréal: Editions Hurtubise Inc., 2011), 206.

42 Correspondence with Charles Bronfman, December 8, 2021.

43 *Les Expos, Nos Amours.*

FROM A (CANADIAN) BASEBALL RESEARCHER'S NOTEBOOK

By David Matchett

Al Kermisch, who joined SABR in 1971, was a baseball researcher for over 60 years. His paper, "Walter Johnson: King of the 1-0 Hurlers," appeared in the first SABR *Baseball Research Journal* in 1972, and in 1975 he debuted "From a Researcher's Notebook": seven small stories covering 4½ pages. This became a regular feature and, starting in 1990, many SABR members read the *Journal* back-to-front as it became the customary last article in the annual publication. The following is a tribute to Mr. Kermisch and his contributions to baseball research, with a Canadian twist.

KING GEORGE V AND THE OTHER ROYALS

From *Sporting Life*, September 14, 1901:

"Base ball is to be among the amusements furnished the Duke of Cornwall and York during his stay in Montréal. The Torontos and Montréalers, the two Canadian Eastern League clubs, will furnish the base ball."[1]

The Duke, son of King Edward VII, ascended to the throne as George V after his father's death in 1910. The Duke and Duchess of Cornwall and York spent much of 1901 touring the British Empire; when asked what he would like to do in Canada, the Duke said, "I want a day's duck shooting, and I want to watch a lacrosse match."[2] Added to the itinerary was the Eastern League baseball game of September 20, when the Toronto Royals played the Montréal Royals.[3]

The visiting Toronto squad, managed by Ed Barrow,[4] scored a run in the top of the first when Jimmy Bannon hit a home run over the left-field fence off Montréal ace Harry Felix. The home team tied it up in the bottom of the fourth off future major-league starter Pop Williams, but Toronto regained the lead in the fifth frame and added insurance runs in the eighth and ninth innings for a 4-1 victory.[5] Thirteen of the 18 players were former or future major leaguers;[6] the game was played in a brisk 1 hour and 20 minutes before 500 fans on a cool, cloudy afternoon.

What were the future King's impressions of the contest? He had none because he wasn't there. The tour's organizing committee was overly enthusiastic in filling the Duke's schedule, and the game was dropped from the program. The governor-general, Lord Minto, justified this by stating, "… baseball is looked upon as an American game and is not at all popular in Canada – moreover it had fallen entirely out of the hands of amateurs and has been taken over by the very low American professional element."[7] The English-born Minto donated a cup that is still being awarded to Canadian lacrosse champions, but he was clearly not a baseball fan.

The Duke got to see a lacrosse match in Ottawa and go duck hunting in Manitoba. He did eventually attend a baseball game in London, England, on July 4, 1918, between teams representing the US Army and Navy,[8] but he missed a good contest at Atwater Park in Montréal in 1901.[9]

THE MONTRÉAL EXPOS' 21-GAME LOSING STREAK

In 1969, their first year, the Montréal Expos were one of the worst teams in major-league history; their 110 losses have been exceeded by only 19 teams, and included in their season was a 20-game losing streak between May 13 and June 7, tied for the third worst stretch in the modern era.[10] But they actually lost 21 in a row if an exhibition game is included.

The Expos ended a homestand on Wednesday, June 4, with their 18th straight loss. They flew to the West Coast the next morning to start a road trip in Los Angeles, but it wasn't a direct flight: They stopped en route in Vancouver for an exhibition game against their Triple-A affiliate.[11]

Coach Bob Oldis quipped, "Go get 'em boys… [t]his is a sudden death game, the winner advancing to complete the remainder of the National League schedule."[12] Pitcher John Glass was called up from West Palm Beach of the Class-A Florida State League to start for the Expos,[13] and he surrendered five runs on eight hits before being lifted in the fourth inning. Three major-league pitchers shut down the Mounties for the rest of the game, and Mack Jones launched what was regarded as

the longest home run ever hit at Capilano Stadium,[14] but it was too little, too late as Vancouver won 5-3 despite Montréal playing most of its regulars.[15]

Disregarding Oldis's edict, the defeated Expos, and not the victorious Mounties, dashed to the airport after the game and arrived in Los Angeles at 3:00 A.M., 23 hours after their first flight left Montréal.[16] Unsurprisingly, they lost their next two games, but on June 8, they held off a late Dodger rally to finally break their 20-game (or really 21-game) losing streak.[17]

WHY DID ERIC MACKENZIE PLAY FOR KANSAS CITY IN 1955?

Eric Hugh MacKenzie, from Glendon, Alberta, had one big-league plate appearance, playing one inning in the field with the Kansas City Athletics in 1955. Other than that day of glory, he never played a game above Single A. What series of events caused this cup of coffee to happen?

After the 1954 season the Athletics franchise shifted from Philadelphia to Kansas City, and this included a managerial change from Eddie Joost to Lou Boudreau. Boudreau went into spring training not knowing any of his players and, as noted in *The Sporting News*, because he had "… a fetish for competition, he has included 12 of his young hopefuls in the squad here."[18] One of the young hopefuls invited to training camp was Eric MacKenzie. MacKenzie had been signed by the Athletics when he was 18, and had started his career in the low minors in 1951. He spent 1954 in Class C with the Drummondville, Québec, team of the Provincial League and, despite a .265 batting average and a slugging percentage below .340, he was given an opportunity to audition for the big team.

In 1954 the Philadelphia Athletics had three players split the catching duties: Joe Astroth (64 starts), Billy Shantz (49), and Jim Robertson (43).

They all returned for 1955, but Boudreau had MacKenzie catch nine spring-training games before he was farmed out at the end of March.[19] When the regular season began, the Athletics' catching duties were split as they had been the year before, but Shantz was injured on April 22, and Robertson was out of town as the defendant in a lawsuit, so, with Astroth as the only remaining catching option, MacKenzie was recalled to be a backup.[20]

One might ask why MacKenzie was promoted from Single A ahead of a catcher from Kansas City's top farm club in Triple-A Columbus. Al Lakeman was that team's regular backstop but, at age 36, he was hardly a prospect. He was in Detroit's organization in 1954, and he didn't appear in any games in the Athletics' 1955 training camp, so he wasn't known to Boudreau. Twenty-four-year-old Mike Roarke was his backup, but his contract was the property of Milwaukee's Triple-A team in Toledo, and he was only playing for Columbus on option. Paul Burris and Canadian Stubby Erautt also caught for Columbus that year, but not until later in the season. With the only Triple-A options being a 36-year-old who was new to the organization and someone who was on loan from another team, it made sense that the Athletics would go to their next highest minor-league affiliate for MacKenzie, especially since he had seen significant action in training camp just a month earlier, and Boudreau was already familiar with him.

MacKenzie arrived in Kansas City on April 23 in time to see one of the biggest offensive outbursts in major-league history as the Chicago White Sox rolled to a 29-6 victory. Boudreau gave Astroth a break late in that game and had MacKenzie pinch-hit in the eighth inning. He grounded out to second base for the last out, then took the field as the Athletics' catcher in the top of the ninth. Fellow Canadian Ozzie Van Brabant was on the mound, and MacKenzie's debut resulted in an all-Canadian battery for three batters as the White Sox went down in order for the only time in the game.

MacKenzie didn't get into another game, and he was returned to Savannah a few days later when Shantz was ready to play. Although he was only 22, he never made it back to the big leagues; in fact, he never even made it to Double A. He played three more seasons in the low minors before retiring as a player, but that was not the end of his baseball career. He moved back to Canada and became heavily involved in amateur baseball, including managing the Canadian National team at the 1984 Summer Olympics in Los Angeles.[21]

It took a long series of unrelated events for Eric MacKenzie to appear in his lone major-league game. One can imagine that had any one of these events not occurred, MacKenzie would never have played in the major leagues.

THE FIRST RED SOX PITCHER

The National League was the lone major league from 1892 through 1900, at which point the big leagues doubled in size with the creation of the American League in 1901.[22] A Canadian who took advantage of this expansion to make his debut with the newly-formed Boston Americans (in 1908 renamed the Red Sox) was pitcher Winford Ansley "Win" Kellum from Waterford, Ontario.

Cy Young was Boston's ace pitcher, but a bout of tonsillitis sidelined him in April, so the honor of starting the team's opener went to Kellum in his major-league debut. Baltimore jumped on him for three runs in the first inning and tacked on seven more for a 10-6 win. All of the runs were earned on 11 hits, including five doubles and three triples, plus four walks. Kellum was removed in the top of the ninth inning for pinch-hitter and fellow Canadian Larry McLean, also making his debut. Kellum's next game was one of the worst pitching performances in team history; He surrendered 14 runs, 11 earned, on 20 hits in a 14-1 loss to Philadelphia on May 1.

Kellum started a total of six games for Boston in 1901, the last of which was on June 14. He was released a few days later with a 2-3 record and a 6.38 ERA, and finished the season with New Orleans of the Southern Association. He won 15 games with Cincinnati in 1904, and pitched for St. Louis the next year to end his big-league career, but he played in the minors until 1909.

Since the team was founded in 1901, 905 players have toed the rubber for the Boston Red Sox, including 14 Hall of Fame pitchers,[23] and the first of them all was Canadian Win Kellum.

TUG THOMPSON IN PHILADELPHIA

From 1877 through 1882 the National League was not represented in the two largest cities of the United States – New York and Philadelphia. The unveiling of the American Association forced the hands of the league's executives, and plans were made to groom teams from New York and Philadelphia to join in 1883. Sporting-goods entrepreneur Al Reach, a former player himself, ran the Philadelphia team in 1882 and they played over 140 games, almost half of them exhibition games against National League teams.

Twenty men appeared for the Philadelphias and most of them played in the major leagues at some point.[24] Finding an adequate catcher, however, was an ongoing issue:

"The position that proved most vexing for Reach to fill was catcher. The club experimented with nine different players at the position during the season, all of whom displayed various shortcomings."[25]

One of these catchers was London, Ontario's John Parkinson "Tug" Thompson. His first appearance for Philadelphia was in a game played on August 9 at home versus a team from Atlantic City. Thompson caught and contributed a single and a run scored to Philadelphia's victory.[26] The local newspapers noted that this game was his debut: "Thompson made his first appearance with the Philadelphias. ..." and "Thompson, the new catcher, made his first appearance. ..."[27]

He played again the next day and appeared in six games in total for Philadelphia. Consistent with the team's season-long revolving door for backstops, on August 29 – two days after his last game and a mere two weeks after his debut with the team, "Thompson was released by the Philadelphia club on Wednesday."[28] He failed to impress either at or behind the bat, as his final statistics included five hits in 23 at-bats (.217 average), 45 putouts, three assists, nine errors (.842 fielding average), and eight passed balls.

Evidence about Thompson's origins appeared in the *New York Clipper* when he joined the Philadelphias: "Thompson, late of the Canadian Tecumsehs, made his first appearance with the Philadelphias. ..."[29] The Tecumseh team was based in London, Ontario, and a review of the local press found a fond adieu being bade to their local hero as he headed south of the border:

"Mr. J. Thompson, who has distinguished himself behind the bat for the Tecumsehs of this city, left to-day to accept a similar position for the remainder of the season with the Philadelphia Base Ball Club."[30]

Thompson started the 1882 baseball season with this amateur team that played at least 16 games. Box scores for nine of them have been found, and those summaries show Thompson appearing primarily as the catcher, with a few games at third base. He also appeared in a game for a team from nearby Petrolia, Ontario, on July 4 at Port Huron, Michigan, and caught for a picked nine who played against London on July 14. He even pulled off the neat trick of catching for both teams in a match between the 7th Band and the Philharmonic Society played in London on July 17.[31] The Tecumseh team doesn't appear to have played any competitive games after July 27, and the team disbanded after a friendly game with a picked nine on August 3.

After Thompson's departure from Philadelphia, the *London Advertiser* welcomed him back home and revealed his next assignment:

"John Thompson, London's famous catcher, just returned from a short engagement with the Philadelphias, has accepted an excellent offer to play with the Cincinnati team for the remainder of the season. He left yesterday."[32]

And the Fourth Estate in Cincinnati introduced him to the local cranks:

"Thompson, the catcher of the Tecumsehs, of London, will join the Cincinnatis at Louisville to catch, provided Snyder should get hurt, or Powers is not able to throw yet."[33]

Thompson debuted with the American Association's Cincinnati team on August 31, playing center field. He caught exhibition games on September 1 and 3, then sat on the bench until his release later in the month:

"Thompson, who was brought to this city from London, Ont., to take Powers' place while the latter was laid up, will return home on Monday next."[34]

Thompson played in the Northwestern League in 1883, and then joined Indianapolis of the American Association for 1884. During that season the press of the cities for whose teams he had played in 1882 acknowledged his return, first Cincinnati in May:

"'Tug' Thompson, who was under engagement to the Cincinnati Club in 1882 for several months, and played "one consecutive" afternoon, is now with the Indianapolis Club."[35]

And then Philadelphia in June:

"'Tug' Thompson, who caught a few games for the Phillies in 1882, is catching now for the Indianapolis Club."[36]

Thompson played his last game with Indianapolis on July 4, 1884, but that didn't end his playing career. He spent a few seasons with teams in London and Hamilton in the Canadian and International Leagues, and finished up with a few games with Rochester of the International Association in 1888.

THE MOST CANADIAN HOME RUN

Over 250 Canadian-born players have appeared in the major leagues, and 89 of them have combined to hit over 3,000 home runs.[37] Which of these is the "most Canadian" home run? This is, of course, a subjective matter, but the following criteria are offered to help answer the question:

1. The player who hit the home run was born in Canada.

2. The game was played in Canada.

3. The home run was hit on Canada Day (July 1).

4. The batter's team was based in Canada.

5. The pitcher's team was based in Canada.

6. The opposing pitcher was born in Canada.

For this to be considered a Canadian home run, the first two criteria must be met. Allowing for that, we can eliminate the third condition because a Canadian-born player has never hit a home run on Canada Day in a major-league game played in Canada. The closest were Larry Walker's June 30, 1990, and June 30, 1993, home runs for the Expos in Montréal, Brett Lawrie's June 30, 2012, home run, and Russell Martin's on July 2, 2015, for the Blue Jays in Toronto.

Through 2021 there have been 207 home runs hit by Canadian-born players in regular-season and playoff games played in Canada. This has been accomplished by 17 batters, led by Larry Walker (58), Russell Martin (36), and Brett Lawrie (23), with Montréal-born Vladimir Guerrero Jr. quickly moving up the leaderboard with 15 and counting. None of these 207 home runs meet each of the last three criteria, but some meet two of the three:

+ The batter's team was based in Canada: This, of course, means that the batter played for either the Montréal Expos (1969 to 2004) or the Toronto Blue Jays (1977 to the present). Of the home runs in question, 110 were hit by Blue Jays and 48 were hit by Expos before that franchise shifted to Washington, DC.

+ The pitcher's team was based in Canada: Toronto Blue Jays pitchers have surrendered 36 home runs to Canadian-born batters in games played in Canada, while Expos pitchers allowed 14 through 2004.

+ Both teams were based in Canada: For this to have happened, the game must have been played between the Expos and the Blue Jays. Interleague play started in 1997, and before the Expos left Montréal, the two teams met 43 times. Three of the Expos' home games were played in San Juan, Puerto Rico, in 2004, so there were only 40 games played in

Canada between the two Canadian teams: 23 in Toronto and 17 in Montréal. Only one Canadian-born player hit a home run in the series: Toronto native Rob Ducey of the Expos hit one off Toronto's Chris Carpenter on June 15, 2001, in Montréal.

+ The opposing pitcher was Canadian: Three of the 207 home runs were surrendered by a Canadian pitcher: Matt Stairs of Oakland hit a grand slam off Toronto's Paul Spoljaric on August 13, 1999; Blue Jay Brett Lawrie took Boston's Ryan Dempster deep on May 2, 2013; and Michael Saunders of Toronto cleared the fences against Seattle's James Paxton on July 22, 2016. All three of these home runs were hit in Toronto.

So which is the most Canadian home run? We have three that were hit by a Canadian-born batter off a Canadian-born pitcher in a game played in Canada, and another one hit by a Canadian-born batter in a game played in Canada between two Canadian-based teams. Any one of these four could take the title.

THE MAJOR LEAGUES COME TO MONTRÉAL – IN 1918?

The following note was found in the *Boston Globe* from Wednesday, July 24, 1918:

"Montréal, July 23 – The Chicago National League team will play the Boston Braves ... a regular scheduled game in Montréal, Sunday. This is the game scheduled to be played in Boston Monday, but the schedule has been advanced and permission granted to play in Montréal Sunday. The net proceeds will be devoted to patriotic purposes and if the attendance warrants it, practically every team in the National and American Leagues, it is expected, will play in Montréal on Sundays."[38]

Major-league baseball arrived in Montréal with the birth of the Expos and the first big-league game played outside of the United States took place on April 14, 1969. Or did it? Is it possible that a regular-season game was played in the city five decades earlier?

Blue laws prevented Sunday baseball in Boston until 1929.[39] The Lord's Day was always an open date on the Braves homestands in that era, and Chicago's July 1918 visit was no different, with games scheduled for Saturday, July 27, plus the following Monday through Wednesday. Raising money for "patriotic purposes" during a war is a reasonable motive for moving a game, and this scheduling change raises the possibility that many of the firsts accomplished by the Expos and their opponents in 1969 were not actually so. Alas, it was not to be. The *Boston Globe* noted a day later:

> "A dispatch from Montréal, saying that the game to be played there Sunday between the Braves and the Cubs was a championship game, being the one scheduled for Boston on Monday, was in error. The game in Montréal will be an exhibition game, although both clubs will use their regular players. ..."[40]

The Cubs beat the Braves in Boston on Saturday and the two teams traveled to Montréal for a 3:00 P.M. game on Sunday. It was played at Delorimier Park, a horserace track about a mile (1.6 kilometers) from the future site of Delorimier Stadium, made famous in 1946 as the home of the Jackie Robinson-led Montréal Royals.[41] Only four starters per team got into the game, despite the promise that the regular players would be used. Most of the other participants were backups, and Chicago even had coach Otto Knabe play second base. Boston's starting pitcher was an enigmatic player known only as Jackson who had previously been pitching for Richmond of the Virginia League. This was actually George

Winn, who wouldn't make his regular-season debut until the following April.[42] The field wasn't in the best condition but the players put on a good show for the packed house. It was a close game, with Chicago taking a 2-1 lead into the bottom of the ninth inning before two bases-loaded walks gave Boston the win.[43]

The Braves returned the following weekend for a Sunday match against the Cincinnati Reds. That game was referred to as "Burlesque Baseball," as the teams disappointed the 2,500 in attendance with a sloppy 11-6 Cincinnati victory with Jackson (aka Winn) again in the box.[44] The Braves started a three-week road trip a few days later, and the season ended on September 2 because of World War I, so there were no more Braves visits to Montréal. Other exhibition contests with big-league teams were played in Montréal over the years,[45] but no regular-season major-league games ensued until the Expos showed up in 1969.[46]

STOCKY BALLPLAYERS IN 1881

From the *New York Clipper*, May 28, 1881:

> "A FATMAN'S TOURNEY. – A team of fat Canadians – none to weigh less than 200 lb – is being organized to take a trip through New York State this Summer, to play against local fatmen's teams of Buffalo, Rochester, Troy, Albany and this city. They will meet with a right royal welcome when they come. Fat men of New York State, to the rescue. Organize your nines at once."[47]

Despite a thorough review of newspapers from the noted cities, no box scores or game stories have been found. It remains to be seen if this planned tour of tubby gentlemen actually took place.

THREE CANADIAN PITCHERS

Through the 2021 season, 134 Canadian-born players have pitched in the major leagues. Seventy teams have had multiple Canadian pitchers in the same season, including five teams that had three.[48] Has there ever been a major-league game in which a team fielded three Canadian moundsmen?

Four of the five teams that had three Canadian pitchers in one season (1885 Baltimore Orioles, 1961 Milwaukee Braves, 1992 Boston Red Sox, and 1999 Toronto Blue Jays) never had all three of these players on the active roster at the same time. The possibility of three Canadians pitching on the same day was therefore left to the fifth team, the 1965 Houston Astros.

Claude Raymond was drafted by Houston from Milwaukee after the 1963 season, and he pitched with the team through mid-1967. His teammate from the 1961 Braves, Ken MacKenzie, had bounced to the Mets, Cardinals, and Giants over the next three seasons before the Astros acquired him for 1965. Raymond was with the team all season and had 33 appearances, including all seven of his career starts; he pitched quite well, accumulating 2.2 bWAR, almost two-thirds of the total he amassed over 12 major-league seasons. MacKenzie was used exclusively out of the bullpen; he pitched 21 times before he was assigned to Triple A on August 6, ending his major-league career. Nine of his appearances were in games in which Raymond also pitched.

The third Canadian pitcher was Ron Taylor. Taylor was acquired in a trade from St. Louis in June; he pitched 32 times over the last 3½ months of the season, all but one game in relief. From Taylor's acquisition on June 15 until MacKenzie's demotion on August 6, a period that included 45 Houston games, the Astros had three Canadian pitchers on the active roster. This didn't go unnoticed; *The Sporting News* published a photograph of the three of them holding the Canadian flag with the caption:

> *"The Houston Astros, only major league club with three Canadian players, lean heavily on Ron Taylor, Ken MacKenzie and Claude Raymond, holding the Canadian flag. Curiously, all of them are pitchers."*[49]

In this period Raymond pitched seven times, including five starts, Taylor made 16 relief appearances, and MacKenzie came in from the bullpen seven times. Taylor and MacKenzie both pitched on July 8 and 31, but Raymond didn't play on those days. Taylor and Raymond both pitched on July 18 without MacKenzie.

But history wouldn't deny them. It all came together on Friday, July 23, 1965, when Houston hosted the Cincinnati Reds. The Astros scored an early run as Raymond, the starting pitcher for the last time in his career, shut the Reds out until Pete Rose hit an RBI triple in the sixth inning to tie it up. Three singles by the first four batters in the seventh gave the Reds a 2-1 lead to end Raymond's day; he was relieved by Taylor, who got out of trouble by inducing a double play from the first batter he faced. The game went to the top of the eighth with Cincinnati clinging to a one-run lead, but then the wheels fell off, and the Canucks were to blame. Taylor faced four batters, giving up two singles and a walk surrounding a sacrifice. With the score then 3-1, he was removed and replaced by MacKenzie, who promptly allowed a fourth run to score on a wild pitch, then surrendered consecutive singles to Vada Pinson, Frank Robinson, and Tony Perez to give the Reds a 6-1 lead. MacKenzie was pulled without retiring a batter, and it was left to US-born Danny Coombs to complete the inning without further damage.[50] The Reds tacked on another three runs in the ninth, and Joey Jay completed the game for Cincinnati's 9-1 win.

It wasn't the best of days for the pitchers, especially Taylor and MacKenzie, but it was the first and, as of 2021, the only major-league game in which a team sent three Canadian pitchers to the mound.

SOURCES

Statistics and roster information from https://www.Baseball-Reference.com/. Transactions data from *The Sporting News Player Contract Cards*, courtesy the LA84 Foundation Digital Library Collections. Constrained player searches typically performed via Stathead Baseball at https://Stathead.com/baseball/.

NOTES

1   "Before Royalty." *Sporting Life*, September 14, 1901: 3.

2   Carl Bridge and Kent Fedorowich, eds., *The British World Diaspora, Culture and Identity* (London: Frank Cass Publishers, 2003), 161-3.

3   Toronto's entries in the Eastern and International Leagues had nicknames including Canucks, Canadians, Maple Leafs, and Beavers. The only season in which they were known as the Royals was 1901. Montréal's teams of the era were always known as the Royals.

4   Barrow managed Toronto from 1900 to 1902, and again in 1905 and 1906.

5   "Last of the Season," *Montréal Gazette*, September 21, 1901: 2.

6   Montréal's major leaguers were Tommy Raub, John Shearon, Joe Delahanty, Fred Odwell, Abbie Johnson, and Harry Felix. The other Montréal players, Charles Dooley, Dan Sheehan, and Larry Quinlan, were never major leaguers. Toronto's major leaguers were George Browne, Jimmy Bannon, Charlie Carr, Frank Bonner, Lew Carr, Harry Bemis, and Pop Williams. The other Toronto players, Billy Hargrove and Bob Schaub, were never major leaguers.

7   Bridge and Fedorowich, 162-3.

8   Jim Leeke, *Nine Innings for the King: The Day Wartime London Stopped for Baseball, July 4, 1918* (Jefferson, North Carolina: McFarland & Company Inc., 2015).

9   Atwater Park was used by Montréal's entries in the Eastern and International Leagues from 1897 through 1923.

10 Nineteen teams had between 111 and 134 losses, led by the 1899 Cleveland Spiders of the National League. Only eight teams have accomplished this dubious feat in the Expansion Era, 1961 to the present. Sarah Langs, "Longest Losing Streaks in MLB History," MLB.com, August 25, 2021, accessed November 15, 2021: https://www.mlb.com/news/longest-losing-streaks-in-mlb-history. Since 1900 only the 1961 Phillies (23 games) and the 1988 Orioles (21 games) have had longer single-season losing streaks. The Expos are one of four teams to have lost 20 in a row.

11 This team was a shared affiliate of the Expos and their fellow first-year franchise, the Seattle Pilots.

12 Ted Blackman, "Funtastic California – Expos Made It in 26 hours," *Montréal Gazette*, June 7, 1969: 30.

13 Clancy Loranger, "Can Glass Cut It?," *Vancouver* (British Columbia) *Province*, June 5, 1969: 19.

14 "A Grand Night at Cap Stadium," *Vancouver Province*, June 6, 1969: 21. "The veteran Jones, who leads the Expos in home runs with nine, hit a ball out of Capilano Stadium off Dick Bates in the sixth inning and precipitated a debate among the pressbox historians. It will probably never be settled satisfactorily, but it may have been the longest home run ever hit in the park since it opened in 1951. The prodigious wallop cleared the centre field fence by a few feet, just to the right of the scoreboard. It's 415 feet to dead centre – and the fence there is about 25 feet high – so you figure it out." Capilano Stadium was built in 1951 and was renamed Nat Bailey Stadium in 1978. It is still in use today as the home of the Vancouver Canadians, the Toronto Blue Jays' affiliate of the High-A West League. "Nat Bailey Stadium," City of Vancouver Park Finder website, accessed November 15, 2021: https://covapp.vancouver.ca/parkfinder/ParkDetail.aspx?inparkid=165.

15 Based on the box score from the *Vancouver Province*, the Expos starting lineup for this game included Gary Sutherland, Manny Mota, Rusty Staub, Mack Jones, Coco Laboy, Bob Bailey, John Boccabella, and Bobby Wine.

16 Ted Blackman, "Funtastic California – Expos Made It in 26 hours." This story notes that the Expos' flight left Montréal at 7:00 A.M. EDT on Friday morning and arrived in Los Angeles at 6:00 A.M. EDT (3:00 A.M. local time).

17 The Expos entered the bottom of the ninth inning with a 4-1 lead, but three singles, a walk and a balk brought the score to 4-3 with one out and runners on second and third. Relief pitcher Roy Face got Ken Boyer to hit a foul popup to third base, then Willie Crawford hit a fly ball to right field to end the game.

18 Ernest Mehl, "Lou's Kiddie Camp First to Show New Spirit Spurring A's," *The Sporting News*, March 9, 1955: 8.

19 MacKenzie's last spring-training appearance with the A's was a start on March 28. He was sent to Triple-A Columbus two days later. Joe McGuff, "A's Squad Is Cut," *Kansas City Times*, April 1, 1955: 40, noted "… Boudreau lopped four more men off his roster, sending all of them to Columbus of the International league … Eric McKenzie [*sic*] …" "Deals of the Week, Class AAA," *The Sporting News*, April 20, 1955: 37 noted that Columbus later assigned MacKenzie to Savannah.

20 Ernest Mehl, "Boudreau Looks Past Cutdown, Sees More Confidence in Squad," *The Sporting News*, May 4, 1955: 18. Regarding the lawsuit, see "Ball Player Charged In FHA Fraud," *Indianapolis Star*, April 13, 1955: 18 which notes: "… Robertson Jr., 27-year-old catcher for the Kansas City Athletics, American League baseball team, was arrested here yesterday on a Federal indictment charging a Federal Housing Administration fraud."

21 Tyler Kuda, "'84 Team Canada Players Surprise Their Manager with a Commemorative Ring," *Sarnia* (Ontario) *Observer*, August 14, 2016. Article accessed online on November 14, 2021: 84 Team Canada players surprise their manager with a commemorative ring | The Sarnia Observer (theobserver.ca).

22 The National League and the American Association each fielded eight teams in 1891. The Association then folded, and four franchises were absorbed into the National League for 1892. The League, with 12 teams, stood alone until the minor-league American League was reclassified as major after the 1900 season.

23 A search of the 905 players for Hall of Famers turned up 18 players, but four of them (Ted Williams, Jimmie Foxx, Tris Speaker, and Harry Hooper) were position players with a single pitching appearance.

24 Eighteen of the 20 players appeared in the major leagues.

25 Robert D. Warrington, "Philadelphia in the 1882 League Alliance", SABR *Baseball Research Journal*, Volume 48, Number 2, Fall 2019, 109.

26 "The 'Quakers' Win Again," *Philadelphia Inquirer*, August 10, 1882: 2.

27 "The 'Quakers' Win Again," and "Philadelphia vs. Atlantic City," *Philadelphia Sunday Item,* August 13, 1882: 7.

28 "Base Ball Gossip," *Philadelphia Sunday Item*, August 27, 1882: 7.

29 "Baseball," *New York Clipper*, August 19, 1882: 346.

30 "Base Ball," *London Advertiser*, August 7, 1882: 3.

31 "Base Ball," *London Advertiser*, July 19, 1882: 1. "At the base ball match on Monday afternoon between the 7th Band and Philharmonic Society J. Thompson, of the Tecumsehs, caught for both teams."

32 "Base Ball," *London Advertiser*, Monday, August 28, 1882: 4.

33 "Notes," *Cincinnati Enquirer*, Sunday, August 27, 1882: 2.

34 "Notes," *Cincinnati Enquirer*, September 21, 1882: 2.

35 "Notes," *Cincinnati Enquirer*, May 7, 1884: 2.

36 "Base Ball Gossip," *Evening Item*, June 13, 1884.

37 The 89 Canadian-born players who have hit at least one major-league home run hit a total of 3,166 from 1876 through 2021. If the National Association of 1871 to 1875 is included, then one extra player (Bob Addy) and one home run are added to the totals.

38 "Braves and Cubs to Play Game in Montréal Sunday," *Boston Globe*, July 24, 1918: 5.

39 Charlie Bevis, *Sunday Baseball* (Jefferson, North Carolina: McFarland & Company Inc., 2003), 240-1. The Boston Braves scheduled their first Sunday home game for April 21, 1929, but it was rained out. The Red Sox played the city's first legal Sunday game on April 28, and the Braves had their inaugural home Sunday contest on May 5, 1929. The ability to play on Sundays in Montréal was not matched in all Canadian cities. Montréal's national rival Toronto could not accommodate similar games because of blue laws that made early twentieth-century Boston look like a latter-day Las Vegas. It took three plebiscites before Sunday sports were first permitted in 1950, and a Torontonian couldn't go to a movie theater on a Sunday until 1961. Allan Levine, *Toronto, Biography of a City* (Madeira Park, British Columbia: Douglas and McIntyre, 2014), 189.

40 "Braves-Cubs Clash at Montréal, an Exhibition," *Boston Globe*, July 25, 1918: 4.

41 "Village De Lorimier – The Plateau Stampede," Linda Sullivan-Simpson, *The Past Whispers* website, accessed November 3, 2021. This article places the racetrack on "a lot of land bordered by Des Érables, Masson, Fullum and Mont-Royal streets." Delorimier Stadium, built in 1928, was at the corner of De Lorimier Avenue and Ontario Street East. According to Google Maps, the walking distance from the intersection of Mont-Royal and Des Érables to De Lorimier and Ontario East is 1.5 kilometers (0.94 miles).

42 Jackson's true identity was revealed the following year when James C. O'Leary of the *Globe* wrote on March 4, 1919: "Winn was playing with Richmond under the name of Jackson."

43 "Boston Club Won Out in the Ninth," *Montréal Gazette*, July 29, 1918: 10.

44 "Big League Clubs Go Through Moves," *Montréal Gazette*, August 4, 1918: 10. "Burlesque Baseball on Interior of Delorimier Park Race Track."

45 The Retrosheet list of In-Season Exhibition Games, accessed on November 3, 2021, lists several games played in Montréal from the 1920s to the 1940s. Examples include the Chicago White Sox on July 23, 1928, the Washington Senators on September 22, 1930, and the Brooklyn Dodgers on July 12, 1948, all versus the local Montréal Royals.

46 The Retrosheet list of Alternate Site Games, accessed on November 3, 2021, confirms that no regular-season major-league games have ever been played in Canada other than the home games of the Montréal Expos and Toronto Blue Jays.

47 "A Fatman's Tourney," *New York Clipper*, May 28, 1881: 154.

48 The Stathead search found six teams, but one should not have been included: the 1889 Philadelphia Quakers. They had three Canadians, but only two of them pitched for the team: Pete Wood and George Wood. The third Canadian was Arthur Irwin, who played only shortstop for Philadelphia. His pitching appearance was after he had been acquired by league rival Washington in June.

49 *The Sporting News*, August 28, 1965: 6.

50 Danny Coombs was born in Lincoln, Maine, only 62 miles (100 kilometers) from the Canadian border crossing at Saint Croix, New Brunswick. The Astros' fifth and final pitcher that day was Dave Giusti from Seneca Falls, New York, 140 miles (225 kilometers) from the Canadian border crossing at Alexandria Bay, Ontario.

CONTRIBUTORS

Richard Armstrong lives in Guelph, Ontario, and is particularly interested in the Deadball Era and Canadians who have played the game. In 2020, along with Martin Healy Jr., he co-authored *George 'Mooney' Gibson: Canadian Catcher for the Deadball Era Pirates*.

Robert K. Barney, an American citizen, has lived and worked in Canada at Western University for 50 years. Educated at the University of New Mexico, he received his PhD in 1968; in 2014 Western University awarded him a doctor of laws, *honoris causa*. Recently he has worked with City of London heritage officials on a proposal to federal authorities for Labatt Memorial Park to be awarded National Heritage Site distinction.

Gary Belleville is a retired information technology professional living in Victoria, British Columbia. He has written articles for SABR's *Baseball Research Journal*, Games Project, and Baseball Biography Project, in addition to contributing to several SABR books. Gary grew up in Ottawa, Ontario, and graduated from the University of Waterloo with a bachelor of mathematics (computer science) degree.

Warren Campbell is a Toronto-based entertainment industry executive. For 30 years he's avoided being on a stage, and spends his free time searching through old publications for curious baseball stories. He still has dreams of owning an Independent baseball team.

Patrick Carpentier is a historian specializing in early Quebec baseball. For the last 30 years, he has researched Quebec baseball parks, the Eastern International League, and the life and achievements of Joe Page. He also has worked extensively on the history of baseball in Saint-Hyacinthe. In the past he has collaborated with Baseball Québec, Le Panthéon des sports and a number of baseball exhibitions in and around Montréal. A SABR member since 1992, he has been the SABR-Quebec chapter leader since 2008.

Stephen Dame is a middle school teacher of Humanities in Toronto. He is a member of the Hanlan's Point chapter of SABR. Stephen regularly presents research papers at the annual conference organized by the Centre for Canadian Baseball Research. He has researched military baseball during Canada's World War efforts, and explored the links between baseball and the prime ministers of Canada.

Historian **Marcel Dugas** is a graduate of the University of Montréal. He's been researching the Montréal Royals since 2012. In 2013 he live-tweeted the team's 1946 season for the benefit of his followers across Canada, the United States, Latin America and elsewhere. In 2019 he published *Jackie Robinson, Un été à Montréal* (*Jackie Robinson's Summer in Montréal*), a deep dive into the historic 1946 season.

Eric Frost is a registered nurse, educator, and doctoral student in Texas. After Eric joined the SABR BioProject, Arthur Irwin was the subject of his first biography.

Larry Gerlach, past president of SABR, is the author of *The Men in Blue: Conversations With Umpires*, and co-editor with Bill Nowlin of *The SABR Book of Umpires and Umpiring*.

Historian and consultant **Gary Gillette** is a nationally known baseball author and the foremost expert on Hall of Famer Turkey Stearnes, the Detroit Stars, and the history of the Negro Leagues in Detroit. As founder and chair of the nonprofit Friends of Historic Hamtramck Stadium, Gillette has led the campaign to restore the historic site. His research was key to the approval of a State of Michigan Historic Marker for Hamtramck Stadium and was the basis for two African American Civil Rights Grants from the National Park Service. In 2021 he was the recipient of the prestigious Tweed Webb Lifetime Achievement Award from SABR's Negro Leagues Committee.

Tom Hawthorn is a speechwriter for British Columbia Premier John Horgan. Hawthorn's most recent book is *The Year Canadians Lost Their Minds and Found Their Country: The Centennial of 1967* (Vancouver: Douglas & McIntyre, 2017). He served as archival researcher for the 2003 National Film Board documentary *Sleeping Tigers: The*

Asahi Baseball Story. He is an honorary member of Havana's Peña Deportivo. Born in Winnipeg, he moved to Montréal as a boy, and used earnings from two paper routes to attend Montréal Expos games at Jarry Park.

The late **Martin Healy Jr.** was from Hamilton, Ontario. A lifelong Toronto Blue Jays fan and Canadian baseball historian, he published his first book, a biography of George "Mooney" Gibson, in March 2020. After his passing in September 2020, Richard Armstrong, his friend and co-author, submitted Marty's essay on Ed Pinnance.

Dr. Colin Howell (B.A., M.A. Dalhousie, PhD, Cincinnati) is professor emeritus in history, recently retired academic director of the Centre for the Study of Sport and Health at Saint Mary's University, and a former co-editor of the *Canadian Historical Review*. He has published widely in the field of sport and health studies, and is the author of *Northern Sandlots* (1995), *Blood, Sweat and Cheers: Sport and the Making of Modern Canada* (2001), and a number of edited collections.

William Humber's five books on baseball include *Diamonds of the North: A Concise History of Baseball in Canada* (1995). He has been a facilitator since 1979 of an in-class and now online subject *Baseball Spring Training for Fans*, is an inductee into Canada's Baseball Hall of Fame (2018), and was appointed to the Order of Canada (2022) for his baseball research. He finds it all a tad overwhelming.

Heidi LM Jacobs is a librarian at the University of Windsor's Leddy Library. She was one of the researchers behind the "Breaking the Colour Barrier: Wilfred 'Boomer' Harding & the Chatham Coloured All-Stars" project. She is a co-editor of the *Journal of Canadian Baseball* and the author of *100 Miles of Baseball: Fifty Games, One Summer* (with Dale Jacobs). Her book *1934: The Barrier-Breaking Year of the Chatham Coloured All-Stars* will be published in 2023 from Biblioasis.

SABR member **Sean Kane** is an artist and designer who incorporates classic baseball gloves in his paintings featuring greats of the game. His work is in the permanent collection of the National Baseball Hall of Fame and Museum and the Negro Leagues Baseball Museum. Sean creates work for major-league teams, Hall of Fame players, institutions, and avid collectors from his studio in Guelph, Ontario.

Maxwell Kates is a chartered accountant who lives and works in Toronto. He has worked in commercial radio in St. Catharines, Ontario, and more recently, wrote a monthly column for the Houston-based *Pecan Park Eagle*. Maxwell's articles and essays have appeared in four issues of *The National Pastime*, and in 2018, he and Bill Nowlin co-edited SABR's *Time for Expansion Baseball*. His speaking credits include SABR engagements in Seattle, Montréal, and Houston, and two presentations at the Canadian Baseball History Conference.

Martin Lacoste has taught high-school music for over 30 years, but has always had a passion for baseball, whether fondly recalling the Expos from the 1980s or digging into the Maple Leafs from the 1880s. Having been a SABR member in the 1990s, he is excited to again be a member (in the digital era) since 2016.

Bill Lamb spent more than 30 years as a state/county prosecutor in New Jersey. He currently serves as editor of the *The Inside Game*, the quarterly newsletter of SABR's Deadball Era Committee, and is the author of *Black Sox in the Courtroom: The Grand Jury, Criminal*

Trial and Civil Proceedings (Jefferson, North Carolina: McFarland, 2013). He can be contacted at wflamb12@yahoo.com.

Len Levin is a longtime newspaper editor in New England, now retired. He lives in Providence with his wife, Linda, and an overachieving orange cat. He now (Len, not the cat) is the grammarian for the Rhode Island Supreme Court and edits its decisions. He also copyedits many SABR books, including this one. He is just down the interstate from Fenway Park, where he has spent many happy hours.

Brian "Chip" Martin lives in London, Ontario. He is the author of six baseball books, including *Baseball's Creation Myth*, *The Tecumsehs of the International Association* and *The Man Who Made Babe Ruth: Brother Matthias of St. Mary's School*. He is a director of the Centre for Canadian Baseball Research and a member of the selection committee for the Canadian Baseball Hall of Fame. He is also a member of SABR's Nineteenth Century Committee, and a repeat presenter at the committee's annual Conference in Cooperstown.

David Matchett grew up in Lachine, Quebec, and had his sixth birthday a month before the Montréal Expos played their first game. He earned a degree in finance and later moved to Toronto to pursue his career, arriving the same day the Blue Jays acquired Dave Winfield for their World Series run in 1992. David first discovered SABR when he bought a few back issues of the *Baseball Research Journal* on his initial trip to Cooperstown in 1981, and he has been a member for over 25 years. He is a certified financial planner and lives in downtown Toronto, a 15-minute walk from Rogers Centre. When he isn't watching a game or doing research, he enjoys travel, movies, and taking in all of Toronto's cultural activities with his friends.

Andy McCue's *Mover and Shaker: Walter O'Malley, the Dodgers and Baseball's Westward Expansion* won the Seymour Medal for the best book of baseball history or biography in 2015. He is a former president of SABR and a recipient of the Bob Davids Award.

David McDonald is a writer, broadcaster, and filmmaker, with a particular interest in the long and colorful history of baseball in Ottawa, where he lives.

When **Peter Morris** first developed a serious interest in baseball at the age of four, it was a transformative event. Up until then, he had been best known for his impetuous decisions and his penchant for napping.

Andrew North is a retired developer of statistical software. He is a director of the Centre for Canadian Baseball Research and serves on the Editorial Board of the *Journal for Canadian Baseball*. A SABR member since 1982, he lives in St. Marys, Ontario, where he maintains the research library at the Canadian Baseball Hall of Fame and Museum.

Bill Nowlin was born in Boston and grew up in Lexington, Massachusetts ("The Birthplace of American Liberty"), where he guided tourists around the Battle Green for summers all through high school and college. The same month he began teaching political science at university in 1970, he founded the Rounder Records label with two friends. In 1997, he joined with Jim Prime of Nova Scotia's Annapolis Valley and coauthored *Ted Williams: A Tribute*, based on 200 interviews of people who knew Ted Williams – and he was hooked. He's helped write or edit just over 100 books on baseball since that time.

Riley Nowokowski is a PhD Candidate at Western University in London, Ontario. He loves all types of sport but takes a particular interest in baseball history. His work largely has focused on sport during the late nineteenth and early twentieth centuries.

Bill Pruden has been a teacher and administrator, primarily at the high-school level, for almost 40 years. A SABR member since 2001, he has contributed to both the BioProject and Games Project, as well as to a number of book projects. A lifetime baseball fan, he also loves to read, research, and write about American history of all kinds, passions undoubtedly fueled by the fact that as a seven-year-old, at only his second major-league game, he witnessed Roger Maris hit his historic 61st home run.

Carl Riechers retired from United Parcel Service in 2012 after 35 years of service. With more free time, he became a SABR member that same year. Born and raised in the suburbs of St. Louis, he became a big fan of the Cardinals. He and his wife, Janet, have three children and are the proud grandparents of two.

David Siegel has been a member of SABR since 2006. After 40 years as a professor of political science and an administrator at Brock University in St. Catharines, Ontario, he has now turned his attention to doing research on baseball.

Paul Sinclair retired after a 38-year career as an investment professional for a leading Canadian life insurance company. A graduate of the University of Toronto, he is a lifelong Toronto resident, baseball player and fan. As a player he tried out for both the Montréal Expos and Toronto Blue Jays. Highlights of his lifelong fandom include watching spring training with the Detroit Tigers in the mid-'70s, enduring the snow and cold of the first Blue Jays game ever, and throwing out the first pitch at a Blue Jays game in August 2015.

Allen Tait has been a SABR member since 1976. A retired fraud investigator, he is chapter leader for the Hanlan's Point (Toronto) chapter and a member of numerous SABR Research Committees.

Dennis Thiessen is a retired professor of education at the University of Toronto. He is the author of *Tip O'Neill and the St. Louis Browns of 1887*, published by McFarland in 2019. A SABR member since 2012, Thiessen has presented papers on the St. Louis Browns, record-keeping, and Sunday baseball at the Frederick Ivor-Campbell Nineteenth Century Base Ball Conference, and papers on Tip O'Neill, the Woodstock Wonder, and Tip O'Neill, Champion Batsman of 1887, at the Canadian Baseball History Conference.

Christian Trudeau is a professor of economics at the University of Windsor. For the last 20 years, he has researched Quebec baseball history. His findings are documented at LesFantomesduStade.ca.

Max Weder is a lawyer who lives on the Sunshine Coast of British Columbia. He has been a member of SABR since 1987. His research and collecting interests focus on the history of baseball in Western Canada and early baseball books.

Daniel Wyatt is Canadian, born and raised on the prairies of Saskatchewan. Currently residing outside Toronto, he is the author of 12 books in the historical and historical fiction genres. He's had articles published in various magazines, including *The Hockey News* and *Baseball Digest*, and has been a steady article contributor to TheNationalPastimeMuseum.com online baseball history website.

Friends of SABR

You can become a Friend of SABR by giving as little as $10 per month or by making a one-time gift of $1,000 or more. When you do so, you will be inducted into a community of passionate baseball fans dedicated to supporting SABR's work.

Friends of SABR receive the following benefits:
- ✓ Annual Friends of SABR Commemorative Lapel Pin
- ✓ Recognition in This Week in SABR, SABR.org, and the SABR Annual Report
- ✓ Access to the SABR Annual Convention VIP donor event
- ✓ Invitations to exclusive Friends of SABR events

SABR On-Deck Circle - $10/month, $30/month, $50/month

Get in the SABR On-Deck Circle, and help SABR become the essential community for the world of baseball. Your support will build capacity around all things SABR, including publications, website content, podcast development, and community growth.

A monthly gift is deducted from your bank account or charged to a credit card until you tell us to stop. No more email, mail, or phone reminders.

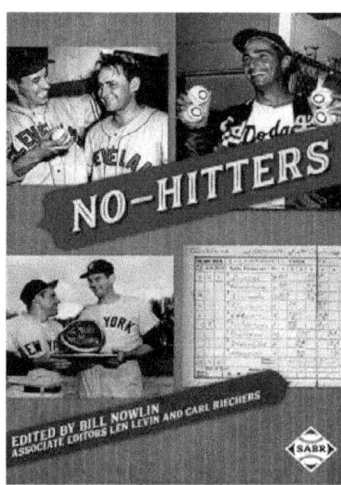

Join the SABR On-Deck Circle

Payment Info: _____Visa _____Mastercard

Name on Card: _____

Card #: _____

Exp. Date: _____ Security Code: _____

Signature: _____

- ○ $10/month
- ○ $30/month
- ○ $50/month
- ○ Other amount _____

Go to sabr.org/donate to make your gift online

New Books from SABR

Part of the mission of the Society for American Baseball Research has always been to disseminate member research. In addition to the *Baseball Research Journal*, SABR publishes books that include player biographies, historical game recaps, and statistical analysis. All SABR books are available in print and ebook formats. SABR members can access the entire SABR Digital Library for free and purchase print copies at significant member discounts of 40 to 50% off cover price.

JEFF BAGWELL IN CONNECTICUT:
A Consistent Lad in the Land of Steady Habits
This volume of articles, interviews, and essays by members of the Connecticut chapter of SABR chronicles the life and career of Connecticut's favorite baseball son, Hall-of-Famer Jeff Bagwell, with special attention on his high school and college years.
Edited by Karl Cicitto, Bill Nowlin, & Len Levin
$19.95 paperback (ISBN 978-1-943816-97-2)
$9.99 ebook (ISBN 978-1-943816-96-5)
7"x10", 246 pages, 45 photos

1995 CLEVELAND INDIANS:
The Sleeping Giant Awakens
After almost 40 years of sub-500 baseball, the Sleeping Giant woke in 1995, the first season in the Indians spent in their new home of Jacob's Field. The biographies of all the players, coaches, and broadcasters from that year are here, sprinkled with personal perspectives, as well as game stories from key matchups during the 1995 season, information about Jacob's Field, and other essays.
Edited by Joseph Wancho
$19.95 paperback (ISBN 978-1-943816-95-8)
$9.99 ebook (ISBN 978-1-943816-94-1)
8.5"X11", 410 pages, 76 photos

TIME FOR EXPANSION BASEBALL
The LA Angels and "new" Washington Senators ushered in MLB expansion in 1960, followed by the Houston Colt .45s and New York Mets. By 1998, 10 additional teams had launched: the Kansas City Royals, Seattle Pilots, Toronto Blue Jays, and Tampa Bay Devil Tays in the AL, and the Montreal Expos, San Diego Padres, Colorado Rockies, Florida Marlins, and Arizona Diamondbacks in the NL. *Time for Expansion Baseball* tells each team's origin and includes biographies of key players.
Edited by Maxwell Kates and Bill Nowlin
$24.95 paperback (ISBN 978-1-933599-89-7)
$9.99 ebook (ISBN 978-1-933599-88-0)
8.5"X11", 430 pages, 150 photos

Base Ball's 19th Century "Winter" Meetings
1857-1900
A look at the business meetings of base ball's earliest days (not all of which were in the winter). As John Thorn writes in his Foreword, "This monumental volume traces the development of the game from its birth as an organized institution to its very near suicide at the dawn of the next century."
Edited by Jeremy K. Hodges and Bill Nowlin
$29.95 paperback (ISBN 978-1-943816-91-0)
$9.99 ebook (ISBN978-1-943816-90-3)
8.5"x11", 390 pages, 50 photos

MET-ROSPECTIVES:
A Collection of the Greatest Games in New York Mets History
This book's 57 game stories—coinciding with the number of Mets years through 2018—are strictly for the eternal optimist. They include the team's very first victory in April 1962 at Forbes Field, Tom Seaver's "Imperfect Game" in July '69, the unforgettable Game Sixes in October '86, the "Grand Slam Single" in the 1999 NLCS, and concludes with the extra-innings heroics in September 2016 at Citi Field that helped ensure a wild-card berth.
edited by Brian Wright and Bill Nowlin
$14.95 paperback (ISBN 978-1-943816-87-3)
$9.99 ebook (ISBN 978-1-943816-86-6)
8.5"X11", 148 pages, 44 photos

CINCINNATI'S CROSLEY FIELD:
A Gem in the Queen City
This book evokes memories of Crosley Field through detailed summaries of more than 85 historic and monumental games played there, and 10 insightful feature essays about the history of the ballpark. Former Reds players Johnny Edwards and Art Shamsky share their memories of the park in introductions.
Edited by Gregory H. Wolf
$19.95 paperback (ISBN 978-1-943816-75-0)
$9.99 ebook (ISBN 978-1-943816-74-3)
8.5"X11", 320 pages, 43 photos

MOMENTS OF JOY AND HEARTBREAK:
66 Significant Episodes in the History of the Pittsburgh Pirates
In this book we relive no-hitters, World Series-winning homers, and the last tripleheader ever played in major-league baseball. Famous Pirates like Honus Wagner and Roberto Clemente—and infamous ones like Dock Ellis—make their appearances, as well as recent stars like Andrew McCutcheon.
Edited by Jorge Iber and Bill Nowlin
$19.95 paperback (ISBN 978-1-943816-73-6)
$9.99 ebook (ISBN 978-1-943816-72-9)
8.5"X11", 208 pages, 36 photos

FROM SPRING TRAINING TO SCREEN TEST:
Baseball Players Turned Actors
SABR"s book of baseball's "matinee stars," a selection of those who crossed the lines between professional sports and popular entertainment. Included are the famous (Gene Autry, Joe DiMaggio, Jim Thorpe, Bernie Williams) and the forgotten (Al Gettel, Lou Stringer, Wally Hebert, Wally Hood), essays on baseball in TV shows and Coca-Cola commercials, and Jim Bouton's casting as "Jim Barton" in the *Ball Four* TV series.
Edited by Rob Edelman and Bill Nowlin
$19.95 paperback (ISBN 978-1-943816-71-2)
$9.99 ebook (ISBN 978-1-943816-70-5)
8.5"X11", 410 pages, 89 photos

To learn more about how to receive these publications for free or at member discount
as a member of SABR, visit the website: sabr.org/join

www.ingramcontent.com/pod-product-compliance
Lightning Source LLC
Chambersburg PA
CBHW080944120626
46546CB00010B/2829